Popular Writing in America

POPULAR WRITING IN AMERICA

THE INTERACTION OF STYLE AND AUDIENCE

SECOND EDITION

Donald McQuade

Queens College
of the City of New York

Robert Atwan

New York   Oxford
OXFORD UNIVERSITY PRESS
1980

Copyright © 1974, 1977, 1980 by Oxford University Press, Inc.

Library of Congress Cataloging in Publication Data
McQuade, Donald, comp.
Popular writing in America.
1. College readers.   2. American prose literature—
20th century.   I. Atwan, Robert.   II. Title.
PE1417.M35   1980   808'.04275   79-20655   ISBN 0-19-502693-4

Second printing, 1980

Printed in the United States of America

For Our Parents

PREFACE

For this second edition of *Popular Writing in America,* we retained the organization and principles of the first edition but made a number of changes that we trust will enhance the book's overall flexibility and usefulness. We have revised the contents considerably. In choosing new reading material, we were guided by a two-fold commitment: 1) to locate *short,* effective representations of each form of popular writing, and 2) to select writing particularly appropriate to the experiences and interests of today's college students. Though the book's historical dimensions have been maintained, its emphasis is now contemporary.

Our choices were also guided by a principle of interconnectedness that we believe is one of the most important features of the book: virtually every selection in *Popular Writing in America* is connected either thematically or stylistically with one or more of the other selections. In addition, the range of thematic interconnections has been expanded and now includes such topics as capital punishment, the American hero, consumerism, and popular entertainment. But perhaps the principal—and most noticeable—change is the inclusion of poetry. We think the generous sampling of poems extends the book's adaptability for the classroom and allows teachers and students the opportunity to explore an even greater diversity of popular and classical writing than did the earlier edition.

We want to remind readers again that selections are not meant to serve only as models for student compositions. The selections are intended in part to stimulate discussion about writing and to help students become more analytically familiar with the diversity of styles and strategies that develop within a contemporary system of communications almost wholly dependent upon corporate enterprise, mass audiences, interlocking media industries, and vast outlays of money. Few acts of writing—and surely student compositions are no exception—exist completely outside of competitive, socio-economic considerations. We assume that the more conscious students are of the public and commercial pressures behind a piece of writing (pressures that can be felt *in* the writing, whether an ad, article, news item or best seller), the more sensitive they will become to whatever institutional styles or "voices" they may inadvertently be underwriting in their own compositions. In order to make this particular interaction of style and audience dramatically visible to students, we have added a considerable number of selections dealing with the ways in which mass-media artists and artifacts determine the shape of our consumer culture.

In general, most of the changes we have made for this new edition—the inclusion of more ads and articles about advertising; more human interest journalism; a greater range of short magazine articles; more best-selling nonfiction; and more accessible modern classics—represent our considered responses to the many instructors throughout the country who have used *Popular Writing in America* and have generously suggested specific ways they thought the book could be improved. We hope that our decisions have resulted in a stronger, more practical book—one that will be welcomed by those who have worked with the book before as well as by those who are trying it for the first time.

Acknowledgments

We are grateful for the many helpful suggestions sent to us over the past few years by instructors who have used *Popular Writing in America*. We have included as many of their recommendations as possible. In particular, we would like to thank: Gail Bounds, Addison Bross, Douglas Butturff, Lyman L. Fink, Jr., Christine Freeman, R. S. Hootman, Lee A. Jacobus, D. G. Kehl, Henry Knepler, Andrea Lundsford, Helen Naugle, Matthew O'Brien, Lori Rath, Harold Schechter, Nancy Sommers, Victor H. Thompson, and Barbara H. Traister. In addition, we appreciate the special assistance of Trudy Baltz, John Clifford, Kent Ekberg, Kate Hirsh, Kay Kier, John McDermott, Paul O'Connell, Sharon Shaloo, and Harvey Wiener.

We would like to acknowledge once again all those who helped us structure our original text and whose influence is still very much felt in this new edition: Paul Bertram, Thomas R. Edwards, Bruce Forer, Christopher Gay, Mark Gibbons, Ron Holland, Daniel F. Howard, Betsy B. Kaufman, Robert E. Lynch, Robert Lyons, C. F. Main, George Mandelbaum, Max and Barbara Maxwell, Kevin McQuade, Frank Moorman, Richard Poirier, Douglas Roehm, Sandra Schor, Gary Tate, Thomas Van Laan, William Vesterman, and Elissa Weaver. John Leypoldt of the Princeton University Library was extremely helpful in producing many of the illustrations.

We continue to value the thoughtful assistance of our editor, John Wright, and the help of the professional staff at Oxford University Press, especially Dale Demy, Ellie Fuchs, Jean Shapiro, and Gerald Mentor. We deeply appreciate the excellent revision of the Teacher's Manual—now a more detailed teaching resource—prepared by our friend and colleague, Christopher Motley. Another friend, Richard Mikita, has given generously of his time and intelligence, and his critical judgment in many ways helped determine the course of this revision. As usual, we owe far too much to Helene Atwan and Susanne McQuade.

New York   D. McQ.
October 1979   R. A.

CONTENTS

Contents

Contents

PRESS   97

Contents

ON THE DEATH PENALTY

MAGAZINES   219

Contents

BEST SELLERS 377

CLASSICS   473

RHETORICAL TABLE OF CONTENTS

DESCRIPTION

NARRATION

FACTUAL AND HISTORICAL

FICTIONAL

EXPOSITION

DEFINITION

CAUSE AND EFFECT

ARGUMENT

PERSUASION

Advertisements

Virtually all of them

INTRODUCTION

This book grew out of our commitment to the notion—one that still might seem peculiar to many people—that *any* form of writing can be made the subject of rewarding critical attention. And because we are most interested in the written products of American culture that are continually shaping the ways we think, talk, and feel, our editorial effort has been to include as great a variety of American themes and prose styles as could be managed within a single text. Along with some traditional selections from such classic American writers as Thoreau, Twain, Crane, and Faulkner, we have brought together an assortment of material from best sellers, popular magazines, newspapers, and advertisements. One critical principle informs our selections: we want to illustrate through historical sequences, thematic cross references, and divergent creative intentions precisely how the most widely read forms of American writing interact with each other and with their audiences to produce that intricate network of artistic and commercial collaboration known as "popular culture."

Popular Writing in America is divided into five parts. The opening section consists of some of the most successful copywriting in the history of American advertising. We have arranged the ads in clusters dealing with similar products (automobiles, cosmetics, clothing, etc.) over a number of decades both to provide a brief historical perspective on the language and rhetorical strategies of advertising and to invite speculation on changes in American culture as they are reflected in the ways our society is talked to in its advertisements. In addition, to demonstrate some of the ways advertising is thought about both inside and outside the industry, we have also included essays on the art of copywriting by two leading practitioners, a well known critique of advertising techniques and their relationship to media, and a series of delightful letters showing a prominent American poet exercising her imagination and vocabulary in an attempt to invent a suitable name for a new automobile.

The examples of newspaper writing we include in the next chapter (Press) range from different styles of headlines through the compressed prose of teletype releases to extended forms of news coverage. Events of such historical magnitude as the Lincoln and Kennedy assassinations and the use of the atom bomb on Japan are interspersed among some of the usual kinds of news stories, feature articles, interviews, and editorials that comprise the substance of the daily American newspaper. Since we want to emphasize in this chapter the stylistic and structural consequences of writing performed under emergency conditions and against competitive deadlines—"Journalism is literature in a hurry," according to Matthew Arnold—we have weighted our selections in favor of the kinds of violence and tragedies that have inspired reporters, made history, and sold newspapers.

Magazines are eclectic by necessity. Represented are a variety of topics from some of the most popular "big" and "little" magazines published in America since the middle of the nineteenth century. With very few exceptions, an article or poem from a particular magazine is intended to be at least fairly typical of the kind of material and tonal quality found in that magazine around the time the article appeared. Our selections in this chapter are limited to nonfiction because a good deal of the fiction in Best Sellers and Classics was originally published in magazines. Consequently, an important periodical like *Scribner's* is not represented by an article in this section but by the short stories of Stephen Crane and Ernest Hemingway that appear in Classics.

The material reprinted in "Best Sellers" affords the reader the opportunity to examine some of the most commercially successful prose in American publishing history. It is, for the most part, writing that the academic community has seldom paid serious attention to—selections from best sellers are rarely made available in textbooks or anthologies. Yet, because of their massive audiences and their frequent interactions with other forms of media, best sellers deserve to be attended to by readers interested in examining the relationship between their own verbal experiences and those of a literate public. Passages such as Tarzan's rescue of Jane in *Tarzan of the Apes* or the shooting of Don Corleone from *The Godfather* were selected not as specimens of mediocre writing—mediocre, that is, *because* they are from best sellers—but as examples of writing that has had enormous impact on the American reading public.

The success of many of the best selling books represented in this section depended, to a great extent, on their public's previous acceptance of similar subjects and verbal strategies in advertisements, newspapers, and magazine articles. To cite but one example, the phenomenal attention Mario Puzo's *The Godfather* received was due, in large measure, to the extensive news coverage given to the felonies and frolics of underworld characters. Popular fiction, in turn, affects other forms of media, as can be seen from the account of the murder of Joey Gallo in *Time* magazine, where the report of a ritualist gangland shooting self-consciously trades on the rendition of a similar event in *The Godfather*. Throughout the book, connections such as this one are signaled in headnotes and discussion questions in order to map out a network of thematic and stylistic interrelations.

Though our emphasis in Classics is on short fiction and poetry, we also include essays, excerpts from autobiographies, and other selected nonfiction from some of America's major authors. We have taken the liberty of designating the work of such contemporary writers as John Updike, Norman Mailer, Flannery O'Connor, and Joyce Carol Oates as "classic" because we feel that the quality of their performances and their critical alertness to the present condition of our language entitle them to be viewed in the same historical perspective as Thoreau, Twain, Crane, and Faulkner. *Classic* is a term we adopt for the sake of convenience; it is not intended to suggest writing that is antiquated, writing that is easily dissociated from popular culture because it sounds serious and elevated, but writing that has, so far, stayed around because it has stayed alive. We want to show from our selections that "classic" authors have not remained socially and intellectually superior to the various ordinary languages of popular culture but have tried to come to terms with those languages by appropriating them, occasionally discarding them, often shaping or extending them so that their writing can reflect the complex interplay between what we call literature and what we recognize as the accents of the life around us.

It might be argued that this type of book is unnecessary since the abundance of ads, newspapers, magazines, and best sellers makes them so available as "texts" that there is really no need to collect samples of them in a separate volume. If our "texts" had been chosen indiscriminately, simply to document different types of writing, that might be the case. But, quite clearly, one way the book can be used is to illustrate a verbal progression from the readily accessible language and strategies of advertising to the more obviously complicated styles of expression that characterize outstanding prose. The risk of this procedure, however, is that it may prove too schematic, may even encourage readers to regard the ads, some of the journalism and magazine articles, and most of the best sellers as blatantly inferior forms of writing, "straw men" set up to be discarded all too easily in favor of the durable excellence of the "great works." It should be noted, therefore, that our categories and sequence were not specially designed to endorse already entrenched hierarchies by setting up fairly obvious gradations in the quality of several particular types of prose and poetry, but were intended to illustrate how various kinds of writing shaped by quite different commercial purposes and intended audiences interact with and modify each other to produce what we can reasonably call a common culture.

It might also be argued that Classics have no place in an anthology devoted to popular writing. Classics are among the finest holdings of an educated minority; popular writing belongs to something as repugnant as "mass culture." That is one way to look at it. Another, and one that this book is premised on, is that Classics are among the best things we have to share with each other, and they ought to be encountered in all their challenging complexity as opportunities to enliven and, if need be, toughen the questions we ask of all the other modes of expression we participate in daily. That is why we have included an excerpt from Norman Mailer's *Of a Fire on the Moon* in Classics. Throughout his comprehensive report on the Apollo expedition, Mailer is critically aware of the ways his own prose interrelates with a variety of other, mainly competing verbal efforts. Mailer's original contract to write about the Apollo XI astronauts was with *Life,* a popular magazine. But Mailer is no ordinary reporter, and for him the moonshot was no ordinary assignment. As a writer, Mailer is so attuned to his own participation in any form of media that it was only natural his coverage of the moon landing would inform us as much about the special tasks of modern journalism as it would tell us about one of the great episodes in American history. As it stands, *Of a Fire on the Moon* is a fascinating social document incorporating the many voices of technology, science, and broadcasting that converged at that particular moment in our culture to produce the moon spectacle. Such responsiveness to the shaping influences of our verbal environment is what we want the word "classic" to suggest.

A word about the introduction to each section. A full survey outlining the history of the various forms of printed media that make up our categories would not have been practical. Also, we wanted to avoid introducing such essentially futile, if not paralyzing, questions as "Is the news truly objective?" and "Is advertising an abuse of language?" Instead, we have tried in each introduction to strike an agreeable balance between saying something general about the type of material in that section and something specific about the verbal qualities of a particular passage. Of course, no single excerpt can typify all the writing in a chapter. Yet, we have chosen to examine closely, though not at great length, those passages that we feel will conveniently clarify the relations between the distinctive features of an individual style and the kind of reader that style seems directed to. We thought that by providing models of the analytic procedure we want to encourage we would, in fact, be offering something of a consistent critical approach to what might seem a bewildering assortment of material.

Any act of composition presupposes an audience. To read a "text" attentively is to discover something specific about the characteristics of the people it is intended to appeal to—their interests and the ways of talking they can respond to most readily. Once we ask the question "Whom is this ad or magazine article addressed to?" we invite statements about the traits of large groups of people. Questions like this one can be best approached not from a reader's preconceived idea of what certain groups of people in America are supposed to be like but from his responsiveness to the specific ways in which a society is talked to in print. Our responses to popular writing will be the more attuned to the culture we live in the more our terms can encompass the aesthetic significance of a particular work and the bearings that significance has on our shared social experiences. In the model analysis we provide in each of our introductions, especially in the one to "Best Sellers," we try to show that it is only when we make an effort to measure the responses of the audience implicit in a specific passage—an audience, it should be noted, that very often *literally* appears in the work as spectators, witnesses, advertising models, etc.—against the quality of our own participation that we can assess more comprehensively the interactions between the various styles and audiences within a single society.

Popular forms of writing pose special challenges to traditional analytical methods. Popular writing is often, or so it would seem, so opaquely simple and ordinary that a standard critical vocabulary might come across as too labored or too imposing for the occasion. Yet, finding an appropriate tone has always been a problem even for traditional literary criticism. It would *sound* wrong to talk about Ernest Hemingway in the highly idiosyncratic critical language of Henry James' "Prefaces" or to take the same psychological approach in a discussion of Allen Ginsberg that we would take for Emily Dickinson. Writers exist for us, unless we know them in other, more personal ways, essentially in the specific qualities of their tone and idiom. This should always be our starting point. If, for example, we try to adopt a standard analytical procedure (e.g., searching for symbols) to discuss *Tarzan of the Apes,* and our method becomes too irritatingly cumbersome, that can be an occasion for testing the critical language we are working with and for re-examining the quality of our literary responses rather than concluding that Tarzan was not worth talking about in the first place.

It should be apparent from our model of analysis in each introduction that we have made an effort to avoid using a language that relies too heavily on the terminology of traditional literary criticism, a terminology that has, for the most part, evolved from allegiances and inveterate responses to only the most highly regarded forms of literature. We certainly do not mean to disqualify any of the standard critical approaches, as we trust our Rhetorical Table of Contents will amply indicate, but we want instead to encourage a lively reciprocity between the academically certified terms of serious literary criticism and the ordinary languages of our popular culture. What we hope will come out of such transactions is a resilient critical language applicable to all forms of public discourse. If we cannot adjust our critical vocabularies and find interesting ways to talk about Tarzan, or advertising, or a newspaper item, then it is doubtful we have found the most spirited ways to approach even the best things in our culture.

ADVERTISING

Advertising is a business of words.

DAVID OGILVY

WE are so accustomed to signs, posters, billboards, songs, jingles, graffiti, circulars, placards, announcements, brochures, packages, commercials, and ads in newspapers and magazines that it is difficult for any of us to imagine a world without public and personal advertisements. Ads are practically inescapable; they literally surround us. Few places are remote enough to be completely free from the appeals of advertising. Suppose we picture ourselves on a secluded tropical beach experiencing a dazzling sunset. Even if we have not noticed any discarded packaging or unobtrusively placed signs, we must still recognize the alluring tropical scene itself as one continually promoted by airlines and travel agencies in newspapers, in magazines, and especially on decorative posters. Efforts to escape advertising, to ''discover'' landscapes removed from the intrusions of advertisements may be merely another way of participating in the kind of world advertisements typically endorse. No place, no object, no life style, and certainly no way of talking can be totally exempt from commercialized public notice. The world we live in is an advertised world.

The business of advertising is to invent methods of addressing massive audiences in a language designed to be easily accessible and immediately persuasive. No advertising agency wants to put out an ad that is not clear and convincing to millions of people. But the agencies, though they would agree that ads should be written to sell products, disagree when it comes down to the most effective methods of doing so. Over the years, advertising firms have developed among themselves a variety of distinctive styles based on their understanding of the different kinds of audiences they want to reach. No two agencies would handle the same product identically. To people for whom advertising is an exacting discipline and a highly competitive profession, an ad is much more than a sophisticated sales pitch, an attractive verbal and visual device to serve manufacturers. In fact, for those who examine ads critically or professionally, products may very well be no more than merely points of departure. Ads often outlive their products, and in the case of early advertisements for products that are no longer available, we cannot help but consider the advertisement independently of our responses to those products. The point of examining ads apart from their announced subjects is not that we ignore the product completely, but that we try to see the product only as it is talked about and portrayed in the full context of the ad. Certainly, it is not necessary to have tried a particular product to be able to appreciate the technique and design used in its advertisement.

The emphasis of the following section is on the advertisements themselves, not the commodities they promote. To illustrate a variety of American advertising strategies and styles, we have included advertisements from the late nineteenth century to the present. Some ads have been grouped according to their products, that is, there are a number of ads regarding smoking, transportation, cosmetics, and fashions. This arrangement will allow you to observe some of the ways both advertisements and audiences have changed over the past one hundred years. Many of these ads have been selected because they represent important developments in advertising methodology. But our intentions are not exclusively historical. Other ads were chosen to display significant aspects of standard advertising procedures. We wanted to introduce advertisements that were both interesting and typical. Nearly all the ads we reprint have achieved a good deal of professional recognition. Many have been frequently singled out as examples of some of the finest copy in the history of American advertising.

A few of the early ads may strike you as unimaginative and typographically crude. They appeared in newspapers and magazines before printing innovations and marketing research radically altered advertising techniques. Yet, given their frequent inelegance, naïveté, and commandeering tones, many early ads remind us how advertisers have persistently played on certain themes despite noticeable changes in decorum, style, and methods of persuasion. Perhaps the early ads only put very bluntly the promises and claims that later on would be more politely disguised. Consider the advertisement for Madame Rowley's Toilet Mask that first appeared in 1887. This ad makes no attempt to introduce its product in a pleasing manner. The advantages of using the toilet mask are delivered in a decisively impersonal and mechanically repetitive fashion. No effort was spent on setting up an attractive backdrop or atmosphere. The only graphic detail we are allowed is the sketch of the curious toilet device in operation, appearing ingenuously at the center of an imposingly designed typographical layout.

If the advertisement for Madame Rowley's Toilet Mask makes little attempt to attract visually, neither does it try very hard to gratify its audience verbally. Even the name of the product is deliberately and unappealingly direct—no charming or engaging brand name suggests that the mask is anything more than what it announces itself to be. The copywriter uses none of the enticing and intimately sensuous language that advertisers so often turned to later when addressing women on matters of personal hygiene and beauty. Realizing that Madame Rowley's beauty apparatus was almost embarrassingly unstylish, the writer must have decided he could promote his client's product best by sounding unadornedly legalistic and scientific. While the copywriter assumes that facial beauty is desirable, he restricts his copy to "claims," "grounds," and "proofs" of the toilet mask's effectiveness, instead of extolling the advantages of a blemish free, "cover girl" complexion. Flattering metaphors that would describe the product or its results more sensitively are avoided, apparently so as not to call into question the speaker's assertions. Only once does the idiom anticipate the language of modern cosmetic advertisements. Facial blemishes are said to "vanish from the skin, leaving it soft, clear, brilliant, and beautiful." Future copywriters would capitalize on words, like "vanish," that suggest magical and instantaneous remedies. Later ads for skin care would also focus more directly on the personal and social advantages of having a "soft, clear, brilliant, and beautiful" complexion. But in Madame Rowley's day, beauty in itself had not yet become an advertising commodity.

Apparently, Madame Rowley's Toilet Mask did not put the cosmetic industry out of business. As early as 1912, we find an advertisement for make-up using what has since become a familiar merchandising tactic. The claims made by Madame Rowley's copywriter stopped at a "brilliant" complexion. The ad promised women nothing more than that. But for the writer of the Pompeian Massage Cream copy, a blemish-free countenance was not all his product could supply. The Pompeian ad is one of the first ads for women to promise along with its product's "beautifying" benefits, the additional advantages of marital love and social acceptance. A beautiful complexion, the ad writer suggests, means little by itself. At the heart of the Pompeian ad lies one of the most important developments in the history of advertising technique—the realization that "grounds" and "claims" restricted to the product alone will not always sell the goods. Since the Pompeian ad, copywriters have concentrated more and more on an audience's psychological needs, its attitudes, and anxieties. In the Pompeian ad, the writer promotes not only an effective way to check the wrinkles and blemishes he poetically calls "Time's

MADAME ROWLEY'S TOILET MASK.

TOILET MASK

OR

FACE GLOVE.

TOILET MASK

OR

FACE GLOVE.

The following are the claims made for Madame Rowley's Toilet Mask, and the grounds on which it is recommended to ladies for Beautifying, Bleaching, and Preserving the Complexion:

First—The **Mask** is **Soft** and **Flexible** in form, and can be **Easily Applied** and **Worn** without **Discomfort** or **Inconvenience.**

Second—It is durable, and does not dissolve or come asunder, but holds its original mask shape.

Third—It has been **Analyzed** by **Eminent Scientists** and **Chemical Experts**, and pronounced **Perfectly Pure and Harmless.**

Fourth—With ordinary care the **Mask** will **last for years**, and its **VALUABLE PROPERTIES Never Become Impaired.**

Fifth—The **Mask** is protected by letters patent, and is the **only Genuine** article of the kind.

Sixth—It is Recommended by **Eminent Physicians** and **Scientific Men** as a **SUBSTITUTE FOR INJURIOUS COSMETICS.**

Seventh—The **Mask** is a **Natural Beautifier**, for **Bleaching** and **Preserving the Skin and Removing Complexional Imperfections.**

Eighth—Its use cannot be detected by the closest scrutiny, and it may be worn with **perfect privacy**, if desired.

Ninth—The **Mask** is sold at a moderate price, and is to be PURCHASED BUT ONCE.

Tenth—Hundreds of dollars uselessly expended for cosmetics, lotions, and like preparations, may be saved its possessor.

Eleventh—**Ladies** in every section of the country are using the **Mask** with gratifying results.

Twelfth—It is safe, simple, cleanly, and effective for beautifying purposes, and never injures the most delicate skin.

Thirteenth—While it is intended that the **Mask** should be **Worn During Sleep**, it may be applied WITH EQUALLY GOOD RESULTS at **any time** to suit the convenience of the wearer.

The Toilet Mask (or Face Glove) in position to the face.

TO BE WORN THREE TIMES IN THE WEEK

Fourteenth—The **Mask** has received the testimony of well-known society and professional ladies, who proclaim it to be the greatest discovery for beautifying purposes ever vouchsafed to womankind.

COMPLEXION BLEMISHES

May be hidden imperfectly by cosmetics and powders, but can only be removed permanently by the Toilet Mask. By its use every kind of spots, impurities, roughness, etc., vanish from the skin, leaving it soft, clear, brilliant, and beautiful. It is harmless, costs little, and saves its user money. It prevents and removes wrinkles, and is both a complexion preserver and beautifier. Famous Society Ladies, actresses, belles, etc., use it.

VALUABLE ILLUSTRATED TREATISE, WITH PROOFS AND PARTICULARS.

—MAILED FREE BY—

TOILET MASK

OR

FACE GLOVE.

THE TOILET MASK COMPANY,

Send for Descriptive Treatise.

1164 BROADWAY,

Send for Descriptive Treatise.

NEW YORK.

☞ Mention this paper when you Write.

TOILET MASK

OR

FACE GLOVE.

[1887]

4

"Mother, here she is".

Of all moments the most trying—when the son brings *her* to his mother, of all critics the most exacting. Mother-love causes her to look with penetrating glance, almost *trying* to find flaws. No quality of beauty so serves to win an older woman as a skin smooth, fresh and healthy *in a natural way*, as easily provided by

POMPEIAN MASSAGE CREAM

Where artificial beautifiers—cosmetics and rouges—would only antagonize; and an uncared-for, pallid, wrinkled skin prove a negative influence—the Pompeian complexion immediately wins the mother, as it does in every other instance in social or business life.

You can have a beautiful complexion—

that greatest aid to woman's power and influence. A short use of Pompeian will surprise you and your friends. It will improve even the best complexion, and retain beauty and youthful appearance against Time's ravages.

"Don't *envy* a good complexion; use Pompeian and *have* one."

Pompeian is not a "cold" or "grease" cream, nor a rouge or cosmetic, and positively can not grow hair on the face. Pompeian simply affords a natural means toward a complete cleanliness of the facial pores. And in pores that are "Pompeian clean" lies skin health.

TRIAL JAR

sent for 6c (stamps or coin). Find out for yourself, now, why Pompeian is used and prized in a million homes where the value of a clear, fresh, youthful skin is appreciated. Clip coupon now.

All dealers 50c, 75c, $1

[1912]

ravages'' but also adopts an attitude toward the nature and effects of feminine appeal: ''a beautiful complexion—that greatest aid to woman's power and influence.'' This comment, obviously made by a male copywriter, is offered after we have been told that a ''Pompeian complexion'' will win over any man's mother, ''as it does in every other instance in social or business life.'' The ad inadvertently acknowledges that beauty is only skin deep, after all. Deeper than a woman's worry about facial blemishes, the copywriter intimates, is her terror of not being loved and approved.

Unlike Madame Rowley's mask, the Pompeian Massage Cream does not appear at the center of its advertisement. To be sure, the brand name (chosen to suggest the shade of red found on the walls of the ''preserved'' ancient city of Pompeii) has been allowed central prominence, and the illustration of the product is barely squeezed into the bottom left corner of the ad. More important than the actual cream is the rendition of the familiar dramatic situation in which a young lady is first introduced to the wary scrutiny of her suitor's mother: ''Of all the moments the most trying—the son brings *her* to his mother, of all critics the most exacting.'' With a tone and diction borrowed from the melodramatic superlatives of soap opera and best-selling fiction, the copywriter maintains that with so much at stake a young woman cannot risk using a cosmetic that would make her look vulgar and unacceptable to such an ''exacting'' critic as a potential mother-in-law. The writer offers, in addition, the ultimate emotional reassurance that the massage cream ''positively can not grow hair on the face.'' The ad leaves little doubt, then, that the ''beautiful complexion'' its product guarantees is not what is finally being promoted. The clear complexion, in this case, ultimately stands for something else, as it did not in the ad for Madame Rowley's Toilet Mask. Pompeian Massage Cream, not of much consequence in itself, merely personifies the real ''product'' of the ad—a natural, artless appearance that will ensure unqualified social approval.

Cosmetic advertisements, for the most part, avoid the slightest allusion to artificiality. Madame Rowley's Toilet Mask, which must have looked like an odd contrivance even in its own time, was nevertheless introduced as a ''natural beautifier.'' To bring home a girl whose make-up looked artificial was, to the copy writer for Pompeian Massage Cream at least, an undeserving affront to American motherhood. In our final example of cosmetic advertising, the ad for Yardley's Next to Nature, the entire copy depends on the single notion that make-up must allow a woman to appear *natural,* to look, that is, as if she were not wearing any cosmetic at all. Though the ad does not associate its product with a comforting aura of love and matrimony, like the Pompeian ad, it still assumes that a fine complexion is not an end in itself but a means of possessing a particular kind of ''look.'' Throughout the Next to Nature ad, the copywriter insists on the product's naturalness. The brand itself bears, as Pompeian did not, more than a loose metaphorical relationship to the product: the name suggests not only that the cosmetic formula is literally close to Nature but also that the product's use will engender an appearance that will be the next best thing to natural beauty. Since Madame Rowley's time, advertisers have discovered that probably no word of copy works so effectively as ''natural.'' The copywriter for Next to Nature appropriately avoids gimmicks and artificiality by adopting a casual manner of speaking and by offering a photograph of a demure and innocent looking woman as evidence of his product's ''transparent'' purity. Apparently, he does not feel that he need convince us of his honesty by citing indisputable ''claims'' and

Of all the make-ups on earth, only one is called Next to Nature.™

One of the freshest things that's happened to girls' faces since sunshine and country air: Yardley's Next to Nature Liquid Make-up.

It's made with vitamin A to moisturize, the purest of waters, and all natural colorings. They're blended into a formula so sheer, you can use it generously and still look like a natural beauty.

Try Next to Nature blushers and new Transparent Pressed Powder too.

Because when it comes to giving you the fresh, wholesome look—there's nobody on earth like Yardley.

yardley

How to make the most of what you have.

©1973, Yardley of London, Inc.

[1973]

"grounds" nor does he bank on his audience's fear of social or parental disapproval. He is confident that his readers will need no more than his own sincere
tone to be persuaded that by using Next to Nature they can have "the fresh,
wholesome look" of natural beauty.

These three cosmetic advertisements furnish a brief record of some of the major
developments of American advertising. A glance at the ads demonstrates vividly
the changes in the layout of advertisements brought about by advances in photography and graphic design. The space apportioned for illustration increases substantially. We move from the cameo-like sketch of the figure in the toilet mask to
the poster-like photograph of an attractive woman which dominates the Next to
Nature advertisement and also conveniently eliminates the copywriter's need to
write a lengthy description of what the product can do. The size of the headlines
increases; the style becomes more informal. The headline for Madame Rowley's
Toilet Mask is intended to do no more than name the product explicitly. In the
Pompeian ad, however, there are actually two headlines. One simply mentions
the product by name, while the other invites a reader's response to a fictional
scene. In the Next to Nature ad, after the reader is introduced directly to the brand
name and the special quality of the product, she is then talked to marginally in a
perky and congenial voice. Few ads in Madame Rowley's day would have taken
the liberty of speaking to their readers in such a casual and ingratiating fashion.
Neither would a nineteenth-century copywriter have violated grammatical decorum by writing the kind of breezy and fragmented sentences that characterize
the brisk style of the Next to Nature copy. Quite clearly, the writing in the Next
to Nature ad is meant to sound as natural, relaxed, and sincere as the copywriter
imagines his audience would like to talk and behave. By examining these advertisements, then, we are introduced not only to three markedly different styles of
writing but also to three noticeably different attitudes toward female beauty.

Even though advertisements represent some of the most expensive and calculated acts of composition in America, the audiences they are directed to seldom
attend to them analytically. No one would deny that ads exert tremendous economic and social pressures. (See, for example, the essays by Marshall McLuhan
in Advertising and Vance Packard in Best Sellers.) Yet, few people, aside from
those in the advertising profession, seldom bother to ask how or why a particular
advertisement happened to be written and designed in a certain way (for one
adman's explanation, see Ron Holland's essay "Why I Wrote This Ad This Way"
in this section). The public generally reacts to advertisements exactly the way
advertising agencies would like them to—as consumers, not critics. Assuming,
however, that "advertising is a business of *words,*" not necessarily of products,
we have included examples of successful copy to invite you to consider more
carefully *how* the language and strategies of advertisements affect the ways we
talk and think. Advertisements constitute a lively repository of American vocabulary, idiom, metaphor, and style, in short a fairly reliable index of the state of
public discourse. They create the one verbal environment in which we all participate, willingly or unwillingly.

WHAT SORT OF MAN READS PLAYBOY?

He's his own man. An individualist. And he can afford to express himself with style—in everything
from the girls he dates to the way he dresses. Facts: PLAYBOY is read by nearly 5,000,000 men
in U. S. households with incomes of $10,000 and over. And when they get ready to buy, they look to
the new looks in PLAYBOY. Which is why it's first among all magazines in apparel advertising revenue. PLAYBOY can work miracles for your ad appearance, too. (Sources: *1968 Simmons* and *P.I.B.*)

New York · Chicago · Detroit · Los Angeles · San Francisco · Atlanta · London · Tokyo

[1969]

PRINT MEDIA

This ad as well as those for all the ads in the Print Media section are addressed to
the advertising community. They represent the publications' own view of their
readership and are designed to attract ads for products suitable to that presumed
audience.

"I wish there were 70 minutes in every hour, 25 hours in every day and 8 days in every week."

—John Bradley Springer
Architect

"When I give, it's usually 110% of myself. And I get a lot back for it."

"I see myself as an active participant in life. I've discovered that the more I participate, even if it means taking risks, the more I get out of each day. This joy I get in my work and personal life has created an expansion of my energy and time that's greater than I ever considered possible. The results are incredible.

"My career is on the threshold of skyrocketing. I can feel it. I know it. I'm good. I'm out there doing it, working harder than ever.

"I'm playing harder than ever, too. Until last year, I hadn't climbed a mountain since the Sierra Nevada back when I was in high school. Now I'm climbing again. The difference is that now I can afford the air ticket to get to the mountain.

"I'm climbing the mountain differently, too. Back then, it was always the challenge. How far could we go in a day? Invariably, we'd complete in four days what we set out to do in a week. Then we'd sit around twiddling our thumbs for three days. Now I take my time and enjoy every minute of the climb. The experience of getting there is more important than reaching the top.

"It's the same with skiing, too. Now I'm just enjoying it and, I must say, my skiing has improved tremendously.

"Instead of being in the future or clinging to the past, I'm finding incredible excitement by participating in what I'm doing right now. For me, reality is a better place to be than fantasy.

"How does PLAYBOY today fit where I am today? Very well. Amazingly well, now that I think about it.

It's as though they knew exactly where I've been and where I am, because it's exactly where they were and where they are."

Right you are, Brad Springer. We've stayed with you all the way. And as you've changed, we've changed. That's why you and millions of men like you read PLAYBOY every month. You're the most vital, alive group of young men to come down the pike in a long time—the most vibrant group of prospects American business has been blessed with since the post–World War II boom.

And American business can reach more of you for their advertising dollar in PLAYBOY than in any other men's magazine, newsweekly or sportsweekly.

81% more male readers for their dollar than in *Time*.

50% more for their dollar than in *Newsweek*.

50% more for their dollar than in *Sports Illustrated*.

The Playboy reader.
His lust is for life.

Source: TGI, Spring 1977, Playboy. © 1977, Playboy.

9

[1977]

"Roger reads Esquire"

Photographed by Francesco Scavullo

Mrs. Roger Davis

"He calls it the only 'men's lib' magazine. Meaning, he says, 'Esquire recognizes the fact that man has a mind as well as a body.' I think that's kind of well put, but then Roger was an English major at Columbia ('61) and taught at UCLA before he became an actor. He has a way of saying things that I find very apt. I think that's one of the main reasons I became Mrs. Roger Davis. Most of the women Roger meets are slightly bowled over by his good looks and the fact that he's a TV star. (Alias Smith & Jones' Hannibal Hayes). But I loved him for his originality and style. He's the only man I know who can get high on 18th century literature in the evening and spend the morning watching a boxer he sponsors work out in the gym. Or, go see how his racehorse, 'Royal Bupers' does at the track with a copy of Robert Frost under his arm. He's that way about places, too. So we live in Beverly Hills and New York — and we'd like to have a home in Rome — Roger's favorite city in Europe. But wherever we are — life is interesting — because my husband is an interesting man."

The Esquire Man: He's got a sense of style.

[1972]

10

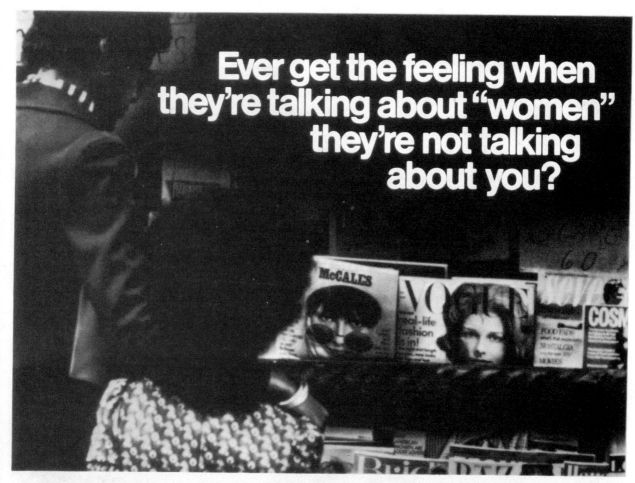

Ever get the feeling when they're talking about "women" they're not talking about you?

Isn't it about time there was a magazine to talk about you, and your life—to tell you what's going down in *your* world and how to deal with it in *your* way?

If you've been waiting, hoping, praying and futilely looking for such a magazine . . . then, look no more. It's finally here.

Black . . . Beautiful . . . and, all yours!

It's ESSENCE—a new and unique magazine created especially for Black women.

ESSENCE talks about things that concern you. It deals with what Black women want, what they are, and what they can be. It's all about your kind of fashion, makeup, home-making, child-raising—and full of pages and pages of prose and poetry to expand your mind (maybe even blow it sometimes). But, most of all, it's an experience. A totally Black Experience.

And, what Black woman's experience is complete without her man? There are articles and features, even fashions, just meant to be shared with your man. ESSENCE opens up a whole new world of ideas and insights for him, too—revealing not only your needs and desires, but showing *him* things about himself you know he should

know, but could never find in any other magazine. And, if your children are mature enough for grownup magazines, reading ESSENCE will bring them a little closer to their own reality, proudly.

Here are just a few recent features.
- Eleanor Holmes Norton—Involved and Committed
- James Baldwin—On Leaving America
- Jesse Jackson—On Politics and Economics
- Alyce Gullattee—On Black Sensuality
- The Black Woman: A Figure in World History

You can't afford to miss another issue. With articles like these, appearing every month, ESSENCE is truly a Black

woman's joy, and a family necessity.

Wouldn't it be nice to have ESSENCE talking about you—to you, and your family, every month? You can. A whole year for only $5, at our special Charter Subscriber rate. Send in the coupon today and begin receiving the first quality magazine ever created *just for you.* Your very own ESSENCE.

[1973]

Should you ever lie? Of
course! People who go
around telling the truth
all the time are a <u>menace</u>.
You have to say a hostess'
quiche is delicious even
when it's soggy and that
somebody's new dress is
pretty even when it's terrible. And sometimes you
have to lie to a man.
Example: If you don't
want to go out with him
anymore, you have to say
there's somebody else in
your life you're serious
about and you can't see
two men at the same time.
My favorite magazine says
you can do a little "social
lying" and still keep your
integrity...just be sure
you keep the facts
straight in your <u>heart</u>.
I love that magazine.
I guess you could say I'm
That COSMOPOLITAN Girl.

Photographed by Francesco Scavullo

If you want to reach me you'll find me reading
COSMOPOLITAN

"The soaps are like Big Macs...a lot of people who won't admit it eat them up."

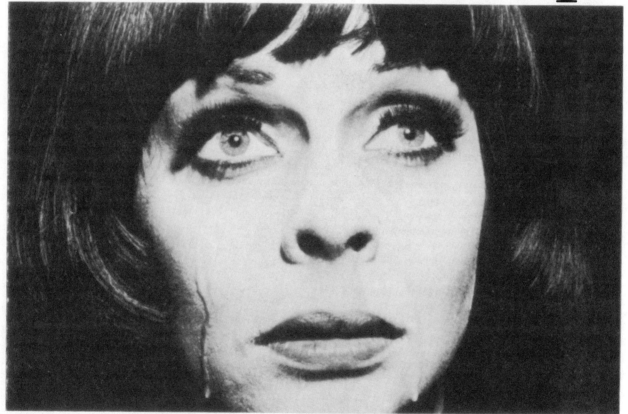

"The symbiosis between audience and show makes soap opera unique, the most powerful entertainment on or off television."

Academic amnesia, vicarious VD, hypothetical hysterectomies: the world of TV soap opera. But TIME readers are among the least avid watchers of daytime television. Why was TIME inspired to devote a cover story to TV soap opera?

Because TIME readers are also insatiably curious. TIME probed the hypnotic appeal

of the soaps, found a whole subculture, discovered the iron hand behind the wet handkerchief. And in so doing, TIME demonstrates once again the rewards of analyzing seriously what seems on the surface to be egregious frivolity.

You know what TIME does. And reading it every week reminds you how well.

[1976]

Scoop McClain?
He doesn't work here anymore.

You remember Scoop McClain—sarcastic and swaggering, a tough guy with a press card in his hat who liked pretty girls and whiskey and telling the world to go to hell. He was something else, Scoop was: a star reporter, streetwise and cynical, but with a heart of gold. He never let the facts get in the way of a good story.

Scoop graduated from the school of hard knocks. He typed with one finger, got news tips from bookies and barmaids and yelled "STOP THE PRESS!" with every fresh exposé. Murder was his specialty, but he fought City Hall, too, and saved widows from eviction. He never forgot a friend and he never told a lie—except to get a story. So here's to Scoop McClain; they don't make 'em like that anymore.

And, of course, they never did. That movie stereotype of American newspaper reporters is part of our folklore; it never had much to do with reality. But there's no question that journalism and the people who practice it have changed over the years.

Today, our reporters and editors come from universities with degrees in economics and sociology, law and public administration, literature and even medicine. Nobody specializes in murder anymore; it's labor and international affairs. politics and education, science and religion. Our exposés take more than a couple of phone calls: months of work by teams of investigators who are more likely to ask help from a computer than a bookie. Our star reporters are streetwise still—but lots smarter than Scoop ever was. They have to be.

Some of the best reporters in the country work for Knight-Ridder newspapers. We're proud of them.

Philadelphia Inquirer • Philadelphia Daily News
Detroit Free Press • Miami Herald
St. Paul Dispatch • St. Paul Pioneer Press
Charlotte Observer • Charlotte News
San Jose Mercury • San Jose News • Wichita Eagle
Wichita Beacon • Akron Beacon Journal
Long Beach Press-Telegram • Long Beach Independent
Lexington Herald • Lexington Leader
Gary Post-Tribune • Duluth News-Tribune
Duluth Herald • Macon Telegraph • Macon News
Columbus Enquirer • Columbus Ledger
Pasadena Star-News • Tallahassee Democrat
Grand Forks Herald • Journal of Commerce
Bradenton Herald • Boulder Daily Camera
Aberdeen American News • Boca Raton News

Knight-Ridder Newspapers

[1977]

14

Her habit of measuring time in terms of dollars gives the woman in business keen insight into the true value of a Ford closed car for her personal use.

This car enables her to conserve minutes, to expedite her affairs, to widen the scope of her activities. Its low first cost, long life and inexpensive operation and upkeep convince her that it is a sound investment value.

And it is such a pleasant car to drive that it transforms the business call which might be an interruption into an enjoyable episode of her busy day.

TUDOR SEDAN, $590   FORDOR SEDAN, $685   COUPE, $525   (All prices f. o. b. Detroit)

Ford

CLOSED CARS

Nagging wives

An eminent Judge recently said that nagging wives lead to more divorces than unfaithful wives, extravagant wives, and "in-laws."

S**HE IS A GOOD LITTLE WOMAN**—and she knows it.

She can hold her head up anywhere—and she does.

She keeps a clean house. She is devoted to her children. She loves her husband—and he loves her.

Life for them should be one sweet song. And it isn't.

Every day is marred by this, or that, or the other thing. Nothing serious. Nothing really wrong.

But she's excitable, and nervous, and tired. And it's remarkable how annoying any little thing can be when one is excitable, and nervous, and tired.

It's remarkable how all these exasperating things are somebody else's fault.

She just *has* to talk about them—to tell the other person they are his fault. So she talks, and talks, and talks.

And sooner or later there is a "scene." And out of many "scenes" there is sometimes a divorce. Tragedy!

* * * *

Women have particularly sensitive nervous systems. They are born that way. Their place in the scheme of things necessitates a highly organized nervous system.

This feminine nervous system is wonderful if it's let alone. But stimulate it a little, and it reacts a lot.

It ceases to be a nervous system and becomes "nerves."

Caffein is perhaps the most widely used stimulant that acts on the nerves. It excites them.

And excited nerves turn trifling annoyances into tragedies. Excited nerves turn wives into nagging wives!

You can avoid caffein so readily! People in millions of homes never use it. And they give up nothing. They still enjoy a delicious hot drink at mealtime.

They use Postum—a drink made of whole wheat and bran. It contains no trace of any stimulant. It has a wonderful flavor. It is easier to prepare, and it costs less.

It is difficult enough for anyone to remain well poised, and calm, and serene, these nervous days. It is particularly difficult in the face of all the exacting problems and crowding cares that are inseparable from the running of a household. Isn't it shortsighted to add to the confusion, by taking into the system an artificial stimulant?

Wives and mothers everywhere are thanking their lucky stars for the thirty-day test of Postum—a test through which they learned how easy and desirable it is to bar caffein from the diet. You make this test, too! Use Postum for thirty days. Judge how much better you look—how much better you feel. *Then* decide!

Carrie Blanchard, famous food demonstrator, makes you this special offer.

Carrie Blanchard's Offer

"Let me give you one week's supply of Postum, free, to start you on the thirty-day test. Carry the test through for a full thirty days, and check results.

"I will also send my personal directions for preparing Postum, both for yourself and, with hot milk, for children. Mothers are enthusiastic about this new drink for the small members of the family.

"If you wish to begin immediately, you can get Postum at your grocer's. It costs only one-half cent a cup.

"For one week's free supply, send me your name and address, and indicate whether you prefer Instant Postum, made instantly in the cup with boiling water or hot (*not boiled*) milk, or Postum Cereal, the kind you boil."

MAIL THIS COUPON NOW!

Postum is one of the Post Health Products, which include also Grape-Nuts, Post Toasties (Double-thick Corn Flakes), Post's Bran Flakes and Post's Bran Chocolate. Your grocer sells Postum in two forms. Instant Postum, made in the cup by adding boiling water, is one of the easiest drinks in the world to prepare. Postum Cereal is also easy to make, but should be boiled 20 minutes.

© 1926, P. C. Co.

[1926]

A woman's instinct tells her

A woman's natural instinct warns her to be on her guard against anything which might detract from her feminine charm.

Perspiration itself cannot be helped—it is one of nature's ways of ridding the body of waste matter. But the unpleasant *odor* of perspiration!—a woman's instinct tells her it must be carefully avoided.

"Mum" is the word! It is so simple to use "Mum", the snow-white cream deodorant. A touch to the underarm, and wherever perspiration is closely confined, assures you that no matter how much you may perspire throughout the day and evening, there can be no unpleasant, unfeminine odor to detract from your charm.

The use of "Mum" is not mere fastidiousness. It is a matter of good breeding and common-sense.

"Mum" is entirely safe to skin and clothing. It can be used immediately after removing superfluous hair. Thousands of women use "Mum" regularly with the sanitary napkin—proof of its effectiveness and entire safety.

Read the pamphlet that comes with every jar. It tells more about the important uses of "Mum" and of our other products.

"Mum" is 25c and 50c at stores. Or see Special Offer.

IMPORTANT: There is an important use of "Mum" that you may not have heard of. "Mum" used on the feet completely neutralizes the *acids* of perspiration, thus greatly lengthening the life of silk stockings. This is well worth learning about. It is fully described in the new pamphlet packed in every jar of "Mum".

"Mum" *is the word!*

17

[1926]

How to Bring Up a Young Daughter

Tips from a teen-ager's smart mama!

Lucy's mother has big dreams for Lucy.

She wants her 13-year-old daughter to have the fun of being pretty and popular right now. And she knows (though Lucy might say "Oh, Moth-errr!" at the thought) that this just leads up to the day Lucy will leave to start a home of her own.

In reading how Lucy's Mother steers her daughter toward a happier life—both now and later—you may run across the name SWAN Soap here and there.

If you do—well, using SWAN is one of the little tricks of know-how that make the bigger things work out better!

1. **Learning to be a smart shopper.** Mother lets Lucy do lots of the family shopping. So Lucy learns to compare. And know a thrifty value when she sees it. Lucy's list doesn't say "soap"—it says SWAN—4 swell soaps in 1!

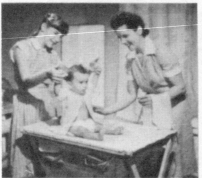

2. **Getting used to handling babies.** Lucy learns on Baby Sis. Feeds her, bathes her, the works. Every bath's a SWAN bath—doctor's orders. For SWAN's pure and mild as fine castiles—agrees with delicate baby skin.

3. **Showing Lucy short cuts on household chores.** Dishwashing's a pest with slow, lazy suds; a hand-ruiner with strong soaps. But Lucy finds dish-doing a breeze with mild, quick-sudsing SWAN!

4. **Blossoming into beauty.** "Complexion is everything," says Lucy's Mother. And the doctors say "Soap-and-water!" for teen-agers. So it's gentle SWAN for Lucy—it takes the bow for Lucy's glowing skin!

5. **Good grooming becomes second nature.** A daily bath—for garden-fresh sweetness. No need to coax Lucy to take her daily Swanning. She feels like a movie queen among SWAN's snow-cloud suds!

6. **Choosing her own wardrobe.** Mother lets Lucy buy some of her clothes—with just a word of advice. And because pretty clothes must be *clean*—Lucy tubs everything in safe SWAN suds! How color-fresh SWAN keeps them!

"Swan is Four Swell Soaps in One!"

[1942]

HER SECRET CAN BE YOURS. You probably know a girl like this. You see faces light as she enters a room . . . note the admiring glances of men. Sometimes you may wonder what is the secret of her appeal.

She's not a beauty. Nice eyes, filled with warmth and animation. A clear, fresh skin. Hair brushed to brightness—to satin smoothness.

Her suit is simple . . . though you notice that it's neatly pressed and settled snugly on her trim shoulders. A blouse of dazzling white—

You grope for phrases to define her appeal . . . and suddenly her secret comes to you. Of course! It's freshness, complete and all pervading. The *freshness* of her costume. The *freshness* of her person.

You know she'd never be guilty of any small, careless neglect. You know that one of her first concerns must be her breath—a thing that only too many otherwise attractive women foolishly take for granted. *This* girl, you're sure, would no more omit Listerine than she would omit her bath. She knows, as every woman should, that a breath like Spring is one of the first require-ments of charm, the first step to Romance. And she also knows how often Listerine Antiseptic can make the breath sweeter and purer.

How About You?

You, yourself, may not know when you have halitosis (bad breath). Isn't it foolish to take chances on offending this way when Listerine Antiseptic with its amazing antiseptic effect is such a delightful precaution? Why not get in the habit of using it night and morning, and between times before meeting others you would like to have think well of you?

While some cases of bad breath are systemic, most cases, in the opinion of some noted authorities, are due to the bacterial fermen-tation of tiny food particles on mouth surfaces. Listerine Antiseptic quickly halts such fermentation and overcomes the odors produced by fermentation. Never omit Listerine from your daily toilette.

LISTERINE ANTISEPTIC *for oral hygiene*

[1942]

19

Should a gentleman offer a Tiparillo to a lab technician?

Behind that pocket of pencils beats the heart of a digital computer. This girl has already cross-indexed Tiparillo® as a cigar with a slim, elegant shape and neat, white tip.

She knows that there are two kinds. Regular Tiparillo, for a mild smoke. Or new Tiparillo M with menthol, for a cold smoke.

She knows. She's programmed.

And she's ready.

But how about you? Which Tiparillo are you going to offer? Or are you just going to stand there and stare at her pencils?

When she gave in to practicality, she didn't give up her individuality.

The first baby moved her to the suburbs. The second one moved her out of her beloved sports car. But not into something square. In fact, into something rather well-rounded. The wide stance AMC Pacer Wagon.

Because a woman who knows anything about cars knows that wide is wonderful. The Pacer Wagon's extra width makes it extra efficient. So you get large size room and comfort in a sensibly sized car. And something even more important, extra stability, to make it ride and handle like a much larger car.

And she doesn't mind that the Pacer Wagon's unique wide design makes it look a little different. That's the way a woman with her own style likes to look.

The exclusive AMC BUYER PROTECTION PLAN® : AMC will fix, or replace free, any part except tires for 12 months or 12,000 miles, whether the part is defective, or just plain wears out under normal use and service.

AMC ◢ Pacer

The room and ride Americans want. The size America needs.

[1978]

"...Guess who's the new Marketing V.P.?"

Peggy Ross. It's time.

Time for the Chase Advantage. Chase has helped a lot of successful people. And Chase knows you need more than just ordinary checking or savings to truly maximize your assets.

So how can Chase really help? To begin with, no bank can give you more imaginative and comprehensive banking than Chase can. With 4 different checking plans. And with a full range of credit and loan services. With 12 different savings plans—including plans that pay extra high interest without tying up your money for years, like our 6 month certificate of deposit, or our 90 day Nest Egg Account.

But most importantly, it's time for the professional and expert guidance you'll get from the world's most knowledgeable bank.

The Chase Advantage means all this and more. That's why, now it's time to put the Chase Advantage to work for you.

The Chase Advantage

Member F.D.I.C

22

Often a bridesmaid but never a bride

EDNA'S case was really a pathetic one. Like every woman, her primary ambition was to marry. Most of the girls of her set were married—or about to be. Yet not one possessed more grace or charm or loveliness than she.

And as her birthdays crept gradually toward that tragic thirty-mark, marriage seemed farther from her life than ever. She was often a bridesmaid but never a bride.

*   *   *

That's the insidious thing about halitosis (unpleasant breath). You, yourself, rarely know when you have it. And even your closest friends won't tell you.

Sometimes, of course, halitosis comes from some deep-seated organic disorder that requires professional advice. But usually—and fortunately—halitosis is only a local condition that yields to the regular use of Listerine as a mouth wash and gargle. It is an interesting thing that this well-known antiseptic that has been in use for years for surgical dressings, possesses these unusual properties as a breath deodorant.

It halts food fermentation in the mouth and leaves the breath sweet, fresh and clean. Not by substituting some other odor but by really removing the old one. The Listerine odor itself quickly disappears. So the systematic use of Listerine puts you on the safe and polite side.

Your druggist will supply you with Listerine. He sells lots of it. It has dozens of different uses as a safe antiseptic and has been trusted as such for a half a century. Read the interesting little booklet that comes with every bottle.
—Lambert Pharmacal Company, Saint Louis, U. S. A.

For HALITOSIS use LISTERINE

ANXIETIES

Your Five Miles of Pores

Are They Open Roads, or Closed?

END on end your millions of pores would make a pipe line five miles long. Are they *open* roads or *closed*? Are they carrying their normal traffic, or is the "closed" sign diverting it to other channels and so causing congestion and lowered vitality? In other words, are you *really* clean or only *nearly* clean?

Real cleanliness is *pore-deep* cleanliness. And pore-deep cleanliness demands a soap which will not leave behind a residue to clog the skin. For this reason more and more people everywhere are adopting

American white cleanliness which calls for *white* soap, a soap that soothes as well as invigorates, a soap which makes every pore an *open road* to health.

So, the ever-growing demand is for Fairy—*the whitest soap in the world*—soap in its purest form. In America's foremost baths, clubs and athletic institutions—*wherever cleanliness is a business*—there you will find Fairy Soap. There may be "prettier" soaps. There may be "smellier" soaps; but when it comes to honest-to-goodness, deep-down cleanliness, the call is for Fairy.

It comes clean, it looks clean, it is clean through and through, and it does a clean job.

Entrust your skin to Fairy. It works no harm—it does great good. It *more* than cleans; it helps the body *breathe*. And every *clean*-thinking man or woman knows how essential that is to well-being. Its shape is handy. It floats. It gives instantly a wealth of cleansing, quick-rinsing lather. It wears without waste to a thin wafer. It is a really-clean soap for really-clean people.

THE N.K. **FAIRBANK** COMPANY
Factories in United States and Canada

The Whitest Soap In the World—The Soap of Really-Clean People

Ritz-Carlton Hotel
Broad and Walnut Streets
Philadelphia Pa.

The N. K. Fairbank Company,
New York City.

Gentlemen:—

The choice of a soap to be used in a representative hotel is a matter of considerable importance. We have found that Fairy Soap meets the particular demands of a high-grade clientele. Its whiteness, quick-cleansing quality and gentle tonic effect on the pores contribute largely to this preference.

Yours very truly,
RITZ-CARLTON HOTEL

Director

FAIRY SOAP
HELPS THE BODY BREATHE

[1923]

Turned down again

—perhaps it's *comedones**

Not a single dance with her. How he envied the other men as they gaily whirled her round the floor! Somehow *he* was always "just too late." He suspected she was purposely declining his invitations. But never for a moment did he guess that the reason was . . . comedones.

A great many young men suffer from comedones—commonly called blackheads. Skin can't be clean-looking, fresh, wholesome, if these disfiguring formations are present.

What's more, you may not even be conscious of *comedones*. But your friends notice them. You may wonder why invitations become fewer—why friends—girls in particular—seem to avoid you. You may never guess. Perhaps it's *comedones*.

Pompeian Massage Cream helps you overcome comedones. It gives you a clean, clear, ruddy complexion. It gets into the pores where comedones form, rolls out all dirt and oily secretions, and stimulates a healthy circulation, keeping skin clean, pores open.

Try this treatment

After you shave, spread Pompeian Massage Cream generously over your face—and *rub*. Continue to rub until the cream rolls out. Note how dark the cream looks. That's the dirt that was in your pores.

No need to have a dirty skin. Don't let comedones form. Use Pompeian Massage Cream every day. It means a healthy, wholesome skin. It means more joy in living.

Use at Home after Shaving

To get full pleasure and benefit, use Pompeian Massage Cream regularly at home after shaving. Your face will feel and look like a million dollars. For sale at all drug stores.

---

*WHAT ARE COMEDONES? (pronounced Cŏm'ē-dōnes)

Dictionary definition: A small plug or mass occluding the excretory duct of a sebaceous gland, occurring frequently upon the face, especially the nose, and consisting of retained semi-liquid glandular secretion or sebum. The outer end is often dark or black, due to accumulation of dust and dirt; hence it is often called blackhead.

SEND FOR
10-DAY TRIAL TUBE

For Men!

For 10c we will send a special trial tube containing sufficient cream for many delightful massages. Positively only one trial tube to a family on this exceptional offer.

Use this coupon now.

Tear off, sign and send

The Pompeian Laboratories, Dept. A-37, Cleveland, Ohio.

Gentlemen. I enclose a dime (10c) for a special trial tube of Massage Cream.

Name...............................

Street Address.....................

City.................State...........

[1923]

Leave home.

It's scary, right?

The family drives off, leaving you hanging five on the edge of your suitcase, along with your stuffed dog, six last-minute doubts, and one of those looks you thought you'd outgrown. Boston is a big city, and at first it doesn't look very much like home. (And home, right about now, never looked better.)

Sure it's scary. But not half so scary as facing that big, complicated world without the tools to live in it.

And that's what Chamberlayne is all about. Giving you tools for life.

"Life" means more than just a job. It means understanding, appreciating, and contributing: *being* something, as well as *doing* something. While we offer you a complete range of good, practical, vocational programs (like Retailing, Interior Design, Secretarial, IBM Data Processing, and Business Administration), we also offer you a thorough grounding in the liberal arts: literature, economics, history, psychology, and all the other towering records of man's ability to think and feel.

Life also means growth. In character, as well as intellect. And if we have anything to do with it, your two years at Chamberlayne will give you the time, and the protection, to let down your hair and do some good, serious soul-searching.

But life, we're continually informed, is also social. Oh, yes.

Chamberlayne is co-educational. And apparently our being a stone's throw from the finest men's schools in the country doesn't bother most of our women, either.

In fact, Chamberlayne is in the very heart of America's college community: Boston's charming Back Bay, laced with dozens of schools and universities, museums, libraries, theaters, symphonies, art galleries — a delightful pocket of social stimulation and gentle sophistication that make Chamberlayne emphatically where it's at.

So look: we know how it is to leave home. How scary it is, how much character it takes, and how much trust you have to muster up in yourself and the college you're bound for. Plenty of girls *never* get over the hurdle.

But some do. They come to Boston, to a fine co-educational junior college, and they learn to live in this complicated world. If you have the self-reliance, the faith in yourself to think about this kind of decision, we'd be happy to help you with it. Just fill out the attached reply card and mail it to us. We'll send you a copy of our catalog, and let you know a bit more about what it would be like to make Chamberlayne your home for two years.

(And don't worry about that "lost little girl" look that sweeps over your face for the first few minutes. You can change it in two short years to a woman who's found herself.)

Chamberlayne
Junior College

[1968]

26

After I realized my Skinny Mini was skinnier than I was, I lost 75 pounds.

BEFORE: Here I am at a whopping 220 pounds. No wonder my little girl couldn't see my Frigidaire Skinny Mini behind me.

AFTER: Down to 145 pounds. I no longer overshadow my Skinny Mini.

I was a whopping two feet, two inches wide hip-wise. And my Frigidaire Skinny Mini was only two feet wide.

So, not surprisingly, my day of fate came as I was standing in front of my Skinny Mini, loading the washer with dirty clothes, and the dryer with just washed clothes.

Mary Ellen, my little three-year-old, asked, "Mommy where's the stinnie-ninnie?" She couldn't see the Skinny Mini behind me.

It's that small! Even though it's got a two-speed, two-cycle washer. With four wash and rinse temperature combinations.

Two feet wide! With three soil settings and a Flo-Through Lint Filter.

And my 120-volt Skinny Mini runs on normal house current.

The dryer even has a two-position fabric selector for all kinds of clothes...both heat and non-heat air fluff settings. It stops when the clothes are dry and buzzes to let me know it's stopped. And both the washer and dryer have Permanent Press cycles!

All this and more, and it was skinnier than me.

Six months later I could look the Skinny Mini controls right in the eye. I think I made it happy because I didn't overshadow it anymore.

F GM
MARK OF EXCELLENCE

Every Frigidaire is not a refrigerator.

[1972]

27

Don't walk when you can ride.

Presenting Another Lesson in How To Kill Yourself.

In an earlier lesson, we told you to eat, drink, be merry, and most important, to overdo it.

Now we are going to suggest that, once you've taken in all those calories, do nothing—absolutely nothing—to burn any of them off.

No matter how short the trip, don't walk when you can ride.

And if walking is out, jogging is unthinkable. Even though your doctor told you you're one of those people who could well invest in some exercise—to get your heart muscle pumping and your blood circulating.

True, you have heard it said that most children in America learn to walk by 16 months and stop walking by 16 years. But then, *you're* no child.

And, anyway, exercise is a big, fat bore.

Why Are America's Doctors Telling You This?

Well, for a long time we've been telling you how to stay alive and healthy. (In fact, about 70% of the annual budget of the American Medical Association goes to health education.) But many of you go do the opposite.

Now we figure we'll tell you how to kill yourselves. In the fervent hope that once again you'll do the exact opposite. If you do, there's every chance we'll be seeing less of you. Just for check-ups. And that's it.

Doing your bit to take care of yourself (such as exercising, but only if your doctor says it's OK) means your doctor can give everyone the best care possible. When *only* his care will do.

For a free booklet on the right kind and right amount of exercise for you, write: Box X, American Medical Association, 535 North Dearborn Street, Chicago, Illinois 60610.

America's Doctors of Medicine

(Our Best Patients Take Care of Themselves)

[1972]   28

Again She Orders —
"A Chicken Salad, Please"

FOR him she is wearing her new frock. For him she is trying to look her prettiest. If only she can impress him—make him like her—just a little.

Across the table he smiles at her, proud of her prettiness, glad to notice that others admire. And she smiles back, a bit timidly, a bit self-conscious.

What wonderful poise he has! What complete self-possession! If only *she* could be so thoroughly at ease.

She pats the folds of her new frock nervously, hoping that he will not notice how embarrassed she is, how uncomfortable. He doesn't—until the waiter comes to their table and stands, with pencil poised, to take the order.

"A chicken salad, please." She hears herself give the order as in a daze. She hears him repeat the order to the waiter, in a rather surprised tone. Why *had* she ordered that again! This was the third time she had ordered chicken salad while dining with him.

He would think she didn't know how to order a dinner. Well, did she? No. She didn't know how to pronounce those French words on the menu. And she didn't know how to use the table appointment as gracefully as she would have liked; found that she couldn't create conversation—and was actually tongue-tied; was conscious of little crudities which she just knew he must be noticing. She wasn't sure of herself, she didn't *know*. And she discovered, as we all do, that there is only one way to have complete poise and ease of manner, and that is to know definitely what to do and say on every occasion.

Are You Conscious of Your Crudities?

It is not, perhaps, so serious a fault to be unable to order a correct dinner. But it is just such little things as these that betray us—that reveal our crudities to others.

Are you sure of yourself? Do you know precisely what to do and say wherever you happen to be? Or are you always hesitant and ill at ease, never quite sure that you haven't blundered?

Every day in our contact with men and women we meet little unexpected problems of conduct. Unless we are prepared to meet them, it is inevitable that we suffer embarrassment and keen humiliation.

Etiquette is the armor that protects us from these embarrassments. It makes us aware instantly of the little crudities that are robbing us of our poise and ease. It tells us how to smooth away these crudities and achieve a manner of confidence and self-possession. It eliminates doubt and uncertainty, tells us exactly what we want to know.

There is an old proverb which says "Good manners make good mixers." We all know how true this is. No one likes to associate with a person who is self-conscious and embarrassed; whose crudities are obvious to all.

Do You Make Friends Easily?

By telling you exactly what is expected of you on all occasions, by giving you a wonderful new ease and dignity of manner, the Book of Etiquette will help make you more popular—a "better mixer." This famous two-volume set of books is the recognized social authority—is a silent social secretary in half a million homes.

Let us pretend that you have received an invitation. Would you know exactly how to acknowledge it? Would you know what sort of gift to send, what to write on the card that accompanies it? Perhaps it is an invitation to a formal wedding. Would you know what to wear? Would you know what to say to the host and hostess upon arrival?

If a Dinner Follows the Wedding—

Would you know exactly how to proceed to the dining room, when to seat yourself, how to create conversation, how to conduct yourself with ease and dignity?

Would you use a fork for your fruit salad, or a spoon? Would you cut your roll with a knife, or break it with your fingers? Would you take olives with a fork? How would you take celery—asparagus—radishes? Unless you are absolutely sure of yourself, you will be embarrassed. And embarrassment *cannot be concealed*.

Book of Etiquette Gives Lifelong Advice

Hundreds of thousands of men and women know and use the Book of Etiquette and find it increasingly helpful. Every time an occasion of importance arises—every time expert help, advice and suggestion is required—they find what they seek in the Book of Etiquette. It solves all problems, answers all questions, tells you exactly what to do, say, write and wear on every occasion.

If you want always to be sure of yourself, to have ease and poise, to avoid embarrassment and humiliation, send for the Book of Etiquette at once. Take advantage of the special bargain offer explained in the panel. Let the Book of Etiquette give you complete self-possession; let it banish the crudities that are perhaps making you self-conscious and uncomfortable when you should be thoroughly at ease.

Mail this coupon *now* while you are thinking of it. The Book of Etiquette will be sent to you in a plain carton with no identifying marks. Be among those who will take advantage of the special offer. Nelson Doubleday, Inc., Dept. 3911, Garden City, New York.

SELF-IMPROVEMENT

[1921]

[1944]

30

Keystone Press Agency photograph of the burning of the books, Berlin, May 10, 1933.

These are the books that Hitler burned

He had to.

These books riddle superstition and viciousness with *truth*.

These thoughts and theories built our democracies and broke the chains of bondage.

These words are more powerful than any Gestapo or thought police.

Here, in 54 superbly bound volumes, you'll find the wisdom of Shakespeare, Plato, Thomas Aquinas, Adam Smith, Tolstoy, Darwin and Freud. The truths of Homer, Augustine and many, many more.

No power-hungry madman could stand for long against these books. That's why Hitler burned them.

Now these Great Books can all be yours, 443 works by 74 immortal authors. Yours, in your own home. To enlighten you, console you, to help you guide your children.

The amazing Syntopicon

With Great Books you receive the two-volume Syntopicon, an *idea* index that took 8 years and over a million dollars to build. With the Syntopicon, you can trace every thought in the Great Books as easily as you look up words in your dictionary.

FREE OFFER...act now

Find out more about Great Books. It's free. Just mail in the attached post card for a profusely illustrated 16-page booklet—*free*. Do it today, no postage required. GREAT BOOKS, Dept. 142-J, 425 No. Michigan, Chicago, Illinois 60611.

GREAT BOOKS

54 superb volumes • 74 immortal authors • 443 works

[1966]

"How I slimmed down to almost nothing."

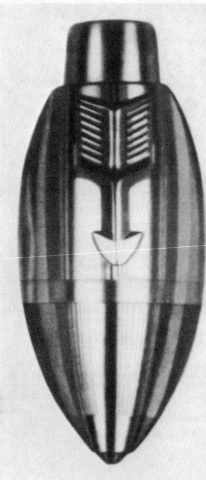

"How I felt before"

Nobody loves a fat pen.

"Look at the knockwurst," people said. "Is it a pen or a balloon?"

"Watch out for Tubby. He'll rip the pocket right off your shirt."

That's all I ever heard, day and night. "Fat pen." "Fat pen." "Fat pen."

I wept bitter ink. After all, I'm sensitive. I'm a writer, you know.

Besides, I wasn't just fat. I was fat for a reason: beneath that lumpy exterior bulged an enormous ink cartridge, that wrote more than any other pen's.

Yes, I was fat. But I also wrote longer than any other ballpoint pen. A lot longer. More than a mile longer.

I felt all mixed up. Proud and ashamed at the same time.

Writing longer meant everything to me. I would never give it up. Never.

But how I envied my pen pals. Those slim, trim jobs. So chic. So elegant.

Short on ink, maybe. But long on looks. So I went right to the top.

"Oh powerful Parker engineers," I pleaded. "Oh skillful Parker designers. Do something. Help me get into shape. Deliver me in a trimmed-down case.

"I don't care what the cost or how sharp the pain. I'll do anything. But touch not a drop of my ink supply."

Well. All the words in my big, fat ink cartridge can't describe the torture.

The pushing, the pulling, the tightening! The stretching, the pummeling, the strain!

It took forever, but they performed a miracle.

A skintight sheath!

No. Even better. *Five* skintight sheaths.

A $6 brushed stainless steel job. A $15 12k gold-filled number. A $17.50 sterling silver version. A $25 14k gold-filled dream. And a dazzling vermeil outfit at $32.50.

I can't believe it's the same me. With exactly the same ink refill.

But it *is*. At last, I'm the pen you love to touch.

Long on ink *and* long on looks.

It's changed my whole life. People want me near them. I feel needed.

I'm writing things I could never write. I'm going places I've never been and doing things I've never done.

I'm one of the beautiful pens.

I even have a jet-set name: the Parker International Classic Ball Pen.

Not bad for a fat little pen from Janesville, Wisconsin.

The Parker International
Classic Ball Pen

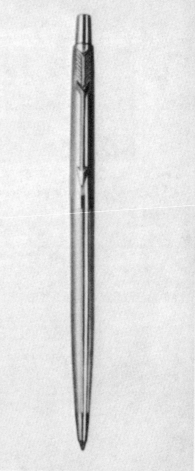

"Look at me now"

[1968]

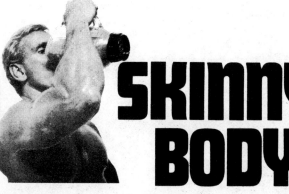

33

[1973]

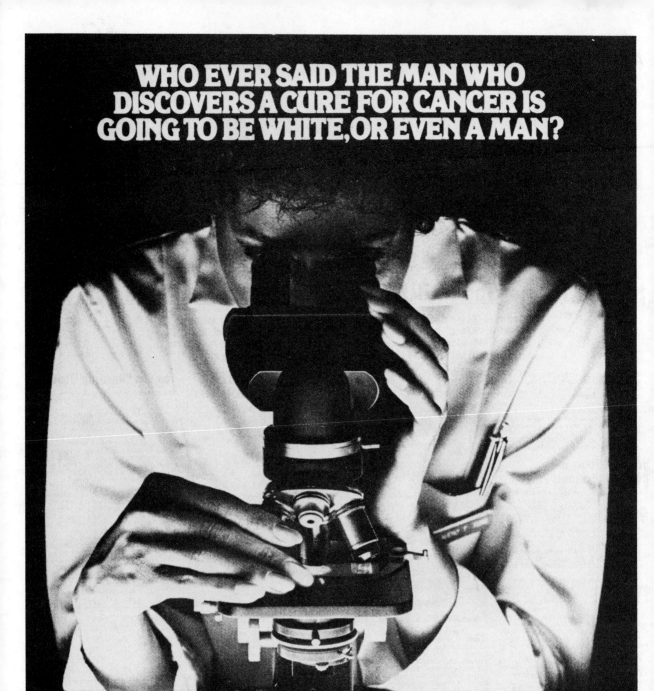

WHO EVER SAID THE MAN WHO DISCOVERS A CURE FOR CANCER IS GOING TO BE WHITE, OR EVEN A MAN?

This black woman could be America's hope...she's a United Negro College Fund graduate who could dedicate her life to finding a cure for cancer. A cure that could save thousands of lives each year. And fill every black person's heart with pride. That's why it's so important that blacks support the United Negro College Fund, 100 percent.

If she discovered the cure, in a sense, it would also be your discovery because the world would recognize it as a major black contribution.

When you give to the United Negro College Fund, you help support 41 private, predominantly black, four-year colleges and universities. Colleges that give us thousands of black graduates each year, who go on to become doctors, lawyers, accountants, engineers and scientists.

So support black education. Because black contributions help make black contributions. Send your check to the United Negro College Fund, Box Q, 500 East 62nd St., New York, N.Y. 10021. We're not asking for a handout, just a hand.

GIVE TO THE UNITED NEGRO COLLEGE FUND.
A mind is a terrible thing to waste.

"Most Automobiles are like most Men"

"They are either all right or all wrong, but seldom one or the other for long at a time."

"That's probably why they call this a Woman's Car, it's so consistent."

"Your intuition, my dear, is perfect. That's just it. You know, I used to call the last car we had, a 'Cook Four,' because it cost more than it was worth, consumed more than it earned, and was always quitting!"

"And what do you call this?"

"Oh, the Overland is like a first-rate cook — popular with the whole family! This is the first Saturday I've had this car to myself since—"

"Heavens, Helen, you went right into that mudhole!"

"Didn't jar you, did it?"

"No, not at all! But isn't it remarkable for so light a car?"

"Yes. Harry calls it a feather bed on wheels. It's some funny new spring they've invented that lets you down easy when the going's hard. How do you like the tan velour upholstery?"

"Just love it, Helen, it is so restrained. But how about gas?"

"That's restrained, too, my dear. Harry says we're averaging twenty-five miles to the gallon."

"Twenty-five miles?"

"Sounds as incredible as a woman's age, but it's true. In fact, I've only one complaint against this Overland Sedan — it's too useful!"

"Too useful?"

"Yes, too useful. So useful that it points a moral."

"For example?"

"Well, all you ever have to do with this Overland Sedan is to step on it. And that is the fate of all useful things and all useful people. Somebody is always stepping on them!"

"Helen, you talk like a Socialist."

"It's true. This little Overland Sedan is like a household drudge — always working and never through!"

"You'd better hurry, Helen, the train's in. We'll miss Harry."

"Don't worry. He'll wait. There he is now.... oh, Harry!"

"Hello, girls! Have you room for a few bundles and may a husband presume to ride home in his wife's car?"

WILLYS-OVERLAND, INC., TOLEDO, OHIO

Sedans, Coupés, Touring Cars, Roadsters

Willys Overland, Limited, Toronto, Canada   The John N. Willys Export Corp., New York

Overland

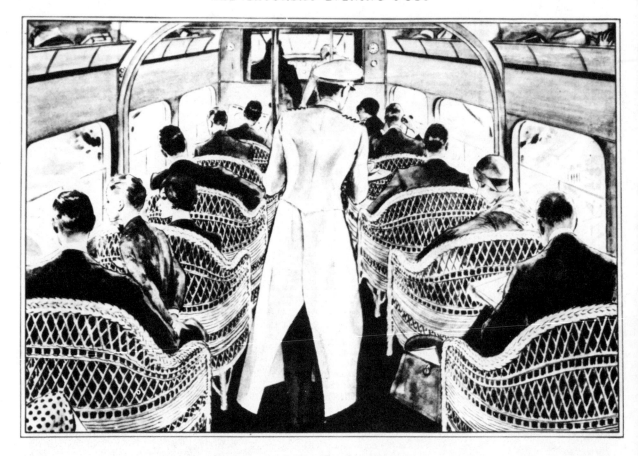

FIRST TIME UP!

You settle back in your wicker chair a little nervously as the engines roar. Then a burst of speed across the flying-field! Forty miles an hour . . . fifty-five! Someone shouts:

"Watch the wheels!"

Unless your eyes are fixed on the great balloon tires no sense perception tells when you have left the earth. There is only an astonishing feeling of stability; then comfortable relaxation as the motors are throttled down. The giant, tri-motored car moves upward on a cushioning ramp of air. . . .

Gradually you experience a sensation that is certainly one of the most extraordinary man has ever felt. You are transcending human nature. You feel immeasurably superior to the crawling beings in the miniature world immersed in silence two thousand feet below. Though ordinarily you may suffer from fear of heights, this fear does not touch you now, *for there are no lines of perspective drawing you earthward!*

Streets, monuments, buildings, vehicles and living creatures, are fractions of inches in size. Hedgerows, fences, and symmetrically plowed fields of red and brown earth form rug-like patterns, while distance gives the raw surfaces a velvety texture.

Boats, moving along a river the color of green onyx, push threads of cotton from their bows. Trains wind through the hills with lazy deliberation. Automobiles creep along ribboned roads. Sheep, cattle, horses graze heads downward in the fields, unaware that you are watching from the sky.

The air of other-worldliness that hangs over the earth below is emphasized by the fact that you are hardly aware of forward motion, *though moving twice as fast as the fastest express trains,* and it is as easy to stand poised on one foot in the cabin as on the floor of your own bedroom. Your fellow passengers move freely about, shifting the ten wicker chairs companionably, to play cards, to typewrite, to make sketches, or, gathering in groups, first on one side of the plane then on the other, to study the panorama below.

You soon accept the truth of the reported safety of these giant commercial planes. What if a motor fails? With two, the plane can continue to its destination! If two fail—the remaining motor can extend the angle of descent to cover an area almost half the size of Delaware. And if all three fail the plane has a gliding range of miles.

Ford tri-motored, all-metal planes have demonstrated railroad efficiency for over a million miles of flight, carrying mail, freight and passengers . . . in tropical regions, in arctic regions, at sea level and over the highest mountain ranges on this continent.

Events of the last twelve months have put commercial flying in America on the level of stable industries. Great businesses have accepted it as a dependable means of swift transport, cutting two-thirds off railroad time. Business men no longer think of the mere thrill of "going up"; they think rather in terms of profitable service.

In the modern business world, the dawn of each new day presents a different scene . . . new products, new competition, new markets. To meet its challenge, you must be prepared.

When the occasion comes for your first time up, it will not be to "joy-ride" in an antiquated and hazardous machine; but far more probably it will be to reach some distant meeting-place in advance of business competition!

FORD MOTOR COMPANY

[1928]

36

They'll know you've *arrived*

when you drive up in an Edsel

Step into an Edsel and you'll learn where the excitement is this year.

Other drivers spot that classic vertical grille a block away—and never fail to take a long look at this year's most exciting car.

On the open road, your Edsel is watched eagerly for its already-famous performance.

And parked in front of your home, your Edsel always gets even more attention—because it always says a lot about you. It says you chose elegant styling, luxurious comfort and such exclusive features as Edsel's famous Teletouch Drive—only shift that puts the buttons where they belong, on the steering-wheel hub.

Your Edsel also means you made a wonderful buy. For of all medium-priced cars, this one really new car is actually priced the lowest.* See your Edsel Dealer this week.

Based on comparison of suggested retail delivered prices of the Edsel Ranger and similarly equipped cars in the medium-price field.

Above: Edsel Citation 2-door Hardtop. Engine: the E-475, with 10.5 to one compression ratio, 345 hp, 475 ft.-lb. torque. Transmission: Automatic with Teletouch Drive. Suspension: Ball-joint with optional air suspension. Brakes: self-adjusting.

EDSEL DIVISION · FORD MOTOR COMPANY

1958 EDSEL

Of all medium-priced cars, the one that's really new is the lowest-priced, too!

[1958]

37

The Rolls-Royce Silver Cloud—$13,550

"At 60 miles an hour the loudest noise in this new Rolls-Royce comes from the electric clock"

What makes Rolls-Royce the best car in the world? "There is really no magic about it— it is merely patient attention to detail," says an eminent Rolls-Royce engineer.

1. "At 60 miles an hour the loudest noise comes from the electric clock," reports the Technical Editor of THE MOTOR. The silence of the engine is uncanny. Three mufflers tune out sound frequencies – acoustically.

2. Every Rolls-Royce engine is run for seven hours at full throttle before installation, and each car is test-driven for hundreds of miles over varying road surfaces.

3. The Rolls-Royce is designed as an *owner-driven* car. It is eighteen inches shorter than the largest domestic cars.

4. The car has power steering, power brakes and automatic gear-shift. It is very easy to drive and to park. No chauffeur required.

5. There is no metal-to-metal contact between the body of the car and the chassis frame—except for the speedometer drive. The entire body is insulated and under-sealed.

6. The finished car spends a week in the final test-shop, being fine-tuned. Here it is subjected to ninety-eight separate ordeals. For example, the engineers use a *stethoscope* to listen for axle-whine.

7. The Rolls-Royce is guaranteed for *three years*. With a new network of dealers and parts-depots from

Coast to Coast, service is no longer any problem

8. The famous Rolls-Royce radiator has never been changed, except that when Sir Henry Royce died in 1933 the monogram RR was changed from red to black.

9. The coachwork is given five coats of primer paint, and hand rubbed between each coat, before *fourteen* coats of finishing paint go on.

10. By moving a switch on the steering column, you can adjust the shock-absorbers to suit road conditions. (The lack of fatigue in driving this car is remarkable.)

11. Another switch defrosts the rear window, by heating a network of 1360 invisible wires in the glass. There are two separate ventilating systems, so that you can ride in comfort with all the windows closed. Air conditioning is optional.

12. The seats are upholstered with eight hides of English leather—enough to make 128 pairs of soft shoes.

13. A picnic table, veneered in French walnut, slides out from under the dash. Two more swing out behind the front seats.

14. You can get such optional extras as an Espresso coffee-making machine, a dictating machine, a bed, hot and cold water for washing, an electric razor.

15. You can lubricate the entire chassis by simply pushing a pedal from the driver's seat. A gauge on the dash shows the level of oil in the crankcase.

16. Gasoline consumption is remarkably low and there is no need to use premium gas; a happy economy.

17. There are two separate systems of power brakes, hydraulic and mechanical. The Rolls-Royce is a very *safe* car—and also a very *lively* car. It cruises serenely at eighty-five. Top speed is in excess of 100 m.p.h.

18. Rolls-Royce engineers make periodic visits to inspect owners' motor cars and advise on service.

ROLLS-ROYCE AND BENTLEY

19. The Bentley is made by Rolls-Royce. Except for the radiators, they are identical motor cars, manufactured by the same engineers in the same works. The Bentley costs $300 less, because its radiator is simpler to make. People who feel diffident about driving a Rolls-Royce can buy a Bentley.

PRICE. The car illustrated in this advertisement— f.o.b. principal port of entry—costs $13,550.

If you would like the rewarding experience of driving a Rolls-Royce or Bentley, get in touch with our dealer. His name is on the bottom of this page. Rolls-Royce Inc., 10 Rockefeller Plaza, New York, N.Y.

JET ENGINES AND THE FUTURE

Certain airlines have chosen Rolls-Royce turbo-jets for their Boeing 707's and Douglas DC8's. Rolls-Royce prop-jets are in the Vickers Viscount, the Fairchild F.27 and the Grumman Gulfstream.

Rolls-Royce engines power more than half the turbo-jet and prop-jet airliners supplied to or on order for world airlines.

Rolls-Royce now employ 42,000 people and the company's engineering experience does not stop at motor cars and jet engines. There are Rolls-Royce diesel and gasoline engines for many other applications.

The huge research and development resources of the company are now at work on many projects for the future, including nuclear and rocket propulsion.

Special showing of the Rolls-Royce and Bentley at Salter Automotive Imports, Inc., 9009 Carnegie Ave., tomorrow through April 26.

© VOLKSWAGEN OF AMERICA, INC.

Which man would you vote for?

Ah yes, what could be more dazzling than watching the candidates parade about, kissing babies and flashing winning smiles.

Consider the man in the top picture.

He promises to spend your tax dollars wisely.

But see how he spends his campaign dollars.

On a very fancy convertible.

Resplendent with genuine leather seats. A big 425-horsepower engine.

And a price tag that makes it one of the most expensive convertibles you can buy.

Now consider his opponent.

He promises to spend your tax dollars wisely.

But see how he spends his campaign dollars.

On a Volkswagen Convertible.

Resplendent with a hand-fitted top.

A warranty and four free diagnostic check-ups that cover you for 24 months or 24,000 miles.*

And a price tag that makes it one of the least expensive convertibles you can buy.

So maybe this year you'll find a politician who'll do what few politicians ever do:

Keep his promises before he's elected.

*If an owner maintains and services his vehicle in accordance with the Volkswagen maintenance schedule any factory part found to be defective in material or workmanship within 24 months or 24,000 miles, whichever comes first (except normal wear and tear and service items), will be repaired or replaced by any U.S. or Canadian Volkswagen Dealer. And this will be done free of charge. See your Volkswagen dealer for details.

[1972]

CITY BOY. Paul spotted him first, just a bouncin' along, an' a grinnin' away like he know'd somethin' everybody else didn't. When he finally got to where we were a settin', Paul winked at me an' ask him real straight-faced, "You lost, city boy?"

"Not necessarily," he smiled.

Bobby ask him what it was that he was ridin', an' city boy said it was a Kawasaki. "A whut?" Bobby said. "A Kawasaki, KE175," city boy told him, real proud. Said it had some kinda new-fangled engine, an' a five-speed transmission, an' all kinds'a other fancy stuff. Said he could ride it just about anywhere he pleased, too…on the road or off — didn't make no difference. Bobby said, "I'll take my palomino any day, he don't get lost." "That's right," Paul said, "horses got brains. Know where they're goin', even if you don't."

City boy just grinned an' said, "Which way's town?"

Well, right away Paul starts ta' pointin' up the road, toward the bunkhouse. An' no sooner'n he had his finger stuck out, an' Bobby was a pointin' up t'other way.

City boy just eyed 'em both for a minute, an' then, with that same grin on his face, he started up his motor-sickle. First kick. Then he pulled out a map an' handed it over ta' Bobby an' said straight-out, "Stick it where your brains are, cowboy…and maybe you'll end up smart as your horse," An' off he rode.

Thought Paul and Bobby's faces were gonna turn redder'n their necks. Good thing that machine didn't stall.

Kawasaki
lets the good times roll.

[1976]

40

DODGE IS INTO PICKUPS LIKE AMERICA'S INTO JEANS.

Both blue jeans and Dodge pickups got their start by being tough. Dependable. And therefore necessary.

Then something happened. Jeans became a whole new style of dressing. A denim philosophy that captured the mood and attitude of an entire country.

And Dodge pickups stopped being just workhorses and found themselves as at home on the town's main drag as on a dusty country road.

The plain Jane Dodge pickup has grown into pickups with Crew Cabs, Club Cabs, two- or four-wheel drive, dual rear wheels, and a variety of carrying capacities.

You can equip them with road wheels, white letter tires, bucket seats, stereos, air conditioning, and special paint jobs.

And you can take your choice of buying or leasing.

Dodge pickups have become an exciting part of America's new style. Get into it yourself...at your local Dodge Dealer's.

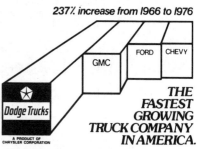

237% increase from 1966 to 1976

GMC   FORD   CHEVY

Dodge Trucks
A PRODUCT OF
CHRYSLER CORPORATION

THE FASTEST GROWING TRUCK COMPANY IN AMERICA.

[1977]

"I thought seeing Italy would teach me more about my father. Instead it taught me more about myself."

Carolyn Berger, Philadelphia, Pa.

"My maiden name is Aquino. A very common name in the town of Monte Fredane, where my father was born. He left there almost 100 years ago, in the steerage section of a boat, to start a new life in America.

"Recently, I went to Italy to visit his hometown. My father's house is still standing. (It's home now to another family.) I visited the church where my father was baptized and was able to see the record of his birth in the Town Hall. You see, the Monte Fredane I saw is very much the same as the one my father left so many years ago.

"Even with a background of hardship and coming to a strange new land, my father and mother managed to raise 12 children. Sometimes with an iron hand. But always with love.

"There were many times that my father and I didn't agree. And many times that I didn't understand his ways. But now I do.

"What formed his personality was the land he left. And through him, the memory of that same land formed mine."

An airline like ours does a lot of things.

But it seems that nothing we do has as much meaning as when we help somebody discover the second heritage every American has.

PAN AM
America's airline to the world.

See your travel agent.

The "Pony's" Last Ride

LAST APRIL, an old man swung into the saddle of a waiting horse and cantered across the rutted field at Newark airport.

And as he rode, the ground about him must have sprouted memories. For this old man was the last of the "Pony" riders—sole survivor of a band whose flying hoofbeats immortalized the Pony Express.

The package he handed to the pilot of an airliner was whisked to California overnight. Yet just 75 years ago, this man and his fellow-riders had startled a nation by cutting 12 days off the coast-to-coast mail time.

No more dramatic example of the progress of transportation has occurred in our day. From Pony Express to Airliner—in the space of one man's lifetime!

In awarding the laurels to those who have quickened the pulse of travel, a fair share should go to the Gulf Refining Company. For Gulf, since its founding, has fought the battle of time versus distance—on land, on sea, and in the air.

New and improved fuels and lubricants for marine engines, for aviation and land motors have come in rapid succession from Gulf's laboratories. With the aid of Gulf products, nearly a score of world's records have been shattered.

Today, many leading ocean and air lines pay high tribute to these Gulf products by using them exclusively. At this very moment, Gulf research scientists are perfecting still better products to help raise the tempo of transportation on land, on sea, and in the air.

And the same skill and foresight which fathered these fuels and lubricants are applied to every one of the 654 petroleum products sold under the sign of the Orange Disc.

GULF REFINING COMPANY

[1935]

NATURE AND TECHNOLOGY

43

It's practically your own island.

Imagine a sun-drenched island that is practically yours to do what you please, when you please, with whom you please. An island with no packaged hotels or motor inns. No hordes of vacationers trying desperately to get away from it all. Imagine sharing with a few like-minded people miles and miles of simplicity and beauty in the Dutch Antilles with all the wonder and freshness of Eden before the apple.

Imagine no more. It's real. It's St. Eustatius. We call it Statia. Come. You'll call it your own.

Just twenty minutes by plane from St. Maarten in the Caribbean, Statia is light years away from crowds and plastic vacations. Golden Rock Resort is your key to Statia. Your personal hideaway where your desires and privacy are assured.

In Statia pick your own special spot in the sun from scores of unspoiled beaches where the mode of dress or undress is your choice to make. Or follow the butterflies

to a place called the Quill, an extinct volcano in whose crater you'll discover a tropical rain forest of indescribable beauty. Amble through the shaded streets of historic Oranjestad, Statia's quaint capital populated with friendly, honest inhabitants.

Unlock the mysteries surrounding the 18th century treasure house ruins; explore the original storehouses that supplied the American Revolutionaries; visit 250 year old Dutch homes; and see the first synagogue in the Western Hemisphere. At day's end, sit on your terrace overlooking the sea and enjoy cocktails before an excellent continental or native style dinner tastefully prepared and graciously served.

And when you're ready, retire in complete privacy and security to sleep with the doors of your villa open if you like, with only the gentle breeze to share your dreams.

Your own island for $35 a day for two.

At Golden Rock Resort, this idyll

in the sun for you and your companion is yours for an astonishing $35 a day per couple, double occupancy on a modified American plan. (Breakfast and dinner included in the daily price, no extra charge) Come to Statia. You'll not only find "your own" island, you'll find each other.

For travel arrangements, information and free brochure contact Golden Rock Resort in New York City at 212-877-5200 or any of these travel agents.
Empress Travel Service
490 Avenue of the Americas
New York, N.Y. 10011/242-4444
Koerner, Liberman, Roland Travel, Inc.
424 Madison Avenue
New York, N.Y. 10017/758-0500
Stark Travel Service
120 Wall Street,
New York, N.Y. 10005/952-7600
Zenith Tours
9 East 40th Street,
New York, N.Y. 10017/725-8812
Austin Travel Co.
560 So. Broadway, Hicksville, L.I.,
N.Y. 11801/(516) 822-2222

Golden Rock Resort on Statia.
Your island in the Caribbean.

[1976]

44

THE URBAN WINDMILLS

Something old is something new — power out of the blue, literally, by harnessing wind, the world's ageless dynamo. An N-M Urban Windmill for her, and one for him, means each can enjoy today's electrical appliances and gadgets without overtaxing public power supplies, family utility bills, or tempers.

Not only do windmills keep on working when all else is in darkness, but they're also non-polluting, noiseless (when properly maintained), and environmentally safe.

In an area with an average wind velocity of 12 mph (Boston, for example), HER WINDMILL would generate more than enough wattage to brew her morning coffee, Benedict an egg, heat her hair rollers, soothe her psyche with stereo, and give her bronze beauty while she relaxes under the sun lamp.

Under the same conditions, HIS WINDMILL would give him the juice to whisk off the morning's stubble, type away at the electric portable, indulge his creative urge with power tools, then blend a pitcher of Daiquiris.

Each windmill operates independently, with its own storage batteries and an alternator to convert to alternating current when needed. For total togetherness, the systems may be linked to provide plug-in potential for Junior's All Electric Guitar Rock Group.

Someday, when the electric car is produced, you can fill yours right at the windmill and be, as they say, home (or elsewhere) free.

137. His or Her Windmill, with batteries and alternator, 16,000.00 each, exclusive of installation, F.O.B. Dallas/ Ft. Worth, Texas. For details: AC 214/741-6911, ext. 1225.

[1977]

A Fable For Now:

Why Elephants Can't Live on Peanuts

The Elephant is a remarkable animal...huge, yet able to move quickly...stronger than any person, yet willing to work hard if properly treated.

One day, an Elephant was ambling through the forest. To her surprise, she found her path to the water hole blocked by a huge pile of sticks, vines, and brambles.

"Hello?" she called out over the barricade. "What gives?"

From behind the pile popped the Monkey. "Buzz off, snake-snoot," the Monkey shouted. "It's an outrage to little folk how much you take in, so the rest of us animals have seized the water hole and the food supply. You're gross, and we're revolting!"

"You certainly give that appearance," the Elephant noted quietly. "What's eating you?"

"It's *you* that's doing too much eating," the Monkey replied, "but we're going to change all that. Strict rations for you, fat friend. No more of your obscene profiteering at the feed trough." Overhead, a Parrot screamed: "From each according to your ability. To each according to our need. Gimme your crackers, gimme *all* your crackers!"

The Elephant was upset at this enormous misunderstanding. Yet, though her heart pounded, between the ears she was quite unflappable. "A moment, please," she said. "Though it may seem that I consume a great deal, it's no more than my share. Because I am large—not fat—it just takes more to keep me going. How can I work hard if you won't let me have the proper nourishment?"

The Monkey sneered. "Knock off that mumbo-jumbo, Dumbo," he said. "You already net more than a million Spiders. You take in more than a thousand Pack Rats. You profit more from the jungle's abundance than a hundred Monkeys!"

"But I also can haul tree trunks too heavy for any other creature," the Elephant said. "I can explore for new food supplies and water holes, and clear paths through the jungle with my strong legs. My feet can crush, my shoulders can pull, my trunk can lift. I am full of energy. I even give rides to the little ones. But I can't survive on peanuts."

Hours passed. The Elephant, denied access to her eating and drinking grounds, felt hungrier and hungrier, thirstier and thirstier. But soon, so did the other animals. For the sticks and vines that the animals had dragged together and woven into a barricade had become a solid dam, diverting the stream that fed the watering hole. "Help, help," the animals shouted, "crisis, crisis!"

The Elephant surveyed the scene. "Friends," she said, "see what a fix we're all in. Thank goodness I still have the energy to help. And, with your permission, I will." They quickly consented, and she set to work on the dam, pushing earth and pulling plants until the water hole again began to fill. "That's nice," the animals cried, greeting her undamming with faint praise.

"You see," the Elephant said, "you need a big beast for a big job, and a big beast has big needs. Not just to stay alive and growing, but to put a bit aside for tomorrow. And to have a bit extra for working especially hard, or for sharing with have-not animals."

She noticed that everybody had resumed drinking thirstily. Well, that tickled her old ivories, for all she really wanted was to be allowed to go on doing her customary work without any new wrinkles. No need for hurt feelings. After all, who ever heard of a thin-skinned Elephant?

Moral: Meeting America's energy needs is a big job and it takes big companies. If an energy company doesn't earn a profit proportionate to its size, it won't be able to seek and produce more energy. And that's no fable.

Mobil

©1979 Mobil Corporation

What do you see when you look at a tree?

It depends on your perspective. You might see a source of jobs.

You might see a source of lumber, plywood, paper, packaging—"need" products as opposed to "want" products.

You might see an ideal base for a growth business, a natural resource that, managed properly, renews itself perpetually.

You might see a splendid example of Nature's artistry.

When we look at a tree, we see all these things, and more. We see our life's blood. Much of what we do depends on trees. So we take care of ours.

We strive to manage them in a way that reconciles your perspectives and ours, so they'll provide jobs, products, profits and splendor forever.

If we succeed, everybody wins. You the worker, consumer, investor and citizen. And we the employees and shareholders of Boise Cascade.

Reason enough to try, don't you think?

Boise Cascade Corporation 🌲
A company worth looking at.

47

Without chemicals, life itself would be impossible.

Some people think anything "chemical" is bad and anything "natural" is good. Yet nature is chemical.

Plant life generates the oxygen we need through a chemical process called photosynthesis. When you breathe, your body absorbs that oxygen through a chemical reaction with your blood.

Life is chemical. And with chemicals, companies like Monsanto are working to help improve the quality of life.

Chemicals help you live longer. Rickets was a common childhood disease until a chemical called Vitamin D was added to milk and other foods.

Chemicals help you eat better. Chemical weed-killers have dramatically increased the supply and availability of our food. But no chemical is totally safe, all the time, everywhere. In nature or the laboratory. The real challenge is to use chemicals properly. To help make life a lot more livable. © Monsanto Company 1977

48

Stanley Jones
Prided himself on having a
Strictly logical masculine mind.
Stanley heard, for example, that Postum
Is drunk by many people who cannot drink coffee.
Therefore, reasoned logical Stanley,
Postum must be a "coffee substitute";
Postum must *taste like coffee*.

Now, Stanley Jones did not care for substitutes;
He did not like to drink something that
Tastes like something else.
Therefore, he, Stanley Jones, decided he
Would not care for Postum.

Period.

Paragraph.

Stanley's wife, on the other hand,
Operated more on the basis of
Her woman's intuition.
Hearing that millions of people drink Postum,
She simply decided to try it herself.
Which she did,
Without any attempt at being logical.

Well!

Mrs. Jones discovered that Postum
Is a perfectly swell hot meal-time drink,
That doesn't taste like coffee
Or any other drink.
She discovered that Postum
Has a rich, full-bodied, satisfying flavor
All its own.
She discovered that Postum, in two words,
Is *downright delicious*.

Well!

"You and your logic!" she said to Mr. Jones.
"Postum is no coffee substitute.
It doesn't even *taste* like coffee.
In fact, Postum tastes no more like coffee
Than coffee tastes like tea.

"Why don't you be illogical for once
And try it?
Particularly, since
The shortages of tea and coffee
Are getting rather serious."

So
Stanley Jones, after considerable hemming and hawing,
Put his logic in his pocket
And tried a hot, steaming cup of Postum.

Whereupon, Mr. Jones smiled cheerfully, and said:
"Let us pursue this subject no longer.
Just pour me another cup of Postum."

THE END

P.S. Postum is a fine drink for all the family, even the children,
Since it contains no caffein, no stimulant of any kind.
Costs less than ½ cent a cup.
Try Postum Cereal, the kind you boil or "perk."
Or Instant Postum, made instantly in the cup.

☆ Listen to The Aldrich Family, Thursday nights
over NBC Network. One of America's
great radio programs, sponsored by Postum.

POSTUM—ONE OF AMERICA'S THREE GREAT MEALTIME DRINKS

[1942]

EATING AND DRINKING

ERNEST HEMINGWAY, who has been called the greatest living American writer, is also internationally famous as a deep-sea fisherman. Since publication of *The Sun Also Rises* in 1926, his novels and short stories have enriched the literature of the English language consistently, year after year. His newest book is *The Old Man and the Sea*.

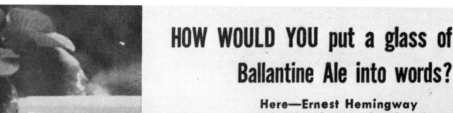

HOW WOULD YOU put a glass of Ballantine Ale into words?

Here—Ernest Hemingway turns his famous hand to it...

Ernest Hemingway

FINCA VIGIA, SAN FRANCISCO DE PAULA, CUBA

Bob Benchley first introduced me to Ballantine Ale. It has been a good companion ever since.

You have to work hard to deserve to drink it. But I would rather have a bottle of Ballantine Ale than any other drink after fighting a really big fish.

We keep it iced in the bait box with chunks of ice packed around it. And you ought to taste it on a hot day when you have worked a big marlin fast because there were sharks after him.

You are tired all the way through. The fish is landed untouched by sharks and you have a bottle of Ballantine cold in your hand and drink it cool, light, and full-bodied, so it tastes good long after you have swallowed it. That's the test of an ale with me: whether it tastes as good afterwards as when it's going down. Ballantine does.

Ernest Hemingway

| More people like it... | More people buy it... | than any other ale... | ...by Four to One! |

BALLANTINE ALE

PURITY · BODY · FLAVOR

Since 1840

P. Ballantine & Sons, Newark

[1952]

51

"You're some tomato. California's written all over you. We could make beautiful Bloody Marys together. I'm different from those other fellows."

"I like you, Wolfschmidt. You've got taste."

Wolfschmidt in a Bloody Mary is a tomato in triumph. Wolfschmidt has the touch of taste that marks genuine old world vodka. It heightens, accents, brings out the best in every drink.

"You sweet California doll. I appreciate you. I've got taste. I'll bring out your inner orange. I'll make you famous. Roll over here and kiss me."

"Who was that tomato I saw you with last week?"

Wolfschmidt in a Screwdriver is an orange in ecstasy. Wolfschmidt has the touch of taste that marks genuine old world vodka. It heightens, accents, brings out the best in every drink.

[1961]

Why husbands leave home:

He gets home from a typically miserable day at the office, and what does he find?

Love? Tender hugs and kisses?

No such thing. He finds a scribbled note, and there, in the freezer, nestled among the roasts—

Let's face it. Run-of-the-mill frozen meals don't do right by him <u>or</u> you.

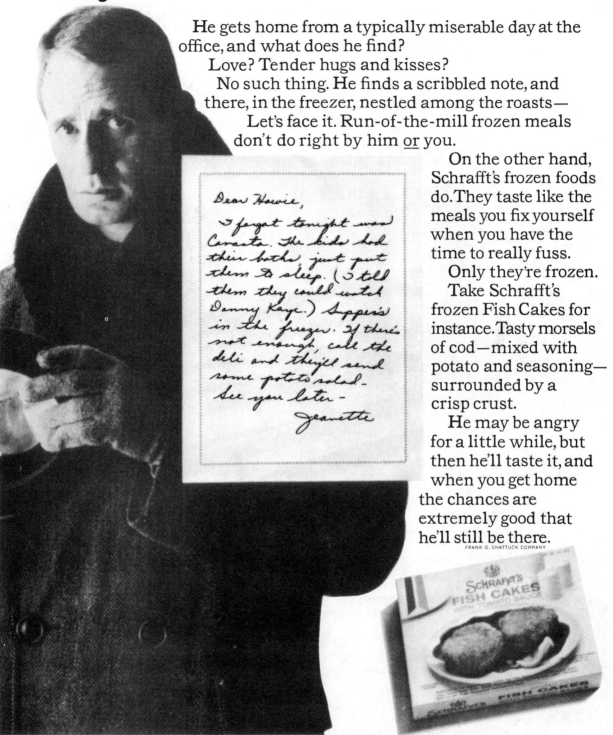

Dear Howie,

I forgot tonight was Canasta. The kids had their baths, just put them to sleep. (I told them they could watch Danny Kaye.) Supper's in the freezer. If there's not enough, call the deli and they'll send some potato salad.

See you later—

Jeanette

On the other hand, Schrafft's frozen foods do. They taste like the meals you fix yourself when you have the time to really fuss.

Only they're frozen.

Take Schrafft's frozen Fish Cakes for instance. Tasty morsels of cod—mixed with potato and seasoning—surrounded by a crisp crust.

He may be angry for a little while, but then he'll taste it, and when you get home the chances are extremely good that he'll still be there.

FRANK G. SHATTUCK COMPANY

HURRY-UP MEALS YOU DON'T HAVE TO MAKE EXCUSES FOR.
SCHRAFFT'S

[1966]

53

Three hours to sunrise.
The time for classes and rapping is past. Now you have to
put it all together. And it isn't easy.
But you have the head for it. And the heart. And
a Pepsi-Cola handy to give you a lift.
Pepsi gives you more than just a big taste. It gives you energy
to keep going. And you're going a long way.

You've got a lot to live. Pepsi's got a lot to give.

Go forth now and cook amongst the Americans.

It's not easy earning the right to feed the people of America.

No, it's no picnic getting admitted to the league of Benihana chefs.

First, you must serve a 2 year apprenticeship in Japan. Then you must be accepted at the Benihana College of Chefs in Tokyo. There you have to spend fifteen gruelling weeks under Master Chef Shinji Fujisaku. You don't graduate unless the Master certifies that you've become an absolute whiz at Benihana's special style of Hibachi cooking (Japanese grill cuisine as opposed to classical Japanese cuisine.)

And what are some of the teachings of the Master?

Well, one of the first has to do with the cutting of the meat. "A Benihana chef is an artist, not a butcher," the Master says. So you must learn to wield a knife with dazzling grace, speed and precision. Your hands should move like Fred Astaire's feet.

You also learn that to a Benihana chef, Hibachi cooking is never solemn. As the Master says "It's an act of pure joy." So joy, really, is what you must bring to the Hibachi table. A joy that the people around you can see and feel. A joy they can catch as you sauté those jumbo shrimps. Or as you dust that chicken with sesame seeds. Or as you slam that pepper shaker against the grill and send the pepper swirling over those glorious chunks of steak.

Perhaps most important of all, is this saying of the Master's: "Benihana has no cooks. Only chefs." Which means that while you should be joyous, you must always strive for perfection. So you learn everything there is to learn about sauces and seasonings. You labor to make your shrimp the most succulent shrimp anyone's ever tasted. Your sirloin the most delicious and juicy. Your every mushroom and bean-sprout a song.

Over and over the Master drills you. Again and again you go through your paces. Fifteen exhausting, perfection-seeking weeks.

But the day comes when you're ready. Ready to bring what you've learned to the people of such faraway places as New York, Chicago and Los Angeles.

It's a great moment.

"Sayonara, Honorable Teacher," you say.

"Knock 'em dead, Honorable Graduate," he replies.

BENIHANA of TOKYO

[1973]

55

America

If you'll stop and think for just a moment, you'll find we have more of the good things in this country than anywhere else in the world.

Think of this land. From the surf at Big Sur to a Florida sunrise. And all the places in between.

The Grand Canyon... the wheat fields of Kansas... Autumn in New Hampshire...

You could go on forever. But America is more than a place of much beauty. It's a place for good times.

It's Saturday night.

It's a trip down a dirt road in a beat up old jalopy.

It's your team winning. It's a late night movie you could enjoy a thousand times.

And, yes, when you're thirsty, it's the taste of ice-cold Coca-Cola. It's the real thing.

In fact, all of the good things in this country are real. They're all around you, plainly visible. We point to many of them in our advertising. But you can discover many, many more without ever seeing a single commercial for Coke.

So have a bottle of Coke... and start looking up.

The Coca-Cola Company

DO YOUR DINNERTIMIN'™ AT McDONALD'S.

McDonald's ®

When you're looking for a different place to have dinner, check out McDonald's. You don't have to get dressed up, there's no tipping and the kids love it.

You can relax and get down with good food that won't keep you waitin'

Dinnertimin' or anytimin', going out is easy at McDonald's.

WE DO IT ALL FOR YOU ™

[1976]

With my cooking, the army that travels on its stomach is facing a pretty bumpy road.

As far as being a rookie cook goes, I was as green as the guys who ate what I cooked.

They said my hamburgers tasted like hockey pucks.

They said my chipped beef stuck to their ribs, permanently.

And what they said about my sloppy joes could have gotten them all arrested.

I finally had to face up to it. No one could stomach my cooking. And my brilliant military career would have gone down the drain then and there if it

wasn't for McCormick/Schilling.

They're the experts on spice and flavor. And they make all kinds of sauces, seasonings and gravies that can really make things taste good. Even the stuff I cook.

So, I tried their sloppy joes mix. All I had to do was brown 1,000 pounds of ground beef, mix in the McCormick/Schilling seasoning; add tomato paste and 150 gallons of water.

And in no time, I had enough to feed an army.

It was easy. And more important, it was good.

Guys were standing in line for seconds. (Before, they never stuck around for firsts).

Matter of fact, they stopped griping about my cooking long enough for me to finally get my stripes.

And I owe it all to McCormick/Schilling.

I guess you could say that when it comes to cooking, they turned me into a seasoned veteran.

My sloppy joes recipe for 6,000:

Brown 1,000 lbs. of ground beef. Mix in 1,000 packages of McCormick/Schilling Sloppy Joes Mix and blend thoroughly. Stir in 1,000 6-ounce cans of tomato paste and 1,250 cups of water. Bring to a boil. Then reduce heat and simmer 10 minutes, stirring occasionally. Spoon over hamburger buns. Makes 6,000 ½-cup servings. (To get 6 servings, divide by 1,000).

McCormick/Schilling flavor makes all the difference in the world.

McCormick/Schilling

[1976]

58

One of the Yank Veterans

"We smash 'em HARD"

WHITE
OWL
▼
Invincible
Shape
7c

OWL
▼
Square-
end
6c

"Did I bayonet my first Hun? Sure! How did it feel? It *doesn't* feel! There *he* is. There *you* are. One of you has got to go. I preferred to stay.

"So when sergeant says, 'Smash 'em, boys'—we do. And we go them one better like good old Yankee Doodle Yanks. For bullets and bayonets are the only kind of lingo that a Hun can *understand!*"

* * * *

The *dependable* Yank, whose photograph appears above, first met the *dependable* Owl Cigar while boosting that *dependable* investment—the Liberty Loan.

We didn't tell him about the $2,000,000 stock of leaf that is always aging for Owl and White Owl. Nor the over 100,000,000 Owls and White Owls sold last year. We just swapped him a White Owl for a smile. And it doesn't look like the smile came hard, does it?

Why don't you, too, try an Owl or White Owl—*today?*

DEALERS:
If your distributor does not sell these dependable cigars, write us.
GENERAL CIGAR CO., INC., 119 West 40th Street, New York City

TWO DEPENDABLE CIGARS

OWL 6¢ white OWL 7¢

Branded
for your

Banded
protection

[1918]

SMOKING

There is a Doctor in the House

—and it took a minimum of $15,000 and 7 years' hard work and study to get him there!

PROUDLY he "hangs out his shingle," symbol of his right to engage in the practice of medicine and surgery. But to a doctor it is more than a right: it is a privilege—the privilege of serving mankind, of helping his fellow man to a longer, healthier, and happier life.

According to a recent Nationwide survey:

MORE DOCTORS SMOKE CAMELS THAN ANY OTHER CIGARETTE!

FAMILY physicians, surgeons, diagnosticians, nose and throat specialists, doctors in every branch of medicine...a total of 113,597 doctors ... were asked the question: "What cigarette do you smoke?"

And more of them named Camel as their smoke than any other cigarette!

Three independent research groups found this to be a fact.

You see, doctors too smoke for pleasure. That full Camel flavor is just as appealing to a doctor's taste as to yours ... that marvelous Camel mildness means just as much to his throat as to yours. Next time, get Camels. Compare them in your "T-Zone" (*see right*).

THE "T-ZONE" TEST WILL TELL YOU

The "T-Zone" – T for taste and T for throat—is your own proving ground for any cigarette. For only your taste and your throat can decide which cigarette tastes best to you... and how it affects your throat. On the basis of the experience of many, many millions of smokers, we believe Camels will suit your "T-Zone" to a "T."

R. J. Reynolds Tobacco Co., Winston-Salem, N. C.

CAMELS *Costlier Tobaccos*

[1946]

60

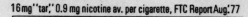

Fashions: Bill Blass

61

[1978]

A word to smokers
(about people who build walls)

It's no secret that there are some folks these days who are trying to build walls between smokers and nonsmokers.

The theory behind all this is that some smokers annoy nonsmokers and, of course, that can happen.

But if you want to get an idea of the ridiculous lengths that some of the wall-builders would like to go to, you have only to consider this:

In one state alone, it was estimated that the first year's cost of administering and enforcing a proposed anti-smoking law and building the physical walls required was nearly $250,000,000.

The proposal was, of course, defeated — for the plain fact is the one you have observed in your own daily life, that the overwhelming majority of smokers and nonsmokers get along very well and don't need or want to be separated.

This infuriates the wall-builders. Since they cannot have their own way in a world of free choice, they would like to eliminate that world by government fiat, by rules and regulations that would tell you where, and with whom, you may work, eat, play and shop. And the enormous burden that would place on all of us, in higher taxes and costs, does not bother them.

Certainly no one, including smokers, can properly object to the common sense rules of, for instance, banning smoking in crowded elevators, poorly ventilated spaces or, indeed, in any place where it is clearly inappropriate. And individual managers in their own interest should see to the mutual comfort of their smoking and nonsmoking patrons. It is only when the long arm, and notoriously insensitive hands, of government regulators start making these private arrangements for us that we all, smoker and nonsmoker alike, begin to lose our freedom of choice.

In the long run, the wall-builders must fail, and the walls will come tumbling down — if not to the sound of a trumpet, then at least to the slower but surer music of common decency and courtesy practiced on both sides of them.

THE TOBACCO INSTITUTE
1776 K St. N.W., Washington, D.C. 20006
Freedom of choice
is the best choice.

A word to nonsmokers
(about people who build walls)

The chances are that you made up your mind about smoking a long time ago—and decided it's not for you.

The chances are equally good that you know a lot of smokers—there are, after all about 60 million of them—and that you may be related to some of them, work with them, play with them, and get along with them very well.

And finally it's a pretty safe bet that you're open-minded and interested in all the various issues about smokers and nonsmokers—or you wouldn't be reading this.

And those three things make you incredibly important today.

Because they mean that yours is the voice— not the smoker's and not the anti-smoker's—that will determine how much of society's efforts should go into building walls that separate us and how much into the search for solutions that bring us together.

For one tragic result of the emphasis on building walls is the diversion of millions of dollars from scientific research on the causes and cures of diseases which, when all is said and done, still strike the nonsmoker as well as the smoker. One prominent health organization, to cite but a single instance, now spends 28¢ of every publicly-contributed dollar on "education" (much of it in anti-smoking propaganda) and only 2¢ on research.

There will always be some who want to build walls, who want to separate people from people, and up to a point, even these may serve society. The anti-smoking wall-builders have, to give them their due, helped to make us all more keenly aware of the value of courtesy and of individual freedom of choice.

But our guess, and certainly our hope, is that you are among the far greater number who know that walls are only temporary at best, and that over the long run, we can serve society's interests better by working together in mutual accommodation.

Whatever virtue walls may have, they can never move our society toward fundamental solutions. People who work together on common problems, common solutions, can.

THE TOBACCO INSTITUTE
1776 K St. N.W., Washington, D.C. 20006
Freedom of choice is the best choice.

[1979]

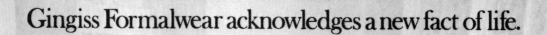

Gingiss Formalwear acknowledges a new fact of life.

Thirty-eight years separate these newlyweds. Which qualify them for special consideraton. She's considered opportunistic and conniving. He's considered a letch. A cradle robber. A dirty old man.

The ceremony is handled like you'd handle a shot-gun wedding. All very hush-hush. And tense. And somber.

Fortunately, these hang-ups are disappearing. In the past couple of years, several of our most distinguished elder statesmen have married women many years their junior. They've done this openly. Unabashedly. With dignity.

Others have followed their lead. (Since we rent more tuxedos than anyone in the world, we deal with a large percentage of these grooms.) They're good men who simply believe that because they'll never see forty or fifty again is no reason to assume they'll never see love or companionship again.

One thing's for sure. You'll be seeing more and more of these marriages in the future. That's a fact of life. And we at Gingiss are proud to play even a small part in it.

gingiss

[1972]

FASHIONS

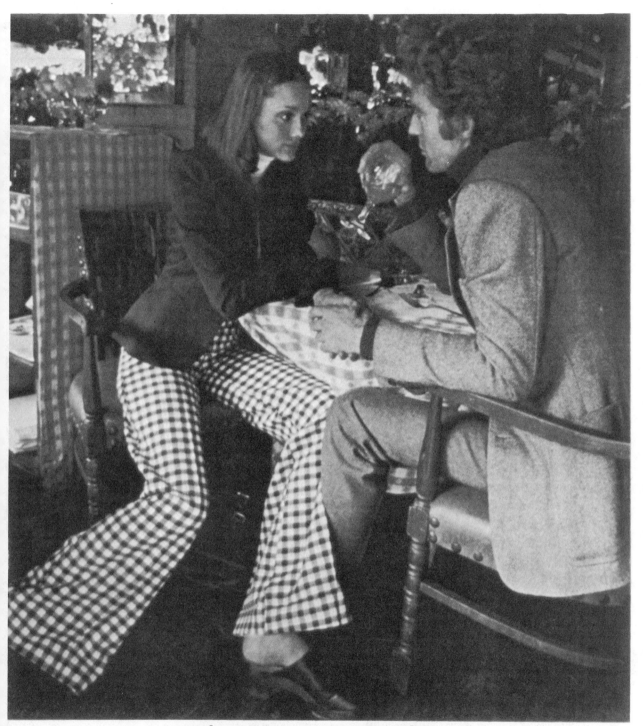

What to wear on Sunday when you won't be home till Monday.

You're on your own. Free to be yourself in everything you do or wear.

That's what Happy Legs is all about. We make things only for spirits like yours. No one else would dig the freedom and taste of our tops and pants. We cut and shape them only for long-legged bodies like yours. In junior sizes. Some day soon, like before next Sunday, just go into a store that knows sportswear and pick out your own look from Happy Legs, Inc., 1407 Broadway, New York 10018, (212) 695-2255. A Spencer Company.

Happy Legs
fits you, fits your life-style.

[1974]

THIS SMUGGLER® COAT DOES EVERYTHING BUT STOP BULLETS.

Like it stops chicks, for instance, dead in their tracks.

Only who's got time for chicks when you got a little business to attend to.

Like lining your pockets with maybe 12 boxes of Cuban cigars, 6 gross Swiss watches, one case good Scotch, 2 snow leopard skins, one German P-38 and 2 solid gold bricks.

Which with a little imagination you can do easy with this coat.

Or take that big collar.

Most guys see it as maybe a pain in the neck, what with keeping it down so it don't mess up your hair.

But any guy sees past his nose sees himself in an open boat in a sudden twister up the Florida Keys, with collar up high to protect the back of his head from taking an awful dousing.

Same goes for the icy blast of a Labrador northeaster down from Fundy.

Or the cold hard stare of a U.S. agent at customs.

There's just about nothing this coat won't do for you when the going gets rough.

Find yourself caught in a tight squeeze on the back of a truck in between a shipment of Picassos and a bunch of Greek vases and you can sleep through the whole night's events and shake off the wrinkles in the AM because the coat's 100% texturized Dacron* polyester.

Or wait for a shipment in the middle of the night in the middle of nowhere and the sky opens up and pours all over you, and it's nice to know you got yourself a coat treated with Scotchgard.†

Now you'd think a coat like this, with and including the zip-in pile lining, would set you back a hundred bills, maybe more.

Not so, only seventy-five.

Which is maybe the hardest part about this Smuggler coat you're going to have to believe.

Colors: Navy, Sand, Rust Plaid and Grey Plaid. $75. Prices slightly higher on the West Coast. At these fine stores: ARNOLD CONSTABLE, New York; JORDAN MARSH CO., Boston; KENNEDY'S, New England and New Jersey; THE HECHT CO., Washington, D.C.; MARSHALL FIELD, Chicago; F&R LAZARUS, Columbus; SHILLITO'S, Cincinnati; BOYD'S, St. Louis; MACY'S, Kansas City. Or write Smuggler: A division of Cable Industries, 130 Auckland St., Boston, Mass.

[1973]

Born to run.

Over twenty eight years ago, adidas gave birth to a new idea in sports shoes. And the people who wear our shoes have been running and winning ever since. In fact, adidas has helped them set over 400 world records in track and field alone.

Maybe that's why more and more football, soccer, basketball, baseball and tennis players are turning to adidas. They know that, whatever their game, they can rely on adidas workmanship and quality in every product we make.

So whether you're pounding the roads on a marathon, or just jogging around the block, adidas should be on your feet.

You were born to run. And we were born to help you do it better. You'll find us anywhere smart sports people buy their shoes.

The all-sports people.

Her shoe: The adidas Runner (3465).
His shoe: The adidas Adistar 2000 (5201).

[1977]

In our family business there's three things you don't mind spending your money on. Copper tubing. Fast cars. And a fine pair of warm, dry boots. And that third one is just as important as the first two. When you're crouching down in some gully with your feet in ice-cold ditch water, never moving a muscle for hours, whilst them damn Treasury agents snoop around with their dogs barking and sniffing, well, that's the time you're glad you didn't cut corners on your boots. These boots we bought are fine boots, well made, need no breaking in. But to us, that don't mean so much compared to the way they're waterproof and warm.

The Timberland Company, Newmarket, NH 03857

[1978]

Marianne Moore / Correspondence with the
Ford Motor Company 1955

In the following exchange of letters, the distinguished American poet, Marianne Moore (1887–1972), a professed "amateur" at the art of copywriting, tries to come up with the best name for a product that the Ford Motor Company thought would revolutionize the automobile industry.

According to Printer's Ink, *the one-time leading advertising trade publication, Ford spent over $350 million "to create and promote the biggest and most expensive new product ever born." (See page 37 for a magazine advertisement for the ill-fated Edsel.)*

OCTOBER 19, 1955

MISS MARIANNE MOORE,
CUMBERLAND STREET,
BROOKLYN 5, NEW YORK

DEAR MISS MOORE:

This is a morning we find ourselves with a problem which, strangely enough, is more in the field of words and the fragile meaning of words than in car-making. And we just wonder whether you might be intrigued with it sufficiently to lend us a hand.

Our dilemma is a name for a rather important new series of cars.

We should like this name to be more than a label. Specifically, we should like it to have a compelling quality in itself and by itself. To convey, through association or other conjuration, some visceral feeling of elegance, fleetness, advanced features and design. A name, in short, that flashes a dramatically desirable picture in people's minds. (Another "Thunderbird" would be fine.)

Over the past few weeks this office has confected a list of three hundred-odd candidates which, it pains me to relate, are characterized by an embarrassing pedestrianism. We are miles short of our ambition. And so we are seeking the help of one who knows more about this sort of magic than we.

As to how we might go about this matter, I have no idea. But, in any event, all would depend on whether you find this overture of some challenge and interest.

Should we be so fortunate as to have piqued your fancy, we will be pleased to write more fully. And, of course, it is expected that our relations will be on a fee basis of an impeccably dignified kind.

Respectfully,
DAVID WALLACE
Special Products Division

OCTOBER 21, 1955

Let me take it under advisement, Mr. Wallace. I am complimented to be recruited in this high matter.

I have seen and admired "Thunderbird" as a Ford designation. It would be hard to match; but let me, the coming week, talk with my brother, who would bring ardor and imagination to bear on the quest.

Sincerely yours,
MARIANNE MOORE

OCTOBER 27, 1955

DEAR MR. WALLACE:

My brother thought most of the names I had considered suggesting to you for your new series too learned or too labored, but thinks I might ask if any of the following approximate the requirements:

THE FORD SILVER SWORD

This plant, of which the flower is a silver sword, I believe grows only on the Hawaiian Island Maui, on Mount Haleakala (House of the Sun); found at an altitude of from 9,500 to 10,000 feet. (The leaves—silver-white—surrounding the individual blossoms—have a pebbled texture that feels like Italian-twist backstitch allover embroidery.)

My first thought was of a bird series—the swallow species—Hirundo, or, phonetically, Aerundo. Malvina Hoffman is designing a device for the radiator of a made-to-order Cadillac, and said in her opinion the only term surpassing Thunderbird would be hurricane; and I then thought Hurricane Hirundo might be the first of a series such as Hurricane Aquila (eagle), Hurricane Accipiter (hawk), and so on. A species that takes its dinner on the wing ("swifts").

If these suggestions are not in character with the car, perhaps you could give me a sketch of its general appearance, or hint as to some of its exciting potentialities—though my brother reminds me that such information is highly confidential.

Sincerely yours,

MARIANNE MOORE

NOVEMBER 4, 1955

DEAR MISS MOORE:

I'm delighted that your note implies that you are interested in helping us in our naming problem.

This being so, procedures in this rigorous business world dictate that we on this end at least document a formal arrangement with provision for a suitable fee or honorarium before pursuing the problem further.

One way might be for you to suggest a figure which could be considered for mutual acceptance. Once this is squared away, we will look forward to having you join us in the continuation of our fascinating search.

Sincerely,

DAVID WALLACE

Special Products Division

NOVEMBER 7, 1955

DEAR MR. WALLACE:

It is handsome of you to consider remuneration for service merely enlisted. My fancy would be inhibited, however, by acknowledgment in advance of performance. If I could be of specific assistance, we could no doubt agree on some kind of honorarium for the service rendered.

I seem to exact participation; but if you could tell me how the suggestions submitted strayed—if obviously—from the ideal, I could then perhaps proceed more nearly in keeping with the Company's objective.

Sincerely yours,

MARIANNE MOORE

DEAR MISS MOORE:

Our office philodendron has just benefitted from an extra measure of water as, pacing about, I have sought words to respond to your recent generous note. Let me state my quandary thus. It is unspeakably contrary to procedure to accept counsel—even needed counsel—without a firm prior agreement of conditions (and, indeed, to follow the letter of things, without a Purchase Notice in quadruplicate and three Competitive Bids). But then, seldom has the auto business had occasion to indulge in so ethereal a matter as this. So, if you will risk a mutually satisfactory outcome with us, we should like to honor your wish for a fancy unencumbered.

As to wherein your earlier suggestions may have "strayed," as you put it—they did not at all. Shipment No. 1 was fine, and we would like to luxuriate in more of same—even those your brother regarded as overlearned or labored. For us to impose an ideal on your efforts would, I fear, merely defeat our purpose. We have sought your help to get an approach quite different from our own. In short, we should like suggestions that we ourselves would not have arrived at. And, in sober fact, have not.

Now we on this end must help you by sending some tangible representation of what we are talking about. Perhaps the enclosed sketches will serve the purpose. They are not IT, but they convey the feeling. At the very least, they may give you a sense of participation should your friend Malvina Hoffman break into brisk conversation on radiator caps.

Sincerely yours,
DAVID WALLACE
Special Products Division

DEAR MR. WALLACE:

The sketches. They are indeed exciting; they have quality, and the toucan tones lend tremendous allure—confirmed by the wheels. Half the magic—sustaining effects of this kind. Looked at upside down, furthermore, there is a sense of fish buoyancy. Immediately your word "impeccable" sprang to mind. Might it be a possibility? The Impeccable. In any case, the baguette lapidary glamour you have achieved certainly spurs the imagination. Car-innovation is like launching a ship—"drama."

I am by no means sure that I can help you to the right thing, but performance with elegance casts a spell. Let me do some thinking in the direction of impeccable, symmechromatic, thunderblender. . . . (The exotics, if I can shape them a little.) Dearborn might come into one.

If the sketches should be returned at once, let me know. Otherwise, let me dwell on them for a time. I am, may I say, a trusty confidante.

I thank you for realizing that under contract esprit could not flower. You owe me nothing, specific or moral.

Sincerely,
MARIANNE MOORE

Some other suggestions, Mr. Wallace, for the phenomenon:

THE RESILIENT BULLET
or Intelligent Bullet
or Bullet Cloisonné or Bullet Lavolta

(I have always had a fancy for THE INTELLIGENT WHALE—the little first Navy submarine, shaped like a sweet potato; on view in our Brooklyn Yard.)

THE FORD FABERGE

(That there is also a perfume Fabergé seems to me to do no harm, for here allusion is to the original silversmith.)

THE ARC-en-CIEL (the rainbow) ARCENCIEL?

Please do not feel that memoranda from me need acknowledgment. I am not working day and night for you; I feel that etymological hits are partially accidental.

The bullet idea has possibilities, it seems to me, in connection with Mercury (with Hermes and Hermes Trismegistus) and magic (white magic).

Sincerely,
MARIANNE MOORE

NOVEMBER 28, 1955

DEAR MR. WALLACE:

MONGOOSE CIVIQUE

ANTICIPATOR

REGNA RACER (couronne à couronne) sovereign to sovereign

AEROTERRE

Fée Rapide (Aérofée, Aéro Faire, Fée Aiglette, Magi-faire) Comme Il Faire

Tonnerre Alifère (winged thunder)

Aliforme Alifère (wing-slender, a-wing)

TURBOTORC (used as an adjective by Plymouth)

THUNDERBIRD Allié (Cousin Thunderbird)

THUNDER CRESTER

DEARBORN Diamante

MAGIGRAVURE

PASTELOGRAM

I shall be returning the sketches very soon.
M.M.

DECEMBER 6, 1955

DEAR MR. WALLACE:
Regina-rex
Taper Racer   Taper Acer
Varsity Stroke

Angelastro
Astranaut

Chaparral

Tir à l'arc (bull's eye)
Cresta Lark
Triskelion (three legs running)

Pluma Piluma (hairfine, feather-foot)

Andante con Moto (description of a good motor?)

My findings thin, so I terminate them and am returning the sketches. Two principles I have not been able to capture: 1, the topknot of the peacock and topnotcher of speed. 2, the swivel-axis (emphasized elsewhere), like the Captain's bed on the whaleship, Charles Morgan—balanced so that it levelled whatever the slant of the ship.

If I stumble on a hit, you shall have it. Anything so far has been pastime. Do not ponder appreciation, Mr. Wallace. That was embodied in the sketches.

M.M.

I cannot resist the temptation to disobey my brother and submit

TURCOTINGA (turquoise cotinga—the cotinga being a South-American finch or sparrow) solid indigo.

(I have a three-volume treatise on flowers that might produce something but the impression given should certainly be unlabored.)

DECEMBER 8, 1955

MR. WALLACE:

May I submit UTOPIAN TURTLE-TOP? Do not trouble to answer unless you like it.
MARIANNE MOORE

DECEMBER 23, 1955

MERRY CHRISTMAS TO OUR FAVORITE TURTLETOPPER.
DAVID WALLACE

DECEMBER 26, 1955

DEAR MR. WALLACE:

An aspiring turtle is certain to glory in spiral eucalyptus, white pine straight from the forest, and innumerable scarlet roses almost too tall for close inspection. Of a temperament susceptible to shock though one may be, to be treated like royalty could not but induce sensations unprecedented august.

Please know that a carfancyer's allegiance to the Ford automotive turtle—extending from the Model T Dynasty to the Wallace Utopian Dynasty—can never waver; impersonal gratitude surely becoming infinite when made personal. Gratitude to unmiserly Mr. Wallace and his idealistic associates.
MARIANNE MOORE

NOVEMBER 8, 1956

DEAR MISS MOORE:

Because you were so kind to us in our early days of looking for a suitable name, I feel a deep obligation to report on events that have ensued.

And I feel I must do so before the public announcement of same come Monday, November 19.

We have chosen a name out of the more than six thousand-odd candidates that we gathered. It fails somewhat of the resonance, gaiety, and zest we were seeking. But it has a personal dignity and meaning to many of us here. Our name, dear Miss Moore, is—Edsel.

I hope you will understand.

Cordially,
DAVID WALLACE
Special Products Division

David Ogilvy / How To Write Potent Copy   1963

> *David Ogilvy was born in England in 1911 and received his education at Christ Church College, Oxford. His professional experiences have been varied: At one time he served as an apprentice chef in the kitchens of the Hotel Majestic in Paris and at another time as a salesman for kitchen stoves. With the founding of Ogilvy, Benson and Mather in 1948, Ogilvy went on to become one of the leading figures of and voices of American advertising. His best known ads—those for Hathaway shirts, Schweppes tonic, and Rolls Royce—have focused on distinctive images of Anglo-American sophistication.*
>
>   *"How to Write Potent Copy"* appeared as a chapter in Ogilvy's best seller, Confessions of an Advertising Man.

I. HEADLINES

The headline is the most important element in most advertisements. It is the telegram which decides the reader whether to read the copy.

On the average, five times as many people read the headline as read the body copy. When you have written your headline, you have spent eighty cents out of your dollar.

If you haven't done some selling in your headline, you have wasted 80 per cent of your client's money. The wickedest of all sins is to run an advertisement *without* a headline. Such headless wonders are still to be found; I don't envy the copywriter who submits one to me.

A change of headline can make a difference of ten to one in sales. I never write fewer than sixteen headlines for a single advertisement, and I observe certain guides in writing them:

> (1) The headline is the "ticket on the meat." Use it to flag down the readers who are prospects for the kind of product you are advertising. If you are selling a remedy for bladder weakness, display the words BLADDER WEAKNESS in your headline; they catch the eye of everyone who suffers from this inconvenience. If you want *mothers* to read your advertisement, display MOTHERS in your headline. And so on.
>
> Conversely, do not say anything in your headline which is likely to *exclude* any readers who might be prospects for your product. Thus, if you are advertising a

product which can be used equally well by men and women, don't slant your headline at women alone; it would frighten men away.

(2) Every headline should appeal to the reader's *self-interest*. It should promise her a benefit, as in my headline for Helena Rubinstein's Hormone Cream: HOW WOMEN OVER 35 CAN LOOK YOUNGER.

(3) Always try to inject *news* into your headlines, because the consumer is always on the lookout for new products, or new ways to use an old product, or new improvements in an old product.

The two most powerful words you can use in a headline are FREE and NEW. You can seldom use FREE, but you can almost always use NEW—if you try hard enough.

(4) Other words and phrases which work wonders are HOW TO, SUDDENLY, NOW, ANNOUNCING, INTRODUCING, IT'S HERE, JUST ARRIVED, IMPORTANT DEVELOPMENT, IMPROVEMENT, AMAZING, SENSATIONAL, REMARKABLE, REVOLUTIONARY, STARTLING, MIRACLE, MAGIC, OFFER, QUICK, EASY, WANTED, CHALLENGE, ADVICE TO, THE TRUTH ABOUT, COMPARE, BARGAIN, HURRY, LAST CHANCE.

Don't turn up your nose at these clichés. They may be shopworn, but they work. That is why you see them turn up so often in the headlines of mail-order advertisers and others who can measure the results of their advertisements.

Headlines can be strengthened by the inclusion of *emotional* words, like DARLING, LOVE, FEAR, PROUD, FRIEND, and BABY. One of the most provocative advertisements which has come out of our agency showed a girl in a bathtub, talking to her lover on the telephone. The headline: *Darling, I'm having the most extraordinary experience . . . I'm head over heels in* DOVE.

(5) Five times as many people read the headline as read the body copy, so it is important that these glancers should at least be told what brand is being advertised. That is why you should always include the brand name in your headlines.

(6) Include your selling promise in your headline. This requires long headlines. When the New York University School of Retailing ran headline tests with the cooperation of a big department store, they found that headlines of ten words or longer, containing news and information, consistently sold more merchandise than short headlines.

Headlines containing six to twelve words pull more coupon returns than short headlines, and there is no significant difference between the readership of twelve-word headlines and the readership of three-word headlines. The best headline I ever wrote contained *eighteen* words: *At Sixty Miles an Hour the Loudest Noise in the New Rolls-Royce comes from the electric clock.*[1]

(7) People are more likely to read your body copy if your headline arouses their curiosity; so you should end your headline with a lure to read on.

(8) Some copywriters write *tricky* headlines—puns, literary allusions, and other obscurities. This is a sin.

In the average newspaper your headline has to compete for attention with 350 others. Research has shown that readers travel so fast through this jungle that they don't stop to decipher the meaning of obscure headlines. Your headline must *telegraph* what you want to say, and it must telegraph it in plain language. Don't play games with the reader.

In 1960 the *Times Literary Supplement* attacked the whimsical tradition in British advertising, calling it "self-indulgent—a kind of middle-class private joke, apparently designed to amuse the advertiser and his client." Amen.

(9) Research shows that it is dangerous to use *negatives* in headlines. If, for example, you write OUR SALT CONTAINS NO ARSENIC, many readers will miss the negative and go away with the impression that you wrote OUR SALT CONTAINS ARSENIC.

---

1. When the chief engineer at the Rolls-Royce factory read this, he shook his head sadly and said, "It is time we did something about that damned clock." [This ad appears on p. 38.]

(10) Avoid *blind* headlines—the kind which mean nothing unless you read the body copy underneath them; most people *don't*.

II. BODY COPY

When you sit down to write your body copy, pretend that you are talking to the woman on your right at a dinner party. She has asked you, "I am thinking of buying a new car. Which would you recommend?" Write your copy as if you were answering that question.

(1) Don't beat about the bush—go straight to the point. Avoid analogies of the "just as, so too" variety. Dr. Gallup has demonstrated that these two-stage arguments are generally misunderstood.

(2) Avoid superlatives, generalizations, and platitudes. Be specific and factual. Be enthusiastic, friendly, and memorable. Don't be a bore. Tell the truth, but make the truth fascinating.

How long should your copy be? It depends on the product. If you are advertising chewing gum, there isn't much to tell, so make your copy short. If, on the other hand, you are advertising a product which has a great many different qualities to recommend it, write long copy: the more you tell, the more you sell.

There is a universal belief in lay circles that people won't read long copy. Nothing could be farther from the truth. Claude Hopkins once wrote five pages of solid text for Schlitz beer. In a few months, Schlitz moved up from fifth place to first. I once wrote a page of solid text for Good Luck Margarine, with most gratifying results.

Research shows that readership falls off rapidly up to fifty words of copy, but drops very little between fifty and 500 words. In my first Rolls-Royce advertisement I used 719 words—piling one fascinating fact on another. In the last paragraph I wrote, "People who feel diffident about driving a Rolls-Royce can buy a Bentley." Judging from the number of motorists who picked up the word "diffident" and bandied it about, I concluded that the advertisement was thoroughly read. In the next one I used 1400 words.

Every advertisement should be a *complete* sales pitch for your product. It is unrealistic to assume that consumers will read a *series* of advertisements for the same product. You should shoot the works in every advertisement, on the assumption that it is the only chance you will ever have to sell your product to the reader— *now or never*.

Says Dr. Charles Edwards of the graduate School of Retailing at New York University, "The more facts you tell, the more you sell. An advertisement's chance for success invariably increases as the number of pertinent merchandise facts included in the advertisement increases."

In my first advertisement for Puerto Rico's Operation Bootstrap, I used 961 words, and persuaded Beardsley Ruml to sign them. Fourteen thousand readers clipped the coupon from this advertisement, and scores of them later established factories in Puerto Rico. The greatest professional satisfaction I have yet had is to see the prosperity in Puerto Rican communities which had lived on the edge of starvation for four hundred years before I wrote my advertisement. If I had confined myself to a few vacuous generalities, nothing would have happened.

We have even been able to get people to read long copy about gasoline. One of our Shell advertisements contained 617 words, and 22 per cent of male readers read more than half of them.

Vic Schwab tells the story of Max Hart (of Hart, Schaffner & Marx) and his advertising manager, George L. Dyer, arguing about long copy. Dyer said, "I'll bet you ten dollars I can write a newspaper page of solid type and you'd read every word of it."

Hart scoffed at the idea. "I don't have to write a line of it to prove my point," Dyer replied. "I'll only tell you the headline: THIS PAGE IS ALL ABOUT MAX HART."

Advertisers who put coupons in their advertisements *know* that short copy doesn't sell. In split-run tests, long copy invariably outsells short copy.

Do I hear someone say that no copywriter can write long advertisements unless his media department gives him big spaces to work with? This question should not arise, because the copywriter should be consulted before planning the media schedule.

> (3) You should always include testimonials in your copy. The reader finds it easier to believe the endorsement of a fellow consumer than the puffery of an anonymous copywriter. Says Jim Young, one of the best copywriters alive today, "Every type of advertiser has the same problem; namely to be believed. The mail-order man knows nothing so potent for this purpose as the testimonial, yet the general advertiser seldom uses it."

Testimonials from celebrities get remarkably high readership, and if they are honestly written they still do not seem to provoke incredulity. The better known the celebrity, the more readers you will attract. We have featured Queen Elizabeth and Winston Churchill in "Come to Britain" advertisements, and we were able to persuade Mrs. Roosevelt to make television commercials for Good Luck Margarine. When we advertised charge accounts for Sears, Roebuck, we reproduced the credit card of Ted Williams, "recently traded by Boston to Sears."

Sometimes you can cast your entire copy in the form of a testimonial. My first advertisement for Austin cars took the form of a letter from an "anonymous diplomat" who was sending his son to Groton with money he had saved driving an Austin—a well-aimed combination of snobbery and economy. Alas, a perspicacious *Time* editor guessed that I was the anonymous diplomat, and asked the headmaster of Groton to comment. Dr. Crocker was so cross that I decided to send my son to Hotchkiss.

> (4) Another profitable gambit is to give the reader helpful advice, or service. It hooks about 75 per cent more readers than copy which deals entirely with the product.

One of our Rinso advertisements told housewives how to remove stains. It was better read (Starch) and better remembered (Gallup) than any detergent advertisement in history. Unfortunately, however, it forgot to feature Rinso's main selling promise—that Rinso washes whiter; for this reason it should never have run.[2]

> (5) I have never admired the *belles lettres* school of advertising, which reached its pompous peak in Theodore F. MacManus' famous advertisement for Cadillac, "The Penalty of Leadership," and Ned Jordan's classic, "Somewhere West of Laramie." Forty years ago the business community seems to have been impressed

---

2. The photograph showed several different kinds of stain—lipstick, coffee, shoe-polish, blood and so forth. The blood was my own; I am the only copywriter who has ever *bled* for his client.

by these pieces of purple prose, but I have always thought them absurd; they did not give the reader a single *fact*. I share Claude Hopkins' view that "fine writing is a distinct disadvantage. So is unique literary style. They take attention away from the subject."

(6) Avoid bombast. Raymond Rubicam's famous slogan for Squibb, "The priceless ingredient of every product is the honor and integrity of its maker," reminds me of my father's advice: when a company boasts about its integrity, or a woman about her virtue, avoid the former and cultivate the latter.

(7) Unless you have some special reason to be solemn and pretentious, write your copy in the colloquial language which your customers use in everyday conversation. I have never acquired a sufficiently good ear for vernacular American to write it, but I admire copywriters who can pull it off, as in this unpublished pearl from a dairy farmer:

> Carnation Milk is the best in the land,
> Here I sit with a can in my hand.
> No tits to pull, no hay to pitch,
> Just punch a hole in the son-of-a-bitch.

It is a mistake to use highfalutin language when you advertise to uneducated people. I once used the word OBSOLETE in a headline, only to discover that 43 per cent of housewives had no idea what it meant. In another headline, I used the word INEFFABLE, only to discover that I didn't know what it meant myself.

However, many copywriters of my vintage err on the side of underestimating the educational level of the population. Philip Hauser, head of the Sociology Department at the University of Chicago, draws attention to the changes which are taking place:

> The increasing exposure of the population to formal schooling . . . can be expected to effect important changes in . . . the style of advertising. . . . Messages aimed at the "average" American on the assumption that he has had less than a grade school education are likely to find themselves with a declining or disappearing clientele.[3]

Meanwhile, all copywriters should read Dr. Rudolph Flesch's *Art of Plain Talk*. It will persuade them to use short words, short sentences, short paragraphs, and highly *personal* copy.

Aldous Huxley, who once tried his hand at writing advertisements, concluded that "any trace of literariness in an advertisement is fatal to its success. Advertisement writers may not be lyrical, or obscure, or in any way esoteric. They must be universally intelligible. A good advertisement has this in common with drama and oratory, that it must be immediately comprehensible and directly moving."[4]

(8) Resist the temptation to write the kind of copy which wins awards. I am always gratified when I win an award, but most of the campaigns which produce *results* never win awards, because they don't draw attention to themselves.

The juries that bestow awards are never given enough information about the *results* of the advertisements they are called upon to judge. In the absence of such information, they rely on their opinions, which are always warped toward the highbrow.

(9) Good copywriters have always resisted the temptation to *entertain*. Their achievement lies in the number of new products they get off to a flying start. In a

3. *Scientific American* (October 1962).

4. *Essays Old And New* (Harper & Brothers, 1927). Charles Lamb and Byron also wrote advertisements. So did Bernard Shaw, Hemingway, Marquand, Sherwood Anderson, and Faulkner—none of them with any degree of success.

class by himself stands Claude Hopkins, who is to advertising what Escoffier is to cooking. By today's standards, Hopkins was an unscrupulous barbarian, but technically he was the supreme master. Next I would place Raymond Rubicam, George Cecil, and James Webb Young, all of whom lacked Hopkins' ruthless salesmanship, but made up for it by their honesty, by the broader range of their work, and by their ability to write civilized copy when the occasion required it. Next I would place John Caples, the mail-order specialist from whom I have learned much.

These giants wrote their advertisements for newspapers and magazines. It is still too early to identify the best writers for television.

Marshall McLuhan / Keeping Upset with the Joneses   1964

Since the publication of The Mechanical Bride *in 1951, Herbert Marshall McLuhan has been a leading figure in the study of mass media and communications. Born in 1911 in Edmonton, Alberta, McLuhan was educated at the University of Manitoba and received his Ph.D. from Cambridge in 1942. His most famous work,* Understanding Media, The Extensions of Man *(1964), a study of the effects of technology and electronics on traditional forms of literacy, has significantly influenced contemporary thought. McLuhan is currently Director of the Center for Culture and Technology at the University of Toronto.*

The following critical assessment of advertising appeared as a chapter in Understanding Media.

The continuous pressure is to create ads more and more in the image of audience motives and desires. The product matters less as the audience participation increases. An extreme example is the corset series that protests that "it is not the corset that you feel." The need is to make the ad include the audience experience. The product and the public response become a single complex pattern. The art of advertising has wondrously come to fulfill the early definition of anthropology as "the science of man embracing woman." The steady trend in advertising is to manifest the product as an integral part of large social purposes and processes. With very large budgets the commercial artists have tended to develop the ad into an icon, and icons are not specialist fragments or aspects but unified and compressed images of complex kind. They focus a large region of experience in tiny compass. The trend in ads, then, is away from the consumer picture of product to the producer image of process. The corporate image of process includes the consumer in the producer role as well.

This powerful new trend in ads toward the iconic image has greatly weakened the position of the magazine industry in general and the picture magazines in particular. Magazine features have long employed the pictorial treatment of themes and news. Side by side with these magazine features that present shots and fragmentary points of view, there are the new massive iconic ads with their compressed images that include producer and consumer, seller and society in a single image. The ads make the features seem pale, weak, and anemic. The features belong to the old pictorial world that preceded TV mosaic imagery.

It is the powerful mosaic and iconic thrust in our experience since TV that explains the paradox of the upsurge of *Time* and *Newsweek* and similar magazines. These magazines present the news in a compressed mosaic form that is a real parallel to the ad world. Mosaic news is neither narrative, nor point of view, nor explanation, nor comment. It is a corporate image in depth of the community in action and invites maximal participation in the social process.

Ads seem to work on the very advanced principle that a small pellet or pattern in a noisy, redundant barrage of repetition will gradually assert itself. Ads push the principle of noise all the way to the plateau of persuasion. They are quite in accord with the procedures of brain-washing. This depth principle of onslaught on the unconscious may be the reason why.

Many people have expressed uneasiness about the advertising enterprise in our time. To put the matter abruptly, the advertising industry is a crude attempt to extend the principles of automation to every aspect of society. Ideally, advertising aims at the goal of a programmed harmony among all human impulses and aspirations and endeavors. Using handicraft methods, it stretches out toward the ultimate electronic goal of a collective consciousness. When all production and all consumption are brought into a pre-established harmony with all desire and all effort, then advertising will have liquidated itself by its own success.

Since the advent of TV, the exploitation of the unconscious by the advertiser has hit a snag. TV experience favors much more consciousness concerning the unconscious than do the hard-sell forms of presentation in the press, the magazine, movie, or radio. The sensory tolerance of the audience has changed, and so have the methods of appeal by the advertisers. In the new cool TV world, the old hot world of hard-selling, earnest-talking salesmen has all the antique charm of the songs and togs of the 1920s. Mort Sahl and Shelley Berman are merely following, not setting, a trend in spoofing the ad world. They discovered that they have only to reel off an ad or news item to have the audience in fits. Will Rogers discovered years ago that any newspaper read aloud from a theater stage is hilarious. The same is true today of ads. Any ad put into a new setting is funny. This is a way of saying that any ad consciously attended to is comical. Ads are not meant for conscious consumption. They are intended as subliminal pills for the subconscious in order to exercise an hypnotic spell, especially on sociologists. That is one of the most edifying aspects of the huge educational enterprise that we call advertising, whose twelve-billion-dollar annual budget approximates the national school budget. Any expensive ad represents the toil, attention, testing, wit, art, and skill of many people. Far more thought and care go into the composition of any prominent ad in a newspaper or magazine than go into the writing of their features and editorials. Any expensive ad is as carefully built on the tested foundations of public stereotypes or "sets" of established attitudes, as any skyscraper is built on bedrock. Since highly skilled and perceptive teams of talent cooperate in the making of an ad for any established line of goods whatever, it is obvious that any acceptable ad is a vigorous dramatization of communal experience. No group of sociologists can approximate the ad teams in the gathering and processing of exploitable social data. The ad teams have billions to spend annually on reasearch and testing of reactions, and their products are magnificent accumulations of material about the shared experience and feelings of the entire community. Of course, if ads were to depart from the center of this shared experience, they would collapse at once, by losing all hold on our feelings.

It is true, of course, that ads use the most basic and tested human experience of a community in grotesque ways. They are as incongruous, if looked at consciously, as the playing of "Silver Threads among the Gold" as music for a strip-tease act. But ads are carefully designed by the Madison Avenue frogmen-of-the-mind for semiconscious exposure. Their mere existence is a testimony, as well as a contribution, to the somnambulistic state of a tired metropolis.

After the Second War, an ad-conscious American army officer in Italy noted with misgiving that Italians could tell you the names of cabinet ministers, but not the names of commodities preferred by Italian celebrities. Furthermore, he said, the wall space of Italian cities was given over to political, rather than commercial, slogans. He predicted that there was small hope that Italians would ever achieve any sort of domestic prosperity or calm until they began to worry about the rival claims of cornflakes and cigarettes, rather than the capacities of public men. In fact, he went so far as to say that democratic freedom very largely consists in ignoring politics and worrying, instead, about the threat of scaly scalp, hairy legs, sluggish bowels, saggy breasts, receding gums, excess weight, and tired blood.

The army officer was probably right. Any community that wants to expedite and maximize the exchange of goods and services has simply got to homogenize its social life. The decision to homogenize comes easily to the highly literate population of the English-speaking world. Yet it is hard for oral cultures to agree on this program of homogenization, for they are only too prone to translate the message of radio into tribal politics, rather than into a new means of pushing Cadillacs. This is one reason that it was easy for the retribalized Nazi to feel superior to the American consumer. The tribal man can spot the gaps in the literate mentality very easily. On the other hand, it is the special illusion of literate societies that they are highly aware and individualistic. Centuries of typographic conditioning in patterns of lineal uniformity and fragmented repeatability have, in the electric age, been given increasing critical attention by the artistic world. The lineal process has been pushed out of industry, not only in management and production, but in entertainment, as well. It is the new mosaic form of the TV image that has replaced the Gutenberg structural assumptions. Reviewers of William Burroughs' *The Naked Lunch* have alluded to the prominent use of the "mosaic" term and method in his novel. The TV image renders the world of standard brands and consumer goods merely amusing. Basically, the reason is that the mosaic mesh of the TV image compels so much active participation on the part of the viewer that he develops a nostalgia for pre-consumer ways and days. Lewis Mumford gets serious attention when he praises the cohesive form of medieval towns as relevant to our time and needs.

Advertising got into high gear only at the end of the last century, with the invention of photoengraving. Ads and pictures then became interchangeable and have continued so. More important, pictures made possible great increases in newspaper and magazine circulation that also increased the quantity and profitability of ads. Today it is inconceivable that any publication, daily or periodical, could hold more than a few thousand readers without pictures. For both the pictorial ad or the picture story provide large quantities of instant information and instant humans, such as are necessary for keeping abreast in our kind of culture. Would it not seem natural and necessary that the young be provided with at least as much training of perception in this graphic and photographic world as they get in the typographic? In fact, they need more training in graphics, because the art of casting and arranging actors in ads is both complex and forcefully insidious.

Some writers have argued that the Graphic Revolution has shifted our culture away from the private ideals to corporate images. That is really to say that the photo and TV seduce us from the *literate* and private "point of view" to the complex and inclusive world of the group icon. That is certainly what advertising does. Instead of presenting a private argument or vista, it offers a way of life that is for everybody or nobody. It offers this prospect with arguments that concern only irrelevant and trivial matters. For example, a lush car ad features a baby's rattle on the rich rug of the back floor and says that it has removed unwanted car rattles as easily as the user could remove the baby's rattle. This kind of copy has really nothing to do with rattles. The copy is merely a punning gag to distract the critical faculties while the image of the car goes to work on the hypnotized viewer. Those who have spent their lives protesting about "false and misleading ad copy" are godsends to advertisers, as teetotalers are to brewers, and moral censors are to books and films. The protestors are the best acclaimers and accelerators. Since the advent of pictures, the job of the ad copy is as incidental and latent, as the "meaning" of a poem is to a poem, or the words of a song are to a song. Highly literate people cannot cope with the nonverbal art of the pictorial, so they dance impatiently up and down to express a pointless disapproval that renders them futile and gives new power and authority to the ads. The unconscious depth-messages of ads are never attacked by the literate, because of their incapacity to notice or discuss nonverbal forms of arrangement and meaning. They have not the art to argue with pictures. When early in TV broadcasting hidden ads were tried out, the literate were in a great panic until they were dropped. The fact that typography is itself mainly subliminal in effect and that pictures are, as well, is a secret that is safe from the book-oriented community.

When the movies came, the entire pattern of American life went on the screen as a nonstop ad. Whatever any actor or actress wore or used or ate was such an ad as had never been dreamed of. The American bathroom, kitchen, and car, like everything else, got the *Arabian Nights* treatment. The result was that all ads in magazines and the press had to look like scenes from a movie. They still do. But the focus has had to become softer since TV.

With radio, ads openly went over to the incantation of the singing commercial. Noise and nausea as a technique of achieving unforgettability became universal. Ad and image making became, and have remained, the only really dynamic and growing part of the economy. Both movie and radio are hot media, whose arrival pepped up everybody to a great degree, giving us the Roaring Twenties. The effect was to provide a massive platform and a mandate for sales promotion as a way of life that ended only with *The Death of a Salesman* and the advent of TV. These two events did not coincide by accident. TV introduced that "experience in depth" and the "do-it-yourself" pattern of living that has shattered the image of the individualist hard-sell salesman and the docile consumer, just as it has blurred the formerly clear figures of the movie stars. This is not to suggest that Arthur Miller was trying to explain TV to America on the eve of its arrival, though he could as appropriately have titled his play "The Birth of the PR Man." Those who saw Harold Lloyd's *World of Comedy* film will remember that surprise at how much of the 1920s they had forgotten. Also, they were surprised to find evidence of how naive and simple the Twenties really were. That age of the vamps, the sheiks, and the cavemen was a raucous nursery compared to our world, in which children read *MAD* magazine for chuckles. It was a world still innocently engaged in expanding and exploding, in separating and teasing and tearing. Today, with TV, we are experiencing the opposite process of integrating and interrelating that is anything but innocent. The simple faith of the salesman in the irresistibility of his line (both talk and goods) now yields to the complex togetherness of the corporate posture, the process and the organization.

Ads have proved to be a self-liquidating form of community entertainment. They came along just after the Victorian gospel of work, and they promised a Beulah land of perfectibility, where it would be possible to "iron shirts without hating your husband." And now they are deserting the individual consumer-product in favor of the all-inclusive and never-ending process that is the Image of any great corporate enterprise. The Container Corporation of America does not feature paper bags and paper cups in its ads, but the container *function,* by means of great art. The historians and archeologists will one day discover that the ads of our time are the richest and most faithful daily reflections that any society ever made of its entire range of activities. The Egyptian hieroglyph lags far behind in this respect. With TV, the smarter advertisers have made free with fur and fuzz, and blur and buzz. They have, in a word, taken a skin-dive. For that is what the TV viewer is. He is a skin-diver, and he no longer likes garish daylight on hard, skiny surfaces, though he must continue to put up with a noisy radio sound track that is painful.

Daniel J. Boorstin / The Rhetoric of Democracy   1974

> *"We are perhaps the first people in history to have a centrally organized mass-produced folk culture,"* writes Daniel J. Boorstin in *"The Rhetoric of Democracy,"* and *"advertising has become the heart of the folk culture and even its very prototype."* In the following essay, which first appeared in Democracy and Its Discontents (*1974) and in 1976 was featured in the advertising trade magazine called* Advertising Age, *Boorstin constructs a historical context for the complex role advertising now plays in contemporary American culture.*
>
> *One of America's leading historians, Daniel J. Boorstin is the author of the critically acclaimed three-volume study,* The Americans. *He has served as director of the National Museum of History and Technology, as senior historian of the Smithsonian Institution, and is currently director of the Library of Congress.*

Advertising, of course, has been part of the mainstream of American civilization, although you might not know it if you read the most respectable surveys of American history. It has been one of the enticements to the settlement of this New World, it has been a producer of the peopling of the United States, and in its modern form, in its world-wide reach, it has been one of our most characteristic products.

Never was there a more outrageous or more unscrupulous or more ill-informed advertising campaign than that by which the promoters for the American colonies brought settlers here. Brochures published in England in the seventeenth century, some even earlier, were full of hopeful overstatements, half-truths, and downright lies, along with some facts which nowadays surely would be the basis for a restraining order from the Federal Trade Commission. Gold and silver, fountains of youth, plenty of fish, venison without limit, all these were promised, and of course some of them were found. It would be interesting to speculate on how long it might have taken to settle this continent if there had not been such promotion by enterprising advertisers. How has American civilization been shaped by the fact that there was a kind of natural selection here of those people who were willing to believe advertising?

Advertising has taken the lead in promising and exploiting the new. This was a new world, and one of the advertisements for it appears on the dollar bill on the Great Seal of the United States, which reads *novus ordo seclorum,* one of the most effective advertising slogans to come out of this country. "A new order of the centuries"—belief in novelty and in the desirability of opening novelty to everybody has been important in our lives throughout our history and especially in this century. Again and again advertising has been an agency for inducing Americans to try anything and everything—from the continent itself to a new brand of soap. As one of the more literate and poetic of the advertising copywriters, James Kenneth Frazier, a Cornell graduate, wrote in 1900 in "The Doctor's Lament":

> This lean M.D. is Dr. Brown
> Who fares but ill in Spotless Town.
> The town is so confounded clean,
> It is no wonder he is lean,
> He's lost all patients now, you know,
> Because they use *Sapolio.*

The same literary talent that once was used to retail Sapolio was later used to induce people to try the Edsel or the Mustang, to experiment with Lifebuoy or Body-All, to drink Pepsi-Cola or Royal Crown Cola, or to shave with a Trac II razor.

And as expansion and novelty have become essential to our economy, advertising has played an ever-larger role: in the settling of the continent, in the expansion of the economy, and in the building of an American standard of living. Advertising has expressed the optimism, the hyperbole, and the sense of community, the sense of reaching which has been so important a feature of our civilization.

Here I wish to explore the significance of advertising, not as a force in the economy or in shaping an American standard of living, but rather as a touchstone of the ways in which we Americans have learned about all sorts of things.

The problems of advertising are of course not peculiar to advertising, for they are just one aspect of the problems of democracy. They reflect the rise of what I have called Consumption Communities and Statistical Communities, and many of the special problems of advertising have arisen from our continuously energetic effort to give everybody everything.

If we consider democracy not just as a political system, but as a set of institutions which do aim to make everything available to everybody, it would not be an overstatement to describe advertising as the characteristic rhetoric of democracy. One of the tendencies of democracy, which Palto and other antidemocrats warned against a long time ago, was the danger that rhetoric would displace or at least overshadow epistemology; that is, *the temptation to allow the problem of persuasion to overshadow the problem of knowledge.* Democratic societies tend to become more concerned with what people believe than with what is true, to become more concerned with credibility than with truth. All these problems become accentuated in a large-scale democracy like ours, which possesses all the apparatus of modern industry. And the problems are accentuated still further by universal literacy, by instantaneous communication, and by the daily plague of words and images.

In the early days it was common for advertising men to define advertisements as a kind of news. The best admen, like the best journalists, were suppose to be those who were able to make their news the most interesting and readable. This was natural enough, since the verb to "advertise" originally meant, intransitively, to take note or to consider. For a person to "advertise" meant originally, in the fourteenth and fifteenth centuries, to reflect on something, to think about something. Then it came to mean, transitively, to call the attention of another to something, to give him notice, to notify, admonish, warn or inform in a formal or impressive manner. And then, by the sixteenth century, it came to mean: to give notice of anything, to make generally known. It was not until the late eighteenth century that the word "advertising" in English came to have a specifically "advertising" connotation as we might say today, and not until the late nineteenth century that it began to have a specifically commercial connotation. By 1879 someone was saying, "Don't advertise unless you have something worth advertising." But even into the present century, newspapers continue to call themselves by the title "Advertiser"—for example, the Boston *Daily Advertiser,* which was a newspaper of long tradition and one of the most dignified papers in Boston until William Randolph Hearst took it over in 1917. Newspapers carried "Advertiser" on their mastheads, not because they sold advertisements but because they brought news.

Now, the main role of advertising in American civilization came increasingly to be that of persuading and appealing rather than that of educating and informing. By 1921, for instance, one of the more popular textbooks, Blanchard's *Essentials of Advertising,* began: "Anything employed to influence people favorably is advertising. The mission of advertising is to persuade men and women to act in a way that will be of advantage to the advertiser." This development—in a country where a shared, a rising, and a democratized standard of living was the national pride and the national hallmark—meant that advertising had become the rhetoric of democracy.

What, then, were some of the main features of modern American advertising—if we consider it as a form of rhetoric? First, and perhaps most obvious, is *repetition.* It is hard for us to realize that the use of repetition in advertising is not an ancient device but a modern one, which actually did not come into common use in American journalism until just past the middle of the nineteenth century.

The development of what came to be called "iteration copy" was a result of a struggle by a courageous man of letters and advertising pioneer, Robert Bonner, who bought the old New York *Merchant's Ledger* in 1851 and turned it into a popular journal. He then had the temerity to try to change the ways of James Gordon Bennett, who of course was one of the most successful of the American newspaper pioneers, and who was both a sensationalist and at the same time an extremely stuffy man when it came to things that he did not consider to be news. Bonner was determined to use advertisements in Bennett's wide-circulating New York *Herald* to sell his own literary product, but he found it difficult to persuade Bennett to allow him to use any but agate type in his advertising. (Agate was the smallest type used by newspapers in that day, only barely legible to the naked eye.) Bennett would not allow advertisers to use larger type, nor would he allow them to use illustrations except stock cuts, because he thought it was undignified.

He said, too, that to allow a variation in the format of ads would be undemocratic. He insisted that all advertisers use the same size type so that no one would be allowed to prevail over another simply by presenting his message in a larger, more clever, or more attention-getting form.

Finally Bonner managed to overcome Bennett's rigidity by leasing whole pages of the paper and using the tiny agate type to form larger letters across the top of the page. In this way he produced a message such as "Bring home the New York Ledger tonight." His were unimaginative messages, and when repeated all across the page they technically did not violate Bennett's agate rule. But they opened a new era and presaged a new freedom for advertisers in their use of the newspaper page. Iteration copy—the practice of presenting prosaic content in ingenious, repetitive form—became common, and nowadays of course is commonplace.

A second characteristic of American advertising which is not unrelated to this is the development of *an advertising style*. We have histories of most other kinds of style—including the style of many unread writers who are remembered today only because they have been forgotten—but we have very few accounts of the history of advertising style, which of course is one of the most important forms of our language and one of the most widely influential.

The development of advertising style was the convergence of several very respectable American traditions. One of these was the tradition of the "plain style," which the Puritans made so much of and which accounts for so much of the strength of the Puritan literature. The "plain style" was of course much influenced by the Bible and found its way into the rhetoric of American writers and speakers of great power like Abraham Lincoln. When advertising began to be self-conscious in the eary years of this century, the pioneers urged copywriters not to be too clever, and especially not to be fancy. One of the pioneers of the advertising copywriters, John Powers, said, for example, "The commonplace is the proper level for writing in business; where the first virtue is plainness, 'fine writing' is not only intellectual, it is offensive." George P. Rowell, another advertising pioneer, said, "You must write your advertisement to catch damned fools—not college professors." He was a very tactful person. And he added, "And you'll catch just as many college professors as you will of any other sort." In the 1920's, when advertising was beginning to come into its own, Claude Hopkins, whose name is known to all in the trade, said, "Brilliant writing has no place in advertising. A unique style takes attention from the subject. Any apparent effort to sell creates corresponding resistance. . . . One should be natural and simple. His language should not be conspicuous. In fishing for buyers, as in fishing for bass, one should not reveal the hook." So there developed a characteristic advertising style in which plainness, the phrase that anyone could understand, was a distinguishing mark.

At the same time, the American advertising style drew on another, and what might seem an antithetic, tradition—the tradition of hyperbole in tall talk, the language of Davy Crockett and Mike Fink. While advertising could think of itself as 99.44 percent pure, it used the language of "Toronado" and "Cutlass." As I listen to the radio in Washington, I hear a celebration of heroic qualities which would make the characteristics of Mike Fink and Davy Crockett pale, only to discover at the end of the paean that what I have been hearing is a description of the Ford dealers in the District of Columbia neighborhood. And along with the folk tradition of hyperbole and tall talk comes the rhythm of folk music. We hear that Pepsi-Cola hits the spot, that it's for the young generation—and we hear other products celebrated in music which we cannot forget and sometimes don't want to remember.

There grew somehow out of all these contradictory tendencies—combining the commonsense language of the "plain style," and the fantasy language of "tall talk"—an advertising style. This characteristic way of talking about things was especially designed to reach and catch the millions. It created a whole new world of myth. A myth, the dictionary tells us, is a notion based more on tradition or convenience than on facts; it is a received idea. Myth is not just fantasy and not just fact but exists in a limbo, in the world of the "Will to Believe," which William James has written about so eloquently and so perceptively. This is the world of the neither true nor false—of the statement that 60 percent of the physicians who expressed a choice said that our brand of aspirin would be more effective in curing a simple headache than any other leading brand.

That kind of statement exists in a penumbra. I would call this the "advertising penumbra." It is not untrue, and yet, in its connotation it is not exactly true.

Now, there is still another characteristic of advertising so obvious that we are inclined perhaps to overlook it. I call that *ubiquity*. Advertising abhors a vacuum and we discover new vacuums every day. The parable, of course, is the story of the man who thought of putting the advertisement on the other side of the cigarette package. Until then, that was wasted space and a society which aims at a democratic standard of living, at extending the benefits of consumption and all sorts of things and services to everybody, must miss no chances to reach people. The highway billboard and other outdoor advertising, bus and streetcar and subway advertising, and skywriting, radio and TV commercials—all these are of course obvious evidence that advertising abhors a vacuum.

We might reverse the old mousetrap slogan and say that anyone who can devise another place to put another mousetrap to catch a consumer will find people beating a path to his door. "Avoiding advertising will become a little harder next January," the *Wall Street Journal* reported on May 17, 1973, "when a Studio City, California, company launches a venture called StoreVision. Its product is a system of billboards that move on a track across supermarket ceilings. Some 650 supermarkets so far are set to have the system." All of which helps us understand the observation attributed to a French man of letters during his recent visit to Times Square. "What a beautiful place, if only one could not read!" Everywhere is a place to be filled, as we discover in a recent *Publishers Weekly* description of one advertising program: "The $1.95 paperback edition of Dr. Thomas A. Harris' million-copy best seller 'I'm O.K., You're O.K.' is in for full-scale promotion in July by its publisher, Avon Books. Plans range from bumper stickers to airplane streamers, from planes flying above Fire Island, the Hamptons and Malibu. In addition, the $100,000 promotion budget calls for 200,000 bookmarks, plus brochures, buttons, lipcards, floor and counter displays, and advertising in magazines and TV."

The ubiquity of advertising is of course just another effect of our uninhibited efforts to use all the media to get all sorts of information to everybody everywhere. Since the places to be filled are everywhere, the amount of advertising is not determined by the *needs* of advertising, but by the *opportunities* for advertising which become unlimited.

But the most effective advertising, in an energetic, novelty-ridden society like ours, tends to be "self-liquidating." To create a cliché you must offer something which everybody accepts. The most successful advertising therefore self-destructs because it becomes cliché. Examples of this are found in the tendency for co-pyrighted names of trademarks to enter the vernacular—for the proper names of products which have been made familiar by costly advertising to become common nouns, and so to apply to anybody's products. Kodak becomes a synonym for camera, Kleenex a synonym for facial tissue, when both begin with a small *k*, and Xerox (now, too, with a small *x*) is used to describe all processes of copying, and so on. These are prototypes of the problem. If you are successful enough, then you will defeat your purpose in the long run—by making the name and the message so familiar that people won't notice them, and then people will cease to distinguish your product from everybody else's.

In a sense, of course, as we will see, the whole of American civilization is an example. When this was a "new" world, if people succeeded in building a civilization here, the New World would survive and would reach the time—in our age—when it would cease to be new. And now we have the oldest written Constitution in use in the world. This is only a parable of which there are many more examples.

The advertising man who is successful in marketing any particular product, then—in our high-technology, well-to-do democratic society, which aims to get everything to everybody—is apt to be diluting the demand for his particular product in the very act of satisfying it. But luckily for him, he is at the very same time creating a fresh demand for his services as advertiser.

And as a consequence, there is yet another role which is assigned to American advertising. This is what I call "erasure." Insofar as advertising is competitive or innovation is widespread, erasure is required in order to persuade consumers that this year's model is superior to last year's. In fact, we consumers learn that we might be risking our lives if we go out on the highway with those very devices that were last year's lifesavers but without whatever special kind of brakes or wipers or seat belt is on this year's model. This is what I mean by "erasure"—and we see it on our advertising pages or our television screen every day. We read in the *New York Times* (May 20, 1973), for example, that "For the price of something small and ugly, you can drive something small and beautiful"—an advertisement for the Fiat 250 Spider. Or another, perhaps more subtle example is the advertisement for shirts under a picture of Oliver Drab: "Oliver Drab. A name to remember in fine designer shirts? No kidding. . . . Because you pay extra money for Oliver Drab. And for all the other superstars of the fashion world. Golden Vee [the name of the brand that is advertised] does not have a designer's label. But we do have designers. . . . By keeping their names *off* our label and simply saying Golden Vee, we can afford to sell our $7 to $12 shirts for just $7 to $12, which should make Golden Vee a name to remember. Golden Vee, you only pay for the shirt."

Having mentioned two special characteristics—the self-liquidating tendency and the need for erasure—which arise from the dynamism of the American economy, I would like to try to place advertising in a larger perspective. The special role of advertising in our life gives a clue to a pervasive oddity in American civilization. A leading feature of past cultures, as anthropologists have explained, is the tendency to distinguish between "high" culture and "low" culture—between the culture of the literate and the learned on the one hand and that of the populace on the other. In other words, between the language of literature and the language of the vernacular. Some of the most useful statements of this distinction have been made by social scientists at the University of Chicago—first by the late Robert

Redfield in his several pioneering books on peasant society, and then by Milton Singer in his remarkable study of Indian civilization. *When a Great Tradition Modernizes* (1972). This distinction between the great tradition and the little tradition, between the high culture and the folk culture, has begun to become a commonplace of modern anthropology.

Some of the obvious features of advertising in modern America offer us an opportunity to note the significance or insignificance of that distinction for us. Elsewhere I have tried to point out some of the peculiarities of the American attitude toward the *high* culture. There is something distinctive about the place of thought in American life, which I think is not quite what it has been in certain Old World cultures.

But what about distinctive American attitudes to *popular* culture? What is our analogue to the folk culture of other peoples? Advertising gives us some clues—to a characteristically American democratic folk culture. Folk culture is a name for the culture which ordinary people everywhere lean on. It is not the writings of Dante and Chaucer and Shakespeare and Milton, the teachings of Machiavelli and Descartes, Locke or Marx. It is, rather, the pattern of slogans, local traditions, tales, songs, dances, and ditties. And of course holiday observances. Popular culture in other civilizations has been for the most part both an area of continuity with the past, a way in which people reach back into the past and out to their community, and at the same time an area of local variations. An area of individual and amateur expression in which a person has his own way of saying, or notes his mother's way of saying or singing, or his own way of dancing, his own view of folk wisdom and the cliché.

And here is an interesting point of contrast. In other societies outside the United States, it is the *high* culture that has generally been an area of centralized, organized control. In Western Europe, for example, universities and churches have tended to be closely allied to the government. The institutions of higher learning have had a relatively limited access to the people as a whole. This was inevitable, of course, in most parts of the world, because there were so few universities. In England, for example, there were only two universities until the early nineteenth century. And there was central control over the printed matter that was used in universities or in the liturgy. The government tended to be close to the high culture, and that was easy because the high culture itself was so centralized and because literacy was relatively limited.

In our society, however, we seem to have turned all of this around. Our high culture is one of the least centralized areas of our culture. And our universities express the atomistic, diffused, chaotic, and individualistic aspect of our life. We have in this country more than twenty-five hundred colleges and universities, institutions of so-called higher learning. We have a vast population in these institutions, somewhere over seven million students.

But when we turn to our popular culture, what do we find? We find that in our nation of Consumption Communities and emphasis on Gross National Product (GNP) and growth rates, advertising has become the heart of the folk culture and even its very prototype. And as we have seen, American advertising shows many characteristics of the folk culture of other societies: repetition, a plain style, hyperbole and tall talk, folk verse, and folk music. Folk culture, wherever it has flourished, has tended to thrive in a limbo between fact and fantasy, and of course, depending on the spoken word and the oral tradition, it spreads easily and tends to be ubiquitous. These are all familiar characteristics of folk culture and they are ways of describing our folk culture, but how do the expressions of our peculiar folk culture come to *us?*

They no longer sprout from the earth, from the village, from the farm, or even from the neighborhood or the city. They come to us primarily from enormous centralized self-consciously *creative* (an overused word, for the overuse of which advertising agencies are in no small part responsible) organizations. They come from advertising agencies, from networks of newspapers, radio, and television, from outdoor-advertising agencies, from the copywriters for ads in the largest-circulation magazines, and so on. These "creators" of folk culture—or pseudo-folk culture—aim at the widest intelligibility and charm and appeal.

But in the United States, we must recall, the advertising folk culture (like all advertising) is also confronted with the problems of self-liquidation and erasure. These are by-products of the expansive, energetic character of our economy. And they, too, distinguish American folk culture from folk cultures elsewhere.

Our folk culture is distinguished from others by being discontinuous, ephemeral, and self-destructive. Where does this leave the common citizen? All of us are qualified to answer.

In our society, then, those who cannot lean on the world of learning, on the high culture of the classics, on the elaborated wisdom of the books, have a new problem. The University of Chicago, for example, in the 1930's and 1940's was the center of a quest for a "common discourse." The champions of that quest, which became a kind of crusade, believed that such a discourse could be found through familiarity with the classics of great literature—and especially of Western European literature. I think they were misled; such works were not, nor are they apt to become, the common discourse of our society. Most people, even in a democracy, and a rich democracy like ours, live in a world of popular culture, our special kind of popular culture.

The characteristic folk culture of our society is a creature of advertising, and in a sense it *is* advertising. But advertising, our own popular culture, is harder to make into a source of continuity than the received wisdom and commonsense slogans and catchy songs of the vivid vernacular. The popular culture of advertising attenuates and is always dissolving before our very eyes. Among the charms, challenges, and tribulations of modern life, we must count this peculiar fluidity, this ephemeral character of that very kind of culture on which other peoples have been able to lean, the kind of culture to which they have looked for the continuity of their traditions, for their ties with the past and with the future.

We are perhaps the first people in history to have a centrally organized mass-produced folk culture. Our kind of popular culture is here today and gone tomorrow—or the day after tomorrow. Or whenever the next semiannual model appears. And insofar as folk culture becomes advertising, and advertising becomes centralized, it becomes a way of depriving people of their opportunities for individual and small-community expression. Our technology and our economy and our democratic ideals have all helped make that possible. Here we have a new test of the problem that is at least as old as Heraclitus—an everyday test of man's ability to find continuity in his experience. And here democratic man has a new opportunity to accommodate himself, if he can, to the unknown.

"The eye, the tooth, the tongue"

(The story behind Market Dining Rooms and Bar, the new restaurant on the World Trade Center Concourse)

Even as New Yorkers are absorbing all the wonders of Windows On The World, we open still another restaurant in the World Trade Center. Why?

Because although the Trade Center now stands on the site of New York's great Washington Market of meat, fish and game, vegetables and fruit, to us it's never disappeared.

At dawn we still feel the rumble of carts, the clamor of vendors, the wondrous variety of provisions awaiting the wide-awake restaurant man. We savor the earthy-pungent-sweet-spicy-briny-herbacious confusion of smells in the market stalls.

And we decide!

We'll give to downtown Manhattan the type of market restaurant that flourished during those delectable days. A restaurant in tireless pursuit of the serious joys of eating. A restaurant where hungry tycoons and discerning workers would gather daily for leisurely, sensual dining. A restaurant where each day's market determines each day's menu. And one where, as you complete your first meal, you already begin, settled back over coffee, to look back over the menu, choosing new dishes, making plans for your second visit.

The better we run our restaurant, the harder it is to explain It.

But we'll give it a try.

Great food purveyors rarely and grudgingly bestow a crisp compliment on a colleague or a customer. When they admit: 'He's got 'the eye, the tooth, the tongue.' They mean, he's got *it*. Few people reach this pinnacle.

And these same purveyors know which restaurant buyers *also* have 'the eye, the tooth, the tongue.' And that's why you'll often catch them having dinner at our place. Choosing for themselves the very products they sold to us that morning…(Indeed, all of our daily specials appear on the menu together with the names of the marketmen who supply them to us.) These men like our Chef's way with food:

"Take all the time that's needed; take as little time as is required." In other words, he understands the natural character of the food he prepares, and labors, contentedly, to bring out all of its fine, full taste.

What is the purpose of cooking?

Only one thing: to make food exactly right for our mouths. In our case, that means a practiced, smooth, painstaking preparation is always followed. We create a menu that changes each day, filled with dishes we know people love, always enhancing taste and appearance, always with natural flavors unmasked.

Is this unbending goal possible?

Yes.

It is the very basis of our convictions. How do we cook vegetables? As little as possible. How do we broil a great steak? Over charcoal. Watchfully. When do we prepare your fish? While its eye still gleams, its scales are still colorful.

To our mind, once people begin tasting, savoring the goodness of the absolute top of the market, they'll come downtown, they'll come crosstown, they'll come in from all over. (And they'll come back!)

Why is our food buyer, Bob Mohel, so numbingly tired by Dinnertime?

Because he's unusual.

Beginning his day before dawn. Picking. Rejecting. Chewing. Squeezing. Frowning. Smiling. Frazzled.

Turning his gimlet-eye on beef. Checking for maturity and marbling. Poking for proper firmness.

At the fish stalls, holding each fish by its open mouth. If it's fresh, its tail stands up. If it droops, let somebody else buy it. (Oh the things Bob Mohel could teach you about shopping.)

Then when other buyers head for home, Bob Mohel stays on in our restaurant. He bought that food. He loves it. He makes sure that the rest of us share his interest. So he's always watching over it, making one last check to see it's served at its finest. He may be exhausted, but he never relaxes.

But if the best the market has to offer doesn't depend on complicated rituals and intricate recipes, why do we need Chef Arnold?

Not so fast.

A humble seafood stew can be complicated.

A perfect calves liver steak is always complicated.

A truly crisp roast duck is *very* complicated.

And behind every great dish is an immaculate, disciplined kitchen. So Chef Arnold is always around. Making certain that all cooking is his cooking, all seasoning his seasoning, all timing *his* timing. Greater responsibility than this hath no man.

How much do we know about running a Bar Room?

We could write a book!

Starting with the sorry-looking fingers of our skillful bartenders at our Market Bar. They won their wrinkled fingerprints by squeezing *groves* of fresh lemons and limes and oranges. (Because fresh juices transform our monumental Bourbon Sours in ways you've never tasted.)

Like all fine bartenders, ours are always on the move. If not checking to see if you're ready for another, they're bringing out more red radishes (with coarse salt alongside) and hot crunchy onions, or french-fried zucchini. (Never the usual peanuts or chips at the Market Bar.)

And, like a true Bar Room, it has its own friendly clatter, its own open pantry where even after midnight you can get yourself a steaming bowl of fish chowder, or a few Cotuit oysters, or smokey beans with peppered duck, or hot mussels with spicy red sauce, or crispy juicy ribs.

What's our policy toward wines?

1. As expected: Good, honest, appropriate wines. And each one ready-to-drink.
2. Less expected: Prices that range from modest to happily low.
3. Completely unexpected: Every wine is available in half-bottles at exactly half the price of a full bottle.

Why do the Market Dining Rooms look the way they do?

Because we think *you'll* think they look just right. Day in, day out, we seek the warmth and welcome those erstwhile market restaurants offered to men of commerce during (and after) their hectic day's work.

Everything about our look bespeaks a restaurant that cares about the pleasures good food can bestow.

That's why our big plates and glasses and flatware are cleanly designed. That's why the salt is coarse, the pepper freshly-ground. That's why unexpected appetizers are plunked down in front of you as soon as you're seated. (Why chewy, crusty, warm bread and chunks of sweet butter arrive at once.) That's why our tablecloths hang deep; why your napkin is huge, starched, pressed and has a buttonhole.

And yes, that's why you'll see quick-stepping waiters carrying live lobsters kitchenward for poaching, or wresting a plump snapper or a silvery bass from their beds of ice, their cover of seaweed. That's why, all about you, baskets and crates of fruits and vegetables from that day's market abound.

That's why our wooden floors and walls are softly burnished, why each table is bathed in a golden glow of light.

Finally, that's why we *want* you to look into our open pantry, our open kitchen, where a dish in preparation might attract you more than a menu description ever could.

You will not be mistaken in our intentions toward you.

Will our Market Dining Rooms & Bar become a day-in, day-out restaurant for you?

We'll say this:

We intend to be one of the great delights of downtown Manhattan. Our restaurant is temptingly easy to come back to. It fits you like a favorite chair.

We're new, you bet, but we already have regular friends. Friends who bring other friends dedicated to leisurely evenings satisfying 'the eye, the tooth, the tongue.' Why not do the same?

Ron Holland / Why I Wrote This Ad This Way   1979

*Advertising has become such a conspicuous part of our everyday lives that al-
though Madison Avenue starts in Manhattan it can now be said to reach every
home in America. Estimates of advertising's impact on American business and
culture range from Will Rogers' wry assertion that it "persuades people to buy
things that they don't need with money they ain't got" to Franklin Delano Roosevelt's surprising confession that "If I were starting my life over again, I would
probably give first thought to making advertising my career . . . because it combines real imagination with a deep study of psychology." Effective advertising, as
Roosevelt sensed, created memorable relationships between products and consumers by blending thorough market research, attractive graphics, and engaging
copywriting.*

*Ron Holland is one of advertising's most prominent copywriters. Born in Paw-
catuck, Connecticut in 1931, Holland worked his way through the University of
Connecticut by peddling Good Humor ice cream. After service in the Army's
counter-intelligence corps, he returned to a brief stint behind the wheel of his
own ice cream truck. At the urging of his brother, who had marvelled at the ads
created by the Papert, Koenig, and Lois Agency, Holland sent a short story and a
job application to Julian Koenig, and he was immediately put to work. Over the
years, Holland has written successful and original advertising for Lestoil, Braniff, the New York* Herald Tribune, *Redbook,* Cutty Sark, The Star, *and Restaurant
Associates. Perhaps his most famous slogan is the one he wrote for Braniff:
"When you got it, flaunt it!" He is now chairman of the board of Holland and
Callaway, an agency that sets the pace for the highly competitive field of restaurant advertising. His ad, "The eye, the tooth, the tongue," demonstrates how a
new restaurant tries to establish a marketing edge on its rivals in a cosmopolitan
community. The ad is premised on his belief that people will read and be influenced by good writing–even when the text is longer than usual.*

*In the following essay, written especially for this volume, Holland analyzes
how effective copywriting can command an audience's attention, create a memorable identity for a product, and increase a client's profits. As such, the essay
confirms Thomas Babington Macauley's dictum that "nothing except the Mint can
make money without advertising."*

Part of the fun of working in advertising is bumping into people who not only
know every nuance of their business, but whose ability is coupled with a genius
that lets them change the direction and goal of their industry. Joe Baum is a
brilliant (and irascible) example.

Joe created The Four Seasons, The Forum of the Twelve Caesars, La Fonda del
Sol, Charley O's, Charlie Brown's, Tower Suite, the Brasserie, Zum Zum, and
many other superior joints in New York. (The pleasure that his spots give New
Yorkers is enhanced a hundred-fold by the awesome standards he imposed on the
restaurant business, to the point where every restaurant buff remains inextricably
in his debt.)

During almost two decades of exhilarating and infuriating working together,

Joe, and George Lois and I tried to change restaurant advertising from routine promises of "steak and Chops our Speciality" or "We're not satisfied until *you're* satisfied" to ads that might prick up your ears. Ads like one for Charley O's that said: "Everybody raves about my Corned Beef and Cabbage. *Any*body can make good Corned Beef and Cabbage." I submit that such an ad tells you more about a restaurant's atmosphere (and about its corned beef and cabbage) than all the puffery in the world.

Right on the footsteps of his creation of Windows on the World (a restaurant so satisfying and successful that it not only changed New Yorkers's feeling about the World Trade Center as some kind of legislative boondoggle, but, in my opinion, gave a nice jolt of pride to the city and helped spark our financial comeback), Joe gave me a call.

"Come on downtown," he said, "and let's talk about a restaurant I'm going to open in the *basement* of the World Trade Center."

The *basement* of the World Trade Center? (As it turned, not the basement, but the ground floor. Still a long way, though, from the 107th floor, where Windows on the World was breaking every restaurant attendance and spending record.) However, since a phone call from Joe easily outranks a summons from the White House, I went down. And listened. And listened. And listened.

The Trade Center, Joe explained, is built on the site of the great Washington Market. During its construction, diggers had even exhumed a time capsule buried in the 1870's containing, among other delightful artifacts, newspapers filled with descriptions and prices of food and fowl, fish and game, fruits and vegetables available at the Washington Market. That gave Joe his leaping-off point. He wanted to open a true market restaurant. And that's a rare bird (except for those that evolved inside actual markets, of course).

Market restaurants are, or should be, as unpredictable as a harvest, or a trawler's catch, or a chef's whimsy. This puts a lot of pressure on the owner, but gives him unparalleled opportunities to excite his patrons, and drag them back, over and over. Of course, the customers he attracts are the most discerning, most critical, most sophisticated eaters who ever crankily assembled for a meal. But when it works, no other restaurant can touch it. And Joe was making it work.

Now.

How about the ad.

OK. My first boss, Julian Koenig (like Joe, a genius) once told me that if you listen to a client long enough, he will write your advertising for you. And since it is an unfailing (and inescapable) pleasure to listen to Joe Baum talk about the restaurant business, that's what I did. And, proving Julian out, when Joe was finished talking, the advertising was right there, waiting to be written.

Here's what I added to the raw material that Joe's enchanting journey through the history (and promise) of market restaurants dumped in my lap. The ad attempts (as all advertising must) to tell the truth and make it interesting.

1. The headline. An attempt to cut through atmosphere and ambiance and panache, and get down to senses and bodily equipment that deal with food. (Not, you will notice, the ear, because, although restaurant sounds can please or dismay, with the exception of celery, noise isn't much part of an eating experience.) And, of course, it's a headline that has to make you at least consider reading on.

2. First subhead. It couldn't hurt, I felt, to pick up a little of the glamour of Windows on the World, but to do so in a way that sounded as if we might be mistaken in opening another important restaurant in the World Trade Center so soon after its fabulous debut.

3. The question and answer format was necessary once we decided to produce what is certainly the longest restaurant ad ever written. It forces the writer to organize his thoughts, and allows him to influence the attitude of the reader. (It's a gratuitous question, but still fun to ask: What is the purpose of cooking?)

4. Thus use of archaic language was obvious enough. We intended the restaurant to be a throw-back, and so it was. Hence (a throw-back word) the use of words like *bestow* or phrases like *to our mind* or awkward descriptions like *to make food exactly right for our mouths* or *bespeaks*. The very indulgence of using words out of currency suggests to the reader that the restaurant itself probably isn't taking many shortcuts, and is, indeed, harking back to a different, more desirable day.

5. The length of the ad is, I must admit, also due to Joe Baum's correct insistence that the restaurant-goer will read information about food as long as it is sensible and to the point. So, at extraordinary length, I went on and on, but always hewing to the point of how much respect this place had for food and its preparation.

6. For all its length, you'll notice (if you plow through the ad) that there is no description of any dish. That's deliberate, and, I'll bet, proper. A restaurant ad, like a menu, shouldn't get into wheedling paean to the goodness of a dish. That's the job of the eye, the tooth, the tongue.

7. But the generosity of a restaurant can, and ought to be, described. And that's why I went to some length to explain the steps the Market Dining Rooms & Bar goes to, to give you your money's worth. Like the fresh-squeezed limes and the buttonhole in the napkin. (And the fact that, for all its simplicity of preparation, enormous skills on the part of the kitchen are necessary.)

8. Other things, like throwing in the names of the Chef (usual) and the food-buyer (usual, but not in the plaintive way it is done here) and the subhead that admits we can't explain the restaurant clearly, just keep the reader moving along. But keep him moving in the direction we want, and help him understand the easy-going, yet highly disciplined attitude of the restaurant.

9. The biggest reason that this huge chunk of copy became digestible is due to the warm design and friendly art direction of Milton Glaser.

Well!

It's bad enough to expect anyone to read an ad this long, but certainly unforgivable to ask you to read such a tortuous argument for its existence.

But I do think that if you read the ad, you will know more about Market Dining Rooms & Bar than you know about any other restaurant. And for a reward, take yourself down there.

The ad is true.

DISCUSSION QUESTIONS

1. Holland says that "the ad attempts (as all advertising must) to tell the truth and make it interesting." Another critic writes that because of the pressures of an overcrowded marketplace copywriters "found themselves indulging first in the use of the "little lie" and later in the " 'big lie'. . . ." Support one or the other of these statements with ads in this book.

2. How do the headlines and subheads in Holland's ad measure up to Ogilvy's ten rules for writing headlines? How nearly does his text conform to Ogilvy's nine guidelines for writing body copy? In an instance where you think Holland's ad runs counter to Ogilvy's suggestions, determine whether the ad is better or worse for having done so. Find other ads that support your answer.

PRESS

Journalism is literature in a hurry.
MATTHEW ARNOLD

NEWS may be America's best-selling product. Despite the intense competition from radio and television broadcasts, where news is delivered instantaneously and free of charge, well over fifty-eight million Americans are still willing to pay for their daily newspaper. Serving this immense market is an industry built around twenty-three thousand daily and weekly newspapers. The industry ranges from the picturesque one room office of a country paper, where the news is gathered, written, edited, and printed by a handful of people, to multi-level, worldwide corporate enterprises employing thousands in the strenuous business of compiling, disseminating, and even occasionally making the news. A news item, whether in a two page rural paper or in that monstrous, practically unfinishable, several hundred page Sunday edition of the *New York Times,* needs to be seen, then, as something more than simply a report of current events. To be comprehended fully, the news should be considered in its largest corporate context—as the result of individual and group writing performed under the pressures of advertising revenue, available space, deadlines, audience surveys, ownership policy, editorial selection, and professional competition. The "news" is not only transmitted information, it is the commodity of newspapers.

The pledge "All the News That's Fit To Print" on the front page of every copy of the *New York Times* reminds us that only news deemed suitable to print has been *selected* for us by editors apparently fastidious in their taste and conscience. The *Times'* motto, however, once prompted the following slightly cynical parody: "All the News That Fits We Print." The joke here works not only at the expense of the *New York Times;* it could easily apply to any large newspaper. A simple experiment shows how relatively small is the percentage of space allotted for what is supposedly a newspaper's main product, news. If you cut out from any newspaper with a fairly large circulation all the commercial and classified advertisements, the theater, movie, radio, and television listings, the national and local gossip, the personal advice columns, the horoscope, the puzzles and games, the cartoons, the letters to the editor, the "human interest" tid-bits, and the fillers, you are left with very few of what are, strictly speaking, genuine news items. In short, little of the shape and essence of a modern newspaper remains. The parody of the *Times'* pledge is right on target. It does seem that readers of most newspapers are given only the news that "fits" between the spaces reserved for more profitable or entertaining pieces.

To make sure that all the news will "fit"—in the sense of meeting editorial standards and conforming to the physical confines of the paper—newspapers impose a strictly regulated system of reportorial procedures and conventions. A person who writes for a newspaper must not only contend with tight deadlines but must also satisfy an experienced copy editor whose job is to see to it that the report will conform to the paper's public image and fit easily into its style. The writer must also be aware that the report will compete with all other news and non-news for prominent display in the layout of each edition. The exigencies of the newspaper business demand that the writer develop a comfortable, transferable, and conveniently alterable prose.

Any respected editor will say that clear and concise writing is encouraged. This usually means prose whittled down to short, simple sentences, the sparing use of adjectives and adverbs, a minimal reliance on synonyms, an avoidance of cumbersome syntactical relations, and brief paragraphs with few transitions. Most of the journalism reprinted in this section illustrates writing that conforms to these editorial strictures. Such standards are double-edged: they ensure the kind of writing generally considered to be most appropriate to rendering factual information quickly and precisely, and they guarantee sentences that are uniform and formulaic enough so as to be easily maneuvered into each newspaper's particular editorial requirements and emphases.

A stylistic uniformity for reporting important news stories (feature articles, editorials, and so on, are not so restricted) is enforced even further by a standardized narrative procedure newspapermen call the "inverted pyramid." The opening of a news story conventionally contains all the significant facts—the who, what, when, where, and occasionally the why—and the story tapers off gradually (picture a pyramid upside down), delivering additional facts and embellishments in a diminishing order of importance. Editors assume that their readers will want all the major details of a story right away, and that they should have the opportunity to move on to another story as soon as they feel they have absorbed enough information. Consequently, the emphasis in news writing is placed on the "lead," the opening sentences or paragraphs. In writing about a major news event, the reporter is obligated to pack in the principal facts in the first few lines. Since each succeeding sentence becomes less significant and, from an editor's point of view, increasingly dispensable, it is not unusual for reporters to let their prose slacken as their story moves further away from the top.

By opening the story with its climax, the writer gives up the possibility of sequential development and narrative suspense so that his readers can focus on the most important details immediately and his editor can lop off, should he need space for something else, the tapered strands of the report without losing any essential points. Therefore, paragraphs in most news stories are not connected to each other within a coherent expository framework. Instead, they can be thought of as self-contained, transferable, and, occasionally, disposable units. As a result, the reporter continually faces a rather disconcerting problem: he must write in such a manner that enables, even encourages, his audience to stop reading after the main points have been made, and, at the same time, he must make his writing compelling enough so that his readers will want to read on.

Yet reporters contend with more than the difficulties of composition. News stories need to be covered before they can be written. Reporters are men and women often entangled in the intricacies and drawn into the pace of the events they are trying to write about. They compose stories under pressure and in a hurry. To be "on the spot" during an event of some magnitude means most often to get caught up in the uncertain movements of participants and in the prevailing mood of the occasion. The inconveniences are many and unpredictable. One famous reporter, Stephen Crane, accompanying a crew of gun runners headed for Cuba during the insurrection at the close of the last century, was shipwrecked off the coast of Florida (see "Stephen Crane's Own Story"), and wound up with a tale far different from the one he had intended to write (see "The Open Boat" in Classics). To illustrate most dramatically the kind of difficulties encountered during a strenuous and emotionally trying reportorial assignment, we have included Tom Wicker's recollections of his efforts to cover the assassination of President Kennedy (see "The Assassination").

November 22, 1963, was for Wicker a day of great confusion and physical exhaustion. Though he was on the spot, Wicker was not close enough to the President's car to witness the shooting directly, nor did he even have the opportunity to view the principal characters afterward for more than a few moments. Covering the story of Kennedy's assassination was mainly an ordeal of getting quickly from one good news position to another and of assimilating the disparate and occasionally contradictory details of the event as rapidly as possible. The information came, as Wicker says, "in bits and pieces," and most of the time he had no way of verifying the data. The news story of the assassination was not "out there" to be copied down leisurely, without risks of inaccuracy. It was a matter of acting on hunches, recovering quickly from wrong turns, finding reliable contacts, getting around physical and bureaucratic obstacles, and all the while trying to put as many details into as coherent a shape as conditions allowed so the story could get to press on time.

Yet the by-line report printed in the *New York Times* the next day (see "Kennedy Is Killed by Sniper") conveys nothing at all of the frantic pace and exasperating confusions Wicker tells us obstructed his coverage. What Wicker went through that day—whatever public and private significances the event had for him—was not news. The conventions of newspaper reporting are exacting on one point: the reporter must not figure as a main character in his own story. If indeed, as Thoreau says, "It is, after all, always the first person that is speaking," we nevertheless need to work quite hard to imagine the "I" who is the eyewitness behind Wicker's writing. Not even an effort to read "between the lines" could help us reconstruct from his prose alone the tensions of Wicker's day as he hustled around Dallas for the news.

Wicker's report provides us with a fine instance of journalistic workmanship. The assassination was far too important an event for Wicker to take stylistic chances. The *Times* got what it wanted: the straightforward, informative account that is the marrow of news reporting. It saved the expressions of personal grief and the emotional record of the public sentiment appropriate to such occasions for its features and editorials. Part of Wicker's accomplishment in this by-line report is his cool, professional manner—he resists the impulse to attract attention to himself as a writer privileged to have been an eyewitness to one of the most sensational news events of the twentieth century. As a narrator, Wicker is never anxious to assure his readers of his presence at the scene. He never pauses in the account to remind us that his perspectives depend on his following the day's developments through several different locations in Dallas. Wicker deliberately avoids commenting on his own emotional connection to an event that we know from his own recollection shocked and grieved him. Nor, as he writes, does he allow himself the liberty of sounding like a worried citizen reflecting on the political and social significance of Kennedy's murder. It is clear that we cannot properly read Wicker's piece as a *personal* account of the assassination. In other words, we can not respond to his writing as if it were—what most of us usually expect writing to be—the disclosure of a particular personality. If Wicker tells us anything at all about himself, it is that he has mastered the discipline of news reporting.

Wicker's prose conforms to all the rules of journalistic style outlined earlier. The writing consists, for the most part, of syntactically simple, declarative sentences. The paragraphs are brief; only one contains as many as five sentences. The first few paragraphs provide the reader with all the crucial information, and the narrative proceeds to register details in what Wicker and his editors presumably considered to be a scale of decreasing importance. Though the narrative procedure would seem to recall the "inverted pyramid" mentioned previously, a closer look at Wicker's prose reveals a movement less narrowing than it would have been had Wicker adhered strictly to that often tyrannizing model. Instead, the narrative proceeds with a spiraling effect, moving from the center outward, moving, that is, away from its "lead" only to return to it repeatedly, though each time with a new angle and a diminishing emphasis.

Wicker, however, is not fully responsible for the narrative shape the story eventually took. He mentions in his retrospective analysis that he sent off to the *Times* information in "a straight narrative" he knew would be cut up by his editors as they decided on the best sequence and appropriate emphases. Although the by-line officially recognizes Wicker as the "author" of the news release, the final report the *Times* printed was, as is usually the case in news writing, the result of a collective activity that included Wicker and several other reporters who assisted him in Dallas, along with a New York staff of rewrite, copy, and managing editors.

While he was writing his report, Wicker must have been acutely conscious of the extensive television coverage given to the assassination. In fact, Wicker tells us that he filled in a few of the gaps in his own report by drawing on some of the information provided by television. Yet, as an antidote to the bewildering discontinuities and the numbing replays of the television reports, Wicker articulated a full, dispassionate recapitulation of the Kennedy assassination, accentuating the official interconnections between people and events rather than the panorama of personalities on location. To illustrate how a journalist responded to a similar incident almost a hundred years earlier, we have included the *New York Herald*'s coverage of President Lincoln's assassination. The April 15, 1865, issue of the *New York Herald* furnishes us with reportorial styles that were beginning to be conditioned by the invention of the telegraph but were not yet forced into competition with radio and television networks.

Tom Wicker's task as a reporter competing with the "live" transmission of news was not nearly so problematic as was Thomas O'Toole's assignment for the *Washington Post* to watch and write about the first landing on the moon in July 1969 (see " 'The Eagle Has Landed': Two Men Walk on the Moon"). Given the hermetic nature of such an electronically engineered event as *Apollo XI*'s flight to the moon, O'Toole could not claim a better vantage point for viewing the episode than could anyone else in the world with access to a television set. If the event O'Toole reported were, as he says in his lead, "a show that will long be remembered by the worldwide television audience," then he must have seen his function as that of a television reviewer rather than a privileged eyewitness commentator. In fact, his report makes it clear that the astronauts spent a good deal of their time transforming the moon into a television studio in which they then performed and improvised before the camera. Overshadowed by television, O'Toole's report could be little more than a public transcript of conversations everyone heard and descriptions of what everyone witnessed, punctuated by hyperbolic remarks that could express only the exclamatory mood of millions. Whether viewed as a technological triumph or as a television spectacular, the moon landing came as no special blessing to the newspaper industry. Upstaged by the extensive, unprecedented television coverage, reporters like O'Toole were left with relatively little to do but gather feature stories, collate information from television broadcasts, and turn NASA press releases into intelligible prose.

Each new day does not supply newspapers with a calamity or a triumph—most days newspapers need to find their news in the ordinary occurrences of life. Though a new headline appears daily, it may be merely perfunctory. Given standard newspaper format, one event must always be given more prominence than others. In our selections, we have tried to represent a good portion of the kind of news material you would normally find in American newspapers. We have included many of the standard forms and predominant styles of journalism: head lines, the "inverted pyramid" of major news stories, the fictional structures of feature stories, the polemical mode of editorials, along with by-lines, personal commentaries and columns, interviews, and humorous and whimsical anecdotes. Still, if the subjects for a good deal of the writing that follows strike you as disproportionately unpleasant, that is because the newspaper business generally thrives on the purveyance of "bad news." Pick up any newspaper, and you will be likely to find some account of individual or public violence, organized crime, political scandal, skirmishes with minorities and subcultures, domestic and international conflicts, the catastrophes of floods, earthquakes, and fires, and the routine disasters of modern transportation.

The material in this section is not intended as an introduction to the profession of journalism. The "texts" are meant to be read as examples of the often special language of the "reported" world. Our purpose is to invite you to consider the compositional procedures and prose styles of various kinds of reporting in order to observe how the reporter's method of writing appropriates public events in a way that makes it especially difficult for any of us to talk or to write about those events independently of the language provided by newspapers.

Walt Whitman / The Death Penalty

Brooklyn Eagle, January 13, 1858

> *I sit and look out upon all the sorrows of the world, and upon all
>   oppression and shame,*
> *I hear secret convulsive sobs from young men at anguish with them-
>   selves, remorseful after deeds done,*
> *I see in low life the mother misused by her children, dying, neglected,
>   gaunt, desperate,*
> *I see the wife misused by her husband, I see the treacherous seducer of
>   young women,*
> *I mark the ranklings of jealousy and unrequited love attempted to be
>   hid, I see these sights on the earth,*
> *I see the workings of battle, pestilence, tyranny, I see martyrs and pris-
>   oners,*
> *I observe a famine at sea, I observe the sailors casting lots who shall be
>   kill'd to preserve the lives of the rest,*
> *I observe the slights and degradations cast by arrogant persons upon
>   laborers, the poor, and upon negroes, and the like;*
> *All these—all the meanness and agony without end I sitting look out
>   upon,*
> *See, hear, and am silent.*

So the poet Walt Whitman wrote in Leaves of Grass *in 1860, but the journalist Whitman was not silent during his years as a reporter and editor. He spoke out*

often from his editorial column in the Brooklyn Eagle *and the* Brooklyn Daily
Times.

*"I was in early life very bigoted in my anti-slavery, anti-capital punishment
and so on, but I have always had a latent toleration for the people who choose a
reactionary course," wrote Whitman, who at another time called out "Let him
hang!" concerning a man convicted of murder. But in 1858, Whitman wrote the
more judicious editorial printed below. (Four recent editorials on the death
penalty appear later in this section.)*

*More biographical information about Whitman can be found in the headnote to
his poem "Crossing Brooklyn Ferry" in Classics.*

The law, or more correctly speaking, the custom, in relation to punishment of capital offenses, is in a very unsatisfactory state. The Southern papers are taunting
New York with the charge, that while fifty or sixty murders have been committed
there during the year, and only one by a negro, only one execution has taken
place, and that in the case of the negro. At present there are three prisoners in
New York awaiting execution. In one case, that of Rogers, a writ of error has
been granted, staying the proceedings. In that of Cancemi, too, it is anticipated
that a respite will be granted; while Shepherd will probably be executed, his case
having no melodramatic atrocity about it, fitted to enlist the sympathy of the soft-
hearted (and soft-headed) prison philanthropists. The law does not seem to have
made up its mind about the death penalty, whether it is proper to exact it in the
case of murderers or not. Hence, when a prisoner is sentenced, the execution is
fixed at a ridiculously distant day, and every facility is given for romantic penny-
a-liners and sympathetic old ladies to visit the cell and get up a fictitious public
opinion which will justify the Executive in pardoning him. And Judges, Counsel,
and every one connected with the administration of justice, exert themselves to
give the condemned every chance of evading punishment that the most hair-split-
ting quibbler can devise. In fact, while adhering to the death penalty, nominally,
our authorities act as if they had a lurking conviction that, after all, it is very questionable whether society is justified in depriving its recreant member of life. This
is not as it should be. Either society has as absolute a right to hang the murderer as
it has to lock up the street brawler; or the life of its worst member is sacred from
its touch. If the former let the doom and execution of the murderers be certain,
swift, prompt and unregretted; if the latter let the death penalty be erased from the
statute book. But, above all, let there be not even the appearance of irresolution in
the action of the law, or any scruple in carrying out to the letter its sternest
provisions.

DISCUSSION QUESTIONS

1. Is Whitman arguing for or against capital punishment in this editorial? Or is he
arguing another point? How can you tell?

2. Both Whitman and *The New York Times* ("Who Gets the Chair," page 204)
mention that capital punishment is not applied equitably. How is that point used
in Whitman's argument? In that of the *Times?*

Staff Correspondent / Important. Assassination
of President Lincoln   *New York Herald,* April 15, 1865

The following series of telegraphic dispatches and reports appeared in the New York Herald *the morning after President Lincoln's assassination.*

IMPORTANT.

.

ASSASSINATION
OF
PRESIDENT LINCOLN.

.

The President Shot at the
Theatre Last Evening.

.

SECRETARY SEWARD
DAGGERED IN HIS BED,
BUT
NOT MORTALLY WOUNDED.

.

Clarence and Frederick Seward Badly Hurt.

.

ESCAPE OF THE ASSASSINS.

.

Intense Excitement in
Washington.

.

Scene at the Deathbed of
Mr. Lincoln.

.

FIRST DISPATCH

Washington, April 14, 1865.

Assassination has been inaugurated in Washington. The bowie knife and pistol have been applied to President Lincoln and Secretary Seward. The former was shot in the throat, while at Ford's theatre to-night. Mr. Seward was badly cut about the neck, while in his bed at his residence.

SECOND DISPATCH

Washington, April 14, 1865.

An attempt was made about ten o'clock this evening to assassinate the President and Secretary Seward. The President was shot at Ford's Theatre. Result not yet known. Mr. Seward's throat was cut, and his son badly wounded.

There is intense excitement here.

Important. Assassination of President Lincoln

DETAILS OF THE ASSASSINATION

Washington, April 14, 1865.

Washington was thrown into an intense excitement a few minutes before eleven o'clock this evening, by the announcement that the President and Secretary Seward had been assassinated and were dead.

The wildest excitement prevailed in all parts of the city. Men, women and children, old and young, rushed to and fro, and the rumors were magnified until we had nearly every member of the Cabinet killed. Some time elapsed before authentic data could be ascertained in regard to the affair.

The President and Mrs. Lincoln were at Ford's theatre, listening to the performance of *The American Cousin,* occupying a box in the second tier. At the close of the third act a person entered the box occupied by the President, and shot Mr. Lincoln in the head. The shot entered the back of his head, and came out above the temple.

The assassin then jumped from the box upon the stage and ran across to the other side, exhibiting a dagger in his hand, flourishing it in a tragical manner, shouting the same words repeated by the desperado at Mr. Seward's house, adding to it, ''The South is avenged,'' and then escaped from the back entrance to the stage, but in his passage dropped his pistol and his hat.

Mr. Lincoln fell forward from his seat, and Mrs. Lincoln fainted.

The moment the astonished audience could realize what had happened, the President was taken and carried to Mr. Peterson's house, in Tenth Street, opposite to the theatre. Medical aid was immediately sent for, and the wound was at first supposed to be fatal, and it was announced that he could not live, but at half-past twelve he is still alive, though in a precarious condition.

As the assassin ran across the stage, Colonel J.B. Stewart, of this city, who was occupying one of the front seats in the orchestra, on the same side of the house as the box occupied by Mr. Lincoln, sprang to the stage and followed him; but he was obstructed in his passage across the stage by the fright of the actors, and reached the back door about three seconds after the assassin had passed out. Colonel Stewart got to the street just in time to see him mount his horse and ride away.

The operation shows that the whole thing was a preconcerted plan. The person who fired the pistol was a man about thirty years of age, about five feet nine, spare built, fair skin, dark hair, apparently bushy, with a large moustache. Laura Keene and the leader of the orchestra declare that they recognized him as J. Wilkes Booth the actor, and a rabid secessionist. Whoever he was, it is plainly evident that he thoroughly understood the theatre and all the approaches and modes of escape to the stage. A person not familiar with the theatre could not have possibly made his escape so well and quickly.

The alarm was sounded in every quarter. Mr. Stanton was notified, and immediately left his house.

All the other members of the Cabinet escaped attack.

Cavalrymen were sent out in all directions, and dispatches sent out to.all the fortifications, and it is thought they will be captured.

About half-past ten o'clock this evening a tall, well dressed man made his appearance at Secretary Seward's residence, and applied for admission. He was refused admission by the servant, when the desperado stated that he had a prescription from the Surgeon General, and that he was ordered to deliver it in person. He was still refused, except upon the written order of the physician. This he pretended to show, and pushed by the servant and rushed up stairs to Mr. Seward's room. He was met at the door by Mr. Fred Seward, who notified him that he was master of the house, and would take charge of the medicine. After a few words had passed between them he dodged by Fred Seward and rushed to the Secretary's bed and struck him in the neck with a dagger, and also in the breast.

It was supposed at first that Mr. Seward was killed instantly, but it was found afterwards that the wound was not mortal.

Major Wm. H. Seward, Jr., paymaster, was in the room, and rushed to the defense of his father, and was badly cut in the *melee* with the assassin, but not fatally.

The desperado managed to escape from the house, and was prepared for escape by having a horse at the door. He immediately mounted his horse, and sung out the motto of the State of Virginia, *"Sic Semper Tyrannis!"* and rode off.

Surgeon General Barnes was immediately sent for, and he examined Mr. Seward and pronounced him safe. His wounds were not fatal. The jugular vein was not cut, nor the wound in the breast deep enough to be fatal.

Washington, April 15—1 A.M.

The streets in the vicinity of Ford's Theatre are densely crowded by an anxious and excited crowd. A guard has been placed across Tenth Street and F and K Streets, and only official persons and particular friends of the President are allowed to pass.

The popular heart is deeply stirred, and the deepest indignation against leading rebels is freely expressed.

The scene at the house where the President lies in *extremis* is very affecting. Even Secretary Stanton is affected to tears.

When the news spread through the city that the President had been shot, the people, with pale faces and compressed lips, crowded every place where there was the slightest chance of obtaining information in regard to the affair.

After the President was shot, Lieutenant Rathbun, caught the assassin by the arm, who immediately struck him with a knife, and jumped from the box, as before stated.

The popular affection for Mr. Lincoln has been shown by this diabolical assassination, which will bring eternal infamy, not only upon its authors, but upon the hellish cause which they desire to avenge.

Vice President Johnson arrived at the White House, where the President lies, about one o'clock, and will remain with him to the last.

The President's family are in attendance upon him also.

As soon as intelligence could be got to the War Department, the electric telegraph and the Signal corps were put in requisition to endeavor to prevent the escape of the assassins, and all the troops around Washington are under arms.

Popular report points to a somewhat celebrated actor of known secession proclivities as the assassin; but it would be unjust to name him until some further evidence of his guilt is obtained. It is rumored that the person alluded to is in custody.

The latest advices from Secretary Seward reveals more desperate work there than at first supposed. Seward's wounds are not in themselves fatal, but, in connection with his recent injuries, and the great loss of blood he has sustained, his recovery is questionable.

It was Clarence A. Seward, instead of William H. Seward, Jr., who was wounded. Fred Seward was also badly cut, as were also three nurses, who were in attendance upon the Secretary, showing that a desperate struggle took place there. The wounds of the whole party were dressed.

One o'clock A.M.

The President is perfectly senseless, and there is not the slightest hope of his surviving. Physicians believe that he will die before morning. All of his Cabinet, except Secretary Seward, are with him. Speaker Colfax, Senator Farwell, of Maine, and many other gentlemen, are also at the house awaiting the termination.

The scene at the President's bedside is described by one who witnessed it as most affecting. He was surrounded by his Cabinet ministers, all of whom were bathed in tears, not even excepting Mr. Stanton, who, when informed by Surgeon General Barnes, that the President could not live until morning, exclaimed, "Oh, no, General; no—no;" and with an impulse, natural as it was unaffected, immediately sat down on a chair near his bedside and wept like a child.

Senator Sumner was seated on the right of the President's couch, near the head, holding the right hand of the President in his own. He was sobbing like a woman, with his head bowed down almost on the pillow of the bed on which the President was lying.

Two o'clock A.M.

The President is still alive, but there is no improvement in his condition.

DISCUSSION QUESTION

1. How does the *Herald* account differ from Wicker's report of President Kennedy's assassination? How is the President described in each? Which account do you think describes the assassination most vividly? Most informatively? With the most feeling?

Ernest Laurence Thayer / Casey at the Bat

San Francisco Examiner, June 3, 1888

Ernest Laurence Thayer (1863–1940) published the humorous poem "Casey at the Bat" in the June 3, 1888 San Francisco Examiner, *using the pseudonym* Phin. *The poem became famous when a well-known entertainer of the time, DeWolf Hopper, made it part of his vaudeville act. So compellingly does "Casey at the Bat" document the drama and idiom of the game that poet-critic Louis Untermeyer has called it "the acknowledged classic of baseball, its anthem and theme song."*

The outlook wasn't brilliant for the Mudville nine that day:
The score stood four to two with but one inning more to play.
And then when Cooney died at first, and Barrows did the same,
A sickly silence fell upon the patrons of the game.

A straggling few got up to go in deep despair. The rest   5
Clung to that hope which springs eternal in the human breast;
They thought if only Casey could but get a whack at that—
We'd put up even money now with Casey at the bat.

But Flynn preceded Casey, as did also Jimmy Blake,
And the former was a lulu and the latter was a cake;   10
So upon that stricken multitude grim melancholy sat,
For there seemed but little chance of Casey's getting to the bat.

But Flynn let drive a single, to the wonderment of all,
And Blake, the much despis-ed, tore the cover off the ball;
And when the dust had lifted, and the men saw what had occurred,   15
There was Jimmy safe at second and Flynn a-hugging third.

Then from 5,000 throats and more there rose a lusty yell;
It rumbled through the valley, it rattled in the dell;
It knocked upon the mountain and recoiled upon the flat,
For Casey, mighty Casey, was advancing to the bat.   20

There was ease in Casey's manner as he stepped into his place;
There was pride in Casey's bearing and a smile on Casey's face.
And when, responding to the cheers, he lightly doffed his hat,
No stranger in the crowd could doubt 'twas Casey at the bat.

Ten thousand eyes were on him as he rubbed his hands with dirt;   25
Five thousand tongues applauded when he wiped them on his shirt.
Then while the writhing pitcher ground the ball into his hip,
Defiance gleamed in Casey's eye, a sneer curled Casey's lip.

And now the leather-covered sphere came hurtling through the air,
And Casey stood a-watching it in haughty grandeur there.   30
Close by the sturdy batsman the ball unheeded sped—
"That ain't my style," said Casey. "Strike one," the umpire said.

From the benches back with people, there went up a muffled roar,
Like the beating of the storm-waves on a stern and distant shore.
"Kill him! Kill the umpire!" shouted some one on the stand;   35
And it's likely they'd have killed him had not Casey raised his hand.

With a smile of Christian charity great Casey's visage shone;
He stilled the rising tumult; he bade the game go on;
He signaled to the pitcher, and once more the spheroid flew;
But Casey still ignored it, and the umpire said, "Strike two."   40

"Fraud!" cried the maddened thousands, and echo answered fraud;
But one scornful look from Casey and the audience was awed.
They saw his face grow stern and cold, they saw his muscles strain,
And they knew that Casey wouldn't let that ball go by again.

The sneer is gone from Casey's lip, his teeth are clenched in hate;   45
He pounds with cruel violence his bat upon the plate.
And now the pitcher holds the ball, and now he lets it go,
And now the air is shattered by the force of Casey's blow.

Oh, somewhere in this favored land the sun is shining bright;
The band is playing somewhere, and somewhere hearts are light,   50
And somewhere men are laughing, and somewhere children shout;
But there is no joy in Mudville—mighty Casey has struck out.

Theodore Dreiser / Burned to Death

St. Louis *Globe-Democrat*, January 22, 1893

Novelist, critic, and magazine editor, Theodore Dreiser (1871–1945), like Mark Twain, was first a journalist. After some brief experience working for the Chicago Globe, *Dreiser joined the* Globe-Democrat *in 1893 as a cub reporter. When word of the disastrous train wreck near Alton, Illinois, first reached the* Globe-Democrat *newsroom, Dreiser rushed to the scene to write what became the only eyewitness account of the dramatic fires and explosions that were claiming an increasing number of victims. Printed without a by-line in the* Globe-Democrat *of January 22, 1893, Dreiser's report nonetheless became a heralded news "scoop" and launched his successful career as a journalist. After writing for newspapers in New York and Pittsburgh, Dreiser turned to fiction and published* Sister Carrie *in 1900. In* An American Tragedy *(1925), his most widely read work, Dreiser drew upon his training as a reporter to produce an impressive fictional report based on a real murder story.*

BURNED TO DEATH.

.

One of the Most Disastrous Railroad
Casualties Ever Recorded.

.

A Collision on the Big Four Followed by
an Explosion of Oil Cars.

.

Thousands of Gallons of the Burning
Fluid Scattered Over the Crowd.

.

Six People Killed Outright and a Score
of Others Will Die.

.

The Fearful Holocaust Brought About by
an Open Switch—Total Destruction of
the Big Four's Southwestern

Press

Limited Express—Heart-
rending Scenes.

One of the most appalling and disastrous wrecks that has occurred in years
followed the negligence of a switchman on the Big Four road at Wann, Ill., yesterday morning. Passenger engine 109, drawing the Southwestern limited express of
four coaches, headed east for New York, crashed into an open switch a half mile
north of Wann, a joint station of the Chicago and Alton and the Big Four roads,
where seven oil tanks stood in line on the side track. The result was a fire, and later
an explosion in which life and property were destroyed. The dead number six and
the wounded twenty-two. . . .

THE EXPLOSION

The crashing of the engine into the sidetracked oil tanks was not disastrous in itself. The consequent explosion and the fire that occurred two hours later caused the
terrible havoc, but not among the passengers. It was the sightseers from Alton, Ill.,
who suffered the loss of life and limb. The Southwestern limited train that leaves St.
Louis in the morning for New York and arrives at Wann at 8:48 A.M., was thirteen
minutes late. At Wann, which is a flag station, there is no side-track, but a half mile
further on, opposite the little cluster of houses known as Alton Junction, several
tracks are laid side by side with the main line to permit switching and the taking on
of cattle from a stock yard which is there. On one of these tracks seven oil tanks
filled with refined lubricating oil and consigned to the Waters-Pierce Oil Company,
of this city, were left standing by the switch engine of the Vandalia Line, which
brought them there from Beardstown, Ill. The switchman who has charge of this
section is R. Gratten, who, it is said, is both a switchman and a barber, managing to
eke out a precarious existence by combining the salaries of the two. To this gentleman's door is laid the entire blame by more than one employee of the Big Four.
Last evening, it is said, he left Alton Junction, his home, for parts unknown.

THE FATAL CRASH

When the limited arrived the switch was still open. Rushing along at a speed of
fully forty miles an hour the limited rushed into the switch and on, fairly over the
tanks, splitting two of them in twain and throwing the rest crushed right and left.
The engineer, Webb Ross, and the fireman, Dick White, both saw the danger.
White swung himself from the side of the flying train and ran out across the fields.
Webb Ross stood manfully to his post, reversed the lever and threw on the air
brakes, but to no avail. The velocity overpowered all opposition. Ross stood the
shock and still found time to leap from the cab. Almost instantly, however, the
burning oil had spread about the engine and the ground was a seething sea of
flames. Into this he plunged—a break for life. The flames burned away his garments and scorched his body into a blackened mass. He emerged from the flames
only to fall dead at the top of the bank that led from the track. Next to the engine
was the baggage car and cafe car, the occupants of which were badly shaken up and

110

thrown to the floor. The same condition affected the passengers of the three remaining palace cars, but further than that no one of the thirty passengers was injured. They rushed to the doors on realizing the catastrophe and made good their escape. The flames soon spread from the tank to the cars, and for several hours they burned fiercely in the morning breeze. In the baggage end of the first car were the mails, eleven pieces of baggage, and a corpse, which was being forwarded from the Southwest to Boston. The body was that of Mrs. Morrison.

THE SECOND EXPLOSION

The passengers gathered about the blazing wreck and began looking for any one who might need assistance. The villagers from the little town of Alton Junction rushed to the scene; word was telegraphed to St. Louis, Alton and neighboring points, and the company ordered a wrecking train with a score of physicians to the scene. The news of the burning wreck brought hundreds of sightseers from Alton, which is only three miles north of the wreck. They gathered about viewing the flames and chatting idly. At 11 o'clock the horrible addition to the already shocking story was made. Two of the remaining tanks, apparently not yet affected, reached the climax of self-containing heat. An explosion followed that shook the ground for miles about. Seething, blazing oil was showered upon the onlookers, thrown high in the air and over on to the comfortable cottages of villagers who lived by the roadside. The scene that followed beggars description. Many forms were instantly transformed to blazing, screaming, running, rolling bodies, crying loudly for mercy and aid. These tortured souls threw themselves to the ground and rolled about on the earth. They threw their burning hands to tortured, flame-lit faces, from which all semblance to humanity had already departed. They clawed and bit the earth, and then, with an agonizing gasp, sunk, faint and dying, into a deathly stillness. The horrible holocaust had been accomplished. Five souls had been burned into eternity and twenty-two had been maimed, blinded, burned into an unsightly condition, that made every face blanch and every heart shudder. In all this awful holocaust distraction and frantic fear held sway.

PARALYZED WITH FEAR

People perfectly safe and unharmed stood wringing their hands, crying out in useless fear or rushing madly to and fro in almost an agony of despair. The explosion gathered together all those who had previously left the wreck, or had as yet not heard of it. They gathered in throngs, but their presence was ineffective and entirely useless. Water would not quench the hissing, flaming oil, and more than that, water was not to be had. The little village of Alton Junction has no water supply except a few wells. The explosion drove the shattered mass of iron with fearful velocity far across the fields. Some of it fell close at hand, however, and pinioned the bystanders beneath its weight of molten heat. The wires overhead leading to St. Louis were melted, fell to the earth, severing all direct connection with the city. The only alternative was to bring aid from Alton, Ill., three miles away. At 11:30 A.M. the train arrived bearing the medical staff of St. Joseph's Hospital. . . . They hurried from the wrecking train to the scene and superintended the removal of the bodies. Shutters and cots were brought from various little homes and the moaning victims were wrapped in blankets and cloths and carried to the Big Four station at Alton Junction. The scene at the little frame depot was exciting. A great crowd stood about and blocked the entrance way to the various rooms. One by one the litters came, borne by strong, willing citizens, who drove back the morbidly curious and filed into the little depot waiting room.

CARING FOR THE INJURED

Here the couches were arranged side by side, and over each one a physician bowed for a few minutes to see just how serious the wounds were. Nothing could be done, for no lint or ointment could be applied that would ease the blackened flesh and bones of the half charred frames. Every now and then the cover was slightly raised to see if life still remained. The gents' waiting room would only hold five bodies, and when that number had been laid side by side the north room was cleared of benches and the coming litters arranged in this also. There were still others, and out on the platform they were tenderly cared for by the self-appointed nurses. The others were carried across the fields to the little cottages, where the families ministered all that could possibly ease their suffering. By 12 o'clock the Mattoon accommodation train was ready to depart for Alton. In the four coaches and baggage car the dead and the dying were deposited. The work of loading the dead and dying was another appalling spectacle. Out from the waiting room were borne the litters and gently lifted into the cars. From out the little cottages the wounded were again borne, followed by all the villagers, talking and gesticulating, but in a mournful, subdued manner. When the train had been filled the signal was given and the hospital train was off. Notice was telegraphed to the Alton Police and Fire Departments, who prepared to assist in removing the bodies from the train to St. Joseph's Hospital, which stands on a hill overlooking the city. The accommodation stopped some seven blocks south of the regular station to permit of a short cut to the hospital. At this point were gathered a score of wagons, prepared to do duty as ambulances. Here, too, had gathered hundreds of the local residents who had heard of the awful wreck. It was with difficulty that the crowd was forced back from the cars and the bodies lowered. Then started the succession of wagon journeys to and from the hospital that in no time lined the way with thousands of people gaping and talking in an anxious, nervous manner. From every window and doorway, in back and front yards, on the stoops and hanging on the fences that lined the way the people looked out and down upon the procession.

AT THE HOSPITAL

From the railroad track to the hospital gate is three straight blocks, ascending very rapidly to the crest of the hill, where St. Joseph's stands. The ascent was necessarily slow and gave ample time for the crowd to satisfy its curiosity. Before the hospital door another immense throng was gathered, anxious and almost determined to view the unrecognizable faces that passed on litters through the entrance-way. Inside all was confusion and hurry. Dr. Haskell, the physician in charge, returned with the train and hurried to and fro, gathering about him his staff and urging his assistants to great speed. The sick of the hospital are attended by the Sisters of Charity, and they busied themselves in taking the suffering to the respective rooms. In a little while three rooms on the main floor were filled with the wounded. The sick that had occupied them were borne out into the hall or carried into other rooms less crowded. The work was lovingly, anxiously done. Each sigh and groan of pain found an echoing response in the heart of the self-sacrificing attendants. One room was cleared for surgical purposes, but was not closed until all of the first train had been cared for. The scenes in the rooms where the wounded were removed from the rough temporary litters into the snowy couches were heartrending. The removal was necessary, however, and much as the victims shrieked and groaned, the work went on. Lying on the couches, the dirty, oil-soaked rags were cut away from the bodies and laid bare the horrible work of the burning oil. The hands and faces of all were scorched, torn and bleeding. The lips and noses were swollen and distorted, and the eyes were either burned out or were flame-eaten and encrusted with blood and dust, the hands of many were burned to a crust, fingers were missing and arms broken. Several of the victims when uncovered were found to be without cuticle, the flames having cooked and burned it until it either clung to the clothing in removal, or fell away of its own accord.

THE SEARCH FOR LOST ONES

When all arrangements had been made the public were admitted. An eager throng of mothers, fathers, wives and daughters hurried along the aisle and into the chambers of suffering. Here they viewed each face, but in many cases without avail, for the forms and faces were unrecognizable. . . . A *Globe-Democrat* reporter entered the chamber of suffering and went from couch to couch inquiring from the distorted occupant his name, age and address. After a long period of waiting and gentle questioning the list was completed and he returned to the hall. To those inquiring the list was read, and as the last name was spoken and "that's all" ejaculated a score of sighs were heard, for many an anxious heart knew that the loved one was not in the list.

A SECOND HOSPITAL TRAIN

At 3:30 P.M. the second hospital train that had been sent to Wann by the railroad company returned to Alton. At Wann the same scenes were re-enacted, and at Alton the same crowd lined the way to watch the progress of the painfully thrilling work. This train brought four bodies from the scene of the disaster. They were those who had since been prepared for the journey, having missed the first train. The progress up the hill was none the less interesting. The throng at the gate, though having watched without food or drink during the long hours of the morning, were none the less eager in their looks nor none the less backward in pressing forward to look at the bodies. More order prevailed inside the hospital with the coming of these bodies. The work of the noon hour had nerved the attendants and practiced their ability in taking care of the unfortunates. . . .

BEGGED TO BE KILLED

Several begged to be killed, that they might be free from their pain. "Oh, I'm blind," moaned one; "I feel that my eyes are gone. Oh, I could stand all, everything, I could be burned with satisfaction, I could be crippled or deformed forever, but to be without eyes, to have the light shut out forever, that is too much. I want to die! I want to die!'' and then a loving mother bowed low over the moaning form and buried her tear-stained face and misery-convulsed form in the clothing that shielded her son. Several little boys were among the victims, and their moanings were the sources of much distress to all the others. Still others were only slightly injured, and deeply congratulated themselves upon their luck in escaping at all. One of these, Charles Hammond, a track-walker for the Big Four, had escaped with the loss of his hair, several severe scalp wounds and a burned hand. He sat in the corridor of the hospital solemnly viewing the proceedings. In reply to questions from a *Globe-Democrat* reporter, Mr. Hammond said: ''I am a track-walker for the Big Four, traveling between Venice and Alton at night time, and my home is at Alton Junction. My work was all done, of course, and I was sleeping soundly when my wife woke me up to tell me of the horrible wreck. I jumped up and ran over to the place. There was nothing that I could do. Water would do no good, and so I stood looking on. I had started to stroll away when the explosion occurred. I intended going north to the Junction Station, but I had not got 70 feet away before I was knocked to my knees by the crash of the tank. I felt the hot oil light on my head and hands and felt the fearful burning sensation. To relieve myself I buried my head in the earth and threw dirt over my hands. Then I ran away. I don't know how fast. Here at the junction I met a physician who bandaged my head and hand. Then they put me on the wrecking train and I came here. The sound wasn't so loud as it was stunning. I didn't look back much. All I wanted was to get away. The man that had charge of the switch at that place was a fellow by the name of R. Gratten. He kept a barber shop and attended the switch at the same time. The company hired him simply because he was cheap. I know that he has gone out of the country already, and they won't find him soon. It's a shame that a railroad company should be allowed to hire men to do work in that manner, risking the lives of passengers, simply because it is cheap.''

SCENES AT THE WRECK

The scene at the wreck late in the afternoon was one of vast destruction. The burning oil had been thrown for a distance of 800 feet and more, and had set fire to two little cottages that stood facing the track. . . . On the track where the seven oil tanks had stood a line of melted, rusted car trucks and piles of ashes lay. Lying in a molten heap among them were the gnarled remnants of engine 109, and back of it the ashes of the four coaches with bars of twisted protruding iron completed the side-track picture. To the east a wrecking train brought from East St. Louis lay, and to this the gang of wreckers carried whatever they saw fit to remove. The work of clearing the debris from the main track was soon accomplished, and trains plied to and fro at will. A small crowd of sightseers was gathered about the place, but always at a discreet distance from an oil tank that had not yet exploded, and which was credited with being perfectly empty. They plodded to and fro, each one bent upon gathering some little stick or piece of iron as a souvenir or memento of the great disaster. A little north at the station the bodies of the six dead lay in order awaiting the coming of the Coroner. One of these was identified by a watch upon his person which bore his name–Edward Miller. A singular feature of his death was that his watch stopped at 11:10, supposedly the time of the great explosion which buried him beneath a mass of heated iron. The telegraph operators and station employees generally were very cautious about their remarks. They professed ignorance of the number and names of the dead, and the extent of the damage. Their order, they said, was to keep still, and that if they talked they were liable to lose their position. . . . The station agent at Wann said that he thought the company had lost something like $200,000 by the fire. "The company won't pay anything to all these sightseers who gathered about here to view the ruins. They have no business here, and, of course, if they come to grief it is no fault of the company's."

AT ALTON

In the city of Alton the news of the wreck was the topic of the hour. The streets there had the appearance of a country seat upon the arrival of some big circus. Everybody was out of doors. The streets were promenaded by the inhabitants; the store fronts were occupied by crowds of gossiping residents who collected together for the sole purpose of recounting the enormity of it and of recalling the great wrecks of the past. The depot station was the resort of another class who vaguely imagined that each incoming train would bear peculiar intelligence relative to the matter that might not be had elsewhere in the city. The offices of the local newspapers were scenes of vast activity, and the floors of the same were strewn with paper on which was scribbled more than a dozen introductions to the wreck. . . .

CHIEF DISPATCHER'S ADVICES

H. M. Stubblefield, Chief Train Dispatcher of the Big Four road in this city, was busy all day in the operating rooms at the Knapp building, in St. Louis. When asked for a statement regarding the wreck he said, briefly: "Train No. 18, leaving the St. Louis Union Depot at 8:05 A.M., ran into an open switch at the west end of the Wann yards and collided with a number of oil-tank cars. Engineer Webb Ross was killed and Fireman Dick White jumped and escaped. The engine and cafe car were destroyed. We do not know who left the switch open. About 11:40 o'clock some of the fire reached the tank cars, and five men and a boy who were standing by were killed. A wrecking train was sent at 9:30 o'clock." . . .

A CONDUCTOR ON THE EXPLOSION

The reports that reached the Union Depot last night of the horrible wreck were very conflicting. Some placed the loss at fifty lives, with almost 100 injured, while others placed the loss at only one killed and about six injured. James H. McClintock, a conductor on the Big Four, was an eye-witness of the explosion. When seen at the depot last night by a *Globe-Democrat* reporter, he said:

"We arrived at Wann Junction on our westward trip about 11:30 o'clock. We then heard of the wreck, which had occurred about 9 o'clock. Webb Ross, the engineer, was the only one reported killed. The cars and oil tanks were then burning only a few blocks away. I was standing on the platform viewing the destruction, when all of a sudden an explosion shook the very ground beneath my feet and rattled the windows in the station. There were hundreds of people standing near, and as a sheet of flame shot into the air over 100 feet high the crowd attempted to escape.

Before they had moved any distance to speak of the burning mass of oil came down upon them. Shrieks of agony, groans and stifled cries met our ears with a sickening effect. Pell-mell scattered the human beings, bereft of all feelings, only endeavoring to get out of reach of a fiery death. Those caught in the burning mass must have perished immediately. People came running in all directions without a shred of clothing on their persons, the fiery liquid having done its work only too well. Their hair singed to a crisp and their bodies a mass of blisters, the wretches presented a heart-rending sight. Taken altogether, it was the most awful sight that was ever pictured. It was a scene impossible to describe. I remember one little boy 13 years old, who ran into the depot utterly naked and crawled under the benches frantic with fear. All blistered as he was, he unhesitatingly asked an anxious gazer to bring a priest. There was none around, and the boy half smiled, closed his eyes and lapsed into unconsciousness. In a spectacular sense the explosion was one of the grandest sights man ever witnessed. Fireworks were never invented which cast such a pretty reflection in the sky as did the burning oil on this disastrous occasion.''

DISCUSSION QUESTIONS

1. The audience Dreiser is writing for is, to a great extent, typified by the ever-present crowd of onlookers (the ''morbidly curious'') eager to view human suffering and mutilation. What influence does his audience's curiosity have on Dreiser's style?

2. Compare Dreiser's description of the victims of the train wreck with Jack London's account of the San Francisco earthquake (see ''The Story of an Eyewitness'' in Magazines). What is the purpose of each article? How does each author ''translate'' bare statistics into compelling scenes? How does each writer sustain a persuasive sense of realism?

Stephen Crane / Stephen Crane's Own Story
[*He Tells How the* Commodore *Was Wrecked and How He Escaped*]

New York Press, January 7, 1897

Though Stephen Crane had not witnessed a single battle before he wrote The Red Badge of Courage *in 1895, the immense popularity of the novel helped to establish a career for him as a leading war correspondent. Crane spent most of his remaining years traveling, despite ill-health, to cover the Greco-Turkish, the Boer, and the Spanish American wars.*

*   ''Stephen Crane's Own Story'' details his experiences during the wreck of the* Commodore, *a cargo ship carrying guns and ammunition to Cuban insurgents. This account served as the basis for Crane's well-known short story, ''The Open Boat'' (see Classics).*

JACKSONVILLE, FLA., Jan. 6.—It was the afternoon of New Year's. The Commodore lay at her dock in Jacksonville and negro stevedores processioned steadily toward her with box after box of ammunition and bundle after bundle of rifles. Her hatch, like the mouth of a monster, engulfed them. It might have been the feeding time of some legendary creature of the sea. It was in broad daylight and the crowd of gleeful Cubans on the pier did not forbear to sing the strange patriotic ballads of their island.

Everything was perfectly open. The Commodore was cleared with a cargo of arms and munition for Cuba. There was none of that extreme modesty about the proceeding which had marked previous departures of the famous tug. She loaded up as placidly as if she were going to carry oranges to New York, instead of Remingtons to Cuba. Down the river, furthermore, the revenue cutter Boutwell, the old isosceles triangle that protects United States interests in the St. John's, lay at anchor, with no sign of excitement aboard her.

EXCHANGING FAREWELLS

On the decks of the Commodore there were exchanges of farewells in two languages. Many of the men who were to sail upon her had many intimates in the old Southern town, and we who had left our friends in the remote North received our first touch of melancholy on witnessing these strenuous and earnest goodbys.

It seems, however, that there was more difficulty at the custom house. The officers of the ship and the Cuban leaders were detained there until a mournful twilight settled upon the St. John's, and through a heavy fog the lights of Jacksonville blinked dimly. Then at last the Commodore swung clear of the dock, amid a tumult of goodbys. As she turned her bow toward the distant sea the Cubans ashore cheered and cheered. In response the Commodore gave three long blasts of her whistle, which even to this time impressed me with their sadness. Somehow, they sounded as wails.

Then at last we began to feel like filibusters. I don't suppose that the most stolid brain could contrive to believe that there is not a mere trifle of danger in filibustering, and so as we watched the lights of Jacksonville swing past us and heard the regular thump, thump, thump of the engines we did considerable reflecting.

But I am sure that there were no hifalutin emotions visible upon any of the faces which fronted the speeding shore. In fact, from cook's boy to captain, we were all enveloped in a gentle satisfaction and cheerfulness. But less than two miles from Jacksonville, this atrocious fog caused the pilot to ram the bow of the Commodore hard upon the mud and in this ignominious position we were compelled to stay until daybreak.

HELP FROM THE BOUTWELL

It was to all of us more than a physical calamity. We were now no longer filibusters. We were men on a ship stuck in the mud. A certain mental somersault was made once more necessary.

But word had been sent to Jacksonville to the captain of the revenue cutter Boutwell, and Captain Kilgore turned out promptly and generously fired up his old triangle, and came at full speed to our assistance. She dragged us out of the mud, and again we headed for the mouth of the river. The revenue cutter pounded along a half mile astern of us, to make sure that we did not take on board at some place along the river men for the Cuban army.

This was the early morning of New Year's Day, and the fine golden southern sunlight fell full upon the river. It flashed over the ancient Boutwell, until her white sides gleamed like pearl, and her rigging was spun into little threads of gold.

Cheers greeted the old Commodore from passing ship and from the shore. It was a cheerful, almost merry, beginning to our voyage. At Mayport, however, we changed our river pilot for a man who could take her to open sea, and again the Commodore was beached. The Boutwell was fussing around us in her venerable way, and, upon seeing our predicament, she came again to assist us, but this time, with engines reversed, the Commodore dragged herself away from the grip of the sand and again headed for the open sea.

The captain of the revenue cutter grew curious. He hailed the Commodore: "Are you fellows going to sea to-day?"

Captain Murphy of the Commodore called back: "Yes, sir."

And then as the whistle of the Commodore saluted him, Captain Kilgore doffed his cap and said: "Well, gentlemen, I hope you have a pleasant cruise," and this was our last word from shore.

When the Commodore came to enormous rollers that flee over the bar a certain light-heartedness departed from the ship's company.

SLEEP IMPOSSIBLE

As darkness came upon the waters, the Commodore was a broad, flaming path of blue and silver phosphorescence, and as her stout bow lunged at the great black waves she threw flashing, roaring cascades to either side. And all that was to be heard was the rhythmical and mighty pounding of the engines. Being an inexperienced filibuster, the writer had undergone considerable mental excitement since the starting of the ship, and in consequence he had not yet been to sleep and so I went to the first mate's bunk to indulge myself in all the physical delights of holding one's-self in bed. Every time the ship lurched I expected to be fired through a bulkhead, and it was neither amusing nor instructive to see in the dim light a certain accursed valise aiming itself at the top of my stomach with every lurch of the vessel.

THE COOK IS HOPEFUL

The cook was asleep on a bench in the galley. He is of a portly and noble exterior, and by means of a checker board he had himself wedged on this bench in such a manner the motion of the ship would be unable to dislodge him. He woke as I entered the galley and delivered himself of some dolorous sentiments: "God," he said in the course of his observations, "I don't feel right about this ship, somehow. It strikes me that something is going to happen to us. I don't know what it is, but the old ship is going to get it in the neck, I think."

"Well, how about the men on board of her?" said I. "Are any of us going to get out, prophet?"

"Yes," said the cook. "Sometimes I have these damned feelings come over me, and they are always right, and it seems to me, somehow, that you and I will both get out and meet again somewhere, down at Coney Island, perhaps, or some place like that.''

ONE MAN HAS ENOUGH

Finding it impossible to sleep, I went back to the pilot house. An old seaman, Tom Smith, from Charleston, was then at the wheel. In the darkness I could not see Tom's face, except at those times when he leaned forward to scan the compass and the dim light from the box came upon his weatherbeaten features.

''Well, Tom,'' said I, ''how do you like filibustering?''

He said ''I think I am about through with it. I've been in a number of these expeditions and the pay is good, but I think if I ever get back safe this time I will cut it.''

I sat down in the corner of the pilot house and almost went to sleep. In the meantime the captain came on duty and he was standing near me when the chief engineer rushed up the stairs and cried hurriedly to the captain that there was something wrong in the engine room. He and the captain departed swiftly.

I was drowsing there in my corner when the captain returned, and, going to the door of the little room directly back of the pilot house, he cried to the Cuban leader:

''Say, can't you get those fellows to work. I can't talk their language and I can't get them started. Come on and get them going.''

HELPS IN THE FIREROOM

The Cuban leader turned to me and said: ''Go help in the fireroom. They are going to bail with buckets.''

The engine room, by the way, represented a scene at this time taken from the middle kitchen of hades. In the first place, it was insufferably warm, and the lights burned faintly in a way to cause mystic and grewsome shadows. There was a quantity of soapish sea water swirling and sweeping and swishing among machinery that roared and banged and clattered and steamed, and, in the second place, it was a devil of a ways down below.

Here I first came to know a certain young oiler named Billy Higgins. He was sloshing around this inferno filling buckets with water and passing them to a chain of men that extended up the ship's side. Afterward we got orders to change our point of attack on water and to operate through a little door on the windward side of the ship that led into the engine room.

NO PANIC ON BOARD

During this time there was much talk of pumps out of order and many other statements of a mechanical kind, which I did not altogether comprehend but understood to mean that there was a general and sudden ruin in the engine room.

There was no particular agitation at this time, and even later there was never a panic on board the Commodore. The party of men who worked with Higgins and me at this time were all Cubans, and we were under the direction of the Cuban leaders. Presently we were ordered again to the afterhold, and there was some hesitation about going into the abominable fireroom again, but Higgins dashed down the companion way with a bucket.

LOWERING BOATS

The heat and hard work in the fireroom affected me and I was obliged to come on deck again. Going forward, I heard as I went talk of lowering the boats. Near the corner of the galley the mate was talking with a man.

"Why don't you send up a rocket?" said this unknown man. And the mate replied: "What the hell do we want to send up a rocket for? The ship is all right."

Returning with a little rubber and cloth overcoat, I saw the first boat about to be lowered. A certain man was the first person in this first boat, and they were handing him in a valise about as large as a hotel. I had not entirely recovered from astonishment and pleasure in witnessing this noble deed when I saw another valise go to him.

HUMAN HOG APPEARS

This valise was not perhaps so large as a hotel, but it was a big valise anyhow. Afterward there went to him something which looked to me like an overcoat.

Seeing the chief engineer leaning out of his little window, I remarked to him:

"What do you think of that blank, blank, blank?"

"Oh, he's a bird," said the old chief.

It was now that was heard the order to get away the lifeboat, which was stowed on top of the deckhouse. The deckhouse was a mighty slippery place, and with each roll of the ship, the men there thought themselves likely to take headers into the deadly black sea.

Higgins was on top of the deckhouse, and, with the first mate and two colored stokers, we wrestled with that boat, which, I am willing to swear, weighed as much as a Broadway cable car. She might have been spiked to the deck. We could have pushed a little brick schoolhouse along a corduroy road as easily as we could have moved this boat. But the first mate got a tackle to her from a leeward davit, and on the deck below the captain corralled enough men to make an impression upon the boat.

We were ordered to cease hauling then, and in this lull the cook of the ship came to me and said: "What are you going to do?"

I told him of my plans, and he said:

"Well, my God, that's what I am going to do."

A WHISTLE OF DESPAIR

Now the whistle of the Commodore had been turned loose, and if there ever was a voice of despair and death, it was in the voice of this whistle. It had gained a new tone. It was as if its throat was already choked by the water, and this cry on the sea at night, with a wind blowing the spray over the ship, and the waves roaring over the bow, and swirling white along the decks, was to each of us probably a song of man's end.

It was now that the first mate showed a sign of losing his grip. To us who were trying in all stages of competence and experience to launch the lifeboat he raged in all terms of fiery satire and hammerlike abuse. But the boat moved at last and swung down toward the water.

Afterward, when I went aft, I saw the captain standing, with his arm in a sling, holding on to a stay with his one good hand and directing the launching of the boat. He gave me a five-gallon jug of water to hold, and asked me what I was going to do. I told him what I thought was about the proper thing, and he told me then that the cook had the same idea, and ordered me to go forward and be ready to launch the ten-foot dingy.

IN THE TEN-FOOT DINGY

I remember well that he turned then to swear at a colored stoker who was prowling around, done up in life preservers until he looked like a feather bed. I went forward with my five-gallon jug of water, and when the captain came we launched the dingy, and they put me over the side to fend her off from the ship with an oar.

They handed me down the water jug, and then the cook came into the boat, and we sat there in the darkness, wondering why, by all our hopes of future happiness, the captain was so long in coming over to the side and ordering us away from the doomed ship.

The captain was waiting for the other boat to go. Finally he hailed in the darkness: "Are you all right, Mr. Graines?"

The first mate answered: "All right, sir."

"Shove off, then," cried the captain.

The captain was just about to swing over the rail when a dark form came forward and a voice said: "Captain, I go with you."

The captain answered: "Yes, Billy; get in."

HIGGINS LAST TO LEAVE SHIP

It was Billy Higgins, the oiler. Billy dropped into the boat and a moment later the captain followed, bringing with him an end of about forty yards of lead line. The other end was attached to the rail of the ship.

As we swung back to leeward the captain said: "Boys, we will stay right near the ship till she goes down."

This cheerful information, of course, filled us all with glee. The line kept us headed properly into the wind, and as we rode over the monstrous waves we saw upon each rise the swaying lights of the dying Commodore.

When came the gray shade of dawn, the form of the Commodore grew slowly clear to us as our little ten-foot boat rose over each swell. She was floating with such an air of buoyancy that we laughed when we had time, and said "What a gag it would be on those other fellows if she didn't sink at all."

But later we saw men aboard of her, and later still they began to hail us.

HELPING THEIR MATES

I had forgot to mention that previously we had loosened the end of the lead line and dropped much further to leeward. The men on board were a mystery to us, of course, as we had seen all the boats leave the ship. We rowed back to the ship, but did not approach too near, because we were four men in a ten-foot boat, and we knew that the touch of a hand on our gunwale would assuredly swamp us.

The first mate cried out from the ship that the third boat had foundered alongside. He cried that they had made rafts, and wished us to tow them.

The captain said, "All right."

Their rafts were floating astern. "Jump in!" cried the captain, but there was a singular and most harrowing hesitation. There were five white men and two negroes. This scene in the gray light of morning impressed one as would a view into some place where ghosts move slowly. These seven men on the stern of the sinking Commodore were silent. Save the words of the mate to the captain there was no talk. Here was death, but here also was a most singular and indefinable kind of fortitude.

Four men, I remember, clambered over the railing and stood there watching the cold, steely sheen of the sweeping waves.

"Jump," cried the captain again.

The old chief engineer first obeyed the order. He landed on the outside raft and the captain told him how to grip the raft and he obeyed as promptly and as docilely as a scholar in riding school.

THE MATE'S MAD PLUNGE

A stoker followed him, and then the first mate threw his hands over his head and plunged into the sea. He had no life belt and for my part, even when he did this horrible thing, I somehow felt that I could see in the expression of his hands, and in the very toss of his head, as he leaped thus to death, that it was rage, rage, rage unspeakable that was in his heart at the time.

And then I saw Tom Smith, the man who was going to quit filibustering after this expedition, jump to a raft and turn his face toward us. On board the Commodore three men strode, still in silence and with their faces turned toward us. One man had his arms folded and was leaning against the deckhouse. His feet were crossed, so that the toe of his left foot pointed downward. There they stood gazing at us, and neither from the deck nor from the rafts was a voice raised. Still was there this silence.

TRIED TO TOW THE RAFTS

The colored stoker on the first raft threw us a line and we began to tow. Of course, we perfectly understood the absolute impossibility of any such thing; our dingy was within six inches of the water's edge, there was an enormous sea running, and I knew that under the circumstances a tugboat would have no light task in moving these rafts.

But we tried it, and would have continued to try it indefinitely, but that something critical came to pass. I was at an oar and so faced the rafts. The cook controlled the line. Suddenly the boat began to go backward and then we saw this negro on the first raft pulling on the line hand over hand and drawing us to him.

He had turned into a demon. He was wild—wild as a tiger. He was crouched on this raft and ready to spring. Every muscle of him seemed to be turned into an elastic spring. His eyes were almost white. His face was the face of a lost man reaching upward, and we knew that the weight of his hand on our gunwale doomed us.

THE COMMODORE SINKS

The cook let go of the line. We rowed around to see if we could not get a line from the chief engineer, and all this time, mind you, there were no shrieks, no groans, but silence, silence and silence, and then the Commodore sank.

She lurched to windward, then swung afar back, righted and dove into the sea, and the rafts were suddenly swallowed by this frightful maw of the ocean. And then by the men on the ten-foot dingy were words said that were still not words— something far beyond words.

The lighthouse of Mosquito Inlet stuck up above the horizon like the point of a pin. We turned our dingy toward the shore.

The history of life in an open boat for thirty hours would no doubt be instructive for the young, but none is to be told here and now. For my part I would prefer to tell the story at once, because from it would shine the splendid manhood of Captain Edward Murphy and of William Higgins, the oiler, but let it suffice at this time to say that when we were swamped in the surf and making the best of our way toward the shore the captain gave orders amid the wildness of the breakers as clearly as if he had been on the quarter deck of a battleship.

John Kitchell of Daytona came running down the beach, and as he ran the air was filled with clothes. If he had pulled a single lever and undressed, even as the fire horses harness, he could not seem to me to have stripped with more speed. He dashed into the water and dragged the cook. Then he went after the captain, but the captain sent him to me, and then it was that he saw Billy Higgins lying with his forehead on sand that was clear of the water, and he was dead.

Staff Correspondent / Flying Machine Soars 3 Miles in Teeth of High Wind
[First Account of the Wright Brothers' Success]
Norfolk *Virginian Pilot*, December 18, 1903

Wilbur and Orville Wright, the owners of a bicycle shop in Dayton, Ohio, where they also at one time edited a weekly newspaper, had been experimenting since their youth on designs for a workable "flying machine." Venturing to the wind-swept coast near Kittyhawk, North Carolina, the Wright brothers set up a primitive monorail-like skid from which to launch their craft. Powered by a twelve horse-power gasoline engine, the "monster bird hovered above the breakers" for almost a minute, traveling a distance of nearly a quarter of a mile. Surrounded by several highly publicized failures, this event, one of the major advances in twentieth cen-

tury science, went practically unnoticed. Only the Norfolk Virginian-Pilot *printed a full story of the world's first successful flight.*

FLYING MACHINE SOARS 3 MILES
IN TEETH OF HIGH WIND OVER SAND HILLS AND WAVES AT KITTY-
HAWK ON CAROLINA COAST.

.

NO BALLOON ATTACHED TO AID IT.

.

The problem of aerial navigation without the use of a balloon has been solved at last.

Over the sand hills of the North Carolina coast yesterday, near Kittyhawk, two Ohio men proved that they could soar through the air in a flying machine of their own construction, with the power to steer and speed it at will.

This, too, in the face of a wind blowing at the registered velocity of twenty-one miles an hour.

Like a monster bird, the invention hovered above the breakers and circled over the rolling sand hills at the command of its navigator and, after soaring for three miles, it gracefully descended to earth again, and rested lightly upon the spot selected by the man in the car as a suitable landing place.

While the United States government has been spending thousands of dollars in an effort to make practicable the ideas of Professor Langley, of the Smithsonian Insti-tute, Wilbur and Orville Wright, two brothers, natives of Dayton, Ohio, have, quietly, even secretly, perfected their invention and put it to a successful test.

They are not yet ready that the world should know the methods they have adopted in conquering the air, but the *Virginian-Pilot* is able to state authentically the nature of their invention, its principles and its chief dimensions.

The idea of the box kite has been adhered to strictly in the basic formation of the flying machine.

A huge framework of light timbers, thirty-three feet wide, five feet deep, and five feet across the top, forms the machine proper.

This is covered with a tough, but light canvas.

In the center, and suspended just below the bottom plane, is the small gasoline engine which furnished the motive power for the propelling and elevating wheels.

There are two six-bladed propellers, one arranged just below the center of the frame, so gauged as to exert an upward force when in motion, and the other extends horizontally to the rear from the center of the car, furnishing the forward impetus.

Protruding from the center of the car is a huge, fan-shaped rudder of canvas, stretched upon a frame of wood. This rudder is controlled by the navigator and may be moved to each side, raised, or lowered.

Wilbur Wright, the chief inventor of the machine, sat in the operator's car, and when all was ready his brother unfastened the catch which held the invention at the top of the slope.

The big box began to move slowly at first, acquiring velocity as it went, and when halfway down the hundred feet the engine was started.

The propeller in the rear immediately began to revolve at a high rate of speed, and when the end of the incline was reached the machine shot out into space without a perceptible fall.

By this time the elevating propeller was also in motion, and keeping its altitude, the machine slowly began to go higher and higher until it finally soared sixty feet above the ground.

Maintaining this height by the action of the under wheel, the navigator increased the revolutions of the rear propeller, and the forward speed of the huge affair increased until a velocity of eight miles was attained.

All this time the machine headed into a twenty-one-mile wind.

The little crowd of fisherfolk and coast guards, who have been watching the construction of the machine with unconcealed curiosity since September, were amazed.

They endeavored to race over the sand and keep up with the thing in the air, but it soon distanced them and continued its flight alone, save the man in the car.

Steadily it pursued its way, first tacking to port, then to starboard, and then driving straight ahead.

"It is a success," declared Orville Wright to the crowd on the beach after the first mile had been covered.

But the inventor waited. Not until he had accomplished three miles, putting the machine through all sorts of maneuvers en route, was he satisfied.

Then he selected a suitable place to land and, gracefully circling, drew his invention slowly to the earth, where it settled, like some big bird, in the chosen spot.

"Eureka!" he cried, as did the alchemists of old.

The success of the Wright brothers in their invention is the result of three years of hard work. Experiment after experiment has been made and failure resulted, but each experiment had its lesson, and finally, when the two reappeared at Kittyhawk last fall, they felt more confident than ever.

The spot selected for the building and perfecting of the machine is one of the most desolate upon the Atlantic seaboard. Just on the southern extremity of that coast stretch known as the graveyard of American shipping, cut off from civilization by a wide expanse of sound water and seldom in touch with the outer world save when a steamer once or twice a week touches at the little wharf to take and leave government mail, no better place could scarcely have been selected to maintain secrecy.

And this is where the failures have grown into success.

The machine which made yesterday's flight easily carried the weight of a man of 150 pounds, and is nothing like so large as the ill-fated *Buzzard* of Potomac River fame.

It is said the Wright brothers intend constructing a much larger machine, but before this they will go back to their homes for the holidays.

Wilbur Wright, the inventor, is a well-groomed man of prepossessing appearance. He is about five feet, six inches tall, weighs about 150 pounds, and is of swarthy complexion. His hair is raven-hued and straight, but a piercing pair of deep-blue eyes peer at you over a nose of extreme length and sharpness.

His brother, Orville, on the other hand, is a blond, with sandy hair and fair complexion, even features, and sparkling black eyes. He is not quite as large as Wilbur, but is of magnificent physique.

The pair have spent almost the entire fall and winter and early spring months of the past three years at Kittyhawk, working upon their invention, leaving when the weather began to grow warm and returning in the early fall to work.

Their last appearance was on September 1, and since then they have been actively engaged upon the construction of the machine which made yesterday's successful flight.

Jack Lait / Dillinger "Gets His"

International News Service, July 23, 1934

On a steamy July evening in 1934, after having seen Clark Gable and William Powell star in a popular gangster film, Manhattan Melodrama, *John Dillinger, "Public Enemy No. 1," left a run-down movie house on Chicago's East Side and walked into the waiting bullets of federal police forces. By all accounts one of the most notorious criminals of modern times, Dillinger had blazed out a legendary "career" for himself that had all the earmarks of best-selling detective fiction: daring bank robberies, raids on police arsenals, bloody shoot-outs, bold escapes from prison, along with disguises, blurred fingerprints, and plastic surgery to help him defy what was then described as "the greatest manhunt in contemporary criminal annals." Yet, like Joey Gallo (see "Death of a Maverick Mafioso," in Magazines), Dillinger eventually found the heat of the limelight deadly. Betrayed by one of the many women he supported, Dillinger finally fell victim to the facts that fed the fictions he provoked.*

Jack Lait, a hard-nosed reporter who later took over as editor of the New York Daily Mirror, turned out this "scoop" for the International News Service, an agency set up by William Randolph Hearst in 1909 to offer news items to a network of morning newspapers.

"Dillinger 'Gets His' " should be compared to David Wagoner's poem on the same subject in Classics.

John Dillinger, ace bad man of the world, got his last night—two slugs through his heart and one through his head. He was tough and he was shrewd, but wasn't as tough and shrewd as the Federals, who never close a case until the end. It took twenty-seven of them to end Dillinger's career, and their strength came out of his weakness—a woman.

Dillinger was put on the spot by a tip-off to the local bureau of the Department of Justice. It was a feminine voice that Melvin H. Purvis, head of the Chicago office, heard. He had waited long for it.

It was Sunday, but Uncle Sam doesn't observe any NRA* and works seven days a week.

The voice told him that Dillinger would be at a little third-run movie house, the Biograph, last night—that he went there every night and usually got there about 7:30. It was almost 7:30 then. Purvis sent out a call for all men within reach and hustled all men on hand with him. They waited more than an hour. They knew from the informer that he must come out, turn left, turn again into a dark alley where he parked his Ford-8 coupé.

Purvis himself stood at the main exit. He had men on foot and in parked inconspicuous cars strung on both sides of the alley. He was to give the signal. He had ascertained about when the feature film, *Manhattan Melodrama,* would end. Tensely eying his wrist watch he stood. Then the crowd that always streams out when the main picture finishes came. Purvis had seen Dillinger when he was

---

* National Recovery Administration, a New Deal Agency that, among other functions, regulated hours of work in industry.

126

brought through from Arizona to Crown Point, Indiana, and his heart pounded as he saw again the face that has been studied by countless millions on the front pages of the world.

Purvis gave the signal. Dillinger did not see him. Public Enemy No. 1 lit a cigarette, strolled a few feet to the alley with the mass of middle-class citizens going in that direction, then wheeled left.

A Federal man, revolver in hand, stepped from behind a telegraph pole at the mouth of the passage. "Hello, John," he said, almost whispered, his voice husky with the intensity of the classic melodrama. Dillinger went with lightning right hand for his gun, a .38 Colt automatic. He drew it from his trousers pocket.

But, from behind, another government agent pressed the muzzle of his service revolver against Dillinger's back and fired twice. Both bullets went through the bandit's heart.

He staggered, his weapon clattered to the asphalt paving, and as he went three more shots flashed. One bullet hit the back of his head, downward, as he was falling, and came out under his eye.

Police cleared the way for the police car which was there in a few minutes. The police were there not because they were in on the capture, but because the sight of so many mysterious men around the theater had scared the manager into thinking he was about to be stuck up and he had called the nearest station.

When the detectives came on the run, Purvis intercepted them and told them what was up. They called headquarters and more police came, but with instructions to stand by and take orders from Purvis.

Dillinger's body was rushed to Alexian Brothers' hospital in a patrol wagon. There were no surgeons in it. But the policeman knew he was dead, and at the entrance of the hospital, where a kindly priest in a long cassock had come to the door to see who might be in need of help, the driver was ordered to the morgue.

I was in a taxi that caught up with the police car at the hospital, and we followed across town to the old morgue. No one bothered us, though we went fifty miles an hour.

There was no crowd then. We pulled in. Strong arms carried the limp, light form of the man who had been feared by a great government through that grim door of many minor tragedies. It lay on a rubber stretcher.

In the basement, the receiving ward of the last public hospice of the doomed, they stripped the fearsome remains.

What showed up, nude and pink, still warm, was the body of what seemed a boy, the features as though at rest and only an ugly, bleeding hole under the left eye, such as a boy might have gotten in a street fight. His arms were bruised from the fall and the bumping in the wagon.

But under the heart were two little black, bleeding holes, clean and fresh. These could not have been anything but what they were. That part of John Dillinger did not look as though it was a boy's hurt—it was the fatal finish of a cold-blooded killer and not half of what he had given Officer O'Malley in East Chicago, Indiana, in the bank robbery when he cut the policeman almost in half with a machine gun.

The marks of the garters were still on the skin of his sturdy calves, the only part of him that looked like any part of a strong man. His arms were slender, even emaciated. But his legs were powerful-looking. His feet were neat and almost womanish, after the white socks and dudish white shoes had been taken from them.

His clothes were shabby with still an attempt at smartness. The white shirt was cheap, the gray flannel trousers, and the uninitialed belt buckle were basement-counter merchandise, his maroon-and-white print tie might have cost half a dollar.

In his pockets were $7.70 and a few keys and a watch in which was the picture of a pretty female.

Two women bystanders were caught in the line of fire and wounded slightly as the Federal men blazed away. They were Miss Etta Natalsky, forty-five, and Miss Theresa Paulus, twenty-nine, both residents of the neighborhood.

Miss Natalsky was taken to the Columbus Memorial Hospital with a wound in the leg and Miss Paulus to the Grant Hospital, but her wound, also in the leg, was found to be only superficial.

The notorious desperado had resorted to facial surgery to disguise himself, and it was only by his piercing eyes—described by crime experts as "the eyes of a born killer"—that he was recognized.

In addition to the facial alterations, he had dyed his hair a jet black from its natural sandy shade, and he wore gold-rimmed glasses. Identification of the fallen man was confirmed by Purvis on the spot. Later, at the morgue, an attempt was made to identify the body from fingerprints, but the tips of the fingers had been scarred, as if with acid.

A recent wound in the chest, which had just healed, was revealed in the morgue examination. It was believed this was a memento of a recent bank robbery.

Dr. Charles D. Parker, coroner's physician, remarked on the alteration in the slain man's features. Scars which he carried on each cheek Dillinger had had smoothed out by facial surgery. Purvis, after closely examining the changed features, said:

"His nose, that originally was pronounced 'pug,' had been made nearly straight. His hair had been dyed recently."

Souvenir hunters among the excited crowds that swarmed to the scene of the shooting frantically dipped newspapers and handkerchiefs in the patch of blood left on the pavement.

Traffic became so jammed that streetcars were rerouted, police lines established, and all traffic finally blocked out of the area.

Unsatiated by their morbid milling around the death spot, the crowds a little later rushed to the morgue to view the body. Denied admittance, they battled police and shouted and yelled to get inside. More than two thousand at one time were struggling to force the doors.

I have indisputable proof that the bureau had information that Dillinger had been here for at least three days. It was the first definite location of the hunted murderer since the affray in the Little Bohemia (Wisconsin) lodge.

"We didn't have time to get him then, but we had time enough this time," Purvis said.

Evidently Purvis not only had enough time, but used it with the traditional efficiency of his department. There has always been open rancor between the Chicago police and the Federals, who have several times done them out of rewards. The Federals are not permitted to accept rewards.

But the East Chicago force—Dillinger had slaughtered three of their outfit in two raids, and the "coincidence" of their presence "when the tip came in" is obvious.

That Dillinger suspected nothing is proven by nothing as much as that the safety catch on his magazine gun was set. It was a new, high-type weapon, so powerful that its slugs would penetrate the bulletproof vests of the sort that Dillinger himself had worn in other spots. The number had been filed off. Close examination indicated it had never been fired. It was fully loaded, and a clip of extra cartridges was in a pocket.

He had no other possible instrument of offense or defense, this desperado, except a slender penknife on the other end of a thin chain that held his watch.

All his possessions lay on the marble slab beside the rubber stretcher in the basement of the morgue as the internes pawed his still warm face and body as they threw his head to this side and that, slung him over on his face, and dabbed the still-wet blood from where the bullets had bitten into him.

I wondered whether, a few brief minutes earlier, they would have had the temerity to treat John Dillinger's flesh so cavalierly.

They pointed to the scar on his shinbone, the one which had been so heavily broadcast as maiming and even killing Dillinger. It was a little bit of a thing and looked more like the result of a stone bruise than a volley from the muzzle of outraged society.

They flopped him over on the slab, quite by a clumsy accident, because the body didn't turn easily within the stretcher, what with its gangly, rubbery legs, and its thin, boneless arms. And as what was left of Dillinger clamped like a clod, face down, upon the slab which had held the clay of hoboes and who knows, a still warm but spent hand knocked off the straw hat which had fallen off his head in the alley and been trampled upon. And a good ten-cent cigar. Strangely intact.

The man who had killed him stood two feet away, smoking a cigar of the same brand. I must not mention his name. Purvis says "keep that a trade secret." With John ("Happy Jack") Hamilton and George ("Baby Face") Nelson, Dillinger's lieutenants, still at large, perhaps that is a fair enough precaution.

The Bureau of Identification men were on the job in a jiffy. They proved up the fingerprints, though they had been treated with a biting acid in an effort to obliterate the telltale. But the deltas and cores were unmistakable.

Behind the ears were well-done scars of a face-lifting job by a skillful plastic specialist. A mole on the forehead had been trimmed off rather well. His hair, by rights sandy, had been painted a muddy black with a poor grade of dye.

So had his mustache. The one identifying mark known around the globe as the Dillinger characteristic was there. And even in death he looked just like the Dillinger we all knew from the photographs. Probably the last breath of his ego.

Dillinger was a ladies' man. He didn't want to be picked up and identified by a rube sheriff. But, still, he wanted to whisper to a new sweetie in the confidences of the night:

"Baby, I can trust you—I'm John Dillinger!"

And she would look, and—he was! That mustache!

Having gone to astonishing lengths to change his inconspicuous identifying marks, with the necessary aid and advice of expert medical men, he had still refused to shave off that familiar trade-mark that every newspaper reader could see with eyes shut.

A scar on his chin had been reopened and smoothed up some, but not very convincingly. The droop at the left corner of his mouth was unmistakably intact. But the most striking facial change was in the tightening of the skin on his chin, almost completely killing his dimple, which was almost as widely known as his mustache.

Gold-rimmed eyeglasses fell off his face as he toppled over. These, one of the most amateurish of elements in disguise, did change his appearance decisively, the officers tell me.

The Federal office, as usual, issued contradictory statements and frankly admitted that certain information would not be given out.

Of the twenty-seven men who worked with Purvis, one was Captain Tim O'Neill of East Chicago, and four others were O'Neill's men. Purvis said they were there quite by chance and he had taken them in on the big adventure. A second statement also gave forth that Purvis had seen Dillinger enter as well as leave the theater.

As Dillinger emerged, walking near him were two youngish women, one of them wearing a red dress. Hundreds were leaving the house at the time, and almost any number of women would naturally have been near him. But the one with the red dress hurried up the alley, and four Federals made a formation between her and Dillinger before the first shot was fired. It is my theory that she was with Dillinger and that she was the tip-off party or in league with Purvis.

DISCUSSION QUESTIONS

1. Compare Lait's report of Dillinger's death with that of David Wagoner in his poem, "The Shooting of John Dillinger Outside the Biograph Theater, July 22, 1934" (see Classics). What do the titles of the two pieces suggest about their differences? How do the details of the shooting differ from news item to poem? What are the effects of those differences?

2. What can you tell about Lait's opinion of Dillinger? From what facts are you able to infer his opinion? What can you tell about Wagoner's opinion of Dillinger? How do they compare? From the style of Lait's news report and Wagoner's poem, how do they expect their respective audiences to feel about Dillinger?

Orson Welles / The War of the Worlds
[An Excerpt from the Radio Broadcast]

October 31, 1938

Born in Kenosha, Wisconsin, in 1915, Orson Welles had earned, by the age of twenty-six, an international reputation as an actor and director in radio, theater, and cinema. Welles' virtuosity includes celebrated performances as a playwright, cartoonist, and journalist. He has written several syndicated columns.

In 1937, Welles launched the Mercury Theater on the Air to present a regular series of radio broadcasts of dramatic adaptation of famous novels. On October 31, 1938, Welles' "splendid purple-velvet voice" came on the radio to announce a story appropriate to a Halloween evening—H. G. Wells' The War of the Worlds, written in 1898, depicting an invasion from Mars. Despite several reminders to the audience that they were listening to an adaptation of a novel, the authentic sounding details and tones of the broadcast, as the following excerpts dramatize, threw a sizable portion of the nation into mass hysteria.

The War of the Worlds

Ladies and gentlemen, here is the latest bulletin from the Intercontinental Radio News. Toronto, Canada: Professor Morse of Macmillan University reports observing a total of three explosions on the planet Mars, between the hours of 7:45 p.m. and 9:20 p.m., eastern standard time. This confirms earlier reports received from American observatories. Now, nearer home, comes a special announcement from Trenton, New Jersey. It is reported that at 8:50 p.m. a huge, flaming object, believed to be a meteorite, fell on a farm in the neighborhood of Grovers Mill, New Jersey, twenty-two miles from Trenton. The flash in the sky was visible within a radius of several hundred miles and the noise of the impact was heard as far north as Elizabeth.

We have dispatched a special mobile unit to the scene, and we will have our commentator, Mr. Phillips, give you a word description as soon as he can reach there from Princeton. In the meantime, we take you to the Hotel Martinet in Brooklyn, where Bobby Millette and his orchestra are offering a program of dance music. (SWING BAND FOR 20 SECONDS . . . THEN CUT)

ANNOUNCER

We take you now to Grovers Mill, New Jersey.
(CROWD NOISES . . . POLICE SIRENS)

PHILLIPS

Ladies and gentlemen, this is Carl Phillips again, at the Wilmuth farm, Grovers Mill, New Jersey. Professor Pierson and myself made the eleven miles from Princeton in ten minutes. Well, I . . . I hardly know where to begin, to paint for you a word picture of the strange scene before my eyes, like something out of a modern Arabian Nights. Well, I just got here. I haven't had a chance to look around yet. I guess that's *it*. Yes, I guess that's the . . . *thing*, directly in front of me, half buried in a vast pit. Must have struck with terrific force. The ground is covered with splinters of a tree it must have struck on its way down. What I can see of the . . . object itself doesn't look very much like a meteor, at least not the meteors I've seen. It looks more like a huge cylinder. It has a diameter of . . . what would you say, Professor Pierson? . . .

ANNOUNCER

Ladies and gentlemen, I have a grave announcement to make. Incredible as it may seem, both the observations of science and the evidence of our eyes lead to the inescapable assumption that those strange beings who landed in the Jersey farmlands tonight are the vanguard of an invading army from the planet Mars. The battle which took place tonight at Grovers Mill has ended in one of the most startling defeats ever suffered by an army in modern times; seven thousand men armed with rifles and machine guns pitted against a single fighting machine of the invaders from Mars. One hundred and twenty known survivors. The rest strewn over the battle area from Grovers Mill to Plainsboro crushed and trampled to death under the metal feet of the monster, or burned to cinders by its heat-ray. The monster is now in control of the middle section of New Jersey and has effectively cut the state through its center. Communication lines are down from Pennsylvania to the Atlantic Ocean. Railroad tracks are torn and service from New York to Philadelphia discontinued except routing some of the trains through Allentown and Phoenixville. Highways to the north, south, and west are clogged with frantic human traffic. Police and army reserves are unable to control the mad flight. By morning the fugitives will have swelled Philadelphia, Camden and Trenton, it is estimated, to twice their normal population.

At this time martial law prevails throughout New Jersey and eastern Pennsylvania. We take you now to Washington for a special broadcast on the National Emergency . . . the Secretary of the Interior. . . .

ANNOUNCER

I'm speaking from the roof of Broadcasting Building, New York City. The bells you hear are ringing to warn the people to evacuate the city as the Martians approach. Estimated in last two hours three million people have moved out along the roads to the north, Hutchison River Parkway still kept open for motor traffic. Avoid bridges to Long Island . . . hopelessly jammed. All communication with Jersey shore closed ten minutes ago. No more defenses. Our army wiped out . . . artillery, air force, everything wiped out. This may be the last broadcast. We'll stay here to the end. . . . People are holding service below us . . . in the cathedral.
(VOICES SINGING HYMN)
Now I look down the harbor. All manner of boats, overloaded with fleeing population, pulling out from docks.
(SOUND OF BOAT WHISTLES)
Streets are all jammed. Noise in crowds like New Year's Eve in city. Wait a minute. . . . Enemy now in sight above the Palisades. Five great machines. First one is crossing river. I can see it from here, wading the Hudson like a man wading through a brook. . . . A bulletin's handed me. . . . Martian cylinders are falling all over the country. One outside Buffalo, one in Chicago, St. Louis . . . seem to be timed and spaced. . . . Now the first machine reaches the shore. He stands watching, looking over the city. His steel, cowlish head is even with the skyscrapers. He waits for the others. They rise like a line of new towers on the city's west side. . . . Now they're lifting their metal hands. This is the end now. Smoke comes out . . . black smoke, drifting over the city. People in the streets see it now. They're running towards the East River . . . thousands of them, dropping in like rats. Now the smoke's spreading faster. It's reached Times Square. People trying to run away from it, but it's no use. They're falling like flies. Now the smoke's crossing Sixth Avenue . . . Fifth Avenue . . . 100 yards away . . . it's 50 feet. . . .

George M. Mahawinney / An Invasion from the Planet Mars

Philadelphia Inquirer, November 1, 1938

George M. Mahawinney, a rewrite man on duty at the Philadelphia Inquirer *the evening of the Welles broadcast, was besieged by frantic telephone calls seeking information about the invasion from Mars. The* Inquirer, *close to the reputed scene of the Martian landing at Grovers Mill, near Princeton, New Jersey, became the focal point for the nation's coverage of the bizarre results of Welles' broadcast. With America's news services clamoring for reports, Mahawinney wrote the following account in less than an hour.*

Terror struck at the hearts of hundreds of thousands of persons in the length and breadth of the United States last night as crisp words of what they believed to be a news broadcast leaped from their radio sets—telling of catastrophe from the skies visited on this country.

Out of the heavens, they learned, objects at first believed to be meteors crashed down near Trenton, killing many.

Then out of the "meteors" came monsters, spreading destruction with torch and poison gas.

It was all just a radio dramatization, but the result, in all actuality, was nationwide hysteria.

In Philadelphia, women and children ran from their homes, screaming. In Newark, New Jersey, ambulances rushed to one neighborhood to protect residents against a gas attack. In the deep South men and women knelt in groups in the streets and prayed for deliverance.

In reality there was no danger. The broadcast was merely a Halloween program in which Orson Welles, actor-director of the Mercury Theater on the Air, related, as though he were one of the few human survivors of the catastrophe, an adaptation of H. G. Wells' *The War of the Worlds.*

In that piece of fiction men from Mars, in meteorlike space ships, come to make conquest of earth. The circumstances of the story were unbelievable enough, but the manner of its presentation was apparently convincing to hundreds of thousands of persons—despite the fact that the program was interrupted thrice for an announcement that it was fiction, and fiction only.

For the fanciful tale was broadcast casually, for all the world like a news broadcast, opening up serenely enough with a weather report.

The realism of the broadcast, especially for those who had tuned in after it had started, brought effects which none—not the directors of the Federal Radio Theater Project, which sponsored it, nor the Columbia Broadcasting Company, which carried it over a coast-to-coast chain of 151 stations, nor Station WCAU, which broadcast it locally—could foresee.

Within a few minutes newspaper offices, radio stations, and police departments everywhere were flooded with anxious telephone calls. Sobbing women sought advice on what to do; broken-voiced men wished to know where to take their families.

Station WCAU received more than four thousand calls and eventually interrupted a later program to make an elaborate explanation that death had not actually descended on New Jersey, and that monsters were not actually invading the world.

But calm did not come readily to the frightened radio listeners of the country.

The hysteria reached such proportions that the New York City Department of Health called up a newspaper and wanted advice on offering its facilities for the protection of the populace. Nurses and physicians were among the telephone callers everywhere. They were ready to offer their assistance to the injured or maimed.

Hundreds of motorists touring through New Jersey heard the broadcast over their radios and detoured to avoid the area upon which the holocaust was focused—the area in the vicinity of Trenton and Princeton.

In scores of New Jersey towns women in their homes fainted as the horror of the broadcast fell on their ears. In Palmyra some residents packed up their worldly goods and prepared to move across the river into Philadelphia.

A white-faced man raced into the Hillside, New Jersey, police station and asked for a gas mask. Police said he panted out a tale of "terrible people spraying liquid gas all over Jersey meadows."

A weeping lady stopped Motorcycle Patrolman Lawrence Treger and asked where she should go to escape the "attack."

A terrified motorist asked the patrolman the way to Route 24. "All creation's busted loose. I'm getting out of Jersey," he screamed.

"Grovers Mill, New Jersey," was mentioned as a scene of destruction. In Stockton more than a half-hundred persons abandoned Colligan's Inn after hearing the broadcast and journeyed to Groveville to view the incredible "damage." They had misheard the name of the hypothetical town of "Grovers Mill," and believed it to be Groveville.

At Princeton University, women members of the geology faculty, equipped with flashlights and hammers, started for Grovers Corners. Dozens of cars were driven to the hamlet by curious motorists. A score of university students were phoned by their parents and told to come home.

An anonymous and somewhat hysterical girl phoned the Princeton Press Club from Grovers Corners and said:

"You can't imagine the horror of it! It's hell!"

A man came into the club and said he saw the meteor strike the earth and witnessed animals jumping from the alien body.

The Trenton police and fire telephone board bore the brunt of the nation's calls, because of its geographical location close to the presumed scene of catastrophe. On that board were received calls from Wilmington, Washington, Philadelphia, Jersey City, and Newark.

North of Trenton most of New Jersey was in the midst of a bad scare.

A report spread through Newark that the city was to be the target of a "gas-bomb attack." Police headquarters were notified there was a serious gas accident in the Clinton Hills section of that city. They sent squad cars and ambulances.

They found only householders, with possessions hastily bundled, leaving their homes. The householders returned to their homes only after emphatic explanations by the police.

Fifteen persons were treated for shock in one Newark hospital.

In Jersey City one resident demanded a gas mask of police. Another telephoned to ask whether he ought to flee the area or merely keep his windows closed and hope for the best.

Many New Yorkers seized personal effects and raced out of their apartments, some jumping into their automobiles and heading for the wide-open spaces.

Samuel Tishman, a Riverside Drive resident, declared he and hundreds of others evacuated their homes, fearing "the city was being bombed."

He told of going home and receiving a frantic telephone call from a nephew.

Tishman denounced the program as "the most asinine stunt I ever heard of" and as "a pretty crumby thing to do."

The panic it caused gripped impressionable Harlemites, and one man ran into the street declaring it was the President's voice they heard, advising: "Pack up and go North, the machines are coming from Mars."

Police in the vicinity at first regarded the excitement as a joke, but they were soon hard pressed in controlling the swarms in the streets.

A man entered the Wadsworth Avenue station uptown and said he heard "planes had bombed Jersey and were headed for Times Square."

A rumor spread over Washington Heights that a war was on.

At Caldwell, New Jersey, an excited parishioner rushed into the First Baptist Church during evening services and shouted that a tremendous meteor had fallen, causing widespread death, and that north Jersey was threatened with a shower of meteors. The congregation joined in prayer for deliverance.

Reactions as strange, or stranger, occurred in other parts of the country. In San Francisco, a citizen called police, crying:

"My God, where can I volunteer my services? We've got to stop this awful thing."

In Indianapolis, Indiana, a woman ran screaming into a church.

"New York is destroyed; it's the end of the world," she cried. "You might as well go home to die."

At Brevard College, North Carolina, five boys in dormitories fainted on hearing the broadcast. In Birmingham, Alabama, men and women gathered in groups and prayed. Women wept and prayed in Memphis, Tennessee.

Throughout Atlanta was a wide-spread belief that a "planet" had struck New Jersey, killing from forty to seven thousand persons.

At Pittsburgh one man telephoned a newspaper that he had returned to his home in the middle of the broadcast and found his wife in the bathroom, clutching a bottle of poison.

"I'd rather die this way than like that," she screamed before he was able to calm her.

Another citizen telephoned a newspaper in Washington, Pennsylvania, that a group of guests in his home playing cards "fell down on their knees and prayed," and then hurried home.

At Rivesville, West Virginia, a woman interrupted the pastor's sermon at a church meeting with loud outcries that there had been "an invasion." The meeting broke up in confusion.

Two heart attacks were reported by Kansas City hospitals, and the Associated Press Bureau there received calls of inquiry from Los Angeles, Salt Lake City, Beaumont, Texas, and St. Joseph, Missouri.

Minneapolis and St. Paul police switchboards were deluged with calls from frightened people.

Weeping and hysterical women in Providence, Rhode Island, cried out for officials of the electric company there to "turn off the lights so that the city will be safe from the enemy."

In some places mass hysteria grew so great that witnesses to the "invasion" could be found.

A Boston woman telephoned a newspaper to say she could "see the fire" from her window, and that she and her neighbors were "getting out of here."

The broadcast began at eight P.M. Within a few minutes after that time it had brought such a serious reaction that New Jersey state police sent out a teletype message to its various stations and barracks, containing explanations and instructions to police officers on how to handle the hysteria.

These and other police everywhere had problems on their hands as the broadcast moved on, telling of a "bulletin from the Intercontinental Radio News Bureau" saying there had been a gas explosion in New Jersey.

"Bulletins" that came in rapidly after that told of "meteors," then corrected that statement and described the Mars monsters.

The march of the Martians was disastrous. For a while they swept everything before them, according to the pseudo-bulletins. Mere armies and navies were being wiped out in a trice.

Actually, outside the radio stations, the Martians were doing a pretty good job on the Halloween imaginations of the citizenry. The radio stations and the Columbia Broadcasting Company spent much of the remainder of the evening clearing up the situation. Again and again they explained the whole thing was nothing more than a dramatization.

In the long run, however, calm was restored in the myriad American homes which had been momentarily threatened by interplanetary invasion. Fear of the monsters from Mars eventually subsided.

There was no reason for being afraid of them, anyway. Even the bulletins of the radio broadcast explained they all soon died. They couldn't stand the earth's atmosphere and perished of pneumonia.

Dorothy Thompson / Mr. Welles and Mass Delusion
New York Herald Tribune, November 2, 1938

Dorothy Thompson (1894–1961) remained one of America's most distinguished columnists for more than a generation. Her syndicated reports, "On the Record," appeared three times a week and discussed such contemporary issues as President Roosevelt's "New Deal" and the emerging Nazi regime—each column marked by her commitment to journalistic candor. In "Mr. Welles and Mass Delusion," Dorothy Thompson, two days after the Welles broadcast, poignantly depicts the malleability of the national psychology on the eve of another world war and reminds us of the terrifying power of mass media.

All unwittingly Mr. Orson Welles and the Mercury Theater on the Air have made one of the most fascinating and important demonstrations of all time. They have proved that a few effective voices, accompanied by sound effects, can so convince masses of people of a totally unreasonable, completely fantastic proposition as to create nation-wide panic.

They have demonstrated more potently than any argument, demonstrated beyond question of a doubt, the appalling dangers and enormous effectiveness of popular and theatrical demagoguery.

They have cast a brilliant and cruel light upon the failure of popular education.

They have shown up the incredible stupidity, lack of nerve and ignorance of thousands.

They have proved how easy it is to start a mass delusion.

They have uncovered the primeval fears lying under the thinnest surface of the so-called civilized man.

They have shown that man, when the victim of his own gullibility, turns to the government to protect him against his own errors of judgment.

The newspapers are correct in playing up this story over every other news event in the world. It is the story of the century.

And far from blaming Mr. Orson Welles, he ought to be given a Congressional medal and a national prize for having made the most amazing and important contribution to the social sciences. For Mr. Orson Welles and his theater have made a greater contribution to an understanding of Hitlerism, Mussolinism, Stalinism, anti-Semitism and all the other terrorisms of our times than all the words about them that have been written by reasonable men. They have made the reductio ad absurdum of mass manias. They have thrown more light on recent events in Europe leading to the Munich pact than everything that has been said on the subject by all the journalists and commentators.

Hitler managed to scare all Europe to its knees a month ago, but he at least had an army and an air force to back up his shrieking words.

But Mr. Welles scared thousands into demoralization with nothing at all.

That historic hour on the air was an act of unconscious genius, performed by the very innocence of intelligence.

Nothing whatever about the dramatization of the "War of the Worlds" was in the least credible, no matter at what point the hearer might have tuned in. The entire verisimilitude was in the names of a few specific places. Monsters were depicted of a type that nobody has ever seen, equipped with "rays" entirely fantastic; they were described as "straddling the Pulaski Skyway" and throughout the broadcast they were referred to as Martians, men from another planet.

A twist of the dial would have established for anybody that the national catastrophe was not being noted on any other station. A second of logic would have dispelled any terror. A notice that the broadcast came from a non-existent agency would have awakened skepticism.

A reference to the radio program would have established that the "War of the Worlds" was announced in advance.

The time element was obviously lunatic.

Listeners were told that "within two hours three million people have moved out of New York"—an obvious impossibility for the most disciplined army moving exactly as planned, and a double fallacy because only a few minutes before, the news of the arrival of the monster had been announced.

And of course it was not even a planned hoax. Nobody was more surprised at the result than Mr. Welles. The public was told at the beginning, at the end and during the course of the drama that it *was* a drama.

But eyewitnesses presented themselves; the report became second hand, third hand, fourth hand, and became more and more credible, so that nurses and doctors and National Guardsmen rushed to defense.

When the truth became known the reaction was also significant. The deceived were furious and of course demanded that the state protect them, demonstrating that they were incapable of relying on their own judgment.

Again there was a complete failure of logic. For if the deceived had thought about it they would realize that the greatest organizers of mass hysterias and mass delusions today are states using the radio to excite terrors, incite hatreds, inflame masses, win mass support for policies, create idolatries, abolish reason and maintain themselves in power.

The immediate moral is apparent if the whole incident is viewed in reason: no political body must ever, under any circumstances, obtain a monopoly of radio.

The second moral is that our popular and universal education is failing to train reason and logic, even in the educated.

The third is that the popularization of science has led to gullibility and new superstitions, rather than to skepticism and the really scientific attitude of mind.

The fourth is that the power of mass suggestion is the most potent force today and that the political demagogue is more powerful than all the economic forces.

For, mind you, Mr. Welles was managing an obscure program, competing with one of the most popular entertainments on the air!

The conclusion is that the radio must not be used to create mass prejudices and mass divisions and schisms, either by private individuals or by government or its agencies, or its officials, or its opponents.

If people can be frightened out of their wits by mythical men from Mars, they can be frightened into fanaticism by the fear of Reds, or convinced that America is in the hands of sixty families, or aroused to revenge against any minority, or terrorized into subservience to leadership because of any imaginable menace.

The technique of modern mass politics calling itself democracy is to create a fear—a fear of economic royalists, or of Reds, or of Jews, or of starvation, or of an outside enemy—and exploit that fear into obtaining subservience in return for protection.

I wrote in this column a short time ago that the new warfare was waged by propaganda, the outcome depending on which side could first frighten the other to death.

The British people were frightened into obedience to a policy a few weeks ago by a radio speech and by digging a few trenches in Hyde Park, and afterward led to hysterical jubilation over a catastrophic defeat for their democracy.

But Mr. Welles went all the politicians one better. He made the scare to end scares, the menace to end menaces, the unreason to end unreason, the perfect demonstration that the danger is not from Mars but from the theatrical demagogue.

Langston Hughes / Family Tree

Chicago Defender, ca. 1942

The author of more than sixty volumes of fiction, poetry, drama, gospel song-plays, opera lyrics, translations, and children's books, Langston Hughes has also written scores of essays and news reports. Born in Joplin, Missouri in 1902, Hughes studied at Columbia University and later signed on as a cook's helper aboard a tramp freighter bound for Africa. He also worked as a cook in a Paris night club, as a busboy in a Washington hotel, and, after his writing had been "discovered" during the Harlem Renaissance of the late 1920s, served as a correspondent for the Baltimore Afro-American *reporting on the Spanish Civil War.*

Hughes' most popular writing features the exploits, opinions, and musings of Jesse B. Semple ("Simple"), a masterful rendition of a battered but resilient character Hughes had met in a Harlem bar in 1942. "Simple" tells a story (see Mark Twain's "How To Tell a Story" in Classics) with an engaging combination of humor and irony, penetrating wit and realistic observation.

Hughes' conversations with "Simple" were recorded for over two decades in the Chicago Defender, *a newspaper addressed to that city's black community, and were subsequently collected in four volumes.*

"Anybody can look at me and tell I am part Indian," said Simple.

"I see you almost every day," I said, "and I did not know it until now."

"I have Indian blood but I do not show it much," said Simple. "My uncle's cousin's great-grandma were a Cherokee. I only shows mine when I lose my temper—then my Indian blood boils. I am quick-tempered just like a Indian. If somebody does something to me, I always fights back. In fact, when I get mad, I am the toughest Negro God's got. It's my Indian blood. When I were a young man, I used to play baseball and steal bases just like Jackie. If the empire would rule me out, I would get mad and hit the empire. I had to stop playing. That Indian temper. Nowadays, though, it's mostly womens that riles me up, especially landladies, waitresses, and girl friends. To tell the truth, I believe in a woman keeping her place. Womens is beside themselves these days. They want to rule the roost."

"You have old-fashioned ideas about sex," I said. "In fact, your line of thought is based on outmoded economics."

"What?"

"In the days when women were dependent upon men for a living, you could be the boss. But now women make their own living. Some of them make more money than you do."

"True," said Simple. "During the war they got into that habit. But boss I am still due to be."

"So you think. But you can't always put your authority into effect."

"I can try," said Simple. "I can say, 'Do this!' And if she does something else, I can raise my voice, if not my hand."

"You can be sued for raising your voice," I stated, "and arrested for raising your hand."

"And she can be annihilated when I return from being arrested," said Simple. "That's my Indian blood!"

"You must believe in a woman being a squaw."

"She better not look like no squaw," said Simple. "I want a woman to look sharp when she goes out with me. No moccasins. I wants high-heel shoes and nylons, cute legs—and short dresses. But I also do not want her to talk back to me. As I said, I am the man. *Mine* is the word, and she is due to hush."

"Indians customarily expect their women to be quiet," I said.

"I do not expect mine to be *too* quiet," said Simple. "I want 'em to sweet-talk me—'Sweet baby, this,' and 'Baby, that,' and 'Baby, you's right, darling,' when they talk to me."

"In other words, you want them both old-fashioned and modern at the same time," I said. "The convolutions of your hypothesis are sometimes beyond cognizance."

"Cog hell!" said Simple. "I just do not like no old loud back-talking chick. That's the Indian in me. My grandpa on my father's side were like that, too, an Indian. He was married five times and he really ruled his roost."

"There are a mighty lot of Indians up your family tree," I said. "Did your granddad look like one?"

"Only his nose. He was dark brownskin otherwise. In fact, he were black. And the womens! Man! They was crazy about Grandpa. Every time he walked down the street, they stuck their heads out the windows and kept 'em turned South—which was where the beer parlor was."

"So your grandpa was a drinking man, too. That must be whom you take after."

"I also am named after him," said Simple. "Grandpa's name was Jess, too. So I am Jesse B. Semple."

"What does the *B* stand for?"

"Nothing. I just put it there myself since they didn't give me no initial when I was born. I am really Jess Semple—which the kids changed around into a nick-name when I were in school. In fact, they used to tease me when I were small, calling me 'Simple Simon.' But I was right handy with my fists, and after I beat the 'Simon' out of a few of them, they let me alone. But my friends still call me 'Simple.' "

"In reality, you are Jesse Semple," I said, "colored."

"Part Indian," insisted Simple, reaching for his beer.

"Jess is certainly not an Indian name."

"No, it ain't," said Simple, "but we did have a Hiawatha in our family. She died."

"She?" I said. "Hiawatha was no *she*."

"She was a *she* in our family. And she had long coal-black hair just like a Creole. You know, I started to marry a Creole one time when I was coach-boy on the L. & N. down to New Orleans. Them Louisiana girls are bee-oou-te-ful! Man, I mean!"

"Why didn't you marry her, fellow?"

"They are more dangerous than a Indian," said Simple, "also I do not want no pretty woman. First thing you know, you fall in love with her—then you got to kill somebody about her. She'll make you so jealous, you'll bust! A pretty woman will get a man in trouble. Me and my Indian blood, quick-tempered as I is. No! I do not crave a pretty woman."

"Joyce is certainly not bad-looking," I said. "You hang around her all the time."

"She is far from a Creole. Besides, she appreciates me," said Simple. "Joyce knows I got Indian blood which makes my temper bad. But we take each other as we is. I respect her and she respects me."

"That's the way it should be with the whole world," I said. "Therefore, you and Joyce are setting a fine example in these days of trials and tribulations. Everybody should take each other as they are, white, black, Indians, Creole. Then there would be no prejudice, nations would get along."

"Some folks do not see it like that," said Simple. "For instant, my landlady—and my wife. Isabel could never get along with me. That is why we are not together today."

"I'm not talking personally," I said, "so why bring in your wife?"

"Getting along *starts* with persons, don't it?" asked Simple. "You *must* include my wife. That woman got my Indian blood so riled up one day I thought I would explode."

"I still say, I'm not talking personally."

"Then stop talking," exploded Simple, "because with me it is personal. Facts, I cannot even talk about my wife if I don't get personal. That's how it is if you're part Indian—everything is personal. *Heap much personal.*"

William L. Laurence / Atomic Bombing of Nagasaki Told by Flight Member

The New York Times, September 9, 1945

Science dominated the life of William L. Laurence from his early youth. When he was growing up in Lithuania, according to a biographical profile in the New Yorker, *Laurence received as a gift a book "that speculated on the possibility of a civilization on Mars, and young [Laurence] was so impressed that he decided to go to the United States when he was old enough, because from there . . . he might most easily be able to establish contact with that planet."*

He arrived in Hoboken, New Jersey, in 1905, and proceeded to study at Harvard and the Boston University Law School. After five years of reporting for the New York World, *Laurence went to work for the* New York Times *where he covered some of the most momentous events in the history of twentieth century science. The only reporter with access to the "top secret" testing and development of the atomic bomb, Laurence also prepared the War Department's press releases on the weapon.*

On August 9, 1945, Laurence flew with the mission to bomb Nagasaki, barely three days after one hundred thousand people had been killed at Hiroshima in what Time *magazine called "The Birth of an Era." Laurence's Pulitzer Prize eyewitness account is underlined by a curious aesthetic sense—one that watches this "thing of beauty" destroy a major Japanese city.*

With the atomic-bomb mission to Japan, August 9 (Delayed)—We are on our way to bomb the mainland of Japan. Our flying contingent consists of three specially designed B-29 Superforts, and two of these carry no bombs. But our lead plane is on its way with another atomic bomb, the second in three days, concentrating in its active substance an explosive energy equivalent to twenty thousand and, under favorable conditions, forty thousand tons of TNT.

We have several chosen targets. One of these is the great industrial and shipping center of Nagasaki, on the western shore of Kyushu, one of the main islands of the Japanese homeland.

I watched the assembly of this man-made meteor during the past two days and was among the small group of scientists and Army and Navy representatives privileged to be present at the ritual of its loading in the Superfort last night, against a background of threatening black skies torn open at intervals by great lightning flashes.

It is a thing of beauty to behold, this "gadget." Into its design went millions of man-hours of what is without doubt the most concentrated intellectual effort in history. Never before had so much brain power been focused on a single problem.

This atomic bomb is different from the bomb used three days ago with such devastating results on Hiroshima.

I saw the atomic substance before it was placed inside the bomb. By itself it is not at all dangerous to handle. It is only under certain conditions, produced in the bomb assembly, that it can be made to yield up its energy, and even then it gives only a small fraction of its total contents—a fraction, however, large enough to produce the greatest explosion on earth.

The briefing at midnight revealed the extreme care and the tremendous amount of preparation that had been made to take care of every detail of the mission, to make certain that the atomic bomb fully served the purpose for which it was intended. Each target in turn was shown in detailed maps and in aerial photographs. Every detail of the course was rehearsed—navigation, altitude, weather, where to land in emergencies. It came out that the Navy had submarines and rescue craft, known as Dumbos and Superdumbos, stationed at various strategic points in the vicinity of the targets, ready to rescue the fliers in case they were forced to bail out.

The briefing period ended with a moving prayer by the chaplain. We then proceeded to the mess hall for the traditional early-morning breakfast before departure on a bombing mission.

A convoy of trucks took us to the supply building for the special equipment carried on combat missions. This included the Mae West, a parachute, a lifeboat, an oxygen mask, a flak suit, and a survival vest. We still had a few hours before take-off time, but we all went to the flying field and stood around in little groups or sat in jeeps talking rather casually about our mission to the Empire, as the Japanese home islands are known hereabouts.

In command of our mission is Major Charles W. Sweeney, twenty-five, of 124 Hamilton Avenue, North Quincy, Massachusetts. His flagship, carrying the atomic bomb, is named *The Great Artiste,* but the name does not appear on the body of the great silver ship, with its unusually long, four-bladed, orange-tipped propellers. Instead, it carries the number 77, and someone remarks that it was "Red" Grange's winning number on the gridiron.

We took off at 3:50 this morning and headed northwest on a straight line for the Empire. The night was cloudy and threatening, with only a few stars here and there breaking through the overcast. The weather report had predicted storms ahead part of the way but clear sailing for the final and climactic stages of our odyssey.

We were about an hour away from our base when the storm broke. Our great ship took some heavy dips through the abysmal darkness around us, but it took these dips much more gracefully than a large commercial air liner, producing a sensation more in the nature of a glide than a "bump," like a great ocean liner riding the waves except that in this case the air waves were much higher and the rhythmic tempo of the glide was much faster.

I noticed a strange eerie light coming through the window high above the navigator's cabin, and as I peered through the dark all around us I saw a startling phenomenon. The whirling giant propellers had somehow become great luminous disks of blue flame. The same luminous blue flame appeared on the plexiglas windows in the nose of the ship, and on the tips of the giant wings. It looked as though we were riding the whirlwind through space on a chariot of blue fire.

It was, I surmised, a surcharge of static electricity that had accumulated on the tips of the propellers and on the di-electric material of the plastic windows. One's thoughts dwelt anxiously on the precious cargo in the invisible ship ahead of us. Was there any likelihood of danger that this heavy electric tension in the atmosphere all about us might set it off?

I expressed my fears to Captain Bock, who seems nonchalant and unperturbed at the controls. He quickly reassured me.

"It is a familiar phenomenon seen often on ships. I have seen it many times on bombing missions. It is known as St. Elmo's fire."

On we went through the night. We soon rode out the storm and our ship was once again sailing on a smooth course straight ahead, on a direct line to the Empire.

Our altimeter showed that we were traveling through space at a height of seventeen thousand feet. The thermometer registered an outside temperature of thirty-three degrees below zero Centigrade, about thirty below Fahrenheit. Inside our pressurized cabin the temperature was that of a comfortable air-conditioned room and a pressure corresponding to an altitude of eight thousand feet. Captain Bock cautioned me, however, to keep my oxygen mask handy in case of emergency. This, he explained, might mean either something going wrong with the pressure equipment inside the ship or a hole through the cabin by flak.

The first signs of dawn came shortly after five o'clock. Sergeant Curry, of Hoopeston, Illinois, who had been listening steadily on his earphones for radio reports, while maintaining a strict radio silence himself, greeted it by rising to his feet and gazing out the window.

"It's good to see the day," he told me. "I get a feeling of claustrophobia hemmed in in this cabin at night."

He is a typical American youth, looking even younger than his twenty years. It takes no mind reader to read his thoughts.

"It's a long way from Hoopeston," I find myself remarking.

"Yep," he replies, as he busies himself decoding a message from outer space.

"Think this atomic bomb will end the war?" he asks hopefully.

"There is a very good chance that this one may do the trick," I assured him, "but if not, then the next one or two surely will. Its power is such that no nation can stand up against it very long." This was not my own view. I had heard it expressed all around a few hours earlier, before we took off. To anyone who had seen this man-made fireball in action, as I had less than a month ago in the desert of New Mexico, this view did not sound overoptimistic.

By 5:50 it was really light outside. We had lost our lead ship, but Lieutenant Godfrey, our navigator, informs me that we had arranged for that contingency. We have an assembly point in the sky above the little island of Yakushima, southeast of Kyushu, at 9:10. We are to circle there and wait for the rest of our formation.

Our genial bombardier, Lieutenant Levy, comes over to invite me to take his front-row seat in the transparent nose of the ship, and I accept eagerly. From that vantage point in space, seventeen thousand feet above the Pacific, one gets a view of hundreds of miles on all sides, horizontally and vertically. At that height the vast ocean below and the sky above seem to merge into one great sphere.

I was on the inside of that firmament, riding above the giant mountains of white cumulus clouds, letting myself be suspended in infinite space. One hears the whirl of the motors behind one, but it soon becomes insignificant against the immensity all around and is before long swallowed by it. There comes a point where space also swallows time and one lives through eternal moments filled with an oppressive loneliness, as though all life had suddenly vanished from the earth and you are the only one left, a lone survivor traveling endlessly through interplanetary space.

My mind soon returns to the mission I am on. Somewhere beyond these vast mountains of white clouds ahead of me there lies Japan, the land of our enemy. In about four hours from now one of its cities, making weapons of war for use against us, will be wiped off the map by the greatest weapon ever made by man: In one tenth of a millionth of a second, a fraction of time immeasurable by any clock, a whirlwind from the skies will pulverize thousands of its buildings and tens of thousands of its inhabitants.

But at this moment no one yet knows which one of the several cities chosen as targets is to be annihilated. The final choice lies with destiny. The winds over Japan will make the decision. If they carry heavy clouds over our primary target, that city will be saved, at least for the time being. None of its inhabitants will ever know that the wind of a benevolent destiny had passed over their heads. But that same wind will doom another city.

Our weather planes ahead of us are on their way to find out where the wind blows. Half an hour before target time we will know what the winds have decided.

Does one feel any pity or compassion for the poor devils about to die? Not when one thinks of Pearl Harbor and of the Death March on Bataan.

Captain Bock informs me that we are about to start our climb to bombing altitude.

He manipulates a few knobs on his control panel to the right of him, and I alternately watch the white clouds and ocean below me and the altimeter on the bombardier's panel. We reached our altitude at nine o'clock. We were then over Japanese waters, close to their mainland. Lieutenant Godfrey motioned to me to look through his radar scope. Before me was the outline of our assembly point. We shall soon meet our lead ship and proceed to the final stage of our journey.

We reached Yakushima at 9:12 and there, about four thousand feet ahead of us, was *The Great Artiste* with its precious load. I saw Lieutenant Godfrey and Sergeant Curry strap on their parachutes and I decided to do likewise.

We started circling. We saw little towns on the coastline, heedless of our presence. We kept on circling, waiting for the third ship in our formation.

It was 9:56 when we began heading for the coastline. Our weather scouts had sent us code messages, deciphered by Sergeant Curry, informing us that both the primary target as well as the secondary were clearly visible.

The winds of destiny seemed to favor certain Japanese cities that must remain nameless. We circled about them again and again and found no opening in the thick umbrella of clouds that covered them. Destiny chose Nagasaki as the ultimate target.

We had been circling for some time when we noticed black puffs of smoke coming through the white clouds directly at us. There were fifteen bursts of flak in rapid succession, all too low. Captain Bock changed his course. There soon followed eight more bursts of flak, right up to our altitude, but by this time were too far to the left.

We flew southward down the channel and at 11:33 crossed the coastline and headed straight for Nagasaki, about one hundred miles to the west. Here again we circled until we found an opening in the clouds. It was 12:01 and the goal of our mission had arrived.

We heard the prearranged signal on our radio, put on our arc welder's glasses, and watched tensely the maneuverings of the strike ship about half a mile in front of us.

"There she goes!" someone said.

Out of the belly of *The Great Artiste* what looked like a black object went downward.

Captain Bock swung around to get out of range; but even though we were turning away in the opposite direction, and despite the fact that it was broad daylight in our cabin, all of us became aware of a giant flash that broke through the dark barrier of our arc welder's lenses and flooded our cabin with intense light.

We removed our glasses after the first flash, but the light still lingered on, a bluish-green light that illuminated the entire sky all around. A tremendous blast wave struck our ship and made it tremble from nose to tail. This was followed by four more blasts in rapid succession, each resounding like the boom of cannon fire hitting our plane from all directions.

Observers in the tail of our ship saw a giant ball of fire rise as though from the bowels of the earth, belching forth enormous white smoke rings. Next they saw a giant pillar of purple fire, ten thousand feet high, shooting skyward with enormous speed.

By the time our ship had made another turn in the direction of the atomic explosion the pillar of purple fire had reached the level of our altitude. Only about forty-five seconds had passed. Awe-struck, we watched it shoot upward like a meteor coming from the earth instead of from outer space, becoming ever more alive as it climbed skyward through the white clouds. It was no longer smoke, or dust, or even a cloud of fire. It was a living thing, a new species of being, born right before our incredulous eyes.

At one stage of its evolution, covering millions of years in terms of seconds, the entity assumed the form of a giant square totem pole, with its base about three miles long, tapering off to about a mile at the top. Its bottom was brown, its center was amber, its top white. But it was a living totem pole, carved with many grotesque masks grimacing at the earth.

Then, just when it appeared as though the thing had settled down into a state of permanence, there came shooting out of the top a giant mushroom that increased the height of the pillar to a total of forty-five thousand feet. The mushroom top was even more alive than the pillar, seething and boiling in a white fury of creamy foam, sizzling upward and then descending earthward, a thousand Old Faithful geysers rolled into one.

It kept struggling in an elemental fury, like a creature in the act of breaking the bonds that held it down. In a few seconds it had freed itself from its gigantic stem and floated upward with tremendous speed, its momentum carrying it into the stratosphere to a height of about sixty thousand feet.

But no sooner did this happen when another mushroom, smaller in size than the first one, began emerging out of the pillar. It was as though the decapitated monster was growing a new head.

As the first mushroom floated off into the blue it changed its shape into a flower-like form, its giant petals curving downward, creamy white outside, rose-colored inside. It still retained that shape when we last gazed at it from a distance of about two hundred miles. The boiling pillar of many colors could also be seen at that distance, a giant mountain of jumbled rainbows, in travail. Much living substance had gone into those rainbows. The quivering top of the pillar was protruding to a great height through the white clouds, giving the appearance of a monstrous prehistoric creature with a ruff around its neck, a fleecy ruff extending in all directions, as far as the eye could see.

DISCUSSION QUESTIONS

1. How does William Laurence respond to the disastrous event he is covering? Does he include in his report his own feelings about what he is witnessing? What rhetorical devices characterize his account? What effects do these devices have on your response to his report?

2. Laurence calls the atomic bomb "a thing of beauty." Does he find any other examples of "beauty" on the mission? Explain. How does his use of detail contribute to (detract from) the aesthetic effects he wants to convey?

3. Does Laurence have any political or moral attitudes toward the bombing? Explain. Point to specific words and phrases to verify your contention. What is the effect of the final image in Laurence's report?

Tom Wicker / Kennedy Is Killed by Sniper as He Rides in Car in Dallas

The New York Times, November 23, 1963

Tom Wicker had a great deal of experience in journalism before he joined the Washington office of the New York Times *in 1960. Born and educated in North Carolina, Wicker worked in his home state as editor of the* Sanhill Citizen *and as managing editor of the* Robesonian. *After serving as copy editor, sports editor, and Washington correspondent for the* Winston-Salem Journal, *Wicker took on the responsibilities of the associate editorship of the* Nashville Tennessean. *Since his report on the assassination of President Kennedy, Wicker has moved from a featured reporter to columnist and associate editor of the* New York Times. *He has also written several novels.*

Tom Wicker's recollections of his coverage of the tumultuous events of November 22, 1963, follow the report below. They are reprinted from Times Talk, *the monthly report circulated to members of the* Times *organization.*

KENNEDY IS KILLED BY SNIPER AS HE RIDES IN CAR
IN DALLAS; JOHNSON SWORN IN ON PLANE.

.

Gov. Connally Shot;
Mrs. Kennedy Safe.

.

President Is Struck Down by a Rifle Shot
From Building on Motorcade Route—
Johnson, Riding Behind, Is Unhurt.

.

Kennedy Is Killed by Sniper as He Rides in Car in Dallas

DALLAS, Nov. 22—President John Fitzgerald Kennedy was shot and killed by an assassin today.

He died of a wound in the brain caused by a rifle bullet that was fired at him as he was riding through downtown Dallas in a motorcade.

Vice President Lyndon Baines Johnson, who was riding in the third car behind Mr. Kennedy's, was sworn in as the 36th President of the United States 99 minutes after Mr. Kennedy's death.

Mr. Johnson is 55 years old; Mr. Kennedy was 46.

Shortly after the assassination, Lee H. Oswald, who once defected to the Soviet Union and who has been active in the Fair Play for Cuba Committee, was arrested by the Dallas police. Tonight he was accused of the killing.

SUSPECT CAPTURED AFTER SCUFFLE

Oswald, 24 years old, was also accused of slaying a policeman who had approached him in the street. Oswald was subdued after a scuffle with a second policeman in a nearby theater.

President Kennedy was shot at 12:30 P.M., Central Standard Time (1:30 P.M., New York time). He was pronounced dead at 1 P.M. and Mr. Johnson was sworn in at 2:39 P.M.

Mr. Johnson, who was uninjured in the shooting, took his oath in the Presidential jet plane as it stood on the runway at Love Field. The body of Mr. Kennedy was aboard. Immediately after the oath-taking, the plane took off for Washington.

Standing beside the new President as Mr. Johnson took the oath of office was Mrs. John F. Kennedy. Her stockings were spattered with her husband's blood.

Gov. John B. Connally, Jr., of Texas, who was riding in the same car with Mr. Kennedy, was severely wounded in the chest, ribs and arm. His condition was serious, but not critical.

The killer fired the rifle from a building just off the motorcade route. Mr. Kennedy, Governor Connally and Mr. Johnson had just received an enthusiastic welcome from a large crowd in downtown Dallas.

Mr. Kennedy apparently was hit by the first of what witnesses believed were three shots. He was driven at high speed to Dallas Parkland Hospital. There, in an emergency operating room, with only physicians and nurses in attendance, he died without regaining consciousness.

Mrs. Kennedy, Mrs. Connally and a Secret Service agent were in the car with Mr. Kennedy and Governor Connally. Two Secret Service agents flanked the car. Other than Mr. Connally, none of this group was injured in the shooting. Mrs. Kennedy cried, "Oh no!" immediately after her husband was struck.

Mrs. Kennedy was in the hospital near her husband when he died, but not in the operating room. When the body was taken from the hospital in a bronze coffin about 2 P.M., Mrs. Kennedy walked beside it.

Her face was sorrowful. She looked steadily at the floor. She still wore the raspberry-colored suit in which she had greeted welcoming crowds in Fort Worth and Dallas. But she had taken off the matching pillbox hat she wore earlier in the day, and her dark hair was windblown and tangled. Her hand rested lightly on her husband's coffin as it was taken to a waiting hearse.

Mrs. Kennedy climbed in beside the coffin. Then the ambulance drove to Love

Field, and Mr. Kennedy's body was placed aboard the Presidential jet. Mrs. Kennedy then attended the swearing-in ceremony for Mr. Johnson.

As Mr. Kennedy's body left Parkland Hospital, a few stunned persons stood outside. Nurses and doctors, whispering among themselves, looked from the window. A larger crowd that had gathered earlier, before it was known that the President was dead, had been dispersed by Secret Service men and policemen.

PRIESTS ADMINISTER LAST RITES

Two priests administered last rites to Mr. Kennedy, a Roman Catholic. They were the Very Rev. Oscar Huber, the pastor of Holy Trinity Church in Dallas, and the Rev. James Thompson.

Mr. Johnson was sworn in as President by Federal Judge Sarah T. Hughes of the Northern District of Texas. She was appointed to the judgeship by Mr. Kennedy in October, 1961.

The ceremony, delayed about five minutes for Mrs. Kennedy's arrival, took place in the private Presidential cabin in the rear of the plane.

About 25 to 30 persons—members of the late President's staff, members of Congress who had been accompanying the President on a two-day tour of Texas cities and a few reporters—crowded into the little room.

No accurate listing of those present could be obtained. Mrs. Kennedy stood at the left of Mr. Johnson, her eyes and face showing the signs of weeping that had apparently shaken her since she left the hospital not long before.

Mrs. Johnson, wearing a beige dress, stood at her husband's right.

As Judge Hughes read the brief oath of office, her eyes, too, were red from weeping. Mr. Johnson's hands rested on a black, leatherbound Bible as Judge Hughes read and he repeated:

"I do solemnly swear that I will perform the duties of the President of the United States to the best of my ability and defend, protect and preserve the Constitution of the United States."

Those 34 words made Lyndon Baines Johnson, one-time farmboy and schoolteacher of Johnson City, the President.

JOHNSON EMBRACES MRS. KENNEDY

Mr. Johnson made no statement. He embraced Mrs. Kennedy and she held his hand for a long moment. He also embraced Mrs. Johnson and Mrs. Evelyn Lincoln, Mr. Kennedy's private secretary.

"O.K.," Mr. Johnson said. "Let's get this plane back to Washington."

At 2:46 P.M., seven minutes after he had become President, 106 minutes after Mr. Kennedy had become the fourth American President to succumb to an assassin's wounds, the white and red jet took off for Washington.

In the cabin when Mr. Johnson took the oath was Cecil Stoughton, an armed forces photographer assigned to the White House.

Mr. Kennedy's staff members appeared stunned and bewildered. Lawrence F. O'Brien, the Congressional liaison officer, and P. Kenneth O'Donnell, the appointment secretary, both long associates of Mr. Kennedy, showed evidences of weeping. None had anything to say.

Other staff members believed to be in the cabin for the swearing-in included David F. Powers, the White House receptionist; Miss Pamela Turnure, Mrs. Kennedy's press secretary; and Malcolm Kilduff, the assistant White House press secretary.

Mr. Kilduff announced the President's death, with choked voice and red-rimmed eyes, at about 1:36 P.M.

"President John F. Kennedy died at approximately 1 o'clock Central Standard Time today here in Dallas," Mr. Kilduff said at the hospital. "He died of a gunshot wound in the brain. I have no other details regarding the assassination of the President."

Mr. Kilduff also announced that Governor Connally had been hit by a bullet or bullets and that Mr. Johnson, who had not yet been sworn in, was safe in the protective custody of the Secret Service at an unannounced place, presumably the airplane at Love Field.

Mr. Kilduff indicated that the President had been shot once. Later medical reports raised the possibility that there had been two wounds. But the death was caused, as far as could be learned, by a massive wound in the brain.

Later in the afternoon, Dr. Malcolm Perry, an attending surgeon, and Dr. Kemp Clark, chief of neurosurgery at Parkland Hospital, gave more details.

Mr. Kennedy was hit by a bullet in the throat, just below the Adam's apple, they said. This wound had the appearance of a bullet's entry.

Mr. Kennedy also had a massive, gaping wound in the back and one on the right side of the head. However, the doctors said it was impossible to determine immediately whether the wounds had been caused by one bullet or two.

RESUSCITATION ATTEMPTED

Dr. Perry, the first physician to treat the President, said a number of resuscitative measures had been attempted, including oxygen, anesthesia, an indotracheal tube, a tracheotomy, blood and fluids. An electrocardiogram monitor was attached to measure Mr. Kennedy's heart beats.

Dr. Clark was summoned and arrived in a minute or two. By then, Dr. Perry said, Mr. Kennedy was "critically ill and moribund," or near death.

Dr. Clark said that on his first sight of the President, he had concluded immediately that Mr. Kennedy could not live.

"It was apparent that the President had sustained a lethal wound," he said. "A missile had gone in and out of the back of his head causing external lacerations and loss of brain tissue."

Shortly after he arrived, Dr. Clark said, "the President lost his heart action by the electrocardiogram." A closed-chest cardiograph massage was attempted, as were other emergency resuscitation measures.

Dr. Clark said these had produced "palpable pulses" for a short time, but all were "to no avail."

IN OPERATING ROOM 40 MINUTES

The President was on the emergency table at the hospital for about 40 minutes, the doctors said. At the end, perhaps eight physicians were in Operating Room No.

1, where Mr. Kennedy remained until his death. Dr. Clark said it was difficult to determine the exact moment of death, but the doctors said officially that it occurred at 1 P.M.

Later, there were unofficial reports that Mr. Kennedy had been killed instantly. The source of these reports, Dr. Tom Shires, chief surgeon at the hospital and professor of surgery at the University of Texas Southwest Medical School, issued this statement tonight:

"Medically, it was apparent the President was not alive when he was brought in. There was no spontaneous respiration. He had dilated, fixed pupils. It was obvious he had a lethal head wound.

"Technically, however, by using vigorous resuscitation, intravenous tubes and all the usual supportive measures, we were able to raise a semblance of a heartbeat."

Dr. Shires was not present when Mr. Kennedy was being treated at Parkland Hospital. He issued his statement, however, after lengthy conferences with the doctors who had attended the President.

Mr. Johnson remained in the hospital about 30 minutes after Mr. Kennedy died.

The details of what happened when shots first rang out, as the President's car moved along at about 25 miles an hour, were sketchy. Secret Service agents, who might have given more details, were unavailable to the press at first, and then returned to Washington with President Johnson.

KENNEDYS HAILED AT BREAKFAST

Mr. Kennedy had opened his day in Fort Worth, first with a speech in a parking lot and then at a Chamber of Commerce breakfast. The breakfast appearance was a particular triumph for Mrs. Kennedy, who entered late and was given an ovation.

Then the Presidential party, including Governor and Mrs. Connally, flew on to Dallas, an eight-minute flight. Mr. Johnson, as is customary, flew in a separate plane. The President and the Vice President do not travel together, out of fear of a double tragedy.

At Love Field, Mr. and Mrs. Kennedy lingered for 10 minutes, shaking hands with an enthusiastic group lining the fence. The group called itself "Grassroots Democrats."

Mr. Kennedy then entered his open Lincoln convertible at the head of the motorcade. He sat in the rear seat on the right-hand side. Mrs. Kennedy, who appeared to be enjoying one of the first political outings she had ever made with her husband, sat at his left.

In the "jump" seat, directly ahead of Mr. Kennedy, sat Governor Connally, with Mrs. Connally at his left in another "jump" seat. A Secret Service agent was driving and the two others ran alongside.

Behind the President's limousine was an open sedan carrying a number of Secret Service agents. Behind them, in an open convertible, rode Mr. and Mrs. Johnson and Texas's senior Senator, Ralph W. Yarborough, a Democrat.

The motorcade proceeded uneventfully along a 10-mile route through downtown Dallas, aiming for the Merchandise Mart. Mr. Kennedy was to address a group of the city's leading citizens at a luncheon in his honor.

In downtown Dallas, crowds were thick, enthusiastic and cheering. The turnout was somewhat unusual for this center of conservatism, where only a month ago

Adlai E. Stevenson was attacked by a rightist crowd. It was also in Dallas, during the 1960 campaign, that Senator Lyndon B. Johnson and his wife were nearly mobbed in the lobby of the Baker Hotel.

As the motorcade neared its end and the President's car moved out of the thick crowds onto Stennonds Freeway near the Merchandise Mart, Mrs. Connally recalled later, "we were all very pleased with the reception in downtown Dallas."

APPROACHING 3-STREET UNDERPASS

Behind the three leading cars were a string of others carrying Texas and Dallas dignitaries, two buses of reporters, several open cars carrying photographers and other reporters, and a bus for White House staff members.

As Mrs. Connally recalled later, the President's car was almost ready to go underneath a "triple underpass" beneath three streets—Elm, Commerce and Main— when the first shot was fired.

That shot apparently struck Mr. Kennedy. Governor Connally turned in his seat at the sound and appeared immediately to be hit in the chest.

Mrs. Mary Norman of Dallas was standing at the curb and at that moment was aiming her camera at the President. She saw him slump forward, then slide down in the seat.

"My God," Mrs. Norman screamed, as she recalled it later, "he's shot!"

Mrs. Connally said that Mrs. Kennedy had reached and "grabbed" her husband. Mrs. Connally put her arms around the Governor. Mrs. Connally said that she and Mrs. Kennedy had then ducked low in the car as it sped off.

Mrs. Connally's recollections were reported by Julian Reade, an aide to the Governor.

Most reporters in the press buses were too far back to see the shootings, but they observed some quick scurrying by motor policemen accompanying the motorcade. It was noted that the President's car had picked up speed and raced away, but reporters were not aware that anything serious had occurred until they reached the Merchandise Mart two or three minutes later.

RUMORS SPREAD AT TRADE MART

Rumors of the shooting already were spreading through the luncheon crowd of hundreds, which was having the first course. No White House officials or Secret Service agents were present, but the reporters were taken quickly to Parkland Hospital on the strength of the rumors.

There they encountered Senator Yarborough, white, shaken and horrified.

The shots, he said, seemed to have come from the right and the rear of the car in which he was riding, the third in the motorcade. Another eyewitness, Mel Crouch, a Dallas television reporter, reported that as the shots rang out he saw a rifle extended and then withdrawn from a window on the "fifth or sixth floor" of the Texas Public School Book Depository. This is a leased state building on Elm Street, to the right of the motorcade route.

Senator Yarborough said there had been a slight pause between the first two shots and a longer pause between the second and third. A Secret Service man riding in the Senator's car, the Senator said, immediately ordered Mr. and Mrs. Johnson to get down below the level of the doors. They did so, and Senator Yarborough also got down.

The leading cars of the motorcade then pulled away at high speed toward Parkland Hospital, which was not far away, by the fast highway.

"We knew by the speed that something was terribly wrong," Senator Yarborough reported. When he put his head up, he said, he saw a Secret Service man in the car ahead beating his fists against the trunk deck of the car in which he was riding, apparently in frustration and anguish.

MRS. KENNEDY'S REACTION

Only White House staff members spoke with Mrs. Kennedy. A Dallas medical student, David Edwards, saw her in Parkland Hospital while she was waiting for news of her husband. He gave this description:

"The look in her eyes was like an animal that had been trapped, like a little rabbit—brave, but fear was in the eyes."

Dr. Clark was reported to have informed Mrs. Kennedy of her husband's death.

No witnesses reported seeing or hearing any of the Secret Service agents or policemen fire back. One agent was seen to brandish a machine gun as the cars sped away. Mr. Crouch observed a policeman falling to the ground and pulling a weapon. But the events had occurred so quickly that there was apparently nothing for the men to shoot at.

Mr. Crouch said he saw two women, standing at a curb to watch the motorcade pass, fall to the ground when the shots rang out. He also saw a man snatch up his little girl and run along the road. Policemen, he said, immediately chased this man under the impression he had been involved in the shooting, but Mr. Crouch said he had been a fleeing spectator.

Mr. Kennedy's limousine—license No. GG300 under District of Columbia registry—pulled up at the emergency entrance of Parkland Hospital. Senator Yarborough said the President had been carried inside on a stretcher.

By the time reporters arrived at the hospital, the police were guarding the Presidential car closely. They would allow no one to approach it. A bucket of water stood by the car, suggesting that the back seat had been scrubbed out.

Robert Clark of the American Broadcasting Company, who had been riding near the front of the motorcade, said Mr. Kennedy was motionless when he was carried inside. There was a great amount of blood on Mr. Kennedy's suit and shirtfront and the front of his body, Mr. Clark said.

Mrs. Kennedy was leaning over her husband when the car stopped, Mr. Clark said, and walked beside the wheeled stretcher into the hospital. Mr. Connally sat with his hands holding his stomach, his head bent over. He, too, was moved into the hospital in a stretcher, with Mrs. Connally at his side.

Robert McNeill of the National Broadcasting Company, who also was in the reporters' pool car, jumped out at the scene of the shooting. He said the police had taken two eyewitnesses into custody—an 8-year-old Negro boy and a white man—for informational purposes.

Many of these reports could not be verified immediately.

EYEWITNESS DESCRIBES SHOOTING

An unidentified Dallas man, interviewed on television here, said he had been waving at the President when the shots were fired. His belief was that Mr. Kennedy had been struck twice—once, as Mrs. Norman recalled, when he slumped in his seat; again when he slid down in it.

"It seemed to just knock him down," the man said.

Governor Connally's condition was reported as "satisfactory" tonight after four hours in surgery at Parkland Hospital.

Dr. Robert R. Shaw, a thoracic surgeon, operated on the Governor to repair damage to his left chest.

Later, Dr. Shaw said Governor Connally had been hit in the back just below the shoulder blade, and that the bullet had gone completely through the Governor's chest, taking out part of the fifth rib.

After leaving the body, he said, the bullet struck the Governor's right wrist, causing a compound fracture. It then lodged in the left thigh.

The thigh wound, Dr. Shaw said, was trivial. He said the compound fracture would heal.

Dr. Shaw said it would be unwise for Governor Connally to be moved in the next 10 to 14 days. Mrs. Connally was remaining at his side tonight.

TOUR BY MRS. KENNEDY UNUSUAL

Mrs. Kennedy's presence near her husband's bedside at his death resulted from somewhat unusual circumstances. She had rarely accompanied him on his trips about the country and had almost never made political trips with him.

The tour on which Mr. Kennedy was engaged yesterday and today was only quasi-political; the only open political activity was to have been a speech tonight to a fund-raising dinner at the state capitol in Austin.

In visiting Texas, Mr. Kennedy was seeking to improve his political fortunes in a pivotal state that he barely won in 1960. He was also hoping to patch a bitter internal dispute among Texas's Democrats.

At 8:45 A.M., when Mr. Kennedy left the Texas hotel in Fort Worth, where he spent his last night, to address the parking lot crowd across the street, Mrs. Kennedy was not with him. There appeared to be some disappointment.

"Mrs. Kennedy is organizing herself," the President said good-naturedly. "It takes longer, but, of course, she looks better than we do when she does it."

Later, Mrs. Kennedy appeared late at the Chamber of Commerce breakfast in Fort Worth.

Again, Mr. Kennedy took note of her presence. "Two years ago," he said, "I introduced myself in Paris by saying that I was the man who had accompanied Mrs. Kennedy to Paris. I am getting somewhat that same sensation as I travel around Texas. Nobody wonders what Lyndon and I wear."

The speech Mr. Kennedy never delivered at the Merchandise Mart luncheon contained a passage commenting on a recent preoccupation of his, and a subject of much interest in this city, where right-wing conservatism is the rule rather than the exception.

"Voices are being heard in the land," he said, "voices preaching doctrines wholly unrelated to reality, wholly unsuited to the sixties, doctrines which apparently assume that words will suffice without weapons, that vituperation is as good as victory and that peace is a sign of weakness.''

The speech went on: "At a time when the national debt is steadily being reduced in terms of its burden on our economy, they see that debt as the greatest threat to our security. At a time when we are steadily reducing the number of Federal employees serving every thousand citizens, they fear those supposed hordes of civil servants far more than the actual hordes of opposing armies.

"We cannot expect that everyone, to use the phrase of a decade ago, will 'talk sense to the American people.' But we can hope that fewer people will listen to nonsense. And the notion that this nation is headed for defeat through deficit, or that strength is but a matter of slogans, is nothing but just plain nonsense.''

DISCUSSION QUESTIONS

1. What is the verb tense at the beginning of the headline for Wicker's story? What effect is created by the use of this particular verb form? Does the tense remain consistent with the verb form used in the remainder of the headline? In the text of the story?

2. Compare the headline to this story with that of the *New York Herald* on the assassination of President Lincoln. What can these examples tell you about the language of headlines in general?

3. How is the first paragraph of each story partly determined by the information presented in the headline? Contrast the leads of each news story. Which do you find most successful? Why? Does each story adhere to the format of the "inverted pyramid" as described in the introduction to Press?

Tom Wicker / The Assassination

Times Talk, December 1963

WASHINGTON

I think I was in the first press bus. But I can't be sure. Pete Lisagor of The Chicago Daily News says he *knows* he was in the first press bus and he describes things that went on aboard it that didn't happen on the bus I was in. But I still *think* I was in the first press bus.

I cite that minor confusion as an example of the way it was in Dallas in the early afternoon of Nov. 22. At first no one knew what happened, or how, or where, much less why. Gradually, bits and pieces began to fall together and within two hours a reasonably coherent version of the story began to be possible. Even now, however, I know no reporter who was there who has a clear and orderly picture of that surrealistic afternoon; it is still a matter of bits and pieces thrown hastily into something like a whole.

It began, for most reporters, when the central fact of it was over. As our press bus eased at motorcade speed down an incline toward an underpass, there was a little confusion in the sparse crowds that at that point had been standing at the curb to see the President of the United States pass. As we came out of the underpass, I saw a motorcycle policeman drive over the curb, across an open area, a few feet up a railroad bank, dismount and start scrambling up the bank.

Jim Mathis of The Advance (Newhouse) Syndicate went to the front of our bus and looked ahead to where the President's car was supposed to be, perhaps ten cars ahead of us. He hurried back to his seat.

"The President's car just sped off," he said. "Really gunned away." (How could Mathis have seen that if there had been another bus in front of us?)

But that could have happened if someone had thrown a tomato at the President. The press bus in its stately pace rolled on to the Trade Mart, where the President was to speak. Fortunately, it was only a few minutes away.

At the Trade Mart, rumor was sweeping the hundreds of Texans already eating their lunch. It was the only rumor that I had ever *seen;* it was moving across that crowd like a wind over a wheatfield. A man eating a grapefruit seized my arm as I passed.

"Has the President been shot?" he asked.

"I don't think so," I said. "But something happened."

With the other reporters—I suppose 35 of them—I went on through the huge hall to the upstairs press room. We were hardly there when Marianne Means of Hearst Headline Service hung up a telephone, ran to a group of us and said, "The President's been shot. He's at Parkland Hospital."

One thing I learned that day; I suppose I already knew it, but that day made it plain. A reporter must trust his instinct. When Miss Means said those eight words— I never learned who told her—I knew absolutely they were true. Everyone did. We ran for the press buses.

Again, a man seized my arm—an official-looking man.

"No running in here," he said sternly. I pulled free and ran on. Doug Kiker of The Herald Tribune barreled head-on into a waiter carrying a plate of potatoes. Waiter and potatoes flew about the room. Kiker ran on. He was in his first week with The Trib, and his first Presidential trip.

I barely got aboard a moving press bus. Bob Pierrepoint of C.B.S. was aboard and he said that he now recalled having heard something that could have been shots—or firecrackers, or motorcycle backfire. We talked anxiously, unbelieving, afraid.

Fortunately again, it was only a few minutes to Parkland Hospital. There at its emergency entrance, stood the President's car, the top up, a bucket of bloody water beside it. Automatically, I took down its license number—GG300 District of Columbia.

The first eyewitness description came from Senator Ralph Yarborough, who had been riding in the third car of the motorcade with Vice President and Mrs. Johnson. Senator Yarborough is an East Texan, which is to say a Southerner, a man of quick emotion, old-fashioned rhetoric.

"Gentlemen," he said, pale, shaken, near tears. "It is a deed of horror."

The details he gave us were good and mostly—as it later proved—accurate. But he would not describe to us the appearance of the President as he was wheeled into the hospital, except to say that he was "gravely wounded." We could not doubt, then, that it was serious.

I had chosen that day to be without a notebook. I took notes on the back of my mimeographed schedule of the two-day tour of Texas we had been so near to concluding. Today, I cannot read many of the notes; on Nov. 22, they were as clear as 60-point type.

A local television reporter, Mel Crouch, told us he had seen a rifle being withdrawn from the corner fifth or sixth floor window of the Texas School Book Depository. Instinct again—Crouch sounded right, positive, though none of us knew him. We believed it and it was right.

Mac Kilduff, an assistant White House press secretary in charge of the press on that trip, and who was to acquit himself well that day, came out of the hospital. We gathered round and he told us the President was alive. It wasn't true, we later learned; but Mac thought it was true at that time, and he didn't mislead us about a possible recovery. His whole demeanor made plain what was likely to happen. He also told us—as Senator Yarborough had—that Gov. John Connally of Texas was shot, too.

Kilduff promised more details in five minutes and went back into the hospital. We were barred. Word came to us secondhand—I don't remember exactly how— from Bob Clark of A.B.C., one of the men who had been riding in the press "pool" car near the President's, that he had been lying face down in Mrs. Kennedy's lap when the car arrived at Parkland. No signs of life.

That is what I mean by instinct. That day, a reporter had none of the ordinary means or time to check and double-check matters given as fact. He had to go on what he knew of people he talked to, what he knew of human reaction, what two isolated "facts" added to in sum—above all on what he felt in his bones. I knew Clark and respected him. I took his report at face value, even at second hand. It turned out to be true. In a crisis, if a reporter can't trust his instinct for truth, he can't trust anything.

When Wayne Hawks of the White House staff appeared to say that a press room had been set up in a hospital classroom at the left rear of the building, the group of reporters began struggling across the lawn in that direction. I lingered to ask a motorcycle policeman if he had heard on his radio anything about the pursuit or capture of the assassin. He hadn't, and I followed the other reporters.

As I was passing the open convertible in which Vice President and Mrs. Johnson and Senator Yarborough had been riding in the motorcade, a voice boomed from its radio:

"The President of the United States is dead. I repeat—it has just been announced that the President of the United States is dead."

There was no authority, no word of who had announced it. But—instinct again— I believed it instantly. It sounded true. I knew it was true. I stood still a moment, then began running.

Ordinarily, I couldn't jump a tennis net if I'd just beaten Gonzales. That day, carrying a briefcase and a typewriter, I jumped a chain fence looping around the drive, not even breaking stride. Hugh Sidey of Time, a close friend of the President, was walking slowly ahead of me.

"Hugh," I said, "the President's dead. Just announced on the radio. I don't know who announced it but it sounded official to me."

Sidey stopped, looked at me, looked at the ground. I couldn't talk about it. I couldn't think about it. I couldn't do anything but run on to the press room. Then I told others what I had heard.

Sidey, I learned a few minutes later, stood where he was a minute. Then he saw two Catholic priests. He spoke to them. Yes, they told him, the President was dead. They had administered the last rites. Sidey went on to the press room and spread that word, too.

Throughout the day, every reporter on the scene seemed to me to do his best to help everyone else. Information came only in bits and pieces. Each man who picked up a bit or a piece passed it on. I know no one who held anything out. Nobody thought about an exclusive; it didn't seem important.

After perhaps 10 minutes when we milled around in the press room—my instinct was to find the new President, but no one knew where he was—Kilduff appeared red-eyed, barely in control of himself. In that hushed classroom, he made the official, the unbelievable announcement. The President was dead of a gunshot wound in the brain. Lyndon Johnson was safe, in the protective custody of the Secret Service. He would be sworn in as soon as possible.

Kilduff, composed as a man could be in those circumstances, promised more details when he could get them, then left. The search for phones began. Jack Gertz, traveling with us for A.T. & T., was frantically moving them by the dozen into the hospital, but few were ready yet.

I wandered down the hall, found a doctor's office, walked in and told him I had to use his phone. He got up without a word and left. I battled the hospital switchboard for five minutes and finally got a line to New York—Hal Faber on the other end, with Harrison Salisbury on an extension.

They knew what had happened, I said. The death had been confirmed. I proposed to write one long story, as quickly as I could, throwing in everything I could learn. On the desk, they could cut it up as they needed—throwing part into other stories, putting other facts into mine. But I would file a straight narrative without worrying about their editing needs.

Reporters always fuss at editors and always will. But Salisbury and Faber are good men to talk to in a crisis. They knew what they were doing and realized my problems. I may fuss at them again sometime, but after that day my heart won't be in it. Quickly, clearly, they told me to go ahead, gave me the moved-up deadlines, told me of plans already made to get other reporters into Dallas, but made it plain they would be hours in arriving.

Salisbury told me to use the phone and take no chances on a wire circuit being jammed or going wrong. Stop reporting and start writing in time to meet the deadline, he said. Pay anyone $50 if necessary to dictate for you.

The whole conversation probably took three minutes. Then I hung up, thinking of all there was to know, all there was I didn't know. I wandered down a corridor and ran into Sidey and Chuck Roberts of Newsweek. They'd seen a hearse pulling up at the emergency entrance and we figured they were about to move the body.

We made our way to the hearse—a Secret Service agent who knew us helped us through suspicious Dallas police lines—and the driver said his instructions were to take the body to the airport. That confirmed our hunch, but gave me, at least, another wrong one. Mr. Johnson, I declared, would fly to Washington with the body and be sworn in there.

We posted ourselves inconspicuously near the emergency entrance. Within minutes, they brought the body out in a bronze coffin.

A number of White House staff people—stunned, silent, stumbling along as if dazed—walked with it. Mrs. Kennedy walked by the coffin, her hand on it, her head down, her hat gone, her dress and stockings spattered. She got into the hearse with the coffin. The staff men crowded into cars and followed.

That was just about the only eyewitness matter that I got with my own eyes that entire afternoon.

Roberts commandeered a seat in a police car and followed, promising to "fill" Sidey and me as necessary. We made the same promise to him and went back to the press room.

There, we received an account from Julian Reade, a staff assistant, of Mrs. John Connally's recollection of the shooting. Most of his recital was helpful and it established the important fact of who was sitting in which seat in the President's car at the time of the shooting.

The doctors who had treated the President came in after Mr. Reade. They gave us copious detail, particularly as to the efforts they had made to resuscitate the President. They were less explicit about the wounds, explaining that the body had been in their hands only a short time and they had little time to examine it closely. They conceded they were unsure as to the time of death and had arbitrarily put it at 1 P.M., C.S.T.

Much of their information, as it developed later, was erroneous. Subsequent reports made it pretty clear that Mr. Kennedy probably was killed instantly. His body, as a physical mechanism, however, continued to flicker an occasional pulse and heartbeat. No doubt this justified the doctors' first account. There also was the question of national security and Mr. Johnson's swearing-in. Perhaps, too, there was a question about the Roman Catholic rites. In any case, until a later doctors' statement about 9 P.M. that night, the account we got at the hospital was official.

The doctors hardly had left before Hawks came in and told us Mr. Johnson would be sworn in immediately at the airport. We dashed for the press buses, still parked outside. Many a campaign had taught me something about press buses and I ran a little harder, got there first, and went to the wide rear seat. That is the best place on a bus to open up a typewriter and get some work done.

On the short trip to the airport, I got about 500 words on paper—leaving a blank space for the hour of Mr. Johnson's swearing-in, and putting down the mistaken assumption that the scene would be somewhere in the terminal. As we arrived at a back gate along the airstrip, we could see Air Force One, the Presidential jet, screaming down the runway and into the air.

Left behind had been Sid Davis of Westinghouse Broadcasting, one of the few reporters who had been present for the swearing-in. Roberts, who had guessed right in going to the airport when he did, had been there too and was aboard the plane on the way to Washington.

Davis climbed on the back of a shiny new car that was parked near where our bus halted. I hate to think what happened to its trunk deck. He and Roberts—true to his promise—had put together a magnificent "pool" report on the swearing-in. Davis read it off, answered questions, and gave a picture that so far as I know was complete, accurate and has not yet been added to.

I said to Kiker of The Trib: "We better go write. There'll be phones in the terminal." He agreed. Bob Manning, an ice-cool member of the White House transportation staff, agreed to get our bags off the press plane, which would return to Washington as soon as possible, and put them in a nearby telephone booth.

Kiker and I ran a half-mile to the terminal, cutting through a baggage-handling room to get there. I went immediately to a phone booth and dictated my 500-word lead, correcting it as I read, embellishing it too. Before I hung up, I got Salisbury and asked him to cut into my story whatever the wires were filing on the assassin. There was no time left to chase down the Dallas police and find out those details on my own.

Dallas Love Field has a mezzanine running around its main waiting room; it is equipped with writing desks for travelers. I took one and went to work. My recollection is that it was then about 5 P.M. New York time.

I would write two pages, run down the stairs, across the waiting room, grab a phone and dictate. Miraculously, I never had to wait for a phone booth or to get a line through. Dictating each take, I would throw in items I hadn't written, sometimes whole paragraphs. It must have been tough on the dictating room crew.

Once, while in the booth dictating, I looked up and found twitching above me the imposing mustache of Gladwin Hill. He was the first Times man in and had found me right off; I was seldom more glad to see anyone. We conferred quickly and he took off for the police station; it was a tremendous load off my mind to have that angle covered and out of my hands.

I was half through, maybe more, when I heard myself paged. It turned out to be Kiker, who had been separated from me and was working in the El Dorado room, a bottle club in the terminal. My mezzanine was quieter and a better place to work, but he had a TV going for him, so I moved in too.

The TV helped in one important respect. I took down from it an eyewitness account of one Charles Drehm, who had been waving at the President when he was shot. Instinct again: Drehm sounded positive, right, sure of what he said. And his report was the first real indication that the President probably was shot twice.

Shortly after 7 P.M., New York time, I finished. So did Kiker. Simultaneously we thought of our bags out in that remote phone booth. We ran for a taxi and urged an unwilling driver out along the dark airstrip. As we found the place, with some difficulty, an American Airlines man was walking off with the bags. He was going to ship them off to the White House, having seen the tags on them. A minute later and we'd have been stuck in Dallas without even a toothbrush.

Kiker and I went to The Dallas News. The work wasn't done—I filed a number of inserts later that night, wrote a separate story on the building from which the assassin had fired, tried to get John Herbers, Don Janson, Joe Loftus on useful angles as they drifted in. But when I left the airport, I knew the worst of it was over. The story was filed on time, good or bad, complete or incomplete, and any reporter knows how that feels. They couldn't say I missed the deadline.

It was a long taxi ride to The Dallas News. We were hungry, not having eaten since an early breakfast. It was then that I remembered John F. Kennedy's obituary. Last June, Hal Faber had sent it to me for updating. On Nov. 22, it was still lying on my desk in Washington, not updated, not rewritten, a monument to the incredibility of that afternoon in Dallas.

Harry Golden / The Individual

Carolina Israelite, ca. 1967

One of five children born to Leib and Nuchama Goldenhurst, Harry Golden was raised in New York City's Lower East Side, a turn-of-the-century haven for thousands of Jewish immigrants from central and eastern Europe. While helping his father edit the Jewish Daily Forward, *Golden attended the City College of the City University of New York. He left in 1920 without a degree, explaining years later: "I majored in America—in books and history and literature—with no attempt to pinpoint anything in particular or to become anything in particular. I just wanted to become what my father would call a learned man."*

In 1939, after years of holding jobs ranging from a blocker of women's hats to a pamphleteer on behalf of Socialist causes and tax reform movements, Golden decided to start fresh and set out for North Carolina, where he worked as a reporter for the Charlotte Observer *and then for the* Hendersonville Times-News. *Within two years he had started his own monthly, the* Carolina Israelite, *a newspaper without headlines, photographs, social notes, sports pages, obituaries, or "hard" news. Golden's sixteen-page, five-column tabloid contains principally a blend of advertisements with his own nostalgic, whimsical, and irreverent observations of the American Scene.*

From an initial subscription list of only 800, the Carolina Israelite *grew modestly over the years, reaching 16,000 by 1958, the year Golden's first bestselling collection of his most memorable columns,* Only in America, *was published. His work is now syndicated in newspapers across the country.*

"The Individual" was reprinted in The Best of Harry Golden *(1967).*

At this precise moment there are one half million Hindus starving. Within the year, most of these Hindus will be dead. Dead children with swollen stomachs will litter the streets and their parents will collapse with dizziness and fatigue, pleading for a handful of rice which they cannot have. Yet these half million Hindus are only statistics to us.

Sometimes we hear people talk about the six million Jews who died in Nazi gas ovens and perhaps because he knows we cannot respond properly the speaker is indignant and rhetorical. And the man who talks of the half million Hindus does so with incredulity.

But the man whose little girl has been hit by a car is the least indignant and rhetorical of all men, and when he sees the crumpled body he is too all-believing.

The great sadness of our history is that the mortal imagination cannot summon the same grief for the casualties of an earthquake that it can for one little girl. It is too hard for the imagination to conceive of a half million Hindus comprising a half million different souls.

It's a lot easier for a college graduate to squeeze a button and release an atomic bomb from the *Enola Gay* over Hiroshima than it is for the same college graduate turned infantry sniper to squeeze the trigger on a lone, unsuspecting Japanese soldier. The people obliterated in the atom blast will not know who dropped the bomb, nor will the bombardier have to watch them die. It is much easier because a city is inanimate and cannot levy blame. But the Japanese infantryman will stand stunned and surprised and regret his carelessness before he sinks to earth. And there will be an instant when American and Japanese are each caught up in the significance of the deed. Because it is only to individuals that compassion and sympathy belong. The desperate fact is that we cannot will our sympathy to the group. Bitter though this truth is, we have not betrayed our heritage. We have made the individual supreme, because that is the only hope of exciting compassion and sympathy.

Perhaps the day will come when our imagination will not be surprised by vast numbers and we will be able to see every individual as integral in himself. If that day comes, it will be because we placed such high value on the single individual.

Thomas O'Toole / "The Eagle Has Landed": Two Men Walk on the Moon

Washington Post, July 24, 1969

On July 20, 1969, Thomas O'Toole, staff writer for the Washington Post, *covered his story by watching Neil Armstrong and Buzz Aldrin participate in what President Richard Nixon called "the greatest moment in history since the Creation."*

HOUSTON, July 20—Man stepped out onto the moon tonight for the first time in his two-million-year history.

"That's one small step for man," declared pioneer astronaut Neil Armstrong at 10:56 P.M. EDT, "one giant leap for mankind."

Just after that historic moment in man's quest for his origins, Armstrong walked on the dead satellite and found the surface very powdery, littered with fine grains of black dust.

A few minutes later, Edwin (Buzz) Aldrin joined Armstrong on the lunar surface and in less than an hour they put on a show that will long be remembered by the worldwide television audience.

AMERICAN FLAG PLANTED

The two men walked easily, talked easily, even ran and jumped happily so it seemed. They picked up rocks, talked at length of what they saw, planted an American flag, saluted it, and talked by radiophone with the President in the White House, and then faced the camera and saluted Mr. Nixon.

"For every American, this has to be the proudest day of our lives," the President told the astronauts. "For one priceless moment in the whole history of man, all the people on this earth are truly one."

Seven hours earlier, at 4:17 P.M., the Eagle and its two pilots thrilled the world as they zoomed in over a rock-covered field, hovered and then slowly let down on the moon. "Houston, Tranquillity base here," Armstrong radioed. "The Eagle has landed."

At 1:10 A.M. Monday—2 hours and 14 minutes after Armstrong first stepped upon the lunar surface—the astronauts were back in their moon craft and the hatch was closed.

In describing the moon, Armstrong told Houston that it was "fine and powdery. I can kick it up loosely with my toe.

"It adheres like powdered charcoal to the boot," he went on, "but I only go in a small fraction of an inch. I can see my footprint in the moon like fine grainy particles."

Armstrong found he had such little trouble walking on the moon that he began talking almost as if he didn't want to leave it.

"It has a stark beauty all its own," Armstrong said. "It's like the desert in the Southwestern United States. It's very pretty out here."

AMAZINGLY CLEAR PICTURE

Armstrong shared his first incredible moments on the moon with the whole world, as a television camera on the outside of the wingless Eagle landing craft sent back an amazingly clear picture of his first steps on the moon.

Armstrong seemed like he was swimming along, taking big and easy steps on the airless moon despite the cumbersome white pressure-suit he wore.

"There seems to be no difficulty walking around," he said. "As we suspected, it's even easier than the one-sixth G that we did in simulations on the ground."

One of the first things he did was to scoop up a small sample of the moon with a long-handled spoon with a bag on its end like a small butterfly net.

"Looks like it's easy," Aldrin said, looking down from the Lem.

"It is," Armstrong told him. "I'm sure I could push it in farther but I can't bend down that far."

GUIDES ALDRIN DOWN LADDER

At 11:11 P.M., Aldrin started down the landing craft's ten-foot ladder to join Armstrong.

Backing down the nine-step ladder, Aldrin was guided the entire way by Armstrong, who stood at the foot of the ladder looking up at him.

"Okay," Armstrong said, "watch your 'pliss' (PLSS, for portable life support system) from underneath. Drop your pliss down. You're clear. About an inch clear on your pliss."

"Okay," Aldrin said. "You need a little arching of the back to come down."

After he stepped onto the first rung of the ladder, Aldrin went back up to the Lem's "front porch" to partially close the Lem's hatch.

"Making sure not to lock it on my way out," he said in comic fashion. "That's our home for the next couple of hours and I want to make sure we can get back in."

"Beautiful," said Aldrin when he met Armstrong on the lunar surface.

"Isn't that something," said Armstrong. "It's a magnificent sight out here."

While Armstrong watched, Aldrin went through some cautious walking experiments to see how difficult it was in his pressure suit.

"Reaching down is fairly easy," he said. "The mass of the backpack does have some effect on inertia. There's a slight tendency, I can see now, to tip backwards."

Aldrin and Armstrong then both walked around the Lem's 31-foot base, inspecting its four legs and undercarriage at the same time that they began looking over the moon's surface.

"These rocks are rather slippery," Armstrong said. "The powdery surface fills up the fine pores on the rocks, and we tend to slide over it rather easily."

While Armstrong got ready to move the television camera out about 30 feet from the Lem, Aldrin did some more experimental walking.

"If I'm about to lose my balance in one direction," said Aldrin, "recovery is quite natural and easy. You've just got to be careful leaning in the direction you want to go in."

At that, Aldrin apparently spotted an interesting rock.

"Hey, Neil," he said. "Didn't I say we'd find a purple rock?"

"Did you find a purple rock?" Armstrong asked him.

"Yep," replied Aldrin.

The next thing Armstrong did was to change lenses on the television camera, putting a telephoto lens on it for a closeup view of what was happening.

"Now we'll read the plaque for those who haven't read it before," Armstrong said, referring to a small stainless steel plaque that had been placed on one of the landing craft's legs.

"It says," Armstrong said, "Here men from the planet Earth first set foot on the moon. July 1969, A.D. We came in peace for all mankind."

"It has the crew members' signatures," Armstrong said, "and the signature of the President of the United States."

BLEAK BUT BEAUTIFUL

Armstrong next took the television camera out to a spot about 40 feet from the Lem, and placed it on a small tripod.

Incredibly clear, the picture showed a distant Lem, squatting on the bleak but beautiful lunar surface like some giant mechanical toy. It appeared to be perfectly level, not at all tilted on the rough lunar terrain.

When he got the camera mounted correctly, he walked back toward the Lem, with the camera view following him all the way.

Just after 11:30, both men removed a pole, flagstaff and a plastic American flag from one of the Lem's legs. They gently pressed the flag into the lunar surface.

After they saluted the flag, astronaut Bruce McCandless commented on the little ceremony from his perch in the Manned Spacecraft center's mission control room.

"The flag is up now," he said. "You can see the stars and stripes on the lunar surface."

At 11:48 McCandless asked both men to stand together near the flag. "The President of the United States would like to talk to you," McCandless said.

Mr. Nixon spoke to the astronauts for almost two minutes, and when he finished, the two astronauts stood erect and saluted directly at the television camera.

During most of their early time on the moon, astronaut Michael Collins not only didn't see them walking on the moon, but was behind the moon and out of radio touch in his orbiting command craft.

When he finally swung around in front of the moon again, Armstrong and Aldrin had been out almost 30 minutes.

"How's it going?" Collins asked plaintively.

"Just great," McCandless told him.

"How's the television?" he asked.

"Just beautiful," he was told.

Armstrong and Aldrin stayed out on the moon for almost two hours, with Aldrin first back into the Lem just before 1 A.M. Monday.

"Adios, Amigos," he said as he pulled himself easily back up the ladder.

Armstrong started back up the ladder a few minutes after 1 A.M. Monday. He took what seemed like the first four rungs with one huge leap upward. At 1:10 A.M., Armstrong had joined Aldrin inside the cabin. "Okay, the hatch is closed and latched," said Aldrin seconds later.

When both men had repressurized their cabin and taken off their helmets and gloves, Collins reappeared over the lunar horizon in his command craft. At once, he asked how everything had gone.

SLEEP, THEN RENDEZVOUS

"Hallelujah," he said when he was told what had happened.

All three astronauts were due to get their first sleep in almost 24 hours, a sleep that was never more richly deserved.

If nothing went wrong—and nobody was expecting anything would—Armstrong and Aldrin were due to lift back off the surface of the moon at 1:55 P.M. EDT Monday.

Burning their ascent engine full-blast for just over seven minutes, they will start a four-hour flight to rejoin Collins and the command craft 70 miles above the lunar surface.

The majestic moment of man's first steps on the moon came about six hours after Armstrong and Aldrin set their four-legged, wingless landing craft down in the moon's Sea of Tranquillity—precisely at 4:17 P.M. EDT.

"Houston, Tranquillity Base here," Armstrong announced to a breathless world. "The Eagle has landed."

"You did a beautiful job," astronaut Charles Duke said from Houston's Manned Spacecraft Center. "Be advised there's lots of smiling faces down here."

"There's two of them down here," Armstrong replied.

The landing apparently was not an easy one. It was about four miles from the target point in the southwestern edge of the Sea of Tranquillity, almost right on the lunar equator.

"We were coming down in a crater the size of a football field with lots of big rocks around and in it," Armstrong said about five minutes after landing. "We had to fly it manually over the rock field to find a place to land."

"EVERY VARIETY OF SHAPES"

A few minutes later, Aldrin gave a waiting world its first eyewitness description on the moon's surface.

"It looks like a collection of just about every variety of shapes and angularity, every variety of rock you could find," Aldrin said.

"There doesn't appear to be too much color," he went on, "except that it looks as though some of the boulders are going to have some interesting color."

Armstrong then described their landing site in a little detail.

"It's a relatively flat plain," he said, "with a lot of craters of the five- to 50-foot variety. Some small ridges 20 to 30 feet high. Thousands of little one- and two-foot craters. Some angular levees in front of us two feet in size. There is a hill in view ahead of us. It might be a half-mile or a mile away."

Armstrong then described what he said were rocks fractured by the exhaust of Eagle's rocket plume.

"Some of the surface rocks in close look like they might have a coating on them," he said. "Where they're broken, they display a very dark gray interior. It looks like it could be country basalt."

"LIKE BEING IN AN AIRPLANE"

Both men seemed to actually enjoy being in the moon's gravity, which is one-sixth that of earth's.

"It's like being in an airplane," Armstrong said. "It seems immediately natural to move around in this environment."

Armstrong and Aldrin apparently felt fine. Armstrong's heart rate went as high as 156 beats per minute at the time of landing, but dropped down into the nineties 15 minutes later.

The time leading up to the landing is difficult to describe, except to say that it was as dramatic a time as any in memory.

It all began at 3:08 P.M. EDT when Armstrong and Aldrin—flying feet first and face down—fired up their landing craft's descent engine for the first time.

Burning the engine for 27 seconds in what amounted to a braking maneuver to slow it down and start it falling, the two men were behind the moon at the time and out of radio touch with earth.

It was not until 3:47 P.M. that the men at the Manned Spacecraft Center heard that Armstrong and Aldrin were on their way down—and they heard it first from Collins, who flew from behind the moon in the command craft above and in front of the landing craft.

"Columbia, Houston," said Duke from the Center. "How did it go?"

"Listen, Babe," replied an excited Collins. "Everything's going just swimmingly. Beautiful."

Two minutes later, Duke made radio contact with Armstrong and Aldrin.

"We're standing by for your burn report," Duke said.

"The burn was on time," Aldrin told him.

"Rog, copy," Duke said. "Looks great."

At this point, the men in Mission Control bent their backs to the toughest jobs they'd ever have—following the two spacecraft at all times, to give them the guidance they would need for the Eagle's descent to the moon.

"JUST PLAY IT COOL"

Looking around the very quiet Mission Control room, flight director Gene Kranz simply said, "We're off to a good start. Just play it cool."

Flying down and westward across the moon's surface, the Eagle suddenly dropped out of radio contact with earth, but in moments was back in touch again.

"I don't know what the problem was," a totally composed Buzz Aldrin said when he came back on. "We started yawing and we're picking up a little oscillation rate now."

Still falling, the Eagle was coming up over the eastern region of the Sea of Tranquillity at an altitude of 53,000 feet and only minutes away from its second critical maneuver—the powered descent to the lunar surface.

"Five minutes to ignition," Duke radioed up. "You are go for a powered descent."

"Roger," Armstrong replied softly. "Understand."

At 4:05, Armstrong began throttling up the engine to slow the Eagle again, to drop it down toward the lunar surface.

"Light's on," he said. "Descent looks good."

Two minutes later, it was plain to everybody listening that they were indeed on their way down to the moon.

"Show an altitude of 47,000 feet," Armstrong said. "Everything looking good."

Still calm, Aldrin said he noticed a few warning lights coming on inside the spacecraft. "I'm getting some AC voltage fluctuations," he said, "and our position checks downrange show us to be a little long."

"You're looking good to us, Eagle," Duke answered. "You are go to continue powered descent. Repeat. You are go to continue powered descent."

FALLING, SLOWING APPROACH

"Altitude 27,000 feet," Aldrin read off. "This throttle down is better than the simulator."

Down they came, still falling but slowing down at the same time. At 21,000 feet, their speed had fallen to 800 miles an hour.

"You're looking great to us, Eagle," Duke said.

A minute later, it was 500 miles an hour, then it was suddenly down to less than 90 miles an hour.

"You're looking great at eight minutes. . . . You're looking great at nine minutes," Duke told them.

At this point, the two explorers began their final approach to the moon surface, coming in sideways and downwardly only 5200 feet above the moon.

When the Eagle dropped to 4200 feet Duke broke in on the radio, his voice tense and excited.

"Eagle, you are go for landing," he said.

"Roger, understand," a calm Armstrong replied. "Go for landing."

"Eagle, you're looking great," Duke said. "You're go at 1600 feet."

At that, Armstrong began to read off rapidly his altitudes and pitch angles—the angle at which the spacecraft was falling toward the lunar surface.

"Three-hundred feet," he said. "Down three and a half. A hundred feet. Three and a half down. Okay. Seventy-five feet. Looking good. Down a half."

"Sixty seconds," Duke said.

"Lights on," Armstrong replied. "Forty feet. Kicking up some dust. Great shadows.

"Four forward. Drifting to the right a little."

His voice then rose a little, as he turned off the engine for the first time and started free-falling to the moon.

"Okay, engine stop," he said. "Overdrive off. Engine arm off."

There was a pause—then the first voice came from the surface of the moon.

"Houston. Tranquillity Base here," Armstrong announced. "The Eagle has landed."

"You've got a bunch of guys about to turn blue," Duke told him. "Now we're breathing again."

"Okay, standby," Armstrong replied. "We're going to be busy for a minute."

Just then, Collins broke in from his lonesome spot 70 miles above the moon, desperately wanting in on the historic conversation.

"He has landed," Duke informed him. "Eagle has landed at Tranquillity."

"Good show," Collins said. "Fantastic."

Five minutes after touchdown, Duke told them things looked good enough for them to stay there a while.

"We thank you," Armstrong answered.

It was then that Armstrong told Houston he had to fly the spacecraft in manually to avoid a football-sized crater and a large rock field.

COULDN'T PINPOINT LOCATION

"It really was rough over the target area," he said. "It was heavily cratered and some of the large rocks may have been bigger than 10 feet around."

He then said he was not sure of his location on the moon either. "Well," he said, "the guys who said we wouldn't be able to tell exactly where we are are the winners today."

Armstrong reported that the four-legged spacecraft had landed on a level plain and appeared to be tilted at an angle no greater than 4.5 degrees.

Their first moments on the moon were truly incredible, but the entire day seemed incredible, as if the scenario for it all had been written by some bizarre science fiction writer.

"We've done everything humanly possible," Manned Spacecraft Center Director Robert C. Gilruth told one newsman, "but boy is this a tense and unreal time for me."

Preparing for the busiest and most historic day of their lives, the three crewmen hadn't even gotten to sleep until after 1 A.M.—and it was the ground that suggested they all go to bed.

"That really winds things up as far as we're concerned," astronaut Owen Garriott said in Houston. "We're ready to go to bed and get a little sleep."

COLLINS WAKES UP FIRST

"Yeah, we're about to join you," Armstrong replied.

Armstrong and Aldrin were the first to go to sleep, and then Collins finally went to sleep two hours later, at just after 3 A.M.

Four hours later, astronaut Ron Evans was manning the radio in Houston and he put in the first wake-up call.

"Apollo 11, Apollo 11," he said. "Good morning from the black team."

It was Collins who answered first, even though he'd had the least sleep. "Oh my, you guys wake up early," he said.

"You're about two minutes early on the wakeup," Evans conceded. "Looks like you were really sawing them away."

"You're right," said Collins.

Everybody got right down to business then. "Looks like the command module's in good shape," Evans told Collins. "Black team's been watching it real closely for you."

"We sure appreciate that," Collins said, "because I sure haven't."

ACTIVATES LANDING CRAFT

Just after 9:30 A.M., as the three men began their 11th orbit of the moon, Aldrin got into the Eagle for the first time—to power it up, start the oxygen flowing into the spacecraft and make sure everything was in working order. Forty-five minutes later, Armstrong joined him.

On the 13th orbit, Eagle undocked from Columbia, moving off about 40 or 50 feet from the command craft, which Collins was piloting alone.

Like most of the maneuvers they've made, this one was done behind the moon and out of contact with earth—so nobody in Houston knew for almost 45 minutes if the separation had been successful.

At 1:50 P.M., the two spacecraft came over the moon's rim.

"Eagle, we see you on the steerable," said Duke, who had just replaced Evans. "How does it look?"

"Eagle has wings," was Armstrong's simple reply.

For a while, all the astronauts did was look each other over, to make sure the two spacecraft were shipshape.

"Check that tracking light, Mike," Armstrong told Collins.

"Okay," Armstrong said next, "I'm ready to start my yaw manuever if it suits you, Mike."

Press

ELABORATE INSTRUMENT CHECK

Aldrin got on next, reading off what seemed like endless instrument checklists. For 15 minutes, he talked on, never once missing a word, sounding totally composed.

At 2:12 P.M., Collins fired his tiny thruster jets to increase distance between the craft.

"Thrusting," Collins said. "Everything's looking real good."

The two spacecraft were 1000 feet away from each other within moments. Collins took a radar check on the distance.

"I got a solid lock on it," he said. "It looks like point 27 miles"—about 1400 feet.

"Hey," Collins said to Armstrong when he'd looked out his window, "you're upside down."

"Somebody's upside down," Armstrong replied.

Just then, Collins asked Armstrong: "Put your tracking light on, please."

"It's on, Mike," answered Aldrin.

"Give us a mark when you're at seven-tenths of a mile," Duke said to Collins from the ground.

Moments later, Duke told Collins the big radars on the ground showed the two spacecraft seven-tenths of a mile apart.

"Rog," Collins said. "I'm oscillating between point 69 and seven-tenths."

At 2:50 P.M. Houston gave the go signal for the first maneuver, the so-called descent orbit insertion burn.

"Eagle," Duke said, "you are go for DOI."

"Roger," replied Aldrin matter-of-factly. "Go for DOI."

And while the whole world listened one of the most majestic dramas in mankind's history began to unfold.

DISCUSSION QUESTION

1. Compare Thomas O'Toole's report of the moon landing with Norman Mailer's account in Classics. How does O'Toole's use of transcripts differ from Mailer's? Why doesn't O'Toole talk about the way the astronauts talk? Why does Mailer do this? What effect does O'Toole want the transcripts to have in his report? What role does television play in his report?

Vivian Gornick / The Next Great Moment in History Is Theirs
[An Introduction to the Women's Liberation Movement]
Village Voice, November 27, 1969

A persuasive introduction to the women's liberation movement, Vivian Gornick's "The Next Great Moment in History Is Theirs" is a closely reasoned, insightful commentary on the acculturated inequities that have entrapped the public and private lives of American women and a record of their continuing struggle for freedom and self-definition.

The Next Great Moment in History Is Theirs

Founded in New York in 1955 by freelance journalist Daniel Wolf, psychologist Edward Fancher, and novelist Norman Mailer, the Village Voice *was the first successful avant-garde, antiestablishment newspaper in what has come to be known as "the underground press." Less expensively designed and printed than mass circulation daily newspapers and with few of their inhibitions or restraints, the* Village Voice *of the late sixties, published weekly with a circulation well over one hundred thousand, could afford to be more eclectic and extensive in its selection and coverage of contemporary events.*

A staff writer for the Voice *for several years, Vivian Gornick has also taught English at Hunter College and at the Stony Brook campus of the State University of New York. She co-edited* Woman in Sexist Society *(1971), an impressive collection of feminist writings.*

One evening not too long ago, at the home of a well-educated and extremely intelligent couple I know, I mentioned the women's liberation movement and was mildly astonished by the response the subject received. The man said: "Jesus, what *is* all that crap about?" The woman, a scientist who had given up 10 working years to raise her children, said: "I can understand if these women want to work and are demanding equal pay. But why on earth do they want to have children too?" To which the man rejoined: "Ah, they don't want kids. They're mostly a bunch of dykes, anyway."

Again: Having lunch with an erudite, liberal editor, trained in the humanist tradition, I was struck dumb by his reply to my mention of the women's liberation movement: "Ah shit, who the hell is oppressing them?"

And yet again: A college-educated housewife, fat and neurotic, announced with arch sweetness, "I'm sorry, I just don't *feel* oppressed."

Over and over again, in educated, thinking circles, one meets with a bizarre, almost determined, ignorance of the unrest that is growing daily and exists in formally organized bodies in nearly every major city and on dozens of campuses across America. The women of this country are gathering themselves into a sweat of civil revolt, and the general population seems totally unaware of what is happening—if, indeed, they realize *anything* is happening—or that there is a legitimate need behind what is going on. How is this possible? Why is it true? What relation is there between the peculiarly unalarmed, amused dismissal of the women's-rights movement and the movement itself? Is this relation only coincidental, only the apathetic response of a society already benumbed by civil rights and student anarchy and unable to rise to yet one more protest movement? Or is it not, in fact, precisely the key to the entire issue?

Almost invariably, when people set out to tell you there is no such thing as discrimination against women in this country, the first thing they hastily admit to is a *minor* degree of economic favoritism shown toward men. In fact, they will eagerly, almost gratefully, support the claim of economic inequity, as though that will keep the discussion within manageable bounds. Curious. But even on economic grounds or grounds of legal discrimination most people are dismally ignorant of the true proportions of the issue. They will grant that often a man will make as much as $100 more than a woman at the same job, and yes, it *is* often difficult for a woman to be hired when a man can be hired instead, but after all, that's really not so terrible.

This is closer to the facts:

Women in this country make 60 cents for every $1 a man makes.

Women do not share in the benefits of the fair employment practices laws because those laws do not specify "no discrimination on the basis of sex."

Women often rise in salary only to the point at which a man starts.

Women occupy, in great masses, the "household tasks" of industry. They are nurses but not doctors, secretaries but not executives, researchers but not writers, workers but not managers, bookkeepers but not promoters.

Women almost never occupy decision—or policy-making positions.

Women are almost non-existent in government.

Women are subject to a set of "protective" laws that restrict their working hours, do not allow them to occupy many jobs in which the carrying of weights is involved, do not allow them to enter innumerable bars, restaurants, hotels, and other public places unescorted.

Women, despite 100 years of reform, exist in the domestic and marriage laws of our country almost literally as appendages of their husbands. Did you know that rape by a husband is legal but that if a woman refuses to sleep with her husband she is subject to legal suit? Did you know that the word domicile in the law refers to the husband's domicile and that if a woman refuses to follow her husband to wherever he makes his home, legal suit can be brought against her to force her to do so? Did you know that in most states the law imposes severe legal disabilities on married women with regard to their personal and property rights? (As a feminist said to me: "The United Nations has defined servitude as necessarily involuntary, but women, ignorant of the law, put themselves into *voluntary* servitude.")

Perhaps, you will say, these observations are not so shocking. After all, women *are* weaker than men, they do need protection, what on earth is so terrible about being protected, for God's sake! And as for those laws, they're never invoked, no woman is dragged anywhere against her will, on the contrary, women's desires rule the middle-class household, and women can work at hundreds of jobs, in fact, a great deal of the wealth of the country is in their hands, and no woman ever goes hungry.

I agree. These observed facts of our national life are not so shocking. The laws and what accrues from them are not so terrible. It is what's behind the laws that is so terrible. It is not the letter of the law but the spirit determining the law that is terrible. It is not what is explicit but what is implicit in the law that is terrible. It is not the apparent condition but the actual condition of woman that is terrible.

"The woman's issue is the true barometer of social change," said a famous political theoretician. This was true 100 years ago; it is no less true today. Women and blacks were and are, traditionally and perpetually, the great "outsiders" in Western culture, and their erratic swellings of outrage parallel each other in a number of ways that are both understandable and also extraordinary. A hundred years ago a great abolitionist force wrenched this country apart and changed its history forever; many, many radical men devoted a fever of life to wrecking a system in which men were bought and sold; many radical women worked toward the same end; the abolitionist movement contained women who came out of educated and liberal 19th century families, women who considered themselves independent thinking beings. It was only when Elizabeth Cady Stanton and Lucretia Mott were not allowed to be seated at a World Anti-Slavery Conference held in the 1840s that the intellectual abolitionist women suddenly perceived that their own political existence resembled that of the blacks. They raised the issue with their radical men and were denounced furiously for introducing an insignificant and divisive issue, one which was sure to weaken the movement. Let's win this war first, they said, and then we'll see about women's rights. But the women had seen, in one swift visionary moment, to the very center of the truth about their own lives, and they knew that first was *now*, that there would never be a time when men would willingly address themselves to the question of female rights, that to strike out now for women's rights could do nothing but strengthen the issue of black civil rights because it called attention to all instances or rights denied in a nation that prided itself on rights for all.

Thus was born the original Women's Rights Movement, which became known as the Women's Suffrage Movement because the single great issue, of course, was legal political recognition. But it was never meant to begin and end with the vote, just as the abolitionist movement was never meant to begin and end with the vote. Somehow, though, that awful and passionate struggle for suffrage seemed to exhaust both the blacks and the women, especially the women, for when the vote finally came at the end of the Civil War, it was handed to black males—but not to women; the women had to go on fighting for 60 bitterly long years for suffrage. And then both blacks and women lay back panting, unable to catch their breath for generation upon generation.

The great civil rights movement for blacks in the 1950s and '60s is the second wind of that monumental first effort, necessary because the legislated political equality of the 1860s was never translated into actual equality. The reforms promised by law had never happened. The piece of paper meant nothing. Racism had never been legislated out of existence; in fact, its original virulence had remained virtually untouched, and, more important, the black in this country had never been able to shake off the slave mentality. He was born scared, he ran scared, he died scared; for 100 years after legal emancipation, he lived as though it had never happened. Blacks and whites did not regard either themselves or each other differently, and so they in no way lived differently. In the 1950s and '60s the surging force behind the renewed civil rights effort has been the desire to eradicate this condition more than any other, to enable the American black to believe in himself as a whole, independent, expressive human being capable of fulfilling and protecting himself in the very best way he knows how. Today, after more than 15 years of unremitting struggle, after a formidable array of reform laws legislated at the federal, state, and local level, after a concentration on black rights and black existence that has traumatized the nation, it is still not unfair to say that the psychology of defeat has not been lifted from black life. Still (aside from the continuance of crime, drugs, broken homes, and all the wretched rest of it), employers are able to say: "Sure, I'd love to hire one if I could find one who qualified," and while true, half the time it *is,* because black life is still marked by the "nigger mentality," the terrible inertia of spirit that accompanies the perhaps irrational but deeply felt conviction that no matter what one does, one is going to wind up a 35-year-old busboy. This "nigger mentality" characterizes black lives. It also characterizes women's lives. And it is this, and this alone, that is behind the second wave of feminism now sweeping the country and paralleling precisely, exactly as it does 100 years ago, the black rights movement. The fight for reform laws is just the beginning. What women are really after this time around is the utter eradication of the "nigger" in themselves.

Most women who feel "niggerized" have tales of overt oppression to tell. They feel they've been put down by their fathers, their brothers, their lovers, their bosses. They feel that in their families, in their sex lives, and in their jobs they have counted as nothing, they have been treated as second-class citizens, their minds have been deliberately stunted and their emotions warped. My own experience with the condition is a bit more subtle, and, without bragging, I do believe a bit closer to the true feminist point.

To begin with, let me tell a little story. Recently, I had lunch with a man I had known at school. He and his wife and I had all been friends at college; they had courted while we were in school and immediately upon graduation they got married. They were both talented art students, and it was assumed both would work in commercial art. But shortly after their marriage she became pregnant, and never did go to work. Within five years they had two children. At first I visited them often; their home was lovely, full of their mutual talent for atmosphere; the wife sparkled, the children flourished; he rose in the field of commercial art; I envied them both their self-containment, and she especially her apparently contented, settled state. But as I had remained single and life took me off in various other directions we soon began to drift apart, and when I again met the husband we had not seen each other in many years. We spoke animatedly of what we had both been doing for quite a while. Then I asked about his wife. His face rearranged itself suddenly, but I couldn't quite tell how at first. He said she was fine, but didn't sound right.

"What's wrong?" I asked. "Is she doing something you don't want her to do? Or the other way around?"

"No, no," he said hastily. "I want her to do whatever she wants to do. Anything. Anything that will make her happy. And get her off my back," he ended bluntly. I asked what he meant and he told me of his wife's restlessness of the last few years, of how sick she was of being a housewife, how useless she felt, and how she longed to go back to work.

"Well?" I asked, "did you object?"

"Of course not!" he replied vigorously. "Why the hell would I do that? She's a very talented woman, her children are half grown, she's got every right in the world to go to work."

"So?" I said.

"It's *her*," he said bewilderedly. "She doesn't seem able to just go out and get a job."

"What do you mean?" I asked. But beneath the surface of my own puzzled response I more than half knew what was coming.

"Well, she's scared, I think. She's more talented than half the people who walk into my office asking for work, but do what I will she won't get a portfolio together and make the rounds. Also, she cries a lot lately. For no reason, if you know what I mean. And then, she can't seem to get up in the morning in time to get a babysitter and get out of the house. This is a woman who was always up at 7 A.M. to feed everybody, get things going; busy, capable, doing 10 things at once." He shook his head as though in a true quandary. "Oh well," he ended up "I guess it doesn't really matter any more."

"Why not?" I asked.

His eyes came up and he looked levelly at me. "She's just become pregnant again."

I listened silently, but with what internal churning! Even though the external events of our lives were quite different, I felt as though this woman had been living inside my skin all these years, so close was I to the essential nature of her experience as I perceived it listening to her husband's woebegone tale. I had wandered about the world, I had gained another degree, I had married twice, I had written, taught, edited, I had no children. And yet I knew that in some fundamental sense we were the same woman. I understood exactly—but exactly—the kind of neurotic anxiety that just beset her, and that had ultimately defeated her; it was a neurosis I shared and had recognized in almost every woman I had ever known—including Monica Vitti, having her Schiaparellied nervous breakdown, stuffing her hand into her mouth, rolling her eyes wildly, surrounded by helplessly sympathetic men who kept saying: "Just tell me what's *wrong.*"

I was raised in an immigrant home where education was worshiped. As the entire American culture was somewhat mysterious to my parents, the educational possibilities of that world were equally unknown for both the boy and the girl in our family. Therefore, I grew up in the certainty that if my brother went to college, I too could go to college; and, indeed, he did, and I in my turn did too. We both read voraciously from early childhood on, and we were both encouraged to do so. We both had precocious and outspoken opinions and neither of us was ever discouraged from uttering them. We both were exposed early to unionist radicalism and neither of us met with opposition when, separately, we experimented with youthful political organizations. And yet somewhere along the line my brother and I managed to receive an utterly different education regarding ourselves and our own expectations from life. He was taught many things but what he learned was the need to develop a kind of inner necessity. I was taught many things, but what I learned, ultimately, was that it was the prime vocation of my life to prepare myself for the love of a good man and the responsibilities of homemaking and motherhood. All the rest, the education, the books, the jobs, that was all very nice and of course, why not? I was an intelligent girl, shouldn't I learn? *make* something of myself! but oh dolly, you'll see, in the end no woman could possibly be happy without a man to love and children to raise. What's more, came the heavy implication, if I *didn't* marry I would be considered an irredeemable failure.

How did I learn this? How? I have pondered this question 1000 times. Was it really that explicit? Was it laid out in lessons strategically planned and carefully executed? Was it spooned down my throat at regular intervals? No. It wasn't. I have come finally to understand that the lessons were implicit and they took place in 100 different ways, in a continuous day-to-day exposure to an *attitude,* shared by all, about women, about what kind of creatures they were and what kind of lives they were meant to live; the lessons were administered not only by my parents but by the men and women, the boys and girls, all around me who, of course, had been made in the image of this attitude.

My mother would say to me when I was very young, as I studied at the kitchen table and she cooked: "How lucky you are to go to school! I wasn't so lucky. I had to go to work in the factory. I wanted so to be a nurse! But go be a nurse in Williamsburg in 1920! Maybe you'll be a nurse. . . ." I listened, I nodded, but somehow the message I got was that I was like her and I would one day be doing what she was now doing.

My brother was the "serious and steady" student, I the "erratic and undisciplined" one. When he studied the house was silenced; when I studied, business as usual.

When I was 14 and I came in flushed and disarrayed my mother knew I'd been with a boy. Her fingers gripped my upper arm; her face, white and intent, bent over me: What did he do to you? *Where* did he do it? I was frightened to death. What was she so upset about? What could he do to me? I learned that I was the keeper of an incomparable treasure and it had to be guarded: it was meant to be a gift for my husband. (Later that year when I read "A Rage to Live" I knew without any instruction exactly what all those elliptical sentences were about.)

When I threw some hideous temper tantrum my mother would say: "What a little female you are!" (I have since seen many little boys throw the same tantrums and have noted with interest that they are not told they are little females.)

The girls on the street would talk forever about boys, clothes, movies, fights with their mothers. The 1000 thoughts racing around in my head from the books I was reading remained secret, no one to share them with.

The boys would be gentler with the girls than with each other when we all played roughly; and our opinions were never considered seriously.

I grew up, I went to school, I came out, wandered around, went to Europe, went back to school, wandered again, taught in a desultory fashion, and at last! got married!

It was during my first marriage that I began to realize something was terribly wrong inside me, but it took me 10 years to understand that I was suffering the classic female pathology. My husband, like all the men I have known, was a good man, a man who wanted my independence for me more than I wanted it for myself. He urged me to work, to do something, anything, that would make me happy; he knew that our pleasure in each other could be heightened only if I was a functioning human being too. Yes, yes! I said, and leaned back in the rocking chair with yet another novel. Somehow, I couldn't do anything. I didn't really know where to start, what I wanted to do. Oh, I had always had a number of interests but they, through an inability on my part to stick with anything, had always been superficial; when I arrived at a difficult point in a subject, a job, an interest, I would simply drop it. Of course, what I really wanted to do was write; but that was an altogether ghastly agony and one I could never come to grips with. There seemed to be some terrible aimlessness at the very center of me, some paralyzing lack of will. My energy, which was abundant, was held in a trap of some sort; occasionally that useless energy would wake up roaring, demanding to be let out of its cage, and then I became "emotional"; I would have hysterical depressions, rage on and on about the meaninglessness of my life, force my husband into long psychoanalytic discussions about the source of my (our) trouble, end in a purging storm of tears, a determination to do "something," and six months later I was right back where I started. If my marriage had not dissolved, I am sure that I would still be in exactly that same peculiarly nightmarish position. But as it happened, the events of life forced me out into the world, and repeatedly I had to come up against myself. I found this pattern of behavior manifesting itself in 100 different circumstances; regardless of how things began, they always seemed to end in the same place. Oh, I worked, I advanced, in a sense, but only erratically and with superhuman effort. Always the battle was internal, and it was with a kind of paralyzing anxiety at the center of me that drained off my energy and retarded my capacity for intellectual concentration. It took me a long time to perceive that nearly every woman I knew exhibited the same symptoms, and when I did perceive it, became frightened. I thought, at first, that perhaps, indeed, we were all victims of some biological deficiency, that some vital ingredient had been deleted in the female of the species, that we were a physiological metaphor for human neurosis. It took me a long time to understand, with an understanding that is irrevocable, that we are the victims of culture, not biology.

Recently, I read a marvelous biography of Beatrice Webb, the English socialist. The book is full of vivid portraits, but the one that is fixed forever in my mind is that of Mrs. Webb's mother, Laurencina Potter. Laurencina Potter was a beautiful, intelligent, intellectually energetic woman of the middle 19th century. She knew 12 languages, spoke Latin and Greek better than half the classics-trained men who came to her home, and was interested in everything. Her marriage to wealthy and powerful Richard Potter was a love match, and she looked forward to a life of intellectual companionship, stimulating activity, lively participation. No sooner were they married than Richard installed her in a Victorian fortress in the country, surrounded her with servants and physical comfort, and started her off with the first of the 11 children she eventually bore. He went out into the world, bought and sold railroads, made important political connections, mingled in London society, increased his powers, and relished his life. She, meanwhile, languished. She sat in the country, staring at the four brocaded walls; her energy remained bottled up, her mind became useless, her will evaporated. The children became symbols of her enslavement and, in consequence, she was a lousy mother: neurotic, self-absorbed, increasingly colder and more withdrawn, increasingly more involved in taking her emotional temperature. She became, in short, the Victorian lady afflicted with indefinable maladies.

When I read of Laurencina's life I felt as though I was reading about the lives of most of the women I know, and it struck me that 100 years ago sexual submission was all for a woman, and today sexual fulfillment is all for a woman, and the two are one and the same.

Most of the women I know are people of superior intelligence, developed emotions, and higher education. And yet our friendships, our conversations, our lives, are not marked by intellectual substance or emotional distance or objective concern. It is only briefly and insubstantially that I ever discuss books or politics or philosophical issues or abstractions of any kind with the women I know. Mainly, we discuss and are intimate about our Emotional Lives. Endlessly, endlessly, we go on and on about our emotional "problems" and "needs" and "relationships." And, of course, because we are all bright and well-educated, we bring to bear on these sessions a formidable amount of sociology and psychology, literature and history, all hoked out so that it sounds as though these are serious conversations on serious subjects, when in fact they are caricatures of seriousness right out of Jonathan Swift. Caricatures, because they have no beginning, middle, end, or point. They go nowhere, they conclude nothing, they change nothing. They are elaborate descriptions in the ongoing soap opera that is our lives. It took me a long time to understand that we were talking about nothing, and it took me an even longer and harder time, traveling down that dark, narrow road in the mind, back back to the time when I was a little girl sitting in the kitchen with my mother, to understand, at last, that the affliction was cultural not biological, that it was because we had never been taught to take ourselves seriously that I and all the women I knew had become parodies of "taking ourselves seriously."

The rallying cry of the black civil rights movement has always been: "Give us back our manhood!" What exactly does that mean? Where is black manhood? How has it been taken from blacks? And how can it be retrieved? The answer lies in one word: responsibility; therefore, they have been deprived of self-respect; therefore, they have been deprived of manhood. Women have been deprived of exactly the same thing and in every real sense have thus been deprived of womanhood. We have never been prepared to assume responsibility; we have never been prepared to make demands upon ourselves; we have never been taught to expect the development of what is best in ourselves because no one has ever expected *anything* of us—or for us. Because no one has ever had any intention of turning over any serious work to us. Both we and the blacks lost the ballgame before we ever got up to play. In order to live you've got to have nerve; and we were stripped of our nerve before we began. Black is ugly and female is inferior. These are the primary lessons of our experience, and in these ways both blacks and women have been kept, not as functioning nationals, but rather as operating objects. But a human being who remains as a child throughout his adult life is an object, not a mature specimen, and the definition of a child is: one without reponsibility.

At the very center of all human life is energy, psychic energy. It is the force of that energy that drives us, that surges continually up in us, that must repeatedly spend and renew itself in us, that must perpetually be reaching for something beyond itself in order to satisfy its own insatiable appetite. It is the imperative of that energy that has determined man's characteristic interest, problem-solving. The modern ecologist attests to that driving need by demonstrating that in a time when all the real problems are solved, man makes up new ones in order to go on solving. He must have work, work that he considers real and serious, or he will die, he will simply shrivel up and die. That is the one certain characteristic of human beings. And it is the one characteristic, above all others, that the accidentally dominant white male asserts is not necessary to more than half the members of the race, i.e., the female of the species. This assertion is, quite simply, a lie. Nothing more, nothing less. A lie. That energy is alive in every woman in the world. It lies trapped and dormant like a growing tumor, and at its center there is despair, hot, deep, wordless.

It is amazing to me that I have just written these words. To think that 100 years after Nora slammed the door, and in a civilization and a century utterly converted to the fundamental insights of that exasperating genius, Sigmund Freud, women could still be raised to believe that their basic makeup is determined not by the needs of their egos but by their peculiar child-bearing properties and their so-called unique capacity for loving. No man worth his salt does not wish to be a husband and father; yet no man is raised to be a husband and father and no man would ever conceive of those relationships as instruments of his prime function in life. Yet every woman is raised, still, to believe that the fulfillment of these relationships is her prime function in life and, what's more, her instinctive choice.

The fact is that women have no special capacities for love, and, when a culture reaches a level where its women have nothing to do but "love" (as occurred in the Victorian upper classes and as is occurring now in the American middle classes), they prove to be very bad at it. The modern American wife is not noted for her love of her husband or of her children; she is noted for her driving (or should I say driven?) domination of them. She displays an aberrated, aggressive ambition for her mate and for her offspring which can be explained only by the most vicious feelings toward the self. The reasons are obvious. The woman who must love for a living, the woman who has no self, no objective external reality to take her own measure by, no work to discipline her, no goal to provide the illusion of progress, no internal resources, no separate mental existence, is constitutionally incapable of the emotional distance that is one of the real requirements of love. She cannot separate herself from her husband and children because all the passionate and multiple needs of her being are centered on them. That's why women "take everything personally." It's all they've got to take. "Loving" must substitute for an entire range of feeling and interest. The man, who is not raised to be a husband and father specifically, and who simply loves as a single function of his existence, cannot understand her abnormal "emotionality" and concludes that this is the female nature. (Why shouldn't he? She does too.) But this is not so. It is a result of a psychology achieved by cultural attitudes that run so deep and have gone on for so long that they are mistaken for "nature" or "instinct."

A good example of what I mean are the multiple legends of our culture regarding motherhood. Let's use our heads for a moment. What on earth is holy about motherhood? I mean, why motherhood rather than fatherhood? If anything is holy, it is the consecration of sexual union. A man plants a seed in a woman; the seed matures and eventually is expelled by the woman; a child is born to both of them; each contributed the necessary parts to bring about procreation; each is responsible to and necessary to the child; to claim that the woman is more so than the man is simply not true; certainly it cannot be proven biologically or psychologically (please, no comparisons with baboons and penguins just now—I am sure I can supply 50 examples from nature to counter any assertion made on the subject); all that can be proven is that someone is necessary to the newborn baby; to have instilled in women the belief that their child-bearing and housewifely obligations supersedes all other needs, that indeed what they fundamentally *want* and need is to be wives and mothers as distinguished from being anything else, is to have accomplished an act of trickery, an act which has deprived women of the proper forms of expression necessary to that force of energy alive in every talking creature, an act which has indeed mutilated their natural selves and deprived them of their womanhood, what*ever* that may be, deprived them of the right to say "I" and have it mean something. This understanding, grasped whole, is what underlies the current wave of feminism. It is felt by thousands of women today, it will be felt by millions tomorrow. You have only to examine briefly a fraction of the women's rights organizations already in existence to realize instantly that they form the nucleus of a genuine movement, complete with theoreticians, tacticians, agitators, manifestos, journals, and thesis papers, running the entire political spectrum from conservative reform to visionary radicalism, and powered by an emotional conviction rooted in undeniable experience, and fed by a determination that is irreversible.

One of the oldest and stablest of the feminist organizations is NOW, the National Organization for Women. It was started in 1966 by a group of professional women headed by Mrs. Betty Friedan, author of *The Feminine Mystique,* the book that was the bringer of the word in 1963 to the new feminists. NOW has more than 3000 members, chapters in major cities and on many campuses all over the country, and was read, at its inception, into the Congressional Record. It has many men in its ranks and it works, avowedly within the system, to bring about the kind of reforms that will result in what it calls a "truly equal partnership between men and women" in this country. It is a true reform organization filled with intelligent, liberal, hardworking women devoted to the idea that America is a reformist democracy and ultimately will respond to the justice of their cause. They are currently hard at work on two major issues: repeal of the abortion laws and passage of the Equal Rights Amendment (for which feminists have been fighting since 1923) which would amend the constitution to provide that "equality of rights under the law shall not be denied or abridged by the United States or by any state on account of sex." When this amendment is passed, the employment and marriage laws of more than 40 states will be affected. Also, in direct conjunction with the fight to have this amendment passed, NOW demands increased child-care facilities to be established by law on the same basis as parks, libraries, and public schools.

NOW's influence is growing by leaps and bounds. It is responsible for the passage of many pieces of legislation meant to wipe out discrimination against women, and certainly the size and number of Women's Bureaus, Women's units, Women's Commissions springing up in government agencies and legislative bodies all over the country reflects its presence. Suddenly, there are Presidential reports and gubernatorial conferences and congressional meetings—all leaping all over each other to discuss the status of women. NOW, without a doubt, is the best established feminist group.

From NOW we move, at a shocking rate of speed, to the left. In fact, it would appear that NOW is one of the few reformist groups, that mainly the feminist groups are radical, both in structure and in aim. Some, truth to tell, strike a bizarre and puzzling note. For instance, there is WITCH (Women's International Terrorists Conspiracy From Hell), an offshoot of SDS, where members burned their bras and organized against the Miss America Pageant in a stirring demand that the commercially useful image of female beauty be wiped out. There is Valerie Solanas and her SCUM Manifesto, which Solanas's penetrating observation on our national life was: "If the atom bomb isn't dropped, this society will hump itself to death." There is Cell 55. God knows what they do.

There are the Redstockings, an interesting group that seems to have evolved from direct action into what they call "consciousness-raising." That means, essentially, that they get together in a kind of group therapy session and the women reveal their experiences and feelings to each other in an attempt to analyze the femaleness of their psychology and their circumstances, thereby increasing the invaluable weapon of self-understanding.

And finally, there are the Feminists, without a doubt the most fiercely radical and intellectually impressive of all the groups. This organization was begun a year ago by a group of defectors from NOW and various other feminist groups, in rebellion against the repetition of the hierarchical structure of power in these other groups. Their contention was: women have always been "led"; if they join the rank and file of a feminist organization they are simply being led again. It will still be someone else, even if only the officers of their own interesting group, making the decisions, doing the planning, the executing, and so on. They determined to develop a leaderless society whose guiding principle was participation by lot. And this is precisely what they have done. The organization has no officers, every woman sooner or later performs every single task necessary to the life and aims of the organization, and the organization is willing to temporarily sacrifice efficiency in order that each woman may fully develop all the skills necessary to autonomous functioning. This working individualism is guarded fiercely by a set of rigid rules regarding attendance, behavior, duties, and loyalties.

The Feminists encourage extensive theorizing on the nature and function of a leaderless society, and this has led the organization to a bold and radical view of the future they wish to work for. The group never loses sight of the fact that its primary enemy is the male-female role system which has ended in women being the oppressed and men being the oppressors. It looks forward to a time when this system will be completely eradicated. To prepare for this coming, it now denounces all the institutions which encourage the system, i.e., love, sex, and marriage. It has a quota on married women (only one-third of their number are permitted to be either married or living in a marriage-like situation). It flatly names all men as the enemy. It looks forward to a future in which the family as we know it will disappear, all births will be extra-uterine, children will be raised by communal efforts, and women once and for all will cease to be the persecuted members of the race.

Although a lot of this is hard to take in raw doses, you realize that many of these ideas represent interesting and important turns of thought. First of all, these experiments with a leaderless society are being echoed everywhere: in student radicalism, in black civil rights, in hippie communes. They are part of a great radical lusting after self-determination that is beginning to overtake this country. This is true social revolution, and I believe that feminism, in order to accomplish its aims now, does need revolution, does need a complete overthrow of an old kind of thought and the introduction of a new kind of thought. Secondly, the Feminists are right: most of what men and women now are is determined by the "roles" they play, and love *is* an institution, full of ritualized gestures and positions, and often void of any recognizable naturalness. How, under the present iron-bound social laws, can one know what is female nature and what is female role? (And that question speaks to the source of the whole female pain and confusion.) It *is* thrilling to contemplate a new world, brave or otherwise, in which men and women may free themselves of some of the crippling sexual poses that now circumscribe their lives, thus allowing them some open and equitable exchange of emotion, some release of the natural self which will be greeted with resentment from no one.

But the Feminists strike a wrong and rather hysterical note when they indicate that they don't believe there is a male or female nature, that all is role. I believe that is an utterly wrong headed notion. Not only do I believe there is a genuine male or female nature in each of us, but I believe that what is most exciting about the new world that may be coming is the promise of stripping down to that nature, of the complementary elements in those natures meeting without anxiety, of our different biological tasks being performed without profit for one at the expense of the other.

The Feminists' position is extreme and many of these pronouncements are chilling at first touch. But you quickly realize that this is the harsh, stripped-down language of revolution that is, the language of icy "honesty," of narrow but penetrating vision. (As one Feminist said sweetly, quoting her favorite author: "In order to have a revolution you must have a revolutionary theory.") And besides, you sue for thousands and hope to collect hundreds.

Many Feminists, though, are appalled by the Feminists (the in-fighting in the movement is fierce), feel they are fascists, "superweak," annihilatingly single-minded, and involved in a power play no matter what they say; but then again you can find feminists who will carefully and at great length put down every single feminist group going. But there's one great thing about these chicks: if five feminists fall out with six groups, within half an hour they'll all find each other (probably somewhere on Bleecker Street), within 48 hours a new splinter faction will have announced its existence, and within two weeks the manifesto is being mailed out. It's the mark of a true movement.

Two extremely intelligent and winning feminists who are about to "emerge" as part of a new group are Shulamith Firestone, an ex-Redstocking, and Anne Koedt, an ex-Feminist, and both members of the original radical group, New York Radical Women. They feel that none of the groups now going has the capacity to build a broad mass movement among the women of this country and they intend to start one that will. Both are dedicated to social revolution and agree with many of the ideas of many of the other radical groups. Each one, in her own words, comes equipped with "impeccable revolutionary credentials." They come out of the Chicago SDS and the New York civil rights movement. Interestingly enough, like many of the radical women in this movement, they were converted to feminism because in their participation in the New Left they met with intolerable female discrimination. ("Yeah, baby, comes the revolution . . . baby, comes the revolution. . . . Meanwhile, you make the coffee and later I'll tell you where to hand out the leaflets." And when they raised the issue of women's rights with their radical young men, they were greeted with furious denunciations of introducing divisive issues! Excuse me, but haven't we been here before?)

The intention of Miss Firestone and Miss Koedt is to start a group that will be radical in aim but much looser in structure than anything they've been involved with; it will be an action group, but everyone will also be encouraged to theorize, analyze, create; it will appeal to the broad base of educated women; on the other hand, it will not sound ferocious to the timid non-militant woman. In other words . . .

I mention these two in particular, but at this moment in New York, in Cambridge, in Chicago, in New Haven, in Washington, in San Francisco, in East Podunk—yes! believe it!—there are dozens like them preparing to do the same thing. They are gathering fire and I do believe the next great moment in history is theirs. God knows, for my unborn daughter's sake, I hope so.

DISCUSSION QUESTIONS

1. Which of the advertisements reprinted in the Advertising section could be used to document the feminist issues discussed in Vivian Gornick's essay?

2. In what ways can Gornick's essay be used to establish an ideological context for the situations dramatized in Kate Chopin's "The Dream of an Hour" and Tillie Olsen's "I Stand Here Ironing" (see Classics)? What attitudes towards the experiences of women do they share? In what ways do they differ?

Staff / The Living Lombardi Legend
Green Bay *Press-Gazette,* September 3, 1970

"Winning isn't everything. It's the only thing." Vince Lombardi took over the Green Bay Packers football team when they were at the bottom of their league and brought them to the top. A man who provoked strong responses from both players and fans, Lombardi captured the interest and imagination of many Americans (see James Dickey's poem "On the Death of Vince Lombardi" in Magazines). As the following obituary from the local Green Bay newspaper shows, Lombardi was indeed a living legend.

The untimely death of Vince Lombardi in the prime of his career as a professional football coach and business administrator takes from the sports scene one of its most dynamic and colorful personalities.

Although his death was not unexpected because of the well-founded but unofficial reports of his deteriorating physical condition following two operations, it still came as a shock. Those who have followed Mr. Lombardi's career certainly felt that here was a man of indomitable will who just would not be felled by a physical ailment. And yet his final illness came with devastating and relentless suddenness and to a man who had so prized physical fitness in himself as well as others.

The details of Mr. Lombardi's success in his chosen vocation are well enough known to require no detailed repetition here. Above and beyond that record, however, was the motivating force, the man's philosophy, which must be equally remembered for its impact on those around him as well as those who did not directly come within that sphere. That philosophy centered on man's striving for perfection within himself. Mr. Lombardi saw failures along the road toward that goal as prods to success, but he recognized success as having its own built-in obstacles toward the effort and dedication necessary to prevent backsliding.

Mr. Lombardi was a hard task-master on the football field because he saw no other way to win. He could understand human failures while demanding perfection. He often was less critical when failures occurred than when success was achieved through less than the complete use of an individual's talents whose complete fulfillment he saw as an obligation. The one human failure he could not forgive was shirking from dedication to reach a goal, even one which seemed beyond human reach.

"Football teaches that work and sacrifice, perseverance and competitiveness, selflessness and respect for authority are the things one must possess if he is to achieve," he frequently said. He saw those qualities also as necessary in man's day-to-day life and as national goals. In evaluating today's national problems he said that "the struggle America faces today is a struggle for the hearts and souls and minds of men" in that "we must walk the tightrope between the consent we must receive and the control we must exert" in accepting the exercise of authority rather than its condemnation.

It was during his coaching tenure in Green Bay that Mr. Lombardi put to the test his belief that loyalty, teamwork, Spartanism with sacrifices and what he called "heart power, not hate power" were the touchstones to success. The result: in nine seasons as head coach, Mr. Lombardi led the Packers to five league championships and two Super Bowl championships. What is sometimes forgotten about him in those successes in football is that he also participated as a leader in many fund-raising efforts for charitable, health and educational organizations. He brought to such participation the same all-out effort which marked his coaching genius.

Green Bay has good reason to be thankful to Mr. Lombardi for taking the Packers from the bottom of the NFL to the heights which may never be matched again by any team in the continuity of their success. In turn, Green Bay provided him with a glittering opportunity to put into practice all of the tenets of his philosophy which he had shaped during his many years as a high school, college and professional coach, primarily as an assistant.

A legend in life, Mr. Lombardi will go down in the history of professional football as one of its greatest coaches and administrators. Just as significant will be the influence he had beyond the football field in his constant emphasis on and the need for man to exercise to the fullest the virtues of loyalty, effort, dedication, appreciation for the dignity of the individual and respect for authority properly and validly exercised.

The man has died but the Lombardi legend will live.

Mike Royko / How To Kick a Machine

Chicago *Daily News*, November 15, 1971

Mike Royko writes a 750-word column for the Chicago Sun-Times *five times every week. He did the same for the Chicago* Daily News *for fourteen years. He has been awarded about every major journalism prize in the business. Author of four books, one a long-time resident of the best-seller list, Royko grew up in the tough North Side of Chicago, and his columns have a street-wise slant on the social and political events of that city.*

In "How To Kick a Machine" Royko gives the "fixers, grafters, schemers, hustlers, loaders and shills" he so often writes about a breather in order to thump the malevolent inanimate objects that afflict us all.

The guy in front of me put his dime in the coffee machine. The cup dropped, the machine whirred, but nothing came out.

He muttered, then started to walk away looking dejected and embarrassed. That's the way many people react when a machine doesn't come through: as if they have been outwitted. They feel foolish.

"Aren't you going to do anything about it?" I asked.

"What's there to do?"

What a question. If he had gone in a bar and ordered a beer, and if the bartender had taken his money but not given him a beer, he'd do something. He'd yell or fight or call the police.

But he let a machine cow him.

"Kick it," I said.

"What good will that do?" he said.

"You'll feel better," I said.

He came back and got in position to kick it, but I stopped him.

"Not like that. You are going to kick it with your toe, but you can hurt yourself that way. Do it this way."

I stepped back and showed him the best way. You use the bottom of your foot, as if you're kicking in a bedroom door.

I stepped aside, and he tried it. The first time he used the ball of his foot. It was a weak effort.

"Use more of the heel," I suggested.

That did it. He gave it two good ones and the machine bounced. He has big feet.

"With feet like that," I told him, "you could knock over a sandwich machine."

He stepped back looking much more self-confident.

Somebody else who had been in line said: "I prefer pounding on it. I'll show you."

Leaning on it with his left hand, he put his forehead close to the machine, as if in deep despair. Then he pounded with his clenched fist.

"Never use the knuckles," he said, "because that hurts. Use the bottom of the fist, the way you'd pound on the table."

"Why just one fist?" someone else said. "I always use two."

He demonstrated, standing close to the machine, baring his teeth, and pounding with both fists, as if trying to break down a bedroom door with his hands.

Just then, another guy with a dime stepped up. Seeing us pounding on the machine, he asked: "Is it out of coffee?"

We told him it had shorted on a cup.

He hesitated, then said: "Sometimes it only skips one, then it works OK."

"It's your money," I told him.

He put in his dime, the cup dropped, the machine whirred, and nothing came out.

All he said was "Hmm," and started to walk away.

"Why don't you kick it?" I said.

He grimaced. "It's only a dime."

Only a dime? I don't know anyone who hasn't been cheated by a machine at least once—usually a lot more than once.

First it was the gumball machine, taking your last penny. Then it was the gum machine on the L platform. Then the peanut machine.

And now they all do it. Coffee machines, soft-drink machines, candy machines, sweet-roll machines, sandwich machines.

Only a dime? There are 200 million Americans. If each of us is taken for a dime, that adds up to $20 million.

And it has to be more, now that machines have appeared in every factory and office, depot and terminal.

I once lost an entire dollar to a dollar-changing machine. I gave it five kicks, and even that wasn't enough. For a dollar, I should have broken a chair over its intake slot.

If everyone in the country is taken for a dollar, as I suspect we all will be eventually, that's $200 million. The empty cup is a giant industry.

Putting up a note, as many people do, saying, "This machine owes me a dime," does little good. The men who service them always arrive before you get to work, or after you leave. They are ashamed to face the people they cheat.

You can put up a note saying, "Out of Coffee," which saves others from losing their dimes. But that doesn't get your dime back.

The answer is to kick and punch them. If you are old, lame, or female, bring a hammer to work with you, or an ax.

I feel better, having got this off my chest. But my foot still hurts.

WOODCHUCKS IN DEATH AND LIFE

Joseph Farkas / One Small Life

The New York Times, September 16, 1972

From its beginning in 1851, The New York Times *has been noted for its well balanced, well edited local, national, and world news coverage. Modeled on the* London Times *rather than on the American papers of the period,* The New York Times *took strong editorial positions and did not shy away from controversy.*

The following article by Joseph Farkas, chief historian for the U.S. Army Munitions Command, caused something of a stir; not the kind of controversy that

results in litigation, legislation, or lots of front-page news, but the kind that
occurs when a number of readers have a deep emotional response to what they
find in their morning paper.

We have inserted after Farkas' essay the selection from Thoreau's Journals that
serves as the background to this op-ed piece. Letters to the editor of The New
York Times *in response to Farkas begin on page 187. Following the letters from*
readers are a letter from Farkas and an excerpt from Thoreau. Both are on the
subject of "Woodchucks in Death and Life," which The New York Times *pub-*
lished as a conclusion to the controversy.

MAPLEWOOD, N. J.—After a period of sweltering weather, a bright cool August
day dawned over Concord, Mass., in 1853, and Henry Thoreau, who had planned
to sit and write in the house all day, decided that it was wiser to spend such a day
outdoors. He went for a sail on the Sudbury River with his friend, William Ellery
Channing. He later memorialized this glorious day in his journal.

After the recent extended hot spell, Aug. 10 similarly arrived in New Jersey as
the first bright day of fall. When I left my desk for a brief outdoor walk I noticed a
woodchuck scuttling across the broad lawn in front of my building. When he stopped, with his back toward me, I decided on impulse to see how close I could get
to him before he became aware of me and scurried away. I walked quickly toward
him until I was about six feet away and stopped. I was surprised that he hadn't detected me, but I soon saw why. He lay there with his head stretched out on the
lawn and his eyes closed. He had obviously settled down for a snooze on the sun-
warmed grass.

I stood there for about a minute before he suddenly raised his head and looked
around at me. After contemplating me over his shoulder awhile, he turned around
to face me. Then he sat up on his haunches, as though to get a better view of me.

After we had faced each other for a while, I swayed to left and right to see what
effect such movement would have on him. He dropped to all fours, lowered his
head, and hissed. His defensive posture indicated a readiness to fight rather than
run. I moved back a few paces and then circled in back of him. He turned his head
to keep me in view but did not move his body.

As I went back to the sidewalk from which I had started my confrontation I saw
a small open truck in the cab of which were three workmen who had been watching the woodchuck and me. When I got alongside the truck one of the men offered
to give me a club to attack the woodchuck. When I asked why I should do that, he
said woodchucks were becoming too numerous and causing too much damage.
They dug up lawns and ate shrubbery.

I said it would nevertheless be nice to leave the woodchuck alone, and walked
away. But then I looked back and saw the man who had offered me the club walking toward the woodchuck with a four-foot metal pipe in his hand. Sensing what
was coming, my first impulse was to turn my back on the scene and continue
walking. But I couldn't. I watched the man get to about ten or twelve feet from
the victim and stop. He waved the pipe but the woodchuck didn't move. Then the
man inexplicably turned around, walked back, and got into the truck, which drove
away.

I walked on, but before returning to my office I decided to have another look at
my friend the woodchuck. He was still on the lawn. While I was about 200 feet
away from him I saw a figure approaching him. It was the man from the truck,
this time carrying a long-handled pitchfork. The truck was at the curb.

The man walked slowly toward the woodchuck. When he was about ten feet away, the woodchuck started running. The man pursued him. The woodchuck reached a small pine whose branches grew down to the ground and he ducked into it.

The man stalked around the pine, his pitchfork at the ready. Several times he lunged forward but apparently missed his prey. But then he was suddenly pushing hard on the pitchfork, his body bent forward.

After holding this position for perhaps half a minute, he let up. But the job was not yet done. He ran around to the other side of the tree and began jabbing again. Then once more he leaned hard on the pitchfork and held his position. When he straightened up I caught a glimpse of a bloody mass writhing at the end of the pine.

The man called to the truck for a shovel. The man from the truck came, not with a shovel but holding a metal pipe. He whacked the woodchuck several times, delivering the *coup de grace*. Then the man with the pitchfork impaled the woodchuck on its tines, held it aloft as he walked back to the truck, and threw it into the back of the truck. The truck drove slowly off.

After dinner I went out to my tree-encircled back yard to savor what was left of this sparkling day. I sat there watching the sunlight playing through the top of the big maple. The sky was cloudless. A helicopter chugged through in one direction and a high-flying airliner passed in another.

After sitting awhile, I reread a section of Thoreau's journal describing his encounter with a woodchuck in the spring of 1852. Although I hadn't realized it at the moment I began the episode with my woodchuck, it was residual memory of Thoreau's woodchuck account that had obviously triggered my own adventure.

Thoreau describes how he came across the woodchuck in the middle of a field, pursued it, and then sat down three feet from it when it stopped. It trembled and gritted its teeth. He touched its snout with a twig and it bit the stick. They sat looking at each other for half an hour. Thoreau talked to it in what he called forest baby talk and soothed it enough to enable him to turn it over on its back and even put his hand on it briefly. He thought that if he had had the right food to offer it he could have tamed it completely. Thoreau said that he respected the woodchuck as one of the natives and thought he might learn some wisdom from him.

I also read the journal entry on the beautiful August day of 1853, a day affecting the spirits of men and worthy of a hymn. Thoreau regretted that so few enjoyed such a day. "What do the laborer ox and the laborer man care for the beautiful days? Will the haymaker when he comes home tonight know that this has been such a beautiful day?" Did the woodchuck executioners know when they got home that afternoon that it had been such a beautiful day?

Henry David Thoreau / From *The Journals of Henry David Thoreau*

1852

April 16 . . . As I turned round the corner of Hubbard's Grove, saw a woodchuck, the first of the season, in the middle of the field, six or seven rods from the fence which bounds the wood, and twenty rods distant. I ran along the fence and cut him off, or rather overtook him, though he started at the same time. When I was only a rod and a half off, he stopped, and I did the same; then he ran again, and I ran up within three feet of him, when he stopped again, the fence being between us. I squatted down and surveyed him at my leisure. His eyes were dull black and rather inobvious, with a faint chestnut iris, with but little expression and that more resignation than of anger. The general aspect was a coarse grayish brown, a sort of grisel. A lighter brown next the skin, then black or very dark brown and tipped with whitish rather loosely. The head between a squirrel and a bear, flat on the top and dark brown, and darker still or black on the tip of the nose. The whiskers black, two inches long. The ears very small and roundish, set far back and nearly buried in the fur. Black feet, with long and slender claws for digging. It appeared to tremble, or perchance shivered with cold. When I moved, it gritted its teeth quite loud, sometimes striking the under jaw against the other chatteringly, sometimes grinding one jaw on the other, yet as if more from instinct than anger. Whichever way I turned, that way it headed. I took a twig a foot long and touched its snout, at which it started forward and bit the stick, lessening the distance between us to two feet, and still held all the ground it gained. I played with it tenderly awhile with the stick, trying to open its gritting jaw. Ever its long incisors, two above and two below, were presented. But I thought it would go to sleep if I stayed long enough. It did not sit upright as sometimes, but *standing* on its fore feet with its head down, i.e. half sitting, half standing. We sat looking at one another about half an hour, till we began to feel mesmeric influences. When I was tired, I moved away, wishing to see him run, but I could not start him. He would not stir as long as I was looking at him or could see him. I walked round him; he turned as fast and fronted me still. I sat down by his side within a foot. I talked to him *quasi* forest lingo, baby-talk, at any rate in a conciliatory tone, and thought that I had some influence on him. He gritted his teeth less. I chewed checkerberry leaves and presented them to his nose at last without a grit; though I saw that by so much gritting of the teeth he had worn them rapidly and they were covered with fine white powder, which, if you measured it thus, would have made his anger terrible. He did not mind any noise I might make. With a little stick I lifted one of his paws to examine it, and held it up at pleasure. I turned him over to see what color he was beneath (darker or more purely brown), though he turned himself back again sooner than I could have wished. His tail was also all brown, though not very dark, rat-tail like, with loose hairs standing out on all sides like a caterpillar brush. He had a rather mild look. I spoke kindly to him. I reached checkerberry leaves to his mouth. I stretched my hands over him, though he turned up his head and still gritted a little. I laid my hand on him, but immediately took it off again, instinct not being wholly overcome. If I had had a few fresh bean leaves, thus in advance of the season, I am sure I should have tamed him completely. It was a frizzly tail. His is a humble, terrestrial color like a partridge's, well concealed where dead wiry grass rises above darker brown or chestnut dead leaves—a modest color. If I had had some food, I should have ended with stroking him at my leisure. Could easily have wrapped him in my handkerchief. He was not fat nor particularly lean. I finally had to leave him without seeing him move from the place. A large, clumsy burrowing squirrel. *Arctomys*, bearmouse. I respect him as one of the natives. He lies there, by his color and habits so naturalized amid the dry leaves, the withered grass, and the bushes. A sound nap, too, he has enjoyed in his native fields, the past winter. I think I might learn some wisdom of him. His ancestors have lived here longer than mine. He is more thoroughly acclimated and naturalized than I. Bean leaves the red man raised for him, but he can do without them.

Letters / And What Would Henry Thoreau Have Thought?

The New York Times, September 1972

To the Editor:

It struck me while reading Joseph Farkas' "One Small Life" [Op-Ed, Aug. 29] that Thoreau would never have stood around and allowed another man to kill a wood chuck 200 feet away from him.

Linda Clarke
New York City

•

To the Editor:

The account of the killing of the woodchuck and the earlier account of the poodle standing guard over his collie friend killed on the highway [Op-Ed, July 11] are sad commentaries on man's destructiveness. But implicit in both stories is an increasingly frequent, linked observation: the passivity in the face of violence of men of better instincts. Could not Mr. Farkas have done more than just watch the pitchforking of the woodchuck?

Jo Coudert
New York City

•

To the Editor:

It is quite apparent Mr. Farkas was not brought up on a farm else he would know that the woodchuck is a rodent capable of much damage to crops.

In my vegetable garden a woodchuck has just destroyed seven out of twelve large cabbage plants and has ruined two rows of Swiss Chard.

I am glad to report the villain has been trapped and his remains put to rest without benefit of clergy.

V. R. Blair
White Plains, N.Y.

•

To the Editor:

Little moments, at times, are beyond themselves, and can be lifetimes in miniature. Joseph Farkas called the woodchuck his friend and yet watched the man destroy him. How could he?

Morton Mecklosky
Stony Brook, N.Y.

•

To the Editor:

I would certainly distinguish between woodchucks and human beings, yet I wonder why Mr. Farkas when in no real danger himself would not act to save the woodchuck. I doubt we could count on him when there might be real danger to his own life to resist a wrong to another human being. The point is not whether woodchucks are good or bad animals, nor that those men chose to kill the animal.

The point is that Mr. Farkas chose not to act but to watch, record what he saw, and no doubt receive a fat fee from The New York Times for his trouble.

The Mylai massacre mentality is not confined to a distant tiny war-torn land; it lives among us. Does the chief historian of the U.S. Army Munitions Command record the despicable results of our munitions in Vietnam with equal lack of involvement?

And he dare speak the name Thoreau in the same breath.

Richard Steinberger
Princeton, N.J.

•

To the Editor:

At the end of the article, Mr. Farkas wonders if the woodchuck's murderers truly appreciated the beauty of the day. I would wonder if Farkas ever questioned his moral responsibility in this matter. Surely Thoreau, whom the author apparently admires, would have acted differently. Assuming that he wanted to avoid a physical confrontation, could not Farkas have been more forceful in his verbal exchange with the workmen? At the very least, he could have chased the animal while the men were choosing their respective weapons.

One cannot help feeling that the author had decided early on to abandon the woodchuck to its fate and to record this event for posterity. To what end?

Judith Zinn
Hempstead, N.Y.

•

To the Editor:

What man would not at least have frightened the animal away with a sound—a stone—something that would have given the animal a chance against the executioner?

Mary F. Peo
Short Hills, N.J.

•

To the Editor:

I sat for a long time mulling over this story of brutality to a small creature and wondering what prompted Mr. Farkas to write it.

Was it, perhaps, an attempt to expiate his sin of omission in not intervening in the woodchuck's behalf, or was he merely recording an event while accepting the right of men to destroy creatures whose habits they do not understand or whose existence inconveniences them slightly?

I noticed that Mr. Farkas is connected with the U.S. Army, which turned my thoughts to Vietnam. I think about Vietnam quite a lot during this period of intensive bombing, and I wondered if he might have intended to produce a parable of our involvement there, in order to make more real the cruelty of a few men destroying living beings while our nation stands by and quietly observes.

If that was his intent I wish him success and a wide audience.

Mary Specht
Huntingdon Valley, Pa.

•

I plead guilty to having stood idly by while a woodchuck was being pitchforked to death. I plead guilty to having done nothing to prevent the killing of over a million people in Vietnam. I plead guilty to countless sins of omission in failing to do anything to correct the injustices, the ugliness, the horrors of the life around us. I respect all those who have actively taken arms against a sea of troubles and attempted, by opposing, to end them. But to the millions who—like me—have out of inertia, cowardice, selfishness, or ignorance given silent assent (or even active support) to the perpetration of evil, I say: Let him who is without sin cast the first stone.

Joseph Farkas
Maplewood, N.J., 1972

As I came home through the woods with my string of fish, trailing my pole, it being now quite dark, I caught a glimpse of a woodchuck stealing across my path, and felt a strange thrill of savage delight, and was strongly tempted to seize and devour him raw; not that I was hungry then, except for that wildness which he represented. Once or twice, however, while I lived at the pond, I found myself ranging the woods, like a half-starved hound, with a strange abandonment, seeking some kind of venison which I might devour, and no morsel could have been too savage for me. The wildest scenes had become unaccountably familiar. I found in myself, and still find, an instinct toward a higher, or, as it is named, spiritual life, as do most men, and another toward a primitive rank and savage one, and I reverence them both.

Henry David Thoreau
Walden, Concord, Mass., 1854

HUMAN-INTEREST STORIES

In the 1870s the New York Sun *named, and afterwards filled the blank spaces in its galleys with, "human-interest" stories: brief articles interesting for the indirect comment they seemed to carry about human nature, rather than for the importance of the event or people involved. Since that time, human-interest stories, or "fillers" as they are sometimes called, have become a staple of newspaper fare. Frequently, the disproportionately long title of these snippets tells the whole story, but in a way that entices one to read on because of its quirkiness or apparent absurdity: "G.S.A. Challenged for Removing Plaque Honoring 1874 Cannibal," or "Jilted Californian Accountant Sues His Date for $38 in Expenses."*

The four stories to follow constitute a small sampler of the human-interest story in journalism.

The New York Times Staff / Smuggling of Drugs in False Legs Laid to Two Colombians

The New York Times, April 4, 1973

Two Colombians hobbled into Federal Court in Brooklyn on crutches yesterday, each with a leg missing and each charged with smuggling cocaine and marijuana stored in the hollowed-out parts of their confiscated artificial limbs.

A third suspect, a Colombian woman, was also accused of taking part in the smuggling of $1-million worth of cocaine from Bogotá to Kennedy International Airport.

Acting on confidential information, customs agents took the three into custody Monday night. They also arrested a fourth member of the group on charges of carrying a false passport.

The agents took one of the suspects, William Ochoa, 25 years old, to St. Vincent's Hospital in Manhattan, where physicians removed his plastic leg. Inside, they said, they found one kilo (2.2 pounds) of cocaine wrapped in plastic bags. The suspect told them he had lost his leg during a guerrilla uprising in Colombia two years ago.

Agents said they found six ounces of marijuana in the artificial right limb worn by Jaime Zapata-Reyes, another suspect.

The woman, identified as Mrs. Lenore Jaramillo, 34, was allegedly found to be wearing three girdles, each concealing quantities of plastic-wrapped cocaine totaling one kilo. Agents reported that each suspect had more than $400 and return tickets to Bogotá.

United States Magistrate Vincent A. Catoggio held each in $100,000 bail. Expressing concern over the missing artificial limbs, which had been described as damaged, he directed that customs agents return them in good condition.

The third man was identified as Oloniel Pineda, 36, who was arrested on charges of carrying a false passport. His arraignment was deferred.

United Press International Staff / Woman Says Husband Divided House Literally
August 4, 1976

CARTERET, N.J., Aug. 4 (UPI)—A woman who is suing her husband for divorce has filed a second suit charging that he went too far in dividing their property equally—he allegedly cut their $80,000 home in half with a chain saw.

Eugene Schneider of Carteret, N.J., has been ordered to appear in court Sept. 15 to answer a suit by his wife of 23 years, Phoebe, who is charging him with maliciously damaging their home last July 23.

The action apparently was Mr. Schneider's response to New Jersey divorce laws, which require equal division of all property between spouses.

Edward J. Dolan, the attorney for Mrs. Schneider, said her husband had used a chain saw to cut through the exterior walls, roof and many of the house's support beams.

The three-family home, which was built by Mr. Schneider has been declared unfit for living by the local housing and health inspectors.

Seth S. King / G.S.A. Challenged for Removing Plaque Honoring 1874 Cannibal
The New York Times, August 10, 1977

WASHINGTON, Aug. 9—Bob Bergland, the Secretary of Agriculture, demanded today to know what legal justification the General Services Administration had for removing the dedication plaque from the department's grill, newly named in honor of Alfred Packer, who was convicted of killing and eating five Colorado prospectors in 1874.

Secretary Bergland announced last week that the dining facility was being named in honor of the early Colorado pioneer and mountain guide because his life "exemplifies the spirit and the fare of this Agriculture Department cafeteria."

Yesterday, however, it was discovered that the plaque, mounted at the grill's entrance just beneath the department's seal, had been removed.

Later, it was found that the plaque had been removed at the direction of Melvin Schick, the G.S.A.'s building manager at the Department of Agriculture, who said he had taken it down because he feared it was "in bad taste."

A BIPARTISAN GESTURE

Mr. Bergland insisted that the decision to name the grill in honor of the 19th-century pioneer was a bipartisan gesture.

Packer was convicted of slaying and devouring the five prospectors, whom he was guiding over a high plateau in Hinsdale County in southwestern Colorado.

In sentencing him, Mr. Bergland said, the judge declared: "There was only six Democrats in all of Hinsdale County and you ate five of them. I sentence you to hang—as a warning against further reducing the Democratic population of this county."

Before he could be executed, leaders in Colorado won parole for him.

"The fact that Packer is considered anti-Democratic in some circles obviously did not enter into his choice for this honor," said Mr. Bergland, a former Democratic Representative from Minnesota.

A FOLK HERO IN COLORADO

The Secretary said Packer became something of a folk hero to the people of Colorado, and, after winning parole, lived quietly in the Denver suburb of Littleton.

"It is said that he was much beloved by the children of Littleton, to whom he distributed candy," the Agriculture Secretary added.

Mr. Schick could not be reached for comment. But an official in the Department of Agriculture said Mr. Schick had insisted he was responsible for maintaining a minimum amount of decency in Federal buildings, and was forced to remove the plaque to do this.

When word of the plaque's removal reached Mr. Bergland, who was touring farms in Iowa today, he immediately sent word to Mr. Schick demanding an explanation for his action.

He also sent a message to Joel Solomon, director of the G.S.A., noting the widespread public approval he said the plaque had received and expressing regret for any embarrassment the action might cause Mr. Solomon.

The plaque has since been returned to Stanley D. Weston, the Agriculture Department's deputy director for public affairs, who was one of the three judges who chose Packer as the person to be honored. Mr. Weston also contributed to the cost of the plaque.

"It was a terrible thing," Mr. Weston said. "It was clearly a confiscation of private property."

A legal ruling will be sought on the dispute, an official in the Department of Agriculture said, if a judge can be found to hear the matter.

"Our research of the law governing the display of plaques in public buildings shows that no part of their installation, maintenance or removal may be at government expense," the official said. "The G.S.A. clearly violated the law in taking it down. But we will await the judge's ruling before putting it back up."

DIRECTOR DEFENDS NAME

The Alfred Packer Grill at the University of Colorado at Boulder has borne its name proudly for nearly 10 years, James Schafer, director of the university's Memorial Center, said yesterday. "We've been doing real well," he added.

"Some students felt the food wasn't up to par and that the name was therefore appropriate," Mr. Schafer said. But he reported that things had improved and that the grill now served 7,500 meals a day, including Packerburgers and Packer-snackers, or hero sandwiches, without hearing any complaints about the association with one of the more notorious persons in Colorado's history.

Mr. Schafer said the Packer legend was part of the state's lore and that the university's students even had an Alfred Packer Day in the spring, featuring books, pictures and even a ballad written about Packer and his times. "We've taken the name and played up on it to get across the historical significance not only of Alfred Packer but also of the state of Colorado," he said.

Les Ledbetter / Jilted California Accountant Sues His Date for $38 in Expenses

The New York Times, July 26, 1978

SAN FRANCISCO, July 25—Tom Horsley had his day in court here last night, trying to force Alyn Chesslet to pay for his time and expenses incurred for a date she did not keep early this year.

A large, red cardboard heart with a symbolic writ at the top was the first thing Mr. Horsley presented to Judge Richard P. Figone in small claims court.

"I'd like to present this as Exhibit A," he said.

The judge grimaced. Those in the courtroom at city hall giggled.

Judge Figone told Mr. Horsley to sit down and state his complaint.

Mr. Horsley said that he sued for $32, later amended to $38 because he felt that Miss Chesslet had failed to make "a good faith effort" to inform him that she was canceling the date for dinner and the theater before he drove to San Francisco from San Jose, 50 miles to the south.

He said that her attempt to call him at work on the afternoon of the date was insufficient since "my service has explicit orders not to accept collect calls." She had two weeks to call him at the office before the date, he said, and could have expected him to leave early on the day of the date.

He then explained that his computation of his costs included 15 cents a mile for the 100-mile round trip, which was later raised to 17 cents a mile when the Internal Revenue Service increased its allowances. Other costs, he said, were two hours at "my minimum rate of $8.50 an hour" as an accountant and court costs.

Then Mr. Horsley presented as Exhibit B a letter from a lawyer explaining the legal grounds for the suit.

"I hope somebody has some legal basis for this," Judge Figone said.

Miss Chesslet told the judge that she canceled the date at the last minute because she had to work an extra shift at Ron Fine's Vesuvio Cafe in North Beach.

"It was not that I was unwilling," she said. "I was unable to keep the date. I tried to call him, but he wasn't in his office."

"Your honor, I object," Mr. Horsley said.

Judge Figone told Mr. Horsley to sit down and keep quiet.

When Miss Chesslet said that Mr. Horsley had been abusive on the night of the broken date and had harassed her later, the accountant again objected. He was again told to sit down and keep quiet.

Afterward, Mr. Horsley said that his cardboard heart was an attempt at levity by "handing the judge my broken heart."

But he insisted that he was serious about his suit against the woman who was his first girl friend more than 13 years ago because "there's too much of this thing, broken dates."

"It shows people are not sincere," he added.

Judge Figone reserved judgment for a later date.

Dennis Farney / Trying To Restore a Sea of Grass

The Wall Street Journal, June 6, 1975

The Wall Street Journal, *the most prestigious business and financial newspaper in the world, was started by an enterprising young stock-market reporter, Charles H. Dow, in 1889. Over the years, the paper has enlarged its concept of business news to include a daily quotient of social and cultural phenomena sometimes only peripherally related to the American economy.*

Dennis Farney's article about efforts to save and restore the midwestern prairies represents the kind of feature included within The Wall Street Journal's *expanded notion of a business paper.*

ALMA, KAN.—Wildflowers and grass, rippling in the wind; a landscape in motion beneath the wide midwestern sky.

That is late spring on the prairie. It is a placid time of meadowlarks singing from sun-splashed hillsides and cattle lowing in a gathering dusk. The prairie then is a gentle landscape, a world of low green hills and little wooded valleys that rolls away toward a far-off horizon.

It seems an unlikely place for anything of significance to be happening. Yet a quiet development hereabouts may tell something about the changing mood of the nation.

People are finally coming to value what Walt Whitman once called "North America's characteristic landscape," the American prairie.

Some think this is a reflection of a deep-felt national anxiety about the dizzying pace of social change in the last decade and a half, a yearning for simple, enduring things. Others think it's just an indication that the environmental movement has matured enough to appreciate unspectacular landscapes as well as spectacular ones. Whatever the reason, there is a growing appreciation for the landscape regarded through most of U.S. history as good only for plowing up or mowing down.

Here in the Kansas Flint Hills, a 50-mile-wide band that runs north-south across the state, environmentalists are struggling to establish a Tallgrass Prairie National Park. It would preserve the kind of prairie the homesteaders crossed and conquered, a sea of grass up to nine feet tall, with a root system so matted that it broke the pioneer plows.

Other types of prairie, which have shorter grasses, still survive in large tracts in the dryer parts of the Great Plains. But the tallgrass prairie, which once occupied more humid country from western Ohio to eastern Kansas, has long since vanished beneath the plow. It has become the Corn Belt—except for here, where it's protected by a topsoil too thin to plow.

It is a widespread misconception that prairies are always flat; most of them have a pitch and roll. Another misconception is that they are monotonous landscapes of grass and only grass. A virgin prairie sparkles with the color of from 200 to 300 kinds of wildflowers from April to October. But above all else, a prairie is an utterly open landscape, a place of lonely windmills turning in a ceaseless wind, of redtailed hawks circling in an empty sky, of endless distances receding toward infinity.

This openness tends either to invigorate people or to terrify them. "Between that earth and that sky, I felt erased, blotted out," Willa Cather wrote in *My Antonia,* her classic novel on the settlement of the prairie. All through such prairie novels, and the letters and diaries of the early sod-busters, there is an eerie ambivalence: the prairie will enchant you with its solitude and its serenity—if it doesn't devour you with its loneliness, its enervating winds, its blizzards and its broiling sun.

Perhaps it is only now, after the prairie has been conquered by the plow, the air conditioner and the interstate highway, that men can safely appreciate its harsh and sharp-edged beauty. Perhaps that is the reason a new movement of sorts has sprung up in recent years, waxing strongest in those states like Illinois and Iowa where the prairie has all but disappeared. It is the prairie restoration movement, composed of a diverse assemblage of people who are trying, with seeds and infinite patience, to recreate—from plowed ground—a semblance of the virgin prairie.

It is no hobby for those who like their payoffs quick and their results guaranteed. The native prairie grasses are difficult to reestablish and many of the wildflowers are next to impossible. Some scientists estimate it may be possible to create a pretty good facsimile of the original prairie in 300 years. Others think 500 years. It's an inexact science.

And yet the prairie restoration movement continues to grow. Practically every college and university in the Midwest seems to have its own little plot of restored prairie now. More surprisingly, a growing collection of individuals are toiling in prairie plantations—everybody from academic types to retired farmers, from little old ladies to Madison Avenue admen.

Maybe all this is part of a broader phenomenon, being one of many ways that Americans are trying to ward off future shock. This, at least is the suspicion of one man who is as much an authority on the subject as anybody.

"People long for something that will give them a sense of security and continuity and permanence," ventures Jim Wilson, a sort of philosopher-activist in the prairie restoration movement. He is an ex-saxophone player, ex-explorer (by motorcycle) of the sub-Sahara region, ex-English professor, ex-farmer and now, late in a life well-spent, a writer and seller of grass and wildflower seeds in Polk, Neb.

For years Jim Wilson and his wife Alice have been selling prairie grass seed to ranchers and farmers, who have been planting it for the usual utilitarian reasons. In recent years, though, they've been flooded with orders from a new kind of customer—people who seem to be planting prairie grass and wildflowers just for the innate rightness of it. "They think in poetry," explains Jim Wilson, "whereas the agricultural people think in prose."

All those prairie restorations may or may not endure for the 300 years, or 500 years, necessary before nature slowly shapes them into something approaching the prairie that Willa Cather knew. And the proposed Tallgrass Prairie National Park for the Flint Hills of Kansas may or may not make it through the congressional labyrinth. It's snagged right now, as usually happens with national park proposals before they ultimately pass.

But something subtle does seem to be happening in lots of unheralded ways and places, all across the country. It may be no coincidence that in city after city the rush is on to restore old houses and warehouses instead of tearing them down; that handicrafts are more than ever in vogue; that for the first time in decades, there is a modest movement from the cities to the small towns and countryside.

People seem to be searching for authentic, enduring things. They seem to want to do things for themselves. They seem to believe that if the world has fragmented into countless problems, people, acting individually and together in countless small ways, may yet be able to knit it back together again.

No doubt it would be a mistake to read too much into these quiet and ephemeral developments having to do with Mason jars and prairie coneflowers. Yet they are hardly insignificant, or pessimistic, developments either. And, at a time when our political leaders seem increasingly befuddled and disheartened by events, they just may be a truer gauge of the national temper.

Art Buchwald / Unreality of TV   Ca. 1977

In college, Art Buchwald was the managing editor of Wampus, *the University of Southern California's humor magazine. He also wrote a regular column for that school's paper before leaving for Paris and parts unknown. When his money ran out, Buchwald began writing for the Paris edition of the* New York Herald-Tribune *and became a correspondent for* Variety *magazine. He observed the European scene for fourteen years before moving to Washington, D.C., in 1962 to write a syndicated newspaper column. Buchwald's incisive observations of contemporary politics and culture have earned him the reputation as the most influential wit in American journalism.*

Dr. Heinrich Applebaum recently completed a study on the effects of television on children. In his case, though, he wasn't concerned with violence, but how television gives children a false sense of reality.

Dr. Applebaum told me, "The greatest danger of television is that it presents a world to children that doesn't exist, and raises expectations that can never be fulfilled."

"I don't understand, Doctor," I said.

"Well, let me cite one example. Have you ever seen a television show where a person in an automobile doesn't immediately find a parking place on the very first try?"

"Come to think of it," I said, "I haven't."

"Not only is there always a parking spot available but the driver doesn't even have to back into it. There are *two* parking spaces available whenever someone in a TV show needs one. Children are being led to believe that when they grow up they will always be able to find a parking place when and where they want it. Can you imagine the trauma when they discover that in real life you can drive around a block for three hours and still not find a place to put your car?"

"I never thought of it but it's true. What else do they show on television which gives a distorted picture of the real world?"

"Have you noticed that whenever a character walks out of a restaurant or office building or apartment and says to the doorman, 'Get me a taxi,' the taxi immediately arrives? Millions of children are under the impression that all a doorman has to do is blow his whistle and a taxi will be there. I have never seen a show where the doorman has said, 'I'm sorry. I can't get you a taxi. You better take the bus.' "

"Of course," I said. "I never knew before what bothered me about those TV action programs, but now I do. There is always a yellow taxi waiting offscreen."

"Now," said Applebaum, "have you ever said to a taxi driver, 'Follow that car and don't lose him'?"

"Not really."

"Well, if you had, the driver would have told you to blow it out your ear. No taxi driver is in a mood to follow another car because that means he's going to get involved. But on TV every cabdriver looks as if he'd like nothing better to do than to drive 90 miles an hour through a rain-swept street trying to keep up with a carful of hoods. And the worst thing is that the kids believe it."

"What else have you discovered?"

"Kids have a perverted sense of what emergency wards of hospitals are really like. On TV shows they take a kid to an emergency ward and four doctors come rushing down to bandage his leg. In a real life situation the kid would be sitting on the bench for two hours before he even saw an intern. On TV there always happens to be a hospital bed available when a kid needs it. What the kids in this country don't know is that sometimes you have to wait three days to get a hospital bed and then you have to put a cash deposit of $500 down before they give it to you."

Applebaum said the cruelest hoax of all is when TV shows a lawyer defending someone innocent of a crime.

"On the screen the lawyer spends day and night digging up the evidence to clear his client. In real life the lawyer says to the defendant, 'Look, I've got 20 minutes. Tell me your story and then I'll plead you guilty and make a deal with the DA.' In real life the defendant might say, 'But I'm innocent.' The lawyer would say, 'So what? I can't afford to find that out. I'm not Perry Mason.' "

"Then what you're saying, Dr. Applebaum, is that it isn't the violence on TV but the fantasy that is doing harm to children."

"Exactly. Even the commercials are taking their toll. Children are led to believe that when they grow up if they use a certain mouthwash they'll find the mate of their dreams. When they don't find him or her after gargling all night, they go into a tailspin and many of them never come out of it."

"What do you think is the biggest fear little girls have?"

"I have no idea."

"That someday when they get married their husbands will have ring around the collar."

"What about boys?"

"Boys worry that they'll only go around once in life and they won't have all the gusto out of their beer that they deserve."

National Enquirer Staff / "Roots": Top Psychiatrists Explain Why It Was Most Popular TV Program of All Time

National Enquirer, February 22, 1977

> *The* National Enquirer, *with a circulation of over three million, is a weekly tabloid sold principally at supermarkets and newsstands. Specializing in what it calls "attention-grabbing" articles and photos, the paper often features celebrity profiles, scandals, the occult, medical "breakthroughs," curiosities, adventure tales, and, like the selection that follows, items offering some special angle on whatever happens to be in the news. The* National Enquirer's *"expert" analysis of the popularity of "Roots" (an excerpt from the book appears in Best Sellers), though fairly brief, received that particular week's typically spectacular front-page headline.*

Why was "Roots" the most popular TV program of all time?

According to top psychiatrists, these are the reasons:

Hope—it was a "black Cinderella story," and proved that even in the most desperate situation we should have hope.

Truth—the story was based on fact, and people have always had a deep curiosity about the lives of others.

Guilt—it helped relieve many of us of our guilt by helping us face the facts about slavery.

Escapism—at a time when the U.S. is in the grip of one of its worst winters, and many Americans are having problems, "Roots" pictured people who have it worse.

Hooray for America!—it appealed to the basic American spirit: the fight for personal freedom.

Family—it hammered home everyone's need for a return to close family ties.

History—in close, factual detail, it revealed a little-known and often suppressed side of America's past.

Triumph—it was about an underdog, and all Americans like to see a man who is down rise above his oppression.

Justice—it reflected every American's personal struggle to see that right and compassion prevail.

Entertainment—the program was well done, and good entertainment sadly is lacking on TV these days.

"The show appealed to the basic American spirit—no matter how much you hit me, no matter how many times you spit in my face, no matter how much you debase me, I'll fight back until I get what's rightfully mine," said Dr. Herbert Modlin, senior psychiatrist at the Menninger Foundation in Topeka, Kansas.

"There's nothing Americans love more than to witness a story in which the underdog becomes the winner. We're a nation of fighters. It's the spirit of America. Through fighting for our rights, we've become the greatest and freest nation on Earth.

"All Americans—black and white—could relate to the story of 'Roots' because our ancestors who settled in this country had to face similar fears and great hardships before achieving success and prosperity."

Added Dr. Gilbert R. Parks, a black staff psychiatrist at Topeka State Hospital in Kansas: "In one highly dramatic story, 'Roots' epitomized every American's fight for personal freedom and prosperity. That was its appeal.

"Even though the show highlighted one particular family's struggle for freedom, it was the story of everyone's fight—not only for freedom, but for prosperity and a higher standard of living."

"Roots" also forced all Americans to take a penetrating look at slavery—and thereby helped whites get rid of their burden of guilt, said Dr. James Comer, professor of psychiatry at Yale Child Study Center.

"Facing up to the true story of what happened during those slave years, helps people absolve some of their guilt about it," he declared.

"They've come to the point where they can say: 'Okay, our ancestors enslaved these people, but it turned out okay.' It was a terribly tragic story but it had a happy outcome, which relieves them tremendously.

"It's a firm psychiatric principle that to relieve one's self of guilt, you must face the facts, discuss what happens and then release it. 'Roots' did that for people regarding the slave experience."

Added Dr. Judd Marmor, professor of psychiatry at the University of Southern California:

"There seems to be a collective guilt in this country about the treatment of blacks . . . and in a way, people adopted this family as their own for one week, and were on their side.

"And not only did people feel for this family—it made them think. The story captured both their minds and their hearts, for it made people ask themselves questions like: 'What would I have done if I'd been living in those times? If I were white, would I be as ugly as the white depicted there? If I were a black husband, how would I react if my wife had to submit to sexual relations for me to survive?' "

The fact that the action in "Roots" centered around one close, loving family added immensely to its success, Dr. Modlin believes.

"Today, more than ever before, Americans need the feeling of security which comes from a close family unit," he said. "In 'Roots,' he witnessed a true story—a gripping story—of how a family stuck together despite adversity."

Dr. Parks, the great-great-grandson of an Alabama slave, agreed. "Every American longs for the type of close family ties which were highlighted in

'Roots,' " he said. "The fascination of watching one family united in its personal struggle against inhumanity was a major appeal of this movie."

The inspiring message offered by "Roots"—that we should have hope in even the most desperate situations—helped make it the most-watched TV show of all time, said Dr. Comer.

"It was a black Cinderella story—something we've never had before," he noted. "It proved that in he most desperate situations, we can have hope. Tragic as the story was, it still carried this uplifting message.

"It showed what a human being can do—he can go from slavery to freedom."

The show's appeal—130 million people, far more than half the U.S. population, saw all or a part of it, according to A. C. Nielsen Co.—was partly due to the fact that it was based on true incidents, added Dr. Comer.

"People are far more fascinated by a true story than by anything made up," he explained. "What people are really interested in is other people—how they live, what problems they face, how they suffer."

The "underdog" theme of the eight-part program, which drew a whopping 71 percent of the audience in its final night, also contributed to its spectacular success, Dr. Marmor told The Enquirer.

"Viewers across the country were rooting for these people, wanting them to get their freedom," he said. "People have always identified with the struggle of someone to be free; that's a universal theme duplicated in other long-lasting stories.

In addition, the show's phenomenal success was partly due to the fact that it "hit the current nostalgia interest, which could be described as a national effort to recapture the past," said Dr. John Spiegel, professor of social psychiatry at Brandeis University in Waltham, Mass.

"There's plenty of evidence people have developed a revived type of ethnic pride, in blacks as well as white ethnic groups," he said. "But it's more than saying: 'We're proud of who we are.' People are seeking their own roots, reviving cultural patterns their parents didn't pay much attention to."

Many Americans watched the show because it took their minds off their own problems—it gave them a form of escape, Dr. Spiegel believes.

" 'Roots' showed a family struggling to survive under the most adverse conditions, and people can identify with this," he said. "Most ordinary people can relate to another family with problems—they can put themselves in the family's shoes.

"The average American today has many problems—prices are going up, there's a continual threat of unemployment, there are fuel shortages, pollution and many pressures—and seeing this African family resist and survive made their own problems less significant.

"They could watch this show and say to themselves: 'Gee whiz, what am I complaining about?'

"Also, the show had all the elements of a good detective thriller . . . plenty of soap opera and sentimentality . . . plenty of sex and violence . . . tragedy and comedy following closely on each other's heels."

INCREDIBLE NUMBER OF PEOPLE WHO WATCHED

The estimated viewing audience for "Roots" started off at a whopping 64.8 million—and mushroomed. When the final episode ran on Sunday evening, January 30, there were nearly 82 million Americans tuned in according to the Nielsen ratings and ABC's own figures. And 130 million Americans saw at least some part of the show. Here are the number of people who watched each ''Roots'' installment:

Sunday, Jan. 23 (2 hrs.)	64,800,000
Monday, Jan. 24 (2 hrs.)	70,400,000
Tuesday, Jan. 25 (1 hr.)	71,700,000
Wednesday, Jan. 26 (1 hr.)	70,100,000
Thursday, Jan. 27 (1 hr.)	72,500,000
Friday, Jan. 28 (2 hrs.)	73,500,000
Saturday, Jan. 29 (1 hr.)	69,700,000
Sunday, Jan. 30 (2 hrs.)	81,800,000

Marise McDermott / Three Legs and a Hooey—City Kid Learns the Ropes

San Angelo *Standard-Times*, November 13, 1978

Marise McDermott was born in New York City in 1953, attended Washington University and Wells College, and graduated from Queens College of the City University of New York. She did graduate work in philosophy before joining the staff of the San Angelo Standard-Times, *where she now serves as editorial page director. As such, she is the youngest member of the newspaper's editorial board. In ''Three Legs and Hooey—City Kid Learns the Ropes,'' she recounts the personal adjustment required when the reverberations of street-life in New York yield to the down-home resonances of the frontier in a West Texas fairground.*

The San Angelo Standard-Times, *part of the Harte-Hanks Communication chain, is distributed in both morning and evening editions to 100,000 people in an area the size of Ohio. Now in its seventy-fifth year, this award-winning daily serves as the voice of agriculture and oil in West Texas.*

As I crept under the fence at the 25th annual Invitational Steer Roping at San Angelo Coliseum Fairgrounds arena, I looked up to see about 30 big-thighed roping cowboys staring at me.

''I'm from the Standard-Times,'' I offered meekly, not realizing that these cowboys were from around the nation and had no idea what I was mumbling. Behind me, a calf suddenly bolted from the pen and a horse broke the barrier behind him. The ground thundered, spit and landed somewhere in my hair.

I realized I was in the wrong place.

I sneaked down the arena and sat amidst a dozen old cowboys nodding and telling each other which young boy was the ''best of his generation.'' Cowchips had already taken over the bottom part of my clothes.

Again, a calf bolted from the pen with a cowboy behind him ready to rope. He threw the rope, bounced off his horse, wrapped the calve's legs and raised his arms.

It was the first calf roping of my life. Living on the streets of New York City, the closest I ever came to a roped calf was on a movie screen. But today, before me, was a calf with its tongue stretched out to scream, a cowboy calmly climbing his horse after roping it in 10 seconds and people on the sidelines yippin', yellin', hootin' and howlin'.

I figured that he'd get points taken off for wrapping only three legs of the calf. Increduously, I asked some cowboys sitting on the ground next to me, "Well, why did he only wrap three legs?"

After several minutes of laughter all around, one of them said, "It's faster that way. It's hard enough to get three of them roped."

John Dublin of San Angelo and vice president of the SA&R asked. "Where are you from, anyway?"

"New York."

More laughter, a couple of "damn yankees," some comforting smiles and then those cowboys tried to teach me what a calf roping is all about.

It took awhile to become acclimated to the sound of tobacco juice as it streamed down beside me. In New York it's a $200 fine to spit anything in public. I kept expecting someone to be hauled off to the corner for a citation. But in Texas, it's a man's rite.

"Look," Dublin said, "It's three wraps and then a hooey."

"Umm—What's a hooey?"

"Well—it's a hitch. That cowboy had a loose hooey and the calf got up an walked away. You've got to have a good hitch."

Like a shot, my calf roping school was halted by all-around cowboy Ed Workman of Mineral Wells. He raced to the back of the arena, roped his calf, threw it on the ground, grappled with its stiffening legs, wrapped it, and threw his hands in the air. At the same time, his horse smoothly moved backward holding the rope taut around the calf's neck.

It was always a relief to see the calf bounce back to life and race away with its tail between its legs.

"What's the hardest part of roping?" I asked studiously. "Isn't a lot of it luck? Some of those calves just lay there and some kick like the devil."

"Hell, yes, some of it's luck," Dublin exclaimed. "You've got to have a calf that will lay down and cross his legs for you."

"That's where you lose most of the time," Dublin continued, pointing to the calf's legs, "You can ride that calf down to the back of the arena in two seconds, but if it won't cooperate on the ground you can lose 10 or 20 seconds. You've got to rope the calf when it's still stunned and before it's legs stiffen."

For me, the highlight of the roping was two world champion ropers, Tom Ferguson and Roy Cooper roping 12 calves. Ferguson alternated with Cooper to rope six calves and then about an hour later, Cooper alternated with Ferguson to rope six calves. Both cowboys would have the chance to wrestle with the same 12 calves and they could choose the order of the calves on the second run.

My sideline teachers taught me how to know the calves and discern which calf would be chosen first for the next run. They pointed to the leather guards on the horses ankles and explained that the horse will never stop again if he gets burned once—the guards protect it from the fast stops and biting rocks. They told me about good horse trainers and great ropers.

Pointing to Ferguson, Jim Corbell of Big Spring said, "Look at that man's thighs—you can tell he's a roper."

At the end of Ferguson's first run, Corbell looked at me with a twinkle in his eyes and said, "That man's just roped six calves in little over a minute. 64 seconds to be exact."

There was nothing else to say. It's an art. I sat in silence. I couldn't believe it. It's really an art.

On Sunday, the steers bolted from their pens and headed straight for my camera lens. The tremoring ground was the steer and the muscled Quarter Horses—not the reverberation of subways. But the cowboys rarely missed roping the steer's horns and once they were down and dragged along the dark soil, unlike the calves, they seemed reconciled to the ground. The art here is to fight their spirit and sheer strength—and pull them to the dirt.

It was one art with which I was content to remain a spectator.

DISCUSSION QUESTIONS

1. What does McDermott gain by making the fact that she is a New Yorker such a prominent part of her story? What does that tell you about who she imagines her audience to be?

2. Mike Gray (see Magazines) mentions the need for reporters covering the Three Mile Island accident to educate themselves quickly about the language and principles of nuclear fission. Compare the part that fact plays in his story with the part McDermott's education about roping plays in hers. How much do subject and purpose have to do with the difference? On what have you based your answer?

ON THE DEATH PENALTY

In the following four editorials from the Miami Herald, The New York Times, *the* Atlanta Constitution, *and the Milwaukee* Journal, *thoughtful men and women consider whether society should or should not impose the death penalty on its most violent criminals. The opinions vary, the arguments differ, but each editorial takes a public stand and defends it. Each responds to an event in Starke, Florida, that was about to happen or had just taken place: the execution on May 25, 1979, of John Spenkelink for murder. Following the editorials are two front-page stories that appeared in the Atlanta* Constitution *the day after the state of Florida executed Spenkelink. Bob Dart, a staff writer for the paper wrote one; Horace G. Davis, Jr., an editor for the Gainsville* Sun *and a witness at the execution, contributed the other as a special report.*

Public attention had been focused on capital punishment since 1977, when convicted murderer Gary Gilmore became the first person ever to be voluntarily executed in America. The "prolonged soul-searching and impassioned debate" engaged in by the editors of the Miami Herald *occurred in newspaper boardrooms throughout the nation as editors determined where their papers would stand on the issue of capital punishment.*

Capital punishment is not simply a matter of recent debate. Writing for the Brooklyn Eagle *in 1858, Walt Whitman addressed himself to the very "unsatisfactory state" of the law and the custom of dealing with capital offenders (see* Press, *page 102).*

An Editorial / Death Penalty Is Right

Miami Herald, May 23, 1979

When he signed death warrants for John Spenkelink and Willie Darden, Gov. Bob Graham fulfilled the most awesome responsibility that a state confers upon its governor. In years past, this newspaper would have said that he was wrong, that the concept of capital punishment was wrong. But today, after prolonged soul-searching and impassioned debate within our Editorial Board, we conclude that the governor was right.

Capital punishment is a question of conscience. No question pierces more thoroughly the heart of the relationship between the individual and the state. No question is as irresolvable by the usual means of proof, because the "proof" exists, finally, only in one's view of whether the state has the right to demand that those who commit heinous murder must forfeit their own lives.

To this question of conscience, which we have debated fully and fervidly, we must answer yes. The state *does* have the right—indeed, the duty—to say to the individual citizen on behalf of all other citizens: "When you murder with deliberation and malice, you shatter the bond that prevents society from becoming a jungle. And that is a trangression that society cannot condone or forgive."

Its opponents argue that capital punishment amounts to murder by the state. If one accepts that view, it therefore follows that the state, in exacting capital punishment, flouts the very sacredness of human life upon which Western civilization is premised.

We respect the wellspring of conscience from which that argument flows, but we cannot drink from it. That cup is tainted by a fundamental illogic. It cheats the victim, and weakens the civilizing bond of law, by implicitly stating that the victim's life is worth less than the life of his murderer.

Human life *is* sacred. And because it is, the society that truly values human life asserts that valuation by imposing on murderers the most extraordinary penalty possible: death. If respect for life and for society's reverence for life is to continue, the inevitability of society's maximum penalty must be clearly understood by all who would wantonly take the life of another.

That is not to say that we accept the theory that capital punishment deters heinous crime. We do not. The evidence of capital punishment's deterrent effect is tenuous at best. Moreover, the deterrence argument is both intellectually specious and irrelevant to the sole purpose of capital punishment.

If executing one murderer deters another murder, that effect is incidental. The state does not execute condemned murderers to make them object lessons for others. The state executes murderers because they have violated the cardinal rule that the people, through their Legislature and their courts, have decreed to be inviolable.

Opponents argue that capital punishment is inherently discriminatory because those condemned to death in the past were too often poor, too often black. That argument, to society's shame, is true—*as applied to the past.* But the conditions that obtained in the past, especially in the segrated South, no longer obtain. The U.S. Supreme Court rectified them in 1972 and 1976.

In those years the High Court struck down some states' death-penalty laws and upheld others' in decisions that imposed uniform standards on them all. No black man ever again will be sentenced to death by a Jim Crow judge upon conviction by a Jim Crow jury. Florida's law complies with the Supreme Court standards, which make death-penalty statutes as fair as any that man has devised.

The fundamental question, then, remains not whether capital punishment is a deterrent, not whether it is fair, but whether a civilized society can justify this ultimate sanction. And that question is, and always will be, answerable only in one's conscience.

Our answer, derived with great difficulty, comes from an institutional conscience cleared by the process of argument and thought. Our answer is yes.

An Editorial / Who Gets the Chair?

The New York Times, May 23, 1979

"There will be less brutality in our society if it is made clear we value human life." So said Governor Graham of Florida as he decreed that John Spenkelink, a drifter who murdered a fellow drifter, and Willie Jasper Darden Jr., who killed a merchant during a holdup, should be executed this morning.

Whether one or both in fact die, the Governor's dictum is not supportable. No one can say with certainty that killing deters killing. Even in symbolic terms, the Governor's words are a kind of gallows humor. What else can "less brutality" mean when used to describe the reactivation of the electric chair after a 15-year lapse? What else can "value human life" mean when a state with 132 people on Death Row, more than any other, starts to clear out the inventory? And as for "made clear," the only thing being clarified is that society values some lives more than others.

It would be easier to defend capital punishment if at least it were applied consistently—if the rich or the notable went to the chair. But that rarely happens, as is newly evident from the violence on the streets of San Francisco. A jury has found Dan White guilty only of manslaughter for gunning down a mayor and a city supervisor. Drifters, even those who get religion, get fried; former county officials, "filled with remorse," get seven years, eight months.

Why is there not more remorse about this "system" of capital punishment? One reason is that all its faces are hooded. There is a division of labor and no person or agency—be it prosecutor, jury, judge, governor, state, nation or hangman—need accept responsibility. And from all this diversity of laws, juries and defendants emerges a pattern of who among guilty murderers is condemned: they are all poor.

We abhor capital punishment because we believe it is wrong for the state so to take life; because it is applied capriciously even among the clearly guilty; because even juries make mistakes; and because we think that, far from deterring, it creates a tolerance for killing. But no argument against capital punishment is more damning than to find out who is condemned.

The way to value human life, Governor Graham, is to do so.

An Editorial / The Supreme Penalty

Atlanta *Constitution*, May 24, 1979

It is time to ask ourselves some hard questions about capital punishment. The first and hardest: do we really believe in it?

Public opinion polls show Americans have, in recent years, reversed a previous trend against capital punishment. Now they *say*, by a considerable margin, that they favor bringing back the electric chair, the gas chamber, the noose and the firing squad. The reason for that change of heart is easy to see. Crime is now one of the half dozen overriding problems in our society. The system protecting us against criminals hasn't been working well. A get tough philosophy always looks good at such times.

Yet the last three executions scheduled in this country have won 11th-hour stays. Two in Florida this week, another in Alabama last month. The only person legally executed in this country since the mid-1960s was Gary Gilmore, and he insisted on his own execution despite a last ditch effort that might have spared him.

Why weren't all the legal questions settled one way or the other long before the 11th hour in the cases of John Spenkelink, Willie Jasper Darden and John Lewis Evans? The questions in Spenkelink's case were whether he was adequately represented and whether state prosecutors acted improperly. There is something seriously wrong with an appeals system that overlooks such questions until a few hours before a man is to be executed.

The practical effect of the death verdict today is not the removal of the condemned criminal from this world but his prolonged torture. Even if our society firmly believes in capital punishment, no one will argue that torture, psychological or otherwise, should be part of the process. Spenkelink was originally scheduled to be executed in September 1977, but an appeal saved him three days before his date with the electric chair. And a classic case, of which our society surely cannot be proud, was that of Caryl Chessman who spent 12 years on death row before finally dying in the gas chamber.

Another disturbing factor is the media circus that now surrounds the condemned man every time an execution appears imminent. The demonstrators outside the Florida prison had a perfect right to be there. The media had a perfect right to cover the demonstrations. But a stay granted under these circumstances is at least open to the suspicion that other than purely legal questions were involved. Were the judges reacting to public pressure? Or did they perhaps act out of some deep personal conviction about capital punishment itself and not merely out of consideration of abstruse legal points?

In short, does our society have whatever it takes to restore the death penalty?

If this last question is a valid one, then what *does* it take? Moral courage? Discipline? A profound sense of justice? Or, perhaps, as some would contend, a simple desire for vengeance—a revision to the "eye-for-an-eye" concept of justice?

The fastidiousness our legal system now displays in capital cases may conceal doubts about the justice of the death penalty. Whether that is true or not, the reluctance to carry out capital sentences is certainly clear. How do we explain that reluctance?

Our Judeo-Christian ethical and moral tradition has always posed a question: is killing another person ever justified? The answer in the past has always been a fairly easy "yes." It is justified in war. In defense of home and family. In protecting society. Today that "yes" is not so easy. Maybe this means that our civilization has a more sophisticated sense of right and wrong—or maybe it means simply that we are morally confused. On such questions, individuals work out their own answers. But society as a whole remains uncertain.

In a new book, *For Capital Punishment*, political scientist Walter Berns argues persuasively that justice itself requires the death penalty. In spite of the arguments that it is cruel and unusual punishment, a throwback to primitive times, an offense against human dignity or a violation of human rights, most people stubbornly continue to believe in it. Most people, Berns insists, are right. He admits that arguments favoring capital punishment—arguments claiming that it deters other criminals, for example—are not proven. But society must demand that the criminal law "be made awesome, a continual reminder of the moral order by which alone we can live as human beings."

The recent Supreme Court decision upheld the death penalty on retributive grounds, Berns writes. "In doing so, it recognized, at least implicitly, that the American people are entitled *as a people* to demand that criminals be paid back, and that the worst of them be made to pay with their lives. In doing this, it gave them the means by which they might strengthen the law that makes them a people, and not a mere aggregation of selfish individuals."

Many of those who now favor the death penalty, including the U.S. Supreme Court itself, are deeply worried about the possibility of unjustly applying it. The court ruled out the death penalty for a few years on precisely those grounds. It was determined that, in practice, capital punishment was reserved for blacks and the poor, mostly. But there are other inequities inherent in the death penalty. Spenkelink was convicted of killing a traveling companion, a petty criminal like himself, in what Spenkelink claimed was a fight over a homosexual proposition. That was murder, and the sentence was death. In California a former city official shot and killed the mayor and another official. That turned out to be manslaughter—maximum penalty eight years, but probably less than five. These terms are, of course, defined in the law, and trials are held to decide whether they apply in specific cases. Still, jurors who are called upon to decide what was in the hearts of an accused man are no wiser than the rest of us. But even if they were the wisest people on the surface of the Earth would they be able to answer such a question with the certainty required in condemning a person to death?

An Editorial / With Blood on Its Hands

Milwaukee *Journal*, May 26, 1979

The clock has been turned back to a more barbarous time.

An American state, with the blessing of the nation's highest court, has deliberately taken the life of a man against his will. The ghastly act, if performed without official sanction, would be defined as cold blooded murder. Is the killing any less dreadful because society committed it collectively? Is the guilt less awful because it is shared? Did John Spenkelink's heinous crime require that the state, too, become a slayer?

We believe that the answer is no in each instance. Spenkelink is no less the victim of a killing than if he had been slain by a fellow criminal, and the taking of a guilty person's life is just as violent as the killing of an innocent. In short, capital punishment is too inhumane an act to have any place in a civilized society.

If a state needs to exact retribution for crimes, as we think it often must to vindicate the rule of law, imprisonment can serve the purpose. If crime is to be deterred, and we agree that it must, there are acceptable ways that do not necessitate official homicide.

The experience of Wisconsin, which decently abolished capital punishment 126 years ago, and of many other states has shown that the extreme penality isn't required in maintaining a system of law and order.

Yet a number of states, taking advantage of retrogressive Supreme Court decisions, are determined to bring back the era of executions. Hundreds of prisoners wait in death row cells.

And civilization weeps.

Horace G. Davis, Jr. / Execution Scene Stark; Death Is Undramatic

Atlanta *Constitution*, May 26, 1979

STARKE, FLA.—The time is 9:51 a.m. The place is a waiting room without the luxury of Muzak.

Or any luxury, for that matter. The room is austerely clinical, measuring 22 by 12 feet with tan walls, unappealing common kitchen tile on the floor, gray folding chairs.

But whoever arranged this waiting room has either a sense of humor or something special in mind. The chairs are arranged in four rows facing a plate glass window. On the other side of the window is a drawn Venetian blind.

Thirteen persons are seated on the front two rows and staring at the Venetian blind. Nine more file in to fill the third row. A huge man with a turned collar, The Rev. Tom Feamster, enters and remains standing in the fourth row. With him is a slight and bespectacled figure, Washington attorney David Kendall. He remains standing also. So do four men in khaki and four in mufti, obviously officials.

There are two doors—one to the corridor, thence to outside. The other is beside the plate glass and has 12 panes and is stenciled in paint with the number 47. When both doors close with finality, 32 persons are in that waiting room. One is a woman, a television reporter from Tampa.

The air is stuffy. Except for the odd seating, except for the snappy mufti, this could be a ghetto medical clinic. Feet shuffle, lips murmur, bodies squirm. It is a waiting room in use.

It is 9:57 a.m. Voices can be heard beyond the plate glass. Somebody jostles the Venetian blind. A man in uniform near the door with panes can view the proceedings. He looks, again and again, fascinated.

It is 9:59. A peculiar rhythmic drumming, more vibration than sound, like pounding on pipes, gently shakes the room.

It is 10:03 a.m. On the other side of the door with panes, hands tape paper over the glass. The waiting 32 shuffle, murmur, squirm.

When the Venetian blind is raised, John A. Spenkelink will be there. He will look peculiar, with shaven head, gone that shock of hair with the distinguishing white forelock swept back. He will be either standing, or sitting—but most probably sitting. He will say a few things about the unequal hand of justice. He will say a few kind things about his mom Lois who did not abandon him. He will thank the hulking Rev. Feamster, the same man who played football with Burt Reynolds at Florida State University and pulled a stint with the L.A. Rams.

He will be strapped into that sturdy three-legged oaken chair hewed with convict labor from the banks of the nearby river in 1924. His right ankle will be moistened and an electrode attached. His scalp will be moistened and a hood with electrode insert will be dropped over his face. He will be zapped with 2,500 volts and 20 amps, pulsating up and down for two minutes. He will be dead.

It is 10:11 a.m. The Venetian blind goes up.

What's this? Madame Tussaud's wax museum? A figure, and it could be John Spenkelink, is strapped bolt upright in Old Sparky only two, at the most three, feet beyond the glass. The figure is rigid, unable to move a fraction of an inch. A chin guard, maybe a football or medical jaw support, is firmly strapped around chin and mouth and seemingly cruelly fastening the head to the chairback. Perched on the head is the hood, brass nut protruding from the top, with the black face flap pulled up. The only flesh visible are the lower arms, a portion of the electrode-wrapped right leg, and four inches of face from nose to mid-forehead.

The scene is a tacky copy of Disney World's haunted mansion.

For maybe 30 seconds, this trussed and immobile figure stares into the waiting room. The eyes are wide open, they do not blink. They look neither calm nor terrified.

The figure shares the somewhat smaller room with seven men, not all readily visible. One carries a white towel, to clean up any mess? The top of the executioner's head is visible through a slit in an alcove wall. He is never identified and is getting $150 for this job. One of the men in a semi-circle around the trussed figure wears a large insulated glove. He reaches out with it and lowers the hood.

It is 10:12 a.m. There is a "thump." The waxen figure jerks, as if subjected to an explosive blast of compressed air. It does not thrash around. The right fist remains clinched. Indeed, if any motion is apparent at all in the next six minutes, it is the curved fingers of the left hand. The index finger is pointing at the chest. Is the waxen figure left-handed? Is it saying something?

The Rev. Feamster says something. He speaks loudly in that hushed room, with a voice that brooks no reply, apparently addressing the witnesses, one of them West Florida weekly newspaper publisher Tommy Green who has declared that usable organs should be removed before destruction in the drama. The Rev. Feamster says, "Gentlemen, I hope you pray in the name of God that this is just and merciful punishment, for our own souls' sake."

The convicts are drumming on the pipes again.

It is 10:14 a.m. The man with the glove unfastens the chest strap. An Oriental, supposedly the prison medical doctor, pops into view for the first time. He unbuttons the shirt of the trussed figure. He has problems loosening the undershirt from the trousers. He applies a stethoscope, murmurs something, steps back out of sight. The chest strap is left unfastened. Nothing else happens.

It is 10:16 a.m. The Oriental pops back into view, uses the stethoscope, murmurs something, steps back out of sight.

It is 10:18 a.m. The Oriental appears again, applies the stethoscope, feels the pulse, pulls back the hood slightly to examine the eyes. The jowls of the seated figure have a tinge of blue. The hands also are tinged. The Oriental nods.

The Venetian blind comes down.

Laying credence to averages, the Lord's laser struck down 5,200 Americans on Friday—all but 75 involuntarily. John Spenkelink was one of the involuntary ones.

He is different only because the laser was directed by the final early arbiter—the government—and done deliberately. He also is the first American executed involuntarily in 12 years. Waiting for their electrical trip in Florida are 131 others, one-fourth of all the condemned in the land.

He also had all the land offers—a jury trial, over five years' delay, four audiences with the U.S. Supreme Court, and a mass of tidy rule-setting paperwork in the Florida Capitol. The finest people did this to him and, in a fashion, the execution can be deemed a bequeath from Harvard. The governor who signed the warrant is a Harvard law graduate; the prison superintendent who performed so efficiently was trained at Harvard.

He had the best the state has to offer in a process which is amazingly sanitized, like the execution itself during the six-minute flash of the Venetian blind. All did their duty, and they did it well—but by shuffling and signing papers so no vote was openly taken, confronting no emotional outburst, sustaining no embarrassments. And they did it with the overwhelming approval of public sentiment, according to the Books of Gallup and Harris.

But the Rev. Feamster, the friend standing, at Spenkelink's request, in the rear of the clinical waiting room, was not reading Gallup and Harris during those six minutes. He was silently reading the fifth chapter of Matthew.

And nowhere better was contrasted the two intellectual strains underlying the raising and lowering of the Venetian blind. One is the ancient, harking back to Moses descending Mount Sinai with that terrible judgment, eye for eye, tooth for tooth, hand for hand, foot for foot, burning for burning, wound for wound, stripe for stripe. And the contrary theme, from a gentle figure also standing on a mount a thousand or two years later, declaring that the higher human achievement is overcoming the curse of vengeance—that, indeed, human perfection lies in extending mercy which others deny.

But the victor in that dispute is plain enough. Irritated with Spenkelink defense tactics back in 1973, the condemning Judge John Rudd said, "This court is not interested in philosophy."

Bob Dart / Witness Says Spenkelink Looked Scared

Atlanta *Constitution*, May 26, 1979

STARKE, FLA.—It was shortly after 10 a.m. Friday. The warden was called to the phone. "There are no more stays at this time," reported Florida Gov. Bob Graham. "May God be with us."

Minutes later, John Spenkelink became the first man to be executed against his will in the United States in more than a decade.

The Spenkelink deathwatch that had dragged on agonizingly for six years ended with a shocking suddenness.

Venetian blinds opened abruptly in a small room in the Florida State Prison near here, and Spenkelink, 30, could be seen through a small window. He was strapped tightly into Florida's electric chair.

"He looked at us and he looked terrified," said Kris Rebillot, one of nine reporters who witnessed the electrocution. "His eyes were opened wide. . . . He was absolutely immobile."

The haunting deep-set eyes, peering from beneath a leather deathcap, "looked to the left, looked to the right, then forward," said Wayne Ezell, another observer. "He never got too good a look at his witnesses."

There were no final words.

"In a matter of seconds, a flap was pulled down over his face," explained Miss Rebillot, a 28-year-old reporter for a Tampa television station.

"Almost immediately, moving unobserved in the background, one of two hooded figures in the tiny death chamber pulled a switch.

"There was no jerking and there was no smoke and there was no hollering and screaming," said official state witness Tommy Green. "We hardly knew when it happened. It looked like (his fist) tightened, but that may have been before the juice hit him. The man was dead within fractions of a second—it was over with."

"I don't think the man ever felt anything," said Ezell, a reporter for the Tallahassee Democrat.

But state Rep. Andy Johnson, another official witness and an outspoken opponent of capital punishment, disagreed. He said it was a terrible death.

"We saw a man sizzled today, sizzled again, then sizzled again," said the Jacksonville Democrat. "The man didn't die instantly."

The first surge of electricity hit Spenkelink at 10:12 a.m., the witness agreed, then two other surges followed and by 10:18, a doctor had declared him dead.

The execution was the first in the U.S. since Gary Gilmore died before a Utah firing squad in 1977. But Gilmore had demanded death. Spenkelink, a California prison escapee who was convicted of killing another drifter in a Tallahassee motel in 1973, fought death right down to the wire. The U.S. Supreme Court refused to grant his final request for a stay only minutes before he died Friday.

So Spenkelink was the first American inmate unwillingly executed since Louis Jose Monge was put to death on June 2, 1967, in Colorado.

With more than 500 inmates now on death row in the 32 states with capital punishment laws, some anti-execution activists predict a legal "bloodbath" during the next few years.

"We're at the beginning of the end," said Joe Ingle, director of the anti-execution Southern Coalition on Prisons and Jails. "I'm trying to prepare people for a decade of executions that may claim 1,000 lives."

Spenkelink's final countdown to death began at 11:40 p.m. Thursday when a three-judge panel of the Fifth Judicial Circuit in New Orleans lifted a stay of execution granted earlier by Judge Elbert Tuttle in Atlanta. The U.S. Supreme Court earlier Thursday voted down a separate attempt at delaying the execution.

Thus, the two legal roadblocks that kept Spenkelink from going to the electric chair at 7 a.m. Wednesday were removed. His lawyers began even more last ditch manuevering early Friday.

Meanwhile, Florida's death machinery was put in motion.

By custom, the state's executioners are anonymous, their identities known only to a few top officials. They are paid $150 plus expenses for their work. Prison officials did not explain why two hooded men were reported in the death chamber. However, there were originally two executions scheduled. Willie Darden, a convicted killer from Lakeland, was granted an indefinite stay on Tuesday. The executioner was told of the New Orleans court decision and prison officials early Friday began final preparations for the electrocution.

Spenkelink's family and close friends were summoned for a tearful, farewell "contact visit"—they were allowed to hug and touch. Lois Spenkelink, the condemned man's heavyset, white-haired mother; Carol Myers, his freckled sister; Tim Myers, his bearded brother-in-law; and Carolotta Key, his 44-year-old girlfriend, met together with Spenkelink from 3 a.m. to 5 a.m.

Then Mrs. Spenkelink, 67, sat with her only son for half an hour alone. Brief private visits with Mrs. Myers and Miss Key followed. Mrs. Myers would later complain that they were subjected to a humiliating "thorough search" by a male prison official before the visit was allowed.

After his family left, Spenkelink talked with the Rev. Tom Feamster, an Episcopal priest from nearby Keystone Heights, who had befriended the prematurely gray-haired killer.

"I gave John communion at 8 o'clock," Rev. Feamster said, adding that Spenkelink's last message was "man is what he chooses to be. He chooses that for himself."

Feamster said he watched the execution at Spenkelink's request.

"I witnessed it because John told me to witness it," he said after describing the procedure as barbaric.

"He said, 'If I can go through with it, you can, too.' "

Feamster said he left at 8:15 a.m. "so they could prepare him."

"He said he loved me. That's the last thing he said to me. And I said I loved him. We shook hands."

The death ritual then called for Spenkelink's head and right calf to be shaved, the special sponge, imported from Greece, was taken from the bucket of salt water where it had been soaking. It would be fitted into the death cap to help conduct the surge of electricity.

The final meal was foregone; Spenkelink ate no breakfast.

Wearing dark blue trousers and a white dress shirt, he was taken to the heavy oak electric chair and tightly strapped in. Prison Superintendent David Brierton had set the execution for 10 a.m.

But the appointed hour passed and Spenkelink still lived.

A prison spokesman said that executions traditionally are five to ten minutes late so that last-ditch appeals can be considered. The U.S. Supreme Court's final decision against Spenkelink was called to the prison at 9:55 a.m. A few minutes later, Brierton got the go-ahead from Graham.

Prison officials said Spenkelink was asked if he had any final words. He said "No."

He was bound in the chair at the chest, leg, stomach and chin, Miss Rebillot said. "It was quieter than I expected, less gruesome. Only his eyes got to me. I was scared, but I tried to remember as much as I could."

It was a cold, impersonal atmosphere, she said. "It was done in such a way that it was as antiseptic as possible. One of his hands made a fist, the other was drawn up like a claw. He couldn't have slumped if he had wanted to. After the first surge, there was no movement.''

H. G. "Buddy" Davis, an editorial writer for the Gainesville Sun, who witnessed the electrocution, said he never even conceived the still figure trussed up in the chair as a human. "And I'm sure that was deliberate.

"The blinds went up and we saw this wax-like figure . . . I thought he would at least say something. It was like a waxworks. . . . Just this thing sitting there."

It ended, he recalled, with the still figure's index finger on his left hand "pointing toward his heart."

State Rep. Tom Woodruff another official witness, was reluctant to discuss details of the electrocution, saying only that it was "not inhumane."

"There was a wisp of steam from the sponge . . ." he said. "That's all I saw."

DISCUSSION QUESTIONS

1. The *Times* editorial says that it "would be easier to defend capital punishment if at least it were applied consistently," whereas the *Herald* claims that "that argument, to society's shame, is true—*as applied to the past*. But conditions that obtained in the past, especially in the segregated South, no longer obtain." How does each paper argue its point? Which is more persuasive? What makes it so? What part in the overall argument of each editorial does this point play?

2. List the points mentioned in common by two of the editorials and describe the different uses to which they are put.

3. The Atlanta *Constitution* argues that the death penalty is needed because it gives the American people in the words of Walter Berns, "the means by which they might strengthen the law that makes them a people, and not a mere aggregation of selfish individuals." The Milwaukee *Journal,* on the contrary, sees the death penalty as an indication of social deterioration: "The clock has been turned back to a more barbarous time." How does each paper support its position? Which is more persuasive? Why? What particular strategies or points can you pick out to support your answer?

4. Compare the account of the Spenkelink execution written by Davis with that written by Dart. What happens to one event when reported by two people?

Russell Baker / Jogging
The New York Times Sunday Magazine, June 18, 1978

Russell Baker began writing his wide-ranging column the "Observer" for The New York Times *in 1962 after many years as a reporter. In 1979, Baker won a Pulitzer Prize for his column, usually humorous, but occasionally elegiac or outraged in tone, which appears three times weekly in 475 newspapers nationwide.*

The first regular humor column in America appeared under the name "Mrs. Silence Dogood" (alias Benjamin Franklin) in Boston's New-England Courant, *one of America's most interesting colonial newspapers. Since then, the humor column has been a regular newspaper feature. Russell Baker, according to a* Time *magazine cover story, has "taken newspaper humor a step further. He has turned it into literature—funny, but full of the pain and absurdity of the age."*

For another columnist's opinion of exercise, see "Justifying Inactivity?" by William F. Buckley, Jr., in this section. The views of James Fixx (see Best Sellers), Janice Kaplan (see Magazines), and the comic-strip comment of G. B. Trudeau (see Press) should also be contrasted.

I don't jog. If this makes people who do jog feel smug about their muscle tone, so be it. One old geezer, a friend who chuffs and wheezes through Manhattan each dawn, assures me that refusal to pound arches on concrete signifies a yearning for the grave.

It pleasures him to visualize the interment of persons who are happily snoozing in their beds while he is chugging through the dawn. Health faddists of all eras have sustained themselves on the belief that people pass to the great beyond only because of perverse refusal to humor their muscles and innards, and it would be petty to disabuse them.

To my observation, the decision about who passes over and who lingers on in the earthly domain is based entirely on whim, but if contemplating imminent demise among the sedentary helps the athletic to endure their suffering, I shall not dispute them. Having been a jogger at one stage, I know too well the dreariness and boredom with which they cope. It is more humane to leave intact any compensating delusions which make their lot easier.

My refusal to join them in shin splints stems from an oath sworn years ago after two seasons on the high-school track team. Mere jogging, of course, doesn't qualify a runner for track, but it is an indispensable part of the program. He jogs before the race, he jogs after the race, he jogs most of the time between races. It is exceedingly dull, although not at all tiring for people of high-school age.

The racing, on the other hand, is worse than tiring, at least for persons to whom torture is more painful than fatigue. The aim is to achieve a complete physical collapse just short of death simultaneously with hitting the finish tape. Not being permitted to die, at least when I was in high school, one was permitted to vomit, after which you jogged a little to "cool off."

I should add that I never actually hit the finish tape. Four or five other runners had usually hit it well ahead of me and were already there writhing and jogging and evacuating their lunches by the time I arrived on the scene.

Why, you will ask, should anyone submit to such torment, particularly after learning that he is never going to be the first to collapse? What a question. This was high school. Why do people contend with algebra in high school? Why do they go on wrestling endlessly with a French that always wins?

Youth is a time of enduring agonies without asking why. I knew that even then. I would endure, I told myself, but when I grew up, I would never run again. Or jog. To me, being grown up meant, besides being able to buy beer without having to prove my age, never having to engage in athletics for which I was inadequately constructed.

Very quickly it became apparent that this included almost all athletics. Pressed into the military, I was placed at the mercy of a cabal of professional coaches who were fighting Fascism by subjecting the short-winded and the spindly-shanked to the zest of All-American sports competition.

Their theory held that everybody could become superior on the battlefield by experiencing the thrill of actual sport. For two weeks we played football. I was placed near the center of the line. Periodically, a dense wad of muscle that had played football for Ohio State would run over me with the determination of a runaway locomotive. I swore never to play football again, and haven't.

During the second two weeks we boxed. I was placed in a ring with a light-heavyweight who had been a finalist in some Marine Corps boxing festivity. My left jaw still aches occasionally. I swore never to lift another fist, and haven't.

Some years later, the papers reported that this Marine had been shot down over China, captured and brainwashed. I was depressed to hear this, for the Chinese had obviously stayed well clear of his right hook, which showed they were smarter than I was.

No need to dwell on the two weeks we spent in gymnastics. Who in his right mind would send a giraffe up against Nadia Comaneci in the cartwheel and back somersault? I swore I would never leap, flip, swing, shinny or dive again, and haven't.

As for wrestling, it was not only humiliating—one was accustomed to that by then—but also terrifying, despite the coach's assurances that gorillas did this sort of thing constantly without ever having their necks broken.

One of the few rewards of being grown up is not having to carry on in this fashion. Now and then I feel an urge to do something vigorous in order to refresh the pleasure of being able to stop doing it, but I am always quick to lie down again.

One owes it to friends who jog. Contemplating the imminence of my demise helps them to endure.

G. B. Trudeau / Doonesbury
[*An Interview with the Author of* Jogger Agonistes]

Ca. 1978

One of the most noticeable results of the United Press Syndicate's merger with the Washington Star Syndicate in May of 1979 was the disappearance of Gary Trudeau's comic strip, Doonesbury, *from the pages of the* Washington Post. *As part of the merger agreement,* Donnesbury *was taken from the* Post *and given to the* Washington Star, *a move that Trudeau reportedly likened to being traded "from the Redskins to the San Diego Padres." During the three week Doonesbury blackout in Washington that resulted because of the trade, the strip was broadcast by local television and radio stations, telexed to at least one senator from his home state, and added to the President's daily news summary by White House staffers.*

Gary Trudeau was the first comic strip artist to win a Pulitzer Prize for editorial cartooning. In 1976 he was awarded the honorary degree of Doctor of Humane Letters by Yale University. The citation read at the ceremony said in part: "Your country will never look at itself quite as self-seriously, certainly not as self-righteously, thanks to your satiric insights into the foibles and pretensions of both the notorious and the obscure." In the following selection, Trudeau takes a look at that great American mania–jogging.

215

William F. Buckley, Jr. / Justifying Inactivity?

Manchester New Hampshire *Courier Leader*, May 24, 1979

*Considered by many one of America's finest debators for and defenders of politi-
cal conservatism, William F. Buckley, Jr., currently writes a syndicated column
that appears three times a week. He is the founder and editor of the* National
Review, *an influential fortnightly magazine, and also the host of a television interview show called "Firing Line."*

*Never one to be taken in by trendiness, Buckley turns his critical attention to
jogging in the following selection.*

The jogging craze shows no sign of diminishing. By now one must suppose that
every American who can read has bought a copy of Mr. Fixx's book on the subject [see the selection from Fixx's *The Complete Book of Running* in Best Sellers.]
I have two, which is on the order of buying an encyclopaedia in order to become
educated. I also have one of those indoor exercise bicycles. I wish I had brought a
model that doesn't come with an odometer. Because mine is a standing reproach
to the weakness of the flesh. It reads 103 miles. I got the cursed thing four years
ago.

Pursuant to the human compulsion for self-justification, my mind has turned to
morbid matters, and last week I had a conversation with my physical mentor. He
is a gentleman of great distinction, huge size, who hasn't gone to bed any day of
his adult life without committing 50 push-ups. I turn myself over to him once a
week for about 45 minutes during which I submit to every form of physical abjec-
tion, including hoisting great barbells, imitating Russian cossack dancers, touching toes, clapping hands over my head, and every other conjugal muscular distortion.

I have also learned to become a lethal instrument. As I once put it, any man
who tries to push me over the edge of the Empire State Building will be positively
the last man who ever tries to push me over the edge of the Empire State Building,
because he will find himself without eyes or teeth or tonsils, or other things,
thanks to my coach.

But the subject inevitably arose about doing some homework, and jogging came
up. He knows about my bicycle. The conversation went something like this:

"You need to bring your pulse beat to between 120 and 137 at your age. Then
keep it there for 12 minutes. That flushes out your cardiovascular system. You
should do that every day."

"What happens if you flush out your cardiovascular system?"

"You don't die of heart attacks."

"What do you then die of?"

The silence was eloquent; and the mood shifts as, suddenly, we are required to
ask ourselves that question seriously. We all know what it is we do not want to die
from. Cancer. Leprosy. Creutzfeld-Jakob disease. The list is very long. We do not
want to die of anything that brings protracted pain.

Having said that, we must ask ourselves more difficult questions. We don't
want, do we, a prolonged sentence? Surely we want to depart this vale of tears

some time before we begin sounding like Arthur Schlesinger Jr.? We don't want—do we?—15 years in a nursing home, with day and night care, failed vision, incontinence, blurry speech, indistinct recall?

Mostly we don't want this because each of us knows and loves someone in such a condition, and we recognize the human paradox that we would fight to the death, spend to the point of bankruptcy, to keep him/her alive. But while we have our health, we can think forward sufficiently to know that we do not wish this for ourselves, even though we are bound by the spiritual commandment not to bring on death by suicide nor decline conventional therapy.

Which brings us back to the cardiovascular point. It is tragic, at age 30, to die of heart disease. But is it tragic at age 75 to die of heart disease? The answer is that it is tragic—provided that, after age 75, in the individual case some pleasure, or serenity, or usefulness is in prospect, followed eventually by . . .

What? We all read of those fortunate few who retire to bed one night after a splendid evening with friends and family, and—in the unforgettable phrase of a nine-year old referring to her great-aunt—"wake up dead." It happens. But will happen with diminishing frequency, it would seem, as the science of geriatrics prospers.

What will we do, to induce ourselves, finally, into a thanatotic state?

A question to consider, during those hours we do not spend jogging.

MAGAZINES

I'm obsessed by Time Magazine.
I read it every week.
Its cover stares at me every time I slink past the corner
    candystore.

ALLEN GINSBERG, ''AMERICA''

FROM an early exposé of child labor violations to an analysis of fast food restaurants, the following selection of American magazine writing illustrates a variety of prose styles and compositional procedures adopted by writers to address many different levels of reading interest and aptitude.

No magazine is addressed to everyone. Though all magazines are eager to increase their circulation, they nevertheless operate with a fairly limited market in mind. A magazine's "image" is often as firmly established as the "brand image" devised by advertisers to ensure a commercially reliable consumer identification with a product. "What Sort of Man Reads *Playboy?*" is, according to that magazine's advertisement, a question easily answered, if not by the details of the photograph in the ad, then certainly by the language describing what the "typical" *Playboy* reader is like (see Advertising). Depending on the issue you look at, he may be "urbane," "stylish," "his own man," "literate," "free-wheeling," "an individualist." "Should You Ever Lie?" (*Cosmopolitan*) and "Roger Reads *Esquire*" (see Advertising) offer further instances, though playfully exaggerated, of a magazine's personification of its public image through characters and voices that supposedly convey the life style, or desired life style, of its readers.

Regardless of the ways a magazine goes about promoting its public identity, the type of audience it wants to attract can be seen in the total environment created by such material as the magazine's fiction and nonfiction, its advertisements, editorial commentary, paper quality, and overall physical design. An article in *The New Yorker,* for example, is forced to compete for its readers' attention with glossy scenes of high fashion, mixed drinks, and the allure of exotic places. Yet not all magazines imagine or address their readers in quite such fashionable terms. An article appearing in either *Good Housekeeping, Harper's, Psychology Today,* or *Scientific American* does not usually take its tone from the modish world that forms the context of magazines like *The New Yorker, Playboy, Cosmopolitan, Vogue* and *Esquire.* For example, advertisements for precision instruments, various types of machinery, automobiles, and corporate accountability, along with mathematical games, puzzles, and instructions for home experiments surround the technical articles published in *Scientific American.* The readers of a magazine like *Good Housekeeping* are expected to be particularly attentive to products, services, and expertise that promise to improve a family's immediate domestic environment.

The "ideal reader" for a given magazine—the reader as "housewife," "playboy," "academic," "outdoorsman"—is a vague entity, invented by the magazine more for simple identification than realistic description. No one is *just* a "housewife" or an "academic," even assuming that we know exactly who or what these categories stand for in the first place. Naturally, labels like these suggest different associations to different people. For example, the audience imagined by Hugh Hefner in his editorial statement for *Playboy* and by Lew Dietz in "The Myth of the Boss Bear" for *True* may both be adventurous males, but they certainly are men who find their sport in different environments. The risks and failure detailed by Dietz in his personal adventure in the outdoors would not be nearly as alluring to the self-described "urban male" readers of *Playboy* who "enjoy mixing up cocktails and an *hors d'oeuvre* or two, putting a little mood on the phonograph and inviting in a female acquaintance for a quiet discussion on Picasso, Nietzsche, jazz, or sex." To contend, then, that the audience for Hefner's and Dietz's articles are both male and to let it go at that, is like arguing that the reader of an article in an issue of *TV Guide* can be described solely as someone who has the capacity to watch television.

Some affinity surely exists between the readership a magazine commercially promotes and the individual reader a particular article within that magazine assumes. But to characterize more accurately the audience addressed by a particular article, we need to go beyond the conveniently stereotyped reader presupposed by the magazine's title or its public image. For instance, *Everybody's,* a popular magazine first published nationwide in 1903, certainly could not appeal to everyone in America. Like any other magazine, it selected articles that approximated most closely the style of talk and the strategies of persuasion it felt its readers were most accustomed to. For a number of years, *Everybody's* played a prominent role in helping to develop the mode of American journalism that Theodore Roosevelt scornfully christened "muckraking." Along with other leading newspapers and periodicals, *Everybody's* featured a number of successful articles devoted to exposing public scandals and attacking vice and corruption in business and politics. Its readers were assumed to be civic-minded, generally well informed people concerned with what they felt was a growing network of moral irresponsibility on the part of public administrators and industrial leaders.

William Hard's article "De Kid Wot Works at Night," which appeared in the January 1908 issue of *Everybody's,* was directed to readers already aware of the abuses of child labor and the insidious corruption of urban life through their reading of some of the very newspapers that Hard's young subjects worked so energetically to sell. The boys Hard investigated earned their living out on the streets at night, where they were sadly vulnerable to the sundry temptations of a big city after dark. Hard argued seriously for legislative reform:

> Mr. J. J. Sloan, when he was superintendent of the John Worthy School (which is the local municipal juvenile reformatory), reported that the newsboys committed to his care were, on the average, one-third below the stature and one-third below the strength of average ordinary boys of the same age. In the face of testimony of this kind, which could be duplicated from every city in the United States, it seems absurd to talk about the educative influence of the street. That it has a certain educative influence in undeniable, but it is equally undeniable that the boys who are exposed to this influence should be prevented, by proper legislation, from exposing themselves to it for too many hours a day and should especially be prevented from exposing themselves to it for even a single hour after seven o'clock in the evening.

The facts are certainly unpleasant, and Hard is confident that his readers will be persuaded by the weight of professional testimony and their own natural sympathy for the plight of such unfortunate children.

Yet Hard himself seems not always convinced that his newsboys and messengers are the hopeless victims of a ruthless economic system. It is precisely "after seven o'clock in the evening" that the children he is writing about come to life. The following description portrays "Jelly," the newsboy Hard chooses as his representative "case," and his little sister in ways not nearly so pathetic as engaging:

> At half past ten he went to an elevated railway station to meet his little sister. She was ten years old. She had dressed herself for the part. From her ragged and scanty wardrobe she had chosen her most ragged and her scantiest clothes.

> Accompanied by his sister, "Jelly" then went to a flower shop and bought a bundle of carnations at closing prices. With these carnations he took his sister to the entrance of the Grand Opera House. There she sold the whole bundle to the people coming out from the performance. Her appearance was picturesque and pitiful. Her net profit from the sale of her flowers was usually about thirty-five cents.

Life on the street surely has its "undeniable educative influence." If roaming the streets at night stunted "Jelly's" growth, it certainly did not cripple his resourcefulness and imagination.

Hard's attitude toward the life style of "Jelly" and his associates is ambivalent. The reader of the article is asked to acknowledge the seriousness of the terrible conditions surrounding the lives of impoverished children in the city and, at the same time, to recognize that such circumstances do not always culminate in the melodramatic ruination of their victims. Hard transforms "Jelly" into an entrepreneur responsive to the fluctuations in the flower market—he buys carnations at "closing prices." "Jelly" also knows how to profit from the "ragged and scanty wardrobe" of his little sister. She, too, willingly participates in the act, choosing only those clothes that will show her poverty to best advantage. Hard's diction ("dressed . . . for the part," "most ragged," "scantiest," "picturesque") alerts the reader to the theatricality implicit in the attempts of these children to earn a living.

It should be clear from the language of the passage that Hard does not think of "Jelly" and his sister simply as "pitiful" figures. In fact, the word "pitiful" works not so much to move his readers to compassion for the abject condition of the children as much as it does to describe the self-conscious ways the children display themselves before a fashionable urban audience. From a sociological standpoint, "Jelly" and his sister may very well be "pitiful," but they are also *acting* "pitiful," and the awareness of that distinction is what makes it so difficult for Hard to write a disinterested report wholly committed to immediate legislative reform. Hard's predicament in this article is that the corruption he is striving to eliminate as a reformer sustains the very set of characters he finds, as a writer, so appealing in their verbal energy and playful perseverance.

The attractiveness of the kids that work at night and Hard's reluctance to render them merely in sociological terms prompt him to fictionalize their lives, treating them more like characters in a short story than as subjects to be documented. He takes us beyond the limits of factual observation by vividly imagining many details of the newsboys' behavior in situations that must have been annoyingly inaccessible to him. Whatever *Everybody's* public image and vested interests, Hard's article presupposes a reader attuned to both the need for legislative action and the nuances of parody. Like Gay Talese's example of "new journalism" that also appears in this section, Hard's piece exists in a territory somewhere between the reportorial prose of newspapers and the inventions of fiction.

With the exception of highly specialized journals and periodicals, most magazines, despite their commercial or artistic differences, want their articles to be both informative and entertaining, responding to those timely topics the renowned American novelist and magazine editor, William Dean Howells, once termed "contemporarnics." Pick up any popular magazine and you will be sure to come across essays offering information about some subject that is a topic of current public interest. Sex, celebrities, success, catastrophes, scandals, the bizarre—it would be difficult to find a magazine that does not contain a single article with a contemporary slant on one of these perennial subjects. Precisely how these sub-jects will be rendered in prose most often depends on the vigorous interplay be-tween an author's style and purpose and whatever specific compositional stan-dards or general "tone" the magazine encourages or requires.

Jack London / The Story of an Eyewitness
[An Account of the San Francisco Earthquake]
Collier's Weekly, May 1906

Jack London (1876–1916), a native of San Francisco, happened to be working near the city when the earthquake struck on the evening of April 16, 1906. An in-ternationally prominent novelist, reporter, and social critic, London telegraphed the following vivid eyewitness account of the disaster to Collier's Weekly *for which he was paid twenty-five cents a word. London's dramatic report, which ap-peared in an issue devoted entirely to photographs and articles on the earth-quake, was perfectly suited to* Collier's *characteristically hard-hitting journalism. With a weekly circulation of well over one million,* Collier's *was the country's leading public affairs magazine and an important precursor of modern pho-tojournalism.*

The earthquake shook down in San Francisco hundreds of thousands of dollars' worth of walls and chimneys. But the conflagration that followed burned up hundreds of millions of dollars' worth of property. There is no estimating within hundreds of millions the actual damage wrought. Not in history has a modern impe-rial city been so completely destroyed. San Francisco is gone! Nothing remains of it but memories and a fringe of dwelling houses on its outskirts. Its industrial section is wiped out. Its social and residential section is wiped out. The factories and warehouses, the great stores and newspaper buildings, the hotels and the palaces of the nabobs, are all gone. Remains only the fringe of dwelling houses on the out-skirts of what was once San Francisco.

Within an hour after the earthquake shock the smoke of San Francisco's burning was a lurid tower visible a hundred miles away. And for three days and nights this lurid tower swayed in the sky, reddening the sun, darkening the day, and filling the land with smoke.

On Wednesday morning at a quarter past five came the earthquake. A minute later the flames were leaping upward. In a dozen different quarters south of Market Street, in the working-class ghetto, and in the factories, fires started. There was no opposing the flames. There was no organization, no communication. All the cun-ning adjustments of a twentieth-century city had been smashed by the earthquake. The streets were humped into ridges and depressions and piled with debris of fallen walls. The steel rails were twisted into perpendicular and horizontal angles. The telephone and telegraph systems were disrupted. And the great water mains had burst. All the shrewd contrivances and safeguards of man had been thrown out of gear by thirty seconds' twitching of the earth crust.

By Wednesday afternoon, inside of twelve hours, half the heart of the city was gone. At that time I watched the vast conflagration from out on the bay. It was dead calm. Not a flicker of wind stirred. Yet from every side wind was pouring in upon the city. East, west, north, and south, strong winds were blowing upon the doomed city. The heated air rising made an enormous suck. Thus did the fire of itself build its own colossal chimney through the atmosphere. Day and night, this dead calm continued, and yet, near to the flames, the wind was often half a gale, so mighty was the suck.

The edict which prevented chaos was the following proclamation by Mayor E. E. Schmitz:

"The Federal Troops, the members of the Regular Police Force, and all Special Police Officers have been authorized to KILL any and all persons found engaged in looting or in the commission of any other crime.

"I have directed all the Gas and Electric Lighting Companies not to turn on gas or electricity until I order them to do so; you may therefore expect the city to remain in darkness for an indefinite time.

"I request all citizens to remain at home from darkness until daylight of every night until order is restored.

"I warn all citizens of the danger of fire from damaged or destroyed chimneys, broken or leaking gas pipes or fixtures, or any like cause."

Wednesday night saw the destruction of the very heart of the city. Dynamite was lavishly used, and many of San Francisco's proudest structures were crumbled by man himself into ruins, but there was no withstanding the onrush of the flames. Time and again successful stands were made by the fire fighters, and every time the flames flanked around on either side, or came up from the rear, and turned to defeat the hard-won victory.

An enumeration of the buildings destroyed would be a directory of San Francisco. An enumeration of the buildings undestroyed would be a line and several addresses. An enumeration of the deeds of heroism would stock a library and bankrupt the Carnegie medal fund. An enumeration of the dead—will never be made. All vestiges of them were destroyed by the flames. The number of the victims of the earthquake will never be known. South of Market Street, where the loss of life was particularly heavy, was the first to catch fire.

Remarkable as it may seem, Wednesday night, while the whole city crashed and roared into ruin, was a quiet night. There were no crowds. There was no shouting and yelling. There was no hysteria, no disorder. I passed Wednesday night in the part of the advancing flames, and in all those terrible hours I saw not one woman who wept, not one man who was excited, not one person who was in the slightest degree panic-stricken.

Before the flames, throughout the night, fled tens of thousands of homeless ones. Some were wrapped in blankets. Others carried bundles of bedding and dear household treasures. Sometimes a whole family was harnessed to a carriage or delivery wagon that was weighted down with their possessions. Baby buggies, toy wagons, and gocarts were used as trucks, while every other person was dragging a trunk. Yet everybody was gracious. The most perfect courtesy obtained. Never in all San Francisco's history were her people so kind and courteous as on this night of terror.

All the night these tens of thousands fled before the flames. Many of them, the poor people from the labor ghetto, had fled all day as well. They had left their homes burdened with possessions. Now and again they lightened up, flinging out upon the street clothing and treasures they had dragged for miles.

They held on longest to their trunks, and over these trunks many a strong man broke his heart that night. The hills of San Francisco are steep, and up these hills, mile after mile, were the trunks dragged. Everywhere were trunks, with across them lying their exhausted owners, men and women. Before the march of the flames were flung picket lines of soldiers. And a block at a time, as the flames advanced, these pickets retreated. One of their tasks was to keep the trunk pullers moving. The exhausted creatures, stirred on by the menace of bayonets, would arise and struggle up the steep pavements, pausing from weakness every five or ten feet.

Often after surmounting a heart-breaking hill, they would find another wall of flame advancing upon them at right angles and be compelled to change anew the line of their retreat. In the end, completely played out, after toiling for a dozen hours like giants, thousands of them were compelled to abandon their trunks. Here the shopkeepers and soft members of the middle class were at a disadvantage. But the workingmen dug holes in vacant lots and back yards and buried their trunks.

At nine o'clock Wednesday evening I walked down through miles and miles of magnificent buildings and towering skyscrapers. Here was no fire. All was in perfect order. The police patrolled the streets. Every building had its watchman at the door. And yet it was doomed, all of it. There was no water. The dynamite was giving out. And at right angles two different conflagrations were sweeping down upon it.

At one o'clock in the morning I walked down through the same section. Every-thing still stood intact. There was no fire. And yet there was a change. A rain of ashes was falling. The watchmen at the doors were gone. The police had been withdrawn. There were no firemen, no fire engines, no men fighting with dynamite. The district had been absolutely abandoned. I stood at the corner of Kearney and Market, in the very innermost heart of San Francisco. Kearney Street was deserted. Half a dozen blocks away it was burning on both sides. The street was a wall of flame. And against this wall of flame, silhouetted sharply, were two United States cavalrymen sitting on their horses, calmly watching. That was all. Not another person was in sight. In the intact heart of the city two troopers sat on their horses and watched.

Surrender was complete. There was no water. The sewers had long since been pumped dry. There was no dynamite. Another fire had broken out further uptown, and now from three sides conflagrations were sweeping down. The fourth side had been burned earlier in the day. In that direction stood the tottering walls of the Examiner Building, the burned-out Call Building, the smoldering ruins of the Grand Hotel, and the gutted, devastated, dynamited Palace Hotel.

The following will illustrate the sweep of the flames and the inability of men to calculate their spread. At eight o'clock Wednesday evening I passed through Union Square. It was packed with refugees. Thousands of them had gone to bed on the grass. Government tents had been set up, supper was being cooked, and the refugees were lining up for free meals.

At half-past one in the morning three sides of Union Square were in flames. The fourth side, where stood the great St. Francis Hotel, was still holding out. An hour later, ignited from top and sides, the St. Francis was flaming heavenward. Union Square, heaped high with mountains of trunks, was deserted. Troops, refugees, and all had retreated.

It was at Union Square that I saw a man offering a thousand dollars for a team of horses. He was in charge of a truck piled high with trunks from some hotel. It had been hauled here into what was considered safety, and the horses had been taken out. The flames were on three sides of the square, and there were no horses.

Also, at this time, standing beside the truck, I urged a man to seek safety in flight. He was all but hemmed in by several conflagrations. He was an old man and he was on crutches. Said he: "Today is my birthday. Last night I was worth thirty thousand dollars. I bought five bottles of wine, some delicate fish, and other things for my birthday dinner. I have had no dinner, and all I own are these crutches."

I convinced him of his danger and started him limping on his way. An hour later, from a distance, I saw the truckload of trunks burning merrily in the middle of the street.

On Thursday morning, at a quarter past five, just twenty-four hours after the earthquake, I sat on the steps of a small residence of Nob Hill. With me sat Japanese, Italians, Chinese, and Negroes—a bit of the cosmopolitan flotsam of the wreck of the city. All about were the palaces of the nabob pioneers of Forty-nine. To the east and south, at right angles, were advancing two mighty walls of flame.

I went inside with the owner of the house on the steps of which I sat. He was cool and cheerful and hospitable. "Yesterday morning," he said, "I was worth six hundred thousand dollars. This morning this house is all I have left. It will go in fifteen minutes." He pointed to a large cabinet. "That is my wife's collection of china. This rug upon which we stand is a present. It cost fifteen hundred dollars. Try that piano. Listen to its tone. There are few like it. There are no horses. The flames will be here in fifteen minutes."

Outside, the old Mark Hopkins residence, a palace, was just catching fire. The troops were falling back and driving refugees before them. From every side came the roaring of flames, the crashing of walls, and the detonations of dynamite.

I passed out of the house. Day was trying to dawn through the smoke pall. A sickly light was creeping over the face of things. Once only the sun broke through the smoke pall, blood-red, and showing quarter its usual size. The smoke pall itself, viewed from beneath, was a rose color that pulsed and fluttered with lavender shades. Then it turned to mauve and yellow and dun. There was no sun. And so dawned the second day on stricken San Francisco.

An hour later I was creeping past the shattered dome of the City Hall. Than it there was no better exhibit of the destructive force of the earthquake. Most of the stones had been shaken from the great dome, leaving standing the naked framework of steel. Market Street was piled high with the wreckage, and across the wreckage lay the overthrown pillars of the City Hall shattered into short crosswise sections.

This section of the city, with the exception of the Mint and the Post Office, was already a waste of smoking ruins. Here and there through the smoke, creeping warily under the shadows of tottering walls, emerged occasional men and women. It was like the meeting of the handful of survivors after the day of the end of the world.

On Mission Street lay a dozen steers, in a neat row stretching across the street, just as they had been struck down by the flying ruins of the earthquake. The fire had passed through afterward and roasted them. The human dead had been carried away before the fire came. At another place on Mission Street I saw a milk wagon. A steel telegraph pole had smashed down sheer through the driver's seat and crushed the front wheels. The milk cans lay scattered around.

All day Thursday and all Thursday night, all day Friday and Friday night, the flames still raged.

Friday night saw the flames finally conquered, though not until Russian Hill and Telegraph Hill had been swept and three quarters of a mile of wharves and docks had been licked up.

The great stand of the fire fighters was made Thursday night on Van Ness Avenue. Had they failed here, the comparatively few remaining houses of the city would have been swept.

Here were the magnificent residences of the second generation of San Francisco nabobs, and these, in a solid zone, were dynamited down across the path of the fire. Here and there the flames leaped the zone, but these fires were beaten out, principally by the use of wet blankets and rugs.

San Francisco, at the present time, is like the crater of a volcano, around which are camped tens of thousands of refugees. At the Presidio alone are at least twenty thousand. All the surrounding cities and towns are jammed with the homeless ones, where they are being cared for by the relief committees. The refugees were carried free by the railroads to any point they wished to go, and it is estimated that over one hundred thousand people have left the peninsula on which San Francisco stood. The government has the situation in hand, and thanks to the immediate relief given by the whole United States, there is not the slightest possibility of a famine. The bankers and businessmen have already set about making preparations to rebuild San Francisco.

DISCUSSION QUESTIONS

1. Having read Jack London's essay carefully, work back over it once more and note the significant words and phrases that you find are repeated. What is the purpose of such repetition? Examine the development of London's sentences. Do they work primarily through logic? Emotion? Accumulation of detail? Does this strategy seem best suited to London's occasion and audience?

2. What terms does London use to measure the disastrous effects of the San Francisco earthquake? Does he see the event from a personal or an objective point of view? Does he use, for example, aesthetic, economic, sociological, or psychological language to define his response?

3. Contrast London's point of view and the effects that perspective elicits from his audience with the eyewitness reports of other disasters written by Theodore Dreiser and William L. Laurence (see Press).

William Hard / De Kid Wot Works at Night

Everybody's Magazine, January 1908

Everybody's Magazine (1899–1929) was a leading advocate of social, economic, and political reform in the early years of the twentieth century. When William Hard's article appeared, the magazine had well over one-half million readers. Although the self-consciously melodramatic and playful tone of Hard's prose may have surprised an audience accustomed to a more earnest style of social crusading, Hard's article nevertheless accomplished its goal by helping to instigate child labor reform legislation in Illinois.

When the shades of night look as if they were about to fall; when the atmosphere of Chicago begins to change from the dull gray of unaided local nature to the brilliant white of artificial illumination; when the Loop District, the central crater of the volcano, is filling up rapidly with large numbers of straps [trolley cars] which have been brought downtown from outlying carbarns for the convenience of those who have had enough and who now wish to withdraw; when the sound of the time clock being gladly and brutally punched is heard through every door and window—

When all these things are happening, and, besides—

When all the fat men in the city get to the streetcars first, and all the lean and energetic and profane men have to climb over them to the inner seats; when the salesladies in the department stores throw the night-covers over bargain ormolu clocks just as you pant up to the counter; when the man who has just bought a suburban house stops at the wholesale meat market and carries home a left-over steak in order to have the laugh on the high-priced suburban butcher; when you are sorry your office is on the fifth floor because there are so many people on the eleventh floor and the elevator goes by you without stopping, while you scowl through the glass partition—

When all these things are happening, and, besides—

When the clocks in the towers of the railway stations are turned three minutes ahead so that you will be sure to be on time and so that you will also be sure to drop into your seat with fractured lungs; when the policeman blows his whistle to make the streetcar stop, and the motorman sounds his gong to make the pedestrian stop, and both the motorman and the pedestrian look timorously but longingly at the area of death just in front of the fender; when the streets are full and the straps are full, and the shoes of the motor-cars of the elevated trains are throwing yellow sparks on the shoulders of innocent bystanders; when the reporters, coming back to their offices from their afternoon assignments, are turning about in their doorways to watch the concentrated agony of an American home-going and are thanking God that they go home at the more convenient hour of 1 A.M.—

When all these things are happening, and when, in short, it is between five and six o'clock in the afternoon, the night newsboy and the night messenger boy turn another page in the book of experience and begin to devote themselves once more to the thronging, picturesque, incoherent characters of the night life of a big American city.

Then it is, at just about five o'clock, that the night messenger boy opens the door of his office by pushing against it with his back, turns around and walks sidewise across the floor, throws himself down obliquely on his long, smooth bench, slides a foot or two on the polished surface, comes to a stop against the body of the next boy, and begins to wait for the telegrams, letters and parcels that will keep him engaged till one o'clock the next morning and that may lead his footsteps either to the heavily curtained drawing rooms of disorderly houses in the Red Light district or to the wet planks of the wharves on the Calumet River twelve miles away, where he will curl up under the stars and sleep till the delayed boat arrives from Duluth.

Then it is that the night messenger boy's friend and ally, the night newsboy, gets downtown from school, after having said good-by to his usually mythical "widowed mother," and after having assumed the usually imaginary burden of the support of a "bereaved family." Then it is, at about five o'clock, that he approaches his favorite corner, grins at the man who owns the corner news stand, receives "ten *Choinals*, ten *Murrikins*, ten *Snoozes*, and five *Posts*"; goes away twenty feet, turns around, watches the corner-man to see if he has marked the papers down in his notebook, hopes that he hasn't marked them down, thinks that perhaps he has forgotten just how many there were, wonders if he couldn't persuade him that he didn't give him any *"Murrikins,"* calculates the amount of his profit if he should be able to sell the *"Murrikins"* without having to pay the corner-man for them, turns to the street, dodges a frenzied automobile, worms his way into a hand-packed street-car (which is the only receptacle never convicted by the city government of containing short measure), disappears at the car door, comes to the surface in the middle of the aisle, and hands a *News* to a regular customer.

From the time when the arc lamps sputter out bravely against the evening darkness to the time when they chatter and flicker themselves into extinction before the cold, reproving rays of the early morning sun, what does the street-boy do? What does he see? What films in the moving picture of a big American city are unrolled before his eyes? These are questions that are important to every American city, to every mission superintendent, to every desk sergeant, to every penitentiary warden, to every father, to every mother.

Night, in these modern times, is like the United States Constitution. It is an admirable institution, but it doesn't know what is happening beneath it. Night comes down on Chicago and spreads its wings as largely and as comfortably now as when the *Tribune* building was a sand dune. You stand on Madison Street and look upward, through the glare of the arc lamps, and you see old Mother Night still brooding about you, calmly, imperturbably, quite unconscious of the fact that her mischievous children have lined her feathers with electricity, kerosene, acetylene, coal gas, water gas, and every other species of unlawful, unnatural illuminating substance. She still spreads her wings, simply, grandly, with the cosmic unconcern of a hen that doesn't know she is hatching out ducks instead of chickens; and in the morning she rises from her nest and flutters away westward, feeling quite sure that she has fulfilled her duty in an ancient, regular and irreproachable manner.

She would be quite maternally surprised if she could know what her newsboys and messenger boys are doing while she (good, proper mother!) is nodding her head beautifully among the stars.

I do not mean by this remark to disparage the newsboy. He occupies in Chicago a legal position superior to that of the president of a railway company. The president of a railway company is only an employee. He receives a weekly, a monthly, or at least a yearly salary. The newsboy does not receive a salary. He is not an employee. He is a merchant. He buys his papers and then resells them. He occupies the same legal position as Marshall Field & Co. Therefore he does not fall within the scope of the child-labor law. Therefore no rascally paternalistic factory inspector may vex him in his pursuit of an independent commercial career.

At about five o'clock he strikes his bargain with the corner-man. The corner-man owns the corner. It is a strange and interesting system, lying totally without the pale of recognized law. Theoretically, Dick Kelly, having read the Fourteenth Amendment to the Constitution of the United States, and having become conscious of his rights, might try to set up a news stand at the southwest corner of Wabash and Madison. Practically, the Constitution does not follow the flag as far as that corner. Mr. Kelly's news stand would last a wonderfully short time. The only person who can have a news stand at the corner of Wabash and Madison is Mr. Heffner.

Mr. Heffner is the recognized owner, holder, occupant, possessor, etc., of some eighty square feet of sidewalk at that point, and his sovereignty extends halfway down the block to the next corner southward, and halfway down the other block to the next corner westward. When Mr. Heffner has been in business long enough he will deed, convey and transfer his rights to some other man for anywhere between $5 and $1,500.

These rights consist exclusively of the fact that the newspapers recognize the corner-man as their only agent at that particular spot. When the corner-man wishes to transfer his corner to somebody else, he must see that the newspapers are satisfied with his choice of a successor.

The newsboy deals, generally speaking, with the corner-man. The corner-man pays the *Daily News* sixty cents for every hundred copies. He then hands out these hundred copies in "bunches" of, say, ten or fifteen or twenty to the newsboys who come to him for supplies. Each newsboy receives, as a commission, a certain number of cents for every hundred copies that he can manage to sell. This commission varies from five to twenty cents. The profit of the corner-man varies therefore with the commission that he pays the newsboy. The public pays one hundred cents for one hundred copies of the *News*. The *News* itself gets sixty cents; the newsboy gets from five to twenty cents, the corner-man gets what is left, namely, from thirty-five down to twenty cents in net profit.

On the basis of this net profit, plus the gross profit on his own sales made directly by himself to his customers, there is more than one corner-man in Chicago who owns suburban property and who could live on the income from his real-estate investments.

From five o'clock, therefore, on to about half past six, the newsboy flips streetcars and yells "turrible murdur" on commission. But pretty soon the corner-man wants to go home. He then sells outright all the papers left on the stand. . . .

The best specimen of the finished type of newsboy, within my knowledge, is an Italian boy named "Jelly." His father's surname is Cella, but his own name has been "Jelly" ever since he can remember.

"Jelly" was born on the great, sprawly West Side. His father worked during the summer, digging excavations for sewers and gas mains. His mother worked during the winter, making buttonholes in coats, vests, and pants. Neither parent worked during the whole year.

This domestic situation was overlooked by the Hull House investigators. In their report on newsboys they found that the number of paper-selling orphans had been grossly overestimated by popular imagination. Out of 1,000 newsboys in their final tabulation, there were 803 who had both parents living. There were 74 who had only a father living. There were 97 who had only a mother living. There were only 26, out of the whole 1,000, who had neither a father nor a mother to care for them.

But "Jelly" occupied a peculiar position. He had both parents living and yet, from the standpoint of economics, he was a half-orphan, since neither parent worked all the year.

At the age of ten, therefore, "Jelly" began selling papers. His uncle had a news stand on a big important corner not far from "Jelly's" house on the West Side. At the age of ten "Jelly" was selling papers from five to eight in the morning and from five to eight in the evening. He was therefore inclined to go to sleep at his desk when he was receiving his lesson in mental arithmetic in the public school where he was an unwilling attendant. Nevertheless, he showed an extraordinary aptitude for mental arithmetic a few hours later when he was handing out change to customers on his uncle's corner.

"Jelly" was a pretty good truant in those days. There was no money to be made by going to school and it looked like a waste of time. His acquaintance among truant officers came to be broad and thorough. He was dragged back to school an indefinite number of times. Yet, with the curious limitations of a newsboy's superficially profound knowledge of human nature, he has confided to me the fact that every truant officer gets $1 for every boy that he returns to the principal of his school.

Besides being a pretty good truant, "Jelly" became also a pretty good fighter.

His very first fight won him the undying gratitude of his uncle.

It happened that at that time the struggle between the circulation departments of the evening newspapers was particularly keen. "Jelly's" uncle allowed himself, unwisely, to be drawn into it. The local circulation experts of the *News* and the *American* noticed that on the news stand kept by "Jelly's" uncle the *Journal* was displayed with excessive prominence and the *News* and the *American* were concealed down below. It was currently reported in the neighborhood that "Jelly's" uncle was receiving $10 a week from the *Journal* for behaving in the manner aforesaid.

In about twenty-four hours the corner owned by "Jelly's" uncle bore a tumultuous aspect. The *News* and the *American* had established a rival stand on the other side of the street. This stand was in charge of a man named Gazzolo. Incidentally, it happened that a man named Gazzolo had beaten and killed a man named Cella in the vicinity of Naples some five years before.

Gazzolo's news stand had confronted Cella's, frowning at it from across the street, for about a week, when it began to be guarded by some six or seven broad-chested persons in sweaters. Meanwhile Cella's news stand had also acquired a few sweaters inhabited by capable young men of a combative disposition.

On the afternoon of the eighth day the sweatered agents of the *News* and the *American* advanced across the street and engaged the willing agents of the *Journal* in a face-to-face and then hand-to-hand combat.

At least three murders have happened in Chicago since that time in similar encounters. "Nigger" Clark, an agent of the *News*, was killed on the South Side, and the Higgins brothers were killed on the Ashland Block corner in the downtown district itself, within view of the worldwide commerce transacted in the heart of Chicago. And a Chicago publisher has told me that these three open murders, recognized by everybody as circulation-department murders, must be supplemented by at least six or seven other clandestine murders before the full story of the homicidal rivalry between the agents of Chicago afternoon newspapers is told.

It was amateur murder before the *American* arrived. Then circulation agents began to be enlisted from the ranks of the pupils in the boxing schools, and since that time the circulation situation has become increasingly pugnacious, until today it has reached the State Attorney's office and has come back to the street in the form of indictments and prosecutions.

Typical of this warfare was the fray that followed when the sweatered agents of the *News* and the *American* came across the street and fell rudely upon the news stand of "Jelly's" uncle.

"Jelly's" uncle had his shoulder-blade broken, but "Jelly" himself, being young and agile, escaped from his pursuers and was instantly and miraculously filled with a beautiful idea.

The agents of the *News* and the *American*, coming across the street to attack "Jelly's" uncle, had left Gazzolo's corner unprotected. "Jelly" traversed the cedar blocks of the street and reached Gazzolo in an ecstatic moment when he was surveying the assault on Cella's shoulder-blade with absorbing glee. Just about one-tenth of a second later Mr. Gazzolo was pierced in the region of the abdomen by the largest blade of a small and blunt pocket-knife in the unhesitating right hand of Mr. Cella's nephew, "Jelly."

It was a slight wound, but in consideration of his thoughtfulness in promptly perceiving Mr. Gazzolo's unprotected situation and in immediately running across the street in order to take advantage of it, "Jelly" was transferred by his uncle to a position of independent responsibility. He was put in charge of a news stand just outside an elevated railway station on the South Side.

Nevertheless, even after this honorable promotion, "Jelly's" father continued to take all his money away from him when he came home at night. And the elder Cella did not desist from this practice till his son had been advanced to the supereminent honor of selling papers in the downtown district.

This final transfer happened to "Jelly" when he was fifteen. He still retained his stand on the South Side, selling papers there from five to ten in the morning, but he also came downtown and sold papers at a stand within the Loop from five to nine at night. His uncle had prospered and had been able to invest $1,000 in a downtown corner, which was on the point of being abandoned by a fellow Italian who desired to return to the hills just south of Naples.

Thereafter, till he was sixteen years old, "Jelly" led a full and earnest life. He rose at four; he reached his South Side stand by five; he sold papers there till ten; he reached the downtown district by eleven; he inspected the five-cent theaters and the penny arcades and the alley restaurants till five in the afternoon; he sold papers for his uncle on commission till half past six; he bought his uncle's left-over papers at half past six and sold them on his own account till nine; and then, before going home at ten in order to get his five hours of sleep, he spent a happy sixty minutes reinspecting the five-cent theaters and the penny arcades and dodging Mr. Julius F. Wengierski.

Mr. Wengierski is a probation officer of the Juvenile Court. At that time he was making nightly tours through the downtown district talking to the children on the streets and trying to induce them to go home. He made a special study of some fifty cases, looking into the home circumstances of each child and gathering notes on the reasons why the child was at work. He was assisted by the agents of a reputable and conscientious charitable society.

In only two instances, out of the whole fifty, was the boy's family in need of the actual necessaries of life. In one instance the boy's father was the owner of his house and lot and was earning $5 a day. He also had several hundred dollars in the bank. In only a few instances did the family, as a family, make any considerable gain, for the purposes of household expenses, from the child's labor.

Some fathers, it is true (notably the one who owned his house and lot), used the child selfishly and cruelly as a worker who required no wages and whose total earnings could be appropriated as soon as he came home. It was the same system as that to which "Jelly" had been subjected from ten to fifteen. But these cases were exceptional.

One of the boys was working in order to get the money for the installment payments on a violin, and another was working in order to pay for lessons on a violin of which he was already the complete and enthusiastic owner.

One little girl was selling late editions in the saloons on Van Buren Street in order to have white shoes for her first communion. Another little girl needed shoes of the same color for Easter. Still a third was working in order that after a while she might have clothes just as good as those of the girl who lived next door.

In at least ten of Mr. Wengierski's cases, the reason for earning money on the street at night was the penny arcade and the five-cent theater. The passion for these amusements among children is intense. They will, some of them, work until they have a nickel, expend it on a moving-picture performance, and then start in and work again until they have another nickel to be spent for the same purpose at another "theatorium."

The earnings of these children, according to the Hull House investigation, which is the only authoritative investigation on record, vary from ten cents a day when the children are five years old up to ninety cents a day when they are sixteen. This is the average, but of course there are many children who make less and many who, because of superior skill, make more. Among these latter is "Jelly."

"Jelly's" high average, which used to reach almost $2 a day, was due partly to his own personal power and partly to the fact that on Saturday night he employed the services of his little sister.

Saturday night was "Jelly's" big time. On other nights he went home by ten o'clock. He had to get up by four and it was necessary for even him to take some sleep. But on Saturday night he gave himself up with almost complete abandon to the opportunities of the street.

On that night he used to close up his stand by eight o'clock and then go down to the river and sell his few remaining papers to the passengers on the lake boats. "Last chanst ter git yer *Murrikin*!" "Only one *Choinal* left! De only *Choinal* on de dock!" "Buy a *Post*, mister! Youse won't be able ter sleep ter-night on de boat! De only paper fer only two cents!" "Here's yer *Noose*! Only one cent! No more *Nooses* till youse comes back! Last chanst! Dey will cost yer ten cents apiece on de boat!" "Git yer *Murrikin*. No papers sold on de boat!" "Git yer *Post*. Dey charges yer five cents w'en youse gits 'em on de boat!"

Slightly contradictory those statements of his used to be, but they attained their object. They sold the papers. And as soon as the boats had swung away from their moorings "Jelly" would come back to the region of the five-cent theaters and the penny arcades and resume his nocturnal inquiries into the state of cheap art.

At half past ten he went to an elevated railway station to meet his little sister. She was ten years old. She had dressed herself for the part. From her ragged and scanty wardrobe she had chosen her most ragged and her scantiest clothes.

Accompanied by his sister, "Jelly" then went to a flower shop and bought a bundle of carnations at closing prices. With these carnations he took his sister to the entrance of the Grand Opera House. There she sold the whole bundle to the people coming out from the performance. Her appearance was picturesque and pitiful. Her net profit from the sale of her flowers was usually about thirty-five cents.

As soon as the flowers were sold and the people had gone away, "Jelly" took his sister back to the elevated station. There he counted the money she had made and put it in his pocket. He then handed her out a nickel for carfare and, in addition, a supplementary nickel for herself. "Jelly" was being rapidly Americanized. If he had remained exactly like his father, he would have surrendered only the nickel for carfare.

It was time now to go to the office of the *American* and get the early morning Sunday editions. "Jelly" began selling these editions at about twelve o'clock. He sold them to stragglers in the downtown streets till two. It was then exactly twenty-two hours since he had left his bed. He began to feel a little bit sleepy. He therefore went down to the river and slept on a dock, next to an old berry crate, till four. At four he rose and took the elevated train to the South Side. There he reached his own news stand and opened it up at about five o'clock. This was his Saturday, Saturday-night, and Sunday-morning routine for a long time. On the other nights "Jelly" slept five hours. On Saturday nights he found that two hours was quite enough. And his ability to get along without sleep is characteristic of newsboys and messenger boys rather than exceptional among them.

The reason why "Jelly" used to dodge Mr. Wengierski is now explainable. To begin with, his opinion of all probation officers is unfavorable. He classes them with truant officers. They are not "on the level." They discriminate between different classes of boys. "Jelly" was once accosted by a probation officer at about ten o'clock at night on Clark Street. He gave this probation officer a good tip about a lot of boys who were staying out nights attending services in the old First Methodist Church. These boys had been seen by "Jelly" going home as late as half past ten. The probation officer took no action in their case while at the same time he advised "Jelly" to stop selling papers at an early hour.

Incidents like this had convinced "Jelly" that probation officers were certainly not on the level and were possibly "on the make." But in Mr. Wengierski's case he had an additional reason. Mr. Wengierski was looking for boys of fourteen and under, and, while "Jelly" was entitled by age to escape Mr. Wengierski's notice, he was not so entitled by size. He was sixteen, but he looked not more than thirteen. The street had given him a certain superficial knowledge, but it had dwarfed his body just as surely as it had dwarfed his mind.

Mr. J. J. Sloan, when he was superintendent of the John Worthy School (which is the local municipal juvenile reformatory), reported that the newsboys committed to his care were, on the average, one-third below the stature and one-third below the strength of average ordinary boys of the same age. In the face of testimony of this kind, which could be duplicated from every city in the United States, it seems absurd to talk about the educative influence of the street. That it has a certain educative influence is undeniable, but it is equally undeniable that the boys who are exposed to this influence should be prevented, by proper legislation, from exposing themselves to it too many hours a day and should especially be prevented from exposing themselves to it for even a single hour after seven o'clock in the evening.

"Jelly" has now become a messenger boy and has been given a new name by his new associates. He will some day go back to the newspaper business because there is more money in it, and "Jelly" is fundamentally commercial. But there seems to be, after all, a certain struggling, unruly bubble of romanticism in his nature and it had to rise to the surface and explode.

"Jelly" first thought of the messenger service when he was attending a five-cent theater. "Jelly" went in. The fleeting pictures on the screen at the farther end of the room were telling a story that filled him with swelling interest. A messenger boy is run over by an automobile. He is taken to the hospital. He regains consciousness in his bed. He remembers his message. He calls for a portable telephone. He phones the message to the young man to whom it was addressed. The young man comes at once to the hospital. The young woman who had sent the message also comes. She wants to find out what has happened to the message. The young man and the young woman meet at the bedside of the messenger boy. They fall into each other's arms and the messenger boy sinks back on his pillow and dies. And it is a mighty good story even if the rough points are not rubbed off.

"Jelly" determined at once to be a messenger boy, without delay. [. . .]

Hugh Hefner / First Editorial Statement

Playboy, December 1953

As the magazine's editor, Hugh Hefner, puts it, Playboy *is intended to "entertain and inform a literate, urban, male audience."*

If you're a man between the ages of 18 and 80, *Playboy* is meant for you. If you like your entertainment served up with humor, sophistication and spice, *Playboy* will become a very special favorite.

We want to make clear from the very start, we aren't a "family magazine." If you're somebody's sister, wife or mother-in-law and picked us up by mistake, please pass us along to the man in your life and get back to your *Ladies Home Companion*.

Within the pages of *Playboy* you will find articles, fiction, picture stories, cartoons, humor and special features culled from many sources, past and present, to form a pleasure-primer styled to the masculine taste.

Most of today's "magazines for men" spend all their time out-of-doors—thrashing through thorny thickets or splashing about in fast flowing streams. We'll be out there too, occasionally, but we don't mind telling you in advance—we plan on spending most of our time inside.

We like our apartment. We enjoy mixing up cocktails and an *hors d'oeuvre* or two, putting a little mood music on the phonograph and inviting in a female acquaintance for a quiet discussion on Picasso, Nietzsche, jazz, sex.

We believe, too, that we are filling a publishing need only slightly less important than the one just taken care of by the Kinsey Report. The magazines now being produced for the city-bred male (there are 2—count 'em—2) have, of late, placed so much emphasis on fashion, travel, and "how-to-do-it" features on everything from avoiding a hernia to building your own steam bath, that entertainment has been all but pushed from their pages. *Playboy* will emphasize entertainment.

Affairs of state will be out of our province. We don't expect to solve any world problems or prove any great moral truths. If we are able to give the American male a few extra laughs and a little diversion from the anxieties of the Atomic Age, we'll feel we've justified our existence.

Ralph Ellison / Living with Music

High Fidelity, December 1955

Ralph [Waldo] Ellison, named by his construction worker father after the illustrious American essayist and poet, Ralph Waldo Emerson, was born in Oklahoma City, Oklahoma, in 1914. He studied music at Tuskegee Institute in the hope of becoming a symphonic composer, but left for New York City in 1936 to learn sculpture. In New York he worked with the Federal Writers Project, a depression relief organization employing out-of-work writers, scholars, editors, and journalists. There he met Richard Wright (see Classics), who encouraged him to take up writing, and within a few years Ellison was publishing essays, short stories, and reviews regularly in a number of periodicals. He served with the United States Merchant Marines during the Second World War and afterwards, with the help of fellowships, concentrated on his first novel, Invisible Man. *A highly acclaimed surrealist exploration into the various landscapes of American racism,* Invisible Man *received the National Book Award in 1953. A collection of essays, interviews, and reviews,* Shadow and Act, *appeared in 1964. A deliberate writer, intensely conscious of the craft of fiction, and one of the most distinguished professional men of letters in America, Ellison has lectured widely on comparative literature and cultural studies at home and abroad. As a visiting professor, he has taught writing at Yale, Bard, Rutgers, and the University of Chicago.*

A hi-fi enthusiast, Ellison has published over the years a number of articles on a variety of musical styles. The following essay originally appeared in High Fidelity, *a magazine devoted to the use and maintainance as well as the technologico-cultural dimensions of phonographic equipment.*

In those days it was either live with music or die with noise, and we chose rather desperately to live. In the process our apartment—what with its booby-trappings of audio equipment, wires, discs and tapes—came to resemble the Collier mansion, but that was later. First there was the neighborhood, assorted drunks and a singer.

We were living at the time in a tiny ground-floor-rear apartment in which I was also trying to write. I say "trying" advisedly. To our right, separated by a thin wall, was a small restaurant with a juke box the size of the Roxy. To our left, a night-employed swing enthusiast who took his lullaby music so loud that every morning promptly at nine Basie's brasses started blasting my typewriter off its stand. Our living room looked out across a small back yard to a rough stone wall to an apartment building which, towering above, caught every passing thoroughfare sound and rifled it straight down to me. There were also howling cats and barking dogs, none capable of music worth living with, so we'll pass them by.

But the court behind the wall, which on the far side came knee-high to a short Iroquois, was a forum for various singing and/or preaching drunks who wandered back from the corner bar. From these you sometimes heard a fair barbershop style "Bill Bailey," free-wheeling versions of "The Bastard King of England," the saga of Uncle Bud, or a deeply felt rendition of Leroy Carr's "How Long Blues." The preaching drunks took on any topic that came to mind: current events, the fate of the long-sunk *Titanic* or the relative merits of the Giants and the Dodgers. Naturally there was great argument and occasional fighting—none of it fatal but all of it loud.

I shouldn't complain, however, for these were rather entertaining drunks, who like the birds appeared in the spring and left with the first fall cold. A more dedicated fellow was there all the time, day and night, come rain, come shine. Up on the corner lived a drunk of legend, a true phenomenon, who could surely have qualified as the king of all the world's winos—not excluding the French. He was neither poetic like the others nor ambitious like the singer (to whom we'll presently come) but his drinking bouts were truly awe-inspiring and he was not without his sensitivity. In the throes of his passion he would shout to the whole wide world one concise command, "Shut up!" Which was disconcerting enough to all who heard (except, perhaps, the singer), but such were the labyrinthine acoustics of courtyards and areaways that he seemed to direct his command at me. The writer's block which this produced is indescribable. On one heroic occasion he yelled his obsessive command without one interruption longer than necessary to take another drink (and with no appreciable loss of volume, penetration or authority) for three long summer days and nights, and shortly afterwards he died. Just how many lines of agitated prose he cost me I'll never know, but in all that chaos of sound I sympathized with his obsession, for I, too, hungered and thirsted for quiet. Nor did he inspire me to a painful identification, and for that I was thankful. Identification, after all, involves feelings of guilt and responsibility, and since I could hardly hear my own typewriter keys I felt in no way accountable for his condition. We were simply fellow victims of the madding crowd. May he rest in peace.

No, these more involved feelings were aroused by a more intimate source of noise, one that got beneath the skin and worked into the very structure of one's consciousness—like the "fate" motif in Beethoven's Fifth or the knocking-at-the-gates scene in *Macbeth*. For at the top of our pyramid of noise there was a singer who lived directly above us; you might say we had a singer on our ceiling.

Now, I had learned from the jazz musicians I had known as a boy in Oklahoma City something of the discipline and devotion to his art required of the artist. Hence I knew something of what the singer faced. These jazzmen, many of them now world-famous, lived for and with music intensely. Their driving motivation was neither money nor fame, but the will to achieve the most eloquent expression of idea-emotions through the technical mastery of their instruments (which, incidentally, some of them wore as a priest wears the cross) and the give and take, the subtle rhythmical shaping and blending of idea, tone and imagination demanded of group improvisation. The delicate balance struck between strong individual personality and the group during those early jam sessions was a marvel of social organization. I had learned too that the end of all this discipline and technical mastery was the desire to express an affirmative way of life through its musical tradition and that this tradition insisted that each artist achieve his creativity within its frame. He must learn the best of the past, and add to it his personal vision. Life could be harsh, loud and wrong if it wished, but they lived it fully, and when they expressed their attitude toward the world it was with a fluid style that reduced the chaos of living to form.

The objectives of these jazzmen were not at all those of the singer on our ceiling, but though a purist committed to the mastery of the *bel canto* style, German *lieder*, modern French art songs and a few American slave songs sung as if *bel canto*, she was intensely devoted to her art. From morning to night she vocalized, regardless of the condition of her voice, the weather or my screaming nerves. There were times when her notes, sifting through her floor and my ceiling, bouncing down the walls and ricocheting off the building in the rear, whistled like tenpenny nails, buzzed like a saw, wheezed like the asthma of a Hercules, trumpeted like an enraged African elephant—and the squeaky pedal of her piano rested plumb center above my typing chair. After a year of non-co-operation from the neighbor on my left I became desperate enough to cool down the hot blast of his phonograph by calling the cops, but the singer presented a serious ethical problem: Could I, an aspiring artist, complain against the hard work and devotion to craft of another aspiring artist?

Then there was my sense of guilt. Each time I prepared to shatter the ceiling in protest I was restrained by the knowledge that I, too, during my boyhood, had tried to master a musical instrument and to the great distress of my neighbors—perhaps even greater than that which I now suffered. For while our singer was concerned basically with a single tradition and style, I had been caught actively between two: that of the Negro folk music, both sacred and profane, slave song and jazz, and that of Western classical music. It was most confusing; the folk tradition demanded that I play what I heard and felt around me, while those who were seeking to teach the classical tradition in the schools insisted that I play strictly according to the book and express that which I was *supposed* to feel. This sometimes led to heated clashes of wills. Once during a third-grade music appreciation class a friend of mine insisted that it was a large green snake he saw swimming down a quiet brook instead of the snowy bird the teacher felt that Saint Saëns' *Carnival of the Animals* should evoke. The rest of us sat there and lied like little black, brown and yellow Trojans about that swan, but our stalwart classmate held firm to his snake. In the end he got himself spanked and reduced the teacher to tears, but truth, reality and our environment were redeemed. For we were all familiar with snakes, while a swan was simply something the Ugly Duckling of the story grew up to be. Fortunately some of us grew up with a genuine appreciation of classical music *despite* such teaching methods. But as an inspiring trumpeter I was to wallow in sin for years before being awakened to guilt by our singer.

Caught mid-range between my two traditions, where one attitude often clashed with the other and one technique of playing was by the other opposed, I caused whole blocks of people to suffer.

Indeed, I terrorized a good part of an entire city section. During summer vacation I blew sustained tones out of the window for hours, usually starting—especially on Sunday mornings—before breakfast. I sputtered whole days through M. Arban's (he's the great authority on the instrument) double- and triple-tonguing exercises—with an effect like that of a jackass hiccupping off a big meal of briars. During school-term mornings I practiced a truly exhibitionist "Reveille" before leaving for school, and in the evening I generously gave the ever-listening world a long, slow version of "Taps," ineptly played but throbbing with what I in my adolescent vagueness felt was a romantic sadness. For it was farewell to day and a love song to life and a peace-be-with-you to all the dead and dying.

On hot summer afternoons I tormented the ears of all not blessedly deaf with imitations of the latest hot solos of Hot Lips Paige (then a local hero), the leaping right hand of Earl "Fatha" Hines, or the rowdy poetic flights of Louis Armstrong. Naturally I rehearsed also such school-band standbys as the *Light Cavalry* Overture, Sousa's "Stars and Stripes Forever," the *William Tell* Overture, and "Tiger Rag." (Not even an after-school job as office boy to a dentist could stop my efforts. Frequently, by way of encouraging my development in the proper cultural direction, the dentist asked me proudly to render Schubert's *Serenade* for some poor devil with his jaw propped open in the dental chair. When the drill got going, or the forceps bit deep, I blew real strong.)

Sometimes, inspired by the even then considerable virtuosity of the late Charlie Christian (who during our school days played marvelous riffs on a cigar box banjo), I'd give whole summer afternoons and the evening hours after heavy suppers of black-eyed peas and turnip greens, cracklin' bread and buttermilk, lemonade and sweet potato cobbler, to practicing hard-driving blues. Such food oversupplied me with bursting energy, and from listening to Ma Rainey, Ida Cox and

Clara Smith, who made regular appearances in our town, I knew exactly how I wanted my horn to sound. But in the effort to make it do so (I was no embryo Joe Smith or Tricky Sam Nanton) I sustained the curses of both Christian and infidel—along with the encouragement of those more sympathetic citizens who understood the profound satisfaction to be found in expressing oneself in the blues.

Despite those who complained and cried to heaven for Gabriel to blow a chorus so heavenly sweet and so hellishly hot that I'd forever put down my horn, there were more tolerant ones who were willing to pay in present pain for future pride.

For who knew what skinny kid with his chops wrapped around a trumpet mouthpiece and a faraway look in his eyes might become the next Armstrong? Yes, and send you, at some big dance a few years hence, into an ecstasy of rhythm and memory and brassy affirmation of the goodness of being alive and part of the community? Someone had to; for it was part of the group tradition—though that was not how they said it.

"Let that boy blow," they'd say to the protesting ones. "He's got to talk baby talk on that thing before he can preach on it. Next thing you know he's liable to be up there with Duke Ellington. Sure, plenty Oklahoma boys are up there with the big bands. Son, let's hear you try those "Trouble in Mind Blues." Now try and make it sound like old Ida Cox sings it."

And I'd draw in my breath and do Miss Cox great violence.

Thus the crimes and aspirations of my youth. It had been years since I had played the trumpet or irritated a single ear with other than the spoken or written word, but as far as my singing neighbor was concerned I had to hold my peace. I was forced to listen, and in listening I soon became involved to the point of identification. If she sang badly I'd hear my own futility in the windy sound; if well, I'd stare at my typewriter and despair that I should ever make my prose so sing. She left me neither night nor day, this singer on our ceiling, and as my writing languished I became more and more upset. Thus one desperate morning I decided that since I seemed doomed to live within a shrieking chaos I might as well contribute my share; perhaps if I fought noise with noise I'd attain some small peace. Then a miracle: I turned on my radio (an old Philco AM set connected to a small Pilot FM tuner) and I heard the words

> *Art thou troubled?*
> *Music will calm thee . . .*

I stopped as though struck by the voice of an angel. It was Kathleen Ferrier, that loveliest of singers, giving voice to the aria from Handel's *Rodelinda*. The voice was so completely expressive of words and music that I accepted it without question—what lover of the vocal art could resist her?

Yet it was ironic, for after giving up my trumpet for the typewriter I had avoided too close a contact with the very art which she recommended as balm. For I had started music early and lived with it daily, and when I broke I tried to break clean. Now in this magical moment all the old love, the old fascination with music superbly rendered, flooded back. When she finished I realized that with such music in my own apartment, the chaotic sounds from without and above had sunk, if not into silence, then well below the level where they mattered. Here was a way out. If I was to live and write in that apartment, it would be only through the grace of music. I had tuned in a Ferrier recital, and when it ended I rushed out for several of her records, certain that now deliverance was mine.

But not yet. Between the hi-fi record and the ear, I learned, there was a new electronic world. In that realization our apartment was well on its way toward becoming an audio booby trap. It was 1949 and I rushed to the Audio Fair. I have, I confess, as much gadget-resistance as the next American of my age, weight and slight income; but little did I dream of the test to which it would be put. I had hardly entered the fair before I heard David Sarser's and Mel Sprinkle's Musician's Amplifier, took a look at its schematic and, recalling a boyhood acquaintance with such matters, decided that I could build one. I did, several times before it measured within specifications. And still our system was lacking. Fortunately my wife shared my passion for music; so we went on to buy, piece by piece, a fine speaker system, a first-rate AM-FM tuner, a transcription turntable and a speaker cabinet. I built half a dozen or more preamplifiers and record compensators before finding a commercial one that satisfied my ear, and, finally, we acquired an arm, a magnetic cartridge and—glory of the house—a tape recorder. All this plunge into electronics, mind you, had as its simple end the enjoyment of recorded music as it was intended to be heard. I was obsessed with the idea of reproducing sound with such fidelity that even when using music as a defense behind which I could write, it would reach the unconscious levels of the mind with the least distortion. And it didn't come easily. There were wires and pieces of equipment all over the tiny apartment (I became a compulsive experimenter) and it was worth your life to move about without first taking careful bearings. Once we were almost crushed in our sleep by the tape machine, for which there was space only on a shelf at the head of our bed. But it was worth it.

For now when we played a recording on our system even the drunks on the wall could recognize its quality. I'm ashamed to admit, however, that I did not always restrict its use to the demands of pleasure or defense. Indeed, with such marvels of science at my control I lost my humility. My ethical consideration for the singer up above shriveled like a plant in too much sunlight. For instead of soothing, music seemed to release the beast in me. Now when jarred from my writer's reveries by some especially enthusiastic flourish of our singer, I'd rush to my music system with blood in my eyes and burst a few decibels in her direction. If she defied me with a few more pounds of pressure against her diaphragm, then a war of decibels was declared.

If, let us say, she were singing *"Depuis le Jour"* from *Louise,* I'd put on a tape of Bidu Sayão performing the same aria, and let the rafters ring. If it was some song by Mahler, I'd match her spitefully with Marian Anderson or Kathleen Ferrier; if she offended with something from *Der Rosenkavalier,* I'd attack her flank with Lotte Lehmann. If she brought me up from my desk with art songs by Ravel or Rachmaninoff, I'd defend myself with Maggie Teyte or Jennie Tourel. If she polished a spiritual to a meaningless artiness I'd play Bessie Smith to remind her of the earth out of which we came. Once in a while I'd forget completely that I was supposed to be a gentleman and blast her with Strauss' *Zarathustra,* Bartók's *Concerto for Orchestra,* Ellington's "Flaming Sword," the famous crescendo from *The Pines of Rome,* or Satchmo scatting, "I'll be Glad When You're Dead" (you rascal you!). Oh, I was living with music with a sweet vengeance.

One might think that all this would have made me her most hated enemy, but not at all. When I met her on the stoop a few weeks after my rebellion, expecting her fully to slap my face, she astonished me by complimenting our music system. She even questioned me concerning the artists I had used against her. After that, on days when the acoustics were right, she'd stop singing until the piece was finished and then applaud—not always, I guessed, without a justifiable touch of sarcasm. And although I was not getting on with my writing, the unfairness of this business bore in upon me. Aware that I could not have withstood a similar comparison with literary artists of like caliber, I grew remorseful. I also came to admire the singer's courage and control, for she was neither intimidated into silence nor goaded into undisciplined screaming; she persevered, she marked the phrasing of the great singers I sent her way, she improved her style.

Better still, she vocalized more softly, and I, in turn, used music less and less as a weapon and more for its magic with mood and memory. After a while a simple twirl of the volume control up a few decibels and down again would bring a live-and-let-live reduction of her volume. We have long since moved from that apartment and that most interesting neighborhood and now the floors and walls of our present apartment are adequately thick and there is even a closet large enough to house the audio system; the only wire visible is that leading from the closet to the corner speaker system. Still we are indebted to the singer and the old environment for forcing us to discover one of the most deeply satisfying aspects of our living. Perhaps the enjoyment of music is always suffused with past experience; for me, at least, this is true.

It seems a long way and a long time from the glorious days of Oklahoma jazz dances, the jam sessions at Halley Richardson's place on Deep Second, from the phonographs shouting the blues in the back alleys I knew as a delivery boy, and from the days when watermelon men with voices like mellow bugles shouted their wares in time with the rhythm of their horses' hoofs and farther still from the washerwomen singing slave songs as they stirred sooty tubs in sunny yards; and a long time, too, from those intense, conflicting days when the school music program of Oklahoma city was tuning our earthy young ears to classical accents— with music appreciation classes and free musical instruments and basic instruction for any child who cared to learn and uniforms for all who made the band. There was a mistaken notion on the part of some of the teachers that classical music had nothing to do with the rhythms, relaxed or hectic, of daily living, and that one should crook the little finger when listening to such refined strains. And the blues and the spirituals—jazz—? they would have destroyed them and scattered the pieces. Nevertheless, we learned some of it all, for in the United States when traditions are juxtaposed they tend, regardless of what we do to prevent it, irresistibly to merge. Thus musically at least each child in our town was an heir of all the ages. One learns by moving from the familiar to the unfamiliar, and while it might sound incongruous at first, the step from the spirituality of the spirituals to that of the Beethoven of the symphonies or the Bach of the chorales is not as vast as it seems. Nor is the romanticism of a Brahms or Chopin completely unrelated to that of Louis Armstrong. Those who know their native culture and love it unchauvinistically are never lost when encountering the unfamiliar.

Living with music today we find Mozart and Ellington, Kirsten Flagstad and Chippie Hill, William L. Dawson and Carl Orff all forming part of our regular fare. For all exalt life in rhythm and melody; all add to its significance. Perhaps in the swift change of American society in which the meanings of one's origin are so quickly lost, one of the chief values of living with music lies in its power to give us an orientation in time. In doing so, it gives significance to all those indefinable aspects of experience which nevertheless help to make us what we are. In the swift whirl of time music is a constant, reminding us of what we were and of that toward which we aspired. Art thou troubled? Music will not only calm, it will ennoble thee.

John Updike / Ex-Basketball Player

The New Yorker, July 6, 1957

*Born in 1932, John Updike graduated from Harvard and spent a year in England
at the Ruskin School of Drawing and Fine Art. Updike has maintained a long association with* The New Yorker—*first as a member of its staff for two years and
then since 1957 as a regular contributor of poems, sketches, short stories, and
book reviews. He is the author of four books of poetry, seven novels, and several
collections of short stories and non-fiction.*

Pearl Avenue runs past the high-school lot,
Bends with the trolley tracks, and stops, cut off
Before it has a chance to go two blocks,
At Colonel McComsky Plaza. Berth's Garage
Is on the corner facing west, and there,   5
Most days, you'll find Flick Webb, who helps Berth out.

Flick stands tall among the idiot pumps—
Five on a side, the old bubble-head style,
Their rubber elbows hanging loose and low.
One's nostrils are two S's, and his eyes   10
An E and O. And one is squat, without
A head at all—more of a football type.

Once Flick played for the high-school team, the Wizards.
He was good: In fact, the best. In '46,
He bucketed three hundred ninety points,   15
A county record still. The ball loved Flick.
I saw him rack up thirty-eight of forty
In one home game. His hands were like wild birds.

He never learned a trade, he just sells gas,
Checks oil, and changes flats. Once in a while,   20
As a gag, he dribbles an inner tube,
But most of us remember anyway.
His hands are fine and nervous on the lug wrench.
It makes no difference to the lug wrench, though.

Off work, he hangs around Mae's Luncheonette.   25
Grease-grey and kind of coiled, he plays pinball,
Sips lemon cokes, and smokes those thin cigars;
Flick seldom speaks to Mae, just sits and nods
Beyond her face towards bright applauding tiers
Of Necco Wafers, Nibs, and Juju Beads.   30

John Updike / Energy: A Villanelle

The New Yorker, June 4, 1979

The log gives back, in burning, solar fire
  green leaves imbibed and processed one by one;
nothing is lost but, still, the cost grows higher.

The ocean's tons of tide, to turn, require
  no more than time and moon; it's cosmic fun.   5
The log gives back, in burning, solar fire.

All microörganisms must expire
  and quite a few became petroleum;
nothing is lost but, still, the cost grows higher.

The oil rigs in Bahrain imply a buyer   10
  who counts no cost, when all is said and done.
The logs give back, in burning, solar fire

but Good Gulf gives it faster; every tire
  is by the fiery heavens lightly spun.
Nothing is lost but, still, the cost grows higher.   15

So guzzle gas, the leaden night draws nigher
  when cinders mark where stood the blazing sun.
The logs give back, in burning, solar fire;
nothing is lost but, still, the cost grows higher.

Gay Talese / The Bridge

Esquire, December 1964

*A 1953 graduate of the University of Alabama, Gay Talese worked as a staff
writer on the* New York Times *for ten years. Currently a contributing editor to*
Esquire, *Talese has written articles for the* Saturday Evening Post, Show *magazine,* Life, *and the* Reader's Digest. *Two of his fictionalized studies have made
the best seller lists:* The Kingdom and the Power (1969), *a history of the* New
York Times *enterprise, and* Honor Thy Father (1971), *an intimate, inside view of
an Italo-American family. Both books are written in a mode of reporting that
fuses the techniques of fiction with the craft of nonfiction. In an introduction to a
collection of his reporting,* Fame and Obscurity, *Talese describes his approach to
journalism:*

> *The new journalism, though often reading like fiction, is not like fic-
> tion. It is, or should be, as reliable as the most reliable reportage al-*

though it seeks a larger truth than is possible through the mere compilation of verifiable facts, the use of direct quotations, and adherence to the rigid organizational style of the older form. The new journalism allows, demands in fact, a more imaginative approach to reporting, and it permits the writer to inject himself into the narrative if he wishes, as many writers do, or to assume the role of a detached observer, as others do, including myself.

I try to follow my subjects unobtrusively while observing them in revealing situations, noting their reactions and the reactions of others to them. I attempt to absorb the whole scene, the dialogue and mood, the tension, drama, conflict, and then I try to write it all from the point of view of the persons I am writing about, even revealing whenever possible what these individuals are thinking *during those moments that I am describing. This latter insight is not obtainable, of course, without the full cooperation of the subject, but if the writer enjoys the confidence and trust of his subjects it is possible, through interviews, by asking the right question at the right time, to learn and to report what goes on within other people's minds.*

The title of Talese's collection, Fame and Obscurity, *also helps describe one of the characteristic features of modern journalism. Celebrities and the oddly insignificant are equally attractive to reporters: the famous because the reporter can then publicize the obscurities behind official appearances, and the anonymous so the reporter can then bestow on the truly obscure the status of celebrities.*

They drive into town in big cars, and live in furnished rooms, and drink whiskey with beer chasers, and chase women they will soon forget. They linger only a little while, only until they have built the bridge; then they are off again to another town, another bridge, linking everything but their lives.

They possess none of the foundation of their bridges. They are part circus, part gypsy—graceful in the air, restless on the ground; it is as if the wide-open road below lacks for them the clear direction of an eight-inch beam stretching across the sky six hundred feet above the sea.

When there are no bridges to be built, they will build skyscrapers, or highways, or power dams, or anything that promises a challenge—and overtime. They will go anywhere, will drive a thousand miles all day and night to be part of a new building boom. They find boom towns irresistible. That is why they are called "the boomers."

In appearance, boomers usually are big men, or if not always big, always strong, and their skin is ruddy from all the sun and wind. Some who heat rivets have charred complexions; some who drive rivets are hard of hearing; some who catch rivets in small metal cones have blisters and body burns marking each miss; some who do welding see flashes at night while they sleep. Those who connect steel have deep scars along their shins from climbing columns. Many boomers have mangled hands and fingers sliced off by slipped steel. Most have taken falls and broken a limb or two. All have seen death.

They are cocky men, men of great pride, and at night they brag and build bridges in bars, and sometimes when they are turning to leave, the bartender will yell after them, "Hey, you guys, how's about clearing some steel out of here?"

Stray women are drawn to them, like them because they have money and no wives within miles—they liked them well enough to have floated a bordello boat beneath one bridge near St. Louis, and to have used upturned hardhats for flowerpots in the red-light district of Paducah.

On weekends some boomers drive hundreds of miles to visit their families, are tender and tolerant, and will deny to the heavens any suggestion that they raise hell on the job—except they'll admit it in whispers, half proud, half ashamed, fearful the wives will hear and then any semblance of marital stability will be shattered.

Like most men, the boomer wants it both ways.

Occasionally his family will follow him, living in small hotels or trailer courts, but it is no life for a wife and child.

The boomer's child might live in forty states and attend a dozen high schools before he graduates, *if* he graduates, and though the father swears he wants no boomer for a son, he usually gets one. He gets one, possibly, because he really wanted one, and maybe that is why boomers brag so much at home on weekends, creating a wondrous world with whiskey words, a world no son can resist because this world seems to have everything: adventure, big cars, big money—sometimes $350 or $450 a week—and gambling on rainy days when the bridge is slippery, and booming around the country with Indians who are sure-footed as spiders, with Newfoundlanders as shifty as the sea they come from, with roaming Rebel riveters escaping the poverty of their small Southern towns, all of them building something big and permanent, something that can be revisited years later and pointed to and said of: "See that bridge over there, son—well one day, when I was younger, I drove twelve hundred rivets into that goddamned thing."

They tell their sons the good parts, forgetting the bad, hardly ever describing how men sometimes freeze with fear on high steel and clutch to beams with closed eyes, or admitting that when they climb down they need three drinks to settle their nerves; no, they dwell on the glory, the overtime, not the weeks of unemployment; they recall how they helped build the Golden Gate and Empire State, and how their fathers before them worked on the Williamsburg Bridge in 1902, lifting steel beams with derricks pulled by horses.

They make their world sound as if it were an extension of the Wild West, which in a way it is, with boomers today still regarding themselves as pioneering men, the last of America's unhenpecked heroes, but there are probably only a thousand of them left who are footloose enough to go anywhere to build anything. And when they arrive at the newest boom town, they hold brief reunions in bars, and talk about old times, old faces: about Cicero Mike, who once drove a Capone whiskey truck during Prohibition and recently fell to his death off a bridge near Chicago; and Indian Al Deal, who kept three women happy out West and came to the bridge each morning in a fancy silk shirt; and about Riphorn Red, who used to paste twenty-dollar bills along the sides of his suitcase and who went berserk one night in a cemetery. And there was the Nutley Kid, who smoked long Indian cigars and chewed snuff and used toilet water and, at lunch, would drink milk and beer—without taking out the snuff. And there was Ice Water Charley, who on freezing wintry days up on the bridge would send apprentice boys all the way down to fetch hot water, but by the time they'd climbed back up, the water was cold, and he would spit it out, screaming angrily, *"Ice water, ice water!"* and send them all the way down for more. And there was that one-legged lecher, Whitey Howard, who, on a rail bridge one day, did not hear the train coming, and so he had to jump the tracks at the last second, holding on to the edge, during which time his wooden leg fell off, and Whitey spent the rest of his life bragging about how he lost his left leg twice.

Sometimes they go on and on this way, drinking and reminiscing about the undramatic little things involving people known only to boomers, people seen only at a distance by the rest of the world, and then they'll start a card game, the first of hundreds to be played in this boom town while the bridge is being built—a bridge many boomers will never cross. For before the bridge is finished, maybe six months before it is opened to traffic, some boomers get itchy and want to move elsewhere. The challenge is dying. So is the overtime. And they begin to wonder: "Where next?" This is what they were asking one another in the early spring of 1957, but some boomers already had the answer: New York.

New York was planning a number of bridges. Several projects were scheduled upstate, and New York City alone, between 1958 and 1964, planned to spend nearly $600,000,000 for, among other things, the double-decking of the George Washington Bridge, the construction of the Throgs Neck Bridge across Long Island Sound—and, finally, in what might be the most challenging task of a boomer's lifetime, the construction of the world's largest suspension span, the Verrazano-Narrows Bridge.

The Verrazano-Narrows, linking Brooklyn and Staten Island (over the futile objections of thousands of citizens in both boroughs), would possess a 4,260-foot center span that would surpass San Francisco's Golden Gate by 60 feet, and would be 460 feet longer than the Mackinac Bridge in upper Michigan, just below Canada.

It was the Mackinac Bridge, slicing down between Lake Huron and Lake Michigan and connecting the cities of St. Ignace and Mackinaw City, that had attracted the boomers between the years 1954 and 1957. And though they would now abandon it for New York, not being able to resist the big movement eastward, there were a few boomers who actually were sorry to be leaving Michigan, for in their history of hell-raising there never had been a more bombastic little boom town than the once tranquil St. Ignace.

Before the boomers had infiltrated it, St. Ignace was a rather sober city of about 2,500 residents, who went hunting in winter, fishing in summer, ran small shops that catered to tourists, helped run the ferryboats across five miles of water to Mackinaw City, and gave the local police very little trouble. The land had been inhabited first by peaceful Indians, then by French bushrangers, then by missionaries and fur traders, and in 1954 it was still clean and uncorrupt, still with one hotel, called the Nicolet—named after a white man, Jean Nicolet, who in 1634 is said to have paddled in a canoe through the Straits of Mackinac and discovered Lake Michigan.

So it was the Nicolet Hotel, and principally its bar, that became the boomers' headquarters, and soon the place was a smoky scene of nightly parties and brawls, and there were girls down from Canada and up from Detroit, and there were crap games along the floor—and if St. Ignace had not been such a friendly city, all the boomers might have gone to jail and the bridge might never have been finished.

But the people of St. Ignace were pleased with the big new bridge going up. They could see how hard the men worked on it and they did not want to spoil their little fun at night. The merchants, of course, were favorably disposed because, suddenly, in this small Michigan town by the sea, the sidewalks were enhanced by six hundred or seven hundred men, each earning between $300 and $500 a week—and some spending it as fast as they were making it.

The local police did not want to seem inhospitable, either, and so they did not raid the poker or crap games. The only raid in memory was led by some Michigan state troopers; and when they broke in, they discovered gambling among the boomers another state trooper. The only person arrested was the boomer who had been winning the most. And since his earnings were confiscated, he was unable to pay the $100 fine and therefore had to go to jail. Later that night, however, he got a poker game going in his cell, won $100, and bought his way out of jail. He was on the bridge promptly for work the next morning.

It is perhaps a slight exaggeration to suggest that, excepting state troopers, everybody else in St. Ignace either fawned upon or quietly tolerated boomers. For there were some families who forbade their daughters to date boomers, with some success, and there were young local men in town who despised boomers, although this attitude may be attributed as much to their envy of boomers' big cars and money as to the fact that comparatively few boomers were teetotalers or celibates. On the other hand, it would be equally misleading to assume that there were not some boomers who were quiet, modest men—maybe as many as six or seven— one of them being, for instance, a big quiet Kentuckian named Ace Cowan (whose wife was with him in Michigan), and another being Johnny Atkins, who once at the Nicolet drank a dozen double Martinis without causing a fuss or seeming drunk, and then floated quietly, happily out into the night.

And there was also Jack Kelly, the tall 235-pound son of a Philadelphia sailmaker, who, despite years of work on noisy bridges and despite getting hit on the head by so much falling hardware that he had fifty-two stitches in his scalp, remained ever mild. And finally there was another admired man on the Mackinac—the superintendent, Art "Drag-Up" Drilling, a veteran boomer from Arkansas who went West to work on the Golden Gate and Oakland Bay bridges in the thirties, and who was called "Drag-Up" because he always said, though never in threat, that he'd sooner drag-up and leave town than work under a superintendent who knew less about bridges than he.

So he went from town to town, bridge to bridge, never really satisfied until he became the top bridgeman—as he did on the Mackinac, and as he hoped to do in 1962 on the Verrazano-Narrows Bridge.

In the course of his travels, however, Drag-Up Drilling sired a son named John. And while John Drilling inherited much of his father's soft Southern charm and easy manner, these qualities actually belied the devil beneath. For John Drilling, who was only nineteen years old when he first joined the gang on the Mackinac, worked as hard as any to leave the boomer's mark on St. Ignace.

John Drilling had been born in Oakland in 1937 while his father was finishing on the Bay bridge there. And in the next nineteen years he followed his father, living in forty-one states, attending two dozen schools, charming the girls—marrying one, and living with her for four months. There was nothing raw nor rude in his manner. He was always extremely genteel and clean-cut in appearance, but, like many boomers' offspring, he was afflicted with what old bridgemen call "rambling fever."

This made him challenging to some women, and frustrating to others, yet intriguing to most. On his first week in St. Ignace, while stopped at a gas station, he noticed a carload of girls nearby and, exuding all the shy and bumbling uncertainty of a new boy in town, addressed himself politely to the prettiest girl in the car—a Swedish beauty, a very healthy girl whose boy friend had just been drafted—and thus began an unforgettable romance that would last until the next one.

Having saved a few thousand dollars from working on the Mackinac, he became, very briefly, a student at the University of Arkansas and also bought a $2,700 Impala. One night in Ola, Ark., he cracked up the car and might have gotten into legal difficulty had not his date that evening been the judge's daughter.

John Drilling seemed to have a charmed life. Of all the bridge builders who worked on the Mackinac, and who would later come East to work on the Verrazano-Narrows Bridge, young John Drilling seemed the luckiest—with the possible exception of his close friend, Robert Anderson.

Anderson was luckier mainly because he had lived longer, done more, survived more; and he never lost his sunny disposition or incurable optimism. He was thirty-four years old when he came to the Mackinac. He had been married to one girl for a dozen years, to another for two weeks. He had been in auto accidents, been hit by falling tools, taken falls—once toppling forty-two feet—but his only visible injury was two missing inside fingers on his left hand, and he never lost its full use.

One day on the north tower of the Mackinac, the section of catwalk upon which Anderson was standing snapped loose, and suddenly it came sliding down like a rollercoaster, with Anderson clinging to it as it bumped and raced down the cables, down 1,800 feet all the way to near the bottom where the cables slope gently and straighten out before the anchorage. Anderson quietly got off and began the long climb up again. Fortunately for him, the Mackinac was designed by David B. Steinman, who preferred long, tapering backspans; had the bridge been designed by O. H. Ammann, who favored shorter, chunkier backspans, such as the type he was then creating for the Verrazano-Narrows Bridge, Bob Anderson would have had a steeper, more abrupt ride down, and might have gone smashing into the anchorage and been killed. But Anderson was lucky that way.

Off the bridge, Anderson had a boomer's luck with women. All the moving around he had done during his youth as a boomer's son, all the shifting from town to town and the enforced flexibility required of such living, gave him a casual air of detachment, an ability to be at home anywhere. Once, in Mexico, he made his home in a whorehouse. The prostitutes down there liked him very much, fought over him, admired his gentle manners and the fact that he treated them all like ladies. Finally the madam invited him in as a full-time house guest and each night Anderson would dine with them, and in the morning he stood in line with them awaiting his turn in the shower.

Though he stands six feet and is broad-shouldered and erect, Bob Anderson is not a particularly handsome fellow; but he has bright alert eyes, and a round, friendly, usually smiling face, and he is very disarming, a sort of Tom Jones of the bridge business—smooth and swift, somewhat gallant, addicted to good times and hot-blooded women, and yet never slick or tricky.

He is also fairly lucky at gambling, having learned a bit back in Oklahoma from his uncle Manuel, a guitar-playing rogue who once won a whole carnival playing poker. Anderson avoids crap games, although one evening at the Nicolet, when a crap game got started on the floor of the men's room and he'd been invited to join, he did.

"Oh, I was drunk that night," he said, in his slow Southwestern drawl, to a friend some days later. "I was so drunk I could hardly see. But I jes' kept rolling them dice, and all I was seeing was sevens and elevens, sevens and elevens,

Jee-sus Kee-rist, all night long it went like that, and I kept winning and drinking and winning some more. Finally lots of other folks came jamming in, hearing all the noise and all, in this men's toilet room there's some women and tourists who also came in—jes' watching me roll those sevens and elevens.

"Next morning I woke up with a helluva hangover, but on my bureau I seen this pile of money. And when I felt inside my pockets they were stuffed with bills, crumpled up like dried leaves. And when I counted it all, it came to more than one thousand dollars. And that day on the bridge, there was guys coming up to me and saying, 'Here, Bob, here's the fifty I borrowed last night,' or, 'Here's the hundred,' and I didn't even remember they borrowed it. Jee-sus Kee-rist, what a night!"

When Bob Anderson finally left the Mackinac job and St. Ignace, he had managed to save five thousand dollars, and, not knowing what else to do with it, he bought a round-trip airplane ticket and went flying off to Tangier, Paris and Switzerland—"whoring and drinking," as he put it—and then, flat broke, except for his return ticket, he went back to St. Ignace and married a lean, lovely brunette he'd been unable to forget.

And not long after that, he packed his things and his new wife, and along with dozens of other boomers—with John Drilling and Drag-Up, with Ace Cowan and Jack Kelly and other veterans of the Mackinac and the Nicolet—he began the long road trip eastward to try his luck in New York. [. . .]

DISCUSSION QUESTIONS

1. Compare Talese's account of the "boomers" with Hard's description of newsboys. Which writer maintains more distance between himself and the working groups? How is that distance expressed in style and tone?

2. Describe the differences in each writer's use of details. Which writer tries harder to give the impression of journalistic objectivity? How are details used in each case to convey a sense of closely-knit working communities: Which community do you feel is described more satisfactorily? Explain.

3. Would the working people described by Talese and Hard be included as part of each writer's imagined audience? Describe the distinctions (if any) you think exist between the audience and subjects of each work. Which writer's style is more suited to the language spoken by his subjects? Do you think the smaller the stylistic margin the more honest the appraisal? Explain.

Pauline Kael / Movies on Television

The New Yorker, June 3, 1967

The New Yorker *has long been one of America's most successful weekly "sophisticated" magazines. It was started in 1925 by Harold Ross, a former newspaperman from Aspen, Colorado. The magazine inserted the following editorial in its first issue:*

> *It will publish facts that it will have to go behind the scenes to get, but it will not deal in scandal for the sake of scandal nor sensation for*

> *the sake of sensation. It will try conscientiously to keep its readers in-*
> *formed of what is going on in the fields in which they are most inter-*
> *ested. It has announced that it is not edited for the old lady in Dubuque.*
> *By this it means that it is not of that group of publications engaged in*
> *tapping the Great Buying Power of the North American steppe region*
> *by trading mirrors and colored beads in the form of our best brands of*
> *hokum.*

An urbane, calmly satirical magazine, The New Yorker *has emphasized a cool, ironic style of writing from the start. Over the years, it has featured such popular writers as James Thurber, J. D. Salinger, Dorothy Parker, John O'Hara, and John Updike. Reviews by Pauline Kael, one of this country's most distinguished movie reviewers, appeared regularly in* The New Yorker. *"Movies on Television" appeared in the* New Yorker *in 1967 and was reprinted in Kael's collection of film criticism,* Kiss Kiss Bang Bang.

A few years ago, a jet on which I was returning to California after a trip to New York was instructed to delay landing for a half hour. The plane circled above the San Francisco area, and spread out under me were the farm where I was born, the little town where my grandparents were buried, the city where I had gone to school, the cemetery where my parents were, the homes of my brothers and sisters, Berkeley, where I had gone to college, and the house where at that moment, while I hovered high above, my little daughter and my dogs were awaiting my return. It was as though my whole life were suspended in time—as though no matter where you'd gone, what you'd done, the past were all still there, present, if you just got up high enough to attain the proper perspective.

Sometimes I get a comparable sensation when I turn from the news programs or the discussion shows on television to the old movies. So much of what formed our tastes and shaped our experiences, and so much of the garbage of our youth that we never thought we'd see again—preserved and exposed to eyes and minds that might well want not to believe that this was an important part of our past. Now these movies are there for new generations, to whom they cannot possibly have the same impact or meaning, because they are all jumbled together, out of historical sequence. Even what may deserve an honorable position in movie history is somehow dishonored by being so available, so meaninglessly present. Everything is in hopeless disorder, and that is the way new generations experience our movie past. In the other arts, something like natural selection takes place: only the best or the most significant or influential or successful works compete for our attention. Moreover, those from the past are likely to be touched up to accord with the taste of the present. In popular music, old tunes are newly orchestrated. A small repertory of plays is continually reinterpreted for contemporary meanings—the great ones for new relevance, the not so great rewritten, tackily "brought up to date," or deliberately treated as period pieces. By contrast, movies, through the accidents of commerce, are sold in blocks or packages to television, the worst with the mediocre and the best, the successes with the failures, the forgotten with the half forgotten, the ones so dreary you don't know whether you ever saw them or just others like them with some so famous you can't be sure whether you actually saw them or only imagined what they were like. A lot of this stuff never really made it with any audience; it played in small towns or it was used to soak up the time just the way TV in bars does.

There are so many things that we, having lived through them, or passed over them, never want to think about again. But in movies nothing is cleaned away, sorted out, purposefully discarded. (The destruction of negatives in studio fires or deliberately, to save space, was as indiscriminate as the preservation and resale.) There's a kind of hopelessness about it: what does not deserve to last lasts, and so it all begins to seem one big pile of junk, and some people say, "Movies never really were any good—except maybe the Bogarts." If the same thing had happened in literature or music or painting—if we were constantly surrounded by the piled-up inventory of the past—it's conceivable that modern man's notions of culture and civilization would be very different. Movies, most of them produced as fodder to satisfy the appetite for pleasure and relaxation, turned out to have magical properties—indeed to *be* magical properties. This fodder can be fed to people over and over again. Yet, not altogether strangely, as the years wear on it doesn't please their palates, though many will go on swallowing it, just because nothing tastier is easily accessible. Watching old movies is like spending an evening with those people next door. They bore us, and we wouldn't go out of our way to see them; we drop in on them because they're so close. If it took some effort to see old movies, we might try to find out which were the good ones, and if people saw only the good ones maybe they would still respect old movies. As it is, people sit and watch movies that audiences walked out on thirty year ago. Like Lot's wife, we are tempted to take another look, attracted not by evil but by something that seems much more shameful—our own innocence. We don't try to reread the girls' and boys' "series" books of our adolescence—the very look of them is dismaying. The textbooks we studied in grammar school are probably more "dated" than the movies we saw then, but we never look at the old schoolbooks, whereas we keep seeing on TV the movies that represent the same stage in our lives and played much the same part in them—as things we learned from and, in spite of, went beyond.

Not all old movies look bad now, of course; the good ones are still good—surprisingly good, often, if you consider how much of the detail is lost on television. Not only the size but the shape of the image is changed, and, indeed, almost all the specifically visual elements are so distorted as to be all but completely destroyed. On television, a cattle drive or a cavalry charge or a chase—the climax of so many a big movie—loses the dimensions of space and distance that made it exciting, that sometimes made it great. And since the structural elements—the rhythm, the buildup, the suspense—are also partly destroyed by deletions and commercial breaks and the interruptions incidental to home viewing, it's amazing that the bare bones of performance, dialogue, story, good directing, and (especially important for close-range viewing) good editing can still make an old movie more entertaining than almost anything new on television. (That's why old movies are taking over television—or, more accurately, vice versa.) The verbal slapstick of the newspaper-life comedies—*Blessed Event, Roxie Hart, His Girl Friday*—may no longer be fresh (partly because it has been so widely imitated), but it's still funny. Movies with good, fast, energetic talk seem better than ever on television—still not great but, on television, better than what *is* great. (And as we listen to the tabloid journalists insulting the corrupt politicians, we respond once again to the happy effrontery of that period when the targets of popular satire were still small enough for us to laugh at without choking.) The wit of dialogue comedies like Preston Sturges's *Unfaithfully Yours* isn't much diminished, nor does a tight melodrama like *Double Indemnity* lose a great deal. Movies like Joseph L. Mankiewicz's *A Letter to Three Wives* and *All About Eve* look practically the same on television as in theatres, because they have almost no visual dimensions to lose. In them the camera serves primarily to show us the person who is going to speak the next presumably bright line—a scheme that on television, as in theatres, is acceptable only when the line *is* bright. Horror and fantasy films like Karl Freund's *The Mummy* or Robert Florey's *The Murders in the Rue Morgue*—even with the loss, through miniaturization, of imaginative special effects—are surprisingly effective, perhaps because they are so primitive in their appeal that the qualities of the imagery matter less than the basic suggestions. Fear counts for more than finesse, and viewing horror films is far more frightening at home than in the shared comfort of an audience that breaks the tension with derision.

Other kinds of movies lose much of what made them worth looking at—the films of von Sternberg, for example, designed in light and shadow, or the subtleties of Max Ophuls, or the lyricism of Satyajit Ray. In the box the work of these men is not as lively or as satisfying as the plain good movies of lesser directors. Reduced to the dead grays of a cheap television print, Orson Welles's *The Magnificent Ambersons*—an uneven work that is nevertheless a triumphant conquest of the movie medium—is as lifelessly dull as a newspaper Wirephoto of a great painting. But when people say of a "big" movie like *High Noon* that it has dated or that it doesn't hold up, what they are really saying is that their judgment was faulty or has changed. They may have overresponded to its publicity and reputation or to its attempt to deal with a social problem or an idea, and may have ignored the banalities surrounding that attempt; now that the idea doesn't seem so daring, they notice the rest. Perhaps it was a traditional drama that was new to them and that they thought was new to the world; everyone's "golden age of movies" is the period of his first moviegoing and just before—what he just missed or wasn't allowed to see. (The Bogart films came out just before today's college kids started going.)

Sometimes we suspect, and sometimes rightly, that our memory has improved a picture—that imaginatively we made it what we knew it could have been or should have been—and, fearing this, we may prefer memory to new contact. We'll remember it better if we don't see it again—we'll remember what it meant to us. The nostalgia we may have poured over a performer or over our recollections of a movie has a way of congealing when we try to renew the contact. But sometimes the experience of reseeing is wonderful—a confirmation of the general feeling that was all that remained with us from childhood. And we enjoy the fresh proof of the rightness of our responses that reseeing the film gives us. We re-experience what we once felt, and memories flood back. Then movies seem magical—all those *madeleines* waiting to be dipped in tea. What looks bad in old movies is the culture of which they were part and which they expressed—a tone of American life that we have forgotten. When we see First World War posters, we are far enough away from their patriotic primitivism to be amused at the emotions and sentiments to which they appealed. We can feel charmed but superior. It's not so easy to cut ourselves off from old movies and the old selves who responded to them, because they're not an isolated part of the past held up for derision and amusement and wonder. Although they belong to the same world as stories in *Liberty,* old radio shows, old phonograph records, an America still divided between hayseeds and city slickers, and although they may seem archaic, their pastness isn't so very past. It includes the last decade, last year, yesterday.

Though in advertising movies for TV the recentness is the lure, for many of us what constitutes the attraction is the datedness, and the earlier movies are more compelling than the ones of the fifties or the early sixties. Also, of course, the movies of the thirties and forties look better technically, because, ironically, the competition with television that made movies of the fifties and sixties enlarge their scope and their subject matter has resulted in their looking like a mess in the box—the sides of the image lopped off, the crowds and vistas a boring blur, the color altered, the epic themes incongruous and absurd on the little home screen. In a movie like *The Robe,* the large-scale production values that were depended on to attract TV viewers away from their sets become a negative factor. But even if the quality of the image were improved, these movies are too much like the ones we can see in theatres to be interesting at home. At home, we like to look at those stiff, carefully groomed actors of the thirties, with their clipped, Anglophile stage speech and their regular, clean-cut features—walking profiles, like the figures on Etruscan vases and almost as remote. And there is the faithless wife—how will she decide between her lover and her husband, when they seem as alike as two wax grooms on a wedding cake? For us, all three are doomed not by sin and disgrace but by history. Audiences of the period may have enjoyed these movies for their action, their story, their thrills, their wit, and all this high living. But through our window on the past we see the actors acting our other dramas as well. The Middle European immigrants had children who didn't speak the king's English and, after the Second World War, didn't even respect it so much. A flick of the dial and we are in the fifties amid the slouchers, with their thick lips, shapeless noses, and shaggy haircuts, waiting to say their lines until they think them out, then mumbling something that is barely speech. How long, O Warren Beatty, must we wait before we turn back to beautiful stick figures like Phillips Holmes?

We can take a shortcut through the hell of many lives, turning the dial from the social protest of the thirties to the films of the same writers and directors in the fifties—full of justifications for blabbing, which they shifted onto characters in oddly unrelated situations. We can see in the films of the forties the displaced artists of Europe—the anti-Nazi exiles like Conrad Veidt, the refugees like Peter Lorre, Fritz Kortner, and Alexander Granach. And what are they playing? Nazis, of course, because they have accents, and so for Americans—for the whole world— they become images of Nazi brutes. Or we can look at the patriotic sentiments of the Second World War years and those actresses, in their orgies of ersatz nobility, giving their lives—or, at the very least, their bodies—to save their country. It was sickening at the time; it's perversely amusing now—part of the spectacle of our common culture.

Probably in a few years some kid watching *The Sandpiper* on television will say what I recently heard a kid say about *Mrs. Miniver:* "And to think they really believed it in those days." Of course, we didn't. We didn't accept nearly as much in old movies as we may now fear we did. Many of us went to see big-name pictures just as we went to *The Night of the Iguana,* without believing a minute of it. The James Bond pictures are not to be "believed," but they tell us a lot about the conventions that audiences now accept, just as the confessional films of the thirties dealing with sin and illegitimacy and motherhood tell us about the sickly-sentimental tone of American entertainment in the midst of the Depression. Movies indicate what the producers thought people would pay to see—which was not always the same as what they *would* pay to see. Even what they enjoyed seeing does not tell us directly what they believed but only indirectly hints at the tone and style of a culture. There is no reason to assume that people twenty or thirty years ago were stupider than they are now. (Consider how *we* may be judged by people twenty years from now looking at today's movies.) Though it may not seem obvious to us now, part of the original appeal of old movies—which we certainly understood and responded to as children—was that, despite their sentimental tone, they helped to form the liberalized modern consciousness. This trash—and most of it was, and is, trash—probably taught us more about the world, and even about values, than our "education" did. Movies broke down barriers of all kinds, opened up the world, helped to make us aware. And they were almost always on the side of the mistreated, the socially despised. Almost all drama is. And, because movies were a mass medium, they had to be on the side of the poor.

Nor does it necessarily go without saying that the glimpses of something really good even in mediocre movies—the quickening of excitement at a great performance, the discovery of beauty in a gesture or a phrase or an image—made us understand the meaning of art as our teachers in appreciation courses never could. And—what is more difficult for those who are not movie lovers to grasp—even after this sense of the greater and the higher is developed, we still do not want to live only on the heights. We still want that pleasure of discovering things for ourselves; we need the sustenance of the ordinary, the commonplace, the almost-good as part of the anticipatory atmosphere. And though it all helps us to respond to the moments of greatness, it is not only for this that we want it. The educated person who became interested in cinema as an art form through Bergman or Fellini or Resnais is an alien to me (and my mind goes blank with hostility and indifference when he begins to talk). There isn't much for the art-cinema person on television; to look at a great movie, or even a poor movie carefully designed in terms of textures and contrasts, on television is, in general, maddening, because those movies lose too much. (Educational television, though, persists in this misguided effort to bring the television viewer movie classics.) There are few such movies anyway. But there are all the not-great movies, which we probably wouldn't bother going to see in museums or in theatre revivals—they're just not that important. Seeing them on television is a different kind of experience, with different values—partly because the movie past hasn't been filtered to conform to anyone's convenient favorite notions of film art. We make our own, admittedly small, discoveries or rediscoveries. There's Dan Dailey doing his advertising-wise number in *It's Always Fair Weather,* or Gene Kelly and Fred Astaire singing and dancing "The Babbitt and the Bromide" in *Ziegfeld Follies.* And it's like putting on a record of Ray Charles singing "Georgia on My Mind" or Frank Sinatra singing "Bim Bam Baby" or Elisabeth Schwarzkopf singing operetta, and feeling again the elation we felt the first time. Why should we deny these pleasures because there are other, more complex kinds of pleasure possible? It's true that these pleasures don't deepen, and that they don't change *us,* but maybe that is part of what makes them seem our own—we realize that we have some emotions and responses that *don't* change as we get older.

People who see a movie for the first time on television don't remember it the same way that people do who saw it in a theatre. Even without the specific visual loss that results from the transfer to another medium, it's doubtful whether a movie could have as intense an impact as it had in its own time. Probably by definition, works that are not truly great cannot be as compelling out of their time. Sinclair Lewis's and Hemingway's novels were becoming archaic while their authors lived. Can *On the Waterfront* have the impact now that it had in 1954? Not quite. And revivals in movie theatres don't have the same kind of charge, either.

There's something a little stale in the air, there's a different kind of audience. At a revival, we must allow for the period, or care because of the period. Television viewers seeing old movies for the first time can have very little sense of how and why new stars moved us when they appeared, of the excitement of new themes, of what these movies meant to us. They don't even know which were important in their time, which were "hits."

But they can discover *something* in old movies, and there are few discoveries to be made on dramatic shows produced for television. In comedies, the nervous tic of canned laughter neutralizes everything; the laughter is as false for the funny as for the unfunny and prevents us from responding to either. In general, performances in old movies don't suffer horribly on television except from cuts, and what kindles something like the early flash fire is the power of personality that comes through in those roles that made a star. Today's high school and college students seeing *East of Eden* and *Rebel Without a Cause* for the first time are almost as caught up in James Dean as the first generation of adolescent viewers was, experiencing that tender, romantic, marvelously masochistic identification with the boy who does everything wrong because he cares so much. And because Dean died young and hard, he is not just another actor who outlived his myth and became ordinary in stale roles—he is the symbol of misunderstood youth. He is inside the skin of moviegoing and television-watching youth—even educated youth—in a way that Keats and Shelley or John Cornford and Julian Bell are not. Youth can respond—though not so strongly—to many of our old heroes and heroines: to Gary Cooper, say, as the elegant, lean, amusingly silent romantic loner of his early Western and aviation films. (And they can more easily ignore the actor who sacrificed that character for blubbering righteous bathos.) Bogart found his myth late, and Dean fulfilled the romantic myth of self-destructiveness, so they look good on television. More often, television, by showing us actors before and after their key starring roles, is a myth-killer. But it keeps acting ability alive.

There is a kind of young television watcher seeing old movies for the first time who is surprisingly sensitive to their values and responds almost with the intensity of a moviegoer. But he's different from the moviegoer. For one thing, he's housebound, inactive, solitary. Unlike a moviegoer, he seems to have no need to discuss what he sees. The kind of television watcher I mean (and the ones I've met are all boys) seems to have extreme empathy with the material in the box (new TV shows as well as old movies, though rarely news), but he may not know how to enter into a conversation, or even how to come into a room or go out of it. He fell in love with his baby-sitter, so he remains a baby. He's unusually polite and intelligent, but in a mechanical way—just going through the motions, without interest. He gives the impression that he wants to withdraw from this human interference and get back to his real life—the box. He is like a prisoner who has everything he wants in prison and is content to stay there. Yet, oddly, he and his fellows seem to be tuned in to each other; just as it sometimes seems that even a teen-ager locked in a closet would pick up the new dance steps at the same moment as other teen-agers, these television watchers react to the same things at the same time. If they can find more intensity in this box than in their own living, then this box can provide *constantly* what we got at the movies only a few times a week. Why should they move away from it, or talk, or go out of the house, when they will only experience that as a loss? Of course, we can see why they should, and their inability to make connections outside is frighteningly suggestive of ways in which we, too, are cut off. It's a matter of degree. If we stay up half the night to watch old movies and can't face the next day, it's partly, at least, because of the fascination of our own movie past; *they* live in a past they never had, like people who become obsessed by places they have only imaginative connections with—Brazil, Venezuela, Arabia Deserta. Either way, there is always something a little shameful about living in the past; we feel guilty, stupid—as if the pleasure we get needed some justification that we can't provide.

For some moviegoers, movies probably contribute to that self-defeating romanticizing of expectations which makes life a series of disappointments. They watch the same movies over and over on television, as if they were constantly returning to the scene of the crime—the life they were so busy dreaming about that they never lived it. They are paralyzed by longing, while those less romantic can leap the hurdle. I heard a story the other day about a man who ever since his school days had been worshipfully "in love with" a famous movie star, talking about her, fantasizing about her, following her career, with its ups and downs and its stormy romances and marriages to producers and agents and wealthy sportsmen and rich businessmen. Though he became successful himself, it never occurred to him that he could enter her terrain—she was so glamorously above him. Last week, he got a letter from an old classmate, to whom, years before, he had confided his adoration of the star; the classmate—an unattractive guy who had never done anything with his life and had a crummy job in a crummy business—had just married her.

Movies are a combination of art and mass medium, but television is so single in its purpose—selling—that it operates without that painful, poignant mixture of aspiration and effort and compromise. We almost never think of calling a television show "beautiful," or even of complaining about the absence of beauty, because we take it for granted that television operates without beauty. When we see on television photographic records of the past, like the pictures of Scott's Antarctic expedition or those series on the First World War, they seem almost too strong for the box, too pure for it. The past has a terror and a fascination and a beauty beyond almost anything else. We are looking at the dead, and they move and grin and wave at us; it's an almost unbearable experience. When our wonder and our grief are interrupted or followed by a commercial, we want to destroy the ugly box. Old movies don't tear us apart like that. They do something else, which we can take more of and take more easily: they give us a sense of the passage of life. Here is Elizabeth Taylor as a plump matron and here, an hour later, as an exquisite child. That charmingly petulant little gigolo with the skinny face and the mustache that seems the most substantial part of him—can he have developed into the great Laurence Olivier? Here is Orson Welles, as a young man, playing a handsome old man, and here is Orson Welles as he has really aged. Here are Bette Davis and Charles Boyer traversing the course of their lives from ingenue and juvenile, through major roles, into character parts—back and forth, endlessly, embodying the good and bad characters of many styles, many periods. We see the old character actors put out to pasture in television serials, playing gossipy neighbors or grumpy grandpas, and then we see them in their youth or middle age, in the roles that made them famous—and it's startling to find how good they were, how vital, after we've encountered them caricaturing themselves, feeding off their old roles. They have almost nothing left of that young actor we responded to—and still find ourselves responding to—except the distinctive voice and a few crotchets. There are those of us who, when we watch old movies, sit there murmuring the names as the actors appear (Florence Bates, Henry Daniell, Ernest Thesiger, Constance Collier, Edna May Oliver, Douglas Fowley), or we recognize them but can't remember their names, yet know how well we once knew them, experiencing the failure of memory as a loss of our own past until we can supply it (Maude Eburne or Porter Hall)—with great relief. After a few seconds, I can always remember them, though I cannot remember the names of my childhood companions or of the prizefighter I once dated, or even of the boy who took me to the senior prom. We are eager to hear again that line we know is coming. We hate to miss anything. Our memories are jarred by cuts. We want to see the movie to the end.

The graveyard of *Our Town* affords such a tiny perspective compared to this. Old movies on television are a gigantic, panoramic novel that we can tune in to and out of. People watch avidly for a few weeks or months or years and then give up; others tune in when they're away from home in lonely hotel rooms, or regularly, at home, a few nights a week or every night. The rest of the family may ignore the passing show, may often interrupt, because individual lines of dialogue or details of plot hardly seem to matter as they did originally. A movie on television is no longer just a drama in itself: it is part of a huge ongoing parade. To a new generation, what does it matter if a few gestures and a nuance are lost, when they know they can't watch the parade on all the channels at all hours anyway? It's like traffic on the street. The television generation knows there is no end; it all just goes on. When television watchers are surveyed and asked what kind of programming they want or how they feel television can be improved, some of them not only have no answers but can't understand the questions. What they get on their sets is television—that's it.

DISCUSSION QUESTIONS

1. Kael writes that movies ''are a combination of art and mass media, but television is so single in its purpose—selling—that it operates without that painful, poignant mixture of aspiration and effort and compromise.'' What happens, then, to that combination when movies are shown on TV? How is that like or unlike what happens when a poem is printed in a magazine?

2. Speaking of old movies, Kael writes that ''this trash—and most of it was, and is, trash—probably taught us more about the world, and even about values, than our 'education' did. Movies broke down barriers of all kinds, opened up the world, helped to make us aware.'' How did they do so? Do you agree or disagree with Kael? Use instances from movies she mentions or others you have seen to support your opinion.

Ellen Willis / Women and the Myth of Consumerism

Ramparts, June 1970

A politically leftist monthly addressed to a national audience of college educated men and women, Ramparts *publishes articles devoted to contemporary affairs with an emphasis on social and political reform. Ellen Willis is a free-lance journalist and reviewer of current cultural phenomena for* The New Yorker *and the*

New York Review of Books. *Here she attacks what has become the conventional notion (see Vance Packard in Best Sellers) of consumers victimized by the psychological manipulations of advertising.*

If white radicals are serious about revolution, they are going to have to discard a lot of bullshit ideology created by and for educated white middle-class males. A good example of what has to go is the popular theory of consumerism.

As expounded by many leftist thinkers, notably Marcuse, this theory maintains that consumers are psychically manipulated by the mass media to crave more and more consumer goods, and thus power an economy that depends on constantly expanding sales. The theory is said to be particularly applicable to women, for women do most of the actual buying, their consumption is often directly related to their oppression (e.g. make-up, soap flakes), and they are a special target of advertisers. According to this view, the society defines women as consumers, and the purpose of the prevailing media image of women as passive sexual objects is to sell products. It follows that the beneficiaries of this depreciation of women are not men but the corporate power structure.

Although the consumerism theory has, in recent years, taken on the invulnerability of religious dogma, like most dogmas its basic function is to defend the interests of its adherents—in this case, the class, sexual and racial privileges of Movement people.

First of all, there is nothing inherently wrong with consumption. Shopping and consuming are enjoyable human activities and the marketplace has been a center of social life for thousands of years. The profit system is oppressive not because relatively trivial luxuries are available, but because basic necessities are not. The locus of the oppression resides in the production function: people have no control over which commodities are produced (or services performed), in what amounts, under what conditions, or how these commodities are distributed. Corporations make these decisions and base them solely on their profit potential. It is more profitable to produce luxuries for the affluent (or for that matter for the poor, on exploitative installment plans) than to produce and make available food, housing, medical care, education, and recreational and cultural facilities according to the needs and desires of the people. We, the consumers, can accept the goods offered to us or we can reject them, but we cannot determine their quality or change the system's priorities.

As it is, the profusion of commodities is a genuine and powerful compensation for oppression. It is a bribe, but like all bribes it offers concrete benefits—in the average American's case, a degree of physical comfort unparalleled in history. Under present conditions, people are preoccupied with consumer goods not because they are brainwashed but because buying is the one pleasurable activity not only permitted but actively encouraged by our rulers. The pleasure of eating an ice cream cone may be minor compared to the pleasure of meaningful, autonomous work, but the former is easily available and the latter is not. A poor family would undoubtedly rather have a decent apartment than a new TV, but since they are unlikely to get the apartment, what is to be gained by not getting the TV?

Radicals who in general are healthily skeptical of facile Freudian explanations have been quick to embrace this theory of media manipulation based squarely on Freud, as popularized by market researchers and journalists like Vance Packard (Marcuse acknowledges Packard's influence in *One Dimensional Man*). In essence, this theory holds that ads designed to create unconscious associations between merchandise and deep-seated fears, sexual desires, and needs for identity and self-esteem, induce people to buy products in search of gratifications no product can provide. Furthermore, the corporations, through the media, deliberately create fears and desires that their products can claim to fulfill. The implication is that women are not merely taken in by lies or exaggerations—as, say, by the suggestion that a certain perfume will make us sexually irresistible—but are psychically incapable of learning from experience and will continue to buy no matter how often we are disappointed, and that in any case our "need" to be sexually irresistible is programmed into us to keep us buying perfume. This hypothesis of psychic distortion is based on the erroneous assumption that mental health and anti-materialism are synonymous.

Although they have to cope with the gyppery inherent in the profit system, people for the most part buy goods for practical, self-interested reasons. A washing machine does make a housewife's work easier (in the absence of socialization of housework); Excedrin does make a headache go away; a car does provide transportation. If one is duped into buying a product because of misleading advertising, the process is called exploitation; it has nothing to do with brainwashing.

Advertising, in fact, is a how-to manual on the consumer economy, constantly reminding us of what is available and encouraging us to indulge ourselves. It works (that is, stimulates sales) *because* buying is the only game in town, not vice versa. Advertising does appeal to morbid fears (e.g. of body odors) and false hopes (of irresistibility) and shoppers faced with indistinguishable brands of a product may choose on the basis of an ad (what method is better?), but this is just the old game of caveat emptor. It thrives on naivete and people learn to resist it through experience. Other vulnerable groups are older people, who had no previous experience—individual or historical—to guide them when the consumer cornucopia suddenly developed after World War II, and poor people, who do not have enough money to learn through years of trial, error and disillusionment to be shrewd consumers. The constant refinement of advertising claims, visual effects and so on, shows that experience desensitizes. No one really believes that smoking Brand X cigarettes will make you sexy. (The function of sex in an ad is probably the obvious one—to lure people into paying closer attention to the ad—rather than to make them "identify" their lust with a product. The chief effect of the heavy sexual emphasis in advertising has been to stimulate a national preoccupation with sex, showing that you can't identify away a basic human drive as easily as all that.) Madison Avenue has increasingly de-emphasized "motivational" techniques in favor of aesthetic ones—TV commercials in particular have become incredibly inventive visually— and even made a joke out of the old motivational ploys (the phallic Virginia Slims ad, for instance, is blatantly campy). We can conclude from this that either the depth psychology approach never worked in the first place, or that it has stopped working as consumers have gotten more sophisticated.

The argument that the corporations create new psychological needs in order to sell their wares is equally flimsy. There is no evidence that propaganda can in itself create a desire, as opposed to bringing to consciousness a latent desire by suggesting that means of satisfying it are available. This idea is superstitious: it implies that the oppressor is diabolically intelligent (he has learned how to control human souls) and that the media have magic powers. It also mistakes effects for causes and drastically oversimplifies the relation between ideology and material conditions. We have not been taught to dislike our smell so that they can sell deodorants; deodorants sell because there are social consequences for smelling. And the negative attitude about our bodies that has made it feasible to invent and market deodorants is deeply rooted in our anti-sexual culture, which in turn has been shaped by exploitive modes of production and class antagonism between men and women.

The confusion between cause and effect is particularly apparent in the consumerist analysis of women's oppression. Women are not manipulated by the media into being domestic servants and mindless sexual decorations, the better to sell soap and hair spray. Rather, the image reflects women as they are forced by men in a sexist society to behave. Male supremacy is the oldest and most basic form of class exploitation; it was not invented by a smart ad man. The real evil of the media image of women is that it supports the sexist status quo. In a sense, the fashion, cosmetics and "feminine hygiene" ads are aimed more at men than at women. They encourage men to expect women to sport all the latest trappings of sexual slavery—expectations women must then fulfill if they are to survive. That advertisers exploit women's subordination rather than cause it can be clearly seen now that *male* fashions and toiletries have become big business. In contrast to ads for women's products, whose appeal is "use this and he will want you" (or "if you don't use this, he won't want you"), ads for the male counterparts urge, "You too can enjoy perfume and bright-colored clothes; don't worry, it doesn't make you feminine." Although advertisers are careful to emphasize how *virile* these products are (giving them names like "Brut," showing the man who uses them hunting or flirting with admiring women—who, incidentally, remain decorative objects when the sell is aimed directly at men), it is never claimed that the product is *essential* to masculinity (as make-up is essential to femininity), only *compatible* with it. To convince a man to buy, an ad must appeal to his desire for autonomy and freedom from conventional restrictions; to convince a woman, an ad must appeal to her need to please the male oppressor.

For women, buying and wearing clothes and beauty aids is not so much consumption as work. One of a woman's jobs in this society is to be an attractive sexual object, and clothes and make-up are tools of the trade. Similarly, buying food and household furnishings is a domestic task; it is the wife's chore to pick out the commodities that will be consumed by the whole family. Appliances and cleaning materials are tools that facilitate her domestic function. When a woman spends a lot of money and time decorating her home or herself, or hunting down the latest in vacuum cleaners, it is not idle self-indulgence (let alone the result of psychic manipulation) but a healthy attempt to find outlets for her creative energies within her circumscribed role.

There is a persistent myth that a wife has control over her husband's money because she gets to spend it. Actually, she does not have much more financial autonomy than the employee of a corporation who is delegated to buy office furniture or supplies. The husband, especially if he is rich, may allow his wife wide latitude in spending—he may reason that since she has to work in the home she is entitled to furnish it to her taste, or he may simply not want to bother with domestic details—but he retains the ultimate veto power. If he doesn't like the way his wife handles his money, she will hear about it. In most households, particularly in the working class, a wife cannot make significant expenditures, either personal or in her role as object-servant, without consulting her husband. And more often than not, according to statistics, it is the husband who makes the final decisions about furniture and appliances as well as about other major expenditures like houses, cars and vacations.

The consumerism theory is the outgrowth of an aristocratic, European-oriented anti-materialism based on upper-class resentment against the rise of the vulgar bourgeoisie. Radical intellectuals have been attracted to this essentially reactionary position (Herbert Marcuse's view of mass culture is strikingly similar to that of conservative theorists like Ernest Van Den Haag) because it appeals both to their dislike of capitalism and to their feeling of superiority to the working class. This elitism is evident in radicals' conviction that they have seen through the system, while the average working slob is brainwashed by the media. (Oddly, no one claims that the ruling class is oppressed by commodities; it seems that rich people consume out of free choice.) Ultimately this point of view leads to a sterile emphasis on individual solutions—if only the benighted would reject their "plastic" existence and move to East Village tenements—and the conclusion that people are oppressed because they are stupid or sick. The obnoxiousness of this attitude is compounded by the fact that radicals can only maintain their dropout existence so long as plenty of brainwashed workers keep the economy going.

Consumerism as applied to women is blatantly sexist. The pervasive image of the empty-headed female consumer constantly trying her husband's patience with her extravagant purchases contributes to the myth of male superiority: we are incapable of spending money rationally; all we need to make us happy is a new hat now and then. (There is an analogous racial stereotype—the black with his Cadillac and his magenta shirts.) Furthermore, the consumerism line allows Movement men to avoid recognizing that they exploit women by attributing women's oppression solely to capitalism. It fits neatly into already existing radical theory and concerns, saving the Movement the trouble of tackling the real problems of women's liberation. And it retards the struggle against male supremacy by dividing women. Just as in the male movement, the belief in consumerism encourages radical women to patronize and put down other women for trying to survive as best they can, and maintains individualist illusions.

If we are to build a mass movement we must recognize that no individual decision, like rejecting consumption, can liberate us. We must stop arguing about whose life style is better (and secretly believing ours is) and tend to the task of collectively fighting our own oppression and the ways in which we oppress others. When we create a political alternative to sexism, racism and capitalism, the consumer problem, if it is a problem, will take care of itself.

DISCUSSION QUESTIONS

1. Of what relevance is Vance Packard's essay on consumerism (see Best Sellers) to Willis' argument? How does she feel her audience regards his essay? Whom is she writing for? What assumptions, for example, does she make about the political awareness of her audience?

2. Find some ads in Advertising that Willis could have used to support her arguments about the relationship between advertising methods and buying habits. How does her theory of advertising differ from Packard's? Which theory attributes more power to advertising methods? Which theory do you find more convincing? Support your case by using some of the ads in this book.

Woody Allen / A Look at Organized Crime

The New Yorker, August 15, 1970

"Comic Genius—Woody Allen Comes of Age," read the cover of Time *magazine in the spring of 1979 after the release of his critically acclaimed film,* Manhattan. *Certainly Allen has come a long way from fifteen when he was paid $25 a week to write jokes on a wholesale basis—50 each day after school for two years, or 25,000 jokes. A succession of television-writing jobs, stand-up comedian gigs, short stories for magazines, and eight movies brought Allen to* Manhattan *and his present popular acclaim as our "comic genius."*

In "A Look at Organized Crime," Allen employs a reportorial style to make statements about the mafia ("Other illicit activities engaged in by the Cosa Nostra members included gambling, narcotics, prostitution, hijacking . . .") which he continually undercuts with absurdities ("and the transportation of a large whitefish across the state line for immoral purposes"). As funny as Allen's material can be, it rarely floats free of the undercurrent of anxiety about the difficult moral choices of life and the inevitable occurrence of death.

It is no secret that organized crime in America takes in over forty billion dollars a year. This is quite a profitable sum, especially when one considers that the Mafia spends very little for office supplies. Reliable sources indicate that the Cosa Nostra laid out no more than six thousand dollars last year for personalized stationery, and even less for staples. Furthermore, they have one secretary who does all the typing, and only three small rooms for headquarters which they share with the Fred Persky Dance Studio.

Last year, organized crime was directly responsible for more than one hundred murders, and *mafiosi* participated indirectly in several hundred more, either by lending the killers carfare or by holding their coats. Other illicit activities engaged in by Cosa Nostra members included gambling, narcotics, prostitution, hijacking, loansharking, and the transportation of a large whitefish across the state line for immoral purposes. The tentacles of this corrupt empire even reach into the government itself. Only a few months ago, two gang lords under federal indictment spent the night at the White House, and the President slept on the sofa.

HISTORY OF ORGANIZED CRIME IN THE UNITED STATES

In 1921, Thomas (The Butcher) Covello and Ciro (The Tailor) Santucci attempted to organize disparate ethnic groups of the underworld and thus take over Chicago. This was foiled when Albert (The Logical Positivist) Corillo assassinated Kid Lipsky by locking him in a closet and sucking all the air out through a straw. Lipsky's brother Mendy (alias Mendy Lewis, alias Mendy Larsen, alias Mendy Alias) avenged Lipsky's murder by abducting Santucci's brother Gaetano (also known as Little Tony, or Rabbi Henry Sharpstein) and returning him several weeks later in twenty-seven separate mason jars. This signalled the beginning of a bloodbath.

Dominick (The Herpetologist) Mione shot Lucky Lorenzo (so nicknamed when a bomb that went off in his hat failed to kill him) outside a bar in Chicago. In return, Corillo and his men traced Mione to Newark and made his head into a wind instrument. At this point, the Vitale gang, run by Giuseppe Vitale (real name Quincy Baedeker), made their move to take over all bootlegging in Harlem from Irish Larry Doyle—a racketeer so suspicious that he refused to let anybody in New York ever get behind him, and walked down the street constantly pirouetting and spinning around. Doyle was killed when the Squillante Construction Company decided to erect their new offices on the bridge of his nose. Doyle's lieutenant, Little Petey (Big Petey) Ross, now took command; he resisted the Vitale takeover and lured Vitale to an empty midtown garage on the pretext that a costume party was being held there. Unsuspecting, Vitale walked into the garage dressed as a giant mouse, and was instantly riddled with machine-gun bullets. Out of loyalty to their slain chief, Vitale's men immediately defected to Ross. So did Vitale's fiancée, Bea Moretti, a showgirl and star of the hit Broadway musical *Say Kaddish,* who wound up marrying Ross, although she later sued him for divorce, charging that he once spread an unpleasant ointment on her.

Fearing federal intervention, Vincent Columbraro, the Buttered Toast King, called for a truce. (Columbraro had such tight control over all buttered toast moving in and out of New Jersey that one word from him could ruin breakfast for two-thirds of the nation.) All members of the underworld were summoned to a diner in Perth Amboy, where Columbraro told them that internal warfare must stop and that from then on they had to dress decently and stop slinking around. Letters formerly signed with a black hand would in the future be signed "Best Wishes," and all territory would be divided equally, with New Jersey going to Columbraro's mother. Thus the Mafia, or Cosa Nostra (literally, "my toothpaste" or "our toothpaste"), was born. Two days later, Columbraro got into a nice hot tub to take a bath and has been missing for the past forty-six years.

MOB STRUCTURE

The Cosa Nostra is structured like any government or large corporation—or group of gangsters, for that matter. At the top is the *capo di tutti capi,* or boss of all bosses. Meetings are held at his house, and he is responsible for supplying cold cuts and ice cubes. Failure to do so means instant death. (Death, incidentally, is one of the worst things that can happen to a Cosa Nostra member, and many prefer simply to pay a fine.) Under the boss of bosses are his lieutenants, each of whom runs one section of town with his "family." Mafia families do not consist of a wife and children who always go to places like the circus or on picnics. They are actually groups of rather serious men, whose main joy in life comes from seeing how long certain people can stay under the East River before they start gurgling.

Initiation into the Mafia is quite complicated. A proposed member is blindfolded and led into a dark room. Pieces of Cranshaw melon are placed in his pockets, and he is required to hop around on one foot and cry out, "Toodles! Toodles!" Next, his lower lip is pulled out and snapped back by all the members of the board, or *commissione;* some may even wish to do it twice. Following this, some oats are put on his head. If he complains, he is disqualified. If, however, he says, "Good, I like oats on my head," he is welcomed into the brotherhood. This is done by kissing him on the cheek and shaking his hand. From that moment on, he is not permitted to eat chutney, to amuse his friends by imitating a hen, or to kill anybody named Vito.

CONCLUSIONS

Organized crime is a blight on our nation. While many young Americans are lured into a career of crime by its promise of an easy life, most criminals actually must work long hours, frequently in buildings without air-conditioning. Identifying criminals is up to each of us. Usually they can be recognized by their large cufflinks and their failure to stop eating when the man sitting next to them is hit by a falling anvil. The best methods of combatting organized crime are:

1. Telling the criminals you are not at home.
2. Calling the police whenever an unusual number of men from the Sicilian Laundry Company begin singing in your foyer.
3. Wiretapping.

Wiretapping cannot be employed indiscriminately, but its effectiveness is illustrated by this transcript of a conversation between two gang bosses in the New York area whose phones had been tapped by the F.B.I.

> ANTHONY: Hello? Rico?
> RICO: Hello?
> ANTHONY: Rico?
> RICO: Hello.
> ANTHONY: Rico?
> RICO: I can't hear you.
> ANTHONY: Is that you, Rico? I can't hear you.
> RICO: What?
> ANTHONY: Can you hear me?
> RICO: Hello?
> ANTHONY: Rico?
> RICO: We have a bad connection.
> ANTHONY: Can you hear me?
> RICO: Hello?
> ANTHONY: Rico?
> RICO: Hello?
> ANTHONY: Operator, we have a bad connection.
> OPERATOR: Hang up and dial again, sir.
> RICO: Hello?

Because of this evidence, Anthony (The Fish) Rotunno and Rico Panzini were convicted and are currently serving fifteen years in Sing Sing for illegal possession of Bensonhurst.

Time Staff / Death of a Maverick Mafioso
[*On the Shooting of Joey Gallo*]

Time, April 1972

For many years, the slogan of Time *magazine was "curt, concise, complete." Founded in 1923 by Henry Luce and Briton Hadden,* Time, *the Weekly News Magazine was intended to appeal to the growing number of American college graduates. Its title was meant to suggest both the scope of the magazine's coverage of current events and its sensitivity to the limited time in which "busy men are able to spend on simply keeping informed." Luce and Hadden rejected the conventional format of objective news reporting and promoted instead a highly idiosyncratic, self-consciously "lively" narrative and a somewhat subjective, though corporate, journalistic style.*

Joey Gallo's murder received national attention. Inevitable were the comparisons with Mario Puzo's The Godfather *(see Best Sellers) to show how ruthlessly life imitates art.*

The scene could have been lifted right out of that movie. First, a night of champagne and laughter at Manhattan's Copacabana as Mobster Joseph ("Crazy Joe") Gallo, one of New York's most feared Mafiosi, celebrated his 43rd birthday. Then on to a predawn Italian breakfast at a gleaming new restaurant in the city's Little Italy area. Seated at his left at a rear table in Umbertos Clam House was his brawny bodyguard, Pete ("The Greek") Diopioulis; at Gallo's right, his sister Carmella. Across the table sat Gallo's darkly attractive bride of just three weeks, Sina, 29, and her daughter Lisa, 10. Quietly, a lone gunman stepped through a rear door and strode toward the table.

Both Gallo and Diopioulis were carelessly facing the wall instead of the door. The triggerman opened fire with a .38-caliber revolver. Women screamed. Joey and Pete were hit instantly. The Greek drew his own gun, began shooting back. So did one Gallo ally, seated at the front clam bar. Within 90 seconds, 20 shots ripped through the restaurant. Tables crashed over, hurling hot sauce and ketchup across the blue-tiled floor to mix with the blood of the wounded. The gunman whirled, ran out the same rear door and into a waiting car.

Gallo, wounded in a buttock, an elbow and his back, staggered toward the front of the café. He lurched through a front door and collapsed, bleeding, on the street. Carmella's screams attracted officers in a passing police car. They rushed Gallo to a hospital, but he died before reaching it.

MUSCLING

That melodramatic end to the short, brutal life of Joey Gallo surprised no one in New York's increasingly fratricidal underworld. There had been a contract out on his life ever since Mafia Boss Joe Colombo had been shot at an Italian Day rally in New York last June (TIME cover, July 12). Police do not believe that Gallo plotted that murder attempt, but friends of Colombo, who remains unable to talk or walk, thought he had. Gallo had been counted among the walking dead ever since he also aroused the anger of the biggest boss of them all, aging Carlo Gambino. Told to stop muscling into Gambino's operations, including the lucrative narcotics traffic in East Harlem, the cocky Gallo hurled the ultimate Mafia insult at Gambino: he spat at him.

If that act seemed foolhardy, it was nevertheless typical of Gallo, who never had the sense to play by the rigid rules of the brotherhood. He grew up with his brothers Larry and Albert in Brooklyn's Bath Beach, where mobsters often dumped their victims. One of his neighbors recalled Joey as "the kind of guy who wanted to grow up to be George Raft. He would stand on the corner when he was 15, flipping a half-dollar, and practice talking without moving his lips."

Joey first witnessed a gang murder in his early teens. After the victim was hauled away, he studied the scene, counted the bullet holes and took notes on how the killing must have been done. He began packing a pistol about the same time. Later, he affected the black shirt and white tie of Killer Richard Widmark in the movie *Kiss of Death.* He saw the movie so many times he knew all its lines. He spent hours in front of a mirror, trying to look as tough as Widmark—and he succeeded. He had a mercurial temper and acted out his movie fantasies as the cruelest of the Gallo brothers.

By the time Joey was 21, he was in trouble with the law, and a court-appointed psychiatrist found him insane. Other mobsters started calling him "Crazy Joe" but never to his face. He was too mean. Joey took pleasure in breaking the arm of one of his clients who was sluggish about paying protection money. He punctured an enemy with ice picks. He had gained his status by serving as one member (Colombo was another) of a five-man execution squad of Mafia Boss Joe Profaci in the late '50s. Police claim they had scored 40 hits. By then he and his brothers had carved out a chunk of the Brooklyn rackets; they turned against Profaci, touching off a gang war in which nine mobsters died and three disappeared.

Over the years, Gallo developed a wise-guy kind of humor that led some naive acquaintances to consider him a sort of folk hero. He was summoned to Robert Kennedy's office in 1959 when Kennedy was counsel to a Senate rackets investigating committee, looked at the rug and said, "Hey, this would be a great spot for a crap game." He once told a courtroom: "The cops say I've been picked up 15, maybe 17 times. That's junk. It was 150 times. I been worked over for nothing until my hat sits on my head like it belongs on a midget." Someone in 1961 overheard him trying to shake down a Brooklyn restaurant owner for a share of the profits. The proprietor asked for time to think about it. "Sure," said Gallo, "take three months in the hospital on me."

That quip cost Gallo nine years for extortion. In Attica state prison, Gallo earned a reputation as a civil rights leader of sorts. He helped lead an inmate drive to force white prison barbers to cut the hair of blacks; he had his own hair cut by a black barber to show his lack of prejudice. Actually, his motive seemed to be to recruit black toughs for his gang. When he got out of prison in March of 1971, he began hiring blacks as "button men" (musclemen)—pricking the ethnic sensibilities of other Mafiosi. He had openly toured Little Italy with four black henchmen a few days before he was hit. Some officials think that may have hastened execution of the contract.

HEARTY HOOD

Gallo's defiance of Mafia tradition did not mark him as particularly savvy. Neither did his open claim that he was about to write his memoirs. Other gangsters do not appreciate such literature. There was, for example, a $100,000 contract—for his death, not his papers—out on Joseph Valachi, who wrote in detail of his life with the Mob (he died of natural causes in prison). But Author Marta Curro, the wife of Actor Jerry Orbach, eagerly agreed to help write the book because she had discovered that Joey was "a great person, brilliant, absolutely charming."

It was at the Orbach apartment that Gallo married Sina Essary, a dental assistant he had met eleven years ago, before he went to jail. He and his first wife Jeffie Lee were divorced a few months ago. Joey and Sina, whose young daughter opened in the Broadway play *Voices* last week, soon became a part of the theatergoing, nightclubbing celebrity set. Crazy Joe, the killer, had become Pal Joey, the hearty hood. That, too, did not go down well with various godfathers.

SCRIPTS

Gallo kept telling his new found friends that he had gone straight. He told Celebrity Columnist Earl Wilson: "I'll never go back there—I think there is nothing out there for me but death." Police insist that Gallo was gulling others; that he actually was as much involved in the rackets as ever.

The truth seems to be that Gallo was leading a schizophrenic life in those last days: a steel-tough gunman in racket circles; a philosophic, warm conversationalist outside the Mob. Whether he was really at home in both roles, or just a good actor, he was clearly convincing. Actress Joan Hackett found him fascinating well before she knew of his Mafia connections. "I liked him completely apart from any grotesque glamorization of the underworld," she recalls. "I thought his attempt to leave that life was genuine. He was the brightest person I've ever known." But Gallo also conceded that "I'll never make it in the straight world."

With the slaying of two other lesser mobsters in New York last week, full gang warfare seemed imminent. The new image of Mafiosi as soft-spoken, smart-dressing businessmen, who shun such crudities as murder and torture as old-fashioned, seemed to be fading. Perhaps the Mob was taking those gory movie scripts about itself too seriously. At any rate, it was exposing the cruelty and ruthlessness of racketeering. Off-screen, murder is brutally final. Indeed, Gallo did not like parts of the *The Godfather*. He told a friend that he thought the death scenes seemed "too flashy."

Lew Dietz / The Myth of the Boss Bear

True, May 1973

Edited for an adult male audience interested in reading about adventure, mysteries, sports, military feats, "masculine" personalities, and the outdoors, True *prefers its nonfiction articles to be anecdotal, carefully documented, and written "with a strong punch." When compared with William Faulkner's* The Bear *(see*

Classics), written some thirty years earlier, the following essay reminds us of how "factual" accounts often depend on the expectations we derive from fiction and myth.

The northern Maine wilds were cloaked by a thick haze on my arrival, and when I flew out a week later there was a mountain-hugging fog. Within that span there was rain, more fog—and a bear called Lonesome George. Actually there were nine black bears sighted that week in June and one brought to earth with a bullet from a .284 Winchester. But only Lonesome George mattered to the hunters of Yankee-tu-laidi.

It was Glenn Wilcox who had dubbed the animal Lonesome George and Wilcox who had had the only confrontation with this seemingly immortal beast, a meeting that had left the bear with an altered forefoot. Mostly the animal was called simply The Bear, as though there were no other of its species in this remote and all but inaccessible region north of the Allagash.

Yankee-tu-laidi is the stream which flashes through this ridged country like a bright scepter. Local woodsmen suggest that the name might be a corruption of *touradie,* the French word for lake trout, but the origin is obscure. It's a fine, gamy hunk of territory, primarily because it is all but impossible to get into, and the hunters of Yankee-tu-laidi would like to keep it that way.

The day's hunting was over when I arrived. I tossed my sleeping bag into the loft, the only vacant nook in the gear-cluttered camp. John, the cook by tacit agreement—his stew was no more than tolerable but he was fastidiously clean—was stirring up the potluck. When a bottle started its rounds, I heard about The Bear.

Buzz Barry, a portly and imperturbable fellow with the dark soulful eyes of an Italian opera tenor, put it simply. "Glenn swears he's bigger than Joey's bear. And you saw Joey's bear."

I'd hunted with Barry and his Yankee-tu-laidi irregulars for a number of years. I knew about Joey Wilcox's bear. The spring before, Joey had come upon this King Kong of bears just a mile up the ridge from camp. The bear was shaking its great head as though bewildered by some awesome experience. It was only after Joey had dropped the bear at close range that he gained a clue to the nature of the drama. The dead bear showed evidence of having been bested in a brawl. Joey's bear went close to 400 pounds dressed, which meant a live weight of nearly 500, a big one, considering that the average mature black bear weighs around 300 pounds.

So what about the bear that was the winner and still champion? It was, as Buzz Barry put it, something to think about.

Barry was my host. Since he had the only camp lease in this 200 square miles of bear country, he might well have been elected top dog by expedient acclamation, like the sandlot kid with the only ball in town. Barry, however, had earned his stripes. He and his hunting partner, Glenn Wilcox, had pioneered bear hunting in this shaggy corner of Maine. In the course of five years, the pair had accounted for many bears and they'd got them the hard way, mostly before the state elevated the black bear to the status of game animal and established a limit of one in a season which extends from June 1 to December 31.

There was no further talk about The Bear that night. What else was there to say? These were Maine men who found ease and joy in the fraternity of hunting. They hunted for the challenge and the love of it, as had their fathers and grandfathers before them. And the ease in the camp was an ease that exists among men who have hunted long years together.

Five other men had come primarily to fish. Buzz Barry, Bob York and the Wilcox brothers were the bear hunters. For these four there was a special feeling about a bear hunt, something about the quest as warming and full-bodied as good bourbon. Until recent years few Maine hunters set out specifically for a bear. Bears were trapped, shot over bait or killed at a camp dump. And each fall a few were shot by deer hunters who came upon them accidentally. Maine has a good supply of bears and they seem to be on the increase. But the fellow who thinks he can walk into the woods any fine day and dispatch a bear has neglected to take this crafty animal into his calculation.

There are woodsmen who have spent a good part of their lives in Maine bear country and have never seen a live bear. A truly wild bear has ears like a lynx and the nose of a truffle hound. And although its eyes are no better than a deer's, a bear can identify a motionless man for what he is at 100 yards. A bear seldom waits to learn more.

The hunters had been in camp two days and, as was their custom, they had devoted the time to scouting the country in an attempt to learn how the bears were moving and where they were feeding. The first few months after leaving their winter dens, bears feed primarily on grass, sedges and herbs. These items, along with grubs and other insects, constitute their diet until the berries ripen in late July. The scouts reported encouraging bear signs but no great concentration in any one section. Our best bet, Buzz Barry thought, would be to hunt the overgrown woods, roads and grassy openings.

I was to hunt with him in his rig the next morning. Wheels are not a prerequisite to hunting bears in that big country but they do help, for while a deer is satisfied to live within a few square miles of territory, the "home" range of a mature black bear in Maine is possibly 700 square miles; a sow with cubs as much as 300. June is the peak of the bear's rut season, at which time both the sows and boars are apt to roam a bit more than normal. Eight years earlier, Barry decided that since there was no all-terrain vehicle available to meet the demanding requirements of Maine bear hunting, he would have to build his own rig.

Essentially his woods buggy is a dune buggy adapted to offer more low-gear pulling power and increased clearance. Bus transaxles solved both these problems. They reduced gear ratios and increased undercarriage clearance. And since there was no worry about making gear ratios too high, the hunters were able to go to over-sized tires for better traction. Reducing tire pressures to six pounds forward and eight in the rear offered additional traction and eased the punishing ride. The year before, I'd made the 30-mile buggy ride into Yankee-tu-laidi and can say that the trip would have made a hairy episode for *Mission Impossible.*

Buzz Barry and I set out shortly after sunup, leaving word of our itinerary and expected return time—an obvious precaution. Machines can break down under the punishing paces they are put through. There is no sleep or drink at the camp until all vehicles are accounted for.

Barry wanted to look over the Landry "road" (the quotes are used advisedly). At one point some busy beaver had created a daunting water hazard. As we broke a few holes in the damn to lower the water, I thought about a dialogue Teddy Roosevelt reported after he and his Maine guide had managed to get a wagon through to a camp on Munsungan Lake in mud season. "How," Teddy asked his guide, "do you Maine folks tell a road from a river?" "No beaver dams on the roads," was the guide's ready answer. Which goes to show that even a Maine guide can be wrong sometimes.

It was a dark day with a threat of rain, which was good, Buzz said, because it would make for soft going. Also it would give the hunter something closer to an even break. A bear can smell a man a country mile away. In wet weather a man can smell a bear, not a country mile perhaps, but a good 50 yards if the wind is right. I'd come to know a bear's rank, amonic scent, much like a skunk's, but less penetrating. Once you've smelled a bear, you'll never forget it.

A mile or so beyond the beaver flowage, we came upon fresh bear scats (in spring, a fresh bear dropping is green, turning brown and then black as it ages). Encouraged, we parked the buggy by a swollen brook. The still hunt on foot began.

Barry went ahead 30 paces or so and I took up the rear as we followed the twisting, grass-choked old-haul road. At each turn, my friend would ease to the outside of the trail and peer ahead before exposing himself. You spot a bear at an opening or you don't spot him at all. And if the bear sees you before you see the bear—well, it's good-bye Charlie.

"The bear has one flaw in his defenses. You might call it a character weakness," Barry said earlier. "A bear is a glutton. A bear's not apt to look up between nips when he's feeding, the way a deer does. If you sight a bear and the wind is right, you can stalk him. It takes patience, though. The biggest bear I ever shot took three hours of stalking.

"Matter of fact, there's one other advantage the bear hunter has. In the spring woods there is nothing in the world blacker than a black bear. You may mistake something in the woods for a bear, but you never mistake a bear for anything else. For one thing, a bear in the spring is seldom still; it moves frequently."

The Maine hunter is essentially a still hunter. He prefers to hunt alone or with a seasoned partner of long-standing. There is an incomparable excitement to a still hunt in gamy country. The hunter becomes a part of the natural realm. He tries to match eyes for eyes, ears for ears and cunning for cunning with his quarry. The fact that his rifle is an equalizer makes still-hunting no less a humbling experience.

We saw no sign of The Bear that day nor did we sight a bear of any stripe. The brothers Glenn and Joey Wilcox had arrived in camp when we trundled in. Glenn, plump as Friar Tuck; Joey, a mild apologetic fellow, make an unlikely looking pair of bear hunters. All the same, you'll have to search a long way to find anyone to match their knowledge of bears and their love of the hunt."

"The bears have begun to grub," Joey said. "They're doing a bit of frogging, too. Saw where a sow and her two cubs crossed the trail this morning below Dodge City."

"Dodge City" was a whimsy certainly, but an in-group place-name as well. This decaying cluster of old logging buildings had a story. A bear had broken into the hovel looking for forgotten oats and had been waylaid while attempting to escape through a window frame. There was "Pole Bridge" and "Mary's Tits," a pair of low knobs where Buzz had made that long stalk; "Trail 49," where one spring they had counted 49 bear scats on a two-mile stretch. And there was "Joey's Bend," that turn above the camp where Joey and his great bear had had their confrontation.

"Been a few bears working on the Loop Trail," Glenn said. "Small ones, yearlings, I'd guess.

Four bears had been sighted that day, only one large enough to be considered respectable. No one, not even Glenn Wilcox, mentioned The Bear, though he was the fiercest of all to get the animal dead to rights. I had the feeling that no one wished to hear the very real possibility that this grizzled lord of Yankee-tu-laidi had renounced his kingdom and departed. Only George, one of the fishermen who delighted in ribbing Lester, a pal, made a glancing reference to the subject.

"Lester and I come upon a bear flop near Fall Brook that two men could have shook hands across. I asked Lester to taste it for freshness, but he declined."

That night we feasted on a mess of fresh-caught brook trout. When the Coleman lamps were lit, Glenn decided it was high time he confessed that a bear had once driven him to water. This was early in his bear-hunting career before he'd learned to forgo mixing it up with a she-bear and her cubs. That afternoon he'd squeezed a shot off at a smallish bear. As he'd stepped into the brush to see what damage he'd done, he'd heard a low growl.

"There was that big sow, ears back, teeth bared, coming right for me. There wasn't time to do much more than shoot from the hip. A howl told me I'd creased her, but she came right on. I tried to take a hasty side step, but I wasn't quite fast enough. She caught me on the shoulder as she went by and sent me flying.

"It was just then that I remembered I'd fired the last round in my clip. As I frisked myself for my spare clip, I had a sinking feeling—I'd left my spare clip in my buggy. As that bear was preparing for a fresh charge, I took off for a beaver pond some 50 paces away. I hardly think my boots ever touched the ground."

For a good two hours Wilcox remained in that beaver pond up to his belly button, empty rifle held over his head. Twice he tried to go ashore and each time was driven back. Finally, with night coming on, he made a run for it.

That next morning Buzz Barry and I saw our first bear. Our plot was to leave the buggy at the beginning of Trail 29 and still-hunt the six miles back to camp on the Ridge Road. We were a mile or so from the trail when we spotted a bear down on its hunkers, feeding on grass.

Buzz eased the buggy to a halt. Stepping out, he slid a cartridge into his magazine. What he carried that day was his light carbine, figuring it would be right for that brushy terrain on the ridge. The bear was just under 200 yards away. My old .303 was under a tarp and little help in the situation. Since the bear had sighted us by then, there was no chance for a stalk. We simply stood there and watched the animal wander across the road and pass from view. Buzz estimated that the bear would have gone around 200 pounds, hardly respectable.

So soft was the going that day that we were able to come to within a few yards of deer; and rounding one twist in the trail we were met by a great bull moose which regarded us with lofty disdain and shuffled off in its own good time.

We saw a fair assortment of bear scats, but they weren't fresh enough to excite what Buzz called his turdometer, an instrument allegedly calibrated to degrees of freshness of bear droppings.

We did see where bears had been working earlier that spring. Here and there the bark of young balsams had been peeled back at their bases by sow bears to offer the treat of resin to their cubs. And we saw where bears had dismembered rotted trees seeking grubs in past seasons. I had my eye out for a bear tree, or what Maine woodsmen call a bear "marking post." When a boss bear feels an urge to express its machismo, it will commonly scribe a set of claw marks on a tree at the fullest extent of its reach for any lesser bear to try to match. Presumably an aspirant failing to meet the test moves on.

Back at camp that afternoon we learned that several yearling bears had been sighted on the back side of Haffey Mountain. Since cubs are dropped in midwinter, a "yearling" bear is nearly a year-and-a-half old in June. This is when the sow bear, ready for her biennial mating, drives off her youngsters to fend for themselves. Freshly out of custody and not yet seasoned to danger, these young bears are sighted more frequently than fully mature animals.

Barry wasn't interested in a yearling, but figured that if young bears were feeding in that area, bigger bears might be lurking not too far off. So Haffey Mountain was our destination as we headed out that next morning.

We were no more than three miles from camp when we saw a wolf. What made the sighting special was that wolves are officially extinct in Maine. Only in very recent years have there been reports of canids variously identified as wild dogs, coydogs, coyotes and wolves. We had a good, if brief, view of that animal as it crossed no more than 25 yards in front of us. Its coat was gray, tinged with red. We estimated its weight at something over 70 pounds, heavier than any coyote. It was similar in size and conformation to the wolf-coyote hybrids I'd seen in East Texas.

As we slogged into Haffey Mountain, it struck me that for these men the machines were every bit as much a challenge as the game. In this operation it's not enough to be a good hunter, you'd better be a damn good Yankee mechanic as well. There were few days that week when at least one buggy didn't come in under juryrig. The year before, a fuel pump had given out 20 miles from base. No problem. The gas tank had been unbolted and we rode home with one man holding the tank over the engine and feeding gas directly into the carburetor.

We did some hard traveling that day. We saw game aplenty, but the closest we came to a bear was a set of fresh droppings no more than three hours old. . . .

There was a bear hanging from a tree at the camp when we got in that night, however. Bob York had come upon it that afternoon near the Pole Bridge. By general agreement, it was a two-year-old that would go around 200 pounds.

Time was running out for most of the hunters. A hunt seldom falls into the classical pattern of beginning, middle and final climax. But there is usually a discernible form to a hunting week. The first days are characterized by dalliance and casual exploration, the savoring of a release from structured life. Then as the hunters get down to the prime business of the hunt, the tempo picks up. The last days of the hunt there is a further quickening. Logic, industry, experience having failed, hunters fall back upon hunches.

Buzz Barry aired his that night as we prepared to hit the sack. "We might try that piece west of Joey's Turn," he said. "No one's been in there this spring."

Glenn grunted. "Nothing in there but bog, puckerbrush and blowdowns. What makes you think . . . ."

"I'm half Irish," Buzz said. "I'm listening to the Irish in me. I say if he's still around, he's got to be there. We've covered just about every other place."

Expectancy is an emotion that can be as tangible as heat. Barry said little as we climbed out of the buggy and began to still-hunt up the trail above Joey's Turn that next morning, but I was aware of his leashed excitement. We eased along for a good 20 minutes without seeing any encouraging sign. We were up among the blowdowns when the first fresh bear scats began to show up.

Suddenly Buzz Barry motioned and I moved up abreast him. His eyes were luminous. "My computer's working," he said.

He grinned at my perplexity. "You've hunted long enough to know what I mean. Call it a hunter's sixth sense. Everything is right. The sign, the weather, the time of day, the wind direction and the look of the terrain. Unconsciously, you feed all this data into your computer. Right now, it comes out bear."

We moved on, climbing up over a steep washout. The rain that had been with us off and on all week began to fall in a fine mist. I could hear the rush of a swollen brook. The croak of a young raven was as sharp as drumfire in the stillness. Then I, too, felt the nerve-twanging feeling of something impending.

We saw The Bear that morning. It was no more than a snatch vision. The great black shape was there and then it was gone, so quickly that I was not at all certain that my eyes hadn't been tricked by imagination.

Ahead, Barry had lowered his half-raised rifle. I waited a full minute, then slid up beside him. Together we stepped into the trees. It was only then that I was sure. The smell of bear was astringent and as real as a solid right to the midsection. Abruptly the wind changed, and there was only the smell of the dank woods.

The hunters were lunching when we stepped into camp. Something in our faces or in our silent deliberation as we stacked our rifles compelled their eyes toward us. I was aware of tension in the room.

Finally Glenn Wilcox snapped, "Well, let's have it."

Barry said, "He was too smart for us. We didn't even get a shot."

The hunters stirred and ease came back into the room.

"There'll be another year," someone said. "Good old Lonesome George."

And in that moment I learned something about the hunters of Yankee-tu-laidi. To a man they prefer the myth to a dead bear. Its passing would have removed something irreplaceable; without say-so, the myth—the symbol of a wilderness they knew—was doomed.

Now at least there would be another year.

DISCUSSION QUESTIONS

1. Compare "The Myth of the Boss Bear" with William Faulkner's rendition of an equally "unsuccessful" bear hunt (see Classics). What are the different expectations made by each writer concerning his audience's knowledge of hunting? The wilderness? Bears? Myths? Other writers? Other literature on the same subject? Which writer spends more time talking about the technical details of a hunting expedition? Why is such information introduced?

2. Characterize Dietz's use of such similes and metaphors as: "as real as a solid right to the midsection," "the dark soleful eyes of an Italian opera tenor," "King Kong of bears." Compare them with Faulkner's figurative language (for example: "like pygmies about the ankles of a drowsing elephant," "a flavor like brass in the sudden run of saliva in his mouth").

Veronica Geng / The Blue Jeans Craze

Cosmopolitan, May 1973

Cosmopolitan, *with a circulation of 1.5 million, is directed to young career women. The editors describe their audience and the kind of articles they want to publish in the following way: "We want pieces that tell a hip, attractive, 18–34 year old, intelligent, good-citizen girl how to have a more rewarding life. . . ."*

Veronica Geng, formerly an editor of children's books, is now a freelance writer (see the ad for Cosmopolitan, *page 12, in the Advertising section).*

CAN A MERE FABRIC ATTRACT CULTISTS? YES, IF IT'S DENIM!

Anybody here remember the fashion forecasts of 1960? As we rounded the half-century mark, frantic clothing designers peered anxiously at the works of Arthur C. Clarke and Marshall McLuhan, and decided to hurtle us prematurely into the year 2000. Hard-edge minis with Wonder Woman boots . . . unisex vinyl jumpsuits . . . plastic-disc dresses . . . Jean Shrimpton floating space-helmeted and aluminum-clad through the pages of *Harper's Bazaar* . . . a world of Trova men and women, sleeked down for intergalactic love.

But this force-fed futurism began to look like the Empress's New Clothes. Who *wanted* to go about with a shaved head and NASA-inspired wardrobe? Meanwhile, insinuating itself into electronic-age psyches was an authentic garment-for-the-times: it was the ultimate in mass production, yet became so personal on the wearer that it could be called a uniform only in the sense that the naked human body is a uniform. By the mid-1960s it seemed clear to everybody but Stanley Kubrick that the now-and-future king of fashion was no arbitrary science-fiction fantasy, but a humble pair of pants dating back to the mid-nineteenth century. Jeans.

The pioneer in the field was, of course, Levi Strauss's blue-denim Western-style classic invented in 1850. Its influence spread like a sagebrush fire, so revolutionizing the sportswear industry that designers and manufacturers now say the distinction between "jeans" and "pants" has become virtually meaningless. Most men's and women's pants, whether high- or low-rise, straight- or flare-legged, cotton or suede, now have the basic jeans cut and details: a fairly tight fit across the backside and upper thighs; patch pockets at rear, slash pockets in front; top-stitching, and outside welt seams (as opposed to the concealed seams on, say, a man's tailored suit trouser).

As jeans-consciousness spread in the 1960s, celebrities, the high-visibility tip of any fashion iceberg, began falling all over each other to be photographed in the phenomenon. Some opted for the people's versions, like New York City's Mayor John Lindsay in his Wrangler work shirt and white denims. Others required something a bit more status-y: Henry Ford's former wife, Anne Johnson, bought a dozen denim shirt-and-pants ensembles at Madison Avenue's glittering Veneziano Boutique; and Ann-Margret, Sophia Loren, Marlene Dietrich, Joan Kennedy and many others appeared custom-jeaned in public. Even the aloof salons of international haute couture, perhaps a little piqued at not having *invented* jeans, picked them up and ran. In 1971, Paris declared blue denim the fabric of the year, and designers like St. Laurent and Givenchy (who designed an entire denim wardrobe for Audrey Hepburn) were inspired by the cut of jeans, the textures and shadings of denim, the Wild West fantasy, and so on into the altitudes of high chic. Latest-comers have been interior and industrial designers, playing with denim wall coverings, furniture and auto upholstery.

Today more than 5,000 stores across the country specialize in jeans. (In 1966 there wasn't *one* such store.) Last year, Americans bought 350 million pairs (men's, boys', women's and girls')—that's about two pairs each—and spent $2 billion on them. (Which is 200 times what it cost to run the Peace Corps in its peak year, and possibly as effective an expenditure, since U.S.-made jeans are a leading nonpartisan goodwill ambassador, their popularity untarnished by anti-Americanism. An additional $1 billion worth of their jeans is marketed abroad.)

No longer the exclusive property of an ephemeral love-generation or a few vestigial cowboys, jeans go everywhere on everybody. *Sure* Princess Yasmin is admitted to a plush Manhattan restaurant in her denim pants and matching jeweled bra—she's a Princess! The *hard* news is that my friend Adrianne's mother, a well coiffed woman from sartorially reactionary Washington, D.C., wore her Lee Riders jacket and jeans to the New York City Ballet and afterward to supper in the Plaza Hotel's Palm Court, and no bouncers jettisoned her for bad taste. My straw-in-the-wind contact in Chicago calls her enviably soft, faded denims "my little black dress." She says, "It's like the ad—'Did You Ever Have a Bad Time In Levi's?' Whenever I can't decide what to wear, I reach for my jeans. I just change tops, shoes, jewelry—like Chanel did with the *original* little black dress—and can go from the office to the very nicest party." Men, who were into jeans *first,* are wearing them more, with or without sports jackets, and liking suits less. (In 1970, manufacturers sold 4 million *fewer* suits than in 1935, the height of the Depression; and more recently, production has fallen off about 20 percent a year.) As Levi Strauss's board chairman, Walter A. Haas, Jr., points out, "Jeans have become a way of life for a lot more people than the so-called jeans generation."

So why, I ask myself, are the financial pages and apparel-trade publications sounding a little like reporters on the press bus in the Muskie Presidential campaign? ("Jeans Have Peaked" . . . "Basic Jeans Cooling Off" . . . "The Boom Is Ending.") Perhaps these hand-wringers don't understand the psychology of the jeans trend. Still imprisoned in the mini-midi-maxi-Muskie mentality, they're scared of waking up one morning to find themselves all alone, wearing a funny hat and wondering where the bandwagon went. They needn't worry; for hard-core jeans consumers, blue denim is a *constant* in the changing fashion world. True, the ultra-fashionables are not a market to be counted on; they didn't initiate the jeans movement, and a lot of them would have dropped their Kenneth Jay Lane blue-wolf-belly-lined denim coats fast if doctor and nurse uniforms were suddenly declared the ticket to a mention by *Women's Wear Daily,* Rona Barrett or Pete Hamill. The real jeans person, though, isn't *found* among these privileged ones; the average American consumer, with his or her private, unphotographed-by-Ron-Galella lifestyle, has made jeans much more than the transient hula-hoop of the apparel industry.

Nobody looks at that person more closely (or with more affection) than the major manufacturers of jeans: Levi Strauss & Co., Blue Bell, Inc. (makers of Mr. Wranglers and Lady Wranglers), and the H. D. Lee Co., Inc. Their sales have doubled and tripled in the past five years, and are still climbing. The two biggest manufacturers, Levi Strauss and Blue Bell, report that in 1972 *alone* their sales ($504 million and $344.5 million, respectively) went up 17 percent over the previous year, and most of the increase was due to jeans.

These enormous companies survive on their ability to distinguish between a fad and a solidly accepted style. Unlike a small high-fashion house, which can rush into production with a few hundred garments for a momentarily with-it look, a volume manufacturer produces tens of thousands of items in a particular style, and so cannot afford to be stuck with them when passions cool a month later. Did you think your Lady Wrangler bell-bottoms were cut out with a pair of shears wielded by an adorable Middle European tailor wearing a cardigan sweater draped with measuring tapes? Fantasy! Machines slice through dozens of *layers* of fabric, and have to be retooled every time the pattern is modified—so frivolous fashion mistakes are costly.

According to these hard-headed industry giants, jeans have settled in for a long, easy ride. The Wrangler people, for instance, spend a lot of time studying population trends; they believe that the young jeans wearers who started the fashion ten years ago, and are now entering the 25-to-30 age group, will continue to wear what they grew up in. *Men's Week,* a trade paper, makes a similar point, criticizing timid retailers who fear that "the 'like father, like son' philosophy will one day prevail," leading the young out of jeans and into traditionally tailored suits. The unintimidated big firms are *certain* this will not happen. While Wrangler and Lee and Levi Strauss may speak of "fashion jeans," varying fabrics and silhouettes from season to season, the basic jeans construction is an article of faith; they plan to stick with it.

In full agreement is another group alert to the future of jeans: the fabric manufacturers. When I spoke to Ben Sampson, vice president in charge of denim and fancy jeans fabric at Cone Mills Corporation, world's biggest maker of denim, he did not act like a man whose job was in danger of being phased out in favor of a vice president in charge of gray-flannel suiting. He was healthily pink-cheeked, smoked an expensive cigar, and handled the denim samples as if they were sensuous sable pelts. "We make projections for five years ahead and longer," he said, "and as far as we can see, jeans will continue to grow in importance." Puff on expensive cigar. Now, there is my idea of a happy man.

What is it about this product that has won the loyalty of so many consumers and warmed the hearts of so many vice presidents in charge of denim? Over the years, jeans became so heavy with myth that when the time was ripe, their power was irresistible. The very invention of jeans was a little fable of Frontier Ingenuity. A 20-year-old Bavarian immigrant named Levi Strauss arrived in San Francisco in 1850, carrying a supply of dry goods—including tent canvas—that he planned to sell for a grubstake in Gold Rush country. When he heard from a prospector that gold mining was tough on pants, he had a tailor make his friend a pair from the roll of canvas. The prospector went around praising his new "pants of Levi's," and soon Strauss had set up shop on San Francisco's Battery Street (not far from the company's present location). Rather quickly he switched from canvas (how did he stitch it . . . with an ice pick?) to a tough cotton fabric originally loomed in the Middle Ages in Nimes, France, called serge *de Nimes* (later Americanized to "denim"), in what would become the traditional color, indigo blue. Cowboys, lumberjacks, and other such folk figures took to Levi's for their durability and fit. (Horsemen prefer close-fitting britches with no bags or wrinkles to rub up saddle sores. In those days, before the advent of pre-shrunk fabrics, they'd make their form-fitting jeans even tighter by sitting in a horse-trough with them on, then wearing them till they dried to body-hugging snugness.) And so, along with the Stetson and the stallion, blue jeans passed into the Western Myth.

As other companies got into the action and the denim-wear business expanded, new symbols became attached to jeans. Blue Bell (Wrangler), whose early strength was in work clothing, outfitted farmers and industrial workers in bib overalls, and during World War II introduced a ladies' dungaree—the "Jeanie"—for females staffing the manless factories. Of course, few of these jeans wearers saw themselves as walking symbols of the mighty fist of American labor, any more than a weary, mud-spattered cowboy felt like Robert Mitchum. (In *Clothes* magazine's analysis, the American-worker "wanted to look not like a laborer but like a sport," so after World War II the bib overall fizzled and work-clothes fashion moved on to matched chino ensembles.) Still, residing in the national consciousness was a potent connection as vital as cowboy culture to the later jeans boom: factory or field hand, American working-class hero meant not only blue-collar, but blue denim.

A third element entered the burgeoning jeans myth during the late 1940s, when a generation of young people got fixed on brutal-but-sensitive movie anti-heroes—figures like Montgomery Clift, Marlon Brando, James Dean. Required anti-hero garb? Leather jacket and blue jeans. The genital-hugging fit made jeans the most erotic male garb since Elizabethan cod-pieces. Furthermore, since *machismo* had not yet bit the dust, jeans looked deliciously tough—weathering gang wars, grueling motorcycle rides, fist fights, gun duels, and emotional crises. The soft look for men's jeans was still years away; Hell's Angels prototypes boasted that they hadn't taken *theirs* off for a washing since point-of-purchase. (It was a while before girls would be welcomed into the rebellion as anything more than decorative sidekicks in circular skirts—Natalie Wood!—but our day was to come.) So, as young people began thinking of themselves as a group (a "class" of sorts), blue jeans became a symbol of physical and psychological freedom from the adult world. Adults responded with predictable displeasure—and in some places even tried to ban denim from public schools.

Eminent sociologists are still trying to figure out what happened during the button-down apathy of the Eisenhower years, so I won't hazard any theories of my own. In any case, when jeans were ready for a risorgimento in the 1960s, they already carried an enormous mythic significance. To a generation that believed a massive military-industrial complex was brutalizing the American dream, jeans symbolized a return to the friendlier, simpler values of the frontier, where each man (so goes wistful legend) had control over his own life, and where people cooperated to survive. To a movement of largely middle-class youth concerned with political and economic justice, jeans evoked an identification with the working class, even the poor and oppressed, and made any economic distinction among young people themselves practically invisible. And to all who simply did not like the way their forebears had managed the world, jeans carried the stamp of rebel-with-a-cause.

There are other theories to help explain the popularity of denim. Desmond Morris, in *The Human Zoo,* says the "youth sub-culture," like the dominant "adult culture," needs stimulation from the environment by means of fashion changes. Going with Morris's theory, you can read the jeans boom as one more transitory ploy in the game of "shifting erogenous zones": blue jeans are popular because they accent the pelvic area and rouse jaded humans who have ceased to be turned on by women's breasts or men's status-display. (According to Morris, one of the most stimulating *male* erogenous zones has been the wallet or stock portfolio.) A less cynical theory (one defended by those who feel a preference for jeans is not a mere fad but a sign of profound change in values) was put forward by Charles Reich in *The Greening of America:* "Jeans make one conscious of the body, not as something separate from the face but as part of the whole individual. . . . [Blue jeans are] a declaration of sensuality, not sensuality-for-display as in Madison Avenue style, but sensuality as part of the natural in man. . . . [They] are a deliberate rejection of the neon colors and artificial, plastic-coated look of the affluent society."

As if *that* weren't enough of a blow to the affluent society, many jeans wearers reject the very notion of a consumer culture with its emphasis on what's new. They like what's old: the ultimate blue jean is weathered to the beauty of a New England barn, and each pair arrives at uniqueness by the fading, tears, patches, and shape-changes created by the wearer's body and personal history. For those too impatient to wait for a personal history to evolve, second-hand jeans are big sellers (if you're not afraid of stealing someone else's karma). Eventually, jeans past repair are "recycled" into shorts, bags, patchwork . . . ecology in action, and scarcely reassuring to those whose god is the Gross National Product.

So far, jeans manufacturers have coexisted with this scary trend by marketing "fashion" jeans in new silhouettes, colors, and fabrics to supplement everybody's old standards—but never at the expense of the basic jeans appeal: practicality and quality at a low price. As *Men's Week* recently said: "[Young people] don't want to be intimidated with a 'you're out of vogue' routine that once worked so well for the apparel industry. . . . This is a sitting-on-the-floor generation. . . . They simply will not spend money for something that has to cause worry. Simplicity is everything. They want to buy with a minimal amount of looking, and once they leave the store they don't want to worry about how the garment will wash or wear or stretch or move. It had better not lose shape. It had better not fall apart. It had better perform."

These demands are not unreasonable, and the major jeans producers have a tradition of meeting them. As a result, the production process is one of the most challenging in the apparel field. And in the case of denim jeans, don't be fooled by the down-home simplicity of the fabric—no, you can't duplicate it at home with your hand loom and a box of Tintex. As Ben Sampson, the denim-and-fancy-jeans-fabrics VP at Cone Mills, explained to me, a denim mill is a highly specialized affair. While most other fabrics are woven, dyed and finished (permanent-pressed, Sanforized, etc.) at separate plants set up to perform those functions, denim needs special equipment, and is made under one roof, from bale of cotton to bolt of cloth.

HOW TO BUY JEANS

All About *Your* Jeans

The women who look stunning in jeans on the job or at soirées are not wearing the same shapeless-but-utilitarian dungarees that factory hands suited up in during World War II, nor the pariah-chic kind that Tom Wolfe describes as "the black, Can't Bust 'Em brand, hod-carrier jeans that have an emblem on the back of a hairy gorilla, real *funky* jeans." No. What's wanted is still beauty, and beauty in jeans is largely fit. Tight but not straining over hips, derriere and upper thighs. No baggy waists, pouchy folds of fabric under the buttocks, or hiked-up wrinkles at the knee. In the past, women and girls often turned to men's or boys' jeans, since they were cut tighter (and were available in heavier weight denim): manufacturers once estimated that from 30 to 70 percent of men's jeans were being bought by females. Even so, men's jeans were often too big in the waist for us, or too short in the leg. A friend of mine complained that all the men's jeans she tried on had a huge fold of fabric at the front of the crotch—presumably to accommodate a penis, which she didn't have.

Recently, manufacturers have begun to fill our requirements. Women's jeans are no longer inferior to men's in value or style range, and most now fit more figure types than the jodhpur-thighed odalisques I once paranoically thought they were exclusively designed for. Wrangler provides stores with charts showing waist and hip measurements for each size of Lady Wranglers, plus their equivalents in men's sizes, and has started individual Wrangler stores, as well as boutiques in some department stores, where you can try on both men's and women's jeans, along with related accessories like shirts and belts.

However, until every department store gets its head together and figures out a way to spare us all that running from department to department, the best bet of the *really* confused shopper may be a unisex jeans store, like the Los Angeles-based Jeans West shops, which stock thousands of pairs in many brands, in a wide price and style range.

Wherever you buy, *try on*. Measurements differ slightly from brand to brand. You *can* find one that fits you. No matter what anybody says, remember that preshrunk jeans (most are, nowadays) shrink slightly in length when washed, so buy them an inch or two long. Make sure you try on jeans in the same kind of shoe you'll wear them with; the final result—after shrinking—should cover most of the shoe heel. (Some people like jeans pants skimming the ground.) Purists can also get the original un-Sanforized "shrink-to-fit" jean. (Levi Strauss still makes them with the old-fashioned buttoned fly.) These must be bought two sizes too large; when washed, they shrink up, then stretch slightly to conform to body contours.

What weight to buy? *Consumer Reports* found that in all-cotton jeans, the heavier the weight, the better the wearability. If you're buying lightweight jeans for summer, part-cotton, part-synthetic ones wear best.

When it comes to fashion, what's in is what *you* like, and the available array looks like the menu at an Edwardian banquet. Jeans come in every leg-opening measurement from the narrow 14″ tuck-into-your-boots style to floppy 28″ palazzos. Imported jeans, like the elegant French NewMan brand, offer a variety of color, fabric and cut that is truly *formidable*. ("We are the fancy jeans people," says NewMan's export manager, Jean-Claude Boussion.) Among the most avant-garde American manufacturers is A. Smile, Inc., started by several young men in their early twenties (the same age as pioneer Levi Strauss when he made *his* contribution). The company made its debut in 1969 with pleated and baggy-legged jeans to the horse-laughs of an industry whose biggest seller today is this same style. A. Smile's fashion sense is likely to stay out in front.

FADING AND SOFTENING YOUR BLUE JEANS

One look that *is* out—at present—is the fresh-from-the-Abercrombie-and-Fitch-box appearance of brand-new denims, stiff with sizing; they make you look like a tenderfoot on her first day at the ranch. Before wearing, machine-wash jeans a couple of times, and douse generously with fabric softener. (If they're permanent press, use warm water and a "gentle" cycle). Machine-dry and remove at once so wrinkles don't set. All-cotton jeans may need a little ironing if you're fastidious, but jeans *are* the original wash 'n' wear garment, and wrinkles ease out with a wearing.

The much-sought-after faded look will be discernible after several washings, and is prettiest when natural; but the impatient can hasten the process. Don't throw bleach into the automatic washer (you can't get subtle color-control with machine-bleaching). Preferable technique: fill the bathtub with enough warm water to cover jeans, and add from half a quart to half a gallon of bleach, depending on how light you want them. Stir well. Add jeans, saturating them thoroughly and turning often. After a half hour or so, begin checking for color, and, when it's right, remove them. (Remember, wet fabrics looks darker.) Machine wash to remove bleach smell.

An even paler look and soft texture can be gotten by rubbing jeans with fine sand paper. Give special attention to backside and knee areas for authenticity.

James Dickey / Delights of the Edge

Mademoiselle, June 1974

Mademoiselle *magazine directs itself to the young college-educated woman with fiction by both known and unknown authors, non-fiction about the arts, travel, careers and fashion, and poetry of "the highest literary quality."*

Speaking as a parent and poet, James Dickey describes his youngest son's "dance with the void" and other "delights of the edge" in the article below.

Biographical information about James Dickey can be found in the headnote to Deliverance *in Best Sellers.*

Henry de Montherlant, the fine, fiery novelist and essayist of the muscles, guts and sex organs, of pride and chance-taking, once said, "If your life ever bores you, then risk it." Montherlant is probably, even more than Hemingway, our philosopher of action, of the delights of the edge. He can tell you of the electric life-spark of the bull's too-close horn, of the high-jumper's controlled all-out. He can throw the body.

I thought of this a couple of years ago in North Georgia, sitting two hundred feet above a dammed river, on pinestraw with my feet at a very real edge. My wife and I were looking down onto a section of the Tallulah River where a story of mine called *Deliverance* was being filmed. Both our sons were below us, far out of the range of our voices, my oldest boy working on the shooting crew, my youngest, thirteen, just visiting. The state-run dam was closed, which meant that the great rocky fall-offs had no water to fall off them. But they had my boys.

We lay at the edge, hoping our mortal children would not do anything foolish, but also intensely interested in what they *would* do, down there beyond us. The filming was taking place on both sides of the river, and, at the edge of a ninety-foot down-river drop, there was a primitive rig where you could walk across the river holding a rope. There was also a place where you had to jump over a kind of trickling gap, presumably still holding the rope. Or not holding the rope. My embryonic movie-making son kept going back and forth, carrying spools of film, makeup kits, impossible messages to Burt Reynolds and God knows what else. Below my son for ninety feet—I kept going up and down the rock-cruelties with field glasses—was nothing but a set of outcroppings designed by the universe eons ago to demonstrate the utter indifference of wild nature to the pain-bearing bodies of human beings; I was shook by the rage of their stillness. Any rock in any Body's descent was certain to be death- or mutilation-dealing. My wife and I said, almost the same second, "I hope Kevin doesn't try it."

But then of course he did. The suffering, hawk-perching parents could do nothing to prevent it: could do nothing, in fact, but watch like strange pinestraw-people the adventures of a beloved creature with the sheer murderousness of Gravity in collaboration with the serious cruelty of random stone.

Our child edged out, one foot staying in front of him, along the rope. He came to the gap in the crossing-stones.

He jumped for the place his brother had mastered, and slipped. Helpless in the higher-up, the field glasses hung fire in our hands, but he had not gone over. He swayed half in and half out of life, and pulled himself back into it. There he was, still in the shaking field glasses, four-eyed from the cliff-top and looking good. Then something broke out in him, down there. He started to dance, or do *something:* something with a lot of energy and motion. But it was not done for us: his mother and father, there at the other edge. It was a silent dance of pure delight: he was dancing with the void, and loving what had just about happened to him, and had not. We, creatures in the rarefied air of bushes at the brink, in the leaves of plants that leaned out over the vanished roar of dammed, gone water, knew that his excitement was not a show for Parent's Day, nor was it for the film crew or even for his brother. The adrenaline had hit like a Heaven-through-the-guts, and he rejoiced in the abyss, dancing back in a gangling, curious, beginning-athlete's way to safety, to his brother, to the crew, and eventually to us, who had no word to say, but only deep images, deep energies based on his.

The dance on the edge is one thing. The other, that makes the edge what it is in terms of my son's abandon, is the wheelchair. Or the bed, and hopeless immobility. It is also the coffin, the quiet plot: what Emily Dickinson called "that bareheaded life under the grass." The principle, if one is indeed involved, has something to do with courting mutilation, paralysis and death. It is of course better to think of oneself as a being who *can* display Hemingway's "grace under pressure," but the grace you might or might not be able to display is not nearly so important as the putting of yourself into a situation in which, far from performing according to a set standard of "grace," skill or blind courage, you don't really know what on earth you *will* do, can do, or what some blind agency outside your control will cause you to do. That is when the void can be danced with.

The heights of Tallulah Gorge are not the only edge. When you begin to look for them and court them in what can become your own way, edges are all over the place. Take the Writing Edge, for example. There are standard ways of saying things in verse. There are also very silly, far-out meaningless ways of saying them. And there are other ways that are, if you like, far-out and (maybe) silly but which also open up not only the void but the world.

> Let me pass by that gate
> Where Eve gnaws the ant
> And Adam impregnates a dazzle of fish.

Though this speaks of the Garden of Eden in some way, and though it is momentarily interesting, verbally and visualistically, to think of Eve, for whatever reason, gnawing the ant, the true creative edge is the third line. A million questions come, are denied by the reader, are pondered, rejected, reconsidered. But no matter. The sense of creative daring remains: the picture stays, and on its own terms. The image is unforgettable, though there is no logical reason for it to be so. *Adam,* the first man, the first consciousness, *impregnates* a *dazzle* of *fish.* The first consciousness, an aborning fecundity, sun-on-water, underwater scales: new, strange life. Sure: as a poet you can make yourself look silly, doing such stuff.

But the *possibility* of something strange and good is there: something absurdly reaching-for-it or giving itself a chance at another dimension, good and strange, strange and good, a chance not for routine proportion but for the thrilling, chance-taking queerness of creation: poetry of the edge.

Looked at from a certain, increasingly personal angle, all existence becomes a search for the edge: the place where one danger or the other charges the physical batteries and brings with it the will to live and search for more of the same. But behind the excitement and the momentary thrill of having done something a little special is always the threat of death, and, even more terrible, that of injury and immobilization, whereafter the excitements will all have to turn inward, and you will not—will never: that is, *never*—run that stretch of white water again, ski that slope, hunt that inoffensive deer, descend beneath the reef and look the moray in his strange, challenging and somehow accepting eye. No; for the edge cuts two ways. If you beat it, you can dance with it in all your fragile mortality. But you can also fall into the indifference of the earth or into a hospital bed with your arms full of life-giving tubes that, though they give the necessary chemicals of existence, can never give you back the life you lost on a whim: the one you gave up at the edge when you were seeking something else: the dance.

But lying—perhaps forever—in the hospital bed because the void and you did not *at that time* suit each other, you can assure yourself that the concept of the edge itself has not gone from you, and it is necessary that it should not: perhaps it is even more crucial now than before. It has become not a matter of cliffs and sports cars, of speed and the teeth of sharks, of high-powered bullets and ele-phants, but has changed itself into ideas and words, and these alone. The heroes of the immobilized mind, of the mind that has been reduced to the grave stillness of the body by the fatal interview, by the action of rocks and gravity, say, on human flesh, by the arm lost to the shark at the edge of the underwater pit, by the lower muscular system lost to the hope of the dance at the edge, can now have full time to take the real chance, which is that of *conceiving* the idea of Adam impreg-nating a dazzle of fish.

Or, again, of entering the universe. If one knows, if one has lost the dance at the edge—but not *finally*—that a philosopher named Anaximander once had an idea that the earth hung free in space, one can also, on that hope for us all, hang free in a hospital bed. And another thinker, a compatriot of Anaximander, specu-lated upon what would happen if one threw a spear outward from the very limit of things (What would—what *will* strike? Where will it *go?*). No matter: one has had to be at the edge to throw.

Death, crippling: they are part of the risk of the dance. I have seen my son take both the risk and take on the dance. They are all part of the same life-attitude, and we need not fall, but in the risk of this possibility there is something for us. If your life ever bores you, risk it. All right.

I was somewhere near West Virginia. I had a bow in my hand and darkness coming into my face. I would see no deer this night. But it was warm, and I was not worried. I was also lost. But, double-also, I was ready. I lay down on the ground and chewed a piece of jerky, and my salt-loving saliva glands never did better. I went to sleep and woke up in the same position, remembering vaguely that a puma had been sighted a few weeks before somewhere or other around here. I cracked my eyes for no reason, and across them, in the lower limbs of about ten trees, a ghostly form went. I was not sure of whether it was something in the world, or something lean and quiet within me, or whether it *was* me. I could have traversed those limbs, though I'm glad I didn't have to try. That edge was the border of West Virginia and Virginia. I'm not sure which I was sleeping and waking in, or whether my left hand was in one state and the right in the other. But when that thing floated across me, I was ready to dance with the void out of which all creation comes, and into which it must—hopefully with joy—go back. I got up, dirty and very hungry in the dawn-dingy forest, and looked slack-jawed at the new sun and the few birds that dared it. Here was one of the edges, and I was there. That non-beast could have torn me apart like a rotten gunny-sack, and left my ridiculous blood all over the strewn inconsequence of twigs. Mine. What I had seen was deathless, even if it had not been there. Adrenaline hit solid. Mine. I rose like the wild king of forever.

James Dickey / For the Death of Vince Lombardi

Esquire, September 1971

The poem, "For the Death of Vince Lombardi," was published in Esquire *within the year following the famed coach's death. Dickey's poem should be read in conjunction with the obituary account of "The Living Lombardi Legend" in* Press.

Biographical information about James Dickey can be found in the headnote to Deliverance *in Best Sellers.*

I never played for you. You'd have thrown
Me off the team on my best day—
No guts, maybe   not enough speed,
Yet running in my mind
As Paul Hornung, I made it here   5
With the others, sprinting down railroad tracks,
Hurdling bushes and backyard Cyclone
Fences, through city after city, to stand, at last, around you,
Exhausted, exalted, pale
As though you'd said "Nice going": pale   10
As a hospital wall. You are holding us
Millions together: those who played for you,
And those who entered the bodies
Of Bart Starr, Donny Anderson, Ray Nitschke, Jerry Kramer
Through the snowing tube on Sunday afternoon,   15
Warm, playing painlessly
In the snows of Green Bay Stadium, some of us drunk
On much-advertised beer   some old   some in other
Hospitals—most, middle-aged
And at home. Here you summon us, lying under   20
The surgical snows. Coach, look up: we are here:
We are held in this room

Like cancer.
The Crab has you, and to him
And to us you whisper   25
Drive, *Drive*. Jerry Kramer's face floats near—real, pale—
We others dream ourselves
Around you, and far away in the mountains, driving hard
Through the drifts, Marshall of the Vikings, plunging, burning
Twenty-dollar bills to stay alive, says, still   30
Alive, "I wouldn't be here
If it weren't for the lessons of football." Vince, they've told us;
When the surgeons got themselves
Together and cut loose
Two feet of your large intestine,   35
The Crab whirled up,   whirled out
Of the lost gut and caught you again
Higher up. Everyone's helpless
But cancer. Around your bed
The knocked-out teeth like hail-pebbles   40
Rattle down miles of adhesive tape from hands and ankles
Writhe in the room like vines   gallons of sweat
Blaze in buckets
In the corners   the blue and yellow of bruises
Make one vast sunset around you. No one understands you.   45
Coach, don't you know that some of us were ruined
For life? Everybody can't win. What of almost all
Of us, Vince? We lost.
And our greatest loss was that we could not survive
Football. Paul Hornung has withdrawn   50
From me, and I am middle-aged and grey like these others.
What holds us here?
Is it that you are dying by the code you made us
What we are by? Yes, Coach, it is true: love-hate is stronger
Than either love or hate. Into the weekly, inescapable dance   55
Of speed, deception, and pain
You led us, and brought us here weeping,
But as men. Or, you who created us as George
Patton created armies, did you discover the worst
In us: aggression, meanness, deception, delight in giving   60
Pain to others, for money? Did you make of us, indeed,
Figments   overspecialized, brutal ghosts
Who could have been real
Men in a better sense? Have you driven us mad
Over nothing? Does your death set us free?   65

Too late. We stand here among
Discarded TV commercials:
Among beer cans and razor blades and hair-tonic bottles,
Stinking with male deodorants: we stand here
Among teeth and filthy miles   70
Of unwound tapes, novocaine needles, contracts, champagne

Mixed with shower water,
Unraveling elastic, bloody face guards,
And the Crab, in his new, high position
Works soundlessly. In dying   75
You give us no choice, Coach,
Either. We've got to believe there's such a thing
As winning. The Sunday spirit-screen
Comes on   the bruise-colors brighten   deepen
On the wall   the last tooth spits itself free   80
Of a linebacker's aging head   knee cartilage cracks,
A boy wraps his face in a red jersey and crams it into
A rusty locker to sob, and we're with you
We're with you all the way
You're going forever, Vince.   85

Nora Ephron / The Boston Photographs

Esquire, November 1975

Reporter, free-lance journalist, magazine contributor, columnist, editor, and author of Wallflower at the Orgy (*1970*), Crazy Salad (*1975*), *and* Scribble, Scribble (*1978*), *Nora Ephron has become well-known for her pert prose style and perspicacious eye. In "The Boston Photographs," Ephron examines the outrage so many people felt towards the papers that printed the photos of a woman and child falling from a burning building and explains why they deserved to be printed in papers all over the country.*

"I made all kinds of pictures because I thought it would be a good rescue shot over the ladder . . . never dreamed it would be anything else. . . . I kept having to move around because of the light set. The sky was bright and they were in deep shadow. I was making pictures with a motor drive and he, the fire fighter, was reaching up and, I don't know, everything started falling. I followed the girl down taking pictures . . . I made three or four frames. I realized what was going on and I completely turned around, because I didn't want to see her hit."

You probably saw the photographs. In most newspapers, there were three of them. The first showed some people on a fire escape—a fireman, a woman and a child. The fireman had a nice strong jaw and looked very brave. The woman was holding the child. Smoke was pouring from the building behind them. A rescue ladder was approaching, just a few feet away, and the fireman had one arm around the woman and one arm reaching out toward the ladder. The second picture showed the fire escape slipping off the building. The child had fallen on the escape and seemed about to slide off the edge. The woman was grasping desperately at the legs of the fireman, who had managed to grab the ladder. The third picture showed the woman and child in midair, falling to the ground. Their arms and legs were outstretched, horribly distended. A potted plant was falling too. The caption

Copyright Boston Herald American, Stanley J. Forman, Boston Newspaper Division of the Hearst Corporation.

said that the woman, Diana Bryant, nineteen, died in the fall. The child landed on the woman's body and lived.

The pictures were taken by Stanley Forman, thirty, of the *Boston Herald American*. He used a motor-driven Nikon F set at 1/250, f 5.6–8. Because of the motor, the camera can click off three frames a second. More than four hundred newspapers in the United States alone carried the photographs; the tear sheets from overseas are still coming in. The *New York Times* ran them on the first page of its second section; a paper in south Georgia gave them nineteen columns; the *Chicago Tribune,* the *Washington Post* and the *Washington Star* filled almost half their

front pages, the *Star* under a somewhat redundant headline that read: SENSA-
TIONAL PHOTOS OF RESCUE ATTEMPT THAT FAILED.

The photographs are indeed sensational. They are pictures of death in action, of
that split second when luck runs out, and it is impossible to look at them without
feeling their extraordinary impact and remembering, in an almost subconscious
way, the morbid fantasy of falling, falling off a building, falling to one's death.
Beyond that, the pictures are classics, old-fashioned but perfect examples of pho-
tojournalism at its most spectacular. They're throwbacks, really, fire pictures,
1930s tabloid shots; at the same time they're technically superb and thoroughly
modern—the sequence could not have been taken at all until the development of
the motor-driven camera some sixteen years ago.

Most newspaper editors anticipate some reader reaction to photographs like Forman's; even so, the response around the country was enormous, and almost all of
it was negative. I have read hundreds of the letters that were printed in letters-to-
the-editor sections, and they repeat the same points. "Invading the privacy of
death." "Cheap sensationalism." "I thought I was reading the *National Enquirer.*" "Assigning the agony of a human being in terror of imminent death to
the status of a side-show act." "A tawdry way to sell newspapers." The *Seattle
Times* received sixty letters and calls; its managing editor even got a couple of
them at home. A reader wrote the *Philadelphia Inquirer: "Jaws* and *Towering Inferno* are playing downtown; don't take business away from people who pay good
money to advertise in your own paper." Another reader wrote the *Chicago Sun-
Times:* "I shall try to hide my disappointment that Miss Bryant wasn't wearing a
skirt when she fell to her death. You could have had some award-winning photographs of her underpants as her skirt billowed over her head, you voyeurs." Several newspaper editors wrote columns defending the pictures: Thomas Keevil of
the *Costa Mesa* (California) *Daily Pilot* printed a ballot for readers to vote on
whether they would have printed the pictures; Marshall L. Stone of Maine's
Bangor Daily News, which refused to print the famous assassination picture of the
Vietcong prisoner in Saigon, claimed that the Boston pictures showed the dangers
of fire escapes and raised questions about slumlords. (The burning building was a
five-story brick apartment house on Marlborough Street in the Back Bay section of
Boston.)

For the last five years, the *Washington Post* has employed various journalists as
ombudsmen, whose job is to monitor the paper on behalf of the public. The *Post*'s
current ombudsman is Charles Seib, former managing editor of the *Washington
Star;* the day the Boston photographs appeared, the paper received over seventy
calls in protest. As Seib later wrote in a column about the pictures, it was "the
largest reaction to a published item that I have experienced in eight months as the
Post's ombudsman. . . .

"In the *Post*'s newsroom, on the other hand, I found no doubts, no second
thoughts . . . the question was not whether they should be printed but how they
should be displayed. When I talked to editors . . . they used words like 'interesting' and 'riveting' and 'gripping' to describe them. The pictures told something
about life in the ghetto, they said (although the neighborhood where the tragedy
occurred is not a ghetto, I am told). They dramatized the need to check on the
safety of fire escapes. They dramatically conveyed something that had happened,
and that is the business we're in. They were news. . . .

"Was publication of that [third] picture a bow to the same taste for the morbidly sensational that makes gold mines of disaster movies? Most papers will not

print the picture of a dead body except in the most unusual circumstances. Does the fact that the final picture was taken a millisecond before the young woman died make a difference? Most papers will not print a picture of a bare female breast. Is that a more inappropriate subject for display than the picture of a human being's last agonized instant of life?'' Seib offered no answers to the questions he raised, but he went on to say that although as an editor he would probably have run the pictures, as a reader he was revolted by them.

In conclusion, Seib wrote: ''Any editor who decided to print those pictures without giving at least a moment's thought to what purpose they served and what their effect was likely to be on the reader should ask another question: Have I become so preoccupied with manufacturing a product according to professional traditions and standards that I have forgotten about the consumer, the reader?''

It should be clear that the phone calls and letters and Seib's own reaction were occasioned by one factor alone: the death of the woman. Obviously, had she survived the fall, no one would have protested; the pictures would have had a completely different impact. Equally obviously, had the child died as well—or instead—Seib would undoubtedly have received ten times the phone calls he did. In each case, the pictures would have been exactly the same—only the captions, and thus the responses, would have been different.

But the questions Seib raises are worth discussing—though not exactly for the reasons he mentions. For it may be that the real lesson of the Boston photographs is not the danger that editors will be forgetful of reader reaction, but that they will continue to censor pictures of death precisely because of that reaction. The protests Seib fielded were really a variation on an old theme—and we saw plenty of it during the Nixon-Agnew years—the ''Why doesn't the press print the good news?'' argument. In this case, of course, the objections were all dressed up and cleverly disguised as righteous indignation about the privacy of death. This is a form of puritanism that is often justifiable; just as often it is merely puritanical.

Seib takes it for granted that the widespread though fairly recent newspaper policy against printing pictures of dead bodies is a sound one; I don't know that it makes any sense at all. I recognize that printing pictures of corpses raises all sorts of problems about taste and titillation and sensationalism; the fact is, however, that people die. Death happens to be one of life's main events. And it is irresponsible—and more than that, inaccurate—for newspapers to fail to show it, or to show it only when an astonishing set of photos comes in over the Associated Press wire. Most papers covering fatal automobile accidents will print pictures of mangled cars. But the significance of fatal automobile accidents is not that a great deal of steel is twisted but that people die. Why not show it? That's what accidents are about. Throughout the Vietnam war, editors were reluctant to print atrocity pictures. Why *not* print them? That's what that war was about. Murder victims are almost never photographed; they are granted their privacy. But their relatives are relentlessly pictured on their way in and out of hospitals and morgues and funerals.

I'm not advocating that newspapers print these things in order to teach their readers a lesson. The *Post* editors justified their printing of the Boston pictures with several arguments in that direction; every one of them is irrelevant. The pictures don't show anything about slum life; the incident could have happened anywhere, and it did. It is extremely unlikely that anyone who saw them rushed out and had his fire escape strengthened. And the pictures were not news—at least they were not national news. It is not news in Washington, or New York, or Los Angeles that a woman was killed in a Boston fire. The only newsworthy thing about the pictures is that they were taken. They deserve to be printed because they are great pictures, breathtaking pictures of something that happened. That they disturb readers is exactly as it should be: that's why photojournalism is often more powerful than written journalism.

Dorothy Gloster / Sadie's Song

Essence, December 1975

Describing itself as addressed to "black women, age 18–34," Essence, *started by three young black businessmen in 1970, chose Gordon Parks, the accomplished photographer, journalist, composer, and film producer, as its first editorial director. It chose its name because "black is the essence of all color." The magazine's circulation grew quickly, topping 350,000 within its first year.* Essence *is now generally regarded as "the most glamour-filled black magazine on the market."*

"Sadie's Song," written by Dorothy Gloster, a freelance writer, photographer, and a doctoral student at the Manhattan Center for Advanced Psychoanalytic Studies, is characteristic of the magazine's many articles on contemporary black social and cultural consciousness.

The Mississippi Delta is a stretch of land that lies between the Mississippi and Yazu rivers and extends about 175 miles north to south and averages 60 miles in width. Its flat fertile land that has been hospitable to year after year of cotton planting was the last stronghold of the cotton kingdom and at the height of the civil rights movement was the setting for some of the most desperate attempts to put the constitution into full effect.

But cotton isn't king anymore. Soybeans and rice are cheaper to produce, and the cotton barons of the Delta announced at the beginning of this year's season that planting and production would be limited to 1,125,000 acres, a fraction of last year's planting. Reductions notwithstanding, the U.S. remains the world's number-one cotton producer. And the economy of the Delta still counts on the long rows of cotton that sit ready for choppin' and pickin'.

Plantations with their small green shacks still exist there though some of the residents are no longer the tenders of the fields. Some of them yearn for the opportunity to support themselves in those traditional ways, the only ones they have known, while machines and weed killers gradually replace them in the fields and farm owners gradually displace them from the land.

Next to cotton the Delta's greatest export has been its native born. The wars took many off the farms and plantations. Many returned to take their families. Others followed suit in flight from poverty and cruelty.

Mrs. Sadie Chissok and the two generations after her have stayed, living on in Clarksdale, one of the Delta's major towns and a community of contrasts. Within a few blocks the comfortable, elegant homes of the few businessmen and teachers sit bordered by tiny modest ones. Government projects and new housing developments have very recently been added, but what remain as more typical and traditional are the little two-room white wood houses, which sit in unobtrusive rows a few feet away from one another.

On Sadie Chissok's street and many others like it, the women of the house get up and go at the work early. When chores are done, neighbors sit in porch swings and rockers musing and chatting, often in garbled tones that spill out over a bottom lip full of snuff. Conversations are much like melodies in that part of the world as time enough to do everything "now" also gives time enough to drawl out words and sing their syllables up and down—time enough to think about the past, which hardly seems to have left.

Many, no, most of the community are the former tillers of the soil, or their children. All have known the experience of the plantation on one level or another. Though the past 15 years have brought change and the external circumstances for many are different, for others they are not, and the imprint of a cruel social structure built on cotton and slavery remains.

Mrs. Chissok's voice has a little rasp to it as she talks. She's a short, pudgy size 16. Sickness and fret have worried her down from the size 20 she was just a few years ago. She moves like she talks, slow and easy; there's no need to rush for anything anymore.

"I'm sickly now, but there's many a year I worked out there in them cotton fields. I have a bad heart n fluid n sugar n a goiter, but if the good Lord has it in mind for me to live til November 19th, I'll be 50 years old this year.

"We been round these parts a long time, right here in this same house for 20 years. All this time we been payin $22.50 a month for this little piece of place. But last year the white man we been rentin from sold these three houses here to a black man n now the rent's $50. Well, he did put a bathroom on, so now we don't have to go outside no more. See here where he put sidin up in these here rooms. Ya know, they used to look like that kitchen in there."

The walls of the kitchen are exposed wood, blackened by grease and wear of time. A single 40-watt bulb suspended from the ceiling midway in the room provides the only light. The kitchen has no cabinets to store food. All that there is sits on the table in cans and boxes, leaving a corner for two plates. The family eats with plates on their laps in the other room or on the porch.

"You shoulda come last year n seen the way it was then. See that hole near the roof up there? Chile, there was holes like that all through here. I do believe that's why my daughter's baby got pneumonia n died. It was cold that winter, colder than it get down here. We put blankets up over the window n tried to keep warm with that little ole heater yonder. But baby took sick n died.

"It's better now, but seem like every little thing raise the rent. The man threw a little white paint up side the house n raised it ten dollars more. When he passed out them raise slips, everybody nearly raised up n passed out." Mrs. Chissok stops. Her bottom lip pushes up in a pout. Her hand rises up to support her head tilted to the side. She punctuates her thoughts that way.

"I got sugar n fluid, n my shortnin of breath come on me. I'm sickly; I can't be out there workin like I used to. Where I'm gonna get the money to pay for this?" She shrugs.

"Now see them houses yonder? They built them for cullid folks [modern roomy houses]. I spect if I got one o them houses, I'd take sick n die. I'd wake up n think I was already in heaven n I'd jus go 'head on n die.

"There was a man, lived up in the hills. He took sick, n they took him down to the hospital. Well, they gave him a bath n next thing he died, fore the doctor could even get to see im. You know when you aint never had nothin n aint been used to nothin . . ." Mrs. Chissok grins a little at her own humor. She looks off in the distance.

There's a constant din of activity as three little ones jump, crawl and tumble about. The space she, her two daughters and their children have to share is two 12 by 16 rooms, a narrow kitchen, a porch and six or seven feet of space before the street. The baby girl, two, runs up and flops over Mrs. Chissok's lap, feet in the air. Mrs. Chissok takes a moment to change mini sneakers to the correct feet and tie the laces. They play together, a little pinching here, poking there, smiling a lot. "Her name's Dalmatia Mandalene Cheresa Ann; we call her 'Duck.' That'un over there crawlin name Wendel. We call im 'Caterpillar.' The dog name Rudolph." Mrs. Chissok watches them for a while then returns to her thoughts.

"I was born in Mound Bayou, 1925. That's an all-cullid town, ya know. [Mound Bayou was established in 1877 by the son of a slave, Isaiah Montgomery, on land he'd bought himself in the Delta to create a community where Blacks could control their own destinies.] They didn't use to let no white folks live there. There's a few poor whites live there now, just moved in lately but aint many. Used to be when I was growin up when a cullid person got in trouble out there, we'd help im get away." She giggles. "Mama was living there then. She was a full-blooded Indian."

Hers was one of the families that survived the waves of the 1820s and thirties that forcibly removed the Indians from the land. They'd refused to negotiate its sale to the aspiring businessmen who'd flocked from the northern colonies to make name and fortune off the fertile lands of the Delta by producing cotton.

"I never saw my daddy. He n my mama separated fore I was born. It was jus Mama n me. She did have a sister. We had some cousins. When I was still little I was sold. Yes, I was. We had went back up in the hills to live when I was jus a baby. One day a white man come down there n went round tellin cullid folks that there was good money up in the Delta, north near Shelby, choppin cotton. Said they was paying ten dollars a day, n in those days that was a whole lots of money. He tole us all that. Well, first Mama said we didn't have no way to get up there. He said we didn't have to worry none; he'd get us there. He loaded all us, all kinds o cullid folks, on the back o his truck to make that trip, n sho nuf, soon as we got to Shelby, they sold us! Jus like they sell some chickens. Right at the railroad station.

"I wasn't nothin but seven, eight years old then. The white man what brought us up here got so much money for each one o us from the man he gave us to, n we had to stay there n work til we earned him his money back on his plantation choppin n pickin his cotton. It wasn't for no ten dollars a day neither.

"I didn't do much myself. I was too little to work much so I jus followed Mama round n put a little cotton in her bag while she was working n draggin it down the row. When it got hot in the afternoon, I'd just curl up n go to sleep.

"Well, after we got out from there—Mama, ya know, was from round here— we came back to Mound Bayou to live. She worked the time plantin season got started right on through the fall when all the work was finished. She always tried to save up a little money to get us through the winter til it was time to start choppin again. I was always with her.

"I never went to school but bout two, three days. Plantin season started early, so the schools let out early, sometimes in February, so there'd be more kids to help. Anyway, the kids could really fight n my mama said she didn't want them

Africans beatin up on her baby. So she jus kept me with her. Choppin n pickin cotton is all I ever known since I was born. Hasn't been nothin much else for cullid people to do.''

And in the Delta there hasn't been. The twentieth state added to the union, Mississippi is running a close last in the standard of living of its population. According to the 1970 census, the median per-capita income for whites is $1,935; for Blacks, $898.

Though the rest of the state began to change to a more modern, varied economy in the late 1930s, industry was kept out of the Delta at the request, some say, of the cotton barons. Only now in a recession economy is consideration being given to new ideas for the use of land and manpower. With hoes attached to the back, the somber gray field buses that still drive the streets of the Black section of town are blatant reminders of the power of the land and the power of the planter aristocracy. The land made the culture, the culture made the people, and its not easily removed from them though things have changed.

Kentucky Fried Chicken, McDonald's and other landmarks of modern life are visible in the Black community. Holiday Inn, just a few blocks away, extends welcome now to all guests, and part of the welcome is made by Black staff.

There are a few jobs for Blacks in supermarkets, gas stations and the Wonder Bread factory. Programs like the Comprehensive Employment and Training Act (CETA) have been added in an attempt to teach former farmers and sharecroppers to read and write while CETA searches for jobs for them—jobs that don't exist yet.

Most of what's available are baby-sitting jobs, and it is those jobs that Blacks shun. Most would like to have jobs in the glamorous new companies just beginning to move south (though they have not yet come to Clarksdale or environs), but barring that, many prefer to live on the fringes of subsistence than ". . . work in white folks' kitchens. . . .''

"I remember all those years I worked for them when we wasn't choppin cotton,'' Mrs. Chissok continued. "They'd tell you it was a baby-sittin job n then when you'd get round there they'd have all that heavy cleanin for you to do, n I mean *heavy*. Scrubbin down floors n walls n washin clothes, sometimes by hand. I mean, for ten hours n you wouldn't get nothing but $2.50 for the whole day.

"That was back in the 1950s. They tell you one price n when you get out there, it's somethin different. I think it was all them years o workin hard like that that got me sickly like I am now. I had to turn round n come home n work in my own house like that. The doctor tole me, 'Mrs. Chissok, you just done wore out, that's all.' You know some o these white doctors is awright. They really help you, but it's $40 every time you go down there. N then you have to pay for the medicine, n I get seven different kinds of pills. Sometimes I just get sick o takin em, n where I'm gonna get the money?

"Now I'm just tired, having so many chilren so close together. My shortnin o breath started jus after the last one was born. I don't know seems like it jus did somethin to me. My husband didn't help much. When the babies was little, everything fell on me, n it was all the arguin n such . . .

"I met him when I was washin dishes in a café down the road, down yonder. He'd been workin in the fields for years. He tole me he only been married once before. A few years ago I found out he been married twice before. Anyway, not long ago he jus picked himself up n lef. Got him a job in a gas station, makin about $25 n jus lef. My girls used to see him on the street n cry n ask him when he was comin back.

"It really hurt us bad when he lef. We'd been together all those years. We'd worked choppin cotton in the fields, n when the white folks stopped givin us work, ya know they got them machines to do it n that stuff what kills the weeds instead of havin to chop em . . . when there wasn't no more work to do, he picked up a nickel here n there doin what he could, n it seemed like it jus got to him.

"He started to drink n got meaner n meaner. All the mens round here took to it after a while. Jus wasn't no work n nothin to do, n what little money folks did make, most of it got drank up. People gave us food. Mrs. Henry took food from her own refrigerator for my children. Anytime people from the North came down here with food, she see to it we got some so we could eat.

"My husband's dead now. Folks say he was drinkin one night n got too near the stove, n it caught him on fire, n when the am'lance got there, he was already half burnt up, half dead already. That was a couple years back. Well, I found me somebody new. He's good to me n my girls. Tole me to stop workin so hard, bein sickly like I am.

"Seemed like I started gettin like that fore my husband lef though. It seemed like everything was over in 1967 when my mama died. Look like the world came to an end then. She was 94.

"I don't have no other people. Mama has some cousins n such n so did my husband; they up north somewhere. Cousin Maggie came here to live with us for a while. She worked in the fields too, n when she couldn't get no work, we jus moved on over n made room for her. Anythin we had she could have. Now that was a lots o people living here then. But it was like that for a lots o folks when they had to leave the farms. Well, things got even worse n she went on back up in the hills. She found her a man now. I guess that's the end o that. I guess if things get too bad, we can just go on out in the hills n live. Lots of folks been doin that lately. Aint no money. No jobs, just a lots o stealin n drinkin n robbin. Folks jus sittin round."

Mississippi's record in social welfare, planning, innovation and payment is one of the poorest. A mother, head of household, receives $30 a month for her first child's support; for two children, a total of $48. Folks must pay New York prices for their food and higher for their clothing. They talk about the army and maybe joining and about other states nearby where the welfare payments are higher and could help them got on their feet. They talk of leaving but few do. They stay on and stay together trying to make it work.

"I don't know. My chilren don't seem to care like I cared for my mama," Mrs. Chissok whines. "I always did everythin I could for her. These uns jus sit n play cards all day with their friends. They don't seem to want to do nothin. My youngest one jus up n quit school after she done had the last baby. She jus don't seem to care no more. Said, 'What's the use?' There won't be no jobs no way. They don't seem to want to do nothin but go out jukin [dancing] at these juke houses round here. It's the café every night on the weekend if they can get there. Juke, juke, juke. Seem like these little yellow boys round here, and the ones aint yellow too, is all they think bout. They got grown now n don't wanna listen. All day long it's that damn record player n them damn records."

She nags at the girls to try to find jobs and to do their chores around the house. Sickness absorbs her but also permits her to be the one attended to. It is frightening for her to think of the time when her children will be away from her and for her to be out of their lives too.

For all of them solace comes in simple forms. There's little activity and entertainment except the fellowship of friends, a card game, the pool hall, a little party-ing, an occasional movie when money permits and, of course, church.

House chores are neglected while the few pleasures there are get indulged in. But sustained stress with seemingly no end has a way of lowering tolerance, and tempers, which get shorter as years go on, flare more readily. Tension builds in such close quarters and is spilled over on those closest. Raised voices, raised fists, children raised with too little to eat, too little love, with one parent angry and trapped. And when people and things outside provide no outlet, rage goes inward. And whatever else each day is taken up with, it includes for Mrs. Chissok long recitations of discomforts: the bottles of pills and liquids and the careful review of the conditions they treat.

"Sometimes I jus feel like gettin up out o here n walkin n walkin til I jus fall over dead. My head feels like it jus gonna come apart, worryin with these chilren. It's always somethin. Jolene's second baby died. They said it was a large heart. The next one died. Said he got pneumonia. We didn't think Duck was gonna make it neither. See them scars? We got her to the hospital jus in time. Said her intestines was all twisted up together inside. She wasn't nothin but eight months old then, but they said she was born that way. I don't know what we did wrong. Maybe cause they didn't get enough to eat or maybe somethin else. She had two operations. They gave her up for dead.

"And them doctor bills. Lord, chile! But they couldn't get from me what I didn't have. They started gettin nasty bout the bills after a while. You know it aint been long since that hospital been takin cullid, jus a couple o years. Everybody from here used to go down to Mound Bayou to the hospital there [28 miles]. They nice to you down there, n you don't have to pay if you don't have it. They give you medicine to take home with you, n you don't have to pay for that either. Most of the time, too, if you can't get down there, they try to have somebody pick you up.

"Most everybody from here had their babies down there. But I heard tell they closin the operatin part n the baby part cause o some somethin. I don't know. I heard it on television n folks been talkin bout it. Maybe the white folks just want it closed so we'll have to come up here n spend more money in that big hospital. They let on the Medicaid who they want to round here. You have to go down there n they ask you personal questions bout everything, n you have to answer all of them jus right n bring all kinds of bills n letters n then you still don't get nothin. These white folks round here is somethin. They ain't gonna let you get much of nothin. They don't tell us nothin n we don't tell them nothin. I hear all the stuff them others what been down there tell me n I'm scared. I just aint goin. You know it aint been long since they stopped being real mean, these white folks. They taught us to be scared n I'm scared of em.

"They used to be always findin some cullid person killed n thrown in the river with somethin tied to im. They'll come get you in a minute. They's always been superstitious about what cullid folks be thinkin bout n gonna do. They always think we up to somethin. So be careful, don't be takin no pictures when they lookin at cha.

"Ya know, they never even used to call us by our names. You was always called uncle or preacher or Suzie. It was Aaron Henry got em callin us miss n mis-ter. They names a boulevard after him. One after Martin Luther King too. But they bombed Aaron Henry's house, n they'd take you right on in if they thought you was up to anythin.

"Sometimes I think about gettin out o here, but I ask myself where I'd go. I don't know nobody. I wish I could just find a decent job, like one o them factory jobs. I heard on television they been thinkin bout startin a program for settled aged women, but it ain't got here yet. Once Mrs. Henry tole me about grown folks school. I was gonna go but I'm jus too old. N ya know how sickly I am. They said a doctor has to examine you, n I jus figured I couldn't pass the test no way so I didn't bother. Anyway, I heard tell some old folks sat up there n studied so hard they jus died sittin there. Jus fell right over!"

But Sadie Chissok hasn't fallen over. She still has a bit of Uncle Remus in her, and when distraction from troubles permits, she forgets herself and flows into stories of family and friends, time and the river. With a little seriousness, a coquettish glint in her eye and a little Geraldine Jones in her voice, she brings each character of her sagas to life with the flare and relish of a seasoned show woman on stage—the porch.

She has an easy "Hey!" for most everybody, and when possible, she does see to her own comfort. When it's nap time, it's nap time, and the television and record player go off.

She is not so sick or so overwhelmed that she doesn't care about the children's relationships. She frets, scolds and curses over her oldest daughter's love problems, over her youngest daughter's withdrawing ways and the fact that she spanks her baby too much in anger.

The girls block their mother out after a while. Sometimes they argue, sometimes they complain and sometimes they just walk out for a while, but no one leaves for good. They all fear the day when they will have to be apart. One will be graduated from high school soon. All preparations were made for the big day this past spring, but only weeks before the ceremony she was called into the guidance office and told she was credits short. She attends the white high school and feels that the riot staged a short time ago by Black students for a Black-studies course influenced the decision about her graduation. She's determined to finish, though. She wants to go to the junior college to learn to be a secretary or a bank teller.

She's been freed. What encouragement there has been in the community, the home and earlier schooling has made its mark, and despite many years to make up for not attending school earlier, she will go on. The lessons of the civil rights movement did take hold on the young, and though most of them did not have direct or active touch with it at the time, it was and still is fashioning their lives; they are left with the feeling that change will come.

Justice in any constitutional sense of it is still not anything hoped for in the minds of these residents although some say that things have changed and that ". . . the younger race won't put up with the things older people went along with." Relationships are distant and seem to have a surface easiness among whites and Blacks here. Yet fear of renewed hatreds entrenched in generations will remain until the mentality of the plantation relinquishes its hold and the economy and industry modernize. But perhaps not even then will the Mrs. Chissoks be convinced of the change and their ability to take a place in it.

Peace and a little comfort before death comes are what Sadie hopes for. And sometimes death doesn't seem as frightening as change.

"I guess everybody can't live in the North. I'm shamed o the way I have to live down here, but there aint much we can do bout it. I wish we could all get jobs n get one of them new houses. That way the kids could have their own rooms to play n put their toys in n they wouldn't worry me so much. N I wouldn't have to wonder if they gonna get hit by a car playin out front. Fore I die, I hope I can get to see one o them cities like New York. What's it like? Would you send me a picture?''

A dip of snuff, an occasional new dress and a laugh here and there with a friend or neighbor will be the luxuries she'll have for a while. The other things that will give her strength and keep her going will be the children and their friends who come to play with the babies, those who play endless card games in the front room and who melt into the household.

There won't be much to share materially, but lives will be shared in the spirit of an extended family. Someone will always be in and out with no apologies, no invitations necessary.

A few will leave for Chicago but most will stay. And when there's no more food and no other way to get it, the girls will get up early, 4:30 or 5 a.m., and stand with the others on the corner where the field bus stops. They'll pay the fare of two dollars from their already low pay, and they'll go to the fields like their mother and their grandmother did, and they'll chop cotton too.

Donna Allegra / A Prayer for My Soul

Essence, September 1978

In addition to being a poet, Donna Allegra is a music and theater critic. A member of Jemima, a writers' collective, Allegra produces women's radio programs aired on WBAI in New York City.

In its first issue in May, 1970, the editors of Essence *announced that their purpose was "to provide black women with a platform from which their voices may be heard wherever they are; to guide, to delight, to celebrate black women in all their uniqueness."*

There are things that taste good
that kill you slowly
we must slowly learn to say no
it takes a long time, very often,
up and down like a dying roller coaster   5
I am learning how to fight
It used to be whenever the obsession called
I rolled over
It was because I was bored
or I hated myself   10
or because I didn't know how not to
or I couldn't stand being free
or because because because
Once I couldn't stand up when that sweet dream in my bones
was scraping off the marrow   15
and there I would be:
doing it
and I couldn't stop it

and didn't want to do it anymore
and yet there I was again doing it   20
and I knew all the reasons why not to
and couldn't stop myself
and I would be somewhere, someplace
doing it again
A slip is not forever   25
Some of us go all the way out
and crawl home wasted
before we can pick up and try again
yesterday I got up to recover from a fall
today I'm going out for the running,   30
trying to find my feet
and seeing very clearly the doggy doo
and that I was out on the street
selling myself again
It takes courage for me to come out   35
of the haze into a simple morning
there is no cast of thousands
watching to applaud
my limbs are stiff to unwind
and the task at hand is to live   40
There are other things to do
besides play suicide,
other fantasies to rehearse
instead of my funeral march
Here is what else I know and want you to learn   45
before it is too late
because you are my friend, my sister
and I love you:
Getting yourself straight
is holding on through the times   50
you don't know where the hell you fit
in this world or the next
it is holding out for the self you don't believe in
and finding out that you are true
The nights can look very bleak   55
but there are all possibilities for mercy
in the morning
This is a life long unwind
it is taking your time giving birth
and not holding onto the tradition of pain   60
Try to realize that you are going through the fire
and it is hot when in passage,
but when you come out you'll be silver,
you'll be gold
you will hear the sunshine in your voice   65
I've been too long wandering in this petrified forest
and don't know one person in the wood who
hasn't come out crying diamonds and pearls.

DISCUSSION QUESTIONS

1. How does the poem make the transition from confessing to advising? Characterize the voice in the beginning and at the end. With what authority does that voice speak?

2. Who is the "you" addressed in the poem? What kind of person? Would your answer be different if you didn't know that the poem appeared in *Essence?*

Annie Dillard / Death of a Moth

Harper's, May 1976

In the midst of a recent resurgence of nostalgia for the outdoors, Annie Dillard has distinguished herself by the clarity of her vision, the tenacity of her refusal to sentimentalize nature, and the forcefulness of her prose. Born Annie Doak in Pittsburgh in 1945, she took B.A. and M.A. degrees at Hollins College in Virginia's Roanoke Valley. A contributing editor to Harper's *magazine and a columnist for the Wilderness Society, Annie Dillard has also written strikingly original essays for such publications as the* Christian Science Monitor, Atlantic Monthly, Travel and Leisure, Cosmopolitan, Sports Illustrated, Prose, *and* American Scholar. *Many of these essays, refashioned from precise observations entered in notebooks during leisurely walks in the countryside, were collected as* Pilgrim at Tinker Creek, *which received the 1974 Pulitzer Prize for nonfiction.*

"If there are any faults to find here," wrote a critic for The New York Times Book Review *about Dillard's journal* Holy the Firm *(1977), "let others find them. This is a rare and precious book." Included in her three-day journal written in a one-room house overlooking Puget Sound is the following essay, "Death of a Moth," which first appeared in* Harper's *magazine.*

Harper's, *one of the oldest (1850) magazines in America, characterizes itself as addressed to "well-educated, socially concerned, widely read men and women who are active in community and political affairs."*

I live alone with two cats, who sleep on my legs. There is a yellow one, and a black one whose name is Small. In the morning I joke to the black one, Do you remember last night? Do you remember? I throw them both out before breakfast, so I can eat.

There is a spider, too, in the bathroom, of uncertain lineage, bulbous at the abdomen and drab, whose six-inch mess of web works, works somehow, works miraculously, to keep her alive and me amazed. The web is in a corner behind the toilet, connecting tile wall to tile wall. The house is new, the bathroom immaculate, save for the spider, her web, and the sixteen or so corpses she's tossed to the floor.

The corpses appear to be mostly sow bugs, those little armadillo creatures who live to travel flat out in houses, and die round. In addition to sow-bug husks, hollow and sipped empty of color, there are what seem to be two or three wingless moth bodies, one new flake of earwig, and three spider carcasses crinkled and clenched.

Death of a Moth

I wonder on what fool's errand an earwig, or a moth, or a sow bug, would visit that clean corner of the house behind the toilet; I have not noticed any blind parades of sow bugs blundering into corners. Yet they do hazard there, at a rate of more than one a week, and the spider thrives. Yesterday she was working on the earwig, mouth on gut; today he's on the floor. It must take a certain genius to throw things away from there, to find a straight line through that sticky tangle to the floor.

Today the earwig shines darkly, and gleams, what there is of him: a dorsal curve of thorax and abdomen, and a smooth pair of pincers by which I knew his name. Next week, if the other bodies are any indication, he'll be shrunk and gray, webbed to the floor with dust. The sow bugs beside him are curled and empty, fragile, a breath away from brittle fluff. The spiders lie on their sides, translucent and ragged, their legs drying in knots. The moths stagger against each other, headless, in a confusion of arcing strips of chitin like peeling varnish, like a jumble of buttresses for cathedral vaults, like nothing resembling moths, so that I would hesitate to call them moths, except that I have had some experience with the figure Moth reduced to a nub.

Two summers ago I was camped alone in the Blue Ridge Mountains of Virginia. I had hauled myself and gear up there to read, among other things, *The Day on Fire,* by James Ullman, a novel about Rimbaud that had made me want to be a writer when I was sixteen; I was hoping it would do it again. So I read every day sitting under a tree by my tent, while warblers sang in the leaves overhead and bristle worms trailed their inches over the twiggy dirt at my feet; and I read every night by candlelight, while barred owls called in the forest and pale moths seeking mates massed round my head in the clearing, where my light made a ring.

Moths kept flying into the candle. They would hiss and recoil, reeling upside down in the shadows among my cooking pans. Or they would singe their wings and fall, and their hot wings, as if melted, would stick to the first thing they touched—a pan, a lid, a spoon—so that the snagged moths could struggle only in tiny arcs, unable to flutter free. These I could release by a quick flip with a stick; in the morning I would find my cooking stuff decorated with torn flecks of moth wings, ghostly triangles of shiny dust here and there on the aluminum. So I read, and boiled water, and replenished candles, and read on.

One night a moth flew into the candle, was caught, burnt dry, and held. I must have been staring at the candle, or maybe I looked up when a shadow crossed my page; at any rate, I saw it all. A golden female moth, a biggish one with a two-inch wingspread, flapped into the fire, dropped abdomen into the wet wax, stuck, flamed, and frazzled in a second. Her moving wings ignited like tissue paper, like angels' wings, enlarging the circle of light in the clearing and creating out of the darkness the sudden blue sleeves of my sweater, the green leaves of jewelweed by my side, the ragged red trunk of a pine; at once the light contracted again and the moth's wings vanished in a fine, foul smoke. At the same time, her six legs clawed, curled, blackened, and ceased, disappearing utterly. And her head jerked in spasms, making a spattering noise; her antennae crisped and burnt away and her heaving mouthparts cracked like pistol fire. When it was all over, her head was, so far as I could determine, gone, gone the long way of her wings and legs. Her head was a hole lost to time. All that was left was the glowing horn shell of her abdomen and thorax—a fraying, partially collapsed gold tube jammed upright in the candle's round pool.

And then this moth-essence, this spectacular skeleton, began to act as a wick. She kept burning. The wax rose in the moth's body from her soaking abdomen to her thorax to the shattered hole where her head should have been, and widened into flame, a saffron-yellow flame that robed her to the ground like an immolating monk. That candle had two wicks, two winding flames of identical light, side by side. The moth's head was fire. She burned for two hours, until I blew her out.

She burned for two hours without changing, without swaying or kneeling—only glowing within, like a building fire glimpsed through silhouetted walls, like a hollow saint, like a flame-faced virgin gone to God, while I read by her light, kindled, while Rimbaud in Paris burnt out his brain in a thousand poems, while night pooled wetly at my feet.

So. That is why I think those hollow shreds on the bathroom floor are moths. I believe I know what moths look like, in any state.

I have three candles here on the table which I disentangle from the plants and light when visitors come. The cats avoid them, although Small's tail caught fire once; I rubbed it out before she noticed. I don't mind living alone. I like eating alone and reading. I don't mind sleeping alone. The only time I mind being alone is when something is funny; then, when I am laughing at something funny, I wish someone were around. Sometimes I think it is pretty funny that I sleep alone.

N. Scott Momaday / A First American Views His Land

National Geographic, July 1976

The National Geographic *magazine was founded in 1888 under the auspices of the National Geographic Society as a professional journal devoted to technical essays on exploration and earth sciences. As the society invested more and more heavily in expeditions that would capture the popular imagination, the editors decided to alter the magazine's contents in the hope of attracting a larger, nonspecialized audience. Over the years, the* National Geographic *has become a popular forum for travel, adventure, anthropology, and geographical research. Its consistently high standard of color photography has been a major factor in the magazine's enormous circulation: now well over nine million.*

N. Scott Momaday's "A First American Views His Land" clearly fulfills the National Geographic's *announced criteria for publication:*

> *First person narratives, making it easy for the reader to share the author's experience and observations. Writing should include plenty of human-interest incident, authentic direct quotation, and a bit of humor where appropriate. Accuracy is fundamental. Contemporary problems such as those of pollution and ecology are treated on a factual basis. The magazine is especially seeking short American place pieces with a strong regional "people" flavor.*

Born in Lawton, Oklahoma in 1934, N. Scott Momaday received his B.A. from the University of New Mexico, his Masters and Ph.D. from Stanford. A professor of English at Stanford, Momaday won the Pulitzer Prize for fiction in 1969 for his novel House of Dawn. *He regularly contributes articles, fiction, and poetry to numerous periodicals and frequently reviews work on American Indian culture. The poem woven into the selection printed below is drawn from his book,* The Gourd Dancer (*1976*).

*First Man
behold:
the earth
glitters
with leaves;
the sky
glistens
with rain.
Pollen
is borne
on winds
that low
and lean
upon
mountains.
Cedars
blacken
the slopes—
and pines.*

One hundred centuries ago. There is a wide, irregular landscape in what is now northern New Mexico. The sun is a dull white disk, low in the south; it is a perfect mystery, a deity whose coming and going are inexorable. The gray sky is curdled, and it bears very close upon the earth. A cold wind runs along the ground, dips and spins, flaking drift from a pond in the bottom of a ravine. Beyond the wind the silence is acute. A man crouches in the ravine, in the darkness there, scarcely visible. He moves not a muscle; only the wind lifts a lock of his hair and lays it back along his neck. He wears skins and carries a spear. These things in particular mark his human intelligence and distinguish him as the lord of the universe. And for him the universe is especially *this* landscape; for him the landscape is an element like the air. The vast, virgin wilderness is by and large his whole context. For him there is no possibility of existence elsewhere.

Directly there is a blowing, a rumble of breath deeper than the wind, above him, where some of the hard clay of the bank is broken off and the clods roll down into the water. At the same time there appears on the skyline the massive head of a long-horned bison, then the hump, then the whole beast, huge and black on the sky, standing to a height of seven feet at the hump, with horns that extend six feet across the shaggy crown. For a moment it is poised there; then it lumbers obliquely down the bank to the pond. Still the man does not move, though the beast is now only a few steps upwind. There is no sign of what is about to happen; the beast meanders; the man is frozen in repose.

Then the scene explodes. In one and the same instant the man springs to his feet and bolts forward, his arm cocked and the spear held high, and the huge animal lunges in panic, bellowing, its whole weight thrown violently into the bank, its hooves churning and chipping earth into the air, its eyes gone wide and wild and white. There is a moment in which its awful, frenzied motion is wasted, and it is mired and helpless in its fear, and the man hurls the spear with his whole strength, and the point is driven into the deep, vital flesh, and the bison in its agony staggers and crashes down and dies.

This ancient drama of the hunt is enacted again and again in the landscape. The man is preeminently a predator, the most dangerous of all. He hunts in order to survive; his very existence is simply, squarely established upon that basis. But he hunts also because he can, because he has the means; he has the ultimate weapon of his age, and his prey is plentiful. His relationship to the land has not yet become a moral equation.

But in time he will come to understand that there is an intimate, vital link between the earth and himself, a link that implies an intricate network of rights and responsibilities. In some unimagined future he will understand that he has the ability to devastate and perhaps destroy his environment. That moment will be one of extreme crisis in his evolution.

The weapon is deadly and efficient. The hunter has taken great care in its manufacture, especially in the shaping of the flint point, which is an extraordinary thing. A larger flake has been removed from each face, a groove that extends from the base nearly to the tip. Several hundred pounds of pressure, expertly applied, were required to make these grooves. The hunter then is an artisan, and he must know how to use rudimentary tools. His skill, manifest in the manufacture of this artifact, is unsurpassed for its time and purpose. By means of this weapon is the Paleo-Indian hunter eminently able to exploit his environment.

Thousands of years later, about the time that Columbus begins his first voyage to the New World, another man, in the region of the Great Lakes, stands in the forest shade on the edge of a sunlit brake. In a while a deer enters into the pool of light. Silently the man fits an arrow to a bow, draws aim, and shoots. The arrow zips across the distance and strikes home. The deer leaps and falls dead.

But this latter-day man, unlike his ancient predecessor, is only incidentally a hunter; he is also a fisherman, a husbandman, even a physician. He fells trees and builds canoes; he grows corn, squash, and beans, and he gathers fruits and nuts; he uses hundreds of species of wild plants for food, medicine, teas, and dyes. Instead of one animal, or two or three, he hunts many, none to extinction as the Paleo-Indian may have done. He has fitted himself far more precisely into the patterns of the wilderness than did his ancient predecessor. He lives on the land; he takes his living from it; but he does not destroy it. This distinction supports the fundamental ethic that we call conservation today. In principle, if not yet in name, this man is a conservationist.

These two hunting sketches are far less important in themselves than is that long distance between them, that whole possibility within the dimension of time. I believe that in that interim there grew up in the mind of man an idea of the land as sacred.

> *At dawn*
> *eagles*
> *lie and*
> *hover*
> *above*
> *the plain*
> *where light*
> *gathers*

> *in pools.*
> *Grasses*
> *shimmer*
> *and shine.*
> *Shadows*
> *withdraw*
> *and lie*
> *away*
> *like smoke.*

"The earth is our mother. The sky is our father." This concept of nature, which is at the center of the Native American world view, is familiar to us all. But it may well be that we do not understand entirely what that concept is in its ethical and philosophical implications.

I tell my students that the American Indian has a unique investment in the American landscape. It is an investment that represents perhaps thirty thousand years of habitation. That tenure has to be worth something in itself—a great deal, in fact. The Indian has been here a long time; he is at home here. That simple and obvious truth is one of the most important realities of the Indian world, and it is integral in the Indian mind and spirit.

How does such a concept evolve? Where does it begin? Perhaps it begins with the recognition of beauty, the realization that the physical world *is* beautiful. We don't know much about the ancient hunter's sensibilities. It isn't likely that he had leisure in his life for the elaboration of an aesthetic ideal. And yet the weapon he made was beautiful as well as functional. It has been suggested that much of the minute chipping along the edges of his weapon served no purpose but that of aesthetic satisfaction.

A good deal more is known concerning that man of the central forests. He made beautiful boxes and dishes out of elm and birch bark, for example. His canoes were marvelous, delicate works of art. And this aesthetic perception was a principle of the whole Indian world of his time, as indeed it is of our time. The contemporary Native American is a man whose strong aesthetic perceptions are clearly evident in his arts and crafts, in his religious ceremonies, and in the stories and songs of his rich oral tradition. This, in view of the pressures that have been brought to bear upon the Indian world and the drastic changes that have been effected in its landscape, is a blessing and an irony.

Consider for example the Navajos of the Four Corners area. In recent years an extensive coal-mining operation has mutilated some of their most sacred land. A large power plant in that same region spews a contamination into the sky that is visible for many miles. And yet, as much as any people of whom I have heard, the Navajos perceive and celebrate the beauty of the physical world.

There is a Navajo ceremonial song that celebrates the sounds that are made in the natural world, the particular voices that beautify the earth:

> *Voice above,*
> *Voice of thunder,*
> *Speak from the*
> *dark of clouds;*
> *Voice below,*
> *Grasshopper voice,*
> *Speak from the*

green of plants;
So may the earth
be beautiful.

There is in the motion and meaning of this song a comprehension of the world that is peculiarly native, I believe, that is integral in the Native American mentality. Consider: The singer stands at the center of the natural world, at the source of its sound, of its motion, of its life. Nothing of that world is inaccessible to him or lost upon him. His song is filled with reverence, with wonder and delight, and with confidence as well. He knows something about himself and about the things around him—and he knows that he knows. I am interested in what he sees and hears; I am interested in the range and force of his perception. Our immediate impression may be that his perception is narrow and deep—vertical. After all, "voice above . . . voice below," he sings. But is it vertical only? At each level of his expression there is an extension of his awareness across the whole landscape. The voice above is the voice of thunder, and thunder rolls. Moreover, it issues from the impalpable dark clouds and runs upon their horizontal range. It is a sound that integrates the whole of the atmosphere. And even so, the voice below, that of the grasshopper, issues from the broad plain and multiplicity of plants. And of course the singer is mindful of much more than thunder and insects; we are given in his song the wide angle of his vision and his hearing—and we are given the testimony of his dignity, his trust, and his deep belief.

This comprehension of the earth and air is surely a matter of morality, for it brings into account not only man's instinctive reaction to his environment but the full realization of his humanity as well, the achievement of his intellectual and spiritual development as an individual and as a race.

In my own experience I have seen numerous examples of this regard for nature. My grandfather Mammedaty was a farmer in his mature years; his grandfather was a buffalo hunter. It was not easy for Mammedaty to be a farmer; he was a Kiowa, and the Kiowas never had an agrarian tradition. Yet he had to make his living, and the old, beloved life of roaming the plains and hunting the buffalo was gone forever. Even so, as much as any man before him, he fitted his mind and will and spirit to the land; there was nothing else. He could not have conceived of living apart from the land.

In *The Way to Rainy Mountain* I set down a small narrative that belongs in the oral tradition of my family. It indicates something essential about the Native American attitude toward the land:

"East of my grandmother's house, south of the pecan grove, there is buried a woman in a beautiful dress. Mammedaty used to know where she is buried, but now no one knows. If you stand on the front porch of the house and look eastward towards Carnegie, you know that the woman is buried somewhere within the range of your vision. But her grave is unmarked. She was buried in a cabinet, and she wore a beautiful dress. How beautiful it was! It was one of those fine buckskin dresses, and it was decorated with elk's teeth and beadwork. That dress is still there, under the ground."

It seems to me that this statement is primarily a declaration of love for the land, in which the several elements—the woman, the dress, and this plain—are at last become one reality, one expression of the beautiful in nature. Moreover, it seems to me a peculiarly Native American expression in this sense: that the concentration of things that are explicitly remembered—the general landscape, the simple, almost abstract nature of the burial, above all the beautiful dress, which is wholly singular in kind (as well as in its function within the narrative)—is especially Indian in character. The things that are *not* explicitly remembered—the woman's name, the exact location of her grave—are the things that matter least in the special view of the storyteller. What matters here is the translation of the woman into the landscape, a translation particularly signified by means of the beautiful and distinctive dress, an *Indian* dress.

When I was a boy, I lived for several years at Jemez Pueblo, New Mexico. The Pueblo Indians are perhaps more obviously invested in the land than are other people. Their whole life is predicated upon a thorough perception of the physical world and its myriad aspects. When I first went there to live, the cacique, or chief, of the Pueblos was a venerable old man with long, gray hair and bright, deep-set eyes. He was entirely dignified and imposing—and rather formidable in the eyes of a boy. He excited my imagination a good deal. I was told that this old man kept the calendar of the tribe, that each morning he stood on a certain spot of ground near the center of the town and watched to see where the sun appeared on the skyline. By means of this solar calendar did he know and announce to his people when it was time to plant, to harvest, to perform this or that ceremony. This image of him in my mind's eye—the old man gazing each morning after the ranging sun—came to represent for me the epitome of that real harmony between man and the land that signifies the Indian world.

One day when I was riding my horse along the Jemez River, I looked up to see a long caravan of wagons and people on horseback and on foot. Men, women, and children were crossing the river ahead of me, moving out to the west, where most of the cultivated fields were, the farmland of the town. It was a wonderful sight to see, this long procession, and I was immediately deeply curious. I wanted to investigate, but it was not in me to do so at once, for that racial reserve, that sense of propriety that is deep-seated in Native American culture, stayed me, held me up. Then I saw someone coming toward me on horseback, galloping. It was a friend of mine, a boy of my own age. "Come on," he said. "Come with us." "Where are you going?" I asked casually. But he would not tell me. He simply laughed and urged me to come along, and of course I was very glad to do so. It was a bright spring morning, and I had a good horse under me, and the prospect of adventure was delicious. We moved far out across the eroded plain to the farthest fields at the foot of a great red mesa, and there we planted two large fields of corn. And afterward, on the edge of the fields, we sat on blankets and ate a feast in the shade of a cottonwood grove. Later I learned it was the cacique's fields we planted. And this is an ancient tradition at Jemez. The people of the town plant and tend and harvest the cacique's fields, and in the winter the hunters give to him a portion of the meat that they bring home from the mountains. It is as if the cacique is himself the translation of man, every man, into the landscape.

I have not forgotten that day, nor shall I forget it. I remember the warm earth of the fields, the smooth texture of seeds in my hands, and the brown water moving slowly and irresistibly among the rows. Above all I remember the spirit in which the procession was made, the work was done, and the feasting was enjoyed. It was a spirit of communion, of the life of each man in relation to the life of the planet and of the infinite distance and silence in which it moves. We made, in concert, an appropriate expression of that spirit.

One afternoon an old Kiowa woman talked to me, telling me of the place in Oklahoma in which she had lived for a hundred years. It was the place in which my grandparents, too, lived; and it is the place where I was born. And she told me of a time even further back, when the Kiowas came down from the north and centered their culture in the red earth of the southern plains. She told wonderful stories, and as I listened, I began to feel more and more sure that her voice proceeded from the land itself. I asked her many things concerning the Kiowas, for I wanted to understand all that I could of my heritage. I told the old woman that I had come there to learn from her and from people like her, those in whom the old ways were preserved. And she said simply: "It is good that you have come here." I believe that her word "good" meant many things; for one thing it meant *right,* or *appropriate.* And indeed it was appropriate that she should speak of the land. She was eminently qualified to do so. She had a great reverence for the land, and an ancient perception of it, a perception that it acquired only in the course of many generations.

It is this notion of the appropriate, along with that of the beautiful, that forms the Native American perspective on the land. In a sense these considerations are indivisible; Native American oral tradition is rich with songs and tales that celebrate natural beauty, the beauty of the natural world. What is more appropriate to our world than that which is beautiful:

> *At noon*
> *turtles*
> *enter*
> *slowly*
> *into*
> *the warm*
> *dark loam.*
> *Bees hold*
> *the swarm.*
> *Meadows*
> *recede*
> *through planes*
> *of heat*
> *and pure*
> *distance.*

Very old in the Native American world view is the conviction that the earth is vital, that there is a spiritual dimension to it, a dimension in which man rightly exists. It follows logically that there are ethical imperatives in this matter. I think: Inasmuch as I am in the land, it is appropriate that I should affirm myself in the spirit of the land. I shall celebrate my life in the world and the world in my life. In the natural order man invests himself in the landscape and at the same time incorporates the landscape into his own most fundamental experience. This trust is sacred.

The process of investment and appropriation is, I believe, preeminently a function of the imagination. It is accomplished by means of an act of the imagination that is especially ethical in kind. We are what we imagine ourselves to be. The Native American is someone who thinks of himself, imagines himself in a particular way. By virtue of his experience his idea of himself comprehends his relationship to the land.

And the quality of this imagining is determined as well by racial and cultural experience. The Native American's attitudes toward this landscape have been formulated over a long period of time, a span that reaches back to the end of the Ice Age. The land, *this* land, is secure in his racial memory.

In our society as a whole we conceive of the land in terms of ownership and use. It is a lifeless medium of exchange; it has for most of us, I suspect, no more spirituality than has an automobile, say, or a refrigerator. And our laws confirm us in this view, for we can buy and sell the land, we can exclude each other from it, and in the context of ownership we can use it as we will. Ownership implies use, and use implies consumption.

But this way of thinking of the land is alien to the Indian. His cultural intelligence is opposed to these concepts; indeed, for him they are all but inconceivable quantities. This fundamental distinction is easier to understand with respect to ownership than to use, perhaps. For obviously the Indian does use, and has always used, the land and the available resources in it. The point is that *use* does not indicate in any real way his idea of the land. "Use" is neither his word nor his idea. As an Indian I think: "You say that I *use* the land, and I reply, yes, it is true; but it is not the first truth. The first truth is that I *love* the land; I see that it is beautiful; I delight in it; I am alive in it."

In the long course of his journey from Asia and in the realization of himself in the New World, the Indian has assumed a deep ethical regard for the earth and sky, a reverence for the natural world that is antipodal to that strange tenet of modern civilization that seemingly has it that man must destroy his environnment. It is this ancient ethic of the Native American that must shape our efforts to preserve the earth and the life upon and within it.

> *At dusk*
> *the gray*
> *foxes*
> *stiffen*
> *in cold;*
> *blackbirds*
> *are fixed*
> *in white*
> *branches.*
> *Rivers*
> *follow*
> *the moon,*
> *the long*
> *white track*
> *of the*
> *full moon.*

Eric Hoffer / What America Means to Me

Reader's Digest, September 1976

A member of both the San Francisco Art Commission and the International Longshoremen's and Warehousemen's Union, self-educated Eric Hoffer did his writing "in railroad yards while waiting for a freight, in the fields while waiting for a truck, and at noon after lunch." Hoffer was nearly blind until the age of 15. After regaining his sight, he began to read ravenously in English and German, and he proudly held cards to libraries in nearly every town he travelled to.

The world's most widely circulated monthly, the Reader's Digest *first appeared on the newsstands in 1922 as a magazine specializing in condensed reprinted material. Though at least half of its current material is original, the* Reader's Digest *still maintains the editorial standards—that articles be brief and easily comprehensible—that marked its first issue.*

For the common man, America is still the best country, where he feels most at home. It is the last chance and the last stop. If he can't make it here, he won't make it anywhere.

I have been poor most of my life, and in my years as a migratory worker I was often but a step ahead of hunger. Yet it never occurred to me that there could be a country where I would be more at ease, more at home.

This certitude was not implanted in me by family or school. I never attended school, because I fell off a flight of stairs at the age of five, and two years later lost my eyesight. I remained blind until the age of 15. When my father died in 1920, I was 18. I had $300 and a train ticket to Los Angles. I was convinced that California was God's gift to the poor: warm enough for a person to sleep outside, oranges everywhere for the hungry. My money did not last long, and I soon found myself on skid row. In a sense, I entered America through the portals of that skid row.

For more than 20 years, until I landed on the San Francisco waterfront in the early 1940s, I lived a life of hardships, of self-education, and of teaching myself to write. I wanted to be left alone to do what I was doing. That is what the millions of immigrants who came to this country also looked for: a chance to do what they wanted to do. Many failed, but there were more chances here than anywhere else.

Though I lived on the edge of subsistence, I did not feel poor, and did not see myself as a member of a particular class. I was a human being first. This is what freedom means: to be able to be a human being first. The rich, the learned and the powerful did not seem to me a superior breed. We all spoke the same language, and there were so many topics on which all of us could talk with equal expertise. I can still savor the joy I used to derive from the fact that while doing dull, repetitive work I could talk with my partner and compose sentences in the back of my mind at the same time. Life seemed glorious.

This, then, is what America meant to me: a chance to grow, to be a human being first and to see my fellow men as my equals.

Now there is no doubt that America changed considerably during the 1960s. Yet it is startling how many vital things have *not* changed. One can still cut oneself off from the pervasive conformity, vulgarity, obscenity, hysterical clamor and other corrupting influences around us. There is plenty of elbow room for people who want to be left alone.

America is still an ideal country for people who want to realize their capacities and talents. Had I entered the mainstream of American life in the 1970s instead of the 1920s, I would still be able to educate myself, learn to write, and have books published. The public libraries are as good as they were, and publishers as hospitable to a manuscript of merit.

Certain things have improved. The camaraderie of the young from all walks of life and their readiness to share what they have are beautiful to behold. It is also true that enterprise and character will take a young person farther now than in the past. Alertness and willingness are quickly noticed and appreciated.

And we have grown wiser. We know now that the adult's failure of nerve is more critical than the young's impulse toward anarchy; that righting wrongs is a perilous undertaking which needs a tightening of discipline; that a sense of usefulness is more vital to the quality of life than abundance.

Maureen Orth / All Shook Up
[*On the Death of Elvis Presley*]

Newsweek, August 29, 1977

> *Thomas J. C. Martyn, the first foreign news editor of* Time *magazine, started* News-Week *in early 1933 as a simpler, less interpretive digest of the week's major events than* Time *had been in its first ten years. Although a merger with* Today *magazine in 1937 changed its title to* Newsweek, The Magazine of News Significance, *the periodical remained uncompetitive with* Time *until it was taken over by the* Washington Post *in the early 1960s.*
>
> *The following account should be contrasted with* Time *magazine's article on the same subject to determine which news magazine was more comprehensive and judicious in its reporting and editorial coverage of the death of Elvis Presley.*

Inside his Memphis mansion, Graceland, the king of rock 'n' roll lay silent in a copper coffin. Women hid tiny cameras in their bras to take one last picture as they filed past. Outside, hundreds of floral arrangements, some shaped like guitars and one like a hound dog, lined the long driveway and thousands of fans kept vigil on the tacky boulevard below in the sweltering heat. They had abandoned jobs, driven all night and flown in from abroad for one last glimpse of their idol. "Don't faint now," a mother warned her faltering daughter, "or I'll just have to leave you." A billboard down the way read "In Memoriam" and the Beef and Liberty Restaurant sign directly across the street carried the message "Rest in Peace." But hardly anyone in Memphis could really believe that Elvis Presley was dead of a heart attack, at the age of 42.

Elvis—"Elvis the Pelvis"—was more than a pop superstar. With his sleepy, sensual looks, his sexy bumps and grinds and his black-sounding voice, he not only changed the course of pop music forever, he may have created the generation gap. Rarely does an entertainer so galvanize the unstated yearnings of an age and serve as a harbinger for the decade to come as Elvis did in the mid-1950s with the first of his long parade of hits, which included "Heartbreak Hotel," "Hound Dog" and "All Shook Up." After his famous first appearance on "The Ed Sullivan Show" in 1956, my aunt told me how foolish I was to sit screaming with joy at the spectacle of that vulgar singer on TV. It was then I knew that she and I lived in different worlds, and it was then that kids' bedroom doors slammed all over America. Boys wore greasy ducktail haircuts and tried to imitate Elvis's moves in front of the mirror. Girls gave up collecting charms for their bracelets for the forbidden charms of his 45-rpm records. Our parents hated Elvis and that was all right with us. From Elvis on, rock was rebellious.

His death aroused the same old frenzy—and pared away the sad spectacle of recent years when Elvis had become fat, reclusive and increasingly paranoid. Memphis florists had to fly in 5 extra tons of flowers to fill the orders going to him. Stores all over the country were sold out of Elvis's records, and the RCA plant in Indianapolis, which can press 250,000 albums a day, was working a 24-hour shift to catch up. Ballantine Books received what might be the largest single order in the history of publishing—for 2 million copies of "Elvis: What Happened?" an exposé by three disgruntled former bodyguards. Radio stations all over the world were playing hours of Elvis music. In Japan, music critics reportedly sobbed on television as they discussed him.

In London, hundreds of Teddy boys and their tattooed girlfriends prayed alongside housewives and their babies in a special church service. In Paris, L'Humanité, the Communist Party newspaper, headlined THE "KING" IS DEAD. And back in Memphis, the reckless frenzy reached tragic proportions when, hours before Elvis's private funeral, a drunk teen-age driver ran into three people keeping vigil outside Graceland, killing two young women and critically injuring another.

When he died, Elvis had sold over 500 million records—more than any other pop star. He was born dirt poor in the small rural town of Tupelo, Miss. His father worked at odd jobs and his mother spoiled her only child as much as their meager earnings allowed. When she died, Elvis was so distraught that local lawmen would try to cheer him up by taking him on daily helicopter rides. From his mother, Elvis, who was always shy and uncomfortable around strangers, learned his lifelong habit of "Sirring" and "Ma'aming" everybody.

In 1953, after the family had moved to Memphis, Elvis, who was 18 and working as a truck driver for $41 a week, had "just an urgin' " that prompted him to pull into Sam Phillips's Sun Records to make a record for his mamma's birthday. Phillips was looking for a certain kind of singer. "If I could find a white man who had the Negro sound and the Negro feel," said Phillips, "I could make a billion dollars." That's what he found, but Phillips eventually setted for $35,000—which RCA paid him for his contract a year after Elvis's first Sun single, a black rhythm-and-blues song called "That's All Right," became a regional hit.

The sale was engineered by Elvis's new manager, "Colonel" Tom Parker, a former carnival pitchman. Parker's credo was "Don't try to explain it, just sell it"—a motto his well-trained concessionaires followed last week when they hawked Elvis T shirts for $5 in front of Graceland. The Colonel, as he was called, took absolute charge of Elvis's career and got top dollar for every job. He knew he had something special.

But Elvis didn't. "I don't think of it as an act," he told an early interviewer. "I just sing. It comes out this way and that's what I do. I never really think about it." But he did like to be different. His tight pants and pink silk shirts were extreme at the time. He experimented for hours with his black ducktail. He wore eye shadow for his first appearance on the Grand Ole Opry and heard an official there tell him, "We don't use niggermusic at the Grand Ole Opry." Within a few years Elvis's style had nearly destroyed country music because every country boy wanted to sing just like Elvis—not like Webb Pierce. "He was white but he sang black," says the noted guitarist Chet Atkins, who was assistant producer on the early records at RCA. "It wasn't socially acceptable for white kids to buy black records at the time. Elvis filled a void."

In 1956, the Colonel parlayed Elvis's hits into a movie career that was enhanced sentimentally when Elvis got drafted and served two years in the Army. Long before Robert Redford, Elvis was earning a million dollars per picture for the corny B movies he later scorned as "Presley travelogues." The Colonel maintained it was his "patriotic duty to keep Elvis in the 90 per cent tax bracket"; he was loath to tamper with a successful formula, and along the way, Elvis never really grew up. "I never understood why he didn't try to make better records or movies," says an RCA executive. "He was like the Colonel, who felt that you don't really need quality because you'll always be popular."

In the '60s, Elvis the rock 'n' roll star was eclipsed by the very groups his music had spawned—the Beatles, the Rolling Stones, the Doors—and to most rock fans, he was nothing more than a golden oldie. For almost nine years, the Colonel kept him away from personal appearances. But in the late '60s, he reemerged with a glittering Las Vegas engagement. In recent years, he toured sporadically, overweight and musically lethargic. But he invariably sold out sports arenas to audiences of all ages.

Offstage, Elvis increasingly isolated himself from the public. He granted no interviews. He surrounded himself with an entourage of good-buddy yes-men, the "Memphis Mafia." He spent hours in his bedroom watching TV. For fun, he'd rent an amusement park or movie theater for himself and his friends. His generosity not just to friends but to strangers—upon whom he would sometimes lavish new Cadillacs—was legendary. But in 1972 his wife, Priscilla, whom he had married in 1967—their daughter, Lisa Marie, is now 9—finally grew tired of being a bird in a gilded cage and left him for her karate instructor. It was a blow he never recovered from.

Recently Elvis took to wearing a bulletproof vest during public appearances. He also collected guns. One day a few years ago in Las Vegas, when he couldn't stand to watch Robert Goulet on television, he shot the screen out of the TV set. "He showed us the set," said Mickey, a blond secretary who knew Elvis in Las Vegas, as she stood at the gate outside Graceland the night before his funeral last week.

"He told me it was OK because the hotel always put it on his bill. Toward the end, though, he was paranoid. He kept in his Bible the police report of two guys who tried to rush him on the stage in 1973. My purse was always searched for weapons before I could go into his suite, and once when the cork of a champagne bottle was popped he ducked for cover and his bodyguards completely surrounded me."

Were the rumors true that Elvis was hooked on pills—speed and downers? "He was so out of it sometimes he couldn't talk," Mickey said. "I was there one morning when he was ready to go to bed and his doctor passed out pills to everybody." Last week former bodyguard Sonny West said another guard tried to stop Elvis from taking drugs by roughing up the boys who delivered them. "He looked Red in the eye," West recalled, "and said, 'I need them. I need it'."

But it was the legend of Elvis that mattered to the fans who came to Memphis to say goodbye. "I read the bodyguards' book and I don't believe it," said Margaret Carver, a 37-year-old housewife from Waldorf, Md. "Whatever's writ-

ten about him, true or false, makes no difference to me. I have no other idols.''
The next day, 150 family members and friends sang ''How Great Thou Art'' at
the private funeral service in Graceland, before the king of rock 'n' roll was laid
to rest in the mausoleum at Forest Hill Cemetery. They heard TV evangelist Rex
Humbard tell of how Elvis had invited him to Las Vegas last December. ''He
talked about religion,'' said Humbard. ''He wanted to know if Jesus would be
coming back soon.''

Jay Cocks / Last Stop on the Mystery Train—
An American Legend: Elvis Presley 1935–1977

Time, August 29, 1977

Time *magazine, like* Newsweek, *featured a by-line obituary for Elvis Presley in
the week following his death. The style and strategies of the two pieces should be
compared and contrasted.*

For information about Time *magazine, see the headnote to ''Death of a Maverick Mafioso'' on page 265.*

Train I ride,
Sixteen
Coaches long
Train I ride.
Sixteen
Coaches long
Well, that long black train
Carry my baby and gone.
—Mystery Train

As the legend goes, Elvis Presley had only a year's passing familiarity with a
recording studio when he cut that record in the winter of 1955. He had wandered
into Sun Records with his guitar, two summers before, plucked down $4 to sing a
couple of tunes to his mother, Gladys, and left carrying a 10-in. acetate for her
birthday present. Sun Secretary Marion Keisker heard a mean, lowdown
sweetness in the baritone voice, made a tape of the session and played it back later
for her boss, Sam Phillips. He had been looking for a ''black sound inside a white
boy'' to make Sun Records a national mark way beyond Memphis.

Phillips listened, thought about Presley, took his time making a decision. There
was no rush. Presley, then 18, was pulling down $35 a week as a truck driver for
the Crown Electric Co. About the only audience who knew him were his high
school classmates who had watched, stunned, as their shy schoolmate hot-wired a
class amateur show. Finally, Phillips called Presley back into the studio, a year
after he had left with his gift for Gladys. That marked the last time in his life
things would go slowly for Elvis Presley.

A song that came out of those first sessions, *That's All Right, Mama*, became a substantial local hit. So did the next four singles. By the time the last, *Mystery Train,* was released, Presley had connected with a deadeye promoter named Colonel Tom Parker, who landed him a national contract with RCA Records for the outlandish sum of $35,000. In the winter of 1956, not six months after *Mystery Train* came out, Elvis Presley released *Heartbreak Hotel* and sent American popular culture into a collective delirium that came, after a while, to be called "the Rock Era."

Time passed to a heavy back beat. In a giddy blur, Presley went on the *Ed Sullivan Show,* intimidated the adults of America and drove their kids into a frenzy. Parents said Elvis was suggestive, lewd, a greaser. To kids that was just the point. Elvis reveled in his performances. He used his music as an open invitation to release, and kids took him up on it.

He inspired scores of imitators, sold millions of records. He got drafted into the Army, got his infamous D.A. and 'burns clipped, served a tour of duty in Germany, sold millions of records. He went to Hollywood, appeared in 33 movies, sold millions of records. He played Vegas, got married, filled amphitheatres, got divorced, lived a gaudy life so high and wide that it seemed like a parody of an American success story. And he kept selling records, well over 500 million in all. The music got slicker and often sillier, turned from rock toward rhinestone country and spangled gospel. Only the pace remained the same. Elvis Aron Presley always lived fast, and last week at the age of 42, that was the way he died.

He was found lying on the bathroom floor in the afternoon. All attempts to revive him failed. Presley had died of "cardiac arrythmia"—a severely irregular heartbeat—brought about by "undetermined causes." Doctors said there was "no evidence of any illegal drug use," although a new book co-authored by three former Presley bodyguards maintains that "E" consumed uppers, downers and a variety of narcotic cough medicines, all obtained by prescription. He also was wrestling halfheartedly with a fearful weight problem and was suffering from a variety of other ailments like hypertension, eye trouble and a twisted colon.

So the legend goes: nothing kills America's culture heroes as quickly and as surely as success. Presley burnt himself out, as if on schedule. He had been thirsty for glory. Born in Tupelo, Miss., he was an only child whose parents scraped along on odd jobs until the family moved to Memphis when Elvis was 13. He was fanatically and unabashedly devoted to his mother. He was buried near her after the kind of awful agonized public wake that attended the passing of Rudolph Valentino and Judy Garland. Eighty thousand fans jammed the street outside his Memphis mansion, Graceland, hoping for a view of the body; 30,000 were admitted to the house. Dozens swooned, cried, keened and passed out from the heat outside the mansion gates. Two people were killed when a drunken driver plowed into the crowd. After the funeral at Graceland, a cortege of 16 white Cadillacs led a slow procession down Elvis Presley Boulevard to the cemetery. There the lawn was banked with some 2,200 floral tributes—an imperial crown of golden mums, hortisculptured hound-dogs and guitars, sunflowers in wine bottles. Memphis ran out of flowers; reinforcements were sent in from California and Colorado.

Rock stars—all Presley step-kids in one way or another—paid him tribute. "I am very sad," said Rod Stewart. "His death is a great loss to rock 'n' roll." Said Brian Wilson of the Beach Boys: "His music was a great inspiration to us. His personality was a great inspiration to us. He was a fine gentleman." Meanwhile, radio stations canceled regular programming and even commercials to play lengthy homage to the fallen king. In Boston a fan lent his own Presley collection to fill the gaps in one station's library. Outside the Las Vegas Hilton, the flag was lowered to half-mast. Instant cottage industries in Elvis T shirts blossomed. Stores everywhere sold out of Presley records, as if one spin on the turntable would keep him alive forever.

In a sense, of course, it will. Presley was not, as he has so often been called, "the father of rock 'n' roll," but he was the first to consolidate all its divergent roots into a single, surly, hard-driving style. Rock had its origins deep in rhythm and blues, which, in a time of strict musical segregation, was black music all the way. Presley gave rock and blues a gloss of country-and-western and a rock-a-billy beat, but he preserved the undertones of insinuating sexuality, accentuated rock's and blues' rough edges of danger from the sharp beat to the streetwise lyrics. "It was like a giant wedding ceremony," Marion Keisker said later, "like two feuding clans who had been brought together by marriage."

Those early Sun sides, typified by the wonderfully spooky, smoky *Mystery Train,* were arguably the best music Elvis ever made. The more familiar songs, like *Heartbreak Hotel, Hound Dog* and *Don't Be Cruel* are great tunes, joyful and sassy. They have become cultural artifacts, but no amount of historical respectability can fully dim their raucous vitality. They also represent a high point. Only four or five years after they came out, Presley's music had virtually become a patented mixture of heavy breathing and hokum.

After his Army hitch, and under the guidance of Colonel Parker, Elvis' new music was confined largely to sanctimonious spirituals and sound-track ditties off the string of brain-rotting movies he turned out, sometimes at the rate of three a year. At first, the movies—like *Jailhouse Rock*—tried for a little of the defiance and vitality Elvis got in his music, but such ambitions were quickly forsaken for formula. Elvis beefed about the scripts, which he once contemptuously dismissed as "travelogues," but Parker could point to the fact that each of the movies turned a profit—often a handsome one—and that the sound track from one of these travelogues, *Blue Hawaii,* was Presley's bestselling album ever. The Colonel was constantly nudging Presley away from rock, stuffing him into an entertainment package that offered a little something for everyone. Audiences stayed loyal, and Presley earned millions each year. No matter that with the coming of the Beatles a lot of rockers deserted him. Elvis had already set their style.

It was style as much as the songs he sang that made Elvis Presley such an immediate, and ultimately irreplaceable, phenomenon. Initially, it was all a matter of attitude, the low lids, the lip that curled up like a whitecap before breaking on the beach, the musky voice that seemed to take its honey coating from a lot of scruffy worldliness and its distinct throb from straight below the waist. His first appearances were small Pop cataclysms. The sensuous movements that headline writers called "gyrations" and that earned Presley nicknames he did not like—Swivel Hips, the Pelvis—had their roots in roistering responses of some fundamentalist congregations.

Offstage his deferential manner toward adults, his shy country-boy come-on to women, made him seem, whatever heights of fame he achieved, strictly and forever down home. He defined himself, as Critic Greil Marcus points out in an excellent Presley essay, "by presenting his authentic multiplicity. I am, he announced, a house rocker, a boy steeped in mother-love, a true son of the church, a matinee idol who's only kidding, a man with too many rough edges for anyone ever to smooth away. Something in me yearns for a settling of affairs, he said with his pale music and his tired movies; on the other hand, he answered with his rock 'n' roll and occasional blues, I may break away at any time."

314

He never did. Not really. His later stage shows were full of intentional self-parody; he took to telling audiences "this lip used to curl easier." Of late he made his entrance at concerts to the thundering strains of *Thus Spake Zarathustra*. He could still rock out when he wanted to cut loose with a fine, jagged version of *Hound Dog*, but he seemed increasingly bored with his music and more absorbed in the lavish trappings of his own celebrity.

In the first flush of his success, Elvis lived with the crazy vigor of a good ole boy who just had the whole world tucked snuggly into the back pocket of his overalls. He surrounded himself with home-town cronies, kept them fed and cared for, dispensed lavish gifts. He gave away luxury cars—particularly the Cadillacs he doted on—like gumdrops. After a while, though, the cronies became heavies—bodyguards, procurers—and the gifts bribes to buy loyalty, or silence. He courted a girl, Priscilla Beaulieu, he had met during his Army hitch. He persuaded her father to let her come over from Germany to live and, when he got out of the Army, to go to school in Memphis. She was not yet 15 when they met. They got married when she was 21, and a year later, in 1968, they had a daughter. After that, Elvis spent a lot of time away from her until they divorced in 1973. Presley became reclusive, paranoid. He immured himself among roomfuls of flamboyant furniture in Graceland. He took up karate, amassed a vast collection of guns and police badges and, according to the trio of tattletale bodyguards, would travel not only with a brace of handguns but such heavy armaments as a Thompson submachine gun and an M-16 rifle.

Earlier, he had rented a Memphis movie theater and a roller rink for afterhours amusement. In recent years, his only forays out into the real world were concert tours that were carefully insulated. The routine was usually the same: private plane to private limo to back entrance of hotel to specially cleared elevator to penthouse suite; then, after a while, off to the concert, onto the stage, back to the hotel, then to the airport. Reality never intruded, except when the schedule faltered. In a 1972 documentary, *Elvis on Tour*, there is a quick scene of Elvis, stranded on an airport runway, waiting for the gangway of his private plane to roll out. He is caught in the glare of sunlight, and he looks up in the sky with startled curiosity, as if surveying an alien planet.

The world he left behind so quickly had still not quite recovered from the changes he brought down on it. In England, the punk rockers who are raising such a ruckus, spooking the music business and intimidating their elders, turn themselves out just like the Elvis of the '50s, in tight pants and defensive snarls. Their unadorned, assaultive music tries for the same fierce simplicity Elvis seemed to achieve so effortlessly. Back in Memphis, hysteria prevailed. Guards were posted outside the mausoleum to keep fans and fanatics from laying waste to the burial grounds. There were to be fresh shipments of Elvis records, re-releases of the old movies, TV retrospectives. Presley mourners talked about trying to reach his spirit through séances.

So the legend goes. And grows. From out of the barrage of funeral images, from the fragmented memory of dozens of Presley lyrics, one reaches for a single last memory, searches for an epitaph. Go way back, to another of those early Sun records and there is one that seems particularly appropriate. "Well," Elvis starts off, in a wild, raw drawl, then rushes into the verse:

> *I heard the news*
> *There's good rockin' tonight*

Now there is, for everyone. Elvis saw to that.

DISCUSSION QUESTIONS

1. Is *Time* or *Newsweek* more comprehensive and judicious in its reporting and editorial coverage of the death of Elvis Presley? From what point of view is each story reported? Both are by-line stories, but which seems more personal? What makes it seem so? What attitude does each author take toward Elvis? Toward his fans?

2. Are there any factual discrepancies between the two stories? Do their respective contexts provide you with a way to resolve any apparent contradictions?

3. Focus for a few moments on the opening of both accounts. How would you describe the strategy used to begin each story? Is the strategy the same? If not, how is it different? Is this framework for the story maintained throughout? If not, when is it abandoned? Why?

4. Is the style of one story more figurative than the other? More allusive? More detailed? Can you determine on the basis of their respective styles any differences in the audiences they imagine?

Joseph Morgenstern / "We Get You to Places You Can't Get to"

Horizon, December 1977

After switching from bimonthly to monthly publication in September 1977, the editors of Horizon *reassured their readers that their magazine still "interprets its mandate to cover cultural affairs as extending not simply to art galleries, concert halls, and the Broadway stage, but also to the well-laid table, the nation's courts, and, ultimately, the polling booth."*

As Star Wars *and* Close Encounters of the Third Kind *captivated moviegoers across America in 1977,* Horizon *presented the following article by Los Angeles writer Joseph Morgenstern about the special-effects wizardry that is largely responsible for the new wave of sci-fi cinema.*

The movies have always had their tricksters, those special effects magicians who tickled our terror bones with giant apes, fought dog fights with midget Spitfires and Messerschmitts, waged epic sea battles in studio tanks, and snapped at our grosser sensibilities with bucktoothed rubber sharks. But the charming old tricks that we knew were fake but enjoyed all the same have given way to effects, like the ones in *Star Wars* and *Close Encounters of the Third Kind,* which go beyond ingenious sleight of hand into a relentless assault on the senses. Where once a magician stood on stage and blithely pulled a rabbit out of his hat, the rabbit now turns into a robot, the hat turns into a flying saucer, the robot boards the saucer, shifts into hyperspace, hovers over our heads, and dazzles our eyes with lasers, befuddles our brains with force fields, and pummels our ears with Dolbyized twin track stereophonic sound.

And the audiences love it, with a passion that borders on religious fervor. When the mother ship in *Close Encounters* finally moves into view, it's not a ship at all but a portable civilization that's bigger than a mountain, more complex than an oil refinery, and more dazzling than Manhattan at its most romantic, and people don't care all that much how the magic is done. They assume, quite rightly, that special effects technology has gone beyond them. All they care about is seeing more.

"There's no violence in *Close Encounters*," says Douglas Trumbull, the man who did the visual effects. "And no sex, unless you want to talk about the flying saucers as foreplay. Yet it's the highest-impact G-rated film ever made." The kids who troop back five and six times to see *Star Wars,* the most popular movie in history, aren't going to see a special effects festival. They're going to see a dazzling live-action comic strip. But there's so much cumulative power in the thundering spaceships, the poignant robots, the teeming extraterrestrial life, the Death Star as big as a planet, that a real leap of faith can take place, right into director George Lucas's long ago in a galaxy far away.

In another long ago, the era of the great Hollywood studios, special effects were the exclusive province of the special effects departments. Teams of well-trained and highly paid technicians spent their lives building marvelously detailed miniatures—battleships to sink, buildings to burn—or making mattes—for the kind of composite photography that put the leopard together with Grant and Hepburn in *Bringing Up Baby*. At one time Warner Brothers alone had over 100 people in its special effects department, and 11 full-time matte artists. The names of the masters—Frank Van Der Veer, Albert Whitlock, Glenn Robinson, Bill Abbott, and others—were familiar to readers of those perennial *Collier's* and *Saturday Evening Post* articles about the secrets of Hollywood's special effects of wizards. But all the wizardry in the world couldn't keep the major studios from disintegrating under the impact of network television in the 1950s. Although Whitlock, Abbott, and a few others continue to work brilliantly as individuals (turning out the effects for the recent *King Kong* and *Logan's Run,* as well as all those disaster sequences in *The Towering Inferno, Earthquake,* and *The Poseidon Adventure*), the special effects departments around them have vanished, one by one, like a flotilla of *Titanics*.

Today's technician-artists serve essentially the same function. "We make what you can't get, we get you to places you can't get to," says John Dykstra, the 30-year-old special photographic effects supervisor of *Star Wars*. But they're a new generation, using potent new tools. In their twenties and thirties, for the most part, they've come to feature films not through the studio ranks but from industrial design, film schools, TV commercial production, and allied black arts.

Their dean, 35-year-old Doug Trumbull, was a young artist doing animation work for NASA and then for the New York World's Fair in the early 1960s when Stanley Kubrick hired him as one of four special effects supervisors for *2001: A Space Odyssey*. Kubrick's film was the seedbed for a whole decade of special effects advances that culminated in *Star Wars* and *Close Encounters*. It was a tinker's heaven from the start. Kubrick, riding high from his recent triumph with *Dr. Strangelove,* set up shop in London, as far as he could get from Hollywood control and still have first-rate technical resources. He created his own research and development department and cloaked the whole enterprise in such secrecy that not even the executives of M-G-M, the company financing the film, had any clear idea of what was going on. "In practical terms we had no schedule and we had no budget,'' Trumbull recalls with a head shake and a grin. "Our only mandate from Kubrick was that everything had to be different."

Everything was. Hordes of surreal ape-men danced across a terrestrial and yet somehow alien landscape in the "Dawn of Man" prologue. Giant spaceships with rich interior lives of their own wheeled and waltzed and even copulated, as Kubrick's bomber and tanker had done in *Strangelove*. Lights blazed on a moon base the size of a small city. Astronauts floated in the void like Peter Pans who'd lost all recollection of home. And in the stargate sequence the camera plunged through a seemingly infinite corridor of color and cataclysm that's been imitated ever since in a seemingly infinite succession of inferior science-fiction movies and TV commercials.

The technical achievements of *2001* were amazing, and all the more so because they were almost handmade, compared to the techniques used in *Star Wars* and *Close Encounters*. To give small models the look of majestic reality it's necessary to shoot at least two and sometimes many more takes: one for the spaceship's exterior, say; another for the pulsating light from its engines; still another for the miniature projection of moving astronauts seen through its windows. All the takes must be identical in terms of camera moves, so they can be superimposed on one another in an optical printer that combines the separate pictures into a whole. If the registration is a few thousandths of an inch out of whack in the filming, it will be hugely so when projected on a theater screen, and a cleverly crafted three-foot model will look exactly like a cleverly crafted three-foot model.

In *2001* Kubrick's people built a camera-animating rig with a 20-foot-long worm gear. The monster gear was needed to move the camera with sufficient accuracy for the unprecedented detail of the shots, and even then the rig could move on only one axis, back or forth. But in *Star Wars*, produced ten years later, after men had landed on the moon and phenomenal little electronic calculators had landed in schoolchildren's pockets, worm gears and other mechanical processes were replaced by electronics. John Dykstra was able to move his camera on seven different axes and repeat every move in perfect registration, thanks to an electronic motion-control device that records the physical data on 12-channel magnetic tape.

Dykstra, a car nut who studied industrial design but never got a degree, started working in special effects under Trumbull in *Silent Running*, an influential though commercially unsuccessful sci-fi feature that Trumbull wrote and directed in 1971. From there Dykstra moved to Berkeley, where he worked with computers in environmental simulations—creating, for example, a 24-mile car trip through Marin County without leaving the laboratory. When Lucas hired him for *Star Wars*, Dykstra gathered together some ten key people—designers, photographers, electronics and optics freaks, model builders, and machinists (including Doug Trumbull's father, Don, a designer and inventor who did special effects for *The Wizard of Oz*)—set up shop in a warehouse in the San Fernando Valley, and dubbed this new company the Industrial Light and Magic Corporation.

These days, when you walk around the warehouse, it seems more industrial than magic. Dykstra is doing a new series called *Galactica* for Universal TV. It will use spaceships reminiscent of those in *Star Wars*—we could be seeing more spaceships than cars on TV in the months or years to come—but on one recent afternoon the spaceships were lying idle on the model makers' benches while some costume people were working on a four-armed alien suit for a small actor to fit into. There was also some discussion of putting a trained monkey into an even smaller space suit. As Dykstra passed a seamstress adjusting the bobbin on an ancient Singer sewing machine, he asked, "Will it sew?" and she said, "Yeah, sure, this little guard in here was chafing a thread, that's all."

Yet this was the very warehouse where stars blazed, moons shone, laser bolts sizzled across light seconds, and planets were rent asunder, where Han Solo's Corellian pirate ship ran the enemy blockade, where Luke Skywalker's X-wing fighter, pursued down an endless trench by Darth Vader, dealt the deathblow to the Death Star. Some of the effects were done simply, almost conventionally. The explosions on the surface of the Death Star were filmed in miniature and in slow motion out in the parking lot, with the sun—our own sweet sun—as the key light. The model spaceships were made of ordinary polyurethane foam and other plastic materials. Were they scientifically correct? Not on your life. They were assemblages of parts from hundreds of model kits bought in hobby shops: Ferrari wheels, battleship turrets, destroyer decks, the common clay of toydom. "We just had fun," Dykstra laughs. "We did whatever we thought had to be done to elicit that first leap of faith."

Other techniques, the ones that involved electronic motion control, were unimaginably complex. In a recent issue of *American Cinematographer* Dykstra took almost 7,000 words of lucid prose to describe the making of a single *Star Wars* shot. The shot combined moving pictures of a dogfight between an X-wing fighter and an enemy fighter (all the space battle maneuvers were inspired by previous film footage of aerial battles: the pilots might just as well have been flying American Mustangs or Japanese Zeros), plus moving pictures of planets, stars, lasers, the Death Star surface, and the engines on the ships. And there were some 365 other special effects shots in the film, leading the spectator to leap upon leap of faith and Dykstra to something like apoplexy over the fact that he got a flat salary instead of a percentage of the film. In the future, Dystra insists, he wants a cut of the profits that is "commensurate with the value of the contribution."

But what does the future of special effects hold for the audience? It could, Dykstra concedes, be just more of the same, "more people in rubber suits, more model airplanes on sticks and strings. It may destroy movies based on special effects. That's perfectly O.K. by me, because I don't think movies should be based on special effects. They've got to be integrated with all the other elements, with the actors and the drama."

For Trumbull, who names his company Future General and feels he understands the future of entertainment, the key word is *impact*. He's fascinated by the amusement park industry, which in many ways is more inventive than the film business. People who've gone to Disneyland and ridden on Space Mountain, a roller coaster that runs in the dark, come back talking as if they've been to the moon. People who visit their local movie theater, with its sloppy projection, smudged screen, scratched prints, and generally half-witted pictures, come back talking as if they've been to the cleaners. Most amusement park thrill rides last only two minutes, but they're high-impact minutes, with frequent spikes on the emotional graph. That's what Trumbull wants for his spectators of the future—lots of emotional spikes in new environments that may bear little resemblance to the theaters of today.

He has already discovered a way to heighten the impact of a projected image. In their infancy the movies were called "flicks" because slow shutter and projection speeds made the image flicker. When the shutter speed increased and the projection rate jumped to today's standard of 24 frames per second, the more obvious flicker effects disappeared and gave the illusion of continuous motion. You don't realize what a fragile illusion it is, however, until you've seen pictures projected with even faster shutter speeds at 60 frames per second in Trumbull's new 70 millimeter process, which he calls Super 70. The effect is astonishing, the visual equivalent of switching a radio from some static-ridden AM station to the crystalline transparency of FM stereo.

Trumbull's sample reel, projected on a mammoth deeply curved screen at his facility in Marina Del Rey, begins with a parody of the old Cinerama process, with Trumbull instead of Lowell Thomas conducting us on the roller coaster ride. There's also helicopter footage of mind-bending beauty. The most surprising moments, however, are the briefest. They're shots of ordinary people speaking a few very ordinary words. You'd hardly notice them under normal circumstances, but here they seem to be speaking with uncommon force and clarity, thanks to the depth and purity produced by the projection process itself. It's enough to turn Clint Eastwood into an actor.

At the moment Trumbull's Future General plans are badly bogged down in the present. His company is owned by Paramount Pictures, which is proceeding very cautiously with the new projection technology. Trumbull is convinced that they sold his services to Columbia Pictures for *Close Enounters* mainly to get him and themselves out of the research and development business. He's also convinced that once the studio decides to use the Super 70 process they'll use it in mundane ways. "You know, they'll take it and get Steve McQueen and Ali MacGraw to chase cars through the streets of New York."

That's the problem with special effects. The entertainment industry flogs us with them until they're not special anymore. Emotional spikes, after all, are what the TV networks have been driving into our brains with ever-increasing force, whether it's through made-for-TV movies with their climaxes every eight minutes or remorselessly clever commercials with their animated doughboys and hebephrenic kitty cats. Some people, not just sensitive plants in the feature film audience but serious artists and critics as well, already feel benumbed by the heightened impact of *Star Wars* and the threat of heavier blows to come.

The great temptation is to define the threat in conventional terms: machines are bad, people are good—or at least less bad—and the technology of special effects is bound to dehumanize everything it touches. But these are confused and confusing times in the entertainment business. It's hard to tell exactly who's dehumanizing whom. The producers of macho-violent exploitation films and TV series turn living actors into androids without special effects. Their secret weapon is the squalid script. Nothing could be more plastic than *Charlie's Angels,* more carefully cloned than the anchor persons on the happy-talk news shows, or more inhuman than canned laughter.

In the supposedly mechanistic sci-fi movies, however, human needs and feelings have been cutting in on the dance of the machines in unexpected ways. At first it was the quasi-religious ending of *2001,* full of psychedelia and rebirth, and the disquieting notion of Hal, the petulant computer, having richer emotions than either of the laid-back astronauts on board ship. Next Doug Trumbull elaborated on that turnabout in *Silent Running* with Huey, Dewey, and Louie, the lovable robots who were the spiritual parents of R2-D2 and C-3PO, the machines who provided most of the human interest in *Star Wars*. Then, in the *Star Wars* climax, with young Luke Skywalker in his X-wing fighter, streaking along the Death Star trench to drop his bomb on target, we hear the voice of Alec Guinness's cosmic sage saying "Use the Force, Luke! Trust your feelings! Let go!" The computerized bomb sight moves into position in front of his eyes, but Luke shoves the gadget aside and aims the bomb himself, by guess and by God. It seems hardly the moment for antitechnology propaganda, but it's there all the same, and it's precisely what confirms Luke as hero rather than a tool of tools. Special effects can get you where you want to go, but it still takes soul to deliver the goods.

Fran Lebowitz / Clothes with Pictures and/or Writing on Them: Yes, Another Complaint

Ca. 1977

After a New York Times Book Review *critic called Fran Lebowitz "an important humorist in the classic tradition," the 6,000-copy first pressrun of her book* Metropolitan Life *was quickly exhausted. In a few months, 85,000 copies had been sold, and the paperback rights had been auctioned for $150,000: not best seller numbers or dollars, but a surprising success for a book that was expected to have only a small parochial readership.*

Fran Lebowitz began her professional writing career with book and movie reviews in the now defunct magazine Changes. *Later she wrote a column for Andy Warhol's* Interview *magazine called "The Best of the Worst," and after a year's absence from* Interview *returned with another called "I Cover the Waterfront." She also contributed "The Lebowitz Report" to* Mademoiselle. *Like her idol, Oscar Wilde, Lebowitz is known for her razor-sharp silver tongue. In response to criticism on her pointedness, she said, "You know, someone once said that Dorothy Parker had wasted her life wisecracking. I really can't think of a better use for a life."*

Now, I'm not just talking about Vuitton bags. Or Gucci wallets. Or Hermès scarves. Designers and/or business concerns who splash their names and initials all over overpriced accoutrements of dubious quality are of course solely lacking in taste, but I am not going to be sidetracked by trivialities. I'm talking about the larger issues. Open-necked Deco-ish shirts with a repeating pattern of middle-sized silhouettes of sailboats. Blue jeans depicting the death of Marilyn Monroe in waterproof pastels. Dresses upon which one (but preferably two) can play Monopoly. Overalls that remind toddlers, through the use of small pink animals spouting comic strip balloons, to brush their teeth. T-shirts that proclaim the illegal sexual preferences of the wearer. Etcetera. Etcetera.

While clothes with pictures and/or writing on them are not entirely an invention of the modern age, they are an unpleasant indication of the general state of things. The particular general state of things that I am referring to is the general state of things that encourages people to express themselves through their clothing.

Frankly, I for one would not be unhappy if most people expressed themselves by marching en masse into the nearest large body of water but, barring that, I wish they would at least stop attempting to tell all by word of jacket. I mean, be realistic. If people don't want to listen to *you,* what makes you think they want to hear from your sweater?

There are two main reasons why we wear clothes. First, to hide figure flaws, of which the average person has at least seventeen. And second, to look cute, which is at least cheering. If some people think that nice, muted solid colors are a bit dull they can add some punch with stripes, plaids, checks, or—if it's summer and they're girls—small dots. And for those of you who feel that this is too restrictive, answer me this: If God meant for people to walk around in coats that have pictures of butterscotch sundaes on them, then why does *he* wear Tattersall shirts?

U.S. News and World Report Staff / Why It's Called the "Me" Generation

U.S. News and World Report, March 27, 1978

U.S. News and World Report is a weekly that advertises itself as "the only news magazine devoted entirely to national and international affairs," which means that readers will not find the kind of "entertainment" columns featured by its competitors. With fewer photos and less color than either Time *or* Newsweek, U.S. News and World Report *encourages readers to consider it the no-nonsense news magazine.*

In the following article a staff writer takes a sober look at a generation apparently drunk with its sense of self.

Many of America's young adults have found new heroes—themselves.

Glittering discos, sex clubs, singles apartments and a seemingly endless variety of techniques for baring their psyches enable young people to celebrate themselves in what writer Tom Wolfe calls the "me" decade of self-gratification and self-improvement.

Many observers of this trend say it has serious social consequences, for young adults as well as their elders, such as a high divorce rate, declining participation in the political process, and relationships devoid of feeling and caring.

But others say alarm is unwarranted. They argue that today's young adults are no more self-centered than past generations were. Even these analysts acknowledge, however, that the "me" message is everywhere in the society.

Television is the primary transmitter of the message through its programing and through advertisements that say "you deserve a break today" and "this I do for me." Psychologist Kenneth Keniston at the Massachusetts Institute of Technology says: "Forget about the future, do things now, do them today. That is what television says to people."

Many best-selling books sound a similar theme, telling people they should be "Looking Out for #1" and "Winning Through Intimidation."

A New York department store even opened a "self center," offering such items as health food and cosmetics.

ANALYSTS' LABEL

Social analysts use the phrase "the new narcissism" to describe these goings-on. Narcissists, they explain, find it difficult to enter into close relationships; a narcissist sees others existing only as a means for maintaining his or her own well-being.

Some experts fear that this trend will lead America to an age of anarchic individualism that could have devastating impact on a society whose orderly functioning depends to a large degree on self-restraint. Taking a different view from those who cite political apathy as a problem, they see an increase in one-issue political groups, many of them divided along ethnic or religious lines, and believe that is a sign of social fragmentation. According to Harvard University sociologist David Riesman: "The growth of grievance groups leads to an increase in the number of individuals who feel they are aggrieved."

The reluctance of many couples to have children and the rise in the number of young people who live alone are viewed as other manifestations of self-centeredness by some social scientists who say these developments reflect an unwillingness to make emotional commitments to others.

Even among couples who choose to have children, there is a change in values. A study by the New York research firm of Yankelovich, Skelly & White, Inc., found that large numbers of parents are self-oriented and are reluctant to make sacrifices for their youngsters.

Today's advertising caters to such attitudes. Says New York advertising man Jerry Della Femina: "Ads today tend to focus on the individual rather than on families."

Usually, it is the more affluent who have the time, the money and the freedom to seek ways of breaking out of traditional restraints in the pursuit of self-satisfaction.

"MY PLEASURE"

In New York, more than 700 couples a week—some middle-aged—pay to visit a club where they can engage in sex with any willing party they happen to meet. Says one participant, a divorced executive: "I'm out seeking my own pleasure and satisfying my needs."

Other couples engage in "swinging," swapping partners for sexual excitement. In the San Francisco area, "hot tubs" are the rage. Long soaks by several people at a time—often in the nude—have replaced poolside parties.

A discotheque owner in Washington sums up the prevailing philosophy of such activities in simple terms: "People are into having a good time."

Some young adults are seeking psychological rather than physical gratification, choosing from an array of programs whose costs run from about $20 into the thousands.

More than 138,000 people have tried est, paying $300 to spend the better part of two weekends with about 250 others in a controlled environment where they share experiences and are criticized and encouraged by a group leader.

"I WAS NOT AFRAID"

Alan Levin, a 26-year-old medical student from Baltimore, says that through est he has become less self-centered. "I had a sense I was dissatisfied with the way my life had been. I had trouble committing myself to other people. The training helped me to experience these fears. Once that happened, I was not afraid anymore."

Patricia Hester, a 31-year-old corporate-operations officer at an Atlanta bank, is one of thousands who have tried group therapy. "I discovered that I liked myself and that I could learn more about my inner strengths," she says. "Now, as a member of the 'me' society, I am committed to looking after my own emotional ego needs."

Others try such remedies as transcendental meditation, assertiveness training and hypnosis that takes them into "past" lives—though enthusiasm for meditation seems to be declining in some places.

Those who prefer a more conventional approach go to "positive thinking" rallies, where they hear speeches from Art Linkletter, Paul Harvey, and other personalities. John Handick, the promoter of a recent rally in the San Francisco area that attracted more than 12,000 people, says: "I feel a lot of people are searching for satisfaction and contentment within themselves."

Despite sampling all the consumer goods and excitement that money can buy, many pleasure seekers are lonely. Says one: "You have few close friends and lots of acquaintances, people whom you meet in a discothèque, say hello to and pass in the night."

FILLING THE VOID

It is the inability to form lasting relationships in this highly mobile society that helps account for the new narcissism, according to some social scientists. They say that individuals who are adrift in alien environments and have no sense of community often turn to exotic therapy to help fill the void. For some, these therapies are almost like a new religion.

Says Frederick Koenig, professor of sociology at Tulane University: "Even in many families today, there are voids. Wives work; husbands are away from home. Much of the time that used to be spent interacting with people is spent with machines, such as television."

Other scholars believe that Vietnam, Watergate and other events in recent years disillusioned many activists of the 1960s, causing them to give up on societal improvement and concentrate on self-improvement. Says MIT's Keniston: "If you live in a society where you believe the public institutions are deeply flawed and not easily improved, that leaves the pursuit of individual happiness in a private way as the main challenge to your energies."

Adds Burton Bradley, an Atlanta psychologist: "People are trying to cope with an insane world. The 'me' idea is really more a question of survival than self-indulgence."

AN ALTERNATIVE VIEW

Still others cite multiple factors for the trend. Christopher Lasch, a University of Rochester historian, says that changes in family life, the impact of the visual media, and the growth of bureaucracy—which puts a premium on manipulating people—are all helping to produce the new narcissism.

Scholars acknowledge that love of self and the zealous pursuit of pleasure are not new in a country where individualism is highly valued. Many who have studied the subject, however, say that today's narcissistic behavior is more widespread than in the past.

But not everyone agrees. Michael Novak, professor of religion at Syracuse University, says: "The only difference between now and the past is that today the means of expression are extraordinary. You can buy attention."

Novak says that for every narcissist, there are many more young people who are engaged in fulfilling lives and care about others.

John Pettinato, 26, of New York, is one such person. He overcame a background of drugs and street violence to go to college and become a cardiac technician at a hospital. Running a youth program at a church, he says, helped change his attitude toward others. He explains: "Unless you are committed to a marriage or to a way of life, you become bored, tired, disgusted. Unless there is a commitment, it is easier to walk away from things than see them through."

BENEFITS CITED

Some who partake of the "me" society contend that it is unfair to say they are self-centered. Says Steve Jones, managing editor of a newspaper in Atlanta that caters to alternate lifestyles: "By discovering things about yourself, you can interact much better with other people, help them to deal with their problems."

But historian Lasch argues that excessive self-scrutiny fuels narcissism.

Many authorities who deplore the trend toward preoccupation with self have worries about the future. Harvard sociologst Riesman says: "When a movement looks the strongest, that usually means it is about to fail. But because of the individualistic nature of this movement, it is hard to see how it will fail."

Others fear that the new narcissism is deflecting people from pursuing societal reforms or that it could lead to a benevolent bureaucratic totalitarianism in which professionals such as psychiatrists and teachers run people's lives.

Writer Malcolm Cowley is less concerned. Society, he says, alternates between looking inward and looking outward. The pendulum, he says, will eventually swing outward.

DISCUSSION QUESTIONS

1. In the advertising section of this book, find recent ads that support and others that undermine the argument that "many of America's young adults have found new heroes—themselves." Who were the heroes in early ads?

2. Which of the expert opinions about the "new narcissism" does the article seem to side with? How can you tell? What part do the other opinions cited play?

Peter Carlson / Food for Thought

Newsweek, May 29, 1978

*Longer than a letter to the editor, the full-page column, "My Turn," provides
readers of* Newsweek *with a spacious arena for their opinions. Cliches are both
the subject and substance of Peter Carlson's following contribution to "My
Turn." In keeping with his essay,* Newsweek *described Peter Carlson as "a poor
but happy, starving writer who lives in Boston, the cradle of liberty." Carlson's
essay reflects the growing interest in the proper use and popular abuse of language.*

The cliché, once a hallowed American tradition occupying a unique place in our
national life, is now poised on the brink of the crossroads—and it may be too late
to turn back.

In these troubled times, the cliché is increasingly under fire from the left and the
right alike. Before we allow it to go the way of the nickel phone call, however,
we as a nation must take a good, hard look at this pressing problem.

The cliché is as American as apple pie. An integral part of our way of life, it
has become an American institution. Passed from generation to generation by
word of mouth, the cliché is among the treasures that make up our rich national
heritage.

MANIFEST DESTINY

As every schoolchild knows, the cliché has a long and glorious history here in
the land of the free. Clichés were here long before I was born and they'll be here
long after I'm dead and buried. Clichés traveled from the Old World to the New to
follow their manifest destiny. They crossed the Great Plains, forded the rushing
rivers and traversed the burning sands of the steaming deserts of this teeming continent until they stretched from sea to shining sea. And each succeeding wave of
immigrants assimilated into the melting pot by learning to mouth our clichés.

And these clichés did not crawl out of the woodwork. Many of our Founding
Fathers added their 2 cents to the nation's great storehouse of clichés. Jefferson,
Lincoln and Roosevelt created enough clichés to choke a horse, and Franklin
coined more phrases than Carter has pills. Since then, these immortal words of
wisdom have become landmarks on the American scene.

Today, however, the cliché is under siege. In an age when traditional values are
falling by the wayside like dominoes, nothing is sacred—not even clichés. During
the tumultuous '60s, social critics attacked the cliché from all angles. They
claimed clichés were outdated and irrelevant, stood in the way of meaningful dialogue and threw monkey wrenches into the social fabric. If we can land a man on
the moon, they asked, why can't we do something about the cliché?

Some of these pointy-headed intellectuals urged us to adopt new, improved
clichés, get our heads together and come up with viable alternatives. Others, ex-

tremists of the lunatic fringe, went one step further. These wild-eyed radicals claimed the cliché was elitist, racist and sexist and urged us to abandon it entirely.

But talk is cheap. It's easy to criticize but it's a whole different kettle of fish to propose a practical alternative. And these critics have been unable or unwilling to come up with a single concrete proposal.

Common sense dictates, therefore, that we hold our horses. If we get rid of the cliché before we find something to replace it with, we will be opening a Pandora's box. Charging into this like a bull in a china shop would be putting the cart before the horse and creating a dangerous precedent.

As the great silent majority of Americans understand all too well, we cannot in good conscience allow this to happen. We cannot straddle the fence on this clear-cut issue. We must act quickly and decisively. The vast majority of average Americans of all races, creeds and colors will have to take the bull by the horns and unite in a rare outpouring of bipartisan support for the beleaguered cliché. We cannot afford to give up the cliché without a fight.

Let's face facts: You can fool some of the people some of the time, but you can't change human nature. This is a free country and a man has a right to say what he pleases—even if it's a hackneyed cliché. In this increasingly complex society, where the only constant is change, clichés still occupy a warm spot in our hearts. They are quicker, easier and more economical than other forms of talk. They also require less energy than thoughtful, carefully constructed sentences. And in this day and age, that's nothing to sneeze at.

HEARTWARMING COEXISTENCE

But don't get me wrong. I'm not advocating that we stand in the way of progress. I'm simply urging red-blooded Americans to show their true colors. While holding fast to the tried-and-true clichés that made this country what it is, we must also be eager to embrace the latest up-to-the-minute clichés hot off the presses. It would be truly heartwarming indeed if the old clichés and the new could learn to live together in peaceful coexistence from Maine to California.

And so, my fellow Americans, in conclusion I humbly submit that we must heed the wishes of the people or we will cease to exist as a free and independent nation. Original thoughts are not a dime a dozen. They are rare as diamonds, coming along but once in a lifetime. Therefore we must return to the time-honored phrases of our forefathers. If they were good enough for Ben Franklin, they're good enough for me. Remember: a cliché saved is a cliché earned.

William Severini Kowinski / The Malling of America
New Times, May 1, 1978

"From the beginning," wrote editor Jonathan Z. Larsen in the final issue of New Times (*January 8, 1979*), *"it was our hope that there was a place out there for a medium-sized magazine that did not have to be sold on the basis of celebrities, sex, or 'service journalism,' but rather on the strength of solid reporting by the*

> *best writers we would find. . . . We were determined to make the magazine a*
> *place where journalists could practice their craft at its best. And on that score we*
> *think we were successful." But as advertisers continued to move to more readily*
> *defined markets,* New Times *failed in the marketplace.*
>
> *The magazine gave most of one 1978 issue to William Severini Kowinski's*
> *"The Malling of America," an article far too long for most other national maga-*
> *zines and excerpted here. Given a mall's worth of magazine space, Kowinski, a*
> *former editor of the Boston* Phoenix *and a now defunct Washington weekly paper*
> *called* Newsworks, *was able to make a detailed analysis of suburban America's*
> *marriage to that contemporary phenomenon–the shopping center.*

New scenario for the end of the world: Four survivors of an unnatural disaster are searching by helicopter for safety and sustenance—my God! What'll we do? Where will we go? Then, just below, they see it, spread out over 100 acres, one million sheltered square feet of food and clothing, not to mention variable-intensity massagers, quick-diet books, Stayfree Maxi-pads, rat poison, hunting rifles and glittering panels of Pong and pinball, all enclosed in a single climate-controlled fortress complete with trees, fountains and neon. Safe at last! Home free! The biggest, best-equipped fallout shelter imaginable, the consumer culture's Eden, the post-urban cradle, the womb, the home, the *mall*.

Such is the premise of director George Romero's new zombie movie, the follow-up to his famous *Night of the Living Dead*. In *Dawn of the Dead,* Romero releases his ghouls in the Monroeville Mall in western Pennsylvania, but it could just as well have been . . . Olde Towne Mall in California with its fully enclosed amusement park rides and carnival midway-style shops; or Sarasota Square mall in Florida with its six-screen cinema; or Olde Mistick Village in Mystic, Connecticut, a whole shopping center representing a New England village circa 1720; or just plain, old Linda Vista Shopping Center in San Diego; or Towne West Square in Wichita, Kansas; or Big Town Mall in Dallas—or anyplace where stores such as Sears, Nieman-Marcus, J. C. Penney and Gimbels glare down long corridors of Slack Shacks, Thom McAns, Magic Pan Creperies, Waldenbooks and Bath Trends. These meticulously planned and brightly enclosed structures, these *ideas* conveniently located just off the great American highway, have taken the concept of one-stop shopping, as old as the ancient public market, and turned it into a virtual one-stop culture, providing a cornucopia of products nestled in an ecology of community, entertainment and societal identity.

Malls try hard to be all things to all people, and they seem to be succeeding. According to a *U.S. News & World Report* survey, Americans spend more time at shopping malls than anywhere outside their homes and jobs. You can buy anything from diamonds to yogurt in them, go to church or college, register to vote, give blood, bet, score, jog and meditate in them, and in some you can get a motel room, apartment or condominium—and live there.

They're big business, too. Something like $60 billion is tied up in American shopping centers, money invested primarily by large insurance companies such as Connecticut General and Prudential, and banks such as Citibank and Continental Illinois. Investors love shopping centers for very direct reasons: They turn enormous profits and hardly ever fail. "Everybody has figured out that a major regional shopping center has got to be one of the best investments known to man," says Lawrence R. Glenn, real estate vice-president of Citibank. Right now centers do about half ($300 billion in 1977) of all retail business and, with 80 percent of new major chain outlets going into them, this share is getting larger every day.

The mall building business has steamrollered over every obstacle in its path so far—recession, the gasoline crisis of 1974, the energy crunch of 1977, the bankruptcy of W. T. Grant Co. which left thousands of stores suddenly vacant (80 percent of them were leased to other tenants within a year), government environmental regulations, the Federal Trade Commission, the Supreme Court—everything. Though construction slowed down considerably during the 1974–75 slump, shopping centers "proved to be a magnificent and resilient asset," according to Mathias DeVito, president of the Rouse Company. Even during the recession, the Rouse centers managed to increase their profits by 11 percent. And now building is again increasing by hefty yearly percentages. Small wonder that Albert Sussman, executive vice-president of the International Council of Shopping Centers—the mall business' own trade and lobbying organization—could crow at their 1976 convention: "The shopping center business is creative, it's exciting, it's challenging. Most of all, it's profitable."

Has all this been passing you by? You're not alone. "Malls are a classic case of something that fills millions of people's needs but is of no interest to sociologists," says Ralph Keyes, writer and social scientist. "People who shop at Bloomingdale's and write our sociology couldn't care less." (Bloomie's itself, in fact, has joined the trend.) Richard Francaviglia, professor of geography at Antioch College, tried to read a paper that took malls seriously at the Popular Culture Association convention in Chicago. "It nearly started a riot," he said. "Quite literally, scholars were yelling back and forth at each other—and me. It was all very stimulating," he added. "But while we were arguing, 20 million people were shopping in malls and generally enjoying themselves."

So if you want to hear the Chicago Symphony, try Woodfield Mall near Schaumburg. The Dallas Symphony was at the edge of extinction before a series of successful concerts at North Park Shopping Center rescued it. A Roy Lichtenstein sculpture stands in the Santa Ana Fashion Park in California, which is not to denigrate the 24-foot-high statue of Sir Walter Raleigh commissioned by North Hills Fashion Mall in Raleigh, North Carolina. You can see a laser show (designed by rock impresario Bill Graham's F.M. Productions) three times a day at Old Chicago mall, and listen to the Old Towne Band in Old Towne Mall. Been wondering where Pat Paulsen has been lately? You can catch him at Maplewood Mall near Minneapolis, sharing the bill with Captain Cookie. If you're celebrity hunting in Chicago, try Watertower Place—Muhammad Ali has been seen there.

Of course, it's not all cash and culture. There's kidnapping, car theft, rape, dope—even dognapping. Terrorist bombs have ripped apart an American-style mall in South Africa. In 1972 George Wallace was gunned down in a shopping center parking lot, and five people caught bullets at a political rally for Senator Benjamin Everett Jordan the same year. But there's love too. Researching a story on women and the bar scene in Washington, D.C., writer Jean Callahan discovered that few women actually met prospective lovers in bars. They met them mostly in shopping malls. And so on, for all ages. . . . A Temple University study shows that malls are the most popular gathering places for teenagers in America. So for the noisy rites of pubescence, for old friends sharing a mall bench quietly, for the mainstream middle-class middle-aged middle Americans, Ralph Keyes says it directly in his book *We, The Lonely People:* "Malls aren't part of the community. They are the community."

Tom Walker, business editor of the *Atlanta Journal,* sums it up just a little differently: "If you had to pick one thing that would typify civilization in the United States in the twentieth century, a front-running candidate would be the suburban shopping mall." Hypnotists and jugglers, disco dancing classes, romance, intrigue and disaster—they've got it all, along with quite a bit of money and quite a bit of the landscape. Almost imperceptibly, the culture of the highway has coalesced in these climate-controlled bubbles. . . . The malling of America is happening now.

NEIGHBORS IN NEVER-NEVER LAND

> . . . to be an American . . . is precisely to *imagine* a destiny rather than to inherit one; since we have always been, insofar as we are American at all, inhabitants of myth rather than history.
> —Leslie Fiedler, "Cross the Border, Close the Gap"

> No problem is insoluble given a large a large enough plastic bag.—Tom Stoppard, *Jumpers*

Walter Johnson High School in Bethesda, Maryland, was once in the middle of what was, literally, a cow pasture. There were cow pastures all around it; the team mascot was "Mighty Moo." But when Marcia was in ninth grade, that suddenly changed. And so did everything else.

Because up the hill from the school the Montgomery Mall appeared. A big two-level shopping mall, with four major department stores and the full lineup of other shops—the usual suburban bread-and-butter mall built in its time, about 10 years ago. Nothing outrageous or spectacular . . . but, suddenly the students at Walter Johnson could not remember what they did on Saturday afternoon besides call each other up around 1:00 p.m. to ask, "Going to the mall?"

The girls would go shopping at Garfinckel's and Hechts and the ladies' specialty and shoe stores for their school outfits and casual clothes, and then the boys would show up at around 3:00 and everybody would walk around. Sometimes they'd meet in Bresler's 33 Flavors for ice cream, giggles, gossip and even to share some of those transcendent adolescent moments when they tried to figure out parents, teachers and God (if any).

Montgomery Mall soon became an intimate and almost institutional part of Walter Johnson High and the focus of Marcia's suburban *American Graffiti* years. Her senior prom and Christmas dance (the Snow Ball) were held in the mall. She spent many of her "open campus" free periods there, having a chef's salad in the afternoon with a friend or just walking around. The mall capitalized on the school as well. When its fountain filled up with the pennies people tossed in for luck, the mall drew crowds to watch Walter Johnson's head cheerleader and drum majorette wade into the water in bikinis and sweep up the coins.

The mall was such a part of Marcia's world that a poem in the 1970 yearbook elegized it along with the rest of the evening landscape:

> It's getting late.
> The sun collapsed behind Montgomery Mall hours ago.
> These halls are empty tunnels interrupted by piles of dust left by previous life.

The difference Montgomery Mall made in Marcia's world isn't unique. There are nearly 18,000 shopping plazas in America. Most are small neighborhood and open strip centers—just lines of stores strung out with nothing more in common than a large parking lot. But about 1,000 are as big or bigger than Montgomery

Mall, and a few hundred are huge, some taking up more than 1 million square feet of store space in a vast landscape that includes parking lots, access roads, prefab landscaping and frequently much more.

In the suburbs, malls have been largely unchallenged as social centers—there simply has been no competition. The suburban landscape as it evolved since World War II, with the assistance of FHA housing loans, federal and state highway programs and a boom in subdivisions and housing "plans," became simply houses and space. The suburbs happened so fast that few foresaw they would become anything but bedroom adjuncts to cities.

But children had to go to school, housewives needed places to shop, and everyone needed some common ground. The malls filled these gaps and fulfilled these needs. In 1973, the Camden County Economic Development Committee evaluated the influence of Cherry Hill Mall, which opened in 1961 in New Jersey. The report concluded that Cherry Hill "revolutionized the retail structure of Camden County. . . . Shopping patterns dramatically changed for thousands." Beyond the business aspect, the report found that Cherry Hill and the other malls that have opened there since "are recognized, too, as more than shopping centers. Their generous contribution of space and facilities have added new dimensions to communal life. They're truly the main street of suburbia."

Mall visionaries understood that their space would be the great common area in suburbs otherwise designed for the privacy of single-family dwellings and the convenience of cars, and they welcomed the opportunity to provide that space. In 1960 pioneer mall designer Victor Gruen wrote that malls "can provide the need, place and opportunity for participation in modern community life that the ancient Greek Agora, the medieval market place, and our own town squares provided in the past."

But that is hardly the whole story. To understand how and how well the mall phenomenon touches new American longings, soothes new fears and satisfies new needs, it is necessary to look at the mall more closely: as a structure, a concept, a medium of magic, safety and myth. See the mall after sunset, when it is empty. See it at night.

From the road, malls don't look like much. In the high bare lights, just long stone mausoleums in a wilderness of asphalt. Inside they are movie soundstages on down-time—still possessing potential magic, like sets for an unknown illusion yet to be performed.

This is Greengate Mall in western Pennsylvania, some miles east of the mall where George Romero is filming, at the end of the day. Only McSorley's bar is open. Young management types are drinking and discussing business; if they linger they may talk about merchandising strategy or sex. Before the evening's over, some of McSorley's more loaded customers may even honor the tradition of sliding down the railing of the dormant escalator.

Walking around now and looking at the mall without the animation of people, you see and sense . . . possibility. The white liquidity of light that suffuses it, the areas of relative darkness. The central court. The fountain and the stairs. The balcony effect from the railing on a landing. The aisles and escalators, the now-bracketed store facades, the live greenery. Inside, at night, you understand what is here: protected space. Removed, enclosed, intelligible yet not fully formulated. The potential is enormous and striking.

Outdoor strip shopping centers were built as early as the 1920s in California and became common elsewhere by the late fifties. The big department store owners, realizing that people wanted to shop nearer their homes, next added their bulk and muscle to the shopping center idea. Then designers came up with two major innovations: the two-level mall (introduced by the Rouse Company in Baltimore), which seemed to halve the psychological distance shoppers had to walk, and the most important stroke—the fully enclosed, temperature-controlled mall, the first of which was Southdale Center, built near Minneapolis in 1956 by Victor Gruen Associates for the Dayton Hudson Company.

Gruen enclosed Southdale because of the extremes of Minnesota weather, but the effect was so dramatic that it revolutionized shopping centers everywhere. The malls that followed, even in the sunny climes of Florida and California, were also enclosed. Paul E. Leyton, vice-president of operations of May Stores shopping centers, explains why: "We discovered that the enclosed mall changed the concept. The idea of having an enclosed mall doesn't relate to weather alone. People go to spend time there—they're equally as interested in eating and browsing as in shopping. So now we build only enclosed malls."

When the centers stopped stretching out in a line and "circled up" to form a protected enclosure, they took a profoundly different attitude toward the highways and cars that made them possible in the first place. No longer open to the road as a sustaining environment and especially as a style—freewheeling, frequently vulgar and above all uncontrollable—the shopping malls turned in on themselves to shut out the noise, dirt and danger of cars, as well as the intrusions of the highway, creating inner-directed environments divorced as much as possible from the world outside. Designing for that—the closing off of the outside world and the orchestration of what goes into this protected environment—is the art and science of malls.

In his study "Main Street USA" (the one that triggered the wild reaction at the Popular Culture Association convention), Richard Francaviglia develops a design analysis to show two things: first, that the man who initially built the perfect small town, though it never in fact existed outside his amusement parks, was named Walt Disney. And second, that where Disney left off, the mall builders took over.

Francaviglia demonstrates that by manipulating design elements such as scale and sight-lines, and by mixing the most attractive features of both small towns and cities while leaving out all the bad stuff ("pool halls, bars, second-hand stores, and the kind of people who patronize them"), Disney created a pleasant and aesthetically successful image of what a small town should be. Shopping malls simply took this concept out of Disneyland and gave it to millions just a few automobile-minutes from their homes.

Francaviglia also talks about Disney scaling down the size of his Main Street shops so they would look nostalgically small to adults and uncommonly inviting to kids. Malls are designed for Disney's children. Stores are pressed close together; they have small, low facades. In fact, everything about malls is minimized. Designers go berserk trying to make sure people don't have to walk more than a few hundred feet from their cars to the center. The mall is laid out with few corners and no unused space along store row so that there are no decisions to make—you just flow on.

Enclosure gives the illusion of safety. There is no buffeting wind, no traffic to dodge. The rest of the world may be comprised of spaces too large to feel safe in, too dirty or weird to walk in, or else of enclosures too small to stroll in—school, work place, home. But the mall is a comfortably sized space—danger is kept out, decisions are designed out, the scale is manageable. All the fearful things about the marketplace are minimized. Malls seem to be made for future-shocked agoraphobes. [. . .]

The success of enclosure has to do with things other than keeping out the weather—but it has something to do with that, too. "I like it because no matter what it's doing outside, it's always the same in here—I don't even know whether it's raining or what," says a young employee at Westmoreland Mall. "It's better for looking at girls, too," his friend adds. "They aren't all bundled up in coats and stuff, even in the winter." The absence of weather in malls is a selling point. In a newspaper sent to consumers by Tamarac Square mall in Denver, there is a cute but pointed weather forecast: "Skies over Tamarac Square's enclosed street scene continued irrelevant through the weekend. Temperatures remained consistent, though thunder was heard through the skylights on at least one occasion. No indoor tornadoes were predicted. Forecast: consistently pleasant."

By keeping weather out and keeping itself always in the present—if not in the future—a mall aspires to create timeless space. Removed from everything else and existing in a world of its own, a mall is also placeless space. And the beauty of the form is that this space can be filled with all kinds of fine-tuned fantasies. Malls can host the ideal image of the small-town street or embody nostalgic themes—an anesthetized version of early America is particularly popular in the Northeast. Or they can create new hybrids with elements otherwise found in amusement parks, public markets, sports arenas and symphony halls—encased in structures that partake of the opulence of grand hotels, European city plazas and the great American railroad stations. (Not surprisingly, malls on the West Coast are the most ebulliently rococo, while the Midwest leans toward a kind of mall classicism and the Sunbelt goes for glassy elegance.)

The mall is simply such an elastic form that virtually anything can be packaged and included, as long as it contributes to the basic consumer fantasy: shopping as entertainment. It's fabulous: controlled as a unit in leasing and operation, politically sealed off from the community to the degree the mall owner wishes, protected from the external environment. The mall is a never-never land, a huge plastic bag in which all the proper factors can be arranged to summon up the right consumer myths so that the mall becomes an absolutely vital part of the lives and lifestyle of the Me People, wherever they may be.

The quality of fantasy is sometimes pushed to the edge of surrealism; even at quiet moments the mall may produce scenes seemingly lifted from paintings by de Chirico or Magritte. This feeing can be better appreciated at some hours than others.

For instance, at a mall called Fashion Island in Newport Beach, California, shortly before sunset. . . . The sun is hanging brightly just above the parking lot in the middle of Newport Center, a planned community of which this mall is the epicenter, the temple. A soft yellow light bathes the white sandstone of the high entrance columns as well-dressed ladies in their soft "neutral-look" separates, clinging short-sleeve sweaters and high-heeled sandals jog neatly up the stone steps. Off to one side maintenance men in their sea-green jump suits and black loafers check the immaculate trees and shrubs. Off to the other, a series of bell-like objects rises several stores up, like some giant wind chimes. But they make no sound; it is very quiet here. The whole place is so perfect that it's eerie. But why, with all this quiescent concrete, does it feel so . . . unreal? And then it dawns on me: Fashion Island is a three-dimensional, life-size Artist's Conception. One of those flawless sketches or scale models that buildings themselves never quite turn out to be . . . except there. [. . .]

Janice Kaplan / Exercise—The New "High"

Glamour, May 1978

Janice Kaplan began her career in sports reporting at the age of eighteen, covering women's events for CBS radio in Boston. Yale University, where she majored in Journalism, awarded her a Murray Fellowship to research a book on women's sports. Her sports articles have appeared in The New York Times, Sports Illustrated *and several national women's magazines. Kaplan's book,* Women and Sports, *was published in 1979.*

Glamour magazine publishes articles which its editors consider to be "helpful, informative material, humorous or serious, on all aspects of a young woman's life." Fashion, beauty, decorating, and entertaining are the mainstays of the magazine.

At a physical fitness seminar held recently in Berkeley, California, about twenty people were asked why they wanted to begin exercising. Most said they hoped to look better or lose weight or improve their cardiovascular system. One woman in her mid-thirties had a different idea. "I'm trying to restructure my life," she said, "and I know the mind can't do anything without the body."

The Greeks talked about mind-body flow centuries ago, but until very recently, few people in this country paid much attention to the idea. Now doctors and psychologists are beginning to amass evidence linking exercise and emotional state. At the Esalen Sports Center in San Francisco, researchers have found that sports training can produce altered states of consciousness. "There's a whole aspect of mind experiences that our culture has denied," says Michael Murphy, the founder of Esalen. "We have evidence now that exercise stimulates the mind to new patterns of awareness."

Part of the evidence is purely physiological. Several years ago, Julius Axelrod, a Nobel laureate, identified certain chemical substances that serve as transmitters between neurons in the brain. It has been shown that a deficiency of one of these chemicals, called norepinephrine, can cause feelings of depression. Since then, psychiatrists have discovered that they can change a patient's emotions by giving drugs that affect these transmitters.

"But nature has provided us with a natural way of keeping our body chemicals in balance," says Dr. Robert S. Brown, a psychiatrist associated with the University of Virginia. A vigorous exercise such as running may stimulate the production of norepinephrine, producing the same results as—without the side effects of—many anti-depressant medications. Even mile-a-day joggers often notice that the first part of their run is the hardest, and their strength actually seems to *increase* as they continue. Many runners describe feelings of euphoria during their exercise—what has come to be known as the "runner's high." One reason may be that norepinephrine is chemically indistinguishable from adrenaline.

Other physiological effects of exercise also contribute to changing your mood. For example, several psychiatrists hypothesize that too much salt in the body can cause depression. One way that the anti-depressant drug lithium works is by replacing sodium.

Similarly, if you exercise hard enough to work up a sweat, you're releasing salt from the body. Premenstrual depression is often related to water and salt retention; women who suffer from this may find that a daily run boosts their spirits.

Other biological changes occur during exercise that help to relieve the body of stress. You actually sleep less when you're active, and more glucose, which is essential to the brain's functioning, begins to circulate in your bloodstream. Exercise provides increased amounts of oxygen and blood to the brain, and that in itself may stimulate new thoughts. "The brain is like a muscle," says Mike Spino, the director of the Esalen Sports Center, "and it needs to be worked to function right."

For reasons that aren't yet understood, people who are especially fit handle cholesterol in their system in a different way than those who are sedentary. Also, their immunological responses are better and their body generally functions more efficiently—probably because the cardiovascular system and skeletal-muscular frame are being exercised.

Vigorous activity also helps rid the body of toxins that can upset the hormonal flow. "Nearly everyone has some trace of mercury, aluminum or lead," says Dyveke Spino, coach to several Olympic athletes and codirector of New Dimensions in Lifestyle, based in Boston and San Francisco. "I know—I have hair and nail samples of the people I work with analyzed by a biochemist." This imbalance in body chemistry can affect mood and behavior. "Something like running helps you detoxify. When your body is not working just to stay alive, more blood can go to your brain. Your mind gets sharper, and you feel incredibly light and clear," says Dyveke.

This state of heightened awareness is what one psychologist calls "the 'fun' in fun." You become totally immersed in an activity so that all parts of your body-mind are synchronized. "You surrender to the moment and realize that what you're experiencing right then is you," says Mike Spino. Tim Gallwey explains in *The Inner Game of Tennis* that the mind can actually get in the way of the body's achievement. Commands from the ego ("You're playing awfully! Get your racket back more!") disturb the body's natural flow. "In some ways your body is a lot smarter than your mind is," says Mike Spino. "When you're running, it's almost never your body that tells you to stop. If you get a pain, you can learn about yourself by experiencing it and realizing that it's part of you."

Many athletes describe having "peak experiences" that occur during their activity when they suddenly feel in total harmony with their environment. It is what several humanistic psychologists are beginning to think of as a kind of Western yoga. "The experiences of the mind that athletes report are similar to those of yogis during meditation," says Mike Spino. "An intense physical activity changes your mood and feeling. You get into different ways of being." Carie Graves, who rowed on the U.S. Olympic crew in 1976, recalls having these moments twice during particularly hard workouts. "I was pushing myself 110 percent," she says, "and all of a sudden the pain was gone and I felt very peaceful. It seemed that I knew things about myself most people never realize."

People involved in intense activity also report creative breakthroughs or flashes of insight that they can't explain later. The experiences may have a simple scientific explanation. The left hemisphere of the brain is believed to be the rational, productive part of the mind, while the right hemisphere is believed to control the intuitive, psychic and creative flow. If you surrender to the natural rhythms of your body while involved in a vigorous sport, you may be able to tune out the thinker and allow the right hemisphere—and a whole new consciousness—to take over. "You can get your mind into that state of transcendence through extreme concentration, drugs or hypnosis," says Dyveke Spino, "but how much better to do it by running, swimming or bicycling!"

Michael Murphy has been collecting stories from athletes who have experienced heightened awareness or changed perceptions during physical activity. One pentathlon champion described the sensation of "rising out of his body" during an event, so that he felt he was doing the activity *and* watching himself do it. Other athletes report a "slowing down" state where each moment seems to lengthen, giving them the ability to do something in a split second that they feel should take longer.

Mr. Murphy isn't yet trying to explain these experiences, but he calls mind-body explorations "a new frontier that is as exciting as space." He points to several mountain climbers and long-distance runners who, he believes, are discovering a new level of human potentiality through their intense discipline. "Every time we set a limit on possibility, someone goes beyond it," he says.

Psychologist Ken Dychtwald, the twenty-eight-year-old author of the recently published BODYMIND (Pantheon), adamantly agrees. "You don't just think life, you feel it," Dr. Dychtwald says. "Every motion of the body is an expression of emotion." Most people would agree, for example, that butterflies in the stomach are a sign of nervous stress, and a stiff neck can usually be related to tension. But beyond these common symptoms, many feelings and attitudes are eventually lodged in specific points in the body. Several psychological and physical therapies, such as Bioenergetic Analysis and Rolfing, work on emotional attitudes by encouraging a person to confront how her body feels. The therapist may prescribe certain exercises or actually manipulate muscles to release emotion and anxieties. The underlying concept is that your body gives you access to your mind, and emotional states are manifest in body structure. Dr. Dychtwald explains that a compulsive or overachieving person often has an inflexible back—a result of literally holding herself rigidly in control. Learning to loosen these muscles can help the person relinquish an over-controlling attitude.

Dr. Alexander Lowen, a psychiatrist and proponent of Bioenergetic Analysis, believes that it's impossible to achieve a true sense of identitiy until the body and its instinctive forces are allowed more of a role. For example, you may have difficulty experiencing orgasm if your rational mind insists on staying in control. Many women report an increase in sexuality once they become involved in athletics. "You start listening more to your instincts," says one skier. "You learn to relax your mind and stop worrying about what will happen if the body takes charge." Dr. Lowen says that many people maintain such tight ego-control that they are afraid to let go, but in a healthy person "the irrational is not always suppressed in favor of the rational."

Several academics have recently taken up the subject of sports and personality, and certain traits emerge about women athletes. Most of them—from high school lacrosse players to Olympic champions—score higher on tests measuring self-sufficiency and assertiveness than inactive women. One psychologist who studied a group of joggers found that creativity and independence rose with physical fitness. When Dr. Robert Brown did personality checks on students before and after they began exercise programs, he found marked increases in self-esteem afterward. Most also displayed more cheerfulness and less tension and anxiety.

Dr. Brown is convinced that exercise can make you feel happier. A few years ago, he took several patients on daily walks or jogs. He discovered that within a short time, many no longer needed the anti-depressant drugs they had been taking. Now he regularly uses exercise as one treatment for depression and has had success with several suicidal patients.

Dr. Brown has worked with more than two thousand students and patients, trying to prove the connection between mood and movement. The results have been startling. For example, a score of fifty or above on the Zung Depression Rating Scale is considered a sign of clinical depression. (Opinions vary, but some psychiatrists estimate that 20 to 30 percent of women between eighteen and thirty-five are clinically depressed.) When Dr. Brown administered the test to members of a women's tennis team before the season began, 40 percent of the players were depressed. After the season, the number dropped to 23 percent. Another test with the members of a women's softball team showed that 35 percent were depressed before they began the season's workouts, and only 12 percent were depressed afterward. Equally significant was the fact that nearly all the students who rated on the "non-depressed" end of the scale before the season moved closer to zero once they had been exercising regularly.

A certain amount of initial commitment and dedication is necessary before you can experience the full joy of an activity. You won't achieve an integration of mind and body by forcing yourself to run around the block once a week. But while it may take some time before you experience an altered mind state through sports, other changes will be more readily noticeable. Dr. Brown feels that many people aren't aware of their own mild depressions until they begin exercising and start feeling more joyful. Fitness helps alleviate signs of depression, such as indecision and lack of zest for daily activities.

Dyveke, a woman who is in her forties, runs eight miles up and down a mountain every morning and encourages those in her program to try something similar. She sees physical activity as one way of taking charge of your life. "Athletics give you a sense of your personal worth, separate from any external acclaim," she says. "It makes you understand that most of your energy and potential are untapped."

Dozens of women who have worked with Dyveke Spino insist they have developed a new sense of self that has carried into other parts of their lives. Several ended a bad marriage or got a new job, one woman started her own business, and others have gone back to college. "You get strong mentally while improving your body, and the whole psyche opens," Dyveke says. "So many women feel inadequate in some way or have a negative self-image, but through sports they learn how much power they really have." Dyveke had training as a clinical psychologist but felt that it provided a limited way of dealing with a person. "You can't work with the mind and emotions unless you pay attention to sports and games and movement because that's the basis for so much."

And Dr. Brown adds, "We have control over so few things in our lives that exercise is one of the only means we have to gain a sense of mastery and self-actualization." He is also convinced that there is no such thing as a purely psychological explanation. "Psychological effects are often based on biological facts, and vice versa. There's no separation between the mind and the body."

Joyce Carol Oates / Adapting Literature for the Screen

TV Guide, October 7, 1978

TV Guide has the largest weekly circulation of any magazine in the world. It publishes, along with local television listings, articles about TV celebrities and shows. Before the Oscar-winning film In the Region of Ice *was broadcast, Joyce Carol Oates, the author of the O. Henry Award winning story it was based on, published an article in* TV Guide *describing her attitude towards film adaptations of literature.*

For more information about the author, see Classics (p. 602).

I have always been puzzled by the supposed enmity between the author of an original work and those who adapt the work for another medium. "How can you bear to see something you've written adapted for the screen?" people ask. "Aren't you afraid it will be simplified, or trivialized—or distorted?"

Indeed, there have been tragicomic adaptations of great works for Hollywood—notoriously, William Faulkner's "The Sound and the Fury" and Feodor Dostoevski's "The Brothers Karamazov"—and very recently F. Scott Fitzgerald's "The Great Gatsby." But the translation of prose into visual images is not only a perfectly legitimate and exciting activity, it is an artistic venture of its own. When the scriptwriter honors the depth and complexity of a work of fiction, and brings to its author's intention his own vision, and perhaps even his own *commentary* upon the original work, we have a new and unique work of art.

There need be no enmity, not even an uneasy rivalry: collaboration, perhaps, is the more accurate term.

When I saw the American Film Institute's adaptation of my short story "In the Region of Ice," I was totally unprepared for the experience. Of course, I have seen productions of my plays, but a play is, after all, written to be staged; the playwright, as he or she composes scenes, must "hear" dialogue and envision stage movement. Even so, it is often a faint shock to see living actors speaking the lines one has composed in one's head.

By temperamant I am a rather solitary, perhaps even shy, person: I have been misinterpreted, I think, as aloof—and so I have always thought it wisest to leave the interpretation of my work to others. So long as they have proven themselves professionals, why should the author of the "original" work interfere with their vision? In the theater, of course, interpretation always rests with the director. He is supreme, a necessary tyrant. The fact that I have always stayed away from rehearsals of my plays, and even from opening nights, is a sign not—I hope—of personal aloofness but of my earnest wish that the director be allowed as much freedom as possible in his interpretation: for a produced play is a new work of art, unique in its special circumstances, its special vision.

Adaptations of stories and novels, however, demand a far more complex and sometimes troublesome strategy. Before the director begins his work, there must be a screenplay. Someone must labor to translate the writer's essentially introspective vision into motion. What is so easily done in prose—think of the long, lovely, marvelously self-indulgent paragraphs of Henry James, Marcel Proust, Faulkner—must be rendered into a new medium.

The challenges are considerable; I imagine there have been many worthy projects that have simply failed. Though I am a lover of films and confess to a predilection for the unusual, even for the quirky, I have sat through adaptations of "great works" that were obviously doomed from the outset because the subtlety of the author's imagination was simply beyond the grasp of the scriptwriter. Yet there have been other occasions when, convinced that no scriptwriter and no director *could* succeed because the original material was too difficult, I have been surprised and tremendously excited by the outcome.

In this context I would like to mention the marvelous adaptations of Flannery O'Connor's "The Displaced Person" and John Updike's "The Music School" (presented on the PBS series *The American Short Story*); the extraordinarily sensuous *Masterpiece Theatre* production of Gustave Flaubert's "Madame Bovary"; and the visually memorable production of a short story by Henry James, "The Author of Beltraffio." (Another misconception, in fact an embarrassing cliche that one hears constantly, is the idea that the more serious and complex and poetic the work of literature, the less likely its chances for successful film adaptation. Joseph Strick's "A Portrait of the Artist as a Young Man," based of course on the novel by James Joyce; and the BBC production of Henry James', "The Golden Bowl," which not even the most sympathetic Jamesians—and I count myself among them—would claim to be an essentially dramatic or visually provocative work, were made into brilliant films, and should have, alone, discounted that particular cliche permanently.)

Since I had seen and approved the screenplay of "In the Region of Ice," done by Peter Werner, and was quite impressed by the young writer's sensitivity, I had no reason to fear that the production would distort the work; and I don't have that somewhat excessive sense of possession, or ego-involvement, with my fiction that certain of my contemporaries—most famously J. D. Salinger—evidently have. Nevertheless I was apprehensive, and the first several minutes of the movie were nearly lost, since I was overcome by a truly extraordinary sensation of—was it astonishment? disbelief?—very nearly a feeling of vertigo. I went to see "In the Region of Ice" at a theater near my home that has an art-film series during the academic year. It is supported by an audience one might call superior—they are intelligent, responsive, articulate members of an academic community who have a special interest in films—and it was partly a consequence of the fact that my first experience of the movie was in this context, in this very vocal and critical context, that I felt so strangely upset.

My initial reaction was a feeling that I had made a mistake; I should not have come to see the film at all. The familiar lines of the dialogue, the characters (who looked bizarrely like the fictional characters I had envisioned), the setting, the story itself—suddenly the reality of the transformation, the uncanny *authority* of the movie screen, were overwhelming.

Literature, after all, is an introspective art. Those who write it tend to be introspective, and most serious readers share this temperament: we are fond of analyzing, and brooding, and thinking and rethinking, and speculating, and imagining things for ourselves; we don't really like to be told, to be instructed; we tend to be critical, sometimes even skeptical, of external authority. In reading, we "see" for ourselves what characters look like; we "hear" voices. It isn't an exaggeration to say that the intelligent and sympathetic reader must help with the creation of the literary work itself—since it demands far more imaginative skill than most other forms of art, and certainly far more than any form of popular entertainment.

The visual arts, however, are altogether different. Images predominate. Action—even motion—draws the eye irresistibly. The importance of words as words is far less; actors communicate in many ways other than through dialogue, and directors (by close-ups and other cinematic techniques) enhance or undercut meaning. There is even—unimaginably for prose fiction—background music. All of which synthesize into a truly different art work.

Even inept films sometimes carry with them a certain mesmerizing authority. Stanley Kubrick's "Barry Lyndon," a flawed work based upon a rather uninspiring novel, can be enjoyed, for instance, simply for its visual effects: sheer photography. And the background music is superb. Something of the same can be said for a recent TV adaptation of one of Scott Fitzgerald's more frivolous short stories, "Bernice Bobs Her Hair," which transcended its insipid material by an excellent screenplay and direction and acting. It's simply the case that film, whether in a movie theater or on television, commands an authority that prose does not, because it renders its audiences *passive* rather than *participatory*. And to see one's own imagined characters, and hear their voices, as if a private dream were suddenly flashing onto an enormous screen, can be an unsettling experience.

And then, curiously, the uncanniness of the occasion lifted: within a few minutes I was simply watching a movie. Which I liked very much. My self-consciousness vanished; I was not at all aware of or concerned about the fact that "In the Region of Ice" had been at one time exclusively my own creation. I found myself in the presence of a new, unique, compelling film that had nothing to do with me at all.

I was moved by the understated, elegiac nature of the film, and carried along with no critical reservations at all by the superb acting of Peter Lempert (who took the role of Allen Weinstein and who looked remarkably as I had pictured him) and Fionnuala Flanagan (who played the rather difficult, because ambiguous, role of Sister Irene, a Catholic nun who is also a professor of English). I noted small scenes and dialogue, not in the original story—and thought them inspired. The relatively modest budget for the film necessitated an economic use of setting, but there was even an original—and very striking—musical score (by Don Peake). But what was most remarkable about the film, for me as the author of the story, was its *autonomy*. In the end it had become a new and independent work of art, and I was simply a viewer, one among many.

Over the years readers have asked why films haven't been made of my novels and stories, and I have tended to say: it's just as well, the results would probably be disastrous. Now I feel differently. Of course, there will always be disappointments, and writers react in wildly disparate ways. I remember being surprised by Larry McMurtry's comments on the film adaptation of his novel "The Last Picture Show," which was such a popular and critical success: McMurtry said quite bluntly that the film was better than the novel! Which is hardly a typical author's response.

It is possible that adaptations of short stories and novels are more likely to be worthwhile than original screenplays, if only for the reason that the scriptwriter, the director, the actors and the audience itself can realize a greater depth of experience by going to the primary source. And, of course, films of literary works lead viewers to books—as the success of *Roots,* and *The Pallisers,* and *Rich Man,*

Poor Man attest, among others. Film and print are, certainly, competitive media; but there are occasions when they complement one another, and bring readers to books that might ordinarily remain read by a relatively few people.

Shall I end by listing a few works I would love to see filmed, for the movies or for television? We all have our fantasies about such things, and mine are: Faulkner's "Light in August"; Proust's "Remembrance of Things Past" (Harold Pinter has done a screenplay); Gabriel Garcia Marquez's "One Hundred Years of Solitude" and "The Autumn of the Patriarch"; Virginia Woolf's "To the Lighthouse"; Iris Murdoch's "Henry and Cato"; and short stories by such writers as I. B. Singer, Eudora Welty, Peter Taylor, Bernard Malamud. But then the possibilities are endless.

Albert Benderson / Birth of a Drive-In
New Jersey Monthly, October 1978

As supplements to Sunday newspapers, regional magazines have been around for quite some time. But free-standing regional monthlies are largely a product of the 1960s. The New Yorker, of course, is the exception. It had been the only truly successful city magazine until recently when many of America's cities and states could finally begin to boast of well-written, brightly-colored magazines that were more than advertisements for tourists.

New Jersey Monthly began publishing in November 1976. Still about 70 percent free-lance written, the magazine features interviews with important residents, exposés of incompetent and unethical bureaucratic activities, and how-to articles about living the "better" life in New Jersey, along with regular columns on sports, media, money, and the arts.

Albert Benderson, author of "Birth of a Drive-In," teaches film at Rider College in New Jersey.

In the grand corporate vision of the American future, stepping behind the wheel of the family car becomes analogous to returning to the womb. Detroit, for one, longs for the day when the American motorist can fulfill all needs and gratify all desires without ever leaving the driver's seat. This vision has given birth to a variety of live-in automobile accessories, such as the car refrigerator, telephone, and tape deck, as well as a number of uniquely American institutions such as the drive-in restaurant, the drive-in bank, and the drive-in funeral parlor. Somehow all these innovations are vaguely associated with California in the popular imagination, as if all schemes to mate man with the motorcar emanate from the West Coast. In fact, however, the granddaddy of them all—the drive-in movie theater—is strictly a product of the New Jersey imagination.

On June 6, 1933, Richard Hollingshead opened the World's First Automobile Movie Theater in Camden, New Jersey. In a single bold stroke, Hollingshead fused the two distinctive contributions of New Jersey to the American scene—the motion pictures (via Thomas Edison) and the turnpike—into a revolutionary theatrical experience that was to reshape the American landscape.

"Sit in your car and enjoy the talkies," the opening night ads proclaimed. "Individual driveways three times the length of your car." The initial advertisement didn't mention the name of the film to be shown that fateful night: *Wife Beware* with Adolphe Menjou. The real attraction was clearly the theater itself.

Newspapers of the period suggest that the theater was an immediate success. On opening night it was jammed to capacity with six hundred cars. The fact that patrons had to pay a hefty twenty-five cents for the privilege of parking their cars at the drive-in, as well as an additional twenty-five cents per person or $1 per family, apparently did not deter these pioneer film buffs on wheels. Indeed, the theater continued to prosper throughout that first summer in the face of competition from conventional theaters attempting to lure audiences with offers of free "Diamond Gold Tableware" or "Beautiful Crystal Glassware."

First-night patrons no doubt found it difficult to hear the premier film above the roar of competing attractions on all sides of the theater, for the drive-in was located in the midst of several rather noisy enterprises surrounding what is now the Admiral Wilson traffic circle. Next door to the theater was a short-lived but equally audacious experiment in motorcar entertainment, the Auto Roller Coaster. Here customers laid down their money for the thrill of piloting their model A's and Pierce Arrows up and down wooden ramps designed to simulate the experience of riding a real roller coaster. One can easily imagine the screams of these thrill seekers punctuating the sound track of the Auto Theater's nightly feature at regular intervals as their cars clattered up and down the ramps of the coaster.

The coaster noise was merely the dominant strain in a cacophony of sounds emitted by nearby establishments. For instance, a dog track was located across the street from the theater. Nearby was the Camden Airport, at that time the only airport serving Philadelphia. The popular Hofbrau Restaurant, which featured dance marathons hosted by an obscure comedian named Red Skelton, was the social centerpiece of the airport. Added to all these distractions was the constant road noise from nearby highways. Clearly, the bedlam concentrated in this small area must have been considerable.

Moreover, in '33 the technology permitting individual car speakers had not yet been developed. After his initial, unsuccessful experiment with three large speakers, Hollingshead strategically placed twelve speakers at various points in the ground throughout the theater and turned them up to full volume so that they could be heard if the audience kept its car windows rolled down. He was unable, however, to drown out the intense background noise generated by his neighbors and was eventually compelled to install individual in-ground speakers over each parking spot. The sound from these hundreds of speakers turned up to full volume apprently was more than sufficient to drown out the competition. In fact, it was so prodigious that when the wind blew the wrong way, residents in Merchantville, two miles from the theater, complained about the noise.

As for the films themselves, Hollingshead seems to have taken a *Reader's Digest* approach to the exhibiting of popular features. According to an article in the June 7 Camden *Courier-Post,* "Abridged features, with all dull or uninteresting parts omitted, will be featured at the theatre, which will give three shows nightly." Hollingshead soon succumbed to the logistical difficulties of cramming three shows, even of abridged features, into a single evening, and bowing to the realization that it took longer to empty a drive-in than a conventional theater, he reduced the schedule to two shows nightly at 8:45 and 10 P.M.

Certainly there are still many in the Camden area who remember warm, summer evenings spent at the Auto Theater, perhaps behind the wheel of a new Buick or in the back seat of Dad's car. Some probably were in that very first audience on June 6 and, therefore, were participants in an event ranking in historic significance somewhere between the first trans-Atlantic flight and the eating of the first Mc-Donald's hamburger. No doubt the first baby conceived during the late show at an American drive-in was born during the spring of '34 in Camden.

After perfecting his sound system during a couple of experimental seasons in Camden, Hollingshead moved his operation to Union, New Jersey, where his Union Drive-In still stands on Route 22. Only a vacant lot remains to remind us of his first, pioneering enterprise. No plaque or monument has yet been erected to celebrate the glorious moment in theatrical and social history that occurred there forty-five years ago. But some local residents maintain that on a warm summer evening, when the wind is right, one can still hear in the distance the tinny, amplified voices of long-departed film stars drifting slowly through the thick New Jersey night on that eternal journey to Merchantville.

Walker Percy / Southern Comfort

Harper's, January 1979

From his Birmingham, Alabama home, Walker Percy came to New York City to study medicine at Columbia, but that career was abandoned after he contracted tuberculosis while an intern. After returning to Alabama, Percy recovered and began writing. He won a National Book Award for The Moviegoer *in 1962 and is the author of a wide variety of philosophical, literary, medical, and general interest articles.*

The essay below was originally delivered as the Ferdinand Phinizy Lecture at the University of Georgia and subsequently printed in The Georgia Review. *The version appearing in* Harper's *is a shorter form of that speech.*

Some changes are boring, others specatcular. An example of a boring change is the Changing South, or Atlanta on the Move, or Houston, Fastest Growing City in the World. After one has heard about the Changing South or the New South for fifty years, the suspicion arises that nothing is really changing, or that if it is, the change may be real and even good but also somehow dispiriting, having to do with the Americanization of the South and such boring items as Economic Progress with a Southern Accent, New Orleans, City of Contrasts (the Vieux Carré in all its charm depicted against a backdrop of the Superdome and the Hyatt).

Progress proclaimed long enough as a thesis generates its antithesis: not only boredom and sadness but a growing sense of progress coming to an end and a relief when it does. The most forlorn progress I can recall was the Century of Progress celebrated by the Chicago World's Fair, which came to an end a few months after Hitler became absolute dictator of Germany in 1934. The irony has been noted before, a century of progress issuing in the greatest orgy of death of all time, but what one tends to forget is the general decrepitude of the Century of Progress itself when it ended, trash blowing up and down past G.M.'s City of Tomorrow like the newspapers in the streets of Sydney at the end of the world in *On the Beach*. Is there not a penultimate wistfulness about such progress and a secret satisfaction when it is all brought down? Sydney deserted is not a good thing, but maybe there is something worse, Sydney progressing as usual.

Such is the nature of boring change. Spectacular change differs only in degree: it takes a little longer to become boring. Henry Grady's proclamation of a New South was probably boring the day it was uttered and has been boring ever since. But it took several years for the exploration of the moon, men walking on it, to become boring. Hundreds of millions of people watched Neil Armstrong set foot on the moon, but who can remember the name of the last astronaut who moonwalked? After Armstrong, all I can remember is that some fellow felt obliged to take a five-iron along and hit a pitch shot to liven things up.

The first time you see the new Atlanta, rolling in on the interstates, the setting sun gilding the cylinder and towers and palaces perched on a hill like Zion, it is indeed a spectacular sight, especially if the last time you saw it was from the old *Southerner* that slid into Peachtree railroad station of an evening, or if you drove in on the old Bankhead highway that ran through most of the junkyards of Alabama and Georgia.

So the new Atlanta appears to the visitor. But how does it appear to native Atlantans? Has a cloud of tender irony already begun to settle like smog among the shining towers? Has Progress already run into its own dialectic? How many Atlantans have headed for mountain cabins in north Georgia?

A spectacular change, now become commonplace, is a Georgian in the White House. What is perhaps most important about President Carter is not that he has this virtue or that shortcoming, but rather that people like him or dislike him for reasons that have nothing to do with his southern origins.

Another change, which I think has been insufficiently noticed, can be expressed by a single proposition, an axiom: The South has entered the mainstream of American life for the first time in perhaps 150 years, that is, in a sense that has not been the case since the 1820s or '30s, and accordingly in a sense that has not yet dawnêd on most southerners. Not only that, but through a strange repetition of history and conjunction of circumstance (perhaps a faltering of national purpose, perhaps the inevitable shift of economic and political power to the Southern Rim, perhaps also because of a southern talent for politics), the burden of national leadership may well fall to the South, for better or worse, just as it did in the early 1800s, then certainly for the better. Now it could as easily be for the worse. The critical dimension of the change is the sudden alarming freedom that is being thrust upon the South and for which the South, despite all the talk about a·New South, may not be prepared.

You drive through Atlanta or Houston or Dallas and you look around and up and you wonder: What is this place? Is this progress, and if it is, will it come to the same bad end as the Century of Progress, so bad that it will be a relief to see vines choke the lobby of the Peachtree Plaza Hotel?

The South in its present state might be compared to a man who has had a bad toothache for as long as he can remember and has all of a sudden gotten over it. So constant and nagging has been the pain that he long ago came to accept it as the normal unpleasant condition of his existence. In fact, it never occurred to him to imagine life without it. How does such a man spend his time, energies, talents, mental capacities? In seeking relief from the pain, by drugs, anesthesia, distraction, games, war, whatever—or, failing that, by actually enjoying the pain, the way one probes an aching tooth with one's tongue.

Then one fine morning he wakes to find the pain gone. At first he doesn't know what has happened except that things are somehow different. Then he realizes what has happened and for a while takes pleasure in it. He can't believe his good fortune. But, as time goes on, he discovers that he is faced with a new and somewhat upsetting problem. The problem is, What is he going to do with himself now that he no longer has the pain to worry about, the tooth to tongue?

What has happened, of course, is that for the first time in 150 years the South and southerners, and I mean both white and black southerners, no longer suffer the unique onus, the peculiar burden of race that came to be part of the very connotation of the word *South*. I am not going to argue about what was good and what was bad about the South's racial experience. We're interested here in what was uniquely oppressive for both white and black and which has now vanished. And to say that it has vanished is not of course to suggest that there do not remain serious, even critical, areas of race relations in all of American society, the South included.

Let me give an instance or two of what I mean by the siphoning off of southern talent, by the obsessive tonguing of this particular tooth. The figure of 150 years I got from the history books. But from my own experience, say the past fifty years, I can give a simple example of what I have in mind. During my lifetime and up until a few years ago, I can recall not a single southern politician—and only the rare writer—who was not obsessed with the problem of the relation of white people and black people. It was, in fact, for better or worse, the very condition of being southern.

The obsession almost invariably took polemical form. One either defended the South or attacked the South. What one did not do, did not have the time to do, was take a good look at the South.

Thus Sen. Richard Russell of Georgia, an extraordinarily able and talented man, a man of great character and rectitude. I am sure he accomplished many and varied legislative goals. Yet the only thing I remember about him was his great skill in devising parliamentary tactics to defeat or delay this or that voting-rights bill.

I think next of my own kinsman, William Alexander Percy, who devoted a large part of his autobiography to defending the South against "northern liberals." He wrote a whole chapter in defense of sharecropping. Again, I am not interested in arguing the issue, beyond admitting that in his place and time I'd have felt the same defensiveness and would probably have written similar polemics.

Then, I think of the novelist Richard Wright, who never really came to terms with his southernness, his Americanness, or for that matter his blackness.

The point of course is that the South does not now need defending. Even George Wallace has trouble working himself up to take on "northern liberals." The astounding dimension of the change is that the virtues and faults of the South are the virtues and faults of the nation, no more and no less. The old enemy is no longer there, or if he is, he is too busy with his own troubles. There is no one throwing punches and no one to counterpunch. At least as far as writers are concerned, it does not now occur to a serious writer in the North to "attack" the South or to a serious southern writer to "defend" the South. Perhaps it is not an unhealthy thing for a satirical writer like me to feel free to take on North and South. And for the first time in my experience a black writer, Toni Morrison, has written a novel that is not about White and Black as such, Black *vs.* White, North and South as such, but about people.

I cannot speak for the politician, but to me as a writer it appears that what needs not so much defending as understanding, reconciling, rejoicing in, ridiculing, cracking jokes about, healing, affirming, is not the southern experience but the American experience. And since every writer must write of his own experience—or else not write at all—the southern writer necessarily writes of the South, but he writes of it in terms that are immediately translatable to the American experience and, if he is good enough, to the human experience.

Consider, for example, two southern writers who lived during this period of the long Southern Obsession and who were great enough to transcend it: William Faulkner and Flannery O'Connor. They had their problems. O'Connor succeeded, I think, largely by steering clear of race—with a couple of notable exceptions. Mainly she stuck to whites—figuring, I guess, that whites had enough trouble with themselves without dragging in white-black troubles. Faulkner wobbled. He was at his best in *The Sound and the Fury* with Dilsey and her relationship with the Compsons. No one will ever surpass him on these grounds. But he could also drift into sentimental paternalism and even at times sound like a Mississippi secessionist.

How, into what channels, will southern energies be directed now that the obsession is behind us? Will southerners have a distinctive contribution to make, say in politics or literature? Or will they simply meld into the great American flux?

One possible future is fairly obvious, is indeed already upon us: the ongoing shift in population and economic power to the so-called Sunbelt. To many this is the future that not only goes without saying but is also desirable. One can simply extrapolate the future from what is happening here and now in the southern United States, from Hilton Head to Dallas and indeed—and this is what worries me—on to Phoenix and Los Angeles. The likeliest and, to me, the not wholly desirable future of the region is an ever more prosperous Southern Rim stretching from coast to coast, an L.A.-Dallas-Atlanta axis (the Atlanta of the Omni and the Peachtree Plaza), an agribusiness-sports-vacation-retirement-show-biz culture with its spiritual center perhaps at Oral Roberts University, its media center in Atlanta, its entertainment industry shared by Disney World, the Superdome, and Hollywood. In this scenario the coastal plain of the old Southeast will be preserved as a kind of museum, much like Williamsburg.

One doesn't have to be a prophet to predict with considerable confidence that sooner or later the failing northern cities must either be abandoned or be bailed out by some kind of domestic Marshall Plan—and why not, after all? Everyone else has benefited: Germany, Italy, Japan, Guatemala—everyone except, of course, the defeated Confederacy after the Civil War. The great cities must be saved, and they will be, and guess who will be paying the freight for the next thirty or forty years, that is, guess who will be paying more than their share of federal taxes while Detroiters, New Yorkers, Bostonians pay less? The taxpayers of the Southern Rim. And perhaps this is only as it should be. It gives a certain satisfaction, the South having to save the Union. After all, it is our turn.

These possibilites represent economic inevitabilities, more or less what was bound to happen once the South, with its advantages in climate, resources, and energy, got past the historic disaster that befell it, mainly as a piece of extremely bad luck when two unlikely and unrelated events turned up at the same time—the invention of the cotton gin and the availability of slave labor—and when it came to pass that the two, put together, were extremely profitable: profitable to some, that is, at the expense of a great many others. And when I say expense, I am thinking not merely of economic exploitation but of the massive expenditure of political, intellectual, literary, and emotional energies required to defend ''the peculiar institution.''

As one speculates about what the future holds, one can't help wondering what it was like to live in the South before the bad thing happened, however one might wish to express the bad thing—getting seduced by the economics of cotton and slavery, or, as Faulkner might have put it in stronger language, an entire nation committing what amounted to its Original Sin and suffering the commensurate curse.

I am thinking of the times in both colonial and revolutionary America and in the early 1800s when southerners felt free to develop their talents and energies, both as southerners and as Americans: business and agricultural talents, political talents, technical talents, artistic and creative talents. I suspect they felt much as southerners are beginning to feel now, that is, conscious of being southerners, yes, and glad of it, not especially self-consciously so, but rather as members of a new society where one is challenged by both a new world and a new freedom to respond to the challenge.

Being no historian, I nevertheless take it as a commonplace that the early southern political and juridical talent was unusual. One thinks particularly of the Virginians: Jefferson, Madison, Monroe, Marshall. (Incidentally, whatever happened to Virginia?) The U.S. Constitution and the Declaration were, in the main, southern creations.

If there was such a thing as a southern gift for politics in the larger sense, not just the knack of getting elected or of filibustering in the Senate, but in the sense of discerning what is the greater good of the people, that is, the commonweal, and how best to bring it to pass, I wonder if we have not now come into a new age when these same energies are once again free to do just that.

The fact is there was never any question about the political talent of the South, even when it was badly sidetracked, and even now there is no difficulty in seeing signs of a renascence in a new breed of southern politicians, white and black.

But it also seems to be the case that the South has not yet had the time—paradoxically enough, for the republic is after all more than 200 years old—to produce those ultimate incarnations of great cultures, its true cultural heroes. What happened was that the South wasted 150 of these 200 years. When I speak of cultural heroes, I'm not talking about politicians and generals. In this connection I'd like to quote a man I greatly admire, James McBride Dabbs of South Carolina. Some years ago he wrote:

> The South could create neither poets nor saints—I mean, great region-shaping poets and saints. For it is such persons as these that shape a region, though first the region must have, by the grace of God, sufficient energy and unconscious purpose to create the poets and saints. . . . They create in art, and in life itself, the image of their world, of their time and their region, seen under the aspect of eternity. . . . The poets and saints offer us a criticism of life, not just of life in the abstract but of our life now. The poets see our world, the saints—usually—live in it, in all its richness, complexity, and ambiguity, against a simplicity that lies at the heart both of the world and of themselves. . . . Since the South was never able to create poets in prose or verse, or saints, it never really quarreled with itself. . . . It became, on the contrary, adept at quarreling with others, and for this purpose it developed the instruments of rhetoric and eloquence.

I think Dabbs was probably right. Lee was the nearest thing we had to a saint—and it was no accident that our saint was a general. Faulkner and Tate are perhaps as close as we have come to cosmos-shaping poets, and it is no accident that what they achieved was done almost in spite of the political passions to which they periodically fell prey.

But since James McBride Dabbs wrote these words, times have changed. Somewhere—in the Sixties, maybe, and thanks to white people like Dabbs and black people like Martin Luther King, Jr.—we got back on the track we either left of our own accord or got pushed off of in the 1830s.

The so-called southern literary renascence appears to be over—that is, the thirty years or so when writers like Faulkner, O'Connor, Welty, Wright, and Caldwell traded on the very exoticness, the uniqueness of the southern phenomenon. It was a rich vein to mine and Faulkner, Warren, Tate, and company pretty well mined it out. Unfortunately there are quite a few writers still picking over this exhausted lode like old sourdoughs at Sutter's Mill. So the southern novelist today finds himself in a transition period analogous to the political situation of the South itself. Like his fellow novelists in the Western world, he finds himself faced with larger questions about the dilemma, not of the poor white or poor black, or decadent gentry or deranged backwoods preachers, but of modern urban and suburban man. He can't imitate Faulkner or O'Connor, or at least he had better not try.

What with the South entering the American mainstream and the old southern vein of oddities and exotica playing out, the southern writer may yet shed his own peculiar light on a familiar dilemma of twentieth-century American literature. The dilemma is the perennial divergence of most writers' view of life from most other Americans', from what I can only think to call the standard humanist-optimist *are-all-modern-writers-crazy?* view. This term is designed to embrace any number of attitudes, from the official chamber-of-commerce allegiance to progress to the more admirable credo of scientific humanism that nothing is wrong with people and things that cannot be studied and set right. The common street expression of this attitude goes something like this: Why do you writers write about nuts, freaks, and assorted rogues doing vile things to each other when in fact most people are pretty decent, et cetera? One might suppose therefore that if the South is, as one often hears, the Bible Belt of the nation, southern writers, whether Christian or not, might have bred in their bones some notion about the fallen nature of man that is at least a coherent theory of evil—which is perhaps more than can be said of the atrocities of Jerzy Kosinski or the musical chairs of Updike's wife-swapping or Jong's sexual acrobatics. Such might have been the legacy of, say, Flannery O'Connor. Yet life is never simple. For it is another Georgia Christian, President Carter, who likes to say how good the American people are, fundamentally decent, sound, sensible, generous, and so forth, certainly better than their politicians, who usually fail them. I find it hard to disagree with him. On the other hand, the American novelist seems to be saying something quite different, namely, that something has gone badly wrong with Americans and American life, indeed modern life, that people generally suffer a deep dislocation in their lives that has nothing to do with poverty and ignorance and discrimination. Indeed, it is the very people who have escaped Tobacco Road and moved to the exurbs who have fallen victim to this malaise. What increasingly engages the southern novelist as much as his Connecticut counterpart are no longer Faulkner's Snopeses or O'Connor's crackers or Wright's black underclass but their successful grandchildren, who are going nuts in Atlanta condominiums.

Then who is right, President Carter or the novelists? It is possible that both are, that it is the politician's function from Jefferson to Carter to inspire people to live up to the best in themselves, and that it is the novelist's vocation from Dostoevsky to Faulkner to explore the darker recesses of the human heart, there to name and affirm the strange admixture of good and evil, the action of the demonic, the action of grace, of courage and cowardice, of courage coming out of cowardice and vice-versa—in a word, the strange human creature himself, an admixture now that is perhaps stranger than ever.

I have no idea whether in the year 2000 we of the Southeast, the old Confederacy, will simply have become a quaint corner of the teeming Southern Rim, some 100 million souls with their population center and spiritual heartland somewhere between Dallas and L.A.; whether our best writers will be doing soap opera in Atlanta or writing up restored houses in *Southern Living,* our best composers turning out country-and-western in Nashville, our best film directors making sequels to *Walking Tall* and *Smokey and the Bandit;* whether our supreme cultural achievement will be the year Alabama ranked number one, the Atlanta Falcons won the Super Bowl, and Bobby Jones III made it a grand slam at Augusta.

There is nothing wrong with any of these achievements. The name of the game has always been excellence—excellence in business, politics, literature, sports, whatever. The difference is that the peculiar isolation and disabilities under which the South labored for so long and which served some southern writers so well and preoccupied all southern politicians are now things of the past. Now the South appears to have won after all, and both the southern writer and politician are somewhat at a loss.

Of course something else could happen in the old Southeast, something besides the building of more Hyatts and Hiltons and the preserving of old buildings, perhaps even something comparable to the astonishing burst of creative energy in Virginia 200 years ago.

At least we have gotten past the point Mr. Dabbs spoke of when he said that the trouble with the South was that it could not quarrel with itself. Not only do I feel free to quarrel with the South, or the North, or the U.S., I feel obliged to. A nice lady in my home town said to me the other day: You're just like certain other southern writers—no sooner do you get published in New York than you turn on the South and criticize it. At the time I didn't have the nerve, but I felt like saying: You're damn right, lady, I sure do.

Whichever way it goes, Sunbelt or southeastern renascence, one thing seems reasonably certain: the southerner will be, is already, much more like his ancestor in 1820 than his ancestor in 1920. That is, he is both southern and American, but much more like other Americans than he is different. If he is black, he may discover to his amazement that he is more like his white countrymen, for better or worse, than he is like Ugandans. Like most of us, he is out to make a life for himself, make money, build a house, raise a family, buy a Winnebago or a Sony Trinitron, go skiing at Aspen.

Yet maybe the southerner will retain a soupçon of difference. And who knows? It might even leaven the lump.

Mike Gray / What Really Happened at Three Mile Island

Rolling Stone, May 17, 1979

Mike Gray completed the first draft of a screenplay called The China Syndrome
*in 1974, the same year the Three Mile Island nuclear reactor was completed.
That first draft was based on an accident at the Dresden II reactor near Chicago
in 1970, where a water gauge needle stuck, leading operators to think there was
too little water in the core when there was already too much. An accident at the
Browns Ferry plant in Albama in 1975, in which a fire crippled the reactor's
cooling system, provided details for the next draft of the screenplay. As Gray
recalls, "I was running out of time. I felt sure there would be a really bad
nuclear accident. I had to beat that accident." Michael Douglas then re-wrote
the script, and the two share both movie and novel credits for the story. The
movie, directed by Jim Bridges, made it to the screen shortly before the Three
Mile Island accident.*

*Rolling Stone, a thick, tabloid sized bi-weekly, started out as a sixteen-page
San Francisco counter-culture music magazine in 1967 on a $7,500 loan. Since
then, Jann Wenner, its founder and editor-in-chief, has brought* Rolling Stone *to
a book value of over $750,000 and a readership projected to reach one million in
1980. "Rock and roll is more than just music," ran a full page ad for the magazine in the* New York Times *in 1967, "it is the energy center of the new culture
and youth revolution." Since then the "new culture" and its celebrities have occupied an increasing number of* Rolling Stone's *pages.*

In the whispering predawn darkness of the Susquehanna valley, the ancient river
flows past the state capital, slowly south toward Chesapeake Bay.

Harrisburg is asleep this Wednesday morning, March 28th. The only sound is
the whining rig of a sleepless trucker gaining on the Pennsylvania Turnpike.

About ten miles south of the capital, the river turns east past Steelton and
Middletown, then rounds a bend, then passes a three-mile-long sandspit that is
about to take the center stage of history.

Rising above the shoreline trees are four towers of such gargantuan scale they
seem to have been set there by visitors from outer space. Sweeping upward for
forty stories with graceful precision, their hourglass shape is designed to squeeze
the water out of rising steam. Tonight there is a torrential rainstorm inside the two
south towers, a cooling rainstorm that wrings the heat out of nearly a million
gallons of scalding water a minute.

The water is coming from a windowless green building with the dimensions of
an aircraft carrier. Inside, four stories above the island, a massive steam turbine is
turning its 880 megawatt generator at ninety-seven-percent capacity.

To the north is a bullet-shaped dome that would itself dominate the landscape,
were it not surrounded by such oversized companions. This heavy bunker, called
the containment, houses the boilers that run the Three Mile Island nuclear plant,
and its construction is an indication of the unimaginable power it contains. Over
twenty stories tall, its steel-shielded concrete walls are designed to withstand the
direct impact of a jetliner.

At the moment, the mighty plant is in the hands of control-room operator Ed Frederick, a young but experienced technician. Frederick and the other control-room operators are having a minor problem with one of the condensate filters. There are seven of these filters—a row of steel tanks standing in the turbine building; it is their job to clean the water before it goes to the boilers.

Like any filters, they must be cleaned sooner or later, and one of them is being cleaned now. The job was begun on an earlier shift by first closing the valves to that particular tank and opening other lines to flush it out.

But the sludge stuck, as it does sometimes, so a second pump was brought on line to help shove it along. And at some point, the operators decided to give it a little kick by means of an air line to the tank. Simply open the air valve a few seconds, and a shot of high-pressure air will usually jolt the sludge and get it moving.

But on this occasion, someone opened the air valve and forgot to close it.

Upstairs in the gleaming light of the control room, Frederick and operator Craig Faust routinely scan the hundreds of dials and recording instruments, unaware that the most frightening nuclear accident in history is only seconds away.

Three Mile Island Unit Two is a brand-new Babcock & Wilcox plant, only a few months in full commercial operation, and it is an impressive example of the most advanced engineering technology in the world. Nearly a billion dollars has gone into the design and construction, and it has taken ten long years to bring it to completion.

Even so, some say that the owners rushed the start-up for certain accounting reasons. To understand the incredible pressures on the management of the owner, Metropolitan Edison, you must realize that starting before the end of the year instead of a few days later would mean $40 million in tax write-offs, and more important, the utility would qualify for a rate increase worth an additional $49 million.

They succeeded in getting under way on December 30th.

Faust and Frederick, like the other operators, have had extensive training on simulators, and they have been briefed on every conceivable emergency procedure. For this is no ordinary steam plant; the power here is created by the direct disintegration of matter into energy, a process that is only marginally understood by the world's best scientists.

Because of these uncertainties, incredible precautions have been taken. Nearly half of the money for the design and construction of the plant was spent on safety systems.

Frederick has already handled one sudden, unscheduled shutdown at this facility and his performance was faultless.

Down below in the bowels of the turbine building, water from the filter tank is inching its way up the open air line.

Finally, a few moments before four a.m. Harrisburg time, the water reaches a junction with another air line that controls the valves to the other filters. The sudden change in pressure causes them all to close.

As the first alarms sound in the control room, Frederick rises from his desk and scans the console. With all seven filter valves now closed, no water can reach the boilers.

But the designers have prepared for every contingency. Each essential system has at least two backups, and most of them are set to take over automatically. The feedwater system for the boilers is no exception. Instantly, not one, not two, but three auxiliary pumps come on to supply water through two independent lines.

What no one in the control room realizes is that the valves on both these lines were closed earlier for maintenance.

Outside, across the river, a farmer stops in the barnyard light to listen and wonder at the sudden rumble of steam venting over Three Mile Island. Startling, but nothing unusual. It frequently happens whenever the plant shuts itself down automatically, and this happens at the slightest hint of trouble. No more remarkable than blowing a fuse.

Instantly the reactor scrams itself: radiation-absorbing control rods are driven into the fuel assemblies and the fission chain reaction is halted. At the same moment, the powerful turbine is taking itself off the line, and the steam, which had been generating about $400,000 worth of electricity a day, is vented into the atmosphere.

This steam is harmless because it never comes in direct contact with the nuclear core. The core is cooled by its own separate water loop that flows to the boilers, where it heats clean water in separate pipes to make steam for the turbine. The radioactive water in the main coolant loop never leaves the dome-shaped containment building.

But for Faust and Frederick, things are not going according to plan. Around the sweeping console, more lights begin to blink and other alarms are sounding. For some reason the pressure is dropping in the core, and while that might sound like a good idea to a layman, it could mean disaster for the nuclear fuel rods.

This design, by the engineering firm of Babcock & Wilcox, is a pressurized water reactor; water is jammed into the main coolant loop tightly—more than 2100 pounds per square inch—so that it carries away the intense heat and keeps the reactor temperature within safe limits.

With the pressure falling and the temperature rising, it is only a question of time before they meet at some point on the chart.

Frederick is perplexed. The sudden temperature increase caused pressure in the main coolant loop to rise dramatically and opened a pressure relief valve. It should have closed by now, but it hasn't.

Suddenly there is another ominous alarm. The boilers are drying out. They check the backup feedwater pumps: nothing the matter there. All three emergency pumps running at speed. Once again they fail to notice the red tags hanging from the valve controls on the console.

Deep down in the massive containment building, shielded from humanity by ten feet of concrete, the core is suspended in an awesome pressure vessel forty feet tall with walls of eight-inch forged steel. Midway between top and bottom hang 36,000 zirconium tubes, each the size of your finger. These tubes contain a hundred tons of radioactive fuel.

Although the nuclear chain reaction was ended the second the control rods slammed home, there is still tremendous heat in the core caused by unstable atomic fragments that continue to fly apart. Even after the reactor is shut down completely, this residual heat must be carried away or the core will melt. And with the boilers now dry, there is nothing to carry the heat away from the main coolant loop.

So the temperature continues to rise dramatically. Two minutes have passed since the first alarm, and the much-debated emergency core cooling system is about to receive its first in-service test.

The emergency core cooling system has been the target of nuclear critics for a decade. The system is essential in controlling core damage during an accident.

As pressure in the reactor drops to 1600 pounds, the system activates as designed, automatically releasing a blast of high pressure water into the main loop. According to the mathematical calculations of the government and the designers, this will prevent boiling in the core, but it doesn't. Unknown to the operators, the first damage to the fuel rods has been done.

Meanwhile, Ed Frederick is at sea in a maelstrom of conflicting information. One of his gauges shows that the water level is rising in the pressurizer—a sort of auxiliary tank connected to the main loop. In moments it is off the scale.

The pressurizer is the highest point in the coolant loop, and it normally contains a bubble of gas that acts as a shock absorber. Without this bubble, the water would be confined everywhere by solid steel and any change in temperature would be accompanied by a dramatic—and possibly damaging-change in pressure.

To reduce the water level in the pressurizer, the operators decide to cutback the flow of emergency water by shutting down one of the three pumps. But their instruments still show that the water in the pressurizer is off the high end of the scale. Down in the containment, a geyser of steam is blasting from the pressure relief valve that has jammed open on top of the pressurizer. This steam is deadly radioactive.

At this instant, as Ed Frederick works his way around the panel trying to make sense out of the blizzard of alarming data, his eye catches something on the console. Two red tags hanging on valves in the emergency feedwater system. *Closed for testing and maintenance.* He lunges for them.

And now the luck of the operators, which had been bad enough during these opening seconds, takes an ugly turn. The pressure in the reactor may be dangerously low, but there is no way of telling, because the instruments are lying. The potential of these instruments to make errors has been the subject of memos between the government regulators and the plant's designers. Unfortunately, these recorded doubts never found their way into the hands of the control-room operators.

A few seconds later the operators notice the pressurizer level still off scale on the high side and they make the fateful decision to shut down the second emergency cooling pump. But they are not aware that the water in the core is already boiling.

Moments later the water level in the pressurizer comes back on the scale and they restart the emergency core cooling pumps.

Even though it's an hour before dawn, there are some sixty people working on this shift, and many of them are curious or alarmed at the rumblings heard throughout the plant. Yet here in the control room things are actually looking much better. The feedwater valves have finally been opened and the boilers are carrying away the heat from the main loop. The water level seems to have stabilized; so has the temperature.

The reactor is now set up for normal cool-down. At last everyone can relax.

But shortly after 5:30 a.m., confidence in the control room is shattered by a new and alarming development. The instruments indicate heavy vibration in the main cooling pumps.

Even though these huge pumps are located deep within the containment, it is possible for the operators to plug a headset into the control-room console and actually listen to noise monitors attached to the pumps. And what they hear is frightening.

By now the operators have been trying desperately to get a handle on things for more than ninety minutes, and like a plane with crossed controls, it seems that everything they touch causes something unexpected.

Perhaps if they had an hour to study the situation over a cup of coffee, their next decision might have been different. Unfortunately they are only human and the pressure has been overwhelming.

The operators decide to save the main pumps by shutting them down. What they don't realize is when the pressure dropped in the main coolant loop, steam bubbles formed in the system; these bubbles are now causing the pumps to vibrate and have also accumulated somewhere in the loop into one huge bubble— a vapor lock—that now blocks the flow of cooling water through the core system.

Immediately, the temperature in the main loop begins to rise dramatically. In fifteen minutes it is off the scale. And then, more ominously, the thermocouples just above the core itself go off the scale as well. And down in the core, many of the zirconium tubes are already bowed or fractured, creating hot spots in the fuel bundles. For the next several hours, the core temperature will be recorded by the computer, with rattling precision, as row after row of question marks.

Over the years there has been considerable discussion about exactly when and under what circumstances the containment should be automatically isolated. The government felt it should happen whenever the emergency core cooling system came on. But there are some cases where this would be the last thing one would want. So the engineers at Babcock & Wilcox settled on another concept: when the pressure reaches a certain level inside the containment, the building will seal itself from the outside world so that radioactive gas cannot escape.

Again, chance is working on the side of the devil. The containment will not isolate itself until sometime after nine a.m., when there is an explosion in the building. But right this moment, there are thousands of gallons of deadly radioactive water on the floor, and it is being sucked automatically out of the safety of this massive structure into an adjacent pump house that has no shielding.

At 6:50 a.m., the operators' nerves are further jangled by a radiation alarm. Abnormal radiation in the containment. The decision is made to let somebody on the outside know it's not going to be just another day at the office.

At 7:05, Kevin Molloy, the Dauphin County Civil Defense director is getting ready for work when he gets a call from his communication center in Harrisburg. The watch supervisor has just received word from officials at Three Mile Island and the state Emergency Management Agency that the power plant has declared an on-site emergency. Molloy jumps in his car and heads for the command post, but before he gets there, he hears on the mobile radio that the situation is worsening. A few minutes before 7:30, the plant declares a general emergency.

The chairman of the Pennsylvania Emergency Management Agency is Lieutenant Governor William Scranton III, son of the former governor and only recently elected to office. Although he might be short on experience, his agency is not. Harrisburg is used to killer floods, and the governmental mechanism for disaster response is like a coiled spring.

Except at the moment, Scranton is getting heavy reassurance from the plant owners, Metropolitan Edison. Utility Vice President Jack Herbein paints an encouraging picture to the lieutenant governor, indicating that Herbein is either amazingly naive or contriving a transparently optimistic picture. It is easier to assume the latter if one understands the incredible pressures converging on him.

First of all, the public has always been a little jumpy about nuclear power—or nuclear anything, for that matter. The press always blows these things out of proportion. And now that goddamn Jane Fonda movie has just opened in Harrisburg.

Herbein has obligations not just to his own company but to the entire industry. If they call for an evacuation and it proves totally unnecessary, the financial fallout will be grim indeed.

By eleven a.m. the rumors are flying, and Scranton decides to call a press conference and get a handle on the situation. Up the sweeping marble stairs of the old Statehouse, past the regimental flags of Pennsylvanians who fought at Gettysburg, the press assembles to hear the lieutenant governor say that there is no substantial radiation at this point and Metropolitan Edison says the problem is well in hand.

But in the miles of complex, interactive piping at Unit Two, the situation continues to worsen. With their hands full in the control room, the operators have failed to notice that the sump pump has been drawing water out of the containment since 4:06 this morning. And now the tank into which it is being pumped has filled. In a short time, thousands of gallons of deadly radioactive water spills out onto the floor of the pump house.

This creates a new and serious problem. The pump house cannot be sealed from the outside, so it's a question of time before highly radioactive gas starts pouring out of the ventilators.

Shortly after noon, Metropolitan Edison official Don Curry issues a statement: "The plant is cooling down in an orderly manner with no consequences to the public." At that moment, the first burst of radioactive gas is rising above Three Mile Island, drifting slowly with the breeze.

Governor Dick Thornburgh, like Scranton, has been in office only a few months. Thornburgh, a lawyer with an engineering degree, wants desperately to believe the technical assurances from the utility, but he was also a sometime state's attorney, and the prosecutor in him senses something fishy. By four that afternoon, the governor's office decides to put some distance between itself and Metropolitan Edison. Scranton calls another press conference. "This situation is more complex than the company first led us to believe," he says. "Metropolitan Edison has given you and us conflicting information."

The conflicting information has in fact come from the first government inspectors from the Nuclear Regulatory Commission (NRC) to reach the scene Wednesday afternoon. They are not nearly as relaxed as the utility management seems to be. It is apparent there has already been damage to the fuel rods.

The local radio and television stations seem compelled to ease everyone's fears, and throughout the afternoon the residents of eastern Pennsylvania receive a steady stream of reassurances. So it is unnerving this evening to hear the network anchormen refer to this as the worst nuclear disaster in U.S. history.

The NRC begins to monitor radiation levels around the plant in the early afternoon. A thirty-millirem-per-hour reading is taken south of the plant. Though the average American is only exposed to about 100 millirems per *year*, an NRC official says the reading taken near the plant is "not an indication of a serious problem." Throughout the night and over the next several days, radioactive gas will continue to seep out of the tall stack on the pump house.

There is no question that radiation is not good for people. Radiation is like shrapnel from a subatomic hand grenade. As unstable atoms fly apart, small particles of energy shoot out in all directions, and if there is a living cell in the way, there is the possibility of wounding the complex strip of molecules that tells it what to do.

With high-level radiation, there is the danger you will be hit with enough shrapnel that many cells will die and so will you. But with low-level radiation, the fear is not that a damaged cell will die, but that it will live and go crazy. If it is a typical body cell, the worst you can count on is cancer. But if it involves the reproductive organs, it can lie in wait for generations like a genetic time bomb.

There is no threshold for radiation damage. The government maintains that less than one rem a year is safe for the average human, but that is a number picked out of the air. It will be many decades before accurate data can be accumulated in this new and uncharted field. In the meantime, it has been necessary to say that such and such an amount of radiation is no worse than this or that. As in: "This punch in the mouth may hurt, but it's no worse than a trip to the dentist."

We receive radiation from many sources—the sun, granite tombstones, the air we breathe—and there are scientists who will tell you all of it is harmful. But the next day, government spokesmen assure people that the cloud around Three Mile Island is no worse than one chest x-ray every six or eight hours. Nonetheless, it is unusual for anyone to get two or three chest x-rays a day, particularly ones that include the genitals.

All day Thursday, there are conflicting reports about the amount of radiation escaping from the island. This is not remarkable. The monitors are dealing with a cloud of gas, and like any cloud, it swirls and eddies with unpredictable hot spots. The utility officials, by now exuding all the confidence of fish sitting in a tree, are striving to maintain their posture. And they have a natural inclination to use the lowest available numbers.

But for the first time, Metropolitan Edison admits there has been fuel damage. It has been limited, they say, to less than one percent. The government inspectors know better. Over the direct line to Bethesda, they advise NRC headquarters that the figure is closer to half. Which means that 18,000 fuel rods in the core are in questionable shape.

On Friday morning an attempt is made to clean up the mess in the pump house. But as the water on the floor is being pumped to a storage tank, the radiation in the tank drives up the temperature and pressure. A safety valve vents the poisonous vapor up the stack. Overhead, the government helicopter peels off as the counter needle swings to 1.2 rem per hour, a figure well over anybody's idea of acceptability.

Soon after, the Commonwealth of Pennsylvania and Metropolitan Edison come to a parting of the ways. The utility officials insist the gas release was not dangerous and that more discharges are possible. But the governor has had enough. He advises the 900,000 people in the four counties surrounding Harrisburg to be ready to move. Then he closes the nearby schools and advises pregnant women and small children within five miles of the plant to get out.

In Middletown, a reporter interviews a housewife packing her car. She speaks not only for herself and other innocent bystanders, but in a sense for the federal government and the nuclear industry as well. "You always hear about these things but you never really expect it to happen," she says. "So I didn't really think it would."

The worst is yet to come.

That evening, Metropolitan Edison confesses that the core is not, in fact, cooling as they had led everyone to believe. Rather, it is riddled with hot spots, some of them as high as 600 degrees.

And in Washington, an NRC spokesman first uses the ugly term that will quickly become a household word. There is, he admits, the possibility of a meltdown. In nuclear jargon, such an event is called a "class nine accident." It is deemed so improbable that it is not taken into consideration in designing these plants.

If the core is uncovered, even now, three days after fission has stopped, the residual heat from unstable atomic fragments will cause it to heat up and melt, and the consequences are in the hands of the gods.

Some say the intense heat would cause chemical explosions that would fracture the containment. Others say the core would melt right through the bottom of the plant, into ground water, and spray an atomic geyser into the atmosphere with the fallout of a local nuclear war.

Ironically, the government's own study of the consequences of a meltdown—a secret study called WASH-740 that was prepared by the Atomic Energy Commission in 1965—says the ultimate accident might cause 45,000 immediate deaths, 100,000 injuries and property damage in excess of $17 billion ". . . and render an area equal to that of the state of Pennsylvania permanently uninhabitable. . . ."

The Nuclear Regulatory Commission now calls this study outdated, and in the light of new information, they say the consequences would not be that severe. But the truth is, nobody knows. We are plowing unknown ground. We can't be certain of the consequences of a nuclear disaster until we have one. It could be half as bad as we think. Or it could be twice as bad.

The White House has been watching the situation and keeping a low profile, but they can see Thornburgh is getting jumpy. Carter calls the governor and offers a Signal Corps communications unit to set up a hot line connecting the plant, the state capital and the White House. Thornburgh accepts, but what he really wants is accurate information, not phone lines. Carter offers to send in a team of experts.

Friday afternoon, the Harrisburg airport is closed briefly because of radiation. The NRC flies in a team of technicians headed by Harold Denton, director of reactor regulation, and a quick tour of the plant reveals that the Metropolitan Edison staff is in over its head. Soon after, Denton orders them not to touch a single valve before checking with him, and he fires off an urgent request for heavy technical assistance. The control room at Three Mile Island is wired directly to the NRC headquarters in Bethesda.

People are now converging on Harrisburg from all over the country and from all over the world. Along with the technical experts, hundreds of journalists have hastily assembled, from blunt New York reporters like Jimmy Breslin, to soft-spoken Japanese TV crews ("We have fourteen reactors in Japan. Our people want to know what's going on here").

Considering the fact that no one really wants to be there—as one reporter puts it, "this is the first disaster without sightseers"—the press behaves with unaccustomed diligence. Assailed at first for inaccurate reporting, the reporters struggle to grasp a story that is not clearly understood by the experts in the plant itself.

Reporters from the networks and the great national papers who were trained on Kennedy and Kissinger suddenly find themselves grappling with a new language: heavy technology couched in bureaucratese, that curious lingo in which nothing is what it is. An accident is not an accident here, but an event. And an explosion is not an explosion, but a rapid disassembly.

But they dig in and do their best to get an instant education in nuclear engineering, and within a few days it is possible to pick up a paper and get an accurate account of the technical situation. By Saturday, Metropolitan Edison has canceled its upbeat press conferences and the official word comes from Denton. And the official word is grim indeed.

It seems that somehow a large bubble of hydrogen gas, among other things, has accumulated in the reactor above the fuel. How this could have happened, they are unsure. This staggering eventuality has somehow been totally unforeseen.

In all the years of painstaking analysis, where seemingly the most unlikely possibilities were dissected and accounted for, the plant's designers and the government have overlooked their high-school chemistry.

Water molecules consist of two hydrogen atoms and one oxygen atom bound together with tremendous force. Under certain circumstances—intense radiation, for example—they will separate. And under certain other circumstances, they will recombine with explosive concussion.

The last historic recombining of hydrogen and oxygen was the Hindenburg disaster. And there is—and they are only guessing, for they have no means of directly measuring it—about 1000 cubic feet of hydrogen under tremendous pressure directly above the core. Also there seems to be an unknown quantity of hydrogen collecting at the top of the containment.

To the experts at NRC headquarters in Bethesda, it seems unlikely that an explosion in the core would leave either the pressure vessel or the building undamaged. And this presents a prospect even more horrifying than the so-called class nine accident. A meltdown gives you some time to get people out of the way. But a hydrogen explosion that ruptures the containment will be instantaneous and carry death in the wind.

On the other hand, as best as they can determine, the ratio of oxygen to hydrogen has not yet reached the danger point. And while it might seem prudent to evacuate in the face of such uncertainty, there are other problems almost as pressing as public safety.

The government is also responsible for the public welfare, and we are confronted with runaway inflation, a staggering and steadily increasing outflow of cash into the Arabian sands and a crushing energy shortage.

And there is the nuclear industry itself, which employs tens of thousands of the brightest engineers and technicians in the country and which generates several billion dollars a year in desperately needed exports.

So it is impossible to call for a precautionary evacuation. The sudden movement of a million people would probably be the death knell of nuclear power, and if it later proved unnecessary, it would be an unforgiveable error.

The ratio of hydrogen and oxygen in the building is climbing slowly toward the explosion point, and if the government is to find a palatable alternative to evacuation, it hasn't any time to waste. At the Bethesda computer complex, surrounded by some of the best minds they can assemble, the NRC officials put together a "Bubble Squad" to analyze the possibilities.

But the bubble proves to be a Catch-22. If the pressure in the reactor is reduced, as it will have to be at some point, the bubble may grow bigger and the fuel rods might be uncovered. And if that happens, the fuel will melt.

As the press reports this new and frightening dilemma, the NRC gets some unusual phone calls. Individuals moved by humanitarianism or heroics are volunteering to go into the reactor building and open the valve to let the deadly hydrogen escape. Unfortunately there is no such valve, and if there were, it would be unreachable. Radiation in the containment is now so high that a man would die before he could get to it.

The approach elected by the Bubble Squad is chancy but less draconian than the alternatives. They will try to slowly siphon the hydrogen from the bubble into the containment and pass it through a chamber called a recombiner. Here it will unexplosively be turned back into water. But since the controls are in the building where the radioactive water has been dumped, they must first erect a lead wall to protect the workmen. This is expected to take several days. According to their calculations, they think they have about five or six days until the mixture becomes explosive.

The people who live in the Susquehanna River basin around Three Mile Island are familiar with disaster. Twice this decade the river has spilled over its banks and forced them to run for higher ground. But where is the higher ground if there is a nuclear holocaust? So when the people of Harrisburg and the surrounding suburbs learn that they are living next-door to a nuclear time bomb, they divide into roughly three camps. Some of them panic and clear out or live with a packed suitcase and full tank of gas. Others are worried but feel they can't leave their homes or their businesses. And then there are those who shrug off the danger. But there is one thing most of them have in common: they don't believe everything Metropolitan Edison and the NRC are telling them.

"I don't know what to believe. Nobody does," says a fifteen-year-old girl who is helping out in Hersheypark Arena, where pregnant women and small children who have been evacuated are sheltered on Friday."

"Those fuckers have been lying to us from the start," says a twenty-seven-year-old Harrisburg woman as she loads her two dogs into the back of a van. "I'm getting out of here."

Chris Becker, a Mennonite dairy farmer whose barn is less than a mile from the plant, is worried, but he isn't about to leave. "What would happen to my cattle if I had to evacuate? They'd stop producing milk. I've got to stay . . . for now."

In the downtown Harrisburg train station, where evacuees are streaming out of the city, another customer is telling the waitress behind the snack counter she should leave town. She throws down her wipe rag in disgust. "Look, if you're afraid, you should get out," she says. "I'm staying. If it melts down, I'll melt with it."

Almost half of the 400,000 people in the Harrisburg area clear out over the next few days. But for those who stay in range of the power plant and choose not to laugh off the danger of a meltdown, the weekend is a nightmare.

The fear is always worse at night. In the darkness of half-deserted towns, after official words of reassurance have dried up, rumors and the imagination take over. Every siren might be a call to evacuate. Could the barking dogs sense a flood of radiation? A young man from Harrisburg says he can't sleep because he feels the walls of his house are invisible. A photographer who has been through three wars sits in his hotel room chain-smoking joints. "I spent three years with the Provos in Northern Ireland," he says. "I've lived with guerrillas in Central America—man, I've *never* been this scared."

Eleven miles south, in Middletown, McDonald's doesn't look too different this Friday night. The usual crowd of high-school kids are there, jabbering about last week's dance. But some of the patrons eating their fishburgers are wearing radiation meters, and when a waitress drops a stack of trays, a young girl jumps and shouts: "I don't want to die!" The teenagers laugh.

Even though there is a nine o'clock curfew in the Three Mile Island area, the bars are packed. At one working-class Middletown watering hole, the regulars are hustling reporters at pool, chugging down Miller Lites and making small talk about radiation.

"You know what's the best thing to do when you've been exposed to radiation?" says a worker who was in the plant during the accident. "Drink a six-pack. It washes all that shit out of your system. You piss it out."

The jukebox is churning out the usual country & western tunes and disco numbers, but the songs that were just background music a week ago suddenly have new meaning. A couple of reporters laugh nervously as they read off the selections: "Disco Inferno" (". . . burn, baby, burn . . ."), "Hot Child in the City," "I Will Survive" and "Hot Line": "The way you flash your eyes looks like lightning, lighting up the sky. . . . This is more than an emergency." The reporters huddle over their drinks and make plans to evacuate. "I'll meet you in New York," one says to the other. "You'll know me, I'll be the one who's glowing."

In a Middletown rooming house, Tom, a former nuclear plant worker, sits with one of his buddies on a threadbare couch and shakes a Bible at a local reporter. "We can all be dead in this house tonight," he says. "We're all being radiated to death!" Tom starts paging through the Bible, scouring the passages with his wild eyes. "It's all in here," he says.

His friend explains that Tom became a Jehovah's Witness on Wednesday and that he's been drinking ever since. "Here, read this," Tom says, handing the reporter a piece of paper he's been using as a bookmark in his Bible. The paper is an official report from Metropolitan Edison stating that Tom received .725 rems of gamma radiation at Three Mile Island in 1977. "Here it is in Job!" Tom screams. "This could be part of the prophecies. You want to know who was in the plant? The Reverend Jim Jones was in there! And people like me. Just like me!"

Later that night the same reporter, who has lived in Harrisburg all of his twenty-one years, decides to head for the mountains. After packing his car, he drives to a friend's house and they raise a beer to the city. The friend is leaving too. "They say it's either going to blow up or blow over," he says. "But I don't feel like sticking around to find out."

The disaster has blown over for now. The people who live near Three Mile Island have returned to their homes and their jobs, and life goes on pretty much the way it did before the accident.

But the issue of nuclear power, something few people gave much thought to before March 28th, remains fixed in everyone's minds. And once again, the people in the area are dividing into camps. Some want to forget the whole thing, call the incident a quirk and trust the nuclear industry to make sure it doesn't happen again. Some voice their support for Metropolitan Edison out of fear that if the power plant shuts down, the loss of jobs and property tax revenues paid by the utility will further cripple the already depressed region. And then there are those who live in fear that the plant will reopen and another accident will happen, and maybe this time they won't be so lucky.

The phone in Three Mile Island Alert's ramshackle Harrisburg office hasn't stopped ringing since the morning of the accident. "People have been calling to ask how they can help stop Metropolitan Edison from reopening the plant," says Bill Vastine, the group's sixty-five-year-old coordinator. "It's funny. You know, people wouldn't believe us before; some of them called us fanatics. Now they're rolling out the red carpet." Three Mile Island Alert membership swelled from twelve to more than 200 a week after the incident.

Vastine and a handful of others started Three Mile Island Alert in 1977 when the power plant was licensed. The group worked closely with Citizens for a Safe Environment and the Environmental Coalition on Nuclear Power, organizations that had been trying since 1971 to block Metropolitan Edison's license to open Three Mile Island Units One and Two. While representatives from the larger groups pointed out safety defects in the plant's design and operation to the Nuclear Regulatory Commission, Three Mile Island Alert worked at the grass-roots level.

"We went around knocking on doors, inviting people to meetings, trying to warn people who lived around Three Mile Island that the plant wasn't safe," says Vastine. "But Met Ed did a good job convincing the community that nuclear energy was good for them." Three Mile Island Alert's meetings in Middletown's Borough Hall usually consisted of a small group of regulars and a roomful of empty chairs.

On August 6th, 1977, the anniversary of the Hiroshima bombing, Three Mile Island Alert staged a rally on the western shore of the Susquehanna across from the power plant. The fifty or so demonstrators were heckled by picnickers and fishermen as they released 500 helium balloons into the summer sky. Each of the balloons carried a post card that read: "This balloon was released near Three Mile Island nuclear plant. Fallout may travel this far—how far did this travel?" About fifty balloons that made it into the air were returned from places like Wilmington, Delaware; Cape May, New Jersey; and Massachusetts. But the sluggish balloons that hovered too long over the Susquehanna were batted down and popped by some of the jeering bystanders.

Since the accident, Bill Vastine expects to have an easier time getting his message across—but he knows he's still got a long way to go.

Take Harrisburg's Tony Citriniti for instance. "I don't feel any differently about nuclear energy than I did before the Three Mile Island accident," he says. "The fact is, people want air conditioners and color TVs. I think nuclear power's here to stay. And look at all these people with their Stop Nuclear Energy signs, marching down in Middletown where the radiation is the worst. Who are they trying to kid?"

But the accident *has* changed the attitudes of some of central Pennsylvania's politicians. State Senator Robert Mellow, a conservative Democrat who supported nuclear energy before the Three Mile Island incident, is calling for a moratorium against the development of new nuclear power plants in Pennyslvania.

And Cumberland County Commissioner Jacob Myers is taking a strong stand against Metropolitan Edison. "Speaking for the people here, I'd say we've always ignored Three Mile Island," says Myers. "We thought there was nothing to be afraid of. So we ignored the so-called nukes and protesters. I changed my mind about Three Mile Island on Friday after the accident." On Tuesday, April 3rd, Myers wrote the following letter to Metropolitan Edison President Walter Creitz: "Your company's actions make me feel, as a public official, that your presence in this area is no longer desired, and you should think about evacuating."

On Sunday, President Carter helicopters in from Washington for a firsthand look. When the first lady steps out with him, it is clear this is to be more than an engineering briefing. Rosalyn Carter dutifully shakes hands with a few Middletown residents remaining, and her presence has a buoying effect on those who stayed behind. Her husband emerges from the plant and addresses the press in a Middletown gymnasium. "I've been assured that the reactor core is indeed stable," he says. "I intend to make sure that an investigation is conducted thoroughly and that the results are made public."

Privately, the president is reported to be outraged with the press for blowing this whole thing out of proportion.

Control-room operator Craig Faust would agree. On Saturday night, as the deadly consequences of the damage are being discussed by Carter's advisers, Faust refuses to call it an accident. He refers to it as an "event." "The only accident is that this thing leaked out," he says. "You could have avoided this whole thing by not saying anything. But because of regulations, it was disclosed."

Nonetheless, the press persists, and Monday morning Denton faces hundreds of shouting newsmen jammed into the tiny Middletown gym.

Denton has now been on the firing line for seventy-two hours, including a presidential visit, and while he tries to put his best face forward, the strain is unbearable. Behind the podium his hands twist a roll of documents until his knuckles are white as he cautiously explains that things in the reactor are perhaps slightly better. Their earlier estimates of the oxygen ratio may have been too high. It looks like they have more time. But these estimates are based on inference and lengthy calculations. No direct measurement is possible.

Unfortunately there is also some bad news. Radiation in the containment is now high enough to kill a man in sixty seconds and high enough to start damaging essential equipment. One instrument has already been lost, and they are confronted with the possibility that as time wears on they will know less and less about what's happening in the reactor.

Tuesday dawns gray and dismal in Harrisburg, but there is a genuine reduction in the level of fear. New measurements and new calculations by the Bubble Squad indicate the hydrogen in the reactor may have diminished dramatically. Why, they aren't sure.

Wednesday in Washington, the five commissioners of the NRC are briefed by their staff about the status at Three Mile Island. Staff members Edson Case and Darrel Eisenhut run through the chronology of the accident, and it is a catalog of design deficiencies, equipment failures, operator error and inadequate regulation and inspection.

In the end, the commissioners agree with the staff recommendation to establish full-time inspectors at all operating Babcock & Wilcox reactors and to forward memoranda about the events at Three Mile Island so no other operators will repeat what happened there.

After the meeting, a reporter asks staff member Case why he thinks a memo will do the job when similar memos failed to warn the people at Metropolitan Edison.

"This time," says Case, "we're sending inspectors with the memos."

A few blocks away, Bob Pollard, a former NRC official who resigned in protest over the agency's slipshod procedures, sits in a cramped office talking to reporters. Pollard has been predicting for some time that there would be serious trouble with pressurized water reactors.

But instead of feeling some pleasure over such total vindication, Pollard seems depressed. "You don't have an ultimate catastrophe out of the blue," he says. "There's always some kind of warning. This was a warning."

DISCUSSION QUESTIONS

1. What fictional techniques does Gray use in his account of the accident at Three Mile Island? What is the effect of doing so in a non-fiction report of an actual occurence?

2. What is Gray's attitude towards the use of nuclear power? How can you tell? What does he assume readers of *Rolling Stone* think about nuclear power? What might he have done differently if the article were to appear in a magazine that supported the use of nuclear energy?

3. Who or what is to blame for the accident according to Gray? Does his account of the accident seem fair?

Ray Bradbury / Beyond 1984

Playboy, January 1979

Futuria Fantasia was the title of the mimeographed quarterly Ray Bradbury began while a high school student in Waukegan, Illinois. He sold his first short story at the age of twenty-one and wrote full time thereafter. Bradbury estimates that he has written well over 1,000 short stories, mostly fantasy and science fiction.
Many of his stories have appeared in The New Yorker, Harper's, Mademoiselle, *and other popular magazines; many more have appeared in science fiction magazines and collections. His work is represented in more than 150 anthologies. In the selection below, we can see Bradbury's lifelong, intense fascination with the future.*

Don't look now, but the Eighties are almost upon us. Which means that the usual Chicken Little end-of-the-world doomsters are rushing in circles, colliding with themselves and shouting, "Head for the hills, the dam is broke." Here comes 1984. Watch out, there's Big Brother.

Bulrushes and sauerkraut.

Nineteen eighty-four will never arrive.

Yes, the year itself will show up but not as a Kremlin in gargoyle or an Orwellian beast. We have for the time being, anyway, knocked Big Brother into the next century. With luck and if we keep our eye on the ballot box and our chameleon politicos, he may never recover. Meanwhile, just beyond 1984, a truly grand year awaits us. Nineteen eighty-six will be a special time. Why special and why grand? If 1984 once symbolized the worst of man, 1986 might just possibly symbolize nothing but the best. For that is the year we earthlings will enjoy a close encounter of the fourth kind.

A visitor from beyond will hark itself on our solar doorstep for some few months, then vanish like some Christmas ghost. We will not see it again for another 76 years. How shall we react? In one scenario, we will toss ourselves high in celebrations to meet this ghost. We will stand forth in space and wave the cold beast in. We will laugh in its face. We will probe its icy flesh and swirl our technological matador's cape as it rushes by us some 100,000 miles per hour. We will pierce its heart with the finest brightest swords that science can forge, then offer to crowds around the world the secret of the birth of the solar system.

In another scenario, we will watch an artist's conception of the event on television, our faces illuminated by the pale light of the tube. A commentator will mourn: "Maybe next time."

The visitor, of course, is Halley's comet. The villain is Congress, which must approve the funds for this grand scheme. And who are the people who would play tag with the cosmic train? The amiable "mad" scientists at the Jet Propulsion Laboratory in Pasadena, California.

Those are the same wild folks who helped bring you Mars Viking landings I and II. The folks who remind me of that old Bob Hope/Jerry Colonna routine in which Hope shouts at the sky:

"Colonna, what are you doing up there?"

"Building a bridge—starting at the top."

"But," cries Hope, "you can't do that!"

Colonna shrugs and turns to his workers:

"All right, boys, tear it down."

But the blueprinters at J.P.L. won't tear anything down. They are used to building imaginary bridges, starting at the top, then riveting a foundation under the dream before it blows away.

Those are the folks who want to build a bridge to Mars, who would send a probe there that would return with samples from the surface. Those are the folks who want to build a bridge to Titan to sample the atmosphere of Saturn's most literary moon. They would orbit Jupiter, land on Mercury and send a robot to summer camp on Mars. They are dreamers who, when they awake, try to sell their dreams to NASA and a skinflint Congress.

If Congress wants to share the dream of a Halley's-comet encounter, it will have to reach into its purse and pull out some $500,000,000. And it will have to do so in the near future. If it waits too long, there won't be time for the experimental draftings, the many test failures and the final successes that plague and reward such grandiose exercises. The bureauracy that made Big Brother possible will kill the dream.

One plan to rendezvous with Halley's comet has already bitten the dust. In 1977, scientists at J.P.L. were toying with the idea of a solar sail, a giant kite, a stringless Mylar wonder, several miles square, with all our souls as its endless tail. The sail was to be powered by the light of the sun.

Pure sunlight can do that? It can. Light rays exert pressure in the form of protons—massless particles. When these particles strike a surface, they are, in effect, a supersonic wind blowing against a sail.

The original comet-intercept plan was simple and elegant. The sail would be a thin breath of Mylar plastic skinned out over some aluminum spider that might well measure as much as half a mile wide. This vast experiment would be tucked in special shuttles and launched into space. There, astronauts would scramble to unfurl the beauty, raise the sail, finish out the kite, then hop back into the shuttles and let the sun push the sail with its massless winds. Set free, the sail would be controlled and balanced by vanes.

Slowly it would build speed, until it reached the 100,000 mph necessary to make the rendezvous. Unlike normal rockets, which are limited in the amount of fuel they can carry, and in their final speed, the solar sail would find its fuel in space.

To reach rendezvous speed, a launch would have to have been made by 1981. The seed money should have been granted in 1978. It didn't happen. NASA looked at the comet-intercept project, compared the benefits with other priority projects (including another comet project) and crossed off the solar sail from its 1978 shopping list.

The scientists at J.P.L. were undaunted. They had an alternative propulsion system on the drawing boards: the ion drive, a galactic butterfly that can spin sunlight into electricity, to emit a soft violet blast. Like the solar sail, it finds its fuel in space. Dr. Ken Atkins, head of the comet-intercept program at J.P.L., pulled the ion drive out of the hat and said, Lo: We can't build up speed to rendezvous, but we can cut across the path of the vsitor and drop an instrument package down the throat of the comet.

And just for a touch of class, the J.P.L. plan offered a two-for-one shot: The ion-drive craft could fly by Halley's comet, then, two years later, rendezvous with Tempel II, a bright little visitor that drops by every 5.3 years. We could pace the comet past Mercury without setting ourselves aflame, then tag along when it moved back out to hide itself in the mine-shaft universe.

The project can be done; the only question is, will it be done?

That depends on the Congress and/or the President. The latter is questionable. Space is low down on their priority scale.

Why *should* we spend half a billion dollars on a comet? Because we must confront the mystery. What *is* a comet? The question runs back beyond Bethlehem, before the birth of the Pharaohs.

Is a comet a somewhat soiled but mighty snowball hurled from the left hand of God some winter morning He has long since forgotten? Is it the breath of some old sun now dead but whose final sigh now comes to whisper round our yard? Is it a halation of dusts and interplanetary cinders, fragments of meteoroid flaked from some chance encounter with a far planetary system?

The commonest theory, advanced by Fred Whipple in 1950, describes cometary bodies as blizzards of frozen gases and small nonvolatile solids. Small comets are a few hundred meters in diameter. The largest measure 20 miles across. As a comet enters the system, the sun heats the frozen sphere. The solar wind blows the debris into a tail, or comma, 1,000,000 miles in length.

The scientific community is very interested in the Comet Rendezvous Program. It is likely that the debris caught in the frozen grasp of the comet head is primordial. As old as the universe. The Halley probe could analyze the dust by spectrometer and magnetometer. Cameras could give us a view of the birth scars of the solar system. It is an opportunity too important to pass up because of mere economics.

Of course, there are other comets. The boys at J.P.L. have come up with several alternative missions between now and the turn of the century. But Halley's comet is so American. Indeed, when I first heard of the project, I suggested calling the probe the Mark Twain. Why?

Well, now, Mark Twain was born in 1835, when Halley's comet tore across the sky to welcome him. Doubtful of miracles, suspicious of heaven, nonetheless, Twain later predicted he would depart this Earth when the comet came back to fetch him. It did, and Twain did, in 1910.

Halley's comet has a power over men's imaginations that far exceeds shuttle diplomacy or the best of prime-time television.

At the core of our Mark Twain celestial explorer would be cameras and multipurpose devices to photograph the comet, take its temperature and, with luck, knife through to its bright interior. The instrument package we would hurl into the face of Halley's comet is doomed—at 57 kilometers per second, the comet devours everything in its path. Another fate awaits the surviving part of the ion-drive craft. It will head out beyond the orbit of Mars, turn tail and play catch-up with Tempel II in 1988. The two will head together for the sun—and for six months, we will listen in on their conversation. The ion-drive craft may be captured by the comet, or it may wander off on a solo journey. It depends on the courtship of gravity.

Then again, perhaps we can hurl these robot devices in such a way as to track the Tempel II comet on its entire circumnavigation of our solar system. Playing dead for a good part of the journey, our sensing machines could be programmed to reactivate in what might be called Project Lazarus. In the far mortuary reaches of space, we could call them awake so as to test the vision of Jupiter's giant red eye, or shake the frost from Pluto's back porch.

Think then when these long-distance runners return to speak in tongues late in the 21st Century to tell us of far attic places where we as living flesh cannot follow. Someday, yes, our flesh will landfall Pluto and beyond. But for now, our riddle-solving electric children must roam the vast star meadows to graph the heartbeat of Halley's cosmic beast.

What's holding up this grand cosmic parade?

As in the past, cash in the box.

With a military budget sucking 129 billion dollars away from cities, away from schools, away from hospitals, that inevitably means away from space, time, comets and our possible future survival.

Plus, we have been in a down cycle from overexposure to moon landings, astronauts and the thousands of hours TV networks poured on us, ladling out multitudinous facts but little insight. We have had our feet and minds, as I have often observed, encased in Cronkite. Without poets, philosophers or even smart political observers such as Eric Sevareid, the cosmic question goes abegging year on year.

Meanwhile, because we are so busy building arms to sell to Arabs to scare the Israelites and selling yet further arms to scared Jews to rescare Saudi Arabia and friends, we have no time to stand and stare. We opt out of being philosophers. To think would seem to be the worst thing we might accuse ourselves of. To think *imaginatively* is beyond comment. Dreamers, we snort, stand aside! Reality is the only tonic. Facts are the only medicine. Yet we are full of facts, we burst with data and are not made well. Our spirit flags on the pole.

Can Halley's coment play doctor to our souls? Can the ion-drive craft we build lift our blood and make us truly care about not just mere existence now but futures yet unplumbed?

Why bother? a voice cries from the balcony. PW Who cares? What's all the fuss and star feathers about?

Very simply: We march back to Olympus.

How's that again?

Well, now, we Earth people are great ones, aren't we, for picking ourselves up by the scruff and heaving ourselves out of the Garden or off the holy Mount? We shake ourselves together some facts and add them up to doom, don't we?

Consider: Two thousand years ago, everything was all right with man's universe. We inhabited a planet around which the sun moved as if we were central to its existence. The stars did the same. We were God's navel and everyone found us good to look upon.

Then along came various theologians and astronomers and, next thing we know, we're evicted, both from Eden and from Mount Olympus. We found ourselves out in the rain with a bunch of demoted Apollos, Aphrodites, Zeuses and Titans. It would take a few thousand years before we got around to naming some rockets for the lost gods.

Meanwhile, the astronomers told us that we were not central to anything. We were, in fact, inhabitants of a rather smallish rabbit pellet whirling about a minor sun in the subbasement of a galaxy that did not much care whether we came or went, lived or died, suffered or survived.

The knock on the head that this seeming fact gave us unsettled our egos for quite a few hundred years.

If Copernicus and Galileo and Kepler told us these things, they must be right. If Darwin added that we were merely a bright chimpanzee wheeling a Maserati or a Pinto along time's highway, well, then, why bother to get out of bed in the morning?

But we have got out of bed, and we have gone to the moon, and then we have reached up and fingerprinted Mars. And to those who look at data and say: Mars is empty, there is no life there, we shout:

There *is* life on Mars, and it is *us*.

We are the Martians.

We give ourselves a gift of us.

We move into the universe. We name ourselves, along with our rockets, after old deities. We make ourselves central to existence, knowing not how far we must travel before we meet other mirrors of God staring back into His vast gaze.

For, you see, while facts are important, interpretation of facts is the final builder or destroyer of man and his dream. If we choose to find ourselves minor, or of no worth, the dust will burn and hide our bones. But if we choose to step back into the Garden, devour the apple, throw the snake out into the ditch and survive forever out beyond the Coalsack nebulae, the choice is ours. We will build Olympus and put on our crowns once more.

That is what our encounter with Halley's comet is all about.

So there you have it: 1986 coming on fast. Here comes our chance to reach up.

We would gently touch the passing face of that cold creature, the looming features of that strange matter and force on its blind way round the cosmos. We would do so with that puzzled, infinite curiosity that is the beginning of love.

Do we miss this chance? Do we let time and space churn by without hastening to leap aboard? Do we keep our giant manmade pterodactyl home and lock our best dreams with it, in a box?

I think not. For some century soon, we will be falling out there ourselves. Our dear flesh will outpace that lovely comet.

Meanwhile, our fabulous machines must go for us, do for us and come back smoking a pipe filled with incredible data, to tamp Mark Twain observations in our ears to lean us toward survival.

If our mind flies now, our machines fly later, and our souls fly to follow both in 21st century Salvation Armies of space. And the higher we fly, the more 1984 will recede like a failed threat, an evil promise disconnected, a hell boarded over, a death done in and buried by life.

We will write a better book then. Its title will be *1986* and its hero will be the Great White Comet and Huck Finn's father's kite will lay itself out on the solar winds to welcome it.

As for the comet, it will arrive like doom.

But it will go back out around with annunciations.

What will it announce?

Ourselves, of course, birthing ourselves back into the lap of God.

Telling Him that soon, soon, oh, very soon, we will drop in for a visit. . . .

And *stay* for ten billion years.

Stephen Harrigan / Speed Freak

Texas Monthly, July 1979

Texas Monthly Magazine *describes its audience as "Texans (in and out of state) with educated interests in politics, culture, and life-styles." With a circulation of 200,000, Texas Monthly prefers informational articles: interviews, personal experience, and how-to pieces. In "Speed Freak," a personal paean to fast-food, Stephen Harrigan wittily unwraps the pre-packaged cant comments about franchise food heard everywhere in America today.*

I used to rent a garage apartment from a ninety-year-old doctor who told me that in his professional opinion the Big Mac was a "perfect nutritional unit." Several evenings a week I would see him doddering along the driveway with a big grin on his face, holding his cowboy hat in one hand and a bag from McDonald's in the other. His wife would meet him at the back door, and together they would silently ascend to their dim upstairs dining room and fulfill their nutritional requirements.

I was invariably touched by this scene, which seemed to me a fast-food version of courtly love, but then I'm a romantic about an institution that many people consider the scourge of civilized dining, if not of civilization itself. I like just about everything about fast food. I like to sit in the dining room of Gargantua Burger, relaxing in a booth made of injection-molded plastic and stainless steel, watching the sullen counter personnel in their perky uniforms processing orders while I open up another Serv-A-Portion™ packet of reconstituted lemon juice and pour it into my iced tea. I've heard it said that the color schemes of fast-food establishments are subliminal signals, meant to convey a sense of hospitality of only a limited duration, but I find the bright oranges and yellows much more soothing than the subdued interior of a mainstream restaurant.

In a more active mood I might wheel into the drive-thru lane, give my order to a fiberglass clown with a speaker in its nose, pick up the food, and eat it without turning off the ignition, with all that horsepower still rumbling beneath me. Such a maneuver creates the illusion of predation, of active procurement of food.

There is no point in arguing that fast food is not vulgar. One has only to think of the homogenous blandness of the product, of all the living beasts that are stunned, shredded, and re-formed into harmless-looking protein modules, the top-of-the-food-chain philosophy, the dubious nutritional value. It is a matter of taste, though, whether one finds this vulgarity vibrant or decadent. I don't like urban blight any more than anyone else, but I must admit there have been times when, hungry and tired, driving through a strange town, I was thrilled to see before me the Central Franchise District—cheap, accessible, certifiably mediocre food as far as the eye could see.

If Walt Whitman were alive today he would eat fast food. He would scarf down his hamburger, french fries, and Coke, then lean back in his chair with his arms folded across his chest and take it all in: the construction workers with lock-back knives in sheaths on their belts, children studying their free puzzle placemats, bureaucrats, beauticians, students; people who eat off-handedly, with splendid indifference, who would not know a Cuisinart from a washing machine.

Even people who despise fast food hold passionate opinions about which chains have the best hamburgers or chicken or tacos. In the field of hamburgers, I find it hard to imagine that any reasonable person would question the superiority of Whataburger, a Texas franchise that has recently begun its conquest of the rest of the nation.

I first encountered the Whataburger in Corpus Christi, the city where it originated. One day the mother of one of my fifth-grade classmates appeared in the classroom at lunchtime and presented her son with a white paper bag stained with grease and giving off a warm fragrance that seriously distracted the entire class. Out of the bag the kid pulled the biggest hamburger I had ever seen.

"What is *that?*" I asked him.

"It's a Waterburger," he said. "It weighs a quarter pound and it costs thirty-five cents."

I watched longingly as he ate it. The fact that I thought it was called a Waterburger only added to its mystique.

A few days later I ate my first Whataburger at one of its three Corpus Christi locations. During this period Whataburger architecture was rather extreme, featuring a giant W incorporated into an orange-and-white A-frame building several stories high. One walked in and gave one's order to an employee above whose head was a sign that read, "Please tell me—how many you want! Next man will ask—how you want 'em." The next man, slapping the meat down on the grill, would inquire, in the most courteous manner, "All the way on your double-double?" It was not exactly fast food, but there was a certain satisfaction in dealing with craftsmen.

As the operation began to expand, the A-frames were replaced by more tasteful buildings, the preparation of the food became more covert, the prices soared, and the employees were made to wear see-through plastic aprons that gave them the look of highly specialized medical technicians. Through all this the quality of the basic Whataburger has remained consistent. I doubt if it bears much analysis—it's just a good greasy hamburger—though a Whataburger spokesman I talked to was very proud that the hamburger meat was never frozen, but was instead freshly ground in the company's two processing centers in Corpus Christi and Fort Worth, and cooked to order. "Our concept is that no Whataburger is cooked until you up and order it, as opposed to the precooked, prewrapped, hand-it-to-you-from-the-warmer concept."

That would be the McDonald's concept. I will admit that McDonald's makes excellent french fries, but their hamburgers, in all their various manifestations, taste like mulch. Perhaps this is because, as the McDonald's Beef Brochure says, the meat is cryogenically frozen "to preserve freshness, texture, wholesomeness, and taste in an absolutely uniform way." To be fair, the quality of the food is a secondary phenomenon at McDonald's, which seems more interested in providing its clientele with some form of spiritual nourishment. If one believes the ads, McDonald's is a place where family love and racial harmony abound, where beautiful post-adolescent girls croon "You, you're the one" to lonely businessmen and frazzled Little League coaches. One is not a customer at McDonald's, one is a communicant, a subscriber to a system of values.

Perhaps it is an extension of this world view that makes McDonald's the only fast-food establishment that is unprepared for individual tastes. Order your Filet-o-fish without tartar sauce or your Big Mac without mustard and you will be stranded on the outskirts of McDonaldland for twenty minutes while the faithful file by and are promptly issued their Styrofoam containers.

Wendy's is more flexible. The service is very efficient and accommodating, and the hamburgers, freshly ground and formed in situ by a "patty machine," are not bad at all. The meat in the hamburgers is square, an interesting diversion. "The reason that it's square," a Wendy's representative told me, "is that Dave Thomas, the founder and chairman of the board of Wendy's International, wanted a custom hamburger. He wanted the meat to hang out over the bun."

Of the other hamburger franchises, Burger King, Burger Chef, Royale Burger, Jack in the Box, little needs to be said. None of them inspire me to any enduring observations, though I will say I miss the big inflatable chef that used to hover over the Whopper Burger at the corner of Hancock Drive and Burnet Road in Austin. The other fast-food beef products—tacos, roast beef sandwiches—lie outside the field of my expertise.

Fried chicken is another matter. I know about that and am, in fact, a casual student of the marketing ploys used to take the consumer's mind off the fact that what he is eating was once the limbs and working parts of living chickens. Unlike hamburger, chicken pieces cannot easily be disguised, hence we have euphemisms like "drumstick" for "leg." At Kentucky Fried Chicken, breasts were once referred to as "keels" in an effort to keep the customers at a polite distance from the carnal enterprise, from the vision of millions of naked chicken carcasses being processed through the Colonel's maw.

Colonel Sanders himself has passed into fast-food iconography, a life-size cardboard cutout no more substantial than the Burger King or Ronald McDonald or Tee and Eff, the two Tastee Freeze totems who are, apparently, animate dollops of ice cream. With the Colonel's original Eleven Secret Herbs and Spices recipe joined now by Crispy- and Barbecue-Style chicken, with his face printed on the lids of an execrable line of products called "The Colonel's Little Bucket Desserts," he is the closest thing to a tragic figure one is likely to find in the world of fast food.

The chicken itself, whether original, crispy, or covered in barbecue sauce, is rather dry but durable. The service is generally prompt, but I have no kind words for the gluelike whipped potatoes or the aerated square of dough that is referred to in-house as a "roll."

Kentucky Fried Chicken's principal competition, Church's, is slick and streamlined. The chicken is crispy, plunged before your eyes into bins of boiling fat. (Is it my imagination, or do all Church's employees have the hair singed off their arms?) Unless the chicken has been sitting under the heatlamp for a while it is still glistening from its immersion and too hot to eat. The facilities for leisurely dining are minimal, the few table and chair combinations reminiscent of unsafe playground equipment. And if one hits Church's at the wrong time—say, around lunch and dinner—the chicken may be depleted, since Church's personnel are notorious for not planning ahead. 'Uh, that'll be fourteen minutes on that chicken, sir," they will tell you, immediately removing their operation from the arena of fast food.

Both companies insist their chicken is never frozen. In the case of Church's, the "birds, as we like to call them," are delivered whole, then cut up at each store into eight pieces and marinated in a secret solution for a "semi-secret" amount of time. Kentucky Fried Chickens-to-be are delivered to each outlet already dismembered into pieces that are, on the average, smaller than Church's.

Only those people whose doctors have placed them on unbalanced, high-cholesterol diets should frequent fish and chips establishments. You can feel your arteries begin to harden as soon as you walk through the door. Everything is fried in the same vats, fish and shrimp and terrible french fries and congealed globules of grease called krispies that look and taste like packing material. I must confess, though, that Long John Silver's, one of the most obnoxious places of business on earth, manages to produce delicious fried fish. The thing to do is batten down your imagination and try not to notice the pirate hats and salt-stained walls and door handles that are shaped like cutlasses. Get your fish, walk the plank, and cut out.

The fish at Alfie's is not equal to that at Long John Silver's, but the atmosphere is less relentless. I've never eaten at Arthur Treacher's Fish and Chips, and as I grow older my desire to do so seems to be waning. I once stopped at another franchise called H. Salt, but when I heard pirate music over the loudspeaker ("Doodle *doot* doot doot"), I got embarrassed and had to leave.

The fast-food industry has its unacceptable conceits—the fried pie, for instance—but in general it needs no defense. It may seem now like a rapacious, uncontrollable phenomenon, but already, along certain overdeveloped commercial thoroughfares one notices the vacant hulks of bankrupt franchises that were once thought invincible. Maybe this has something to do with the gas shortage, or with poor marketing decisions, but it is just as likely to be the normal course of things. Fast food won't be around forever, a thought that both comforts and saddens me. I'll be among those who cherish the memory of driving down the highway with a Coke nestled between my legs, a double-double in my hand, and the secure knowledge that should I get hungry again, there will be Dairy Queens at forty-mile intervals all the way to the horizon.

Joan Didion / A Letter from Manhattan

New York Review of Books, August 16, 1979

A former associate feature editor at Vogue *and contributing editor to the* National Review, The Saturday Evening Post, *and* Esquire, *Joan Didion has written for* Mademoiselle, Holiday, The American Scholar, *and* Life *Magazine. Interviews and self-assertion are not her journalistic forte:*

> *My only advantage as a reporter is that I am so physically small, so temperamentally unobtrusive, and so neurotically inarticulate that people tend to forget that my presence runs counter to their best interests. And it always does. That is one last thing to remember: writers are always selling somebody out.*

The author of two novels, Run River (*1963*) and Play It as It Lays (*1970*), *Joan Didion has most recently published a collection of essays titled* The White Album (*1979*).

*"A Letter from Manhattan" is Joan Didion's response to three of Woody Allen's films—*Annie Hall, Interiors, *and* Manhattan. *The essay appeared in the* New York Review of Books, *a biweekly publication founded in 1963 that publishes lengthy reviews and occasional special features by leading critics and literary figures.*

Self-absorption is general, as is self-doubt. In the large coastal cities of the United States this summer many people wanted to be dressed in "real linen," cut by Calvin Klein to wrinkle, which implies real money. In the large coastal cities of the United States this summer many people wanted to be served the perfect vegetable terrine. It was a summer in which only have-nots wanted a cigarette or a vodka-and-tonic or a charcoal-broiled steak. It was a summer in which the more hopeful members of the society wanted roller skates, and stood in line to see Woody Allen's *Manhattan,* a picture in which, toward the end, the Woody Allen character makes a list of reasons to stay alive. "Groucho Marx" is one reason, and "Willie Mays" is another. The second movement of Mozart's "Jupiter" Symphony. Louis Armstrong's "Potato Head Blues." Flaubert's *A Sentimental Education.* This list is modishly eclectic, a trace wry, definitely OK with real linen; and notable, as *raisons d'être* go, in that every experience it evokes is essentially passive. This list of Woody Allen's is the ultimate consumer report, and the extent to which it has been quoted approvingly suggests a new class in America, a subworld of people rigid with apprehension that they will die wearing the wrong sneaker, naming the wrong symphony, preferring *Madame Bovary.*

What is arresting about these recent "serious" pictures of Woody Allen's, about *Annie Hall* and *Interiors* as well as *Manhattan,* is not the way they work as pictures but the way they work with audiences. The people who go to see these pictures, who analyze them and write about them and argue the deeper implications in their texts and subtexts, seem to agree that the world onscreen pretty much mirrors the world as they know it. This is interesting, and rather astonishing, since the peculiar and hermetic self-regard in *Annie Hall* and *Interiors* and *Manhattan* would seem nothing with which large numbers of people would want to identify. The characters in these pictures are, at best, trying. They are morose. They have bad manners. They seem to take long walks and go to smart restaurants only to ask one another hard questions. "Are you serious about Tracy?" the Michael Murphy character asks the Woody Allen character in *Manhattan*. "Are you still hung up on Yale?" the Woody Allen character asks the Diane Keaton character. "I think I'm still in love with Yale," she confesses several scenes later. "You are?" he counters, "or you think you are?" All of the characters in Woody Allen pictures not only ask these questions but actually answer them, on camera, and then, usually in another restaurant, listen raptly to third-party analyses of their own questions and answers.

"How come you guys got divorced?" they ask each other with real interest, and, on a more rhetorical level, "why are you so hostile," and "why can't you just once in a while consider my needs." ("I'm sick of your needs" is the way Diane Keaton answers this question in *Interiors*, one of the few lucid moments in the picture.) *What does she say*, these people ask incessantly, what does she say and what does he say and, finally, inevitably, "what does your analyst say." These people have, on certain subjects, extraordinary attention spans. When Natalie Gittelson of *The New York Times Magazine* recently asked Woody Allen how his own analysis was going after twenty-two years, he answered this way: "It's very slow . . . but an hour a day, talking about your emotions, hopes, angers, disappointments, with someone who's trained to evaluate this material—over a period of years, you're bound to get more in touch with feelings than someone who makes no effort."

Well, yes and (apparently) no. Over a period of twenty-two years "you're bound" only to get older, barring nasty surprises. This notion of oneself as a kind of continuing career—something to work at, work on, "make an effort" for and subject to an hour a day of emotional Nautilus training, all in the interests not of attaining grace but of improving one's "relationships"—is fairly recent in the world, at least in the world not inhabited entirely by adolescents. In fact the paradigm for the action in these recent Woody Allen movies is high school. The characters in *Manhattan* and *Annie Hall* and *Interiors* are, with one exception, presented as adults, as sentient men and women in the most productive years of their lives, but their concerns and conversations are those of clever children, "class brains," acting out a yearbook fantasy of adult life. (The one exception is "Tracy," the Mariel Hemingway part in *Manhattan*, another kind of adolescent fantasy. Tracy actually is a high-school senior, at the Dalton School, and has perfect skin, perfect wisdom, perfect sex, and no visible family. Tracy's mother and father are covered in a single line: they are said to be in London, finding Tracy an apartment. When Tracy wants to go to JFK she calls a limo. Tracy put me in mind of an American-International Pictures executive who once advised me, by way of pointing out the absence of adult characters in AIP beach movies, that nobody ever paid $3 to see a parent.)

These *faux* adults of Woody Allen's have dinner at Elaine's, and argue art versus ethics. They share sodas and wonder "what love is." They have "interesting" occupations, none of which intrudes in any serious way on their dating. Many characters in these pictures "write," usually on tape recorders. In *Manhattan*, Woody Allen quits his job as a television writer and is later seen dictating an "idea" for a short story, an idea which, I am afraid, is also the "idea" for the picture itself: "People in Manhattan are constantly creating these real unnecessary neurotic problems for themselves that keep them from dealing with more terrifying unsolvable problems about the universe.''

In *Annie Hall,* Diane Keaton sings from time to time, at a place like Reno Sweeney's. In *Interiors* she seems to be some kind of celebrity poet. In *Manhattan* she is a magazine writer, and we actually see her typing once, on a novelization, and talking on the telephone to "Harvey," who, given the counterfeit "insider" shine to the dialogue, we are meant to understand is Harvey Shapiro, the editor of *The New York Times Book Review.* (Similarly, we are meant to know that the "Jack and Anjelica" to whom Paul Simon refers in *Annie Hall* are Jack Nicholson and Anjelica Huston, and to feel somehow flattered by our inclusion in this little joke on those who fail to get it.) A writer in *Interiors* is said to be "taking his rage out in critical pieces." "Have you thought any more about having kids?" a wife asks her husband in *Manhattan.* "I've got to get the O'Neill book finished," the husband answers. "I could talk about my book all night," one character says. "Viking loved my book," another says.

These are not possible constructions, but they reflect exactly the false and desperate knowingness of the smartest kid in the class. "When it comes to relationships with women I'm the winner of the August Strindberg Award," the Woody Allen character tells us in *Manhattan;* later, in a frequently quoted and admired line, he says, to Diane Keaton, "I've never had a relationship with a woman that lasted longer than the one between Hitler and Eva Braun." These lines are meaningless, and not funny: they are simply "references," the way Harvey and Jack and Anjelica and *A Sentimental Education* are references, smart talk meant to convey the message that the speaker knows his way around Lit and History, not to mention Show Biz.

In fact the sense of social reality in these pictures is dim in the extreme, and derives more from show business than from anywhere else. The three sisters in *Interiors* are named, without comment, "Renata," "Joey," and "Flyn." That "Renata," "Joey," and "Flyn" are names from three different parts of town seems not to be a point in the picture, nor does the fact that all the characters, who are presented as overeducated, speak an odd and tortured English. "You implied that a lot," one says. "Political activity is not my interest." "Frederick has finished what I've already told him is his best work by far." The particular cadence here is common among actors but not, I think, in the world outside.

"Overeducation" is something Woody Allen seems to discern more often than the rest of us might. "I know so many people who are well-educated and supereducated," he told an interviewer for *Time* recently. "Their common problem is that they have no understanding and no wisdom; without that, their education can only take them so far." In other words they have problems with their "relationships," they have failed to "work through" the material of their lives with a trained evaluator, they have yet to perfect the quality of their emotional consumption. Wisdom is hard to find. Happiness takes research. The message that large numbers of people are getting from *Manhattan* and *Interiors* and *Annie Hall* is that this kind of emotional shopping around is the proper business of life's better students, that adolescence can now extend to middle age. Not long ago I shared, for three nights, a hospital room with a young woman named Linda. I was being watched for appendicitis and was captive to Linda's telephone conversations, which were constant. Linda had two problems, only one of which, her "relationship," had her attention. Linda spoke constantly about this relationship, about her "needs," about her "partner," about the "quality of his nurturance," about the "low frequency of his interaction." Linda's other problem, one which tried her patience because it was preventing her from working on her relationship, was acute and unexplained renal failure. "I'm not relating to this just now," she said to her doctor when he tried to discuss continuing dialysis.

You could call that "overeducation," or you could call it one more instance of "people constantly creating these real unnecessary neurotic problems for themselves that keep them from dealing with more terrifying unsolvable problems about the universe," or you could call it something else. Woody Allen often tells interviewers that his original title for *Annie Hall* was "Anhedonia," which is a psychoanalytic term meaning the inability to experience pleasure. Wanting to call a picture "Anhedonia" is "cute," and implies that the *auteur* and his audience share a superiority to those jocks who need to ask what it means. Superior people suffer. "My emptiness set in a year ago," Diane Keaton is made to say in *Interiors*. "What do I care if a handful of my poems are read after I'm dead . . . is that supposed to be some compensation?" (The notion of compensation for dying is novel.)

Most of us remember very well these secret signals and sighs of adolescence, remember the dramatic apprehension of our own mortality and other "more terrifying unsolvable problems about the universe," but eventually we realize that we are not the first to notice that people die. "Even with all the distractions of my work and my life," Woody Allen was quoted as saying in a cover story (the cover line was "Woody Allen Comes of Age") in *Time*, "I spend a lot of time face to face with my own mortality." This is actually the first time I have ever heard anyone speak of his own life as a "distraction."

BEST SELLERS

*I concluded at length that the People were the best
Judges of my Merit; for they buy my Works . . .*

BENJAMIN FRANKLIN

FEW scenes in best-selling fiction can compare with the one from *Tarzan of the Apes* (1914) in which Tarzan, the son of a shipwrecked British aristocrat, raised from infancy by a tribe of apes in the African jungle, rescues Jane, the comely daughter of an American professor, from the evil clutches of the cruel and capricious ape-king Terkoz:

> Jane—her lithe, young form flattened against the trunk of a great tree, her hands tight pressed against her rising and falling bosom, and her eyes wide with mingled horror, fascination, fear, and admiration—watched the primordial ape battle with the primeval man for possession of a woman—for her.
>
> As the great muscles of the man's back and shoulders knotted beneath the tension of his efforts, and the huge biceps and forearm held at bay those mighty tusks, the veil of centuries of civilization and culture was swept from the blurred vision of the Baltimore girl.

Passion, violence, vengeance, and a melodramatic rescue—the passage is a paradigm of popular fiction.

After killing Terkoz, Tarzan carries off the reluctantly yielding Jane "deeper and deeper into the savage fastness of the untamed forest" to the security of his bower of bliss. What does he do when they get there?

> Tarzan had long since reached a decision as to what his future procedure should be. He had had time to recollect all that he had read of the ways of men and women in the books at the cabin. He would act as he imagined the men in the books would have acted were they in his place.

Apparently, even a situation so geographically and imaginatively far-fetched as that depicting an ape-man entertaining a captivating young woman from Baltimore cannot be entirely free from the guidance, if not the directions, of literature. In a moment obviously more threatening for him than any of his daily adventures in the unchartered jungle, Tarzan can offer no instinctive, spontaneous response. Instead, the "natural" man rescues himself by ponderously turning to the lessons of fiction. Though Tarzan does not tell us what books he had in his cabin library, he will undoubtedly model his future social behavior on the same late nineteenth century popular romances from which his creator, Edgar Rice Burroughs, derived his literary style.

Burroughs, like most best-selling novelists, knew what a reading public wanted. In the Tarzan books he satisfied a contemporary interest in imperialistic adventures and a psychological need for violent, bestial conflicts. A large part of his continuing success is attributable also to his grasp of a fundamental mythic element—that the popular masculine ideal of the twentieth century would be a sensitive brute, a natural aristocrat, a killer with a tender heart. As a type of masculine hero, Tarzan is intended to be not only alluringly primitive (a "woodland demi-god") but also the kind of man that heroines of American fiction have conventionally desired—a cultivated gentleman, preferably a foreign aristocrat.

The image, with variations of course, dominates twentieth century popular fiction and advertising. Michael Rossi, the hero of Grace Metalious' *Peyton Place* (1956), is "a massive boned man with muscles that seemed to quiver every time he moved. . . . His arms, beneath sleeves rolled above the elbow, were knotted powerfully, and the buttons of his work shirts always seemed about to pop off under the strain of trying to cover his chest." Though built like Tarzan, Michael Rossi is not going to wrestle wild beasts. Instead, he arrives in Peyton Place a stranger about to take on the job of headmaster at the local high school, for he "had a mind as analytical as a mathematician's and as curious as a philosopher's." Styles and idioms may change (though in these passages it may not seem so), but a successful formula for fiction is hard to let go of.

Not all best sellers, of course, are so masculinely aggressive, though even a predominately sentimental book like *Uncle Tom's Cabin* (1852) contains its whip wielding Simon Legree. Moreover, *Tarzan of the Apes* and *Peyton Place*, for all their self-conscious primitivism and casual disregard for "centuries of civilization and culture," never really stray very far from the unassailable proprieties and the cozy gentility to which their authors and readers finally subscribe. At the end of *Peyton Place*, Michael Rossi is a vigorous, comfortable, middle-aged married man. And the final scene in *Tarzan of the Apes* finds an educated, love-lorn "demi-god" in conversation at a train station in Wisconsin: " 'I am Monsieur Tarzan,' said the ape-man."

One reason readers respond so positively to a best-selling novel is that it invariably reaffirms in easily accessible language its audience's attitudes, values, and collective fantasies and identifies reassuringly with its anxieties. Novels like *Tarzan of the Apes* and *Peyton Place* become best sellers, then, because, along with excursions into fantasy, they return to what are essentially nonnegotiable domestic standards. In that sense they resemble a great many other American best sellers that have insisted on the inviolability of family bonds. Consider, for instance, a recent best seller by Mario Puzo, *The Godfather* (1969), in which a world of official corruption, blurred loyalties, and misdirected justice is contrasted with a closely knit patriarchal "family" carrying out its obligations and vendettas in a style that ensures the dignity and personal honor of all its members. Another best seller, Harriet Beecher Stowe's *Uncle Tom's Cabin*, fiercely opposes the institution of slavery, not entirely on political or legal grounds, but because it mercilessly breaks up the home by separating children from their parents, husbands from their wives.

Best-selling nonfiction also corroborates its readers' collective values. Many very successful volumes of nonfiction have taken the form of ready-reference compilations of practical advice. Dale Carnegie's *How To Win Friends and Influence People* (1936), Funk and Lewis' *Thirty Days to a More Powerful Vocabulary* (1942), Dr. Benjamin Spock's *Common Sense Book of Baby Care* (1946) and Wayne Dyer's *Your Erroneous Zones* (1976) exemplify the kinds of self-improvement and "how-to-do-it" books that offer their readers guidance that will presumably help them deal successfully with their feelings of ineptitude, confusion, and inferiority and reaffirm their yearnings for an uncomplicated life. Most best sellers offer their characters, and vicariously their readers, a way out of public and private dilemmas by providing them with the possibilities of wealth, sexual gratification, justice or vengeance, romance and adventure, a hard-won optimistic philosophy, or a return to traditional loyalties and uncomplicated codes of behavior.

Like advertisements, newspapers, and magazines, best sellers are frequently written in response to the pressures of contemporary events, issues, and tastes. They capitalize on the public's interests. Some best-selling authors "hit" on or invent something (be it practical advice for self-improvement, a timely exposé, or an extraordinary private eye) that a great number of people want to read about. Others design their books to attract readers predisposed to certain kinds of material by

news coverage and magazine articles. Harriet Beecher Stowe, a dedicated abolitionist, recognized that the much debated issue of slavery, or, more precisely, the
Fugitive Slave Law, was a suitable subject for fiction and wrote what became
America's first major best-selling novel. The enormous popularity of Mario
Puzo's *The Godfather,* one of the fastest-selling novels in the history of American
publishing, can be partly explained by pointing to a reading public fascinated by
the news coverage of the personalities, stratagems, and violence of organized
crime.

Yet books like *Uncle Tom's Cabin* and *The Godfather* did not become best
sellers merely because of their responsiveness to newsworthy public events. If
readers were interested only in the events or issues detailed in these books, they
could have satisfied that need more easily and less expensively by reading newspapers and magazines. But these best sellers, like many of the others we have included, offer readers something more than reportage or polemics; they combine
an awareness of topical subjects with the conventions and techniques of fiction.
Readers can feel that they are learning about the management of the slave trade in
the South or the operations of organized crime while, at the same time, they are
being entertained by the invented characters, situations, and plots that give
factual information the shape of fiction.

The excerpts from best sellers appearing in this section are meant to characterize the kinds of writing that millions of readers have found and still find informative, entertaining, or both.[1] Perhaps the best way for you to read the following
passages is to imagine yourself in a role opposite that of an editor who examines a
piece of writing to try to decide whether it will be commercially successful. Instead, you have material that has been demonstrably successful, and you want to
try to account for that success. What is it about the *writing* that has made it so
popular? To what extent is the book's success attributable to the quality of its
prose? To the types of characters rendered? To the kinds of themes dramatized?
To the information proposed? To the particular psychological, social, or political
issues involved? These and similar questions can, of course, be asked about any
literary work, popular or unpopular, significant or insignificant. But because a
best seller attracts such a large audience, the answers to questions about its compositional strategies and its overall verbal performance suggest a great deal about
the nature of popular writing and the characteristics of the people who read it.

You are being invited to look closely at the following selections from what might
be called a socio-aesthetic point of view. That is, you are being asked to infer from
the distinctive features of the author's prose the kind of people he expects will attend to his writing. By doing so, you will establish the identity of the book's "ideal
reader"—the type of person you imagine the writer would feel most comfortable
talking to. You will have also constructed a criterion against which you can measure your own response to the work. Whatever your final judgment about the relative worth of the material you have read, your criticism will be more attuned to the
particular verbal characteristics of the work the more carefully you can determine
how *you,* as the reader and individual you imagine yourself to be, are taken into account by the author's act of writing.

The audience presupposed by the author's style can become, if the book is a best
seller, the critical justification of his creative efforts. Mickey Spillane, author of the
extraordinarily successful Mike Hammer detective novels, made this point clear

---

1. Margaret Mitchell's *Gone With The Wind,* one of America's most important best selling novels,
has been omitted because the author's estate refuses to allow the book to be excerpted.

when asked in an interview what he thought of the literary criticism of his fiction: "The public is the only critic. And the only *literature* is what the public reads. The first printing of my last book was more than two million copies—that's the kind of opinion that interests me." This way of talking tough is characteristic of Spillane's literary manner. It is a style he worked out before he became a celebrity, so his assurance is not necessarily the result of his having sold over seventy-five million copies of his novels. In fact, the Spillane we hear speaking as a professional writer in the interview quoted above is most likely being playfully imitative of the Spillane who talks to us in the guise of his detective-narrator, Mike Hammer, in the following passage from *I, The Jury:*

> I said no more. I just sat there and glowered at the wall. Someday I'd trigger the bastard that shot Jack. In my time I've done it plenty of times. No sentiment. That went out with the first. After the war I've been almost anxious to get to some of the rats that make up the section of humanity that prey on people. People. How incredibly stupid they could be sometimes. A trial by law for a killer. A loophole in the phrasing that lets a killer crawl out. But in the end the people have their justice. They get it through guys like me once in a while. They crack down on society and I crack down on them. I shoot them like the mad dogs they are and society drags me to court to explain the whys and wherefores of the extermination. They investigate my past, check my fingerprints and throw a million questions my way. The papers make me look like a kill-crazy shamus, but they don't bear down too hard because Pat Chambers [Hammer's police detective friend] keeps them off my neck. Besides, I do my best to help the boys out and they know it. And I'm usually good for a story when I wind up a case.

In this angry internal monologue, Hammer does not talk to himself any differently than he talks to anyone else in the novel. This is his characteristic voice: tough, vindictive, self-assured. It is the voice of a man (rarely do women talk like this in fiction) who refuses to mince his words, who thinks that a more complicated way of talking would invariably associate him with the legalistic language that permits those "loopholes" in phrasing through which killers are allowed to escape justice.

The language in this passage carries with it an authority that would gratify those readers who feel that their own lives are helplessly trapped in bureaucratic labyrinths and compromising civilities, and who consequently seldom, if ever, have the occasion to talk to anybody in the way Mike Hammer does. If Hammer recognizes in this passage that he is forced occasionally to make concessions to the police, the courts, and the press, he does so without compromising his role as a self-appointed arbiter of social justice. He does so also without ever having to modify unwillingly his deliberately aggressive, hard-boiled tone to suit the different types of characters he is obliged to confront. Hammer's is a voice that never interrupts itself to reconsider what it has said. It is a language without hesitations or unnecessary qualifications.

Hammer's style disassociates him from the official language of law enforcement, a language traditionally dependent upon a complicated system of qualifications and constraints. By taking the law into his own hands, Hammer essentially transforms the law into his own language. If, as the self-assertion of the title indicates, Hammer *is* the jury, then he symbolically embodies the "People," whose expectations of justice he considers it is his mission in life to fulfill. The overwhelming public approval that Spillane confidently refers to as the most legitimate criticism of his

fiction has been anticipated in the public approbation he allowed his most successful character to take for granted.

It is not unusual for best selling authors to find a confirmation of their talent in
sales figures. Harriet Beecher Stowe, an author whose literary intentions differ radically from Spillane's, and who would have been offended even by his idiom, acknowledged her enthusiasm for the public's approval of America's first major best
selling novel in terms Spillane would surely understand. Writing in the third person
for an introduction to one of the many editions of *Uncle Tom's Cabin*, she remarks,

> The despondency of the author as to the question whether anybody would
> read or attend to her appeal was soon dispelled. Ten thousand copies
> were sold in a few days, and over three hundred thousand within a year;
> and eight power-presses, running day and night, were barely able to keep
> pace with the demand for it. It was read everywhere, apparently, and by
> everybody; and she soon began to hear echoes of sympathy all over the
> land. The indignation, the pity, the distress, that had long weighed upon
> her soul seemed to pass off from her into the readers of the book.

It would be difficult to find a more apt description of the merger of writer and reader
in the collective enterprise that makes a book a best seller.

Harriet Beecher Stowe / *Uncle Tom's Cabin*   1852

*The daughter of a New England Congregational pastor, Harriet Beecher Stowe
(1811–96) moved to Cincinnati when her father was appointed head of the Lane
Theological Seminary. She began writing sketches for magazines, but after her
marriage to Calvin Ellis Stowe, a professor of Biblical Literature at her father's
seminary, she abandoned the idea of a literary career. At the time, Lane Theological Seminary was a center of antislavery sentiment, and in this environment, plus
occasional visits to the slave state Kentucky, Mrs. Stowe gradually formed the abolitionist opinions that were given full expression in* Uncle Tom's Cabin. *After a
successful serialization in a Washington, D.C., antislavery weekly,* The National
Era, *the novel was brought out in two volumes in 1852. It was a momentous
publishing event: thirty thousand copies were sold in the first year, and by 1856 the
sales in England alone were well over a million. Translations were worldwide.
Mrs. Stowe, then living in Brunswick, Maine, where her husband had a teaching
position at Bowdoin, found herself the most famous literary figure in America and
an international celebrity. Though she continued to write (averaging nearly a book
a year for the next thirty years), none of her later novels ever attained the success
of her first.*

SELECT INCIDENT OF LAWFUL TRADE

> *"In Ramah there was a voice heard,—weeping, and lamentation, and great mourning;
> Rachel weeping for her children, and would not be comforted."*
> —Jeremiah, 31 : 15

Mr. Haley and Tom jogged onward in their wagon, each, for a time, absorbed in his
own reflections. Now, the reflections of two men sitting side by side are a curious

thing,—seated on the same seat, having the same eyes, ears, hands and organs of all sorts, and having pass before their eyes the same objects,—it is wonderful what a variety we shall find in these same reflections!

As, for example, Mr. Haley: he thought first of Tom's length, and breadth, and height, and what he would sell for, if he was kept fat and in good case till he got him into market. He thought of how he should make out his gang; he thought of the respective market value of certain supposititious men and women and children who were to compose it, and other kindred topics of the business; then he thought of himself, and how humane he was, that whereas other men chained their ''niggers'' hand and foot both, he only put fetters on the feet, and left Tom the use of his hands, as long as he behaved well; and he sighed to think how ungrateful human nature was, so that there was even room to doubt whether Tom appreciated his mercies. He had been taken in so by ''niggers'' whom he had favored; but still he was astonished to consider how good-natured he yet remained!

As to Tom, he was thinking over some words of an unfashionable old book, which kept running through his head, again and again, as follows: ''We have here no continuing city, but we seek one to come; wherefore God himself is not ashamed to be called our God; for he hath prepared for us a city.'' These words of an ancient volume, got up principally by ''ignorant and unlearned men,'' have, through all time, kept up, somehow, a strange sort of power over the minds of poor, simple fellows, like Tom. They stir up the soul from its depths, and rouse, as with trumpet call, courage, energy, and enthusiasm, where before was only the blackness of despair.

Mr. Haley pulled out of his pocket sundry newspapers, and began looking over their advertisements, with absorbed interest. He was not a remarkably fluent reader, and was in the habit of reading in a sort of recitative half-aloud, by way of calling in his ears to verify the deductions of his eyes. In this tone he slowly recited the following paragraph:

''EXECUTOR'S SALE,—NEGROES!—*Agreeably to order of court, will be sold, on Tuesday, February 20, before the Court-house door, in the town of Washington, Kentucky, the following negroes: Hagar, aged 60; John, aged 30; Ben, aged 21; Saul, aged 25; Albert, aged 14. Sold for the benefit of the creditors and heirs of the estate of Jesse Blutchford, Esq.*

SAMUEL MORRIS,
THOMAS FLINT,
Executors''

''This yer I must look at,'' said he to Tom, for want of somebody else to talk to.

''Ye see, I'm going to get up a prime gang to take down with ye, Tom; it'll make it sociable and pleasant like,—good company will, ye know. We must drive right to Washington first and foremost, and then I'll clap you into jail, while I does the business.''

Tom received this agreeable intelligence quite meekly; simply wondering, in his own heart, how many of these doomed men had wives and children, and whether they would feel as he did about leaving them. It is to be confessed, too, that the naïve, off-hand information that he was to be thrown into jail by no means produced an agreeable impression on a poor fellow who had always prided himself on a strictly honest and upright course of life. Yes, Tom, we must confess it, was rather proud of his honesty, poor fellow,—not having very much else to be proud of;—if he had belonged to some of the higher walks of society, he, perhaps, would never have been reduced to such straits. However, the day wore on, and the evening saw Haley and Tom comfortably accommodated in Washington,—the one in a tavern, and the other in a jail.

About eleven o'clock the next day, a mixed throng was gathered around the court-house steps,—smoking, chewing, spitting, swearing, and conversing, according to their respective tastes and turns,—waiting for the auction to commence. The men and women to be sold sat in a group apart, talking in a low tone to each other. The woman who had been advertised by the name of Hagar was a regular African in feature and figure. She might have been sixty, but was older than that by hard work and disease, was partially blind, and somewhat crippled with rheumatism. By her side stood her only remaining son, Albert, a bright-looking little fellow of fourteen years. The boy was the only survivor of a large family, who had been successively sold away from her to a southern market. The mother held on to him with both her shaking hands, and eyed with intense trepidation every one who walked up to examine him.

"Don't be feared, Aunt Hagar," said the oldest of the men, "I spoke to Mas'r Thomas 'bout it, and he thought he might manage to sell you in a lot both together."

"Dey needn't call me worn out yet," said she, lifting her shaking hands. "I can cook yet, and scrub, and scour,—I'm wuth a buying, if I come cheap;—tell em dat ar,—you *tell* em," she added, earnestly.

Haley here forced his way into the group, walked up to the old man, pulled his mouth open and looked in, felt of his teeth, made him stand and straighten himself, bend his back, and perform various evolutions to show his muscles; and then passed on to the next, and put him through the same trial. Walking up last to the boy, he felt of his arms, straightened his hands, and looked at his fingers, and made him jump, to show his agility.

"He an't gwine to be sold widout me!" said the old woman, with passionate eagerness; "he and I goes in a lot together; I 's rail strong yet, Mas'r and can do heaps o' work,—heaps on it, Mas'r."

"On plantation?" said Haley, with a contemptuous glance. "Likely story!" and, as if satisfied with his examination, he walked out and looked, and stood with his hands in his pocket, his cigar in his mouth, and his hat cocked on one side, ready for action.

"What think of 'em?" said a man who had been following Haley's examination, as if to make up his own mind from it.

"Wal," said Haley, spitting, "I shall put in, I think, for the youngerly ones and the boy."

"They want to sell the boy and the old woman together," said the man.

"Find it a tight pull;—why, she's an old rack o'bones,—not worth her salt."

"You wouldn't then?" said the man.

"Anybody 'd be a fool 't would. She's half blind, crooked with rheumatis, and foolish to boot."

"Some buys up these yer old critturs, and ses there's a sight more wear in 'em than a body 'd think," said the man, reflectively.

"No go, 't all," said Haley; "wouldn't take her for a present,—fact,—I've *seen,* now."

"Wal, 't is kinder pity, now, not to buy her with her son,—her heart seems so sot on him,—s'pose they fling her in cheap."

"Them that's got money to spend that ar way, it's all well enough. I shall bid off on that ar boy for a plantation-hand;—wouldn't be bothered with her, no way,—not if they'd give her to me," said Haley.

"She'll take on desp't," said the man.

"Nat'lly, she will," said the trader, coolly.

The conversation was here interrupted by a busy hum in the audience; and the auctioneer, a short, bustling, important fellow, elbowed his way into the crowd. The old woman drew in her breath, and caught instinctively at her son.

"Keep close to yer mammy, Albert,—close,—dey'll put us up togedder," she said.

"O, mammy, I'm feard they won't," said the boy.

"Dey must, child; I can't live, no ways, if they don't," said the old creature, vehemently.

The stentorian tones of the auctioneer, calling out to clear the way, now announced that the sale was about to commence. A place was cleared, and the bidding began. The different men on the list were soon knocked off at prices which showed a pretty brisk demand in the market; two of them fell to Haley.

"Come, now, young un," said the auctioneer, giving the boy a touch with his hammer, "be up and show your springs, now."

"Put us two up togedder, togedder,—do please, Mas'r," said the old woman, holding fast to her boy.

"Be off," said the man, gruffly, pushing her hands away; "you come last. Now, darkey, spring;" and, with the word, he pushed the boy toward the block, while a deep, heavy groan rose behind him. The boy paused, and looked back; but there was no time to stay, and dashing the tears from his large, bright eyes, he was up in a moment.

His fine figure, alert limbs, and bright face, raised an instant competition, and half a dozen bids simultaneously met the ear of the auctioneer. Anxious, half-frightened, he looked from side to side, as he heard the clatter of contending bids,—now here, now there,—till the hammer fell. Haley had got him. He was pushed from the block toward his new master, but stopped one moment, and looked back, when his poor old mother, trembling in every limb, held out her shaking hands toward him.

"Buy me too, Mas'r, for de dear Lord's sake!—buy me,—I shall die if you don't!"

"You'll die if I do, that's the kink of it," said Haley,—"no!" And he turned on his heel.

The bidding for the poor old creature was summary. The man who had addressed Haley, and who seemed not destitute of compassion, bought her for a trifle, and the spectators began to disperse.

The poor victims of the sale, who had been brought up in one place together for years, gathered round the despairing old mother, whose agony was pitiful to see.

"Couldn't dey leave me one? Mas'r allers said I should have one,—he did," she repeated over and over, in heart-broken tones.

"Trust in the Lord, Aunt Hagar," said the oldest of the men, sorrowfully.

"What good will it do?" said she, sobbing passionately.

"Mother, mother,—don't! don't!" said the boy. "They say you's got a good master."

"I don't care—I don't care. O, Albert! oh, my boy! you's my last baby. Lord, how ken I?"

"Come, take her off, can't some of ye?" said Haley, dryly; "don't do no good for her to go on that ar way."

The old men of the company, partly by persuasion and partly by force, loosed the poor creature's last despairing hold, and, as they led her off to her new master's wagon, strove to comfort her.

"Now!" said Haley, pushing his three purchases together, and producing a bundle of handcuffs, which he proceeded to put on their wrists; and fastening each handcuff to a long chain, he drove them before him to the jail.

A few days saw Haley, with his possessions, safely deposited on one of the Ohio boats. It was the commencement of his gang, to be augmented, as the boat moved on, by various other merchandise of the same kind, which he, or his agent, had stored for him in various points along shore.

The La Belle Rivière, as brave and beautiful a boat as ever walked the waters of her namesake river, was floating gayly down the stream, under a brilliant sky, the stripes and stars of free America waving and fluttering over head; the guards crowded with well-dressed ladies and gentlemen walking and enjoying the delightful day. All was full of life, buoyant and rejoicing;—all but Haley's gang, who were stored, with other freight, on the lower deck, and who, somehow, did not seem to appreciate their various privileges, as they sat in a knot, talking to each other in low tones.

"Boys," said Haley, coming up, briskly, "I hope you keep up good heart, and are cheerful. Now, no sulks, ye see; keep stiff upper lip, boys; do well by me, and I'll do well by you."

The boys addressed responded the invariable "Yes, Mas'r," for ages the watchword of poor Africa; but it's to be owned they did not look particularly cheerful; they had their various little prejudices in favor of wives, mothers, sisters, and children, seen for the last time,—and though "they that wasted them required of them mirth," it was not instantly forthcoming.

"I've got a wife," spoke out the article enumerated as "John, aged thirty," and he laid his chained hand on Tom's knee,—"and she don't know a word about this, poor girl!"

"Where does she live?" said Tom.

"In a tavern a piece down here," said John; "I wish, now, I *could* see her once more in this world," he added.

Poor John! It *was* rather natural; and the tears that fell, as he spoke, came as naturally as if he had been a white man. Tom drew a long breath from a sore heart, and tried, in his poor way, to comfort him.

And over head, in the cabin, sat fathers and mothers, husbands and wives; and merry, dancing children moved round among them, like so many little butterflies, and everything was going on quite easy and comfortable.

"O, mamma," said a boy, who had just come up from below, "there's a negro trader on board, and he's brought four or five slaves down there."

"Poor creatures!" said the mother, in a tone between grief and indignation.

"What's that?" said another lady.

"Some poor slaves below," said the mother.

"And they've got chains on," said the boy.

"What a shame to our country that such sights are to be seen!" said another lady.

"O, there's a great deal to be said on both sides of the subject," said a genteel woman, who sat at her state-room door sewing, while her little girl and boy were playing round her. "I've been south, and I must say I think the negroes are better off than they would be to be free."

"In some respects, some of them are well off, I grant," said the lady to whose remark she had answered. "The most dreadful part of slavery, to my mind, is its outrages on the feelings and affections,—the separating of families, for example."

"That *is* a bad thing, certainly," said the other lady, holding up a baby's dress she had just completed, and looking intently on its trimmings; "but then, I fancy, it don't occur often."

"O, it does," said the first lady, eagerly; "I've lived many years in Kentucky and Virginia both, and I've seen enough to make any one's heart sick. Suppose, ma'am, your two children, there, should be taken from you, and sold?"

"We can't reason from our feelings to those of this class of persons," said the other lady, sorting out some worsteds on her lap.

"Indeed, ma'am, you can know nothing of them, if you say so," answered the first lady, warmly. "I was born and brought up among them. I know they *do* feel, just as keenly,—even more so, perhaps,—as we do."

The lady said "Indeed!" yawned, and looked out the cabin window, and finally repeated, for a finale, the remark with which she had begun,—"After all, I think they are better off than they would be to be free."

"It's undoubtedly the intention of Providence that the African race should be servants,—kept in a low condition," said a grave-looking gentleman in black, a clergyman, seated by the cabin door. " 'Cursed be Canaan; a servant of servants shall he be,' the Scripture says."

"I say, stranger, is that ar what that text means?" said a tall man, standing by.

"Undoubtedly. It pleased Providence, for some inscrutable reason, to doom the race to bondage, ages ago; and we must not set up our opinion against that."

"Well, then, we'll all go ahead and buy up niggers," said the man, "if that's the way of Providence,—won't we, Squire?" said he, turning to Haley, who had been standing, with his hands in his pockets, by the stove and intently listening to the conversation.

"Yes," continued the tall man, "we must all be resigned to the decrees of Providence. Niggers must be sold, and trucked round, and kept under; it's what they's made for. 'Pears like this yer view 's quite refreshing, ain't it, stranger?" said he to Haley.

"I never thought on 't," said Haley. "I couldn't have said as much, myself; I ha'nt no larning. I took up the trade just to make a living; if 'tan't right, I calculated to 'pent on 't in time, *ye* know."

"And now you'll save yerself the trouble, won't ye?" said the tall man. "See what 't is, now, to know scripture. If ye'd only studied yer Bible, like this yer good man, ye might have know'd it before, and saved ye a heap o' trouble. Ye could jist have said, 'Cussed be'—what's his name?—'and 't would all have come right.' "
And the stranger, who was no other than the honest drover whom we introduced to our readers in the Kentucky tavern, sat down, and began smoking, with a curious smile on his long, dry face.

A tall, slender young man, with a face expressive of great feeling and intelligence, here broke in, and repeated the words, " 'All things whatsoever ye would that men should do unto you, do ye even so unto them.' I suppose," he added, "*that* is scripture, as much as 'Cursed be Canaan.' "

"Wal, it seems quite *as* plain a text, stranger," said John the drover, "to poor fellows like us, now;" and John smoked on like a volcano.

The young man paused, looked as if he was going to say more, when suddenly the boat stopped, and the company made the usual steamboat rush, to see where they were landing.

"Both them ar chaps parsons?" said John to one of the men, as they were going out.

The man nodded.

As the boat stopped, a black woman came running wildly up the plank, darted into the crowd, flew up to where the slave gang sat, and threw her arms round that unfortunate piece of merchandise before enumerated—"John, aged thirty," and with sobs and tears bemoaned him as her husband.

But what needs tell the story, told too oft,—every day told,—of heart-strings rent and broken,—the weak broken and torn for the profit and convenience of the strong! It needs not to be told;—every day is telling it,—telling it, too, in the ear of One who is not deaf, though he be long silent.

The young man who had spoken for the cause of humanity and God before stood with folded arms, looking on this scene. He turned, and Haley was standing at his side. "My friend," he said, speaking with thick utterance, "how can you, how dare you, carry on a trade like this? Look at those poor creatures! Here I am, rejoicing in my heart that I am going home to my wife and child; and the same bell which is a signal to carry me onward towards them will part this poor man and his wife forever. Depend upon it, God will bring you into judgment for this."

The trader turned away in silence.

"I say, now," said the drover, touching his elbow, "there's differences in parsons, an't there? 'Cussed be Cannan' don't seem to go down with this 'un, does it?"

Haley gave an uneasy growl.

"And that ar an't the worst on 't," said John; "mabbee it won't go down with the Lord, neither, when ye come to settle with Him, one o' these days, as all on us must, I reckon."

Haley walked reflectively to the other end of the boat.

"If I make pretty handsomely on one or two next gangs," he thought, "I reckon I'll stop off this yer; it's really getting dangerous." And he took out his pocketbook, and began adding over his accounts,—a process which many gentlemen besides Mr. Haley have found a specific for an uneasy conscience.

The boat swept proudly away from the shore, and all went on merrily, as before. Men talked, and loafed, and read, and smoked. Women sewed, and children played, and the boat passed on her way.

One day, when she lay to for a while at a small town in Kentucky, Haley went up into the place on a little matter of business.

Tom, whose fetters did not prevent his taking a moderate circuit, had drawn near the side of the boat, and stood listlessly gazing over the railing. After a time, he saw the trader returning, with an alert step, in company with a colored woman, bearing in her arms a young child. She was dressed quite respectably, and a colored man followed her, bringing along a small trunk. The woman came cheerfully onward, talking, as she came, with the man who bore her trunk, and so passed up the plank into the boat. The bell rung, the steamer whizzed, the engine groaned and coughed, and away swept the boat down the river.

The woman walked forward among the boxes and bales of the lower deck, and, sitting down, busied herself with chirruping to her baby.

Haley made a turn or two about the boat, and then, coming up, seated himself near her, and began saying something to her in an indifferent undertone.

Tom soon noticed a heavy cloud passing over the woman's brow; and that she answered rapidly, and with great vehemence.

"I don't believe it,—I won't believe it!" he heard her say. "You're jist a foolin with me."

"If you won't believe it, look here!" said the man, drawing out a paper; "this yer 's the bill of sale, and there's your master's name to it; and I paid down good solid cash for it, too, I can tell you,—so, now!"

"I don't believe Mas'r would cheat me so; it can't be true!" said the woman, with increasing agitation.

"You can ask any of these men here, that can read writing. Here!" he said, to a man that was passing by, "jist read this yer, won't you! This yer gal won't believe me, when I tell her what 't is."

"Why, it's a bill of sale, signed by John Fosdick," said the man, "making over to you the girl Lucy and her child. It's all straight enough, for aught I see."

The woman's passionate exclamations collected a crowd around her, and the trader briefly explained to them the cause of the agitation.

"He told me that I was going down to Louisville, to hire out as cook to the same tavern where my husband works,—that's what Mas'r told me, his own self; and I can't believe he'd lie to me," said the woman.

"But he has sold you, my poor woman, there's no doubt about it," said a good-natured looking man, who had been examining the papers; "he has done it, and no mistake."

"Then it's no account talking," said the woman, suddenly growing quite calm; and, clasping her child tighter in her arms, she sat down on her box, turned her back round, and gazed listlessly into the river.

"Going to take it easy, after all!" said the trader. "Gal's got grit, I see."

The woman looked calm, as the boat went on; and a beautiful soft summer breeze passed like a compassionate spirit over her head,—the gentle breeze, that never inquires whether the brow is dusky or fair that it fans. And she saw sunshine sparkling on the water, in golden ripples, and heard gay voices, full of ease and pleasure, talking around her everywhere; but her heart lay as if a great stone had fallen on it. Her baby raised himself up against her, and stroked her cheeks with his little hands; and, springing up and down, crowing and chatting, seemed determined to arouse her. She strained him suddenly and tightly in her arms, and slowly one tear after another fell on his wondering, unconscious face; and gradually she seemed, and little by little, to grow calmer, and busied herself with tending and nursing him.

The child, a boy of ten months, was uncommonly large and strong of his age, and very vigorous in his limbs. Never, for a moment, still, he kept his mother constantly busy in holding him, and guarding his springing activity.

"That's a fine chap!" said a man, suddenly stopping opposite to him, with his hands in his pockets. "How old is he?"

"Ten months and a half," said the mother.

The man whistled to the boy, and offered him part of a stick of candy, which he eagerly grabbed at, and very soon had it in a baby's general depository, to wit, his mouth.

"Rum fellow!" said the man. "Knows what's what!" and he whistled, and walked on. When he had got to the other side of the boat, he came across Haley, who was smoking on top of a pile of boxes.

The stranger produced a match, and lighted a cigar, saying, as he did so,

"Decentish kind o' wench you've got round there, stranger."

"Why, I reckon she *is* tol'able fair," said Haley, blowing the smoke out of his mouth.

"Taking her down south?" said the man.

Haley nodded, and smoked on.

"Plantation hand?" said the man.

"Wal," said Haley, "I'm fillin' out an order for a plantation, and I think I shall put her in. They told me she was a good cook; and they can use her for that, or set her at the cotton-picking. She's got the right fingers for that; I looked at 'em. Sell well, either way;" and Haley resumed his cigar.

"They won't want the young 'un on the plantation," said the man.

"I shall sell him, first chance I find," said Haley, lighting another cigar.

"S'pose you'd be selling him tol'able cheap," said the stranger, mounting the pile of boxes, and sitting down comfortably.

"Don't know 'bout that," said Haley; "he's a pretty smart young 'un,—straight, fat, strong; flesh as hard as a brick!"

"Very true, but then there's the bother and expense of raisin'."

"Nonsense!" said Haley; "they is raised as easy as any kind of critter there is going; they an't a bit more trouble than pups. This yer chap will be running all around, in a month."

"I've got a good place for raisin', and I thought of takin' in a little more stock," said the man. "One cook lost a young 'un last week,—got drownded in a wash-tub while she was a hangin' out clothes,—and I reckon it would be well enough to set her to raisin' this yer."

Haley and the stranger smoked a while in silence, neither seeming willing to broach the test question of the interview. At last the man resumed:

"You wouldn't think of wantin' more than ten dollars for that ar chap, seeing you *must* get him off yer hand, any how?"

Haley shook his head, and spit impressively.

"That won't do, no ways," he said, and began his smoking again.

"Well, stranger, what will you take?"

"Well, now," said Haley, "I *could* raise that ar chap myself, or get him raised; he's oncommon likely and healthy, and he'd fetch a hundred dollars, six months hence; and, in a year or two, he'd bring two hundred, if I had him in the right spot;—so I shan't take a cent less nor fifty for him now."

"O, stranger! that's rediculous, altogether," said the man.

"Fact!" said Haley, with a decisive nod of his head.

"I'll give thirty for him," said the stranger, "but not a cent more."

"Now, I'll tell ye what I will do," said Haley, spitting again, with renewed decision. "I'll split the difference, and say forty-five; and that's the most I will do."

"Well, agreed!" said the man, after an interval.

"Done!" said Haley, "Where do you land?"

"At Louisville," said the man.

"Louisville," said Haley. "Very fair, we get there about dusk. Chap will be asleep,—all fair,—get him off quietly, and no screaming,—happens beautiful,—I like to do everything quietly,—I hates all kind of agitation and fluster." And so, after a transfer of certain bills had passed from the man's pocket-book to the trader's, he resumed his cigar.

It was a bright, tranquil evening when the boat stopped at the wharf at Louisville. The woman had been sitting with her baby in her arms, now wrapped in a heavy sleep. When she heard the name of the place called out, she hastily laid the child down in a little cradle formed by the hollow among the boxes, first carefully spreading under it her cloak; and then she sprung to the side of the boat, in hopes that, among the various hotel-waiters who thronged the wharf, she might see her husband. In this hope, she pressed forward to the front rails, and, stretching far over them, strained her eyes intently on the moving heads on the shore, and the crowd pressed in between her and the child.

"Now's your time," said Haley, taking the sleeping child up, and handing him to the stranger. "Don't wake him up, and set him to crying, now; it would make a devil of a fuss with the gal." The man took the bundle carefully, and was soon lost in the crowd that went up the wharf.

When the boat, creaking, and groaning, and puffing, had loosed from the wharf, and was beginning slowly to strain herself along, the woman returned to her old seat. The trader was sitting there,—the child was gone!

"Why, why,—where?" she began, in bewildered surprise.

"Lucy," said the trader, "your child's gone; you may as well know it first as last. You see, I know'd you couldn't take him down south; and I got a chance to sell him to a first-rate family, that'll raise him better than you can."

The trader had arrived at that stage of Christian and political perfection which has been recommended by some preachers and politicians of the north, lately, in which he had completely overcome every humane weakness and prejudice. His heart was exactly where yours, sir, and mine could be brought, with proper effort and cultivation. The wild look of anguish and utter despair that the woman cast on him might have disturbed one less practised; but he was used to it. He had seen that same look hundreds of time. You can get used to such things, too, my friend; and it is the great object of recent efforts to make our whole northern community used to them, for the glory of the Union. So the trader only regarded the mortal anguish which he saw working in those dark features, those clenched hands, and suffocating breathings, as necessary incidents of the trade, and merely calculated whether she was going to scream, and get up a commotion on the boat; for, like other supporters of our peculiar institution, he decidedly disliked agitation.

But the woman did not scream. The shot had passed too straight and direct through the heart, for cry or tear.

Dizzily she sat down. Her slack hands fell lifeless by her side. Her eyes looked straight forward, but she saw nothing. All the noise and hum of the boat, the groaning of the machinery, mingled dreamily to her bewildered ear; and the poor, dumb-stricken heart had neither cry nor tear to show for its utter misery. She was quite calm.

The trader, who, considering his advantages, was almost as humane as some of our politicians, seemed to feel called on to administer such consolation as the case admitted of.

"I know this yer comes kinder hard, at first, Lucy," said he; "but such a smart, sensible gal as you are, won't give way to it. You see it's *necessary,* and can't be helped!"

"O! don't, Mas'r, don't!" said the woman, with a voice like one that is smothering.

"You're a smart wench, Lucy," he persisted; "I mean to do well by ye, and get ye a nice place down river; and you'll soon get another husband,—such a likely gal as you—"

"O! Mas'r, if you *only* won't talk to me now," said the woman, in a voice of such quick and living anguish that the trader felt that there was something at present in the case beyond his style of operation. He got up, and the woman turned away, and buried her head in her cloak.

The trader walked up and down for a time, and occasionally stopped and looked at her.

"Takes it hard, rather," he soliloquized, "but quiet, tho';—let her sweat a while; she'll come right, by and by!"

Tom had watched the whole transaction from first to last, and had a perfect understanding of its results. To him, it looked like something unutterably horrible and cruel, because, poor, ignorant black soul! he had not learned to generalize, and to take enlarged views. If he had only been instructed by certain ministers of Christianity, he might have thought better of it, and seen in it an every-day incident of a lawful trade; a trade which is the vital support of an institution which an American divine [1] tells us has *"no evils but such as are inseparable from any other relations in social and domestic life."* But Tom, as we see, being a poor, ignorant fellow, whose reading had been confined entirely to the New Testament, could not comfort and solace himself with views like these. His very soul bled within him for what seemed to him the *wrongs* of the poor suffering thing that lay like a crushed reed on the boxes; the feeling, living, bleeding, yet immortal *thing,* which American state law coolly classes with the bundles, and bales, and boxes, among which she is lying.

Tom drew near, and tried to say something; but she only groaned. Honestly, and with tears running down his own cheeks, he spoke of a heart of love in the skies, of a pitying Jesus, and an eternal home; but the ear was deaf with anguish, and the palsied heart could not feel.

Night came on,—night calm, unmoved, and glorious, shining down with her innumerable and solemn angel eyes, twinkling, beautiful, but silent. There was no speech nor language, no pitying voice or helping hand, from that distant sky. One after another, the voices of business or pleasure died away; all on the boat were sleeping, and the ripples at the prow were plainly heard. Tom stretched himself out on a box, and there, as he lay, he heard, ever and anon, a smothered sob or cry from the prostrate creature,—"O! what shall I do? O Lord! O good Lord, do help me!" and so, ever and anon, until the murmur died away in silence.

At midnight, Tom waked, with a sudden start. Something black passed quickly by him to the side of the boat, and he heard a splash in the water. No one else saw or heard anything. He raised his head,—the woman's place was vacant! He got up, and sought about him in vain. The poor bleeding heart was still, at last, and the river rippled and dimpled just as brightly as if it had not closed above it.

Patience! patience! ye whose hearts swell indignant at wrongs like these. Not one throb of anguish, not one tear of the oppressed, is forgotten by the Man of Sorrows, the Lord of Glory. In his patient, generous bosom he bears the anguish of a world. Bear thou, like him, in patience, and labor in love; for sure as he is God, "the year of his redeemed *shall* come."

1. Dr. Joel Parker of Philadelphia.

The trader waked up bright and early, and came out to see to his live stock. It was now his turn to look about in perplexity.

"Where alive is that gal?" he said to Tom.

Tom, who had learned the widom of keeping counsel, did not feel called upon to state his observations and suspicions, but said he did not know.

"She surely couldn't have got off in the night at any of the landings, for I was awake, and on the look-out, whenever the boat stopped. I never trust these yer things to other folks."

This speech was addressed to Tom quite confidentially, as if it was something that would be specially interesting to him. Tom made no answer.

The trader searched the boat from stem to stern, among boxes, bales and barrels, around the machinery, by the chimneys, in vain.

"Now, I say, Tom, be fair about this yer," he said, when, after a fruitless search, he came where Tom was standing. "You know something about it, now. Don't tell me,—I know you do. I saw the gal stretched out here about ten o'clock, and ag'in at twelve, and ag'in between one and two; and then at four she was gone, and you was a sleeping right there all the time. Now, you know something,—you can't help it."

"Well, Mas'r," said Tom, "towards morning something brushed by me, and I kinder half woke; and then I hearn a great splash, and then I clare woke up, and the gal was gone. That's all I know on 't."

The trader was not shocked nor amazed; because, as we said before, he was used to a great many things that you are not used to. Even the awful presence of Death struck no solemn chill upon him. He had seen Death many times,—met him in the way of trade, and got acquainted with him,—and he only thought of him as a hard customer, that embarrassed his property operations very unfairly; and so he only swore that the gal was a baggage, and that he was devilish unlucky, and that, if things went on in this way, he should not make a cent on the trip. In short, he seemed to consider himself an ill-used man, decidedly; but there was no help for it, as the woman had escaped into a state which *never will* give up a fugitive,—not even at the demand of the whole glorious Union. The trader, therefore, sat discontentedly down, with his little account-book, and put down the missing body and soul under the head of *losses!*

"He's a shocking creature, isn't he,—this trader? so unfeeling! It's dreadful, really!"

"O, but nobody thinks anything of these traders! They are universally despised,—never received into any decent society."

But who, sir makes the trader? Who is most to blame? The enlightened, cultivated, intelligent man, who supports the system of which the trader is the inevitable result, or the poor trader himself? You make the public statement that calls for his trade, that debauches and depraves him, till he feels no shame in it; and in what are you better than he?

Are you educated and he ignorant, you high and he low, you refined and he coarse, you talented and he simple?

In the day of a future Judgment, these very considerations may make it more tolerable for him than for you.

In concluding these little incidents of lawful trade, we must beg the world not to think that American legislators are entirely destitute of humanity, as might, perhaps, be unfairly inferred from the great efforts made in our national body to protect and perpetuate this species of traffic.

Who does not know how our great men are outdoing themselves, in declaiming against the *foreign* slave-trade. There are a perfect host of Clarksons and Wilber-forces risen up among us on that subject, most edifying to hear and behold. Trading negroes from Africa, dear reader, is so horrid! It is not to be thought of! But trading them from Kentucky,—that's quite another thing!

Edgar Rice Burroughs / *Tarzan of the Apes*
[*Tarzan Meets Jane; or Girl Goes Ape*]   1914

A one-time soldier, policeman, cowboy, Sears-Roebuck department store man-ager, advertising copywriter, gold miner, salesman, and business failure, Edgar Rice Burroughs (1875–1950) began one of the most successful writing careers in the history of popular literature with the publication of Tarzan of the Apes. *The first of a series of twenty-six novels,* Tarzan of the Apes *initially appeared in* The All Story *magazine for October 1912 and, when no publisher would touch it, was serialized in the* New York Evening World. *The newspaper serialization triggered a demand for the story in book form, and* Tarzan of the Apes *was finally published in 1914.*

Tarzan provided exactly the kind of material the new movie industry was looking for. The first Tarzan film was released in 1918, and the series remained popular until the 1960s. Burroughs' fantasies posed a challenge to "realism" that Holly-wood must have delighted in, as the following description of the technical efforts that went into producing Tarzan's barbaric yawp so perfectly demonstrates:

> *M-G-M spared no expense on the Tarzan yell. Miles of sound track of human, animal and instrument sounds were tested in collecting the ingredients of an unearthly howl. The cry of a mother camel robbed of her young was used until still more mournful sounds were found. A combination of five different sound tracks is used today for the Tarzan yell. There are: 1. Sound track of Weissmuller yelling amplified. 2. Track of hyena howl, run backward and volume diminished. 3. Soprano note sung by Lorraine Bridges, recording on sound track at reduced speed; then rerecorded at varying speeds to give a "flutter" in sound. 4. Growl of dog, recorded very faintly. 5. Raspy note of violin G-string, recorded very faintly. In the experimental stage the five sound tracks were played over five different loud speakers. From time to time the speed of each sound track was varied and the volume amplified or di-minished. When the orchestration of the yell was perfected, the five loudspeakers were played simultaneously and the blended sounds re-corded on the master sound track. By constant practice Weissmuller is now able to let loose an almost perfect imitation of the sound track.*

From the time Tarzan left the tribe of great anthropoids in which he had been raised, it was torn by continual strife and discord. Terkoz proved a cruel and capricious king, so that, one by one, many of the older and weaker apes, upon whom he was particularly prone to vent his brutish nature, took their families and sought the quiet and safety of the far interior.

But at last those who remained were driven to desperation by the continued truculence of Terkoz, and it so happened that one of them recalled the parting admonition of Tarzan:

"If you have a chief who is cruel, do not do as the other apes do, and attempt, any one of you, to pit yourself against him alone. But, instead, let two or three or four of you attack him together. Then, if you will do this, no chief will dare to be other than he should be, for four of you can kill any chief who may ever be over you."

And the ape who recalled this wise counsel repeated it to several of his fellows, so that when Terkoz returned to the tribe that day he found a warm reception awaiting him.

There were no formalities. As Terkoz reached the group, five huge, hairy beasts sprang upon him.

At heart he was an arrant coward, which is the way with bullies among apes as well as among men; so he did not remain to fight and die, but tore himself away from them as quickly as he could and fled into the sheltering boughs of the forest.

Two more attempts he made to rejoin the tribe, but on each occasion he was set upon and driven away. At last he gave it up, and turned, foaming with rage and hatred, into the jungle.

For several days he wandered aimlessly, nursing his spite and looking for some weak thing on which to vent his pent anger.

It was in this state of mind that the horrible, man-like beast, swinging from tree to tree, came suddenly upon two women in the jungle.

He was right above them when he discovered them. The first intimation Jane Porter had of his presence was when the great hairy body dropped to the earth beside her, and she saw the awful face and the snarling, hideous mouth thrust within a foot of her.

One piercing scream escaped her lips as the brute hand clutched her arm. Then she was dragged toward those awful fangs which yawned at her throat. But ere they touched that fair skin another mood claimed the anthropoid.

The tribe had kept his women. He must find others to replace them. This hairless white ape would be the first of his new household, and so he threw her roughly across his broad, hairy shoulders and leaped back into the trees, bearing Jane away.

Esmeralda's scream of terror had mingled once with that of Jane, and then, as was Esmeralda's manner under stress of emergency which required presence of mind, she swooned.

But Jane did not once lose consciousness. It is true that that awful face, pressing close to hers, and the stench of the foul breath beating upon her nostrils, paralyzed her with terror; but her brain was clear, and she comprehended all that transpired.

With what seemed to her marvelous rapidity the brute bore her through the forest, but still she did not cry out or struggle. The sudden advent of the ape had confused her to such an extent that she thought now that he was bearing her toward the beach.

For this reason she conserved her energies and her voice until she could see that they had approached near enough to the camp to attract the succor she craved.

She could not have known it, but she was being borne farther and farther into the impenetrable jungle.

The scream that had brought Clayton and the two older men stumbling through the undergrowth had led Tarzan of the Apes straight to where Esmeralda lay, but it was not Esmeralda in whom his interest centered, though pausing over her he saw that she was unhurt.

For a moment he scrutinized the ground below and the trees above, until the ape that was in him by virtue of training and environment, combined with the intelligence that was his by right of birth, told his wondrous woodcraft the whole story as plainly as though he had seen the thing happen with his own eyes.

And then he was gone again into the swaying trees, following the high-flung spoor which no other human eye could have detected, much less translated.

At boughs' ends, where the anthropoid swings from one tree to another, there is most to mark the trail, but least to point the direction of the quarry; for there the pressure is downward always, toward the small end of the branch, whether the ape be leaving or entering a tree. Nearer the center of the tree, where the signs of passage are fainter, the direction is plainly marked.

Here, on this branch, a caterpillar has been crushed by the fugitive's great foot, and Tarzan knows instinctively where that same foot would touch in the next stride. Here he looks to find a tiny particle of the demolished larva, ofttimes not more than a speck of moisture.

Again, a minute bit of bark has been upturned by the scraping hand, and the direction of the break indicates the direction of the passage. Or some great limb, or the stem of the tree itself has been brushed by the hairy body, and a tiny shred of hair tells him by the direction from which it is wedged beneath the bark that he is on the right trail.

Nor does he need to check his speed to catch these seemingly faint records of the fleeing beast.

To Tarzan they stand out boldly against all the myriad other scars and bruises and signs upon the leafy way. But strongest of all is the scent, for Tarzan is pursuing up the wind, and his trained nostrils are as sensitive as a hound's.

There are those who believe that the lower orders are specially endowed by nature with better olfactory nerves than man, but it is merely a matter of development.

Man's survival does not hinge so greatly upon the perfection of his senses. His power to reason has relieved them of many of their duties, and so they have, to some extent, atrophied, as have the muscles which move the ears and scalp, merely from disuse.

The muscles are there, about the ears and beneath the scalp, and so are the nerves which transmit sensations to the brain, but they are under-developed because they are not needed.

Not so with Tarzan of the Apes. From early infancy his survival had depended upon acuteness of eyesight, hearing, smell, touch, and taste far more than upon the more slowly developed organ of reason.

The least developed of all in Tarzan was the sense of taste, for he could eat luscious fruits, or raw flesh, long buried with almost equal appreciation; but in that he differed but slightly from more civilized epicures.

Almost silently the ape-man sped on in the track of Terkoz and his prey, but the sound of his approach reached the ears of the fleeing beast and spurred it on to greater speed.

Three miles were covered before Tarzan overtook them, and then Terkoz, seeing that further flight was futile, dropped to the ground in a small open glade, that he might turn and fight for his prize or be free to escape unhampered if he saw that the pursuer was more than a match for him.

He still grasped Jane in one great arm as Tarzan bounded like a leopard into the arena which nature had provided for this primeval-like battle.

When Terkoz saw that it was Tarzan who pursued him, he jumped to the conclusion that this was Tarzan's woman, since they were of the same kind—white and hairless—and so he rejoiced at this opportunity for double revenge upon his hated enemy.

To Jane the strange apparition of this god-like man was as wine to sick nerves.

From the description which Clayton and her father and Mr. Philander had given her, she knew that it must be the same wonderful creature who had saved them, and she saw in him only a protector and a friend.

But as Terkoz pushed her roughly aside to meet Tarzan's charge, and she saw the great proportions of the ape and the mighty muscles and the fierce fangs, her heart quailed. How could any vanquish such a mighty antagonist?

Like two charging bulls they came together, and like two wolves sought each other's throat. Against the long canines of the ape was pitted the thin blade of the man's knife.

Jane—her lithe, young form flattened against the trunk of a great tree, her hands tight pressed against her rising and falling bosom, and her eyes wide with mingled horror, fascination, fear, and admiration—watched the primordial ape battle with the primeval man for possession of a woman—for her.

As the great muscles of the man's back and shoulders knotted beneath the tension of his efforts, and the huge biceps and forearm held at bay those mighty tusks, the veil of centuries of civilization and culture was swept from the blurred vision of the Baltimore girl.

When the long knife drank deep a dozen times of Terkoz' heart's blood, and the great carcass rolled lifeless upon the ground, it was a primeval woman who sprang forward with outstretched arms toward the primeval man who had fought for her and won her.

And Tarzan?

He did what no red-blooded man needs lessons in doing. He took his woman in his arms and smothered her upturned, panting lips with kisses.

For a moment Jane lay there with half-closed eyes. For a moment—the first in her young life—she knew the meaning of love.

But as suddenly as the veil had been withdrawn it dropped again, and an outraged conscience suffused her face with its scarlet mantle, and a mortified woman thrust Tarzan of the Apes from her and buried her face in her hands.

Tarzan had been surprised when he had found the girl he had learned to love after a vague and abstract manner a willing prisoner in his arms. Now he was surprised that she repulsed him.

He came close to her once more and took hold of her arm. She turned upon him like a tigress, striking his great breast with her tiny hands.

Tarzan could not understand it.

A moment ago and it had been his intention to hasten Jane back to her people, but that little moment was lost now in the dim and distant past of things which were but can never be again, and with it the good intention had gone to join the impossible.

Since then Tarzan of the Apes had felt a warm, lithe form close pressed to his. Hot, sweet breath against his cheek and mouth had fanned a new flame to life within his breast, and perfect lips had clung to his in burning kisses that had seared a deep brand into his soul—a brand which marked a new Tarzan.

Again he laid his hand upon her arm. Again she repulsed him. And then Tarzan of the Apes did just what his first ancestor would have done.

He took his woman in his arms and carried her into the jungle. . . .

When Jane realized that she was being borne away a captive by the strange forest creature who had rescued her from the clutches of the ape she struggled desperately to escape, but the strong arms that held her as easily as though she had been but a day-old babe only pressed a little more tightly.

So presently she gave up the futile effort and lay quietly, looking through half-closed lids at the face of the man who strode easily through the tangled undergrowth with her.

The face above her was one of extraordinary beauty.

A perfect type of the strongly masculine, unmarred by dissipation, or brutal or degrading passions. For, though Tarzan of the Apes was a killer of men and of beasts, he killed as the hunter kills, dispassionately, except on those rare occasions when he had killed for hate—though not the brooding, malevolent hate which marks the features of its own with hideous lines.

When Tarzan killed he more often smiled than scowled, and smiles are the foundation of beauty.

One thing the girl had noticed particularly when she had seen Tarzan rushing upon Terkoz—the vivid scarlet band upon his forehead, from above the left eye to the scalp; but now as she scanned his features she noticed that it was gone, and only a thin white line marked the spot where it had been.

As she lay more quietly in his arms Tarzan slightly relaxed his grip upon her.

Once he looked down into her eyes and smiled, and the girl had to close her own to shut out the vision of that handsome, winning face.

Presently Tarzan took to the trees, and Jane, wondering that she felt no fear, began to realize that in many respects she had never felt more secure in her whole life than now as she lay in the arms of this strong, wild creature, being borne, God alone knew where or to what fate, deeper and deeper into the savage fastness of the untamed forest.

When, with closed eyes, she commenced to speculate upon the future, and terrifying fears were conjured by a vivid imagination, she had but to raise her lids and look upon that noble face so close to hers to dissipate the last remnant of apprehension.

No, he could never harm her; of that she was convinced when she translated the fine features and the frank, brave eyes above her into the chivalry which they proclaimed.

On and on they went through what seemed to Jane a solid mass of verdure, yet ever there appeared to open before this forest god a passage, as by magic, which closed behind them as they passed.

Scarce a branch scraped against her, yet above and below, before and behind, the view presented naught but a solid mass of inextricably interwoven branches and creepers.

As Tarzan moved steadily onward his mind was occupied with many strange and new thoughts. Here was a problem the like of which he had never encountered, and he felt rather than reasoned that he must meet it as a man and not as an ape.

The free movement through the middle terrace, which was the route he had followed for the most part, had helped to cool the ardor of the first fierce passion of his new found love.

Now he discovered himself speculating upon the fate which would have fallen to the girl had he not rescued her from Terkoz.

He knew why the ape had not killed her, and he commenced to compare his intentions with those of Terkoz.

True, it was the order of the jungle for the male to take his mate by force; but could Tarzan be guided by the laws of the beasts? Was not Tarzan a Man? But what did men do? He was puzzled; for he did not know.

He wished that he might ask the girl, and then it came to him that she had already answered him in the futile struggle she had made to escape and to repulse him.

But now they had come to their destination, and Tarzan of the Apes with Jane in his strong arms, swung lightly to the turf of the arena where the great apes held their councils and danced the wild orgy of the Dum-Dum.

Though they had come many miles, it was still but midafternoon, and the amphitheater was bathed in the half light which filtered through the maze of encircling foliage.

The green turf looked soft and cool and inviting. The myriad noises of the jungle seemed far distant and hushed to a mere echo of blurred sounds, rising and falling like the surf upon a remote shore.

A feeling of dreamy peacefulness stole over Jane as she sank down upon the grass where Tarzan had placed her, and as she looked up at his great figure towering above her, there was added a strange sense of perfect security.

As she watched him from beneath half-closed lids, Tarzan crossed the little circular clearing toward the trees upon the further side. She noted the graceful majesty of his carriage, the perfect symmetry of his magnificent figure and the poise of his well-shaped head upon his broad shoulders.

What a perfect creature! There could be naught of cruelty or baseness beneath that godlike exterior. Never, she thought had such a man strode the earth since God created the first in his own image.

With a bound Tarzan sprang into the trees and disappeared. Jane wondered where he had gone. Had he left her there to her fate in the lonely jungle?

She glanced nervously about. Every vine and bush seemed but the lurking-place of some huge and horrible beast waiting to bury gleaming fangs into her soft flesh. Every sound she magnified into the stealthy creeping of a sinuous and malignant body.

How different now that he had left her!

For a few minutes that seemed hours to the frightened girl, she sat with tense nerves waiting for the spring of the crouching thing that was to end her misery of apprehension.

She almost prayed for the cruel teeth that would give her unconsciousness and surcease from the agony of fear.

She heard a sudden, slight sound behind her. With a cry she sprang to her feet and turned to face her end.

There stood Tarzan, his arms filled with ripe and luscious fruit.

Jane reeled and would have fallen, had not Tarzan, dropping his burden, caught her in his arms. She did not lose consciousness, but she clung tightly to him, shuddering and trembling like a frightened deer.

Tarzan of the Apes stroked her soft hair and tried to comfort and quiet her as Kala had him, when, as a little ape, he had been frightened by Sabor, the lioness, or Histah, the snake.

Once he pressed his lips lightly upon her forehead, and she did not move, but closed her eyes and sighed.

She could not analyze her feelings, nor did she wish to attempt it. She was satisfied to feel the safety of those strong arms, and to leave her future to fate; for the last few hours had taught her to trust this strange wild creature of the forest as she would have trusted but few of the men of her acquaintance.

As she thought of the strangeness of it, there commenced to dawn upon her the realization that she had, possibly, learned something else which she had never really known before—love. She wondered and then she smiled.

And still smiling, she pushed Tarzan gently away; and looking at him with a half-smiling, half-quizzical expression that made her face wholly entrancing, she pointed to the fruit upon the ground, and seated herself upon the edge of the earthen drum of the anthropoids, for hunger was asserting itself.

Tarzan quickly gathered up the fruit, and, bringing it, laid it at her feet; and then he, too, sat upon the drum beside her, and with his knife opened and prepared the various fruits for her meal.

Together and in silence they ate, occasionally stealing sly glances at one another, until finally Jane broke into a merry laugh in which Tarzan joined.

"I wish you spoke English," said the girl.

Tarzan shook his head, and an expression of wistful and pathetic longing sobered his laughing eyes.

Then Jane tried speaking to him in French, and then in German; but she had to laugh at her own blundering attempt at the latter tongue.

"Anyway," she said to him in English, "you understand my German as well as they did in Berlin."

Tarzan had long since reached a decision as to what his future procedure should be. He had had time to recollect all that he had read of the ways of men and women in the books at the cabin. He would act as he imagined the men in the books would have acted were they in his place.

Again he rose and went into the trees, but first he tried to explain by means of signs that he would return shortly, and he did so well that Jane understood and was not afraid when he had gone.

Only a feeling of loneliness came over her and she watched the point where he had disappeared, with longing eyes, awaiting his return. As before, she was appraised of his presence by a soft sound behind her, and turned to see him coming across the turf with a great armful of branches.

Then he went back again into the jungle and in a few minutes reappeared with a quantity of soft grasses and ferns. Two more trips he made until he had quite a pile of material at hand.

Then he spread the ferns and grasses upon the ground in a soft flat bed, and above it leaned many branches together so that they met a few feet over its center. Upon these he spread layers of huge leaves of the great elephant's ear, and with more branches and more leaves he closed one end of the little shelter he had built.

Then they sat down together again upon the edge of the drum and tried to talk by signs.

The magnificent diamond locket which hung about Tarzan's neck, had been a source of much wonderment to Jane. She pointed to it now, and Tarzan removed it and handed the pretty bauble to her.

She saw that it was the work of a skilled artisan and that the diamonds were of great brilliancy and superbly set, but the cutting of them denoted that they were of a former day.

She noticed too that the locket opened, and, pressing the hidden clasp, she saw the two halves spring apart to reveal in either section an ivory miniature.

One was of a beautiful woman and the other might have been a likeness of the man who sat beside her, except for a subtle difference of expression that was scarcely definable.

She looked up at Tarzan to find him leaning toward her gazing on the miniatures with an expression of astonishment. He reached out his hand for the locket and took it away from her, examining the likenesses within with unmistakable signs of surprise and new interest. His manner clearly denoted that he had never before seen them, nor imagined that the locket opened.

This fact caused Jane to indulge in further speculation, and it taxed her imagination to picture how this beautiful ornament came into the possession of a wild and savage creature of the unexplored jungles of Africa.

Still more wonderful was how it contained the likeness of one who might be a brother, or, more likely, the father of this woodland demi-god who was even ignorant of the fact that the locket opened.

Tarzan was still gazing with fixity at the two faces. Presently he removed the quiver from his shoulder, and emptying the arrows upon the ground reached into the bottom of the bag-like receptacle and drew forth a flat object wrapped in many soft leaves and tied with bits of long grass.

Carefully he unwrapped it, removing layer after layer of leaves until at length he held a photograph in his hand.

Pointing to the miniature of the man within the locket he handed the photograph to Jane, holding the open locket beside it.

The photograph only served to puzzle the girl still more, for it was evidently another likeness of the same man whose picture rested in the locket beside that of the beautiful young woman.

Tarzan was looking at her with an expression of puzzled bewilderment in his eyes as she glanced up at him. He seemed to be framing a question with his lips.

The girl pointed to the photograph and then to the miniature and then to him, as though to indicate that she thought the likenesses were of him, but he only shook his head, and then shrugging his great shoulders, he took the photograph from her and having carefully rewrapped it, placed it again in the bottom of his quiver.

For a few moments he sat in silence, his eyes bent upon the ground, while Jane held the little locket in her hand, turning it over and over in an endeavor to find some further clue that might lead to the identity of its original owner.

At length a simple explanation occurred to her.

The locket had belonged to Lord Greystoke, and the likenesses were of himself and Lady Alice.

This wild creature had simply found it in the cabin by the beach. How stupid of her not to have thought of that solution before.

But to account for the strange likeness between Lord Greystoke and this forest god—that was quite beyond her, and it is not strange that she could not imagine that this naked savage was indeed an English nobleman.

At length Tarzan looked up to watch the girl as she examined the locket. He could not fathom the meaning of the faces within, but he could read the interest and fascination upon the face of the live young creature by his side.

She noticed that he was watching her and thinking that he wished his ornament again she held it out to him. He took it from her and taking the chain in his two hands he placed it about her neck, smiling at her expression of surprise at his unexpected gift.

Jane shook her head vehemently and would have removed the golden links from about her throat, but Tarzan would not let her. Taking her hands in his, when she insisted upon it, he held them tightly to prevent her.

At last she desisted and with a little laugh raised the locket to her lips.

Tarzan did not know precisely what she meant, but he guessed correctly that it was her way of acknowledging the gift, and so he rose, and taking the locket in his hand, stooped gravely like some courtier of old, and pressed his lips upon it where hers had rested.

It was a stately and gallant little compliment performed with the grace and dignity of utter unconsciousness of self. It was the hall-mark of his aristocratic birth, the natural out-cropping of many generations of fine breeding, an hereditary instinct of graciousness which a lifetime of uncouth and savage training and environment could not eradicate.

It was growing dark now, and so they ate again of the fruit which was both food and drink for them; then Tarzan rose, and leading Jane to the little bower he had erected, motioned her to go within.

For the first time in hours a feeling of fear swept over her, and Tarzan felt her draw away as though shrinking from him.

Contact with this girl for half a day had left a very different Tarzan from the one on whom the morning's sun had risen.

Now, in every fiber of his being, heredity spoke louder than training.

He had not in one swift transition become a polished gentleman from a savage ape-man, but at last the instincts of the former predominated, and over all was the desire to please the woman he loved, and to appear well in her eyes.

So Tarzan of the Apes did the only thing he knew to assure Jane of her safety. He removed his hunting knife from its sheath and handed it to her hilt first, again motioning her into the bower.

The girl understood, and taking the long knife she entered and lay down upon the soft grasses while Tarzan of the Apes stretched himself upon the ground across the entrance.

And thus the rising sun found them in the morning.

When Jane awoke, she did not at first recall the strange events of the preceding day, and so she wondered at her odd surroundings—the little leafy bower, the soft grasses of her bed, the unfamiliar prospect from the opening at her feet.

Slowly the circumstances of her position crept one by one into her mind. And then a great wonderment arose in her heart—a mighty wave of thankfulness and gratitude that though she had been in such terrible danger, yet she was unharmed.

She moved to the entrance of the shelter to look for Tarzan. He was gone; but this time no fear assailed her for she knew that he would return.

In the grass at the entrance to her bower she saw the imprint of his body where he had lain all night to guard her. She knew that the fact that he had been there was all that had permitted her to sleep in such peaceful security.

With him near, who could entertain fear? She wondered if there was another man on earth with whom a girl could feel so safe in the heart of this savage African jungle. Even the lions and panthers had no fears for her now.

She looked up to see his lithe form drop softly from a near-by tree. As he caught her eyes upon him his face lighted with that frank and radiant smile that had won her confidence the day before.

As he approached her Jane's heart beat faster and her eyes brightened as they had never done before at the approach of any man.

He had again been gathering fruit and this he laid at the entrance of her bower. Once more they sat down together to eat.

Jane commenced to wonder what his plans were. Would he take her back to the beach or would he keep her here? Suddenly she realized that the matter did not seem to give her much concern. Could it be that she did not care!

She began to comprehend, also, that she was entirely contented sitting here by the side of this smiling giant eating delicious fruit in a sylvan paradise far within the remote depths of an African jungle—that she was contented and very happy.

She could not understand it. Her reason told her that she should be torn by wild anxieties, weighted by dread fears, cast down by gloomy forebodings; but instead, her heart was singing and she was smiling into the answering face of the man beside her.

When they had finished their breakfast Tarzan went to her bower and recovered his knife. The girl had entirely forgotten it. She realized that it was because she had forgotten the fear that prompted her to accept it.

Motioning her to follow, Tarzan walked toward the trees at the edge of the arena, and taking her in one strong arm swung to the branches above.

The girl knew that he was taking her back to her people, and she could not understand the sudden feeling of loneliness and sorrow which crept over her.

For hours they swung slowly along.

Tarzan of the Apes did not hurry. He tried to draw out the sweet pleasure of that journey with those dear arms about his neck as long as possible, and so he went far south of the direct route to the beach.

Several times they halted for brief rests, which Tarzan did not need, and at noon they stopped for an hour at a little brook, where they quenched their thirst, and ate.

So it was nearly sunset when they came to the clearing, and Tarzan, dropping to the ground beside a great tree, parted the tall jungle grass and pointed out the little cabin to her.

She took him by the hand to lead him to it, that she might tell her father that this man had saved her from death and worse than death, that he had watched over her as carefully as a mother might have done.

But again the timidity of the wild thing in the face of human habitation swept over Tarzan of the Apes. He drew back, shaking his head.

The girl came close to him, looking up with pleading eyes. Somehow she could not bear the thought of his going back into the terrible jungle alone.

Still he shook his head, and finally he drew her to him very gently and stooped to kiss her, but first he looked into her eyes and waited to learn if she were pleased, or if she would repulse him.

Just an instant the girl hesitated, and then she realized the truth, and throwing her arms about his neck she drew his face to hers and kissed him—unashamed.

"I love you—I love you," she murmured.

From far in the distance came the faint sound of many guns. Tarzan and Jane raised their heads.

From the cabin came Mr. Philander and Esmeralda.

From where Tarzan and the girl stood they could not see the two vessels lying at anchor in the harbor.

Tarzan pointed toward the sounds, touched his breast and pointed again. She understood. He was going, and something told her that it was because he thought her people were in danger.

Again he kissed her.

"Come back to me," she whispered. "I shall wait for you—always."

Dale Carnegie / *How To Win Friends and Influence People* 1936

One of the most successful nonfiction books in the history of American publishing,
How To Win Friends and Influence People *was the culmination of Dale Carnegie's experiences in training thousands of business and professional people in the art of public speaking and in the techniques of "handling people." A compilation of popular psychology, etiquette rules, and after-dinner speech ancedotes,* How To Win Friends and Influence People *suggests that the fuzzy areas of social relationships and human discourse can be gotten through effectively and profitably with elocutionary acumen, a little shrewdness, and the application of proper procedures.*

FUNDAMENTAL TECHNIQUES IN HANDLING PEOPLE

CHAPTER 1: "IF YOU WANT TO GATHER HONEY, DON'T KICK OVER THE BEEHIVE"

On May 7, 1931, New York City witnessed the most sensational man-hunt the old town had ever known. After weeks of search, "Two Gun" Crowley—the killer, the gunman who didn't smoke or drink—was at bay, trapped in his sweetheart's apartment on West End Avenue.

One hundred and fifty policemen and detectives laid siege to his top-floor hideaway. Chopping holes in the roof, they tried to smoke out Crowley, the "cop killer," with tear gas. Then they mounted their machine guns on surrounding buildings, and for more than an hour one of New York's fine residential sections reverberated with the crack of pistol fire and the rat-tat-tat of machine guns. Crowley, crouching behind an overstuffed chair, fired incessantly at the police. Ten thousand excited people watched the battle. Nothing like it had ever been seen before on the sidewalks of New York.

When Crowley was captured, Police Commissioner Mulrooney declared that the two-gun desperado was one of the most dangerous criminals ever encountered in the history of New York. "He will kill," said the Commissioner, "at the drop of a feather."

But how did "Two Gun" Crowley regard himself? We know, because while the police were firing into his apartment, he wrote a letter addressed "To whom it may concern." And, as he wrote, the blood flowing from his wounds left a crimson trail on the paper. In this letter Crowley said: "Under my coat is a weary heart, but a kind one—one that would do nobody any harm."

A short time before this, Crowley had been having a necking party on a country road out on Long Island. Suddenly a policeman walked up to the parked car and said: "Let me see your license."

Without saying a word, Crowley drew his gun, and cut the policeman down with a shower of lead. As the dying officer fell, Crowley leaped out of the car, grabbed the officer's revolver, and fired another bullet into the prostrate body. And that was the killer who said: "Under my coat is a weary heart, but a kind one—one that would do nobody any harm."

Crowley was sentenced to the electric chair. When he arrived at the death house at Sing Sing, did he say, "This is what I get for killing people?" No, he said: "This is what I get for defending myself."

The point of the story is this: "Two Gun" Crowley didn't blame himself for anything.

Is that an unusual attitude among criminals? If you think so, listen to this:

"I have spent the best years of my life giving people the lighter pleasures, helping them have a good time, and all I get is abuse, the existence of a hunted man."

That's Al Capone speaking. Yes, America's erstwhile Public Enemy Number One—the most sinister gang leader who ever shot up Chicago. Capone doesn't condemn himself. He actually regards himself as a public benefactor—an unappreciated and misunderstood public benefactor.

And so did Dutch Schultz before he crumpled up under gangster bullets in Newark. Dutch Schultz, one of New York's most notorious rats, said in a newspaper interview that he was a public benefactor. And he believed it.

I have had some interesting correspondence with Warden Lawes of Sing Sing on this subject, and he declares that "few of the criminals in Sing Sing regard themselves as bad men. They are just as human as you and I. So they rationalize, they explain. They can tell you why they had to crack a safe or be quick on the trigger finger. Most of them attempt by a form of reasoning, fallacious or logical, to justify their anti-social acts even to themselves, consequently stoutly maintaining that they should never have been imprisoned at all."

If Al Capone, "Two Gun" Crowley, Dutch Schultz, the desperate men behind prison walls don't blame themselves for anything—what about the people with whom you and I come in contact?

The late John Wanamaker once confessed: "I learned thirty years ago that it is foolish to scold. I have enough trouble overcoming my own limitations without fretting over the fact that God has not seen fit to distribute evenly the gift of intelligence."

Wanamaker learned this lesson early; but I personally had to blunder through this old world for a third of a century before it even began to dawn upon me that ninety-nine times out of a hundred, no man ever criticizes himself for anything, no matter how wrong he may be.

Criticism is futile because it puts a man on the defensive, and usually makes him strive to justify himself. Criticism is dangerous, because it wounds a man's precious pride, hurts his sense of importance, and arouses his resentment.

The German army won't let a soldier file a complaint and make a criticism immediately after a thing has happened. He has to sleep on his grudge first and cool off. If he files his complaint immediately, he is punished. By the eternals, there ought to be a law like that in civil life too—a law for whining parents and nagging wives and scolding employers and the whole obnoxious parade of fault-finders.

You will find examples of the futility of criticism bristling on a thousand pages of history. Take, for example, the famous quarrel between Theodore Roosevelt and President Taft—a quarrel that split the Republican Party, put Woodrow Wilson in the White House, and wrote bold, luminous lines across the World War and altered the flow of history. Let's review the facts quickly: When Theodore Roosevelt stepped out of the White House in 1908, he made Taft president, and then went off to Africa to shoot lions. When he returned, he exploded. He denounced Taft for his conservatism, tried to secure the nomination for a third term himself, formed the Bull Moose Party, and all but demolished the G.O.P. In the election that followed,

William Howard Taft and the Republican Party carried only two states—Vermont and Utah. The most disastrous defeat the old party had ever known.

Theodore Roosevelt blamed Taft; but did President Taft blame himself? Of course not. With tears in his eyes, Taft said: "I don't see how I could have done any differently from what I have."

Who was to blame? Roosevelt or Taft? Frankly, I don't know, and I don't care. The point I am trying to make is that all of Theodore Roosevelt's criticism didn't persuade Taft that he was wrong. It merely made Taft strive to justify himself and to reiterate with tears in his eyes: "I don't see how I could have done any differently from what I have."

Or, take the Teapot Dome Oil scandal. Remember it? It kept the newspapers ringing with indignation for years. It rocked the nation! Nothing like it had ever happened before in American public life within the memory of living men. Here are the bare facts of the scandal: Albert Fall, Secretary of the Interior in Harding's cabinet, was entrusted with the leasing of government oil reserves at Elk Hill and Teapot Dome—oil reserves that had been set aside for the future use of the Navy. Did Secretary Fall permit competitive bidding? No sir. He handed the fat, juicy contract outright to his friend, Edward L. Doheny. And what did Doheny do? He gave Secretary Fall what he was pleased to call a "loan" of one hundred thousand dollars. Then, in a high-handed manner, Secretary Fall ordered United States Marines into the district to drive off competitors whose adjacent wells were sapping oil out of the Elk Hill reserves. These competitors, driven off their ground at the ends of guns and bayonets, rushed into court—and blew the lid off the hundred million dollar Teapot Dome scandal. A stench arose so vile that it ruined the Harding administration, nauseated an entire nation, threatened to wreck the Republican Party, and put Albert B. Fall behind prison bars.

Fall was condemned viciously—condemned as few men in public life have ever been. Did he repent? Never! Years later Herbert Hoover intimated in a public speech that President Harding's death had been due to mental anxiety and worry because a friend had betrayed him. When Mrs. Fall heard that, she sprang from her chair, she wept, she shook her fists at fate, and screamed: "What! Harding betrayed by Fall? No! My husband never betrayed anyone. This whole house full of gold would not tempt my husband to do wrong. He is the one who has been betrayed and led to the slaughter and crucified."

There you are; human nature in action, the wrong-doer blaming everybody but himself. We are all like that. So when you and I are tempted to criticize someone tomorrow, let's remember Al Capone, "Two Gun" Crowley, and Albert Fall. Let's realize that criticisms are like homing pigeons. They always return home. Let's realize that the person we are going to correct and condemn will probably justify himself, and condemn us in return; or, like the gentle Taft, he will say: "I don't see how I could have done any differently from what I have."

On Saturday morning, April 15, 1865, Abraham Lincoln lay dying in a hall bedroom of a cheap lodging house directly across the street from Ford's Theatre, where Booth had shot him. Lincoln's long body lay stretched diagonally across a sagging bed that was too short for him. A cheap reproduction of Rosa Bonheur's famous painting, "The Horse Fair," hung above the bed, and a dismal gas jet flickered yellow light.

As Lincoln lay dying, Secretary of War Stanton said, "There lies the most perfect ruler of men that the world has ever seen."

What was the secret of Lincoln's success in dealing with men? I studied the life of Abraham Lincoln for ten years, and devoted all of three years to writing and rewriting a book entitled *Lincoln the Unknown*. I believe I have made as detailed and exhaustive a study of Lincoln's personality and home life as it is possible for any human being to make. I made a special study of Lincoln's method of dealing with men. Did he indulge in criticism? Oh, yes. As a young man in the Pigeon Creek Valley of Indiana, he not only criticized but he wrote letters and poems ridiculing people and dropped these letters on the country roads where they were sure to be found. One of these letters aroused resentments that burned for a lifetime.

Even after Lincoln had become a practicing lawyer in Springfield, Illinois, he attacked his opponents openly in letters published in the newspapers. But he did this just once too often.

In the autumn of 1842, he ridiculed a vain, pugnacious Irish politician by the name of James Shields. Lincoln lampooned him through an anonymous letter published in the *Springfield Journal*. The town roared with laughter. Shields, sensitive and proud, boiled with indignation. He found out who wrote the letter, leaped on his horse, started after Lincoln, and challenged him to fight a duel. Lincoln didn't want to fight. He was opposed to dueling; but he couldn't get out of it and save his honor. He was given the choice of weapons. Since he had very long arms, he chose cavalry broad swords, took lessons in sword fighting from a West Point graduate; and, on the appointed day, he and Shields met on a sand bar in the Mississippi River, prepared to fight to the death; but, at the last minute, their seconds interrupted and stopped the duel.

That was the most lurid personal incident in Lincoln's life. It taught him an invaluable lesson in the art of dealing with people. Never again did he write an insulting letter. Never again did he ridicule anyone. And from that time on, he almost never criticized anybody for anything.

Time after time, during the Civil War, Lincoln put a new general at the head of the Army of the Potomac, and each one in turn—McClellan, Pope, Burnside, Hooker, Meade—blundered tragically, and drove Lincoln to pacing the floor in despair. Half the nation savagely condemned these incompetent generals, but Lincoln, "with malice towards none, with charity for all," held his peace. One of his favorite quotations was "Judge not, that ye be not judged."

And when Mrs. Lincoln and others spoke harshly of the Southern people, Lincoln replied: "Don't criticize them; they are just what we would be under similar circumstances."

Yet, if any man ever had occasion to criticize, surely it was Lincoln. Let's take just one illustration:

The Battle of Gettysburg was fought during the first three days of July, 1863. During the night of July 4, Lee began to retreat southward while storm clouds deluged the country with rain. When Lee reached the Potomac with his defeated army, he found a swollen, impassable river in front of him, and a victorious Union army behind him. Lee was in a trap. He couldn't escape. Lincoln saw that. Here was a golden, heaven-sent opportunity—the opportunity to capture Lee's army and end the war immediately. So, with a surge of high hope, Lincoln ordered Meade not to call a council of war but to attack Lee immediately. Lincoln telegraphed his orders and then sent a special messenger to Meade demanding immediate action.

And what did General Meade do? He did the very opposite of what he was told to do. He called a council of war in direct violation of Lincoln's orders. He hesitated.

He procrastinated. He telegraphed all manner of excuses. He refused point blank to attack Lee. Finally the waters receded and Lee escaped over the Potomac with his forces.

Lincoln was furious. "What does this mean?" Lincoln cried to his son Robert. "Great God! What does this mean? We had them within our grasp, and had only to stretch forth our hands and they were ours; yet nothing that I could say or do could make the army move. Under the circumstances, almost any general could have defeated Lee. If I had gone up there, I could have whipped him myself."

In bitter disappointment, Lincoln sat down and wrote Meade this letter. And remember, at this period of his life he was extremely conservative and restrained in his phraseology. So this letter coming from Lincoln in 1863 was tantamount to the severest rebuke.

"My dear General,

"I do not believe you appreciate the magnitude of the misfortune involved in Lee's escape. He was within our easy grasp, and to have closed upon him would, in connection with our other late successes, have ended the war. As it is, the war will be prolonged indefinitely. If you could not safely attack Lee last Monday, how can you possibly do so south of the river, when you can take with you very few—no more than two-thirds of the force you then had in hand? It would be unreasonable to expect and I do not expect that you can now effect much. Your golden opportunity is gone, and I am distressed immeasurably because of it."

What do you suppose Meade did when he read that letter?

Meade never saw that letter. Lincoln never mailed it. It was found among Lincoln's papers after his death.

My guess is—and this is only a guess—that after writing that letter, Lincoln looked out of the window and said to himself, "Just a minute. Maybe I ought not to be so hasty. It is easy enough for me to sit here in the quiet of the White House and order Meade to attack; but if I had been up at Gettysburg, and if I had seen as much blood as Meade has seen during the last week, and if my ears had been pierced with the screams and shrieks of the wounded and dying, maybe I wouldn't be so anxious to attack either. If I had Meade's timid temperament, perhaps I would have done just what he has done. Anyhow, it is water under the bridge now. If I send this letter, it will relieve my feelings but it will make Meade try to justify himself. It will make him condemn me. It will arouse hard feelings, impair all his further usefulness as a commander, and perhaps force him to resign from the army."

So, as I have already said, Lincoln put the letter aside, for he had learned by bitter experience that sharp criticisms and rebukes almost invariably end in futility.

Theodore Roosevelt said that when he, as President, was confronted with some perplexing problem, he used to lean back and look up at a large painting of Lincoln that hung above his desk in the White House and ask himself, "What would Lincoln do if he were in my shoes? How would he solve this problem?"

The next time we are tempted to give somebody "hail Columbia," let's pull a five-dollar bill out of our pocket, look at Lincoln's picture on the bill, and ask, "How would Lincoln handle this problem if he had it?"

Do you know someone you would like to change and regulate and improve? Good! That is fine. I am all in favor of it. But why not begin on yourself? From a purely selfish standpoint, that is a lot more profitable than trying to improve others—yes, and a lot less dangerous.

"When a man's fight begins within himself," said Browning, "he is worth something." It will probably take from now until Christmas to perfect yourself. You can then have a nice long rest over the holidays and devote the New Year to regulating and criticizing other people.

But perfect yourself first.

"Don't complain about the snow on your neighbor's roof," said Confucius, "when your own doorstep is unclean."

When I was still young and trying hard to impress people, I wrote a foolish letter to Richard Harding Davis, an author who once loomed large on the literary horizon of America. I was preparing a magazine article about authors; and I asked Davis to tell me about his method of work. A few weeks earlier, I had received a letter from someone with this notation at the bottom: "Dictated but not read." I was quite impressed. I felt the writer must be very big and busy and important. I wasn't the slightest bit busy; but I was eager to make an impression on Richard Harding Davis so I ended my short note with the words: "Dictated but not read."

He never troubled to answer the letter. He simply returned it to me with this scribbled across the bottom: "Your bad manners are exceeded only by your bad manners." True, I had blundered, and perhaps I deserved his rebuke. But, being human, I resented it. I resented it so sharply that when I read of the death of Richard Harding Davis ten years later, the one thought that still persisted in my mind—I am ashamed to admit—was the hurt he had given me.

If you and I want to stir up a resentment tomorrow that may rankle across the decades and endure until death, just let us indulge in a little stinging criticism—no matter how certain we are that it is justified.

When dealing with people, let us remember we are not dealing with creatures of logic. We are dealing with creatures of emotion, creatures bristling with prejudices and motivated by pride and vanity.

And criticism is a dangerous spark—a spark that is liable to cause an explosion in the powder magazine of pride—an explosion that sometimes hastens death. For example, General Leonard Wood was criticized and not allowed to go with the army to France. That blow to his pride probably shortened his life.

Bitter criticism caused the sensitive Thomas Hardy, one of the finest novelists that ever enriched English literature, to give up the writing of fiction forever. Criticism drove Thomas Chatterton, the English poet, to suicide.

Benjamin Franklin, tactless in his youth, became so diplomatic, so adroit at handling people that he was made American Ambassador to France. The secret of his success? "I will speak ill of no man," he said, ". . . and speak all the good I know of everybody."

Any fool can criticize, condemn, and complain—and most fools do.

But it takes character and self-control to be understanding and forgiving.

"A great man shows his greatness," said Carlyle, "by the way he treats little men."

Instead of condemning people, let's try to understand them. Let's try to figure out why they do what they do. That's a lot more profitable and intriguing than criticism; and it breeds sympathy, tolerance, and kindness. "To know all is to forgive all."

As Dr. Johnson said: "God Himself, sir, does not propose to judge man until the end of his days."

Why should you and I?

DISCUSSION QUESTIONS

1. Discuss whether Dale Carnegie's prose style is an implementation of his contention that "When dealing with people, let us remember we are not dealing with creatures of logic. We are dealing with creatures of emotion, creatures bristling with prejudices and motivated by pride and vanity." How does Carnegie try to convince his audience of the benefits gained by refraining from personal criticism?

2. Compare the sense of an audience implicit in *How To Win Friends and Influence People* with the audience imagined for Funk and Lewis' *Thirty Days to a More Powerful Vocabulary*. What characteristics are common to the audiences anticipated by these writers? What distinctions can you make between these audiences? Show how each writer's particular way of talking is indicative of the reader he imagines for his prose. How does the fact that these writers achieved a great deal of success affect the voices they adopt when addressing their readers?

Wilfred Funk and Norman Lewis / *Thirty Days to a More Powerful Vocabulary*   1942

Written in 1942 by Wilfred Funk, lexicographer, publisher, and author, and Norman Lewis, instructor in English at the City College of New York and New York University, Thirty Days to a More Powerful Vocabulary, *has been one of the most widely used "how-to-do-it" books published in this country. As an introductory "pep talk," "Give Us Fifteen Minutes A Day" started millions of students and adults off on a self-improvement regimen that promised nothing less than success and personal fulfillment when the exercises were completed.*

FIRST DAY: GIVE US 15 MINUTES A DAY

Your boss has a bigger vocabulary than you have.

That's one good reason why he's your boss.

This discovery has been made in the word laboratories of the world. Not by theoretical English professors, but by practical, hard-headed scholars who have been searching for the secrets of success.

After a host of experiments and years of testing they have found out:

That if your vocabulary is limited your chances of success are limited.

That one of the easiest and quickest ways to get ahead is by consciously building up your knowledge of words.

That the vocabulary of the average person almost stops growing by the middle twenties.

And that from then on it is necessary to have an intelligent plan if progress is to be made. No haphazard hit-or-miss methods will do.

It has long since been satisfactorily established that a high executive does not have a large vocabulary merely because of the opportunities of his position. That would be putting the cart before the horse. Quite the reverse is true. His skill in words was a tremendous help in getting him his job.

Dr. Johnson O'Connor of the Human Engineering Laboratory of Boston and of the Stevens Institute of Technology in Hoboken, New Jersey, gave a vocabulary test to 100 young men who were studying to be industrial executives.

Five years later those who had passed in the upper ten per cent *all,* without exception, had executive positions, while *not a single young man of the lower twenty-five per cent had become an executive.*

You see, there are certain factors in success that can be measured as scientifically as the contents of a test-tube, and it has been discovered that the most common characteristic of outstanding success is "an extensive knowledge of the exact meaning of English words."

The extent of your vocabulary indicates the degree of your intelligence. Your brain power will increase as you learn to know more words. Here's the proof.

Two classes in a high school were selected for an experiment. Their ages and their environment were the same. Each class represented an identical cross-section of the community. One, the control class, took the normal courses. The other class was given special vocabulary training. At the end of the period the marks of the latter class surpassed those of the control group, not only in English, but in every subject, including mathematics and the sciences.

Similarly it has been found by Professor Lewis M. Terman, of Stanford University, that a vocabulary test is as accurate a measure of intelligence as any three units of the standard and accepted Stanford-Binet I. Q. tests.

The study of words is not merely something that has to do with literature. Words are your tools of thought. *You can't even think at all without them.* Try it. If you are planning to go down town this afternoon you will find that you are saying to yourself: "I think I will go down town this afternoon." You can't make such a simple decision as this without using words.

Without words you could make no decisions and form no judgments whatsoever. A pianist may have the most beautiful tunes in his head, but if he had only five keys on his piano he would never get more than a fraction of these tunes out.

Your words are *your* keys for *your* thoughts. And the more words you have at your command the deeper, clearer and more accurate will be your thinking.

A command of English will not only improve the processes of your mind. It will give you assurance; build your self-confidence; lend color to your personality; increase your popularity. Your words are your personality. Your vocabulary is you.

Your words are all that we, your friends, have to know and judge you by. You have no other medium for telling us your thoughts—for convincing us, persuading us, giving us orders.

Words are explosive. Phrases are packed with TNT. A simple word can destroy a friendship, land a large order. The proper phrases in the mouths of clerks have quadrupled the sales of a department store. The wrong words used by a campaign orator have lost an election. For instance, on one occasion the four unfortunate words, "Rum, Romanism and Rebellion" used in a Republican campaign speech threw the Catholic vote and the presidential victory to Grover Cleveland. Wars are won by words. Soldiers fight for a phrase. "Make the world safe for Democracy." "All out for England." "V for Victory." The "Remember the Maine" of Spanish war days has now been changed to "Remember Pearl Harbor."

Words have changed the direction of history. Words can also change the direction of your life. They have often raised a man from mediocrity to success.

If you consciously increase your vocabulary you will unconsciously raise yourself to a more important station in life, and the new and higher position you have won will, in turn, give you a better opportunity for further enriching your vocabulary. It is a beautiful and successful cycle.

It is because of this intimate connection between words and life itself that we have organized this small volume in a new way. We have not given you mere lists of unrelated words to learn. We have grouped the words around various departments of your life.

This book is planned to enlist your active cooperation. The authors wish you to read it with a pencil in your hand, for you will often be asked to make certain notations, to write answers to particular questions. The more you use your pencil, the more deeply you will become involved, and the deeper your involvement the more this book will help you. We shall occasionally ask you to use your voice as well as your pencil—to say things out loud. You see, we really want you to keep up a running conversation with us.

It's fun. And it's so easy. And we've made it like a game. We have filled these pages with a collection of devices that we hope will be stimulating. Here are things to challenge you and your friends. Try these tests on your acquaintances. They will enjoy them and it may encourage them to wider explorations in this exciting field of speech. There are entertaining verbal calisthenics here, colorful facts about language, and many excursions among the words that keep our speech the rich, flexible, lively means of communication that it is.

Come to this book every day. Put the volume by your bedside, if you like. A short time spent on these pages before you turn the lights out each night is better than an irregular hour now and then. If you can find the time to learn only two or three words a day—we will still promise you that at the end of thirty days you will have found a new interest. Give us *fifteen minutes a day,* and we will guarantee, at the end of a month, when you have turned over the last page of this book, that your words and your reading and your conversation and your life will all have a new and deeper meaning for you.

For words can make you great!

Benjamin Spock / *The Common Sense Book of Baby Care*   1945

Pediatrician, psychiatrist, former columnist for Ladies' Home Journal *and* Redbook, *and Vietnam antiwar activist, Dr. Benjamin Spock became America's most influential authority on child care soon after the publication of* The Common Sense Book of Baby Care *in 1945. The book was meant to counter some of the absurd notions promulgated by Spock's predecessors, including Dr. John B. Watson who had asserted in his widely distributed text,* Psychological Care of Infant and Child *(1928): "Never, never kiss your child. Never hold it on your lap. Never rock its carriage." Spock's reassuring "common sense," evident in his Preface reprinted below, encourages a more relaxed approach to the difficulties of parenthood. Millions of Americans have been raised according to Spock's principles, the book having enjoyed greater total sales than any other work, except the Bible and Shakespeare's plays.*

TRUST YOURSELF

1. You know more than you think you do. Soon you're going to have a baby. Maybe you have him already. You're happy and excited, but if you haven't had much experience, you wonder whether you are going to know how to do a good job. Lately you have been listening more carefully to your friends and relatives when they talk about bringing up a child. You've begun to read articles by experts in the magazines and newspapers. After the baby is born, the doctor and nurses will begin to give you instructions, too. Sometimes it sounds like a very complicated business. You find out all the vitamins a baby needs and all the inoculations. One mother tells you that egg should be given early because of its iron, and another says that egg should be delayed to avoid allergy. You hear that a baby is easily spoiled by being picked up too much but also that a baby must be cuddled plenty; that fairy tales make children nervous, and that fairy tales are a wholesome outlet.

Don't take too seriously all that the neighbors say. Don't be overawed by what the experts say. Don't be afraid to trust your own common sense. Bringing up your child won't be a complicated job if you take it easy, trust your own instincts and follow the directions that your doctor gives you. We know for a fact that the natural loving care that kindly parents give their children is a hundred times more valuable than their knowing how to pin a diaper on just right or how to make a formula expertly. Every time you pick your baby up, even if you do it a little awkwardly at first, every time you change him, bathe him, feed him, smile at him, he's getting a feeling that he belongs to you and that you belong to him. Nobody else in the world, no matter how skillful, can give that to him.

It may surprise you to hear that the more people have studied different methods of bringing up children, the more they have come to the conclusion that what good mothers and fathers instinctively feel like doing for their babies is usually best, after all. Furthermore, all parents do their best job when they have a natural, easy confidence in themselves. Better to make a few mistakes from being natural than to do everything letter-perfect out of a feeling of worry.

Ogden Nash / Kindly Unhitch That Star, Buddy   1945

Few writers, especially in the twentieth century, have been able to earn a living exclusively by writing poetry. Ogden Nash is one who has. The Pocket Book of Ogden Nash *(1935) ranks among the top ten poetry bestsellers of the last eighty years and nearly every volume of his poetry from* Free Wheeling *(1931) to* Boy Is a Boy *(1960) have found highly receptive audiences.*

Nash (1902–71) is a master of what is usually termed "light verse"—poetry that is witty, humorous, often sophisticated, and not without a slight sting of satire. Nash brought to light verse an exceptionally playful imagination, one that enjoyed challenging the conventions of language and poetry without surrendering a stroke of technical virtuosity. Like the Depression film comedies that were popular just around the time his first volumes began to appear, Nash's verse succeeded in striking a fine balance between tough-talk and innocence, urbanity and absurdity.

The following poem, which takes its lead from Ralph Waldo Emerson's advice that we "hitch our wagon to a star," appeared in Many Long Years Ago *(1945). For two other poetic versions of this distinctively American theme see Emily Dickinson's "Success Is Counted Sweetest" and Robert Frost's "Provide, Provide" in Classics.*

I hardly suppose I know anybody who wouldn't rather be a success than a failure,
Just as I suppose every piece of crabgrass in the garden would much rather be an azalea,
And in celestial circles all the run-of-the-mill angels would rather be archangels or at least cherubim and seraphim,
And in the legal world all the little process-servers hope to grow up into great big bailiffim and sheriffim.
Indeed, everybody wants to be a wow,
But not everybody knows exactly how.
Some people think they will eventually wear diamonds instead of rhinestones
Only by everlastingly keeping their noses to their ghrine-stones,
And other people think they will be able to put in more time at Palm Beach and the Ritz
By not paying too much attention to attendance at the office but rather in being brilliant by starts and fits.
Some people after a full day's work sit up all night getting a college education by correspondence,
While others seem to think they'll get just as far by devoting their evenings to the study of the difference in temperament between brunettance and blondance.
In short, the world is filled with people trying to achieve success,
And half of them think they'll get it by saying No and half of them by saying Yes,
And if all the ones who say No said Yes, and vice versa, such is the fate of humanity that ninety-nine per cent of them still wouldn't be any better off than they were before,
Which perhaps is just as well because if everybody was a success nobody could be contemptuous of anybody else and everybody would start in all over again trying to be a bigger success than everybody else so they would have somebody to be contemptuous of and so on forevermore,
Because when people start hitching their wagons to a star,
That's the way they are.

Mickey Spillane / *I, the Jury*
[*Mike Hammer Plots Revenge*]   1947

Born in 1918 in Brooklyn, the son of an Irish bartender, Mickey Spillane grew up in what he calls a "very tough neighborhood in Elizabeth, New Jersey." He attended Kansas State College, worked summers as captain of lifeguards at Breezy Point, New York, and supplemented his income by writing comic books. In 1935, Spillane began selling stories to detective magazines, and after flying fighter mis-

sions in the Second World War, he worked as a trampoline artist for the Ringling Brothers Circus. Since his first novel, I, the Jury, *published in 1947, Spillane's books have had extraordinary sales. At one time seven of Mickey Spillane's novels were included in a list of the top ten best-selling fiction works of the last fifty years. Many of the novels have been turned into movies, a few with Spillane playing the role of Mike Hammer.*

CHAPTER ONE

I shook the rain from my hat and walked into the room. Nobody said a word. They stepped back politely and I could feel their eyes on me. Pat Chambers was standing by the door to the bedroom trying to steady Myrna. The girl's body was racking with dry sobs. I walked over and put my arms around her.

"Take it easy, kid," I told her. "Come on over here and lie down." I led her to a studio couch that was against the far wall and sat her down. She was in pretty bad shape. One of the uniformed cops put a pillow down for her and she stretched out.

Pat motioned me over to him and pointed to the bedroom. "In there, Mike," he said.

In there. The words hit me hard. In there was my best friend lying on the floor dead. The body. Now I could call it that. Yesterday it was Jack Williams, the guy that shared the same mud bed with me through two years of warfare in the stinking slime of the jungle. Jack, the guy who said he'd give his right arm for a friend and did when he stopped a bastard of a Jap from slitting me in two. He caught the bayonet in the biceps and they amputated his arm.

Pat didn't say a word. He let me uncover the body and feel the cold face. For the first time in my life I felt like crying. "Where did he get it, Pat?"

"In the stomach. Better not look at it. The killer carved the nose off a forty-five and gave it to him low."

I threw back the sheet anyway and a curse caught in my throat. Jack was in shorts, his one hand still clutching his belly in agony. The bullet went in clean, but where it came out left a hole big enough to cram a fist into.

Very gently I pulled the sheet back and stood up. It wasn't a complicated setup. A trail of blood led from the table beside the bed to where Jack's artificial arm lay. Under him the throw rug was ruffled and twisted. He had tried to drag himself along with his one arm, but never reached what he was after.

His police positive, still in the holster, was looped over the back of the chair. That was what he wanted. With a slug in his gut he never gave up.

I pointed to the rocker, overbalanced under the weight of the .38. "Did you move the chair, Pat?"

"No, why?"

"It doesn't belong there. Don't you see?"

Pat looked puzzled. "What are you getting at?"

"That chair was over there by the bed. I've been here often enough to remember that much. After the killer shot Jack, he pulled himself toward the chair. But the killer didn't leave after the shooting. He stood here and watched him grovel on the floor in agony. Jack was after that gun, but he never reached it. He could have if the killer didn't move it. The trigger-happy bastard must have stood by the door laughing while Jack tried to make his last play. He kept pulling the chair back, inch by inch, until Jack gave up. Tormenting a guy who's been through all sorts of hell.

Laughing. This was no ordinary murder, Pat. It's as cold-blooded and as deliberate as I ever saw one. I'm going to get the one that did this."

"You dealing yourself in, Mike?"

"I'm in. What did you expect?"

"You're going to have to go easy."

"Uh-uh. Fast, Pat. From now on it's a race. I want the killer for myself. We'll work together as usual, but in the homestretch, I'm going to pull the trigger."

"No, Mike, it can't be that way. You know it."

"Okay, Pat," I told him. "You have a job to do, but so have I. Jack was about the best friend I ever had. We lived together and fought together. And by Christ, I'm not letting the killer go through the tedious process of the law. You know what happens, damn it. They get the best lawyer there is and screw up the whole thing and wind up a hero! The dead can't speak for themselves. They can't tell what happened. How could Jack tell a jury what it was like to have his insides ripped out by a dumdum? Nobody in the box would know how it felt to be dying or have your own killer laugh in your face. One arm. Hell, what does that mean? So he has the Purple Heart. But did they ever try dragging themselves across a floor to a gun with that one arm, their insides filling up with blood, so goddamn mad to be shot they'd do anything to reach the killer. No, damn it. A jury is cold and impartial like they're supposed to be, while some snotty lawyer makes them pour tears as he tells how his client was insane at the moment or had to shoot in self-defense. Swell. The law is fine. But this time I'm the law and I'm not going to be cold and impartial. I'm going to remember all those things."

I reached out and grabbed the lapels of his coat. "And something more, Pat. I want you to hear every word I say. I want you to tell it to everyone you know. And when you tell it, tell it strong, because I mean every word of it. There are ten thousand mugs that hate me and you know it. They hate me because if they mess with me I shoot their damn heads off. I've done it and I'll do it again."

There was so much hate welled up inside me I was ready to blow up, but I turned and looked down at what was once Jack. Right then I felt like saying a prayer, but I was too mad.

"Jack, you're dead now. You can't hear me any more. Maybe you can. I hope so. I want you to hear what I'm about to say. You've known me a long time, Jack. My word is good just as long as I live. I'm going to get the louse that killed you. He won't sit in the chair. He won't hang. He will die exactly as you died, with a .45 slug in the gut, just a little below the belly button. No matter who it is, Jack, I'll get the one. Remember, no matter who it is, I promise."

When I looked up, Pat was staring at me strangely. He shook his head. I knew what he was thinking. "Mike, lay off. For God's sake don't go off half-cocked about this. I know you too well. You'll start shooting up anyone connected with this and get in a jam you'll never get out of."

"I'm over it now, Pat. Don't get excited. From now on I'm after one thing, the killer. You're a cop, Pat. You're tied down by rules and regulations. There's someone over you. I'm alone. I can slap someone in the puss and they can't do a damn thing. No one can kick me out of my job. Maybe there's nobody to put up a huge fuss if I get gunned down, but then I still have a private cop's license with the privilege to pack a rod, and they're afraid of me. I hate hard, Pat. When I latch on to the one behind this they're going to wish they hadn't started it. Some day, before long, I'm going to have my rod in my mitt and the killer in front of me. I'm going to watch the killer's face. I'm going to plunk one right in his gut, and when he's dying on the floor I may kick his teeth out.

"You couldn't do that. You have to follow the book because you're a Captain of Homicide. Maybe the killer will wind up in the chair. You'd be satisfied, but I wouldn't. It's too easy. That killer is going down like Jack did."

There was nothing more to say. I could see by the set of Pat's jaw that he wasn't going to try to talk me out of it. All he could do was to try to beat me to him and take it from there. We walked out of the room together. The coroner's men had arrived and were ready to carry the body away.

I didn't want Myrna to see that. I sat down on the couch beside her and let her sob on my shoulder. That way I managed to shield her from the sight of her fiancé being carted off in a wicker basket. She was a good kid. Four years ago, when Jack was on the force, he had grabbed her as she was about to do a Dutch over the Brooklyn Bridge. She was a wreck then. Dope had eaten her nerve ends raw. But he had taken her to his house and paid for a full treatment until she was normal. For the both of them it had been a love that blossomed into a beautiful thing. If it weren't for the war they would have been married long ago.

When Jack came back with one arm it had made no difference. He no longer was a cop, but his heart was with the force. She had loved him before and she still loved him. Jack wanted her to give up her job, but Myrna persuaded him to let her hold it until he really got settled. It was tough for a man with one arm to find employment, but he had many friends.

Before long he was part of the investigating staff of an insurance company. It had to be police work. For Jack there was nothing else. Then they were happy. Then they were going to be married. Now this.

Pat tapped me on the shoulder. "There's a car waiting downstairs to take her home."

I rose and took her by the hand. "Come on, kid. There's no more you can do. Let's go."

She didn't say a word, but stood up silently and let a cop steer her out the door. I turned to Pat. "Where do we start?" I asked him.

"Well, I'll give you as much as I know. See what you can add to it. You and Jack were great buddies. It might be that you can add something that will make some sense."

Inwardly I wondered. Jack was such a straight guy that he never made an enemy. Even while on the force. Since he'd gotten back, his work with the insurance company was pretty routine. But maybe an angle there, though.

"Jack threw a party last night," Pat went on. "Not much of an affair."

"I know," I cut in, "he called me and asked me over, but I was pretty well knocked out. I hit the sack early. Just a group of old friends he knew before the army."

"Yeah. We got their names from Myrna. The boys are checking on them now."

"Who found the body?" I asked.

"Myrna did. She and Jack were driving out to the country today to pick a building site for their cottage. She got here at eight A.M. or a little after. When Jack didn't answer, she got worried. His arm had been giving him trouble lately and she thought it might have been that. She called the super. He knew her and let her in. When she screamed the super came running back and called us. Right after I got the story about the party from her, she broke down completely. Then I called you."

"What time did the shooting occur?"

"The coroner places it about five hours before I got here. That would make it about three fifteen. When I get an autopsy report we may be able to narrow it down even further."

"Anyone hear a shot?"

"Nope. It probably was a silenced gun."

"Even with a muffler, a .45 makes a good-sized noise."

"I know, but there was a party going on down the hall. Not loud enough to cause complaints, but enough to cover up any racket that might have been made here."

"What about those that were here?" Pat reached in his pocket and pulled out a pad. He ripped a leaf loose and handed it to me.

"Here's a list Myrna gave me. She was the first to arrive. Got here at eight thirty last night. She acted as hostess, meeting the others at the door. The last one came about eleven. They spent the evening doing some light drinking and dancing, then left as a group about one."

I looked at the names Pat gave me. A few of them I knew well enough, while a couple of the others were people of whom Jack had spoken, but I had never met.

"Where did they go after the party, Pat?"

"They took two cars. The one Myrna went in belonged to Hal Kines. They drove straight up to Westchester, dropping Myrna off on the way. I haven't heard from any of the others yet."

Both of us were silent for a moment, then Pat asked, "What about a motive, Mike?"

I shook my head. "I don't see any yet. But I will. He wasn't killed for nothing. I'll bet this much, whatever it was, was big. There's a lot here that's screwy. You got anything?"

"Nothing more than I gave you, Mike. I was hoping you could supply some answers."

I grinned at him, but I wasn't trying to be funny. "Not yet. Not yet. They'll come though. And I'll relay them on to you, but by that time I'll be working on the next step."

"The cops aren't exactly dumb, you know. We can get our own answers."

"Not like I can. That's why you buzzed me so fast. You can figure things out as quickly as I can, but you haven't got the ways and means of doing the dirty work. That's where I come in. You'll be right behind me every inch of the way, but when the pinch comes I'll get shoved aside and you slap the cuffs on. That is, if you can shove me aside. I don't think you can."

"Okay, Mike, call it your own way. I want you in all right. But I want the killer, too. Don't forget that. I'll be trying to beat you to him. We have every scientific facility at our disposal and a lot of men to do the leg work. We're not short in brains, either," he reminded me.

"Don't worry, I don't underrate the cops. But cops can't break a guy's arm to make him talk, and they can't shove his teeth in with the muzzle of a .45 to remind him that you aren't fooling. I do my own leg work, and there are a lot of guys who will tell me what I want to know because they know what I'll do to them if they don't. My staff is strictly ex officio, but very practical."

That ended the conversation. We walked out into the hall where Pat put a patrolman on the door to make sure things stayed as they were. We took the self-operated elevator down four flights to the lobby and I waited while Pat gave a brief report to some reporters.

My car stood at the curb behind the squad car. I shook hands with Pat and climbed into my jalopy and headed for the Hackard Building, where I held down a two-room suite to use for operation.

CHAPTER TWO

The office was locked when I got there. I kicked on the door a few times and Velda clicked the lock back. When she saw who it was she said, "Oh, it's you."

"What do you mean—'Oh, it's you'! Surely you remember me, Mike Hammer, your boss."

"Poo! You haven't been here in so long I can't tell you from another bill collector." I closed the door and followed her into my sanctum sanctorum. She had million-dollar legs, that girl, and she didn't mind showing them off. For a secretary she was an awful distraction. She kept her coal-black hair long in a page-boy cut and wore tight-fitting dresses that made me think of the curves in the Pennsylvania Highway every time I looked at her. Don't get the idea that she was easy, though. I've seen her give a few punks the brush off the hard way. When it came to quick action she could whip off a shoe and crack a skull before you could bat an eye.

Not only that, but she had a private op's ticket and on occasions when she went out with me on a case, packed a flat .32 automatic—and she wasn't afraid to use it. In the three years she worked for me I never made a pass at her. Not that I didn't want to, but it would be striking too close to home.

Velda picked up her pad and sat down. I plunked myself in the old swivel chair, then swung around facing the window. Velda threw a thick packet on my desk.

"Here's all the information I could get on those that were at the party last night." I looked at her sharply.

"How did you know about Jack? Pat only called my home." Velda wrinkled that pretty face of hers up into a cute grin.

"You forget that I have an in with a few reporters. Tom Dugan from the *Chronicle* remembered that you and Jack had been good friends. He called here to see what he could get and wound up by giving me all the info he had—and I didn't have to sex him, either." She put that in as an afterthought. "Most of the gang at the party were listed in your files. Nothing sensational. I got a little data from Tom who had more personal dealings with a few of them. Mostly character studies and some society reports. Evidently they were people whom Jack had met in the past and liked. You've even spoken about several yourself."

I tore open the package and glanced at a sheaf of photos. "Who are these?" Velda looked over my shoulder and pointed them out.

"Top one is Hal Kines, a med student from a university upstate. He's about twenty-three, tall, and looks like a crew man. At least that's the way he cuts his hair." She flipped the page over. "These two are the Bellemy twins. Age, twenty-nine, unmarried. In the market for husbands. Live off the fatta the land with dough their father left them. A half interest in some textile mills someplace down South."

"Yeah," I cut in, "I know them. Good lookers, but not very bright. I met them at Jack's place once and again at a dinner party."

She pointed to the next one. A newspaper shot of a middle-aged guy with a broken nose. George Kalecki. I knew him pretty well. In the roaring twenties he was a bootlegger. He came out of the crash with a million dollars, paid up his income tax, and went society. He fooled a lot of people but he didn't fool me. He still had his finger in a lot of games just to keep in practice. Nothing you could pin on him though. He kept a staff of lawyers on their toes to keep him clean and they were doing a good job. "What about him?" I asked her.

"You know more than I do. Hal Kines is staying with him. They live about a mile above Myrna in Westchester." I nodded. I remembered Jack talking about him. He had met George through Hal. The kid had been a friend of George ever since the older man had met him through some mutual acquaintance. George was the guy that was putting him through college, but why, I wasn't sure.

The next shot was one of Myrna with a complete history of her that Jack had given me. Included was a medical record from the hospital when he had made her go cold turkey, which is dope-addict talk for an all-out cure. They cut them off from the stuff completely. It either kills them or cures them. In Myrna's case, she made it. But she made Jack promise that he would never try to get any information from her about where she got the stuff. The way he fell for the girl, he was ready to do anything she asked, and so far as he was concerned, the matter was completely dropped.

I flipped through the medical record. Name, Myrna Devlin. Attempted suicide while under the influence of heroin. Brought to emergency ward of General Hospital by Detective Jack Williams. Admitted 3-15-40. Treatment complete 9-21-40. No information available on patient's source of narcotics. Released into custody of Detective Jack Williams 9-30-40. Following this was a page of medical details which I skipped.

"Here's one you'll like, chum," Velda grinned at me. She pulled out a full-length photo of a gorgeous blonde. My heart jumped when I saw it. The picture was taken at a beach, and she stood there tall and languid-looking in a white bathing suit. Long solid legs. A little heavier than the movie experts consider good form, but the kind that make you drool to look at. Under the suit I could see the muscles of her stomach. Incredibly wide shoulders for a woman, framing breasts that jutted out, seeking freedom from the restraining fabric of the suit. Her hair looked white in the picture, but I could tell that it was a natural blonde. Lovely, lovely yellow hair. But her face was what got me. I thought Velda was a good looker, but this one was even lovelier. I felt like whistling.

"Who is she?"

"Maybe I shouldn't tell you. That leer on your face could get you into trouble, but it's all there. Name's Charlotte Manning. She's a female psychiatrist with offices on Park Avenue, and very successful. I understand she caters to a pretty ritzy clientele."

I glanced at the number and made up my mind that right here was something that made this business a pleasurable one. I didn't say that to Velda. Maybe I'm being conceited, but I've always had the impression that she had designs on me. Of course she never mentioned it, but whenever I showed up late in the office with lipstick on my shirt collar, I couldn't get two words out of her for a week.

I stacked the sheaf back on my desk and swung around in the chair. Velda was leaning forward ready to take notes. "Want to add anything, Mike?"

"Don't think so. At least not now. There's too much to think about first. Nothing seems to make sense."

"Well, what about motive? Could Jack have had any enemies that caught up with him?"

"Nope. None I know of. He was square. He always gave a guy a break if he deserved it. Then, too, he never was wrapped up in anything big."

"Did he own anything of any importance?"

"Not a thing. The place was completely untouched. He had a few hundred dollars in his wallet that was lying on the dresser. The killing was done by a sadist. He tried to reach his gun, but the killer pulled the chair it hung on back slowly, making him crawl after it with a slug in his gut, trying to keep his insides from falling out with his hand."

"Mike, please."

I said no more. I just sat there and glowered at the wall. Someday I'd trigger the bastard that shot Jack. In my time I've done it plenty of times. No sentiment. That went out with the first. After the war I've been almost anxious to get to some of the rats that make up the section of humanity that prey on people. People. How incredibly stupid they could be sometimes. A trial by law for a killer. A loophole in the phrasing that lets a killer crawl out. But in the end the people have their justice. They get it through guys like me once in a while. They crack down on society and I crack down on them. I shoot them like the mad dogs they are and society drags me to court to explain the whys and wherefores of the extermination. They investigate my past, check my fingerprints and throw a million questions my way. The papers make me look like a kill-crazy shamus, but they don't bear down too hard because Pat Chambers keeps them off my neck. Besides, I do my best to help the boys out and they know it. And I'm usually good for a story when I wind up a case.

Velda came back into the office with the afternoon edition of the sheets. The kill was spread all over the front page, followed by a four-column layout of what details were available. Velda was reading over my shoulder and I heard her gasp.

"Did you come in for a blasting! Look." She was pointing to the last paragraph. There was my tie-up with the case, but what she was referring to was the word-for-word statement that I had made to Jack. My promise. My word to a dead friend that I would kill this murderer as he had killed him. I rolled the paper into a ball and threw it viciously at the wall.

"The louse! I'll break his filthy neck for printing that. I meant what I said when I made that promise. It's sacred to me, and they make a joke out of it. Pat did that. And I thought he was a friend. Give me the phone."

Velda grabbed my arm. "Take it easy. Suppose he did. After all, Pat's still a cop. Maybe he saw a chance of throwing the killer your way. If the punk knows you're after him for keeps he's liable not to take it standing still and make a play for you. Then you'll have him."

"Thanks, kid," I told her, "but your mind's too clean. I think you got the first part right, but your guess on the last part smells. Pat doesn't want me to have any part of him because he knows the case is ended right there. If he can get the killer to me you can bet your grandmother's uplift bra that he'll have a tail on me all the way with someone ready to stop in when the shooting starts."

"I don't know about that, Mike. Pat knows you're too smart not to recognize when you're being tailed. I wouldn't think he'd do that."

"Oh, no? He isn't dumb by any means. I'll bet you a sandwich against a marriage license he's got a flatfoot downstairs covering every exit in the place ready to pick me up when I leave. Sure, I'll shake them, but it won't stop there. A couple of experts will take up where they leave off."

Velda's eyes were glowing like a couple of hot brands. "Are you serious about that? About the bet, I mean?"

I nodded. "Dead serious. Want to go downstairs with me and take a look?" She grinned and grabbed her coat. I pulled on my battered felt and we left the office, but not before I had taken a second glance at the office address of Charlotte Manning.

Pete, the elevator operator, gave me a toothy grin when we stepped into the car. "Evening, Mr. Hammer," he said.

I gave him an easy jab in the short ribs and said, "What's new with you?"

"Nothing much, 'cepting I don't get to sit down much on the job anymore." I had to grin. Velda had lost the bet already. That little piece of simple repartee between Pete and myself was a code system we had rigged up years ago. His answer meant that I was going to have company when I left the building. It cost me a fin a week but it was worth it. Pete could spot a flatfoot faster than I can. He should. He had been a pickpocket until a long stretch up the river gave him a turn of mind.

For a change I decided to use the front entrance. I looked around for my tail but there was none to be seen. For a split second my heart leaped into my throat. I was afraid Pete had gotten his signals crossed. Velda was a spotter, too, and the smile she was wearing as we crossed the empty lobby was a thing to see. She clamped onto my arm ready to march me to the nearest justice of the peace.

But when I went through the revolving doors her grin passed as fast as mine appeared. Our tail was walking in front of us. Velda said a word that nice girls don't usually use, and you see scratched in the cement by some evil-minded guttersnipe.

This one was smart. We never saw where he came from. He walked a lot faster than we did, swinging a newspaper from his hand against his leg. Probably, he spotted us through the windows behind the palm, then seeing what exit we were going to use, walked around the corner and came past us as we left. If we had gone the other way, undoubtedly there was another ready to pick us up.

But this one had forgotten to take his gun off his hip and stow it under his shoulder, and guns make a bump look the size of a pumpkin when you're used to looking for them.

When I reached the garage he was nowhere to be seen. There were a lot of doors he could have ducked behind. I didn't waste time looking for him. I backed the car out and Velda crawled in beside me. "Where to now?" she asked.

"The automat, where you're going to buy me a sandwich."

Grace Metalious / *Peyton Place*
[*Michael Rossi Comes to Peyton Place*]   1956

One of the greatest selling novels in American publishing history was written by a New Hampshire housewife with little formal education and no literary background or cultural advantages. Born in Manchester, New Hampshire, in 1924, Grace Marie Antoinette Jeanne d'Arc de Repentigny was the daughter of parents who had not much more to give her than her fancy name. At seventeen she married George Metalious, a mill worker, who later put himself through college to become a school teacher only to lose his job as a result of the public scandal caused by his wife's novel. What is perhaps most remarkable about Peyton Place, *for all its faults of gracelessness and composition, is not that the book became a best seller so unexpectedly and rapidly, but that a generally uneducated young woman, with three small children and very little money, had the literary ambition and steady application needed to write publishable fiction.*

> *Grace Metalious was a tough-talking, hard-working, hard-drinking woman. Like many authors of best sellers, she was often defensive about her work: "If I'm a lousy writer," she once said, "a hell of a lot of people have got lousy taste." She died at the age of thirty-nine of a severe liver ailment.*

A few days later, Michael Rossi stepped off the train in front of the Peyton Place railroad station. No other passenger got off with him. He paused on the empty platform and looked around thoroughly, for it was a habit with him to fix a firm picture of a new place in his mind so that it could never be erased nor forgotten. He stood still, feeling the two heavy suitcases that he carried pulling at his arm muscles, and reflected that there wasn't much to see, nor to hear, for that matter. It was shortly after seven o'clock in the evening, but it might have been midnight or four in the morning for all the activity going on. Behind him there was nothing but the two curving railroad tracks and from a distance came the long-drawn-out wail of the train as it made the pull across the wide Connecticut River. And it was cold.

For April, thought Rossi, shrugging uncomfortably under his topcoat, it was damned cold.

Straight ahead of him stood the railroad station, a shabby wooden building with a severely pitched roof and several thin, Gothic-looking windows that gave it the air of a broken-down church. Nailed to the front of the building, at the far left of the front door, was a blue and white enameled sign. PEYTON PLACE, it read. POP. 3675.

Thirty-six seventy-five, thought Rossi, pushing open the railroad station's narrow door. Sounds like the price of a cheap suit.

The inside of the building was lit by several dim electric light bulbs suspended from fixtures which obviously had once burned gas, and there were rows of benches constructed of the most hideous wood obtainable, golden oak. No one was sitting on them. The brown, roughly plastered walls were trimmed with the same yellow wood and the floor was made of black and white marble. There was an iron-barred cage set into one wall and from behind this a straight, thin man with a pinched-looking nose, steel-rimmed glasses and a string tie stared at Rossi.

"Is there a place where I can check these?" asked the new principal, indicating the two bags at his feet.

"Next room," said the man in the cage.

"Thank you," said Rossi and made his way through a narrow archway into another, smaller room. It was a replica of the main room, complete with golden oak, marble and converted gas fixtures, but with the addition of two more doors. These were clearly labeled. MEN, said one. WOMEN, said the other. Against one wall there was a row of pale gray metal lockers, and to Rossi, these looked almost friendly. They were the only things in the station even faintly resembling anything he had ever seen in his life.

"Ah," he murmured, "shades of Grand Central," and bent to push his suitcases into one of the lockers. He deposited his dime, withdrew his key and noticed that his was the only locker in use.

Busy town, he thought, and walked back to the main room. His footsteps rang disquietingly on the scrubbed marble floor.

Leslie Harrington had instructed Rossi to call him at his home as soon as he got off the train, but Rossi by-passed the solitary telephone booth in the railroad station. He wanted to look at the town alone first, to see it through no one's eyes but his own. Besides, he had decided the night that Harrington had called long-distance that the chairman of the Peyton Place School Board sounded like a man puffed up with his own importance, and must therefore be a pain in the ass.

"Say, Dad," began Rossi, addressing the man in the cage.

"Name's Rhodes," said the old man.

"Mr. Rhodes," began Rossi again, "could you tell me how I can get into town from here? I noticed a distressing lack of taxicabs outside."

"Be damned peculiar if I couldn't."

"If you couldn't what?"

"Tell you how to get uptown. Been living here for over sixty years."

"That's interesting."

"You're Mr. Rossi, eh?"

"Admitted."

"Ain't you goin' to call up Leslie Harrington?"

"Later. I'd like to get a cup of coffee first. Listen, isn't there a cab to be had anywhere around here?"

"No."

Michael Rossi controlled a laugh. It was beginning to look as if everything he had ever heard about these sullen New Englanders was true. The old man in the cage gave the impression that he had been sucking lemons for years. Certainly sourness had not been one of the traits in that little Pittsburgh secretary who claimed to be from Boston, but she said herself that she was East Boston Irish, and therefore not reliably representative of New England.

"Do you mind, then, telling me how I can walk into town from here, Mr. Rhodes?" asked Rossi.

"Not at all," said the stationmaster, and Rossi noticed that he pronounced the three words as one: Notatall. "Just go out this front door, walk around the depot to the street and keep on walking for two blocks. That will bring you to Elm Street."

"Elm Street? Is that the main street?"

"Yes."

"I had the idea that the main streets of all small New England towns were named Main Street."

"Perhaps," said Mr. Rhodes, who prided himself, when annoyed, on enunciating his syllables, "it is true that the main streets of all *other* small towns are named Main Street. Not, however, in Peyton Place. Here the main street is called Elm Street."

Period. Paragraph, thought Rossi. Next question. "Peyton Place is an odd name," he said. "How did anyone come to pick that one?"

Mr. Rhodes drew back his hand and started to close the wooden panel that backed the iron bars of his cage.

"I am closing now, Mr. Rossi," he said. "And I suggest that you be on your way if you want to obtain a cup of coffee. Hyde's Diner closes in half an hour."

"Thank you," said Rossi to the wooden panel which was suddenly between him and Mr. Rhodes.

Friendly bastard, he thought, as he left the station and began to walk up the street labeled Depot.

Michael Rossi was a massively boned man with muscles that seemed to quiver every time he moved. In the steel mills of Pittsburgh he had looked, so one smitten secretary had told him, like a color illustration of a steelworker. His arms, beneath sleeves rolled above the elbow, were knotted powerfully, and the buttons of his work shirts always seemed about to pop off under the strain of trying to cover his chest. He was six feet four inches tall, weighed two hundred and twelve pounds, stripped, and looked like anything but a schoolteacher. In fact, the friendly secretary in Pittsburgh had told him that in his dark blue suit, white shirt and dark tie, he looked like a steelworker disguised as a schoolteacher, a fact which would not inspire trust in the heart of any New Englander.

Michael Rossi was a handsome man, in a dark-skinned, black-haired, obviously sexual way, and both men and women were apt to credit him more with attractiveness than intellect. This was a mistake, for Rossi had a mind as analytical as a mathematician's and as curious as a philosopher's. It was his curiosity which had prompted him to give up teaching for a year to go to work in Pittsburgh. He had learned more about economics, labor and capital in that one year than he had learned in ten years of reading books. He was thirty-six years old and totally lacking in regret over the fact that he had never stayed in one job long enough to "get ahead," as the Pittsburgh secretary put it. He was honest, completely lacking in diplomacy, and the victim of a vicious temper which tended to loosen a tongue that had learned to speak on the lower East Side of New York City.

Rossi was halfway through the second block on Depot Street, leading to Elm, when Parker Rhodes, at the wheel of an old sedan, passed him. The stationmaster looked out of the window on the driver's side of his car and looked straight through Peyton Place's new headmaster.

Sonofabitch, thought Rossi. Real friendly sonofabitch to offer me a lift in his junk heap of a car.

Then he smiled and wondered why Mr. Rhodes had been so sensitive on the subject of his town's name. He would ask around and see if everyone in this godforsaken place reacted the same way to his question. He had reached the corner of Elm Street and paused to look about him. On the corner stood a white, cupola-topped house with stiff lace curtains at the windows. Silhouetted against the light inside, he could see two women sitting at a table with what was obviously a checkerboard between them. The women were big, saggy bosomed and white haired, and Rossi thought that they looked like a pair who had worked too long at the same girls' school.

I wonder who they are? he asked himself, as he looked in at the Page Girls. Maybe they're the town's two Lizzies.

Reluctantly, he turned away from the white house and made his way west on Elm Street. When he had walked three blocks, he came to a small, clean-looking and well-lighted restaurant. *Hyde's Diner* said a polite neon sign, and Rossi opened the door and went in. The place was empty except for one old man sitting at the far end of the counter, and another man who came out of the kitchen at the sound of the door opening.

"Good evening, sir," said Corey Hyde.

"Good evening," said Rossi. "Coffee, please, and a piece of pie. Any kind."

"Apple, sir?"

"Any kind is O.K."

"Well, we have pumpkin, too."

"Apple is fine."

"I think there's a piece of cherry left, also."

"Apple," said Rossi, "will be fine."

"You're Mr. Rossi, aren't you?"

"Yes."

"Glad to meet you, Mr. Rossi. My name is Hyde. Corey Hyde."

"How do you do?"

"Quite well, as a rule," said Corey Hyde. "I'll keep on doing quite well, as long as no one starts up another restaurant."

"Look, could I have my coffee now?"

"Certainly. Certainly, Mr. Rossi."

The old man at the end of the counter sipped his coffee from a spoon and looked surreptitiously at the newcomer to town. Rossi wondered if the old man could be the village idiot.

"Here you are, Mr. Rossi," said Corey Hyde. "The best apple pie in Peyton Place."

"Thank you."

Rossi stirred sugar into his coffee and sampled the pie. It was excellent.

"Peyton Place," he said Corey Hyde, "is the oddest name for a town I've ever heard. Who is it named for?"

"Oh, I don't know," said Corey, making unnecessary circular motions with a cloth on his immaculate counter. "There's plenty of towns have funny names. Take that Baton Rouge, Louisiana. I had a kid took French over to the high school. Told me Baton Rouge means Red Stick. Now ain't that a helluva name for a town? Red Stick, Louisiana. And what about that Des Moines, Iowa? What a crazy name that is."

"True," said Rossi. "But for whom is Peyton Place named, or for what?"

"Some feller that built a castle up here back before the Civil War. Feller by the name of Samuel Peyton," said Corey reluctantly.

"A castle!" exclaimed Rossi.

"Yep. A real, true, honest-to-God castle, transported over here from England, every stick and stone of it."

"Who was this Peyton?" asked Rossi. "An exiled duke?"

"Nah," said Corey Hyde. "Just a feller with money to burn. Excuse me, Mr. Rossi. I got things to do in the kitchen."

The old man at the end of the counter chuckled. "Fact of the matter, Mr. Rossi," said Clayton Frazier in a loud voice, "is that this town was named for a friggin' nigger. That's what ails Corey. He's delicate like, and just don't want to spit it right out."

While Michael Rossi sipped his coffee and enjoyed his pie and conversation with Clayton Frazier, Parker Rhodes arrived at his home on Laurel Street. He parked his ancient sedan and entered the house where, without first removing his coat and hat, he went directly to the telephone.

"Hello," he said, as soon as the party he had called answered. "That you, Leslie? Well, he's here, Leslie. Got off the seven o'clock, checked his suitcases and walked uptown. He's sitting down at Hyde's right now. What's that? No, he can't get his bags out of the depot until morning, you know that. What? Well, goddamn it, he didn't ask me, that's why. He didn't ask for information about when he could get them out. He just wanted to know where he could check his bags, so I told him. What'd you say, Leslie? No, I did not tell him that no one has used those lockers since they were installed five years ago. What? Well, goddamn it, he didn't ask me, that's why. Yes. Yes, he is, Leslie. *Real* dark, and big. Sweet Jesus, he's as big as the side of a barn. Yes. Down at Hyde's. Said he wanted a cup of coffee."

If Michael Rossi had overheard this conversation, he would have noticed again that Rhodes pronounced his last three words as one: Kupakawfee. But at the moment, Rossi was looking at the tall, silver-haired man who had just walked through Hyde's front door.

My God! thought Rossi, awed. This guy looks like a walking ad for a Planter's Punch. A goddamned Kentucky colonel in this place!

"Evenin', Doc," said Corey Hyde, who had put his head out of the kitchen at the sound of the door, looking, thought Rossi, rather like a tired turtle poking his head out of his shell.

"Evenin', Corey," and Rossi knew as soon as the man spoke, that this was no fugitive Kentucky colonel but a native.

"Welcome to Peyton Place, Mr. Rossi," said the white-haired native. "It's nice to have you with us. My name is Swain. Matthew Swain."

"Evenin', Doc," said Clayton Frazier. "I just been tellin' Mr. Rossi here some of our local legends."

"Make you want to jump on the next train out, Mr. Rossi?" asked the doctor.

"No, sir," said Rossi, thinking that there was, after all, one goddamned face in this godforsaken town that looked human.

"I hope you'll enjoy living here," said the doctor. "Maybe you'll let me show you the town after you get settled a little."

"Thank you, sir. I'd enjoy that," said Rossi.

"Here comes Leslie Harrington," said Clayton Frazier.

The figure outside the glass door of the restaurant was clearly visible to those inside. The doctor turned to look.

"It's Leslie, all right," he said. "Come to fetch you home, Mr. Rossi."

Harrington strode into the restaurant, a smile like one made of molded ice cream on his face.

"Ah, Mr. Rossi," he cried jovially, extending his hand. "It is indeed a pleasure to welcome you to Peyton Place."

He was thinking, Oh, Christ, he's worse and more of it than I'd feared.

"Hello, Mr. Harrington," said Rossi, barely touching the extended hand. "Made any long-distance calls lately?"

The smile on Harrington's face threatened to melt and run together, but he rescued it just in time.

"Ha, ha, ha," he laughed. "No, Mr. Rossi, I haven't had much time for telephoning these days. I've been too busy looking for a suitable apartment for our new headmaster."

"I trust you were successful," said Rossi.

"Yes. Yes, I was, as a matter of fact. Well, come along. I'll take you over in my car."

"As soon as I finish my coffee," said Rossi.

"Certainly, certainly," said Harrington. "Oh, hello, Matt. 'Lo, Clayton."

"Coffee, Mr. Harrington?" asked Corey Hyde.

"No, thanks," said Harrington.

When Rossi had finished, everyone said good night carefully, all the way around, and he and Harrington left the restaurant. As soon as the door had closed behind them, Dr. Swain began to laugh.

"Goddamn it," he roared, "I'll bet my sweet young arse that Leslie has met his match this time!"

"There's one schoolteacher that Leslie ain't gonna shove around," observed Clayton Frazier.

Corey Hyde, who owed money at the bank where Leslie Harrington was a trustee, smiled uncertainly.

"The textile racket must be pretty good," said Rossi, as he opened the door of Leslie Harrington's new Packard.

"Can't complain," said Harrington. "Can't complain," and the mill-owner shook himself angrily at this sudden tendency to repeat all his words.

Rossi stopped in the act of getting into the car. A woman was walking toward them, and as she stepped under the street light on the corner, Rossi got a quick glimpse of blond hair and a swirl of dark coat.

"Who's that?" he demanded.

Leslie Harrington peered through the darkness. As the figure drew nearer, he smiled.

"That's Constance MacKenzie," he said. "Maybe you two will have a lot in common. She used to live in New York. Nice woman; good looking, too. Widow."

"Introduce me," said Rossi, drawing himself up to his full height.

"Certainly. Certainly, be glad to. Oh, Connie!"

"Yes, Leslie?"

The woman's voice was rich and husky, and Rossi fought down the urge to straighten the knot in his tie.

"Connie," said Harrington, "I'd like you to meet our new headmaster, Mr. Rossi. Mr. Rossi, Constance MacKenzie."

Constance extended her hand and while he held it, she gazed at him full in the eyes.

"How do you do?" she said at last, and Michael Rossi was puzzled, for something very much like relief showed through her voice.

"I'm glad to know you, Mrs. MacKenzie," said Rossi, and he thought, Very glad to know you, baby. I want to know you a lot better, on a bed, for instance, with that blond hair spread out on a pillow.

Vance Packard / *The Hidden Persuaders*　　　　1957

With the publication of The Hidden Persuaders, *Vance Packard, a former columnist for the* Boston Daily Record *and a staff writer for* American Magazine *and* Collier's, *became the most widely read analyst of America's shopping habits. Based on motivational research and the techniques of depth psychology, Packard's findings served as a popular exposé of the manipulations of Madison Avenue. In "Babes in Consumerland," he focuses on the way the "goods" are packaged and positioned in supermarkets to ensure impulse buying.*

BABES IN CONSUMERLAND

"You have to have a carton that attracts and hypnotizes this woman, like waving a flashlight in front of her eyes."
　　—Gerald Stahl, executive vice-president, Package Designers Council

For some years the DuPont company has been surveying the shopping habits of American housewives in the new jungle called the supermarket. The results have been so exciting in the opportunities they suggest to marketers that hundreds of leading food companies and ad agencies have requested copies. Husbands fretting over the high cost of feeding their families would find the results exciting, too, in a dismaying sort of way.

The opening statement of the 1954 report exclaimed enthusiastically in display type: "Today's shopper in the supermarket is more and more guided by the buying philosophy—'If somehow your product catches my eye—and for some reason it looks especially good—I WANT IT.' " That conclusion was based on studying the shopping habits of 5,338 shoppers in 250 supermarkets.

DuPont's investigators have found that the mid-century shopper doesn't bother to make a list or at least not a complete list of what she needs to buy. In fact less than one shopper in five has a complete list, but still the wives always manage to fill up their carts, often while exclaiming, according to DuPont: "I certainly never intended to get that much!" Why doesn't the wife need a list? DuPont gives this blunt answer: "Because seven out of ten of today's purchases are decided in the store, where the shoppers buy on impulse!!!"

The proportion of impulse buying of groceries has grown almost every year for nearly two decades, and DuPont notes that this rise in impulse buying has coincided with the growth in self-service shopping. Other studies show that in groceries where there are clerks to wait on customers there is about half as much impulse buying as in self-service stores. If a wife has to face a clerk she thinks out beforehand what she needs.

The impulse buying of pungent-odored food such as cheese, eye-appealing items like pickles or fruit salad in glass jars, and candy, cake, snack spreads, and other "self-gratifying items" runs even higher than average, 90 per cent of all purchases. Other investigators have in general confirmed the DuPont figures on impulse buying. The Folding Paper Box Association found that two-thirds of all purchases were completely or partially on impulse; the *Progressive Grocer* put the impulse figure about where DuPont does: seven out of ten purchases. And *Printer's Ink* observed with barely restrained happiness that the shopping list had become obsolescent if not obsolete.

One motivational analyst who became curious to know why there had been such a great rise in impulse buying at supermarkets was James Vicary. He suspected that some special psychology must be going on inside the women as they shopped in supermarkets. His suspicion was that perhaps they underwent an increase in tension when confronted with so many possibilities that they were forced into making quick purchases. He set out to find out if this was true. The best way to detect what was going on inside the shopper was a galvanometer or lie detector. That obviously was impractical. The next best thing was to use a hidden motion-picture camera and record the eye-blink rate of the women as they shopped. How fast a person blinks his eyes is a pretty good index of his state of inner tension. The average person, according to Mr. Vicary, normally blinks his eyes about thirty-two times a minute. If he is tense he blinks them more frequently, under extreme tension up to fifty or sixty times a minute. If he is notably relaxed on the other hand his eye-blink rate may drop to a subnormal twenty or less.

Mr. Vicary set up his cameras and started following the ladies as they entered the store. The results were startling, even to him. Their eye-blink rate, instead of going up to indicate mounting tension, went down and down, to a very subnormal fourteen blinks a minute. The ladies fell into what Mr. Vicary calls a hypnoidal trance, a light kind of trance that, he explains, is the first stage of hypnosis. Mr. Vicary has decided that the main cause of the trance is that the supermarket is packed with products that in former years would have been items that only kings and queens could afford, and here in this fairyland they were available. Mr. Vicary theorizes: "Just in this generation, anyone can be a king or queen and go through these stores where the products say 'Buy me, buy me.' "

Interestingly many of these women were in such a trance that they passed by neighbors and old friends without noticing or greeting them. Some had a sort of glassy stare. They were so entranced as they wandered about the store plucking things off shelves at random that they would bump into boxes without seeing them and did not even notice the camera although in some cases their face would pass within a foot and a half of the spot where the hidden camera was clicking away. When the wives had filled their carts (or satisfied themselves) and started toward the check-out counter their eye-blink rate would start rising up to a slightly subnormal twenty-five blinks per minute. Then, at the sound of the cash-register bell and the voice of the clerk asking for money, the eye-blink rate would race up past normal to a high abnormal of forty-five blinks per minute. In many cases it turned out that the women did not have enough money to pay for all the nice things they had put in the cart.

In this beckoning field of impulse buying psychologists have teamed up with merchandising experts to persuade the wife to buy products she may not particularly need or even want until she happens to see it invitingly presented. The 60,000,000 American women who go into supermarkets every week are getting "help" in their purchases and "splurchases" from psychologists and psychiatrists hired by the food merchandisers. On May 18, 1956, *The New York Times* printed a remarkable interview with a young man named Gerald Stahl, executive vice-president of the Package Designers Council. He stated: "Psychiatrists say that people have so much to choose from that they want help—they will like the package that hypnotizes them into picking it." He urged food packers to put more hypnosis into their package designing, so that the housewife will stick out her hand for it rather than one of many rivals.

Mr. Stahl has found that it takes the average woman exactly twenty seconds to cover an aisle in a supermarket if she doesn't tarry; so a good package design should hypnotize the woman like a flashlight waved in front of her eyes. Some colors such as red and yellow are helpful in creating hypnotic effects. Just putting the name and maker of the product on the box is old-fashioned and, he says, has absolutely no effect on the mid-century woman. She can't read anything, really, until she has picked the box up in her hands. To get the woman to reach and get the package in her hands designers, he explained, are now using "symbols that have a dreamlike quality." To cite examples of dreamlike quality, he mentioned the mouth-watering frosted cakes that decorate the packages of cake mixes, sizzling steaks, mushrooms frying in butter. The idea is to sell the sizzle rather than the meat. Such illustrations make the woman's imagination leap ahead to the end product. By 1956 package designers had even produced a box that, when the entranced shopper picked it up and began fingering it, would give a soft sales talk, or stress the brand name. The talk is on a strip that starts broadcasting when a shopper's finger rubs it.

The package people understandably believe that it is the package that makes or breaks the impulse sale, and some more objective experts agree. A buyer for a food chain told of his experience in watching women shopping. The typical shopper, he found, "picks up one, two, or three items, she puts them back on the shelf, then she picks up one and keeps it. I ask her why she keeps it. She says, 'I like the package.' " (This was a buyer for Bohack.)

The Color Research Institute, which specializes in designing deep-impact packages, won't even send a package out into the field for testing until it has been given ocular or eye-movement tests to show how the consumer's eye will travel over the package on the shelf. This is a gauge of the attention-holding power of the design.

According to some psychologists a woman's eye is most quickly attracted to items wrapped in red; a man's eye to items wrapped in blue. Students in this field have speculated on the woman's high vulnerability to red. One package designer, Frank Gianninoto, has developed an interesting theory. He has concluded that a majority of women shoppers leave their glasses at home or will never wear glasses in public if they can avoid it so that a package to be successful must stand out "from the blurred confusion."

Other merchandisers, I should add, have concluded that in the supermarket jungle the all-important fact in impulse buying is shelf position. Many sharp merchandisers see to it that their "splurge" items (on which their profit margin is highest) tend to be at eye level.

Most of the modern supermarkets, by the mid-fifties, were laid out in a carefully calculated manner so that the high-profit impulse items would be most surely noticed. In many stores they were on the first or only aisle the shopper could enter. Among the best tempters, apparently, are those items in glass jars where the contents can be seen, or where the food is actually out in the open, to be savored and seen. Offering free pickles and cubes of cheese on toothpicks has proved to be reliable as a sales booster. An Indiana supermarket operator nationally recognized for his advanced psychological techniques told me he once sold a half ton of cheese in a few hours, just by getting an enormous half-ton wheel of cheese and inviting customers to nibble slivers and cut off their own chunks for purchase. They could have their chunk free if they could guess its weight within an ounce. The mere massiveness of the cheese, he believes, was a powerful influence in making the sales. "People like to see a lot of merchandise," he explained. "When there are only three or four cans of an item on a shelf, they just won't move." People don't want the last package. A test by *The Progressive Grocer* showed that customers buy 22 per cent more if the shelves are kept full. The urge to conformity, it seems, is profound with many of us.

People also are stimulated to be impulsive, evidently, if they are offered a little extravagance. A California supermarket found that putting a pat of butter on top of each of its better steaks caused sales to soar 15 per cent. The Jewel Tea Company set up "splurge counters" in many of its supermarkets after it was found that women in a just-for-the-heck-of-it mood will spend just as freely on food delicacies as they will on a new hat. The Coca-Cola Company made the interesting discovery that customers in a supermarket who paused to refresh themselves at a soft-drink counter tended to spend substantially more. The Coke people put this to work in a test where they offered customers free drinks. About 80 per cent accepted the Cokes and spent on an average $2.44 more than the store's average customer had been spending.

Apparently the only people who are more prone to splurging when they get in a supermarket than housewives are the wives' husbands and children. Supermarket operators are pretty well agreed that men are easy marks for all sorts of impulse items and cite cases they've seen of husbands who are sent to the store for a loaf of bread and depart with both their arms loaded with their favorite snack items. Shrewd supermarket operators have put the superior impulsiveness of little children to work in promoting sales. The Indiana supermarket operator I mentioned has a dozen little wire carts that small children can push about the store while their mothers are shopping with big carts. People think these tiny carts are very cute; and the operator thinks they are very profitable. The small children go zipping up and down the aisles imitating their mothers in impulse buying, only more so. They reach out, hypnotically I assume, and grab boxes of cookies, candies, dog food, and everything else that delights or interests them. Complications arise, of course, when mother and child come out of their trances and together reach the check-out counter. The store operator related thus what happens: "There is usually a wrangle when the mother sees all the things the child has in his basket and she tries to make him take the stuff back. The child will take back items he doesn't particularly care about such as coffee but will usually bawl and kick before surrendering cookies, candy, ice cream, or soft drinks, so they usually stay for the family."

All these factors of sly persuasion may account for the fact that whereas in past years the average American family spent about 23 per cent of its income for food it now spends nearly 30 per cent. The Indiana operator I mentioned estimates that any supermarket shopper could, by showing a little old-fashioned thoughtfulness and preplanning, save 25 per cent easily on her family's food costs.

The exploration of impulse buying on a systematic basis began spreading in the mid-fifties to many other kinds of products not available in food stores. Liquor stores began organizing racks so that women could browse and pick up impulse items. This idea was pioneered on New York's own "ad alley," Madison Avenue, and spread to other parts of the country. Department and specialty stores started having counters simply labeled, "Why Not?" to promote the carefree, impulsive purchasing of new items most people had never tried before. One store merchandiser was quoted as saying: "Just give people an excuse to try what you are selling and you'll make an extra sale."

One of the most daring ventures into impulse selling was that launched by a Chicago insurance firm, Childs and Wood, which speculated that perhaps even insurance could be sold as an impulse item. So it set up a counter to sell insurance to passers-by at the department store Carson Pirie Scott and Company. Women who happened to be in that area, perhaps to shop for fur coats or a bridal gown, could buy insurance (life, automobile, household, fire, theft, jewelry, hospital) from an assortment of firms. The experiment was successful and instituted on a permanent basis. Auto, household, and fire insurance were reported to be the most popular impulse items.

Social scientists at the Survey Research Center at the University of Michigan made studies of the way people make their decisions to buy relatively expensive durable items such as TV sets, refrigerators, washing machines, items that are usually postponable. It concluded: "We did *not* find that all or most purchases of large household goods are made after careful consideration or deliberation . . . that much planning went into the purchasing . . . nor much seeking of information. About a quarter of these purchases of large household goods were found to lack practically all features of careful deliberation."

In a study that was made on the purchasing of homes in New London, Connecticut,[1] investigators were amazed that even with this, the most important purchase a family is likely to make in the year if not the decade, the shopping was lethargic and casual. On an average the people surveyed looked at less than a half-dozen houses before making a decision; 10 per cent of the home buyers looked at only one house before deciding; 19 per cent looked at only two houses before choosing one of them.

1. Ruby T. Norris, "Processes and Objectives in the New London Area," *Consumer Behavior,* ed. Lincoln Clark (New York: New York University Press, 1954), pp. 25–29.

Dr. Warren Bilkey, of the University of Connecticut, and one of the nation's authorities on consumer behavior, systematically followed a large (sixty-three) group of families for more than a year as they wrestled with various major purchasing decisions. He learned that he could chart after each visit the intensity of two opposing factors, "desire" and "resistance." When one finally overwhelmed the other, the decision, pro or con, was made. He found that these people making major decisions, unlike the ladies in the supermarket, did build up a state of tension within themselves. The longer they pondered the decision, the higher the tension. He found that very often the people became so upset by the indecision that they often threw up their hands and decided to make the purchase just to find relief from their state of tension.

DISCUSSION QUESTIONS

1. What are the sources of Packard's data on consumerism? Does personal observation play any role in the development of his argument? Explain how his attitudes toward the "data" are different from the attitudes of those who supply the data. What means does Packard use to suggest these differences?

2. What is the effect of calling the supermarket a "new jungle"? One source Packard cites calls it a "fairyland." Which metaphor seems closest to the data that Packard is using? Which image do you agree with?

3. What image of women is conveyed by the title of Packard's essay? Compare his attitude towards women with the images of women in the Advertising section.

Phyllis McGinley / A Threnody   1958

"The line between light verse and poetry is very thin," wrote Phyllis McGinley, "the appeal of light verse is to the intellect and the appeal of serious verse is to the emotions." McGinley's work falls on both sides of that line, and much of it balances carefully upon it. Winner of a Pulitzer Prize for poetry in 1961, McGinley also wrote a Broadway review, narration for films, and many books for children. In a foreword to one of her collections of verse, the poet W. H. Auden wrote that "Phyllis McGinley needs no puff. Her poems are known and loved by tens of thousands. They call for no learned exegesis." But they do lend themselves to inquiries into the ways McGinley interprets aspects of popular culture.

One of the ads in the Rolls-Royce campaign that prompted "A Threnody" can be found in the Advertising section.

"The new Rolls-Royce is designed to be owner driven. No chauffeur required."
—From an advertisement in *The New Yorker*

Grandeur, farewell.
Farewell, pomp, glory, wealth's indulgent voice.

Tyre turned to dust in time. Great Carthage fell.
And owner-driven is the new Rolls-Royce.

Behold it, democratic front to back;   5
Nimble when traffic pinches;
Steered, braked by power; briefer than Cadillac
By eighteen inches;
Humming at sixty with an eerie purr
But needing no chauffeur.   10

What does it signify if radiator
(Altered but once, and that in '33,
When, at Sir Henry's death, or a little later,
The red R R was re-
Placed by a less conspicuous ebony)   15
Keeps still its ancient shape? What matter whether
The seats no minion now will ever use
Come padded in eight hides of English leather—
Enough for one hundred and twenty-eight pairs of shoes?
That the paint glistens and the brasses shine   20
More lusterful than hope?
That engineers have listened for axle-whine
With a stethoscope?

Splendor decays, despite the walnut table
Sliding from under the dash. Who now will stow   25
The wicker hampers away? For ladies in sable,
Who'll spread the cloth, uncork the Veuve Clicquot?
Who'll clean
The optional-special espresso coffee machine,
From folding bed whip off the cover of baize, or   30
Guard the electric razor?

Who but the owner-driver, squinting ahead
Through the marvelous glass, fretting when lights are red,
Studying on his lap
The cryptic, cross-marked, wife-defeating map?   35
He, it is he,
Tooling toward Cambridge, say (or Yale or Colgate),
On football afternoons, must nervously
Fumble for change at the tollgate,
Curse the careering drivers of both genders   40
Whose rods are hot,
Fear for his fouteen-times-enameled fenders,
Search out the parking lot,
Remember the chains of winter, wrench the round wheel
Against the arrogant trucks, nor ever feel   45
Less mortal than man in Minx or Oldsmobile.

No one remains to touch a decorous forelock
Or fold a monogrammed blanket over the knees.
Gone the chauffeur—gone like Merlin the Warlock
And the unmourned chemise.   50
Gone newsboy's Grail, all that is rich and choice
And suave as David Niven.
Grandeur, a long farewell. The new Rolls-Royce
Is owner-driven.

Stephen E. Whitfield and Gene Roddenberry / *The Making of* Star Trek

[*The Creation of* Star Trek]   1968

On September 8, 1966, NBC launched one of the most popular weekly television series ever produced. The adventures of a futuristic spacecraft on a five-year exploratory mission to discover new worlds and galaxies, Star Trek *was developed and produced by Gene Roddenberry, a former military and commercial pilot and successful screen writer. Though the series currently exists only in re-runs, a cult following has grown up around it.* Star Trek *books, posters, maps, technical manuals, equipment and uniforms are sold widely to members of local* Star Trek *clubs. Many fans also attend national conventions dedicated to the dissemination of* Star Trek *lore.*

The following account of Gene Roddenberry's initial production plans for the new science-fiction television series is taken from Stephen E. Whitfield's popular book, The Making of *Star Trek.*

3 myths in developing a S.F.

I started off writing shows for Ziv. They were very bad shows, "Mr. District Attorney," "Highway Patrol," and so forth. Which was fine, because they didn't require much knowledge or ability in order to sell a script, and in the meantime you learned about writing. What "dissolve into" means, and that sort of thing.
GENE RODDENBERRY

Roddenberry's interest in science fiction dated back to his junior high school days when a classmate lent him a battered copy of *Astounding Stories*. He never seriously considered becoming a writer of science fiction or anything else until the late 1940's, when he found himself a pilot for Pan American Airways' New York–Calcutta run with a lot of time on his hands.

His first sales were to flying magazines. In 1949 he left the airways to move to Los Angeles and investigate the possibilities in the new medium called television. He discovered to his chagrin that there was precious little television going on in Los Angeles at that time.

Having a family to support, he looked for a job and found it with the Los Angeles Police Department. He wrote his first script for television in 1951, under an assumed name, since moonlighting was frowned upon.

The following year he wrote a science-fiction script called "The Secret Defense of 117," which was later aired on Chevron Theater.*

During the years that followed, Gene's interest in science fiction continued. From time to time he would jot down ideas and file them away. In the back of his mind, he began to toy around with the idea of doing a science fiction series someday.

In 1954 Gene suddenly discovered that his TV-writing hobby was earning him four times the amount he was then receiving as a police sergeant. He promptly quit the department and turned to writing full time. A writing stint on "West Point" was followed by an assignment to "Have Gun, Will Travel." † He eventually became head writer on that show. In the years that followed, he wrote scripts for such shows as "Kaiser Aluminum Hour," "Four Star Theater," "Naked City," "Dr. Kildare," and just about every other show that was going on, at one time or another.

By 1963 he had created and was producing (at MGM) his first television series, "The Lieutenant."

When a writer begins to hit well as a free-lance writer, he rapidly develops new strengths and abilities. If lucky, he becomes very much in demand. He can pick up a phone and have an assignment at any time he wishes.

Eventually the realization begins to set in that, although he knows the business and is doing well at it, he is still doing piecework. If he stops writing, the money stops coming in. The money may be great, but there is damned little security in it for his family.

In television the only way to get that security is to own a piece of the action. To own a series so that when there are royalties and profits someday, you will have them. But security was only part of the reason why I made the jump from writer to writer-producer.

Prior to "The Lieutenant" I had written some other pilots. They were produced by other people, and none of them sold. I began to see that to create a program idea and write a script simply wasn't enough.

The story is not "told" until it's on celluloid. Telling that final story involves sound, music, casting, costumes, sets, and all the things that a producer is responsible for. Therefore it became apparent to me that if you want the film to reflect accurately what you felt when you wrote the script, then you have to produce it, too.

This is why television writers tend to become producers.

Producing in television is like storytelling. The choice of the actor, picking the right costumes, getting the right flavor, the right pace—these are as much a part of storytelling as writing out that same description of a character in a novel.

Although the director plays an important role in this, the director in television comes on a show to prepare for a week, shoots for a week, and then goes on to another show. Unlike the producer, he is neither there at the beginning of the script nor rarely there for long after you end up with some 25,000 feet of film which now has to be cut and pasted together into something unified.

---

* Ricardo Montalban starred in this show and many years later was a guest star in a STAR TREK episode.

† His episode titled "Helen of Abajinian" won him a Writer's Guild Award for Best Western. By then he was beginning to be regarded as one of the outstanding writers in television.

There is immense creative challenge and pleasure in taking all of these things and putting them together into something that works. In a show such as Star Trek, almost everything you do . . . from the fashioning of garments, to figuring out what a bed looks like centuries from now, and so on . . . is even more challenging and exciting to do.

During 1963 MGM asked Gene to come up with an idea for a new series. They were afraid (a fear later justified) that "The Lieutenant" would not be picked up for another season.

For some reason television seems to run in cycles. At that time, programming was nearing the end of the "true-to-life-Defenders" type of cycle. All trends indicated a cycle back to action-adventure. This cycle later spawned such shows as "I Spy" and "The Man From U.N.C.L.E." When Gene suggested he'd been playing with a science-fiction adventure script idea, MGM expressed a willingness to look at it.

As production on "The Lieutenant" neared its end, Gene began to finalize the series format he had been developing.

In creating STAR TREK, Gene was, in fact, attempting to destroy three widely accepted Hollywood myths.

First that "science fiction" and "fantasy" were the same. He insisted that the television audience was ready to accept the first, but that the difference between the two was important.

Science fiction is based either on fact or well-thought-out speculation. It is an extension of current knowledge or of a theory worked out in enough detail to seem at least "possible." Once having established known or theoretical scientific ground rules, the true science fiction story adheres to them all the way. With fantasy, on the other hand, you can say, "This man has the power to blink his left eye and he will disappear," and never explain how or why he can do that. For that reason the audience finds it difficult to identify with characters and situations in a fantasy. Roddenberry was convinced that they would identify with science-fiction characters if he set believable ground rules and stuck to them.

The second myth (one of the things that has made science fiction shows so bad in the past) is that most writers and producers viewed science fiction as an entirely separate branch of literature in which the basic rules of drama do not apply. In doing a police show or a hospital show or a Western, they followed the essentials of drama and worked to create belief in the character, build ascending climaxes in the story, orchestrate the characters around a basic theme, and so on. Yet when those same people approached science fiction, they ignored all those dramatic principles. Thus, most science fiction shows were littered with gadgets and bug-eyed monsters and mad scientists, but rarely included realistic characters, believable story situations, or any real drama.

Roddenberry insisted that literature is literature, be it called science fiction, Shakespeare, or Cowboys and Indians. You must work to make your characters come to life whether riding a horse in Dodge City or sitting in a captain's chair far out in space. The audience must think, "I am there." They must believe they are sitting in that saddle or in that chair and it's all happening to *them.*

What's been wrong with science fiction in television and in motion pictures for years is that whenever a monster was used, the tendency was to say, "Ah, ha! Let's have a big one that comes out, attacks, and kills everyone." Nobody ever

asked "Why?" in any other story, if something attacks (a bear, a man, or what-
ever), the author is expected to explain, "Here is why it is the way it is, here are
the things that led it to do this, here is what it wants."

A classic example of doing this right was one of our most popular episodes,
written by Gene Coon,* entitled "The Devil in the Dark." The "Horta" was an
underground creature which attacked a group of miners. In the end they find out
that it attacked because—surprise—it was a mother! It was protecting its eggs
because the miners were destroying them in the belief that they were just strange-
looking mineral formations.

With this understood, the Horta suddenly became understandable, too. It
wasn't just a monster—it was someone. And the audience could put themselves in
the place of the Horta . . . identify . . . feel! That's what drama is all about.
And that's its importance, too . . . if you can learn to feel for a Horta, you may
also be learning to understand and feel for other humans of different colors, ways,
and beliefs.

The third myth involved the belief that it was impossible to weave continuing
characters into television science fiction. Until STAR TREK, all television's science
fiction had been anthologies.

Yet, Roddenberry noted, virtually every other television series on the air, with
mass audience appeal, had a cast of familiar, continuing characters. "Bonanza" is
a classic example. A family group. You get to know them, feel comfortable with
them. One of the earliest examples was "Gunsmoke." Chester, Doc, Kitty, and
Matt. Chester became a familiar figure to people everywhere. Many sent him
worried advice about his bad leg. Others wondered if Matt and Kitty had an "understanding." Some argued whether Doc was drinking too much, considering his
responsibilities.

In addition to the familiar faces, television found familiar surroundings important, too. In the case of "Have Gun, Will Travel," Paladin's home base was the
Carlton Hotel, San Francisco, 1872. Whatever his incredible adventures, he ended
up back there. And it was somehow comfortable to know that he (and the audience who lived the adventures with him) had a home.

These were the elements that Gene set about weaving into the STAR TREK format: science fiction which adhered to the proven rules of drama, a cast of continuing characters, and a familiar home base from which to operate.

As the last days of "The Lieutenant" drew to a close, Gene submitted the completed STAR TREK series format to MGM. Their reaction was not enthusiastic.
They did say they liked the idea enough to consider it and perhaps do something
about it . . . sometime.

Gene waited for a decision. And waited. And waited.

After three or four months it became obvious that nothing would happen with
MGM. The format was submitted to several other studios. The wording may have
varied slightly, but the answers always boiled down to: "It's an interesting idea,
but it's not only too different, it's physically and financially impossible to do as a
weekly television series."

Then Gene's agent called with the rumor that Desilu Studios was desperate for
television properties. He suggested that Gene submit the STAR TREK format to
them. In April, 1964, on the basis of the STAR TREK format, plus several other

---

* Coon took over STAR TREK producer chores after Roddenberry moved to executive producer.

series ideas Gene outlined verbally, Desilu signed Gene to a three-year contract to make television pilots * for them.

Almost immediately STAR TREK was to be dealt a setback.

The ink had hardly dried on the contract before Oscar Katz (at the time, Executive Vice President in Charge of Television Production at Desilu) announced a meeting had been arranged with CBS. Format in hand, Gene prepared to sell his idea.

Present at the meeting were James Aubrey (then President of CBS) and a dozen other CBS vice presidents and executives. The meeting was by no means a "special audience." There were at least fifteen other people waiting outside to explain their proposed series ideas to the CBS officials.

Gene talked for almost two hours, outlining his ideas for the series, explaining ways in which a science-fiction series could be made on budget, and ways it could be made to appeal to a mass audience. He discussed the problems with science fiction in the past, outlined his suggestions for solving them. Aubrey and the others expressed a great deal of interest in what he said. They were particularly interested in his ideas on spaceship design, the types of stories to do, how to cut costs, and other technical aspects that Gene had developed. At the end of the two hours, and after having been questioned closely by most of those present, he thought he had sold them. Then they said, "Thank you very much. We have one of our own that we like better.† But we do appreciate your coming in."

My attitude was, "You S.O.B.'s, why didn't you tell me that after the first ten minutes? If you want technical advice and help, hire me and pay me for it!" It's like calling a doctor and having him analyze you for two hours and then telling him, "Thank you very much for pinpointing what's wrong, and I've decided to go to another doctor for the treatment."

Although Gene was understandably angry, CBS may have simply felt that his idea of an adult science fiction series would not reach a mass audience (it almost didn't) and therefore was not commercial enough. Television is in the business of advertising products to a mass audience. Since advertising rates depend on the size of the audience, there is a tendency to "play it safe."

Television has become "big business," with tens of millions at stake on each program. It takes an extraordinary network executive to gamble on a "special" kind of show that might have only a limited audience.‡

As one highly placed network executive said, "Roddenberry, I like you, I like the kind of ideas you talk. I'm a rebel myself. But I'm responsible to stockholders who expect to see a profit every year. If we try to make a television series out of this idea of yours and the series bombs out, we stand to lose a lot of money and I'll be blamed for trying something too different. If the stockholders get upset, I might find myself out of a job."

There are only three major networks, three markets. And one had already turned STAR TREK down. The proposed series had not gotten off to a very encouraging start.

---

* A "pilot" is like a sample episode from the proposed series and contains all of the normal elements of that series—setting, main characters, type of story, etc. Until recently when sky-rocketing production costs made it impractical, a pilot film was usually required in order to sell a series to one of the networks.

† "Lost in Space."

‡ If one has to choose, the college-level audience must be ignored, since they are a minority.

Mario Puzo / *The Godfather*
[*The Shooting of Don Corleone*] 1969

*Mario Puzo was born in New York City and educated at City College, Columbia,
and the New School for Social Research. In two novels before* The Godfather, The
Dark Arena *(1955) and* The Passionate Pilgrim *(1965), both of which he claims are
better books, Puzo explored generational conflicts and the New York Italo-
American community. Puzo disclaims any Mafia connections:*

> *I'm ashamed to admit that I wrote* The Godfather *entirely from research.
> I never met a real honest-to-god gangster. I knew the gambling world
> pretty good, but that's all. After the book became "famous," I was in-
> troduced to a few gentlemen related to the material. They were flattering.
> They refused to believe that I had never been in the rackets. They refused
> to believe that I had never had the confidence of a Don. But all of them
> loved the book.*

That evening, Hagen went to the Don's house to prepare him for the important
meeting the next day with Virgil Sollozzo. The Don had summoned his eldest son to
attend, and Sonny Corleone, his heavy Cupid-shaped face drawn with fatigue, was
sipping at a glass of water. He must still be humping that maid of honor, Hagen
thought. Another worry.

Don Corleone settled into an armchair puffing his Di Nobili cigar. Hagen kept a
box of them in his room. He had tried to get the Don to switch to Havanas but the
Don claimed they hurt his throat.

"Do we know everything necessary for us to know?" the Don asked.

Hagen opened the folder that held his notes. The notes were in no way incrimi-
nating, merely cryptic reminders to make sure he touched on every important detail.
"Sollozzo is coming to us for help," Hagan said. "He will ask the family to put up
at least a million dollars and to promise some sort of immunity from the law. For
that we get a piece of the action, nobody knows how much. Sollozzo is vouched for
by the Tattaglia family and they may have a piece of the action. The action is narcotics. Sollozzo has the contacts in Turkey, where they grow the poppy. From there
he ships to Sicily. No trouble. In Sicily he has the plant to process into heroin. He
has safety-valve operations to bring it down to morphine·and bring it up to heroin if
necessary. But it would seem that the processing plant in Sicily is protected in every
way. The only hitch is bringing it into this country, and then distribution. Also initial capital. A million dollars cash doesn't grow on trees." Hagen saw Don Corleone grimace. The old man hated unnecessary flourishes in business matters. He
went on hastily.

"They call Sollozzo the Turk. Two reasons. He's spent a lot of time in Turkey
and is supposed to have a Turkish wife and kids. Second. He's supposed to be very
quick with the knife, or was, when he was young. Only in matters of business,
though, and with some sort of reasonable complaint. A very competent man and his
own boss. He has a record, he's done two terms in prison, one in Italy, one in the
United States, and he's known to the authorities as a narcotics man. This could be a
plus for us. It means that he'll never get immunity to testify, since he's considered
the top and, of course, because of his record. Also he has an American wife and

three children and he is a good family man. He'll stand still for any rap as long as he knows that they will be well taken care of for living money.''

The Don puffed on his cigar and said, "Santino, what do you think?"

Hagen knew what Sonny would say. Sonny was chafing at being under the Don's thumb. He wanted a big operation of his own. Something like this would be perfect.

Sonny took a long slug of scotch. "There's a lot of money in that white powder," he said. "But it could be dangerous. Some people could wind up in jail for twenty years. I'd say that if we kept out of the operations end, just stuck to protection and financing, it might be a good idea."

Hagen looked at Sonny approvingly. He had played his cards well. He had stuck to the obvious, much the best course for him.

The Don puffed on his cigar. "And you, Tom, what do you think?"

Hagen composed himself to be absolutely honest. He had already come to the conclusion that the Don would refuse Sollozzo's proposition. But what was worse, Hagen was convinced that for one of the few times in his experience, the Don had not thought things through. He was not looking far enough ahead.

"Go ahead, Tom," the Don said encouragingly. "Not even a Sicilian *Consigliori* always agrees with the boss." They all laughed.

"I think you should say yes," Hagen said. "You know all the obvious reasons. But the most important one is this. There is more money potential in narcotics than in any other business. If we don't get into it, somebody else will, maybe the Tattaglia family. With the revenue they earn they can amass more and more police and political power. Their family will become stronger than ours. Eventually they will come after us to take away what we have. It's just like countries. If they arm, we have to arm. If they become stronger economically, they become a threat to us. Now we have the gambling and we have the unions and right now they are the best things to have. But I think narcotics is the coming thing. I think we have to have a piece of that action or we risk everything we have. Not now, but maybe ten years from now."

The Don seemed enormously impressed. He puffed on his cigar and murmured, "That's the most important thing of course." He sighed and got to his feet. "What time do I have to meet this infidel tomorrow?"

Hagen said hopefully, "He'll be here at ten in the morning." Maybe the Don would go for it.

"I'll want you both here with me," the Don said. He rose, stretching, and took his son by the arm. "Santino, get some sleep tonight, you look like the devil himself. Take care of yourself, you won't be young forever."

Sonny, encouraged by this sign of fatherly concern, asked the question Hagen did not dare to ask. "Pop, what's your answer going to be?"

Don Corleone smiled. "How do I know until I hear the percentages and other details? Besides I have to have time to think over the advice given here tonight. After all, I'm not a man who does things rashly." As he went out the door he said casually to Hagen, "Do you have in your notes that the Turk made his living from prostitution before the war? As the Tattaglia family does now. Write that down before you forget." There was just a touch of derision in the Don's voice and Hagen flushed. He had deliberately not mentioned it, legitimately so since it really had no bearing, but he had feared it might prejudice the Don's decision. He was notoriously straitlaced in matters of sex.

Virgil "the Turk" Sollozzo was a powerfully built, medium-sized man of dark complexion who could have been taken for a true Turk. He had a scimitar of a nose and cruel black eyes. He also had an impressive dignity.

Sonny Corleone met him at the door and brought him into the office where Hagen and the Don waited. Hagen thought he had never seen a more dangerous-looking man except for Luca Brasi.

There were polite handshakings all around. If the Don ever asks me if this man has balls, I would have to answer yes, Hagen thought. He had never seen such force in one man, not even the Don. In fact the Don appeared at his worst. He was being a little too simple, a little too peasantlike in his greeting.

Sollozzo came to the point immediately. The business was narcotics. Everything was set up. Certain poppy fields in Turkey had pledged him certain amounts every year. He had a protected plant in France to convert into morphine. He had an absolutely secure plant in Sicily to process into heroin. Smuggling into both countries was as positively safe as such matters could be. Entry into the United States would entail about five percent losses since the FBI itself was incorruptible, as they both knew. But the profits would be enormous, the risk nonexistent.

"Then why do you come to me?" the Don asked politely. "How have I deserved your generosity?"

Sollozzo's dark face remained impassive. "I need two million dollars cash," he said. "Equally important, I need a man who has powerful friends in the important places. Some of my couriers will be caught over the years. That is inevitable. They will all have clean records, that I promise. So it will be logical for judges to give light sentences. I need a friend who can guarantee that when my people get in trouble they won't spend more than a year or two in jail. Then they won't talk. But if they get ten and twenty years, who knows? In this world there are many weak individuals. They may talk, they may jeopardize more important people. Legal protection is a must. I hear, Don Corleone, that you have as many judges in your pocket as a bootblack has pieces of silver."

Don Corleone didn't bother to acknowledge the compliment. "What percentage for my family?" he asked.

Sollozzo's eyes gleamed. "Fifty percent." He paused and then said in a voice that was almost a caress, "In the first year your share would be three or four million dollars. Then it would go up."

Don Corleone said, "And what is the percentage of the Tattaglia family?"

For the first time Sollozzo seemed to be nervous. "They will receive something from my share. I need some help in the operations."

"So," Don Corleone said, "I receive fifty percent merely for finance and legal protection. I have no worries about operations, is that what you tell me?"

Sollozzo nodded. "If you think two million dollars in cash is 'merely finance,' I congratulate you, Don Corleone."

The Don said quietly, "I consented to see you out of my respect for the Tattaglias and because I've heard you are a serious man to be treated also with respect. I must say no to you but I must give you my reasons. The profits in your business are huge but so are the risks. Your operation, if I were part of it, could damage my other interests. It's true I have many, many friends in politics, but they would not be so friendly if my business were narcotics instead of gambling. They think gambling is something like liquor, a harmless vice, and they think narcotics a dirty business. No, don't protest. I'm telling you their thoughts, not mine. How a man makes his living is not my concern. And what I am telling you is that this business of yours is too risky. All the members of my family have lived well the last ten years, without danger, without harm. I can't endanger them or their livelihoods out of greed.''

The only sign of Sollozzo's disappointment was a quick flickering of his eyes around the room, as if he hoped Hagen or Sonny would speak in his support. Then he said, ''Are you worried about security for your two million?''

The Don smiled coldly. ''No,'' he said.

Sollozzo tried again. ''The Tattaglia family will guarantee your investment also.''

It was then that Sonny Corleone made an unforgivable error in judgment and procedure. He said eagerly, ''The Tattaglia family guarantees the return of our investment without any percentage from us?''

Hagen was horrified at this break. He saw the Don turn cold, malevolent eyes on his eldest son, who froze in uncomprehending dismay. Sollozzo's eyes flickered again but this time with satisfaction. He had discovered a chink in the Don's fortress. When the Don spoke his voice held a dismissal. ''Young people are greedy,'' he said. ''And today they have no manners. They interrupt their elders. They meddle. But I have a sentimental weakness for my children and I have spoiled them. As you see. Signor Sollozzo, my no is final. Let me say that I myself wish you good fortune in your business. It has no conflict with my own. I'm sorry that I had to disappoint you.''

Sollozzo bowed, shook the Don's hand and let Hagen take him to his car outside. There was no expression on his face when he said good-bye to Hagen.

Back in the room, Don Corleone asked Hagen, ''What did you think of that man?''

''He's a Sicilian,'' Hagen said dryly.

The Don nodded his head thoughtfully. Then he turned to his son and said gently, ''Santino, never let anyone outside the family know what you are thinking. Never let them know what you have under your fingernails. I think your brain is going soft from all that comedy you play with that young girl. Stop it and pay attention to business. Now get out of my sight.''

Hagen saw the surprise on Sonny's face, then anger at his father's reproach. Did he really think the Don would be ignorant of his conquest, Hagen wondered. And did he really not know what a dangerous mistake he had made this morning? If that were true, Hagen would never wish to be the *Consigliori* to the Don of Santino Corleone.

Don Corleone waited until Sonny had left the room. Then he sank back into his leather armchair and motioned brusquely for a drink. Hagen poured him a glass of anisette. The Don looked up at him. ''Send Luca Brasi to see me,'' he said.

Three months later, Hagen hurried through the paper work in his city office hoping to leave early enough for some Christmas shopping for his wife and children. He was interrupted by a phone call from a Johnny Fontane bubbling with high spirits. The picture had been shot, the rushes, whatever the hell they were, Hagen thought, were fabulous. He was sending the Don a present for Christmas that would knock his eyes out, he'd bring it himself but there were some little things to be done in the movie. He would have to stay out on the Coast. Hagen tried to conceal his impatience. Johnny Fontane's charm had always been lost on him. But his interest was aroused. ''What is it?'' he asked. Johnny Fontane chuckled and said, ''I can't tell, that's the best part of a Christmas present.'' Hagen immediately lost all interest and finally managed, politely, to hang up.

Ten minutes later his secretary told him that Connie Corleone was on the phone and wanted to speak to him. Hagen sighed. As a young girl Connie had been nice, as a married woman she was a nuisance. She made complaints about her husband. She kept going home to visit her mother for two or three days. And Carlo Rizzi was turning out to be a real loser. He had been fixed up with a nice little business and was running it into the ground. He was also drinking, whoring around, gambling and beating his wife up occasionally. Connie hadn't told her family about that but she had told Hagen. He wondered what new tale of woe she had for him now.

But the Christmas spirit seemed to have cheered her up. She just wanted to ask Hagen what her father would really like for Christmas. And Sonny and Fred and Mike. She already knew what she would get her mother. Hagen made some suggestions, all of which she rejected as silly. Finally she let him go.

When the phone rang again, Hagen threw his papers back into the basket. The hell with it. He'd leave. It never occurred to him to refuse to take the call, however. When his secretary told him it was Michael Corleone he picked up the phone with pleasure. He had always liked Mike.

"Tom," Michael Corleone said, "I'm driving down to the city with Kay tomorrow. There's something important I want to tell the old man before Christmas. Will he be home tomorrow night?"

"Sure," Hagen said. "He's not going out of town until after Christmas. Anything I can do for you?"

Michael was as closemouthed as his father. "No," he said. "I guess I'll see you Christmas, everybody is going to be out at Long Beach, right?"

"Right," Hagen said. He was amused when Mike hung up on him without any small talk.

He told his secretary to call his wife and tell her he would be home a little late but to have some supper for him. Outside the building he walked briskly downtown toward Macy's. Someone stepped in his way. To his surprise he saw it was Sollozzo.

Sollozzo took him by the arm and said quietly, "Don't be frightened. I just want to talk to you." A car parked at the curb suddenly had its door open. Sollozzo said urgently, "Get in, I want to talk to you."

Hagen pulled his arm loose. He was still not alarmed, just irritated. "I haven't got time," he said. At that moment two men came up behind him. Hagen felt a sudden weakness in his legs. Sollozzo said softly, "Get in the car. If I wanted to kill you you'd be dead now. Trust me."

Without a shred of trust Hagen got into the car.

Michael Corleone had lied to Hagen. He was already in New York, and he had called from a room in the Hotel Pennsylvania less than ten blocks away. When he hung up the phone, Kay Adams put out her cigarette and said, "Mike, what a good fibber you are."

Michael sat down beside her on the bed. "All for you, honey; if I told my family we were in town we'd have to go there right away. Then we couldn't go out to dinner, we couldn't go to the theater, and we couldn't sleep together tonight. Not in my father's house, not when we're not married." He put his arms around her and kissed her gently on the lips. Her mouth was sweet and he gently pulled her down on the bed. She closed her eyes, waiting for him to make love to her and Michael felt an enormous happiness. He had spent the war years fighting in the Pacific, and on those bloody islands he had dreamed of a girl like Kay Adams. Of a beauty like hers. A fair and fragile body, milky-skinned and electrified by passion. She opened her eyes and then pulled his head down to kiss him. They made love until it was time for dinner and the theater.

After dinner they walked past the brightly lit department stores full of holiday shoppers and Michael said to her, "What shall I get you for Christmas?"

She pressed against him. "Just you," she said. "Do you think your father will approve of me?"

Michael said gently, "That's not really the question. Will your parents approve of me?"

Kay shrugged. "I don't care," she said.

Michael said, "I even thought of changing my name, legally, but if something happened, that wouldn't really help. You sure you want to be a Corleone?" He said it only half-jokingly.

"Yes," she said without smiling. They pressed against each other. They had decided to get married during Christmas week, a quiet civil ceremony at City Hall with just two friends as witnesses. But Michael had insisted he must tell his father. He had explained that his father would not object in any way as long as it was not done in secrecy. Kay was doubtful. She said she could not tell her parents until after the marriage. "Of course they'll think I'm pregnant," she said. Michael grinned. "So will my parents," he said.

What neither of them mentioned was the fact that Michael would have to cut his close ties with his family. They both understood that Michael had already done so to some extent and yet they both felt guilty about this fact. They planned to finish college, seeing each other weekends and living together during summer vacations. It seemed like a happy life.

The play was a musical called *Carousel* and its sentimental story of a braggart thief made them smile at each other with amusement. When they came out of the theater it had turned cold. Kay snuggled up to him and said, "After we're married, will you beat me and then steal a star for a present?"

Michael laughed. "I'm going to be a mathematics professor," he said. Then he asked, "Do you want something to eat before we go to the hotel?"

Kay shook her head. She looked up at him meaningfully. As always he was touched by her eagerness to make love. He smiled down at her, and they kissed in the cold street. Michael felt hungry, and he decided to order sandwiches sent up to the room.

In the hotel lobby Michael pushed Kay toward the newsstand and said, "Get the papers while I get the key." He had to wait in a small line; the hotel was still short of help despite the end of the war. Michael got his room key and looked around impatiently for Kay. She was standing by the newsstand, staring down at a newspaper she held in her hand. He walked toward her. She looked up at him. Her eyes were filled with tears. "Oh, Mike," she said, "oh, Mike." He took the paper from her hands. The first thing he saw was a photo of his father lying in the street, his head in a pool of blood. A man was sitting on the curb weeping like a child. It was his brother Freddie. Michael Corleone felt his body turning to ice. There was no grief, no fear, just cold rage. He said to Kay, "Go up to the room." But he had to take her by the arm and lead her into the elevator. They rode up together in silence. In their room, Michael sat down on the bed and opened the paper. The headlines said, VITO CORLEONE SHOT. ALLEGED RACKET CHIEF CRITICALLY WOUNDED. OPERATED ON UNDER HEAVY POLICE GUARD. BLOODY MOB WAR FEARED.

Michael felt the weakness in his legs. He said to Kay, "He's not dead, the bastards didn't kill him." He read the story again. His father had been shot at five in the afternoon. That meant that while he had been making love to Kay, having dinner, enjoying the theater, his father was near death. Michael felt sick with guilt.

Kay said, "Shall we go down to the hospital now?"

Michael shook his head. "Let me call the house first. The people who did this are crazy and now that the old man's still alive they'll be desperate. Who the hell knows what they'll pull next."

Both phones in the Long Beach house were busy and it was almost twenty minutes before Michael could get through. He heard Sonny's voice saying, "Yeah."

"Sonny, it's me," Michael said.

He could hear the relief in Sonny's voice. "Jesus, kid, you had us worried. Where the hell are you? I've sent people to that hick town of yours to see what happened."

"How's the old man?" Michael said. "How bad is he hurt?"

"Pretty bad," Sonny said. "They shot him five times. But he's tough." Sonny's voice was proud. "The doctors said he'll pull through. Listen, kid, I'm busy, I can't talk, where are you?"

"In New York," Michael said. "Didn't Tom tell you I was coming down?"

Sonny's voice dropped a little. "They've snatched Tom. That's why I was worried about you. His wife is here. She don't know and neither do the cops. I don't want them to know. The bastards who pulled this must be crazy. I want you to get out here right away and keep your mouth shut. OK?"

"OK," Mike said, "do you know who did it?"

"Sure," Sonny said. "And as soon as Luca Brasi checks in they're gonna be dead meat. We still have all the horses."

"I'll be out in a hour," Mike said. "In a cab." He hung up. The papers had been on the streets for over three hours. There must have been radio news reports. It was almost impossible that Luca hadn't heard the news. Thoughtfully Michael pondered the question. Where was Luca Brasi? It was the same question that Hagen was asking himself at that moment. It was the same question that was worrying Sonny Corleone out in Long Beach.

At a quarter to five that afternoon, Don Corleone had finished checking the papers the office manager of his olive oil company had prepared for him. He put on his jacket and rapped his knuckles on his son Freddie's head to make him take his nose out of the afternoon newspaper. "Tell Gatto to get the car from the lot," he said. "I'll be ready to go home in a few minutes."

Freddie grunted. "I'll have to get it myself. Paulie called in sick this morning. Got a cold again."

Don Corleone looked thoughtful for a moment. "That's the third time this month. I think maybe you'd better get a healthier fellow for this job. Tell Tom."

Fred protested. "Paulie's a good kid. If he says he's sick, he's sick. I don't mind getting the car." He left the office. Don Corleone watched out the window as his son crossed Ninth Avenue to the parking lot. He stopped to call Hagen's office but there was no answer. He called the house at Long Beach but again there was no answer. Irritated, he looked out the window. His car was parked at the curb in front of his building. Freddie was leaning against the fender, arms folded, watching the throng of Christmas shoppers. Don Corleone put on his jacket. The office manager helped him with his overcoat. Don Corleone grunted his thanks and went out the door and started down the two flights of steps.

Out in the street the early winter light was failing. Freddie leaned casually against the fender of the heavy Buick. When he saw his father come out of the building Freddie went out into the street to the driver's side of the car and got in. Don Corleone was about to get in on the sidewalk side of the car when he hesitated and then turned back to the long open fruit stand near the corner. This had been his habit lately, he loved the big out-of-season fruits, yellow peaches and oranges, that glowed in their green boxes. The proprietor sprang to serve him. Don Corleone did not handle the fruit. He pointed. The fruit man disputed his decisions only once, to show him that one of his choices had a rotten underside. Don Corleone took the paper bag in his left hand and paid the man with a five-dollar bill. He took his change and, as he turned to go back to the waiting car, two men stepped from around the corner. Don Corleone knew immediately what was to happen.

The two men wore black overcoats and black hats pulled low to prevent identification by witnesses. They had not expected Don Corleone's alert reaction. He dropped the bag of fruit and darted toward the parked car with startling quickness for a man of his bulk. At the same time he shouted, "Fredo, Fredo." It was only then that the two men drew their guns and fired.

The first bullet caught Don Corleone in the back. He felt the hammer shock of its impact but made his body move toward the car. The next two bullets hit him in the buttocks and sent him sprawling in the middle of the street. Meanwhile the two gunmen, careful not to slip on the rolling fruit, started to follow in order to finish him off. At that moment, perhaps no more than five seconds after the Don's call to his son, Frederico Corleone appeared out of his car, looming over it. The gunmen fired two more hasty shots at the Don lying in the gutter. One hit him in the fleshy part of his arm and the second hit him in the calf of his right leg. Though these wounds were the least serious they bled profusely, forming small pools of blood beside his body. But by this time Don Corleone had lost consciousness.

Freddie had heard his father shout, calling him by his childhood name, and then he had heard the first two loud reports. By the time he got out of the car he was in shock, he had not even drawn his gun. The two assassins could easily have shot him down. But they too panicked. They must have known the son was armed, and besides too much time had passed. They disappeared around the corner, leaving Freddie alone in the street with his father's bleeding body. Many of the people thronging the avenue had flung themselves into doorways or on the ground, others had huddled together in small groups.

Freddie still had not drawn his weapon. He seemed stunned. He stared down at his father's body lying face down on the tarred street, lying now in what seemed to him a blackish lake of blood. Freddie went into physical shock. People eddied out again and someone, seeing him start to sag, led him to the curbstone and made him sit down on it. A crowd gathered around Don Corleone's body, a circle that shattered when the first police car sirened a path through them. Directly behind the police was the *Daily News* radio car and even before it stopped a photographer jumped out to snap pictures of the bleeding Don Corleone. A few moments later an ambulance arrived. The photographer turned his attention to Freddie Corleone, who was now weeping openly, and this was a curiously comical sight, because of his tough, Cupid-featured face, heavy nose and thick mouth smeared with snot. Detectives were spreading through the crowd and more police cars were coming up. One detective knelt beside Freddie, questioning him, but Freddie was too deep in shock to answer. The detective reached inside Freddie's coat and lifted his wallet. He looked at the identification inside and whistled to his partner. In just a few seconds

Freddie had been cut off from the crowd by a flock of plainclothesmen. The first detective found Freddie's gun in its shoulder holster and took it. Then they lifted Freddie off his feet and shoved him into an unmarked car. As that car pulled away it was followed by the *Daily News* radio car. The photographer was still snapping pictures of everybody and everything.

DISCUSSION QUESTIONS

1. How does Puzo go about making Don Corleone an attractive figure? For example, compare the characterization of Don Corleone to that of Sollozzo the Turk? In what ways are the Don's criminal activities given a kind of legitimacy? In this sense, how do Don Corleone's activities compare with those of Joey Gallo (see Magazines)?

2. What is the literary effect of having Don Corleone's death first reported in the newspapers? How do the newspapers determine Puzo's description of the shooting? Compare his description with the account of Joey Gallo's death (see "Death of a Maverick Mafioso" in Magazines).

James Dickey / *Deliverance*   1970

"I wished to write a novel having to do with the violence that is at the periphery of all modern experience," wrote James Dickey of his novel, Deliverance *(1970). He went on to note that we "all fear being set upon by strangers. In fact that feeling is so strong among us that it might well be identified as the characteristic* Angst *of twentieth-century man, particularly the American variety." The success of* Deliverance *attests to our fascination with that fear.*

Born in Atlanta, Georgia in 1923, James Dickey has taught English, written advertising copy, served as poetry consultant to the Library of Congress, and has been poet-in-residence at several universities. He has won numerous awards, including a National Book Award for his poetry. (See his poem "For the Death of Vince Lombardi" and his article "Delights of the Edge" in Magazines.)

Everything around me changed. I put my left arm between the bowstring and the bow and slid the bow back over my shoulder with the broadheads turned down. Then I walked to the gorge side and put a hand on it, the same hand that had been cut by the arrow in the river, as though I might be able to feel what the whole cliff was like, the whole problem, and hold it in my palm. The rock was rough, and a part of it fell away under my hand. The river sound loudened as though the rocks in the channel had shifted their positions. Then it relaxed and the extra sound died or went away again into the middle distance, the middle of the stream.

I knew that was the sign, and I backed off and ran with a hard scramble at the bank, and stretched up far enough to get an elbow over the top side of the first low overhang. Scraping my sides and legs, I got up on it and stood up. Bobby and Lewis were directly beneath me, under a roof of stone, and might as well not have been there. I was standing in the most entire aloneness that I had ever been given.

My heart expanded with joy at the thought of where I was and what I was doing. There was a new light on the water; the moon was going up and up, and I stood watching the stream with my back to the rock for a few minutes, not thinking of anything, with a deep feeling of nakedness and helplessness and intimacy.

I turned around with many small foot movements and leaned close to the cliff, taking on its slant exactly. I put my cheek against it and raised both hands up into the darkness, letting the fingers crawl independently over the soft rock. It was this softness that bothered me more than anything else; I was afraid that anything I would stand on or hold to would give way. I got my right hand placed in what felt like a crack, and began to feel with my left toes for something, anything. There was an unevenness—a bulge—in the rock and I kicked at it and worried it to see how solid it was, then put my foot on it and pulled hard with my right arm.

I rose slowly off the top of the overhang, the bow dropping back further over my left shoulder—which made it necessary to depend more on my right arm than my left—got my right knee and then my foot into some kind of hole. I settled as well as I could into my new position and began to feel upward again. There was a bulge to the left, and I worked toward it, full of wonder at the whole situation.

The cliff was not as steep as I had thought, though from what I had been able to tell earlier, before we spilled, it would probably get steeper toward the top. If I had turned loose it would have been a slide rather than a fall back down to the river or the overhang, and this reassured me a little—though not much—as I watched it happen in my mind.

I got to the bulge and then went up over it and planted my left foot solidly on it and found a good hold on what felt like a root with my right hand. I looked down.

The top of the overhang was pale now, ten or twelve feet below. I turned and forgot about it, pulling upward, kneeing and toeing into the cliff, kicking steps into the shaly rock wherever I could, trying to position both hands and one foot before moving to a new position. Some of the time I could do this, and each time my confidence increased. Often I could only get one handhold and a foothold, or two handholds. Once I could only get one handhold, but it was a strong one, and I scrambled and shifted around it until I could get a toe into the rock and pull up.

The problem-interest of it absorbed me at first, but I began to notice that the solutions were getting harder and harder: the cliff was starting to shudder in my face and against my chest. I became aware of the sound of my breath, whistling and humming crazily into the stone: the cliff was steepening, and I was laboring backbreakingly for every inch. My arms were tiring and my calves were not so much trembling as jumping. I knew now that not looking down or back—the famous advice to people climbing things—was going to enter into it. Panic was getting near me. Not as near as it might have been, but near. I concentrated everything I had to become ultrasensitive to the cliff, feeling it more gently than before, though I was shaking badly. I kept inching up. With each shift to a newer and higher position I felt more and more tenderness toward the wall.

Despite everything, I looked down. The river had spread flat and filled with moonlight. It took up the whole of space under me, bearing in the center of itself a long coiling image of light, a chill, bending flame. I must have been seventy-five or a hundred feet above it, hanging poised over some kind of inescapable glory, a bright pit.

I turned back into the cliff and leaned my mouth against it, feeling all the way out through my nerves and muscles exactly how I had possession of the wall at four random points in a way that held the whole thing together.

It was about this time that I thought of going back down, working along the bank and looking for an easier way up, and I let one foot down behind me into the void. There was nothing. I stood with the foot groping for a hold in the air, then pulled it back to the place on the cliff where it had been. It burrowed in like an animal, and I started up again.

I caught something—part of the rock—with my left hand and started to pull. I could not rise. I let go with my right hand and grabbed the wrist of the left, my left-hand fingers shuddering and popping with weight. I got one toe into the cliff, but that was all I could do. I looked up and held on. The wall was giving me nothing. It no longer sent back any pressure against me. Something I had come to rely on had been taken away, and that was it. I was hanging, but just barely. I concentrated all my strength into the fingers of my left hand, but they were leaving me. I was on the perpendicular part of the cliff, and unless I could get over it soon I would just peel off the wall. I had what I thought of as a plan if this should happen; this was to kick out as strongly as I could from the cliff face and try to get clear of the overhang and out into the river, into the bright coiling of the pit. But even if I cleared the rocks, the river was probably shallow near the bank where I would land, and it would be about as bad as if I were to hit the rocks. And I would have to get rid of the bow.

I held on. By a lot of small tentative maneuvers I swapped hands in the crevice and touched upward with my left hand, weighted down by the bow hanging over my shoulder, along the wall, remembering scenes in movies where a close-up of a hand reaches desperately for something, through a prison grate for a key, or from quicksand toward someone or something on solid ground. There was nothing there. I swapped hands again and tried the wall to my right. There was nothing. I tried the loose foot, hoping that if I could get a good enough foothold, I could get up enough to explore a little more of the wall with my hands, but I couldn't find anything there either, though I searched as far as I could with the toe and the knee, up and down and back and forth. The back of my left leg was shaking badly. My mind began to speed up, in the useless energy of panic. The urine in my bladder turned solid and painful, and then ran with a delicious sexual voiding like a wet dream, something you can't help or be blamed for. There was nothing to do but fall. The last hope I had was that I might awaken.

I was going, but anger held me up a little longer. I would have done something desperate if I had had a little more mobility, but I was practically nailed in one position; there was nothing desperate I could do. Yet I knew that if I were going to try something, I had better do it now.

I hunched down into what little power was left in my left leg muscles and drove as hard as it was possible for me to do; harder than it was possible. With no holds on the cliff, I fought with the wall for anything I could make it give me. For a second I tore at it with both hands. In a flash inside a flash I told myself not to double up my fists but to keep my hands open. I was up against a surface as smooth as monument stone, and I still believe that for a space of time I was held in the air by pure will, fighting an immense rock.

Then it seemed to spring a crack under one finger of my right hand; I thought surely I had split the stone myself. I thrust in other fingers and hung and, as I did, I got the other hand over, feeling for a continuation of the crack; it was there. I had both hands in the cliff to the palms, and strength from the stone flowed into me. I pulled up as though chinning on a sill and swung a leg in. I got the middle section of my body into the crevice as well, which was the hardest part to provide for, as it had been everywhere else. I wedged into the crack like a lizard, not able to get far enough in. As I flattened out on the floor of the crevice, with all my laborious verticality gone, the bow slid down my arm and I hooked upward just in time to stop it with my wrist. I pulled it into the cliff with me, the broadheads at my throat.

DISCUSSION QUESTION

1. How does Dickey build suspense in this scene? What is your relation to the man climbing the cliff as he begins? When he finally reaches safety? Describe the climber's changing relationship to the cliff. What happens to the "joy at the thought of where I was and what I was doing" that he felt at the start of his climb? How is that feeling like the "dance with the void" Dickey describes in his magazine article, "Delights of the Edge"?

Studs Terkel / *Working: People Talk About What They Do All Day and How They Feel About What They Do* 1974

Studs Terkel has held nearly as many jobs as all the people he has tape recorded for his ongoing oral history of everyday working America. Before, during, and after earning advanced degrees in literature and law at the University of Chicago, Terkel worked as a government statistician, news commentator, sportscaster, disc jockey, jazz critic, host of music festivals, playwright, stage and radio actor (he played the ganster on the popular thirties soap operas Ma Perkins *and* Road of Life), *and talk show host. Born in New York City in 1912, he moved to Chicago at eleven and has been associated ever since with both the city's blue-collar workers and its celebrities. His identification with working class Chicago was perhaps further enhanced when he borrowed the nickname of the protagonist of James T. Farrell's celebrated trilogy of the Prohibition and Depression eras,* Studs Lonigan.*

Wielding a portable tape recorder to capture what he calls "the man of inchoate thought," Terkel has turned out three impressive volumes of best-selling nonfiction. Division Street, America *(1966) records the bitterness and anguish that flared in urban America during the sixties.* Hard Times: An Oral History of the Great Depression *(1970) is a "memory book" of the "hard facts," the still smoldering sense of guilt and failure, and the "small triumphs" of both the rich and poor who survived that protracted decade.*

Working: People Talk About What They Do All Day and How They Feel About What They Do *(1974), a tape-recorded exploration of the collective consciousness of American workers, is drawn from 133 interviews conducted over three years, almost exclusively with nonprofessional, seemingly anonymous Americans, most of whom repeatedly startled Terkel with what he has characterized as a search for "daily meaning as well as daily bread, for recognition as well as cash, for astonishment rather than torpor; in short, for a sort of life rather than a Monday through Friday sort of dying." In a recent interview, Terkel clarified his motivation for recording such a range of American attitudes towards work:*

> *. . . today we keep hearing about the dissatisfaction of man with his work—not the wages or hours, but the nature of the work itself. . . . I talked to Pauline Kael. She says you never see people working in films, there's no interest in showing what people do for a living. Most people's work has no connection with any kind of meaning, with life. There's no longer the idea of a calling—work is just something you do eight hours a day, and then you go and do something else. Many of the men I talked to called themselves machines, robots, mules. It's incredible how these men even survive the day. So I wanted to give these people a chance to talk, because more articulate people have their own forums.*

BABE SECOLI

She's a checker at a supermarket. She's been at it for almost thirty years. "I started at twelve—a little, privately owned grocery store across the street from the house. They didn't have no cash registers. I used to mark the prices down on a paper bag.

"When I got out of high school, I didn't want no secretary job. I wanted the grocery job. It was so interesting for a young girl. I just fell into it. I don't know no other work but this. It's hard work, but I like it. This is my life."

We sell everything here, millions of items. From potato chips and pop—we even have a genuine pearl in a can of oysters. It sells for two somethin'. Snails with the shells that you put on the table, fanciness. There are items I never heard of we have here. I know the price of every one. Sometimes the boss asks me and I get a kick out of it. There isn't a thing you don't want that isn't in this store.

You sort of memorize the prices. It just comes to you. I know half a gallon of milk is sixty-four cents; a gallon, $1.10. You look at the labels. A small can of peas, Raggedy Ann. Green Giant, that's a few pennies more. I know Green Giant's eighteen and I know Raggedy Ann is fourteen. I know Del Monte is twenty-two. But lately the prices jack up from one day to another. Margarine two days ago was forty-three cents. Today it's forty-nine. Now when I see Imperial comin' through, I know it's forty-nine cents. You just memorize. On the register is a list of some prices, that's for the part-time girls. I never look at it.

I don't have to look at the keys on my register. I'm like the secretary that knows her typewriter. The touch. My hand fits. The number nine is my big middle finger. The thumb is number one, two and three and up. The side of my hand uses the bar for the total and all that.

I use my three fingers—my thumb, my index finger, and my middle finger. The right hand. And my left hand is on the groceries. They put down their groceries. I got my hips pushin' on the button and it rolls around on the counter. When I feel I have enough groceries in front of me, I let go of my hip. I'm just movin'—the hips, the hand, and the register, the hips, the hand, and the register . . . (As she demonstrates, her hands and hips move in the manner of an Oriental dancer.) You just keep goin', one, two, one, two. If you've got that rhythm, you're a fast checker. Your feet are flat on the floor and you're turning your head back and forth.

Somebody talks to you. If you take your hand off the item, you're gonna forget what you were ringin'. It's the feel. When I'm pushin' the items through I'm always having my hand on the items. If somebody interrupts to ask me the price, I'll answer while I'm movin'. Like playin' a piano.

I'm eight hours a day on my feet. It's just a physical tire of standing up. When I get home I get my second wind. As far as standin' there, I'm not tired. It's when I'm roamin' around tryin' to catch a shoplifter. There's a lot of shoplifters in here. When I see one, I'm ready to run for them.

When my boss asks me how I know, I just know by the movements of their hands. And with their purses and their shopping bags and their clothing rearranged. You can just tell what they're doin' and I'm never wrong so far.

The best kind shoplift. They're not doin' this because they need the money. A very nice class of people off Lake Shore Drive. They do it every day—men and women. Lately it's been more or less these hippies, livin' from day to day . . .

It's meats. Some of these women have big purses. I caught one here last week. She had two big packages of sirloin strips in her purse. That amounted to ten dollars. When she came up to the register, I very politely said, "Would you like to pay for anything else, without me embarrassing you?" My boss is standing right there. I called him over. She looked at me sort of on the cocky side. I said, "I know you have meat in your purse. Before your neighbors see you, you either pay for it or take it out." She got very snippy. That's where my boss stepped in. "Why'd you take the meat?" She paid for it.

Nobody knows it. I talk very politely. My boss doesn't do anything drastic. If they get rowdy, he'll raise his voice to embarrass 'em. He tells them not to come back in the store again.

I have one comin' in here, it's razor blades. He's a very nice dressed man in his early sixties. He doesn't need these razor blades any more than the man in the moon. I've been following him and he knows it. So he's layin' low on the razor blades. It's little petty things like this. They're mad at somebody, so they have to take their anger out on something.

We had one lady, she pleaded with us that she wanted to come back—not to have her husband find out. My boss told her she was gonna be watched wherever she went. But that was just to put a little fright in her. Because she was just an elderly person. I would be too embarrassed to come into a store if this would happen. But I guess it's just the normal thing these days—any place you go. You have to feel sorry for people like this. I like 'em all.

My family gets the biggest kick out of the shoplifters: "What happened today?" (Laughs.) This is about the one with the meat in her purse. She didn't need that meat any more than the man in the moon.

Some of 'em, they get angry and perturbed at the prices, and they start swearin' at me. I just look at 'em. You have to consider the source. I just don't answer them, because before you know it I'll get in a heated argument. The customer's always right. Doesn't she realize I have to buy the same food? I go shopping and pay the same prices. I'm not gettin' a discount. The shoplifters, they say to me, "Don't you want for something?" Yes, I want and I'm standing on my feet all day and I got varicose veins. But I don't walk out of here with a purse full of meat. When I want a piece of steak I buy a piece of steak.

My feet, they hurt at times, very much so. When I was eighteen years old I put the bathing suit on and I could see the map on my leg. From standing, standing. And not the proper shoes. So I wear like nurse's shoes with good inner sole arch support, like Dr. Scholl's. They ease the pain and that's it. Sometimes I go to bed, I'm so tired that I can't sleep. My feet hurt as if I'm standing while I'm in bed.

I love my job. I've got very nice bosses. I got a black manager and he's just beautiful. They don't bother you as long as you do your work. And the pay is terrific. I automatically get a raise because of the union. Retail Clerks. Right now I'm ready for retirement as far as the union goes. I have enough years. I'm as high up as I can go. I make $189 gross pay. When I retire I'll make close to five hundred dollars a month. This is because of the union. Full benefits. The business agents all know me by name. The young kids don't stop and think what good the union's done.

Sometimes I feel some of these girls are overpaid. They don't do the work they're supposed to be doin'. Young girls who come in, they just go plunk, plunk, so slow. All the old customers, they say, "Let's go to Babe," because I'm fast. That's why I'm so tired while these young girls are going dancin' at night. They don't really put pride in their work. To me, this is living. At times, when I feel sick, I come to work feelin' I'll pep up here. Sometimes it doesn't. (Laughs.)

I'm a checker and I'm very proud of it. There's some, they say, "A checker—ugh!" To me, it's like somebody being a teacher or a lawyer. I'm not ashamed that I wear a uniform and nurse's shoes and that I got varicose veins. I'm makin' an honest living. Whoever looks down on me, they're lower than I am.

What irritates me is when customers get very cocky with me. "Hurry up," or "Cash my check quick." I don't think this is right. You wait your time and I'll give you my full, undivided attention. You rush and you're gonna get nothin'. Like yesterday, I had two big orders on my counter and I push the groceries down, and she says, "I have to be somewhere in ten minutes. Hurry up and bag that." You don't talk that way to me or any other checker.

I'm human, I'm working for a living. They belittle me sometimes. They use a little profanity sometimes. I stop right there and I go get the manager. Nobody is gonna call me a (cups hand over mouth, whispers) b-i-t-c-h. These are the higher class of people, like as if I'm their housekeeper or their maid. You don't even talk to a maid like this.

I make mistakes, I'm not infallible. I apologize. I catch it right there and then. I tell my customers, "I overcharged you two pennies on this. I will take it off of your next item." So my customers don't watch me when I ring up. They trust me. But I had one this morning—with this person I say, "How are you?" That's the extent of our conversation. She says to me, "Wait. I want to check you." I just don't bother. I make like I don't even know she's there or I don't even hear her. She's ready for an argument. So I say, "Stop right there and then. I'll give you a receipt when I'm through. If there's any mistakes I'll correct them." These people, I can't understand them—and I can't be bothered with their little trifles because I've got my next customer that wants to get out . . .

It hurts my feelings when they distrust me. I wouldn't cheat nobody, because it isn't going in my pocket. If I make an honest mistake, they call you a thief, they call you a ganef. I'm far from bein' a ganef.

Sometimes I feel my face gettin' so red that I'm so aggravated, I'm a total wreck. My family says, "We better not talk to her today. She's had a bad day." They say, "What happened?" I'll look at 'em and I'll start laughin', because this is not a policy to bring home your work. You leave your troubles at the store and vice versa. But there's days when you can't cope with it. But it irons out.

"When you make a mistake, you get three chances. Then they take it out of your pay, which is right. You can't make a ten-dollar mistake every week. It's fishy. What's this nonsense? If I give a customer ten dollars too much, it's your own fault. That's why they got these registers with the amounts tendered on it. You don't have to stop and count. I've never had such mistakes. I happens mostly with some of these young kids."

Years ago it was more friendlier, more sweeter. Now there's like tension in the air. A tension in the store. The minute you walk in you feel it. Everybody is fightin' with each other. They're pushin', pushin'—"I was first." Now it's an effort to say, "Hello, how are you?" It must be the way of people livin' today. Everything is so rush, rush, rush, and shovin'. Nobody's goin' anywhere. I think they're pushin' themselves to a grave, some of these people.

A lot of traffic here. There's bumpin' into each other with shoppin' carts. Some of 'em just do it intentionally. When I'm shoppin', they just jam you with the carts. That hits your ankle and you have a nice big bruise there. You know who does this the most? These old men that shop. These *men*. They're terrible and just *jam* you. Sometimes I go over and tap them on the shoulder: "Now why did you do this?" They look at you and they just start *laughin'*. It's just hatred in them, they're bitter. They hate themselves, maybe they don't feel good that day. They gotta take their anger out on somethin', so they just *jam* you. It's just ridiculous.

I know some of these people are lonesome. They have really nobody. They got one or two items in their cart and they're just shoppin' for an hour, just dallying along, talkin' to other people. They tell them how they feel, what they did today. It's just that they want to get it out, these old people. And the young ones are rushin' to a PTA meeting or somethin', and they just glance at these people and got no time for 'em.

We have this little coffee nook and we serve free coffee. A lot of people come in for the coffee and just walk out. I have one old lady, she's got no place to go. She sits in front of the window for hours. She'll walk around the store, she'll come back. I found out she's all alone, this old lady. No family, no nothin'. From my register I see the whole bit.

I wouldn't know how to go in a factory. I'd be like in a prison. Like this, I can look outside, see what the weather is like. I want a little fresh air, I walk out the front door, take a few sniffs of air, and come back in. I'm here forty-five minutes early every morning. I've never been late except for that big snowstorm. I never thought of any other work.

I'm a couple of days away, I'm very lonesome for this place. When I'm on a vacation, I can't wait to go, but two or three days away, I start to get fidgety. I can't stand around and do nothin'. I have to be busy at all times. I look forward to comin' to work. It's a great feelin'. I enjoy it somethin' terrible.

DISCUSSION QUESTIONS

1. Why do you think Terkel reprinted tape-recorded interviews with his subjects instead of re-cycling them into a sociological study written in his own words? How does this procedure affect the various roles of writer, subject, and audience? Using Dorothy Gloster's "Sadie's Song" (see Magazines) as an example, describe the differences authorial intervention makes in a similar situation.

2. Does the ungrammatical, rambling style of Terkel's subject bother you? Do you think different criteria other than "Standard English" should be used to evaluate oral compositions? Explain what criteria you think should apply, if any. How does the language John Updike uses to describe supermarket employment (see Classics) differ from Babe Secoli's? What are the advantages and disadvantages of each style? Which do you think more adequately portrays an occupation and the social status that goes with it?

Erica Jong / Paper Cuts   1975

Starting with a line from Theodore Roethke's famous poem "Dolor" (see Classics), Erica Jong re-imagines that poem from quite another perspective in "Paper Cuts." Born in 1942, Jong is the author of the best-selling novel, Fear of Flying *(1973) and a number of highly successful volumes of poetry, all of which explore candidly and sometimes graphically the sexual ups and downs of a contemporary young woman.*

"Paper Cuts" first appeared in Ms. *magazine and was later reprinted in one of her best selling books of poetry,* Half-Lives *(1975).*

for Bob Phillips

Endless duplication of lives and objects . . .
            —Theodore Roethke

I have known the imperial power of secretaries,
the awesome indifference of receptionists,
I have been intimidated by desk & typewriter,
by the silver jaws of the stapler
& the lecherous kiss of the mucilage,   5
& the unctuousness of rubber cement
before it dries.

I have been afraid of telephones,
have put my mouth to their stale tobacco breath,
have been jarred to terror   10
by their jangling midnight music,
& their sudden blackness
even when they are white.

I have been afraid in elevators
amid the satin hiss of cables   15
& the silky lisping of air conditioners
& the helicopter blades of fans.
I have seen time killed in the office jungles
of undeclared war.

My fear has crept into the paper guillotine   20
& voyaged to the Arctic Circle of the water cooler.

456

My fear has followed me into the locked Ladies Room,
& down the iron fire stairs
to the postage meter.

I have seen the mailroom women like lost letters   25
frayed around the edges.
I have seen the xerox room men
shuffling in & out among each other
like cards in identical decks.

I have come to tell you I have survived.   30
I bring you chains of paperclips instead of emeralds.
I bring you lottery tickets instead of poems.
I bring you mucilage instead of love.

I lay my body out before you on the desk.
I spread my hair amid a maze of rubber stamps   35
RUSH. SPECIAL DELIVERY. DO NOT BEND.
I am open—will you lick me like an envelope?
I am bleeding—will you kiss my paper cuts?

Elizabeth L. Post / *Emily Post's Etiquette* ·   1975

*The most influential voice in determining acceptable standards of social conduct
for several generations of Americans, Emily Price was born into a well-to-do Baltimore family in 1873. After the customary education here and abroad, she became a debutante and a bride in the same year, 1892. Divorced in 1901, Emily
Price Post gradually turned to writing as a means of support for her two children, publishing* Flight of a Moth *in 1904—a recounting of her childhood training in Europe. Her later, romantic fiction featured mannered occasions and stylish scenes on the continent. Encouraged to draw on her background and prepare
a book of etiquette, Emily Post was at first repulsed by the notion, but after reading what was available on the subject, she agreed to the project. First published
in 1922 under the title* Etiquette in Society, in Business, in Politics, and at Home,
her book has since gone through more than ninety-five printings.

Elizabeth L. Post, wife of Mrs. Post's grandson, prepared the 1975 edition of
Emily Post's Etiquette *and wrote the following Preface to it.*

PREFACE

It is not uncommon today to hear someone ask, "Are manners still important?
Isn't etiquette outdated, or hypocritical?" Or even, "Do manners and etiquette, as
we used to recognize them, exist at all?"

Of course they do! And they are just as important to us now as they were to
previous generations. But they are different manners, new manners, and this is as
it should be, because our life-style is new. Yesterday, privacy, self-discipline, and

formality were the rule. Today, openness, freedom, and informality are the qualities that we live with. The formalities that our parents worked hard to learn are
outdated, and the informalities that we practice seem right for *now*—so natural to
us that we are scarcely conscious of the difference. Manners evolve of their own
accord, influenced by current life-style, and the best survive until that style
changes again, and they become obsolete.

To be able to answer the question "Is etiquette important?" one must have an
understanding of the true meaning of the word. There is no simple definition or
synonym, but to me "consideration" comes the closest. All good manners are
based on thoughtfulness for others, and if everyone lived by the Golden Rule—
"Do unto others as you would have others do unto you"—there would be no bad
manners in the world. There have been many attempts to define "etiquette" over
the years, but my own particular favorite was found in an old grammar book. It is,

> Politeness is to do and say
> The kindest thing in the kindest way.

The type of person for whom books on etiquette hold an interest has changed almost as much as manners themselves. Until the first edition of *Etiquette* was
printed in 1922, the idea prevailed that manners held little interest for anyone
other than the rich, or members of so-called "society." An etiquette book printed
in Chicago in 1882, for example, stated that the rich needed good manners "to
give finish and éclat to their homes and their wealth"; the middle class needed
manners "to gain admittance to the homes of the rich"; and the poor needed manners "to help find solace for the 'sting of poverty.' " Today, fortunately, our attitude toward manners is far more sensible. As Peg Bracken writes, "Once a proof
of your breeding, manners are now an indication of your warm heart and good intentions as well."

A knowledge of etiquette—and good manners—carries many advantages. It im-
parts a comfortable feeling of security, self-confidence, and self-respect. Unques-
tionably, we enjoy every experience more if we feel that we need not worry about
how to face it—if we know that instinctively we are doing the right thing.

There is a deep basic need in all of us to conform and to be liked. Acting according to accepted standards helps us to avoid criticism and to become popular
members of society. Of course, it is most important that certain standards be
maintained. Just because "everyone does it" does not make an action correct or
even acceptable. Each standard that is lowered or forgotten must be replaced by
another—one that is more suitable to life today. The fact that we live less formally
does not mean that we need live less agreeably. But it does mean that we must
have a knowledge of what is considered right, or wrong, for our times. It was true
many years ago, and it is still true today—we are open to criticism if we flaunt
convention too defiantly.

Finally, good manners simply make one more attractive, and who does not,
"deep down," want to be as attractive as possible? Manners—those that are described in this book, and, perhaps, some that are not—have survived or become
accepted because they have proved over many years to be the pleasantest, most
practical, most considerate, or least offensive way of doing something. They are
not, as some people think, "rules," but rather "guideposts on the road to good
taste."

This new book, then, is designed to *help* you. In no way is it intended to
complicate your life, to make it more difficult or less fun. Rather, it should make

life easier and smoother. Nor is every reader expected to follow all the suggestions to the letter. Each person must read it, consider what advice is applicable to his circumstances, and then adopt those parts of the book that will be of most help to him.

In a comparison of Emily Post's original *Etiquette* with this edition, certain facts emerge. First, and most obvious, *manners* have changed tremendously in fifty years. The clothes we wear, the way we talk, the parties we give, our ideas on how to bring up our children are as different as night from day. (Running throughout this book are some short excerpts from the original edition which will show just how different). The second, and more important, is that *etiquette* has not changed. It is a code of behavior, based on consideration and kindness, and manners are the outward evidence that we live by that code. The conclusion, then, is that, while manners and each individual "manner" must be constantly redefined and revised, Emily Post's definition of etiquette is as valid today as it was in 1922. She wrote: "Beneath its myriad rules, the fundamental purpose of etiquette is to make the world a pleasanter place to live in, and you a more pleasant person to live with." There is no need to redefine that. The way of life of those who accept the code has not changed over many centuries—and, I hope, never will.

Wayne Dyer / *Your Erroneous Zones*   1976

> *"I feel a mission to change the mental health of our country," announced Wayne Dyer, author of professional books on counseling and of two enormously popular works:* Your Erroneous Zones *(1976) and* Pulling Your own Strings *(1978). After two years of research, Dyer reportedly completed the first draft of* Your Errone-ous Zones *in thirteen days. He defines erroneous zones as areas of self-defeating behavior and claims that ridding oneself of them need not involve Freudian, fashionable, or arcane therapies: "Mental health is not complex, expensive or involved, hard work. It is only common sense."*
>
> *In the selection below, Dyer attempts to remove etiquette from the erroneous zone. For another interpretation of etiquette in today's society, see Elizabeth L. Post's Preface to* Emily Post's Etiquette *in this section.*

ETIQUETTE AS A SHOULD

Etiquette is a beautiful example of useless and unhealthy enculturation. Think of all the little meaningless rules you've been encouraged to adopt simply because an Emily Post, Amy Vanderbilt, or Abigail van Buren has so written. Eat your corn on the cob this way, always wait for the hostess to start before eating, introduce the man to the woman, sit on that side of the church at a wedding, tip this, wear that, use these words. Don't consult yourself; look it up in the book. While good manners are certainly appropriate—they simply entail consideration for other people—about ninety percent of all the etiquette guidelines are meaningless rules that were composed arbitrarily at one time. There is no proper way for you; there is only what you decide is right for you—as long as you don't make it hard for others to get along. You can choose how you'll introduce people, what you'll tip, what you'll wear, how you'll speak, where you'll sit, how you'll eat, and so on, strictly on the basis of what you want. Anytime you fall into the trap of "What *should* I wear," or "How *should* I do it," you're giving up a chunk of yourself. I'm not making a case here for being a social rebel since that would be a form of approval-seeking through nonconformity, but rather this is a plea for being self- rather than other-directed in the everyday running of your life. Being true to your- self means being devoid of the need for an external support system.

Alex Haley / *Roots*
[*What Are Slaves*]

1976

A former magazine writer and Coast Guard Chief Journalist, Alex Haley had a modest reputation until the publication of his mammoth work, Roots: The Saga of an American Family, *first in a condensed version by* Reader's Digest *in 1974 and then published in its entirety by Doubleday in 1976. Twelve years in the making,* Roots *won for Haley international fame and personal fortune. An eight part ABC television dramatization of* Roots *drew 130 million viewers. The last episode at- tracted 80 million alone, making it the most popular television program ever aired.*

Kunta Kinte, Haley's African ancestor, born in Gambia in 1750 and carried to America as a slave in 1767, is the most vividly portrayed character in the book. His story fills more than half of Roots' *688 pages. In the following selection, young Kunta Kinte and his brother, Lamin, learn from their father, Omoro, the meaning of slavery.*

"What are slaves?" Lamin asked Kunta one afternoon. Kunta grunted and fell silent. Walking on, seemingly lost in thought, he was wondering what Lamin had overheard to prompt that question. Kunta knew that those who were taken by toubob became slaves, and he had overheard grown-ups talking about slaves who were owned by people in Juffure. But the fact was that he really didn't know what slaves *were*. As had happened so many other times, Lamin's question embarrassed him into finding out more.

The next day, when Omoro was getting ready to go out after some palm wood to build Binta a new food storehouse, Kunta asked to join his father; he loved to go off anywhere with Omoro. But neither spoke this day until they had almost reached the dark, cool palm grove.

Then Kunta asked abruptly, "Fa, what are slaves?"

Omoro just grunted at first, saying nothing, and for several minutes moved about in the grove, inspecting the trunks of diffrent palms.

"Slaves aren't always easy to tell from those who aren't slaves," he said fi- nally. Between blows of his bush ax against the palm he had selected, he told Kunta that slaves' huts were roofed with nyantang jongo and free peoples' huts with nyantang foro, which Kunta knew was the best quality of thatching grass.

"But one should never speak of slaves in the presence of slaves," said Omoro, looking very stern. Kunta didn't understand why, but he nodded as if he did.

When the palm tree fell, Omoro began chopping away its thick, tough fronds. As Kunta plucked off for himself some of the ripened fruits, he sensed his father's mood of willingness to talk today. He thought happily how now he would be able to explain to Lamin all about slaves.

"Why are some people slaves and others not?" he asked.

Omoro said that people became slaves in different ways. Some were born of slave mothers—and he named a few of those who lived in Juffure, people whom Kunta knew well. Some of them were the parents of some of his own kafo mates. Others, said Omoro, had once faced starvation during their home villages' hungry season, and they had come to Juffure and begged to become the slaves of someone who agreed to feed and provide for them. Still others—and he named some of Juffure's older people—had once been enemies and been captured as prisoners. "They become slaves, being not brave enough to die rather than be taken," said Omoro.

He had begun chopping the trunk of the palm into sections of a size that a strong man could carry. Though all he had named were slaves, he said, they were all respected people, as Kunta well knew. "Their rights are guaranteed by the laws of our forefathers," said Omoro, and he explained that all masters had to provide their slaves with food, clothing, a house, a farm plot to work on half shares, and also a wife or husband.

"Only those who permit themselves to be are despised," he told Kunta—those who had been made slaves because they were convicted murderers, thieves, or other criminals. These were the only slaves whom a master could beat or otherwise punish as he felt they deserved.

"Do slaves have to remain slaves always?" asked Kunta.

"No, many slaves buy their freedom with what they save from farming on half share with their masters." Omoro named some in Juffure who had done this. He named others who had won their freedom by marrying into the family that owned them.

To help him carry the heavy sections of palm, Omoro made a stout sling out of green vines, and as he worked, he said that some slaves, in fact, prospered beyond their masters. Some had even taken slaves for themselves, and some had become very famous persons.

"Sundiata was one!" exclaimed Kunta. Many times, he had heard the grandmothers and the griots speaking of the great forefather slave general whose army had conquered so many enemies.

Omoro grunted and nodded, clearly pleased that Kunta knew this, for Omoro also had learned much of Sundiata when he was Kunta's age. Testing his son, Omoro asked, "And who was Sundiata's mother?"

"Sogolon, the Buffalo Woman!" said Kunta proudly.

Omoro smiled, and hoisting onto his strong shoulders two heavy sections of the palm pole within the vine sling, he began walking. Eating his palm fruits, Kunta followed, and nearly all the way back to the village, Omoro told him how the great Mandinka Empire had been won by the crippled, brilliant slave general whose army had begun with runaway slaves found in swamps and other hiding places.

"You will learn much more of him when you are in manhood training," said Omoro—and the very thought of that time sent a fear through Kunta, but also a thrill of anticipation.

Omoro said that Sundiata had run away from his hated master, as most slaves did who didn't like their masters. He said that except for convicted criminals, no slaves could be sold unless the slaves approved of the intended master.

"Grandmother Nyo Boto also is a slave," said Omoro, and Kunta almost swallowed a mouthful of palm fruit. He couldn't comprehend this. Pictures flashed across his mind of beloved old Nyo Boto squatting before the door of her hut, tending the village's twelve or fifteen naked babies while weaving baskets of wigs, and giving the sharp side of her tongue to any passing adult—even the elders, if she felt like it. "That one is nobody's slave," he thought.

The next afternoon, after he had delivered his goats to their pens, Kunta took Lamin home by a way that avoided their usual playmates, and soon they squatted silently before the hut of Nyo Boto. Within a few moments the old lady appeared in her doorway, having sensed that she had visitors. And with but a glance at Kunta, who had always been one of her very favorite children, she knew that something special was on his mind. Inviting the boys inside her hut, she set about the brewing of some hot herb tea for them.

"How are your papa and mama?" she asked.

"Fine. Thank you for asking," said Kunta politely. "And you are well, Grandmother?"

"I'm quite fine, indeed," she replied.

Kunta's next words didn't come until the tea had been set before him. Then he blurted, "Why are you a slave, Grandmother?"

Nyo Boto looked sharply at Kunta and Lamin. Now it was she who didn't speak for a few moments. "I will tell you," she said finally.

"In my home village one night, very far from here and many rains ago, when I was a young woman and wife," Nyo Boto said, she had awakened in terror as flaming grass roofs came crashing down among her screaming neighbors. Snatching up her own two babies, a boy and a girl, whose father had recently died in a tribal war, she rushed out among the others—and awaiting them were armed white slave raiders with their black slatee helpers. In a furious battle, all who didn't escape were roughly herded together, and those who were too badly injured or too old or too young to travel were murdered before the others' eyes. Nyo Boto began to sob, "—including my own two babies and my aged mother."

As Lamin and Kunta clutched each other's hands, she told them how the terrified prisoners, bound neck-to-neck with thongs, were beaten and driven across the hot, hard inland country for many days. And every day, more and more of the prisoners fell beneath the whips that lashed their backs to make them walk faster. After a few days, yet more began to fall of hunger and exhaustion. Some struggled on, but those who couldn't were left for the wild animals to get. The long line of prisoners passed other villages that had been burned and ruined, where the skulls and bones of people and animals lay among the burned-out shells of thatch and mud that had once been family huts. Fewer than half of those who had begun the trip reached the village of Juffure, four days from the nearest place on the Kambi Bolongo where slaves were sold.

"It was here that one young prisoner was sold for a bag of corn," said the old woman. "That was me. And this was how I came to be called Nyo Boto," which Kunta knew meant "bag of corn." The man who bought her for his own slave died before very long, she said, "and I have lived here ever since."

Lamin was wriggling in excitement at the story, and Kunta felt somehow ever greater love and appreciation than he had before for old Nyo Boto, who now sat smiling tenderly at the two boys, whose father and mother, like them, she had once dandled on her knee.

"Omoro, your papa, was of the first kafo when I came to Juffure," said Nyo Boto, looking directly at Kunta. "Yaisa, his mother, who was your grandmother, was my very good friend. Do you remember her?" Kunta said that he did and added proudly that he had told his little brother all about their grandma.

"That is good!" said Nyo Boto. "Now I must get back to work. Run along, now."

Thanking her for the tea, Kunta and Lamin left and walked slowly back to Binta's hut, each deep in his own private thoughts.

The next afternoon, when Kunta returned from his goatherding, he found Lamin filled with questions about Nyo Boto's story. Had any such fire ever burned in Juffure? he wanted to know. Well, he had never heard of any, said Kunta, and the village showed no signs of it. Had Kunta ever seen one of those white people? "Of course not!" he exclaimed. But he said that their father had spoken of a time when he and his brothers had seen the toubob and their ships at a point along the river.

Kunta quickly changed the subject, for he knew very little about toubob, and he wanted to think about them for himself. He wished that he could *see* one of them—from a safe distance, of course, since everything he'd ever heard about them made it plain that people were better off who never got too close to them.

Only recently a girl out gathering herbs—and before her two grown men out hunting—had disappeared, and everyone was certain that toubob had stolen them away. He remembered, of course, how when drums of other villages warned that toubob had either taken somebody or was known to be near, the men would arm themselves and mount a double guard while the frightened women quickly gathered all of the children and hid in the bush far from the village—sometimes for several days—until the toubob was felt to be gone.

Kunta recalled once when he was out with his goats in the quiet of the bush, sitting under his favorite shade tree. He had happened to look upward and there, to his astonishment, in the tree overhead, were twenty or thirty monkeys huddled along the thickly leaved branches as still as statues, with their long tails hanging down. Kunta had always thought of monkeys rushing noisily about, and he couldn't forget how quietly they had been watching his every move. He wished that now *he* might sit in a tree and watch some toubob on the ground below him.

The goats were being driven homeward the afternoon after Lamin had asked him about toubob when Kunta raised the subject among his fellow goatherds—and in no time they were telling about the things they had heard. One boy, Demba Conteh, said that a very brave uncle had once gone close enough to *smell* some toubob, and they had a peculiar stink. All of the boys had heard that toubob took people away to eat them. But some had heard that the toubob claimed the stolen people were not eaten, only put to work on huge farms. Sitafa Silla spat out his grandfather's answer to that: "White man's lie!"

The next chance he had, Kunta asked Omoro, "Papa, will you tell me how you and your brothers saw the toubob at the river?" Quickly, he added, "The matter needs to be told correctly to Lamin." It seemed to Kunta that his father nearly smiled, but Omoro only grunted, evidently not feeling like talking at that moment. But a few days later, Omoro casually invited both Kunta and Lamin to go with him out beyond the village to collect some roots he needed. It was the naked Lamin's first walk anywhere with his father, and he was overjoyed. Knowing that

Kunta's influence had brought this about, he held tightly onto the tail of his big brother's dundiko.

Omoro told his sons that after their manhood training, his two older brothers Janneh and Saloum had left Juffure, and the passing of time brought news of them as well-known travelers in strange and distant places. Their first return home came when drumtalk all the way from Juffure told them of the birth of Omoro's first son. They spent sleepless days and nights on the trail to attend the naming ceremony. And gone from home so long, the brothers joyously embraced some of their kafo mates of boyhood. But those few sadly told of others gone and lost—some in burned villages, some killed by fearsome firesticks, some kidnaped, some missing while farming, hunting, or traveling—and all because of toubob.

Omoro said that his brothers had then angrily asked him to join them on a trip to see what the toubob were doing, to see what might be done. So the three brothers trekked for three days along the banks of the Kamby Bolongo, keeping carefully concealed in the bush, until they found what they were looking for. About twenty great toubob canoes were moored in the river, each big enough that its insides might hold all the people of Juffure, each with a huge white cloth tied by ropes to a treelike pole as tall as ten men. Nearby was an island, and on the island was a fortress.

Many toubob were moving about, and black helpers were with them, both on the fortress and in small canoes. The small canoes were taking such things as dried indigo, cotton, beeswax, and hides to the big canoes. More terrible than he could describe, however, said Omoro, were the beatings and other cruelties they saw being dealt out to those who had been captured for the toubob to take away.

For several moments, Omoro was quiet, and Kunta sensed that he was pondering something else to tell him. Finally he spoke: "Not as many of our people are being taken away now as then." When Kunta was a baby, he said, the King of Barra, who ruled this part of The Gambia, had ordered that there would be no more burning of villages with the capturing or filling of all their people. And soon it did stop, after the soldiers of some angry kings had burned the big canoes down to the water, killing all the toubob on board.

"Now," said Omoro, "nineteen guns are fired in salute to the King of Barra by every toubob canoe entering the Kamby Bolongo." He said that the King's personal agents now supplied most of the people whom the toubob took away—usually criminals or debtors, or anyone convicted for suspicion of plotting against the king—often for little more than whispering. More people seemed to get convicted of crimes, said Omoro, whenever toubob ships sailed in the Kamby Bolongo looking for slaves to buy.

"But even a king cannot stop the stealings of some people from their villages," Omoro continued. "You have known some of those lost from our village, three from among us just within the past few moons, as you know, and you have heard the drumtalk from other villages." He looked hard at his sons, and spoke slowly. "The things I'm going to tell you now, you must hear with more than your ears—for not to do what I say can mean your being stolen away forever!" Kunta and Lamin listened with rising fright. "Never be alone when you can help it," said Omoro. "Never be out at night when you can help it. And day or night, when you're alone, keep away from any high weeds or bush if you can avoid it."

For the rest of their lives, "even when you have come to be men," said their father, they must be on guard for toubob. "He often shoots his firesticks, which can be heard far off. And wherever you see much smoke away from any villages, it is probably his cooking fires, which are too big. You should closely inspect his signs to learn which way the toubob went. Having much heavier footsteps than we do, he leaves signs you will recognize as not ours: He breaks twings and grasses. And when you get close where he has been, you will find that his scent remains there. It's like a wet chicken smells. And many say a toubob sends forth a nervousness that we can feel. If you feel that, become quiet, for often he can be detected at some distance."

But it's not enough to know the toubob, said Omoro. "Many of our own people work for him. They are slatee *traitors*. But without knowing them, there is no way to recognize them. In the bush, therefore, trust *no* one you don't know."

Kunta and Lamin sat frozen with fear. "You cannot be told these things strongly enough," said their father. "You must know what your uncles and I saw happening to those who had been stolen. It is the difference between slaves among ourselves and those whom toubob takes away to be slaves for him." He said that they saw stolen people chained inside long, stout, heavily guarded bamboo pens along the shore of the river. When small canoes brought important-acting toubob from the big canoes, the stolen people were dragged outside their pens onto the sand.

"Their heads had been shaved, and they had been greased until they shined all over. First they were made to squat and jump up and down," said Omoro. "And then, when the toubob had seen enough of that, they ordered the stolen people's mouths forced open for their teeth and their throats to be looked at."

Swiftly, Omoro's finger touched Kunta's crotch, and as Kunta jumped, Omoro said, "Then the men's foto was pulled and looked at. Even the women's private parts were inspected." And the toubob finally made the people squat again and stuck burning hot irons against their backs and shoulders. Then, screaming and struggling, the people were shipped toward the water, where small canoes waited to take them out to the big canoes.

"My brothers and I watched many fall onto their bellies, clawing and eating the sand, as if to get one last hold and bite of their own home," said Omoro. "But they were dragged and beaten on." Even in the small canoes out in the water, he told Kunta and Lamin, some kept fighting against the whips and the clubs until they jumped into the water among terrible long fish with gray backs and white bellies and curved mouths full of thrashing teeth that reddened the water with their blood.

Kunta and Lamin had huddled close to each other, each gripping the other's hands. "It's better that you know these things than that your mother and I kill the white cock one day for you." Omoro looked at his sons. "Do you know what that means?"

Kunta managed to nod, and found his voice. "When someone is missing, Fa?" He had seen families frantically chanting to Allah as they squatted around a white cock bleeding and flapping with its throat slit.

"Yes," said Omoro. "If the white cock dies on its breast, hope remains. But when a white cock flaps to death on its back, then *no* hope remains, and the whole village joins the family in crying to Allah."

"Fa—" Lamin's voice, squeaky with fear, startled Kunta, "where do the big canoes take the stolen people?"

"The elders say to Jong Sang Doo," said Omoro, "a land where slaves are sold to huge cannibals called toubabo koomi, who eat us. No man knows any more about it."

James F. Fixx / *The Complete Book of Running*

The Complete Book of Running by James F. Fixx came out just as interest in jogging was limbering up. A compendium of almost every aspect of running—from "What Happens to Your Mind," to "The Mythology of the Woman Runner," and further on to "Boston and/or Bust"—The Complete Book of Running has proved itself to be a marathoner on the non-fiction best seller list.

Since becoming a runner rather late in life, Fixx has run the equivalent of once around the earth. A former magazine editor and author of Games for the Superintelligent *and* More Games for the Superintelligent, *Fixx now spends his time writing and running ten miles each day through Connecticut.*

[WHAT HAPPENS TO YOUR MIND]

Few psychological frontiers are more fascinating than the changes that occur in your mind as a result of running. Profound and far-reaching, these changes provide clues to the intricate relationship between our minds and our bodies. For several months, as I did research for this book, I traveled a great deal, talking with all sorts of runners and other people whom I hoped could supply me with information about various aspects of running.

In almost every case I would start the discussion with a specific subject in mind—running following a heart attack, say, or racing tactics, or the types of muscle tissue involved in running—and for a while we would stick to that subject. But at some point the conversation would invariably slip off into a topic I had not even brought up: the psychology of running. Everyone, it seemed, was secretly interested in—in a surprising number of cases obsessed by—what goes on in runners' minds and how the sport changes people. I found this such a curious phenomenon that I finally asked Joe Henderson, the editor of *Runner's World* and a man who has thought as deeply as anyone alive about the running process, what he made of it. "I'm not surprised," he told me. "I think the mental aspects of running are going to be the next big field of investigation. That's where the breakthroughs will come."

I agree. Currently our society puts considerable emphasis on personal development and the maximizing of one's potential. Zen, transcendental meditation, assertiveness training, est and similar movements are all directed at making us fulfilled human beings. Sometimes, to judge by the testimony of their adherents, they work well. Sometimes, however, they do not, and I suspect the reason in many cases is that they fail to mesh with the inescapable peculiarities and idiosyncrasies of individual character. In contrast, while running often alters a person profoundly, the changes all come from within and are therefore tightly integrated with the total personality.

In this chapter I plan to discuss the psychological changes that result from running. First, we will examine some of the emotions runners report they feel as a result of running. Then we will look at the ways in which the psychological phenomena of running work to change lives.

Most of the people I talked with told me they felt they had benefited psychologically from running. This did not surprise me, for I myself have long known that I have. Some of the benefits, as already indicated, are easily described: a sense of enhanced mental energy and concentration, a feeling of heightened mental acuity (You don't necessarily notice these things every day, or after every run. But most of the time they're there.) Because our everyday language is not often called upon to describe such phenomena, other benefits are more difficult to put into words. To cite only one example, the qualities and capacities that are important in running—such factors as will power, the ability to apply effort during extreme fatigue, and the acceptance of pain—have a radiating power that subtly influences one's life.

The people I spoke with described these phenomena in persuasive and even poetic terms. Their articulateness did not seem to depend on intelligence or vocabulary. As soon as the subject turned to the mental aspects of running, they all displayed an impressive eloquence.

Nancy Gerstein, for example, is a young editor who was working at *The New Yorker* when I spoke with her (she has since left to join George Plimpton's staff). Nancy runs six miles four or five times a week. She told me: "Running gives me a sense of controlling my own life. I feel I'm doing something for myself, not depending on anyone else to do it for me. I like the finiteness of my runs, the fact that they have a clear beginning and end: I set a goal and I achieve it. I like the fact, too, that there's real difficulty in running; when you have to push yourself to finish a run, you feel wonderful afterward. A good run makes you feel sort of holy."

Allan Ripp is in his early twenties. For years he was bothered by asthma. ("Every gasp was terrible," he told me. "I couldn't think about anything else.") Then he took up running. Although he is careful not to claim that running cured his asthma, he does say that it made it easier to tolerate the attacks when they come. Ripp said: "Running is the greatest thing that ever happened to me. It's the focus of my daily routine, the source of everything. It gives my life a sense of rhythm. It's not just a game or a sport, something *outside* of life; it's *part* of life. It's an adjective—something that defines me."

Ted Corbitt was a member of the 1952 Olympic marathon team, and two years later became marathon champion of the United States. He has competed in nearly 190 marathons, many longer races and innumerable shorter ones—enough, certainly, to have squashed any lingering romanticism about running. Yet when I talked with him he said in his soft-spoken, understated manner: "People get a relief of tension from running. It's like having your own psychiatrist. You have various feelings. Sometimes it's joyous. Everyone benefits from running, both in ways they recognize and in ways they don't. One thing that almost always happens is that your sense of self-worth improves. You accept yourself a little better."

Nina Kuscsik is another veteran runner who in 1972 won the women's division of the Boston Marathon. She told me: "There isn't much freedom in our lives any more. Running gives you freedom. When you run, you can go at your own speed. You can go where you want to go and think your own thoughts. Nobody has any claim on you." And Joe Henderson: "Running is a childish and a primitive thing to do. That's its appeal, I think. You're moving like a child again. You strip away all the chains of civilization. While you're running, you go way back in history."

No one, however, put the matter as simply or as briefly as a runner from Millburn, New Jersey, named Mark Hanson. "To run is to live," he told me. "Everything else is just waiting."

Hanson is not the only person who equates running with living fully. As I talked with people all over the country I discovered that many of them thought of their running hours as their happiest, partly because running is such a powerful antidote to anxiety, depression and other unpleasant mental states. A Brooklyn, New York, runner named Monte Davis told me: "Running long and hard is an ideal antidepressant, since it's hard to run and feel sorry for yourself at the same time. Also, there are those hours of clearheadedness that follow a long run." Beth Richardson, a Boston runner, said, "I feel less cranky and bitchy when I run." A witty Sarasota, Florida, newspaper columnist named Bill Copeland, whose bon mots are often quoted in *Reader's Digest* and elsewhere, spoke evocatively about running on the beach: "As you run, you sink your bare feet into the moistly yielding sand along the surf and invoke the known benefit of sole massage, the next best thing to soul massage for curing the uglies." Finally, another New Jersey runner, Russel Gallop, said, "Several years after college I was struck with both a failing marriage and a leg injury. I had to face a psychologically debilitating divorce and the physical limitations that come with knee surgery. I was in a physical and psychological rut. Running seemed a logical way to get my knee back to its normal function. The unexpected dividend was that I got my head together, too."

The feelings these runners describe have been scientifically documented. Richard Driscoll, a psychologist at Eastern State Psychiatric Hospital in Knoxville, Tennessee, found that running makes people less anxious, particularly if they think pleasant thoughts as they work out. Dr. Michael B. Mock of the National Heart, Lung and Blood Institute told me that "in a society where for many reasons there is a tendency for a large majority of people to have depression, exercise has been found to counter depressed feelings by increasing one's feeling of self-esteem and independence." I even came across one psychiatrist, Dr. John Greist of the University of Wisconsin, who, having assigned a group of abnormally depressed patients to either a ten-week running program or ten weeks of traditional psychotherapy, found the running to be more effective.

The sense of well-being that comes with running is corroborated by still other observers. Dr. Fredrick D. Harper of Howard University's School of Education reports on a semester-long research project designed to assess, among other things, the psychological changes that occurred when students worked their way up from a quarter-mile to several miles of running. Among the results reported by the participants were decreased anxiety, greater sexual appreciation and a better feeling about themselves—including, in Dr. Harper's words, "positive feelings about their body." He also reports on some side effects of the project: "By jogging on the athletic track, the students were subject to spectators, including the football team, which practiced around the same time. Some of the girls felt self-conscious in the beginning because of wisecracks from male bystanders. At the end of the jogging project, the girls had gained respect for their ability and perseverance in getting up to a distance of four and five miles. Some of the football players even commented that the joggers inspired them to practice harder."

The same diminution of anxiety cited by Dr. Harper and others has also been reported in a study carried out by Dr. Herbert A. deVries of the University of Southern California's School of Medicine and Gene M. Adams of the same university's Gerontology Center. DeVries and Adams solicited volunteers from a retirement community, Leisure World, at Laguna Hills, California. The volunteers ranged in age from fifty-two to seventy, and all had such symptoms as nervous tension, sleeplessness, irritability, continual worry and feelings of panic in every-day situations. The researchers tested the volunteers after 400-milligram doses of meprobamate, a widely used tranquilizer; after taking an identical-looking pla-cebo; and after exercising moderately for fifteen minutes. The exercise, it turned out reduced the volunteers' tension more effectively than the tranquilizer did.* Dr. Terence Kavanagh, medical director of the Toronto Rehabilitation Center in Canada, asserts that most heart patients in his running program report "a great im-provement in mood and morale." And Dr. Alan Clark of St. Joseph's Infirmary in Atlanta says, "It is well known that exercise is the best tranquilizer. I refuse to medicate patients with simple neurotic anxiety until they give aerobic exercises an adequate trial."

In a classic study at Purdue University, sixty middle-aged faculty and staff members, all of them in sedentary jobs, participated in a four-month exercise pro-gram consisting chiefly of running. Their personalities were evaluated, both before and after the program by a standard test, the Cattell 16 Personality Factor Ques-tionnaire. As they became more fit, the subjects were found to become more emo-tionally stable, more self-sufficient, more imaginative and more confident.

While I was looking into the mental dimensions of running, I noticed that many writers have in fact been circling the subject for some time. Roger Bannister, the first person ever to run a mile in less than four minutes once wrote:

> I can still remember quite vividly a time when as a child I ran barefoot along damp, firm sand by the seashore. The air there had a special quality, as if it had a life of its own. The sound of breakers on the shore shut out all others, and I was startled and almost frightened by the tremendous excitement a few steps could create. It was an intense moment of discovery of a source of power and beauty that one previously hardly dreamt existed. . . . The sense of exercise is an extra sense, or perhaps a subtle combination of all the others.

Another runner, a woman, says: "My jogging is very symbolic of my active par-ticipation in my life." And still another woman runner, Annette McDaniels of Bethesda, Maryland: "I experience a complete unification of body and mind."

Finally, a runner named David Bradley, writing in New York's *Village Voice,* describes one of his runs in these words:

> I am producing alpha brain waves. I am hurting far more than most people ever do unless they are sick or injured, yet feel relaxed, almost happy. I am deeply in-side myself and yet totally aware of my surroundings. . . . I no longer touch the ground: I am moving through the air, floating. The incline is not a hill, it is just air that is a little thicker, and I can breathe deeply and draw myself up without ef-fort. My body is producing draughts of a hormone called epinephrine, which researchers have linked with feelings of euphoria. This, combined with the alpha

---

* Even without the benefit of a formal study, most runners come to value the tranquilizing effect of their sport. Robert Gene Fineberg of Beaverton, Oregon, reports: "My vocation, market analysis, keeps me under extreme pressure each day, but nothing seems too big when I know that these miles after work will be as smooth as silk. Running gives the mind a boost worth all the tranquilizers in the world." Similarly, Dr. Stephen D. Storey, an orthopedic surgeon in Salinas, California, said: "I find that running allows me to escape from the numerous pressures of private practice. I usually do my run-ning during the noon hour, and I feel much less hassled during the afternoon. I have been through a transcendental meditation program and for a period of time meditated regularly. Running has much the same effect on me as TM."

waves and the repetitive motion of running which acts as a sort of mantra, makes me higher than is legally possible in any other way.

Many of the states these people describe are, of course, much like those that occur occasionally in the lives of all of us, whether we run or not. The important difference is that running makes them more predictable; if you are a runner, you can summon them whenever you want to.

Some runners even argue that running brings about mental states so remote from those of everyday life as to be unimaginable to most of us. The founder of Esalen, Michael Murphy, says many athletes are "closet mystics," people who have had paranormal experiences during competition.* And Mike Spino, Esalen's sports director, has written: "Running . . . can be a way of discovering our larger selves. I am finding that average people as well as superstars touch spiritual elements when they least expect it."

New Zealand's John Walker, who as I write this is history's fastest miler (3:49.4), has in these remarkable words described his victory in an Olympic 1,500-meter race: "When I hit the front I got a flash of compelling certainty. I didn't look over my shoulder, but I sensed someone coming up on me fast. And I knew it was Rick Wohlhuter of the United States, even though I couldn't see who it was. I just knew it. I was already at full stretch. But I went into a sort of mental overdrive, and my subconscious mind took over completely. I've experienced it in races before, and I can't explain it. I burned Wohlhuter off."

In rereading William James's *Varieties of Religious Experience* not long ago, I was struck by how similar runners' language was to that of many of the mystics whose minds James explores. And is it pure accident that, as mentioned earlier, more races are held on Sunday mornings than at any other time? Probably so. Yet it is not difficult to find explicit references to the religious qualities of running. A thirty-year-old runner in Arizona, Coreen Nasenbeny, told me of having become a "true convert" to running in 1976. Then she added: "And I don't think I'm far off in equating my experience with a conversion."

Significantly, no one has yet undertaken a comprehensive investigation of the mental changes that occur as a result of running. Although several writers—Roger Bannister, Joe Henderson, George Sheehan and the psychiatrist Thaddeus Kostrubala prominent among them—have touched upon the subject, no one has yet attempted a full-scale description of the mental phenomena associated with running. In the *The Madness in Sports,* Arnold R. Beisser suggests a reason for the neglect: "The reluctance to penetrate into comprehending the meaning of sports is understandable. We prefer not to know too much about what we treasure. . . . The lover of a beautiful woman protects his cherished concept of her from anything which may detract from her beauty. 'Better let well enough alone,' he feels. This is the prevailing attitude of Americans toward their love affair with sports."

Nonetheless, a few adventurous thinkers have tried to figure out what it is about sports that tugs at us so strongly. Let us see how much light their thoughts shed on the running experience.

Any decently thorough inquiry into the meaning of sport will eventually bring us to the source of much of present-day thinking on the matter: Johan Huizinga's profound *Homo Ludens: A Study of the Play Element in Culture,* mentioned earlier. Published in 1949, the book argues that man is not best defined as *Homo*

---

*A professional football player, for example, has described a game in which all the players were inexplicably surrounded by "auras." By looking at a player's aura, he reported, he could tell which way the man was planning to move.

sapiens (man the wise) or *Homo faber* (man the maker) but as *Homo ludens* (man the game player). This is so, Huizinga says, because we have a propensity for turning all aspects of life, no matter how serious, into games. Beethoven, writing his Fifth Symphony, was playing a game. Faulkner, writing his complex Yoknapatawpha County novels, was playing a different game. Whether corporation president, general or surgeon, when we are at work we are playing games.

If we accept the idea that our lives are games, might not it also be true that what we call our games are in fact a deeper part of our lives than we may hitherto have suspected? This would help explain the frenzied intensity of the hockey fan, the monklike concentration of the chess player, the scholarly zeal with which some people devote themselves to batting averages.

However, none of this would explain why sport penetrates our lives so deeply. For that, we need to turn to another clue in another book, Paul Weiss's *Sport: A Philosophic Inquiry*. Weiss holds that champion athletes are more than merely themselves; they are excellence in human form. We like to watch a Rosewall backhand not just for what it is but for what it represents: pure, idealized, platonic perfection.* So it is with running, both the running of champions and our own. The champion—Bill Rodgers or Filbert Bayi, let us say—is excellence in human form, and we just as surely are our own excellence. When you next watch a race, notice the expressions of ecstasy on the faces of those who cross the finish line many minutes or—in the case of very long races like the marathon—even hours after the winner. These slower runners have pushed themselves just as hard as the winner and, like him, have overcome fatigue and the agony of too much pain too long endured. In the context of the race, they have become as excellent as they are capable of being. It is a rare and wonderful feeling.

Sport also does other things if we let it. For example, it teaches us lessons in human limits. Because sport offers no hiding places, it also teaches honesty and authenticity. In short, it teaches us something about personal wholeness and integrity. And if we give it the respect and attention it deserves, it teaches us something about joy.

These are not lessons in any formal, schoolroom sense. Rather, they are scraps of knowledge received piecemeal through Bannister's "extra sense." Because they are won by so much effort, they are that much more impressive and memorable. In *Leisure: The Basis of Culture*, Josef Pieper remarks that people mistrust rewards that come with too little effort: "[Man] can only enjoy, with a good conscience, what he has acquired with toil and trouble." There is enough "toil and trouble" in running to ease the conscience of the most puritanical of athletes, and this is one of running's clearest pleasures.

The simplest way to understand this apparent paradox is to consider the pain of running. It is possible to run without pain, but as soon as you start trying to improve, pain—or at least some mild distress—will be your companion. Let's assume you are accustomed to running a mile a day. You want to increase that distance, so one day you decide to try running two miles. No doubt you will be able to do it, but toward the end you will be tired and your legs will feel heavy. Then, as you push on, you will feel worse. Pain is the result of a struggle between your mind ("Keep running," it tells your body) and your legs ("For God's sake, let us stop!" they plead).

The severity of pain in running depends on the intensity of the mind-body

---

*This is why we care so little about an athlete's moral character or his or her "niceness." In the face of athletic excellence, such considerations are irrelevant.

struggle. If you just want to cover the two miles, you can slow down, ease the discomfort, and probably experience nothing more than a persistent ache. But if you try to run really hard despite the pain—the way you might, for example, if you were battling a rival in a race—it can be fairly intense. (One doctor has compared it with the pain of childbirth: not unbearable but not particularly pleasant, either.)

Yet pain of that intensity or greater is something runners regularly experience. Rick Wohlhuter once declared, ''I'm willing to accept any kind of pain to win a race.'' Still, to assert that discomfort is a reasonable price to pay for the fruits of victory doesn't get to the heart of the pain question. In most races, even important ones, the prizes are inconsequential—an inexpensive trophy or medal, a round of applause. And in a training run the prize is only what you make it—a rest, a long, cold drink, the satisfaction of finally being home.

Why, then, do runners so willingly accept and even embrace pain? I suspect that it is because there is a close kinship between pain and pleasure. Almost two thousand years ago, Seneca remarked that ''there is a certain pleasure which is akin to pain.'' And Socrates said, ''How singular is the thing called pleasure, and how curiously related to pain, which might be thought to be the opposite of it . . . yet he who pursues either is generally compelled to take the other; their bodies are two but they are joined by a single head.'' In his book: *Pain: Why It Hurts, Where It Hurts, When It Hurts,* Richard Stiller sheds light on the pain-pleasure phenomenon: ''We think of [pain and pleasure] as opposites. Yet our language betrays the confusion that can exist between the two. We describe pleasure as being so intense as to be 'unendurable,' something we 'can't stand.' We talk of 'exquisite' pain. From the physiological point of view, agony and ecstasy seem remarkably similar.''

The pleasure that conceals itself in pain is familiar to most runners. At the finish line of the 1975 Boston Marathon a spectator named Kitty Davis noticed a runner crying. His face was contorted like a child's, and tears were running down his weather-tanned cheeks.

''Why are you crying, sir?'' Mrs. Davis asked. ''Are you hurt?''

''No,'' the runner replied, ''I'm crying because I'm so happy.''

DISCUSSION QUESTIONS

1. Compare James Fixx's description of the psychological changes that take place during running with that of Janice Kaplan in ''Exercise—The New 'High' '' (see Magazines). Does the fact that Fixx is writing for a general audience and Kaplan primarily for an audience of women affect their descriptions? In what ways? Who makes larger claims? Who is more cautious?

2. Does Fixx assume his audience is composed of people who already are runners? How can you tell? Does he assume his audience will be accepting or skeptical of the claims he makes for running? What evidence can you point to in support of your answer?

CLASSICS

Literature is news that stays news.

EZRA POUND

N its popular sense, "classic" means something that remains in style. The word often comes up in talk about a particular cut of clothing, the movements of dancers and athletes, someone's features, the lines of a building or an automobile, and even the preparation of food. "Classic," in such instances, describes certain qualities of craftsmanship, performance, or appearance that remain constant despite changes in fashion, taste, doctrine, or government. Unlike most of the ads, best sellers, articles, and journalism you have read in previous chapters of this book, the prose and poetry reprinted in the following pages represents the work of many writers who have been read continuously over the years, writers who have remained in style. A classic is durable; it is writing that stays in print.

Why do some works preserve a lively reputation for generations while others are forgotten by the end of a season? Surely it is not because the writers of what eventually become classics attend to different subjects than do the authors of even those best sellers whose popularity does not endure very much beyond their arrival in paperback at local bookstores. Adventure and romance, love and death, individual freedom and social order, innocence and experience, success and failure are, for example, often "themes" of classics and best sellers as well as, for that matter, most journalism and advertising. If what makes a work a classic is not simply the author's choice of material—all material is, strictly speaking, in the public domain—then the best place to find the reason for a work's continuing success is in the quality of its writing.

In general, our selections from American classics will provide you with more complicated uses of language than most of the other forms of writing you have encountered in earlier sections of this book. It should be added, however, that the authors of classics are not necessarily hostile to those other, less complicated forms of writing. If anything, they are probably more willing to incorporate the multiplicity of styles and voices surrounding them than are writers who must, because of a greater commercial investment, appeal to quite specific audiences. Journalists, for example, may be reluctant to record the interferences and intrusions they may have encountered in their attempted news coverage. (They have only a limited amount of newspaper space for their "stories" and copy editors to satisfy.) So too, authors of best sellers may not want to, may not know how to, or may not even dare to risk unsettling their readers with sudden shifts in tone or point of view or subtle maneuvers into irony or parody.

From the philosophical manner of Henry David Thoreau to the Beat poetics of Allen Ginsberg, the writing collected here is meant to suggest the variety and complexity of classic American literature. It is literature whose authors, for the most part, have been receptive, at times competitively responsive, to whatever environment of language they chose to work in. Mark Twain, who told many good stories in his own lifetime, makes it clear that telling a story well is a performance of tone and nuance that ought to rival the most successful forms of contemporary entertainment. Twain wants his audience to delight, as he does, in the art of mimicry and parody. "How To Tell a Story" is much more than an enjoyable training manual for delivering effective jokes; it is also a fine critical statement reminding us that the art of reading well is also the art of listening attentively. John Updike in "A & P," Ernest Hemingway in "The Killers," Joyce Carol Oates in "Stalking," and Allen Ginsberg in "A Supermarket in California,'' expect (as Twain does) their audiences to be fully attuned to the ways their styles embody the nonliterary idioms and intonations of American advertising, popular music, and film.

Along with Mark Twain, such writers as Stephen Crane, Ernest Hemingway, and Norman Mailer are competitively aware of how the techniques and verbal formulations of journalism can be exploited and even parodied in their own efforts to render events distinctively. Having been reporters themselves, they have experienced first hand the advantages and limitations of writing the kind of prose that newspapers consistently promote. For example, a comparison of Mailer's account with the newspaper report of the astronauts' walk on the moon will demonstrate what a major novelist considers to be the obligations of a literary consciousness contending with an event that is surrounded, if not dominated, by the machinery of news coverage. In Stephen Crane's ''The Open Boat,'' we can observe how a writer transforms the raw data of a journalistic ''scoop'' (see ''Stephen Crane's Own Story'' in Press) into the complex arrangements of classic fiction.

It should be clear from the following selections that the writers of classics use language in the most demanding and selective ways possible. Theirs is a prose that requires its audience to have attained a more highly developed reading aptitude than that needed to respond to much of the writing appearing earlier in this book. A classic expects its readers to be more than simply ''literate.'' Readers of classics are obliged to engage in difficult, sometimes highly complicated verbal experiences and, at the same time, are encouraged in the act of reading, to refer these verbal experiences to a wide network of accumulated literary responses. In fact, the writers of classic prose (whether it be fiction or nonfiction) very often imagine for themselves readers who take delight in having such demands made on them.

Few authors are more exacting in the demands their writing makes on their audience than William Faulkner. Take, for example, the following passage from *The Bear,* in which Faulkner describes the culmination of young Ike McCaslin's nearly obsessive, increasingly solitary search for the elusive, indomitable bear, Old Ben:

> Then he saw the bear. It did not emerge, appear: it was just there, immobile, fixed in the green and windless noon's hot dappling, not as big as he had dreamed it but as big as he had expected, bigger, dimensionless against the dappled obscurity, looking at him. Then it moved. It crossed the glade without haste, walking for an instant into the sun's full glare and out of it, and stopped again and looked back at him across one shoulder. Then it was gone. It didn't walk into the woods. It faded, sank back into the wilderness without motion as he had watched a fish, a huge old bass, sink back into the dark depths of its pool and vanish without even any movement of its fins.

Faulkner allows Ike his long-awaited confrontation with the bear only after the boy has willingly surrendered himself to the woods by relinquishing his gun, watch, and compass. Bereft of weapon and instruments, those ''tainted'' items of civilization, Ike can *know* the wilderness in ways that permit him to go further than even his mastery of the technique of woodmanship could take him. When Ike finally encounters Old Ben, it is because he has entered into a new relation with the woods, one that has superseded the boundaries set up by the rules and rituals of hunting and tracking.

As a factual account of a hunting incident, this passage is rather unremarkable, surely anticlimactic. Nothing much seems to happen. The boy sees the bear. The bear sees the boy. The bear disappears into the woods. There is no kill, no breathtaking capture or escape. Furthermore, the reader is given few of the details that might be anticipated in such an encounter. Nothing is told of the bear's size, color, or smell; there is none of the usual metaphorical approximations hunters like to make of an animal's brute power. What is perhaps even more surprising, the reader is told nothing at all about the boy's emotional response to the one moment he has trained and waited for through so many hunting seasons.

If the reader cannot easily picture this episode within the frame of a glossy photograph from *Field and Stream* or *True,* it is because Faulkner's writing resists the kind of imagination that would want to reduce the scene to one more clearly and conventionally focused. The total effect produced by the blurring of the bear and woods, the amorphous presence of the boy, the uncertainty of movement, and the confusing shifts of sunlight and shadow is not the result of a verbal or pictorial incompetence but, on the contrary, is the consequence of a deliberate and complex effort of intelligence. Faulkner's style demands that the reader participate in that complexity. The reliance on negatives ("It did not emerge . . . not as big . . . It didn't walk"), the sudden modification of syntax ("but as big as he had expected, bigger, dimensionless"), the struggle to find adequate verbs or adjectives ("emerge, appear . . . immobile, fixed . . . faded, sank"), the process of expansion ("a fish, a huge old bass"), and the apparently reluctant concessions to narrative sequence ("Then he saw the bear . . . Then it moved . . . Then it was gone.") force the reader into suspending temporarily his expectations of the dimensions of an experience and the conduct of sentences. The style, in effect, compels the reader to experience a dislocation and conversion analogous to those that made Ike McCaslin's initiation into the wilderness possible.

A writer's style attests to the quality of his perceptions. Though Faulkner's verbal expansiveness in *The Bear* may seem difficult, even discouragingly so, the demands he makes on his readers are not necessarily any greater than those of writers like Thoreau, Crane, Wright, or Hemingway whose difficulties may seem, at first, much less apparent. The writing in "The Killers" certainly looks "easy," but that does not mean the tale is a "simple" one. Hemingway's stylistic reticence, his self-conscious artistic control, is the consequence of a literary acuity that is perhaps only slightly less remarkable than Faulkner's. If the styles of writers like Hemingway and Faulkner are based on perceptions that happen to be intricate, even unsettling, that is only because each writer struggles to master in his own way the countless verbal options at his disposal. Such writing presupposes an energetic reader, one who is willing to work almost as hard at reading as the author worked at writing. The readers imagined by the writers of the selections that follow would not be intimidated by the kind of rigorous training that, according to Henry David Thoreau, they must undergo if they are to read proficiently:

> To read well, that is, to read books in a true spirit, is a noble exercise, and one that will task the reader more than any exercise which the customs of the day esteem. It requires a training such as the athletes underwent, the steady intention almost of the whole life to this object. Books must be read as deliberately and reservedly as they were written. ("Reading," from *Walden*)

Thoreau's metaphor is, we think, an appropriate one. By comparing the exertion of reading to the "exercise" of athletics, Thoreau converts what is ordinarily regarded as an idle occasion into a tough and invigorating practice. To read well is to do something more than just be a spectator to what Robert Frost terms "the feat of words."

Nathaniel Hawthorne / Wakefield   1835

Throughout his literary career, Nathaniel Hawthorne (1804–64) was acutely conscious of his Puritan ancestors, one of whom presided at the infamous Salem witchcraft trials. After graduating from Bowdoin College in 1825, Hawthorne spent the next twelve years in relative seclusion at his home in Salem, researching and brooding over the chronicles and annals of New England local history that were to supply him with material for the sketches and tales he published continually in the popular periodicals of the day. In 1836, Hawthorne went to Boston, where he edited the American Magazine of Useful and Entertaining Knowledge. *Three years later he was offered a political appointment in the Boston Custom House, where he was able to support himself for a number of years while writing short stories and his first novel,* The Scarlet Letter *(1850).*

First published in the New England Magazine *for May, 1835, "Wakefield" was later included in* Twice-Told Tales *(1837).*

In some old magazine or newspaper I recollect a story, told as truth, of a man—let us call him Wakefield—who absented himself for a long time from his wife. The fact, thus abstractedly stated, is not very uncommon, nor—without a proper distinction of circumstances—to be condemned either as naughty or nonsensical. Howbeit, this, though far from the most aggravated, is perhaps the strangest, instance on record, of marital delinquency; and, moreover, as remarkable a freak as may be found in the whole list of human oddities. The wedded couple lived in London. The man, under pretence of going a journey, took lodgings in the next street to his own house, and there, unheard of by his wife or friends, and without the shadow of a reason for such self-banishment, dwelt upwards of twenty years. During that period, he beheld his home every day, and frequently the forlorn Mrs. Wakefield. And after so great a gap in his matrimonial felicity—when his death was reckoned certain, his estate settled, his name dismissed from memory, and his wife, long, long ago, resigned to her autumnal widowhood—he entered the door one evening, quietly, as from a day's absence, and became a loving spouse till death.

This outline is all that I remember. But the incident, though of the purest originality, unexampled, and probably never to be repeated, is one, I think, which appeals to the generous sympathies of mankind. We know, each for himself, that none of us would perpetrate such a folly, yet feel as if some other might. To my own contemplations, at least, it has often recurred, always exciting wonder, but with a sense that the story must be true, and a conception of its hero's character. Whenever any subject so forcibly affects the mind, time is well spent in thinking of it. If the reader choose, let him do his own meditation; or if he prefer to ramble with me through the twenty years of Wakefield's vagary, I bid him welcome; trusting that there will be a pervading spirit and a moral, even should we fail to find them, done up neatly, and condensed into the final sentence. Thought has always its efficacy, and every striking incident its moral.

What sort of a man was Wakefield? We are free to shape out our own idea, and call it by his name. He was now in the meridian of life; his matrimonial affections, never violent, were sobered into a calm, habitual sentiment; of all husbands, he was likely to be the most constant, because a certain sluggishness would keep his heart at rest, wherever it might be placed. He was intellectual, but not actively so; his mind occupied itself in long and lazy musings, that ended to no purpose, or had not vigor to attain it; his thoughts were seldom so energetic as to seize hold of words. Imagination, in the proper meaning of the term, made no part of Wakefield's gifts. With a cold but not depraved nor wandering heart, and a mind never feverish with riotous thoughts, nor perplexed with originality, who could have anticipated that our friend would entitle himself to a foremost place among the doers of eccentric deeds? Had his acquaintances been asked, who was the man in London the surest to perform nothing today which should be remembered on the morrow, they would have thought of Wakefield. Only the wife of his bosom might have hesitated. She, without having analyzed his character, was partly aware of a quiet selfishness, that had rusted into his inactive mind; of a peculiar sort of vanity, the most uneasy attribute about him; of a disposition to craft, which had seldom produced more positive effects than the keeping of petty secrets, hardly worth revealing; and, lastly, of what she called a little strangeness, sometimes, in the good man. This latter quality is indefinable, and perhaps non-existent.

Let us now imagine Wakefield bidding adieu to his wife. It is the dusk of an October evening. His equipment is a drab great-coat, a hat covered with an oilcloth, top-boots, an umbrella in one hand and a small port-manteau in the other. He has informed Mrs. Wakefield that he is to take the night coach into the country. She would fain inquire the length of his journey, its object, and the probable time of his return; but, indulgent to his harmless love of mystery, interrogates him only by a look. He tells her not to expect him positively by the return coach, nor to be alarmed should he tarry three or four days; but, at all events, to look for him at supper on Friday evening. Wakefield himself, be it considered, has no suspicion of what is before him. He holds out his hand, she gives her own, and meets his parting kiss in the matter-of-course way of a ten years' matrimony; and forth goes the middle-aged Mr. Wakefield, almost resolved to perplex his good lady by a whole week's absence. After the door has closed behind him, she perceives it thrust partly open, and a vision of her husband's face, through the aperture, smiling on her, and gone in a moment. For the time, this little incident is dismissed without a thought. But, long afterwards, when she has been more years a widow than a wife, that smile recurs, and flickers across all her reminiscences of Wakefield's visage. In her many musings, she surrounds the original smile with a multitude of fantasies, which make it strange and awful: as, for instance, if she imagines him in a coffin, that parting look is frozen on his pale features; or, if she dreams of him in heaven, still his blessed spirit wears a quiet and crafty smile. Yet, for its sake, when all others have given him up for dead, she sometimes doubts whether she is a widow.

But our business is with the husband. We must hurry after him along the street, ere he lose his individuality, and melt into the great mass of London life. It would be vain searching for him there. Let us follow close at his heels, therefore, until, after several superfluous turns and doublings, we find him comfortably established by the fireside of a small apartment, previously bespoken. He is in the next street to his own, and at his journey's end. He can scarcely trust his good fortune, in having got thither unperceived—recollecting that, at one time, he was delayed by the throng, in the very focus of a lighted lantern; and, again, there were footsteps that seemed to tread behind his own, distinct from the multitudinous tramp around him; and, anon, he heard a voice shouting afar, and fancied that it called his name. Doubtless, a dozen busybodies had been watching him, and told his wife the whole affair. Poor Wakefield! Little knowest thou thine own insignificance in this great world! No mortal eye but mine has traced thee. Go quietly to thy bed, foolish man; and, on the morrow, if thou wilt be wise, get thee home to good Mrs. Wakefield, and tell her the truth. Remove not thyself, even for a little week, from thy place in her chaste bosom. Were she, for a single moment, to deem thee dead, or lost, or lastingly divided from her, thou wouldst be wofully conscious of a change in thy true wife forever after. It is perilous to make a chasm in human affections; not that they gape so long and wide—but so quickly close again!

Almost repenting of his frolic, or whatever it may be termed, Wakefield lies down betimes, and starting from his first nap, spreads forth his arms into the wide and solitary waste of the unaccustomed bed. "No,"—thinks he, gathering the bedclothes about him—"I will not sleep alone another night."

In the morning he rises earlier than usual, and sets himself to consider what he really means to do. Such are his loose and rambling modes of thought that he has taken this very singular step with the consciousness of a purpose, indeed, but without being able to define it sufficiently for his own contemplation. The vagueness of the project, and the convulsive effort with which he plunges into the execution of it, are equally characteristic of a feeble-minded man. Wakefield sifts his ideas, however, as minutely as he may, and finds himself curious to know the progress of matters at home—how his exemplary wife will endure her widowhood of a week; and, briefly, how the little sphere of creatures and circumstances, in which he was a central object, will be affected by his removal. A morbid vanity, therefore, lies nearest the bottom of the affair. But, how is he to attain his ends? Not, certainly, by keeping close in this comfortable lodging, where, though he slept and awoke in the next street to his home, he is as effectually abroad as if the stage-coach had been whirling him away all night. Yet, should he reappear, the whole project is knocked in the head. His poor brains being hopelessly puzzled with this dilemma, he at length ventures out, partly resolving to cross the head of the street, and send one hasty glance towards his forsaken domicile. Habit—for he is a man of habits—takes him by the hand, and guides him, wholly unaware, to his own door, where, just at the critical moment, he is aroused by the scraping of his foot upon the step. Wakefield! whither are you going?

At that instant his fate was turning on the pivot. Little dreaming of the doom to which his first backward step devotes him, he hurries away, breathless with agitation hitherto unfelt, and hardly dares turn his head at the distant corner. Can it be that nobody caught sight of him? Will not the whole household—the decent Mrs. Wakefield, the smart maid servant, and the dirty little footboy—raise a hue and cry, through London streets, in pursuit of their fugitive lord and master? Wonderful escape! He gathers courage to pause and look homeward, but is perplexed with a sense of change about the familiar edifice, such as affects us all, when, after a separation of months or years, we again see some hill or lake, or work of art, with which we were friends of old. In ordinary cases, this indescribable impression is caused by the comparison and contrast between our imperfect reminiscences and the reality. In Wakefield, the magic of a single night has wrought a similar transformation, because, in that brief period, a great moral change has been effected. But this is a secret from himself. Before leaving the spot, he catches a far and momentary glimpse of his wife, passing athwart the front window, with her face turned towards the head of the street. The crafty nincompoop takes to his heels, scared with the idea that, among a thousand such atoms of mortality, her eye must have detected him. Right glad is his heart, though his brain be somewhat dizzy, when he finds himself by the coal fire of his lodgings.

So much for the commencement of this long whimwham. After the initial conception, and the stirring up of the man's sluggish temperament to put it in practice, the whole matter evolves itself in a natural train. We may suppose him, as the result of deep deliberation, buying a new wig, of reddish hair, and selecting sundry garments, in a fashion unlike his customary suit of brown, from a Jew's old-clothes bag. It is accomplished. Wakefield is another man. The new system being now established, a retrograde movement to the old would be almost as difficult as the step that placed him in his unparalleled position. Furthermore, he is rendered obstinate by a sulkiness occasionally incident to his temper, and brought on at present by the inadequate sensation which he conceives to have been produced in the bosom of Mrs. Wakefield. He will not go back until she be frightened half to death. Well; twice or thrice has she passed before his sight, each time with a heavier step, a paler cheek, and more anxious brow; and in the third week of his non-appearance he detects a portent of evil entering the house, in the guise of an apothecary. Next day the knocker is muffled. Towards nightfall comes the chariot of a physician, and deposits its big-wigged and solemn burden at Wakefield's door, whence, after a quarter of an hour's visit, he emerges, perchance the herald of a funeral. Dear woman! Will she die? By this time, Wakefield is excited to something like energy of feeling, but still lingers away from his wife's bedside, pleading with his conscience that she must not be disturbed at such a juncture. If aught else restrains him, he does not know it. In the course of a few weeks she gradually recovers; the crisis is over; her heart is sad, perhaps, but quiet; and, let him return soon or late, it will never be feverish for him again. Such ideas glimmer through the midst of Wakefield's mind, and render him indistinctly conscious that an almost impassable gulf divides his hired apartment from his former home. "It is but in the next street!" he sometimes says. Fool! it is in another world. Hitherto, he has put off his return from one particular day to another; henceforward, he leaves the precise time undetermined. Not tomorrow—probably next week—pretty soon. Poor man! The dead have nearly as much chance of revisiting their earthly homes as the self-banished Wakefield.

Would that I had a folio to write, instead of an article of a dozen pages! Then might I exemplify how an influence beyond our control lays its strong hand on every deed which we do, and weaves its consequences into an iron tissue of necessity. Wakefield is spell-bound. We must leave him, for ten years or so, to haunt around his house, without once crossing the threshold, and to be faithful to his wife, with all the affection of which his heart is capable, while he is slowly fading out of hers. Long since, it must be remarked, he had lost the perception of singularity in his conduct.

Now for a scene! Amid the throng of a London street we distinguish a man, now waxing elderly, with few characteristics to attract careless observers, yet bearing, in his whole aspect, the handwriting of no common fate, for such as have the skill to read it. He is meagre; his low and narrow forehead is deeply wrinkled; his eyes, small and lustreless, sometimes wander apprehensively about him, but oftener seem to look inward. He bends his head, and moves with an indescribable obliquity of gait, as if unwilling to display his full front to the world. Watch him long enough to see what we have described, and you will allow that circumstances—which often produce remarkable men from nature's ordinary handiwork—have produced one such here. Next, leaving him to sidle along the footwalk, cast your eyes in the opposite direction, where a portly female, considerably in the wane of life, with a prayer-book in her hand, is proceeding to yonder church. She has the placid mien of settled widowhood. Her regrets have either died away, or have become so essential to her heart, that they would be poorly exchanged for joy. Just as the lean man and well-conditioned woman are passing, a slight obstruction occurs, and brings these two figures directly in contact. Their hands touch; the pressure of the crowd forces her bosom against his shoulder; they stand, face to face, staring into each other's eyes. After a ten years' separation, thus Wakefield meets his wife!

The throng eddies away, and carries them asunder. The sober widow, resuming her former pace, proceeds to church, but pauses in the portal, and throws a perplexed glance along the street. She passes in, however, opening her prayer-book as she goes. And the man! with so wild a face that busy and selfish London stands to gaze after him, he hurries to his lodgings, bolts the door, and throws himself upon the bed. The latent feelings of years break out; his feeble mind acquires a brief energy from their strength; all the miserable strangeness of his life is revealed to him at a glance: and he cries out, passionately, "Wakefield! Wakefield! You are mad!"

Perhaps he was so. The singularity of his situation must have so moulded him to himself, that, considered in regard to his fellow-creatures and the business of life, he could not be said to possess his right mind. He had contrived, or rather he had happened, to dissever himself from the world—to vanish—to give up his place and privileges with living men, without being admitted among the dead. The life of a hermit is nowise parallel to his. He was in the bustle of the city, as of old; but the crowd swept by and saw him not; he was, we may figuratively say, always beside his wife and at his hearth, yet must never feel the warmth of the one nor the affection of the other. It was Wakefield's unprecedented fate to retain his original share of human sympathies, and to be still involved in human interests, while he had lost his reciprocal influence on them. It would be a most curious speculation to trace out the effect of such circumstances on his heart and intellect, separately, and in unison. Yet, changed as he was, he would seldom be conscious of it, but deem himself the same man as ever; glimpses of the truth, indeed, would come, but only for the moment; and still he would keep saying, "I shall soon go back!"—nor reflect that he had been saying so for twenty years.

I conceive, also, that these twenty years would appear, in the retrospect, scarcely longer than the week to which Wakefield had at first limited his absence. He would look on the affair as no more than an interlude in the main business of his life. When, after a little while more, he should deem it time to reënter his parlor, his wife would clap her hands for joy, on beholding the middle-aged Mr. Wakefield. Alas, what a mistake! Would Time but await the close of our favorite follies, we should be young men, all of us, and till Doomsday.

One evening, in the twentieth year since he vanished, Wakefield is taking his customary walk towards the dwelling which he still calls his own. It is a gusty night of autumn, with frequent showers that patter down upon the pavement, and are gone before a man can put up his umbrella. Pausing near the house, Wakefield discerns, through the parlor windows of the second floor, the red glow and the glimmer and fitful flash of a comfortable fire. On the ceiling appears a grotesque shadow of good Mrs. Wakefield. The cap, the nose and chin, and the broad waist, form an admirable caricature, which dances, moreover, with the up-flickering and down-sinking blaze, almost too merrily for the shade of an elderly widow. At this instant a shower chances to fall, and is driven, by the unmannerly gust, full into Wakefield's face and bosom. He is quite penetrated with its autumnal chill. Shall he stand, wet and shivering here, when his own hearth has a good fire to warm him, and his own wife will run to fetch the gray coat and small-clothes, which, doubtless, she has kept carefully in the closet of their bed chamber? No! Wakefield is no such fool. He ascends the steps—heavily!—for twenty years have stiffened his legs since he came down—but he knows it not. Stay, Wakefield! Would you go to the sole home that is left you? Then step into your grave! The door opens. As he passes in, we have a parting glimpse of his visage, and recognize the crafty smile, which was the precursor of the little joke that he has ever since been playing off at his wife's expense. How unmercifully has he quizzed the poor woman! Well, a good night's rest to Wakefield!

This happy event—supposing it to be such—could only have occurred at an unpremeditated moment. We will not follow our friend across the threshold. He has left us much food for thought, a portion of which shall lend its wisdom to a moral, and be shaped into a figure. Amid the seeming confusion of our mysterious world, individuals are so nicely adjusted to a system, and systems to one another and to a whole, that, by stepping aside for a moment, a man exposes himself to a fearful risk of losing his place forever. Like Wakefield, he may become, as it were, the Outcast of the Universe.

Edgar Allan Poe / The Man of the Crowd   1840

In his efforts to elevate the craft of magazine journalism, Edgar Allan Poe attempted to blend the techniques of fiction, the theories of scholarship, and the special skills of reporting. In the process, Poe produced some of the finest and strangest short stories in American literature. "The Man of the Crowd" first appeared in a popular miscellany of tales, articles, and oddities called The Casket *(December 1840). The tale introduces us to a character who may well be the first "private eye" in literature, a man in search of both a crime and a vocation.*

Ce grand malheur, de ne pouvoir être seul.
        —La Bruyère

It was well said of a certain German book that *"es lässt sich nicht lesen"*—it does not permit itself to be read. There are some secrets which do not permit themselves to be told. Men die nightly in their beds, wringing the hands of ghostly confessors, and looking them piteously in the eyes—die with despair of heart and convulsion of throat, on account of the hideousness of mysteries which will not *suffer themselves* to be revealed. Now and then, alas, the conscience of man takes up a burthen so heavy in horror that it can be thrown down only into the grave. And thus the essence of all crime is undivulged.

Not long ago, about the closing in of an evening in autumn, I sat at the large bow window of the D—— Coffee-House in London. For some months I had been ill in health, but was now convalescent, and, with returning strength, found myself in one of those happy moods which are so precisely the converse of *ennui*—moods of the keenest appetency, when the film from the mental vision departs—the ἀχλὺς ἣ πρὶν ἐπῆεν—and the intellect, electrified, surpasses as greatly its everyday conditions, as does the vivid yet candid reason of Leibnitz, the mad and flimsy rhetoric of Gorgias. Merely to breathe was enjoyment; and I derived positive pleasure even from many of the legitimate sources of pain. I felt a calm but inquisitive interest in every thing. With a cigar in my mouth and a newspaper in my lap, I had been amusing myself for the greater part of the afternoon, now in poring over advertisements, now in observing the promiscuous company in the room, and now in peering through the smoky panes into the street.

This latter is one of the principal thoroughfares of the city, and had been very much crowded during the whole day. But, as the darkness came on, the throng momently increased; and, by the time the lamps were well lighted, two dense and continuous tides of population were rushing past the door. At this particular period of the evening I had never before been in a similar situation, and the tumultuous sea of human heads filled me, therefore, with a delicious novelty of emotion. I gave up, at length, all care of things within the hotel, and became absorbed in contemplation of the scene without.

At first my observations took an abstract and generalizing turn. I looked at the passengers in masses, and thought of them in their aggregate relations. Soon, however, I descended to details, and regarded with minute interest the innumerable varieties of figure, dress, air, gait, visage, and expression of countenance.

By far the greater number of those who went by had a satisfied business-like demeanor, and seemed to be thinking only of making their way through the press. Their brows were knit, and their eyes rolled quickly; when pushed against by fellow-wayfarers they evinced no symptom of impatience, had adjusted their clothes and hurried on. Others, still a numerous class, were restless in their movements, had flushed faces, and talked and gesticulated to themselves, as if feeling in solitude on account of the very denseness of the company around. When impeded in their progress, these people suddenly ceased muttering, but redoubled their gesticulations, and awaited, with an absent and overdone smile upon the lips, the course of the persons impeding them. If jostled, they bowed profusely to the jostlers, and appeared overwhelmed with confusion.—There was nothing very distinctive about these two large classes beyond what I have noted. Their habiliments belonged to that order which is pointedly termed the decent. They were undoubtedly noblemen, merchants, attorneys, tradesmen, stock-jobbers—the Eupatrids and the commonplaces of society—men of leisure and men actively engaged in affairs of their own—conducting business upon their own responsibility. They did not greatly excite my attention.

The tribe of clerks was an obvious one; and here I discerned two remarkable divisions. There were the junior clerks of flash houses—young gentlemen with tight coats, bright boots, well-oiled hair, and supercilious lips. Setting aside a certain dapperness of carriage, which may be termed *deskism* for want of a better word, the manner of these persons seemed to me an exact facsimile of what had been the perfection of *bon ton* about twelve or eighteen months before. They wore the cast-off graces of the gentry;—and this, I believe, involves the best definition of the class.

The division of the upper clerks of staunch firms, or of the "steady old fellows," it was not possible to mistake. These were known by their coats and pantaloons of black or brown, made to sit comfortably, with white cravats and waistcoats, broad solid-looking shoes, and thick hose or gaiters.—They had all slightly bald heads, from which the right ears, long used to pen-holding, had an odd habit of standing off on end. I observed that they always removed or settled their hats with both hands, and wore watches, with short gold chains of a substantial and ancient pattern. Theirs was the affectation of respectability;—if indeed there be an affectation so honorable.

There were many individuals of dashing appearance, whom I easily understood as belonging to the race of swell pick-pockets, with which all great cities are infested. I watched these gentry with much inquisitiveness, and found it difficult to imagine how they should ever be mistaken for gentlemen by gentlemen themselves. Their voluminousness of wristband, with an air of excessive frankness, should betray them at once.

The gamblers, of whom I descried not a few, were still more easily recognisable. They wore every variety of dress, from that of the desperate thimble-rig bully, with velvet waistcoat, fancy neckerchief, gilt chains, and filagreed buttons, to that of the scrupulously inornate clergyman than which nothing could be less liable to suspicion. Still all were distinguished by a certain sodden swarthiness of complexion, a filmy dimness of eye, and pallor and compression of lip. There were two other traits, moreover, by which I could always detect them;—a guarded lowness of tone in conversation, and a more than ordinary extension of the thumb in a direction at right angles with the fingers.—Very often, in company with these sharpers, I observed an order of men somewhat different in habits, but still birds of a kindred feather. They may be defined as the gentlemen who live by their wits. They seem to prey upon the public in two battalions—that of the dandies and that of the military men. Of the first grade the leading features are long locks and smiles; of the second frogged coats and frowns.

Descending in the scale of what is termed gentility, I found darker and deeper themes for speculation. I saw Jew pedlars, with hawk eyes flashing from countenances whose every other feature wore only an expression of abject humility; sturdy professional street beggars scowling upon mendicants of a better stamp, whom despair alone had driven forth into the night for charity; feeble and ghastly invalids, upon whom death had placed a sure hand, and who sidled and tottered through the mob, looking every one beseechingly in the face, as if in search of some chance consolation, some lost hope; modest young girls returning from long and late labor to a cheerless home, and shrinking more tearfully than indignantly from the glances of ruffians, whose direct contact, even, could not be avoided; women of the town of all kinds and of all ages—the unequivocal beauty in the prime of her womanhood, putting one in mind of the statue in Lucian, with the surface of Parian marble, and the interior filled with filth—the loathsome and utterly lost leper in rags—the wrinkled, bejewelled and paint-begrimed beldame, making a last effort at youth—the mere child of immature form, yet, from long association, an adept in the dreadful coquetries of her trade, and burning with a rabid ambition to be ranked the equal of her elders in vice; drunkards innumerable and indescribable—some in shreds and patches, reeling, inarticulate, with bruised visage and lack-lustre eyes—some in whole although filthy garments, with a slightly unsteady swagger, thick sensual lips, and hearty-looking rubicund faces—others clothed in materials which had once been good, and which even now were scrupulously well brushed—men who walked with a more than naturally firm and springy step, but whose countenances were fearfully pale, whose eyes hideously wild and red, and who clutched with quivering fingers, as they strode through the crowd, at every object which came within their reach; beside these, pie-men, porters, coal-heavers, sweeps; organ-grinders, monkey-exhibiters and ballad mongers, those who vended with those who sang; ragged artizans and exhausted laborers of every description, and all full of a noisy and inordinate vivacity which jarred discordantly upon the ear, and gave an aching sensation to the eye.

As the night deepened, so deepened to me the interest of the scene; for not only did the general character of the crowd materially alter (its gentler features retiring in the gradual withdrawal of the more orderly portion of the people, and its harsher ones coming out into bolder relief, as the late hour brought forth every species of infamy from its den,) but the rays of the gas-lamps, feeble at first in their struggle with the dying day, had now at length gained ascendancy, and threw over every thing a fitful and garish lustre. All was dark yet splendid—as that ebony to which has been likened the style of Tertullian.

The wild effects of the light enchained me to an examination of individual faces; and although the rapidity with which the world of light flitted before the window, prevented me from casting more than a glance upon each visage, still it seemed that, in my then peculiar mental state, I could frequently read, even in that brief interval of a glance, the history of long years.

With my brow to the glass, I was thus occupied in scrutinizing the mob, when suddenly there came into view a countenance (that of a decrepit old man, some sixty-five or seventy years of age,)—a countenance which at once arrested and absorbed my whole attention, on account of the absolute idiosyncracy of its expression. Any thing even remotely resembling that expression I had never seen before. I well remember that my first thought, upon beholding it, was that Retszch, had he viewed it, would have greatly preferred it to his own pictural incarnations of the fiend. As I endeavored, during the brief minute of my original survey, to form some analysis of the meaning conveyed, there arose confusedly and paradoxically within my mind, the ideas of vast mental power, of caution, of penuriousness, of avarice, of coolness, of malice, of blood-thirstiness, of triumph, of merriment, of excessive terror, of intense—of extreme despair. I felt singularly aroused, startled, fascinated. "How wild a history," I said to myself, "is written within that bosom!" Then came a craving desire to keep the man in view—to know more of him. Hurriedly putting on an overcoat, and seizing my hat and cane, I made my way into the street, and pushed through the crowd in the direction which I had seen him take; for he had already disappeared. With some little difficulty I at length came within sight of him, approached, and followed him closely, yet cautiously, so as not to attract his attention.

I had now a good opportunity of examining his person. He was short in stature, very thin, and apparently very feeble. His clothes, generally, were filthy and ragged; but as he came, now and then, within the strong glare of a lamp, I perceived that his linen, although dirty, was of beautiful texture; and my vision deceived me, or, through a rent in a closely-buttoned and evidently second-handed *roquelaire* which enveloped him, I caught a glimpse both of a diamond and of a dagger. These observations heightened my curiosity, and I resolved to follow the stranger whithersoever he should go.

It was now fully night-fall, and a thick humid fog hung over the city, soon ending in a settled and heavy rain. This change of weather had an odd effect upon the crowd, the whole of which was at once put into new commotion, and overshadowed by a world of umbrellas. The waver, the jostle, and the hum increased in a tenfold degree. For my own part I did not much regard the rain—the lurking of an old fever in my system rendering the moisture somewhat too dangerously pleasant. Tying a handkerchief about my mouth, I kept on. For half an hour the old man held his way with difficulty along the great thoroughfare; and I here walked close at his elbow through fear of losing sight of him. Never once turning his head to look back, he did not observe me. By and bye he passed into a cross street, which, although densely filled with people, was not quite so much thronged as the main one he had quitted. Here a change in his demeanor became evident. He walked more slowly and with less object than before—more hesitatingly. He crossed and re-crossed the way repeatedly without apparent aim; and the press was still so thick, that, at every such movement, I was obliged to follow him closely. The street was a narrow and long one, and his course lay within it for nearly an hour, during which the passengers had gradually diminished to about that number which is ordinarily seen at noon in Broadway near the Park—so vast a difference is there between a London populace and that of the most frequented American city. A second turn brought us into a square, brilliantly lighted, and overflowing with life. The old manner of the stranger reappeared. His chin fell upon his breast, while his eyes rolled wildly from under his knit brows, in every direction, upon those who hemmed him in. He urged his way steadily and perseveringly. I was surprised, however, to find, upon his having made the circuit of the square, that he turned and retraced his steps. Still more was I astonished to see him repeat the same walk several times—once nearly detecting me as he came round with a sudden movement.

In this exercise he spent another hour, at the end of which we met with far less interruption from passengers than at first. The rain fell fast; the air grew cool; and the people were retiring to their homes. With a gesture of impatience, the wanderer passed into a by-street comparatively deserted. Down this, some quarter of a mile long, he rushed with an activity I could not have dreamed of seeing in one so aged, and which put me to much trouble in pursuit. A few minutes brought us to a large and busy bazaar, with the localities of which the stranger appeared well acquainted, and where his original demeanor again became apparent, as he forced his way to and fro, without aim, among the host of buyers and sellers.

During the hour and a half, or thereabouts, which we passed in this place, it required much caution on my part to keep him within reach without attracting his observation. Luckily I wore a pair of caoutchouc over-shoes, and could move about in perfect silence. At no moment did he see that I watched him. He entered shop after shop, priced nothing, spoke no word, and looked at all objects with a wild and vacant stare. I was now utterly amazed at his behaviour, and firmly resolved that we should not part until I had satisfied myself in some measure respecting him.

A loud-toned clock struck eleven, and the company were fast deserting the bazaar. A shop-keeper, in putting up a shutter, jostled the old man, and at the instant I saw a strong shudder come over his frame. He hurried into the street, looked anxiously around him for an instant, and then ran with incredible swiftness through many crooked and people-less lanes, until we emerged once more upon the great thoroughfare whence we had started—the street of the D—— Hotel. It no longer wore, however, the same aspect. It was still brilliant with gas; but the rain fell fiercely, and there were few persons to be seen. The stranger grew pale. He walked moodily some paces up the once populous avenue, then, with a heavy sigh, turned in the direction of the river, and, plunging through a great variety of devious ways, came out, at length, in view of one of the principal theatres. It was about being closed, and the audience were thronging from the doors. I saw the old man gasp as if for breath while he threw himself amid the crowd; but I thought that the intense agony of his countenance had, in some measure, abated. His head again fell upon his breast; he appeared as I had seen him at first. I observed that he now took the course in which had gone the greater number of the audience—but, upon the whole, I was at a loss to comprehend the waywardness of his actions.

As he proceeded, the company grew more scattered, and his old uneasiness and vacillation were resumed. For some time he followed closely a party of some ten or twelve roisterers; but from this number one by one dropped off, until three only remained together, in a narrow and gloomy lane little frequented. The stranger paused, and, for a moment, seemed lost in thought; then, with every mark of agitation, pursued, rapidly a route which brought us to the verge of the city, amid regions very different from those we had hitherto traversed. It was the most noisome quarter of London, where everything wore the worst impress of the most deplorable poverty, and of the most desperate crime. By the dim light of an accidental lamp, tall, antique, worm-eaten, wooden tenements were seen tottering to their fall, in directions so many and capricious that scarce the semblance of a passage was discernible between them. The paving-stones lay at random, displaced from their beds by the rankly growing grass. Horrible filth festered in the dammed-up gutters. The whole atmosphere teemed with desolation. Yet, as we proceeded, the sounds of human life revived by sure degrees, and at length large bands of the most abandoned of a London populace were seen reeling to and fro. The spirits of the old man again flickered up, as a lamp which is near its death-hour. Once more he strode onward with elastic tread. Suddenly a corner was turned, a blaze of light burst upon our sight, and we stood before one of the huge suburban temples of Intemperance—one of the palaces of the fiend, Gin.

It was now nearly day-break; but a number of wretched inebriates still pressed in and out of the flaunting entrance. With a half shriek of joy the old man forced a passage within, resumed at once his original bearing, and stalked backward and forward, without apparent object, among the throng. He had not been thus long occupied, however, before a rush to the doors gave token that the host was closing them for the night. It was something even more intense than despair that I then observed upon the countenance of the singular being whom I had watched so pertinaciously. Yet he did not hesitate in his career, but, with a mad energy, retraced his steps at once, to the heart of the mighty London. Long and swiftly he fled, while I followed him in the wildest amazement, resolute not to abandon a scrutiny in which I now felt an interest all-absorbing. The sun arose while we proceeded, and, when we had once again reached that most thronged mart of the populous town, the street of the D—— Hotel, it presented an appearance of human bustle and activity scarcely inferior to what I had seen on the evening before. And here, long, amid the momently increasing confusion, did I persist in my pursuit of the stranger. But, as usual, he walked to and fro, and during the day did not pass from out the turmoil of that street. And, as the shades of the second evening came on, I grew wearied unto death, and, stopping fully in front of the wanderer, gazed at him steadfastly in the face. He noticed me not, but resumed his solemn walk, while I, ceasing to follow, remained absorbed in contemplation. "This old man," I said at length, "is the type and the genius of deep crime. He refuses to be alone. *He is the man of the crowd*. It will be in vain to follow; for I shall learn no more of him, nor of his deeds. The worst heart of the world is a grosser book than the 'Hortulus Animae,' and perhaps it is but one of the great mercies of God that *es lässt sich nicht lesen*."

Henry David Thoreau / *Walden*   1854

Although Henry David Thoreau participated very deeply in American political and cultural life, his name has become synonymous with the archetypal voluntary exile who rejects a crass materialistic world in favor of a rugged, self-reliant outdoor existence and a "career" as an amateur naturalist. The image is partly true: Thoreau consistently endorses a simple, independent, organic life. But it is important to remember that Thoreau was also an outspoken abolitionist, a defender of John Brown even after the bloody raid on Harper's Ferry, and a conscientious dissenter who devised a highly influential philosophy of civil disobedience.

Born in Concord, Massachusetts, son of a pencil manufacturer, Thoreau graduated from Harvard having mastered Greek in 1837. He was also a master of many trades, though all his life he worked only sporadically: at chores, at surveying, at tutoring, at his father's shop, at lecturing, at odd jobs. He never made a good living, although he apparently lived a good life. Only two of his books were published in his lifetime: A Week on the Concord and Merrimack Rivers *(1849) and* Walden *(1854). He never married; he left parties early; he seldom traveled beyond Concord. He died of tuberculosis, a disappointment to his family and friends, when he was forty-four.*

At a time in American history when thousands voluntarily exiled themselves in tiny cabins on the slopes of western mountains to search for gold, Thoreau searched for a different kind of wealth along the gentle edges of a small Massachusetts pond. The book he wrote describing his twenty-six month retreat has long been considered a classic account of a peculiarly American consciousness. The following section, "Where I Lived and What I Lived for," is an excerpt from the second chapter of Walden.

WHERE I LIVED, AND WHAT I LIVED FOR

I went to the woods because I wished to live deliberately, to front only the essential facts of life, and see if I could not learn what it had to teach, and not, when I came to die, discover that I had not lived. I did not wish to live what was not life, living is so dear; nor did I wish to practise resignation, unless it was quite necessary. I wanted to live deep and suck out all the marrow of life, to live so sturdily and Spartan-like as to put to rout all that was not life, to cut a broad swath and shave close, to drive life into a corner, and reduce it to its lowest terms, and, if it proved to be mean, why then to get the whole and genuine meanness of it, and publish its meanness to the world; or if it were sublime, to know it by experience, and be able to give a true account of it in my next excursion. For most men, it appears to me, are in a strange uncertainty about it, whether it is of the devil or of God, and have *somewhat hastily* concluded that it is the chief end of man here to "glorify God and enjoy him forever."

Still we live meanly, like ants; though the fable tells us that we were long ago changed into men; like pygmies we fight with cranes; it is error upon error, and clout upon clout, and our best virtue has for its occasion a superfluous and evitable wretchedness. Our life is frittered away by detail. An honest man has hardly need to count more than his ten fingers, or in extreme cases he may add his ten toes, and lump the rest. Simplicity, simplicity, simplicity! I say, let your affairs be as two or three, and not a hundred or a thousand; instead of a million count half a dozen, and keep your accounts on your thumb-nail. In the midst of this chopping sea of civilized life, such are the clouds and storms and quicksands and thousand-and-one items to be allowed for, that a man has to live, if he would not founder and go to the bottom and not make his port at all, by dead reckoning, and he must be a great calculator indeed who succeeds. Simplify, simplify. Instead of three meals a day, if it be necessary eat but one; instead of a hundred dishes, five; and reduce other things in proportion. Our life is like a German Confederacy, made up of petty states, with its boundary forever fluctuating, so that even a German cannot tell you how it is bounded at any moment. The nation itself, with all its so-called internal improvements, which, by the way, are all external and superficial, is just such an unwieldy and overgrown establishment, cluttered with furniture and tripped up by its own traps, ruined by luxury and heedless expense, by want of calculation and a worthy aim, as the million households in the land; and the only cure for it, as for them, is in a rigid economy, a stern and more than Spartan simplicity of life and elevation of purpose. It lives too fast. Men think that it is essential that the *Nation* have commerce, and export ice, and talk through a telegraph, and ride thirty miles an hour, without a doubt, whether *they* do or not; but whether we should live like baboons or like men, is a little uncertain. If we do not get out sleepers, and forge rails, and devote days and nights to the work, but go to tinkering upon our *lives* to improve *them,* who will build railroads? And if railroads are not built, how shall we get to Heaven in season? But if we stay at home and mind our business, who will want railroads? We do not ride on the railroad; it rides upon us. Did you ever think what those sleepers are that underlie the railroad? Each one is a man, an Irishman, or a Yankee man. The rails are laid on them, and they are covered with sand, and the cars run smoothly over them. They are sound sleepers, I assure you. And every few years a new lot is laid down and run over; so that, if some have the pleasure of riding on a rail, others have the misfortune to be ridden upon. And when they run over a man that is walking in his sleep, a supernumerary sleeper in the wrong position, and wake him up, they suddenly stop the cars, and make a hue and cry about it as if this were an exception. I am glad to know that it takes a gang of men for every five miles to keep the sleepers down and level in their beds as it is, for this is a sign that they may sometime get up again.

Why should we live with such hurry and waste of life? We are determined to be starved before we are hungry. Men say that a stitch in time saves nine, and so they take a thousand stitches to-day to save nine tomorrow. As for *work,* we haven't any of any consequence. We have the Saint Vitus' dance, and cannot possibly keep our heads still. If I should only give a few pulls at the parish bell-rope, as for a fire, that is, without setting the bell, there is hardly a man on his farm in the out-skirts of Concord, notwithstanding that press of engagements which was his ex-cuse so many times this morning, nor a boy, nor a woman, I might almost say, but would forsake all and follow that sound, not mainly to save property from the flames, but, if we will confess the truth, much more to see it burn, since burn it must, and we, be it known, did not set it on fire,—or to see it put out, and have a hand in it, if that is done as handsomely; yes, even if it were the parish church it-self. Hardly a man takes a half-hour's nap after dinner, but when he wakes he holds up his head and asks, "What's the news?" as if the rest of mankind had stood his sentinels. Some give directions to be waked every half-hour, doubtless for no other purpose; and then, to pay for it, they tell what they have dreamed. After a night's sleep the news is as indispensable as the breakfast. "Pray tell me anything new that has happened to a man anywhere on this globe,"—and he reads it over his coffee and rolls, that a man has had his eyes gouged out this morning on the Wachito River; never dreaming the while that he lives in the dark un-fathomed mammoth cave of this world, and has but the rudiment of an eye him-self.

For my part, I could easily do without the post-office. I think that there are very few important communications made through it. To speak critically, I never re-ceived more than one or two letters in my life—I wrote this some years ago—that were worth the postage. The penny-post is, commonly, an institution through which you seriously offer a man that penny for his thoughts which is so often safely offered in jest. And I am sure that I never read any memorable news in a newspaper. If we read of one man robbed, or murdered, or killed by accident, or one house burned, or one vessel wrecked, or one steamboat blown up, or one cow run over on the Western Railroad, or one mad dog killed, or one lot of grasshop-pers in the winter,—we never need read of another. One is enough. If you are acquainted with the principle, what do you care for a myriad instances and appli-cations? To a philosopher all *news*, as it is called, is gossip and they who edit and read it are old women over their tea. Yet not a few are greedy after this gossip. There was such a rush, as I hear, the other day at one of the offices to learn the foreign news by the last arrival, that several large squares of plate glass belonging to the establishment were broken by the pressure,—news which I seriously think a ready wit might write a twelvemonth, or twelve years, beforehand with sufficient accuracy. As for Spain, for instance, if you know how to throw in Don Carlos and the Infanta, and Don Pedro and Seville and Granada, from time to time in the right proportions,—they may have changed the names a little since I saw the papers,—and serve up a bull-fight when other entertainments fail, it will be true to the letter, and give us as good an idea of the exact state or ruin of things in Spain as the most succinct and lucid reports under this head in the newspapers: and as for England, almost the last significant scrap of news from that quarter was the revolution of 1649; and if you have learned the history of her crops for an average year, you never need attend to that thing again, unless your speculations are of a merely pecuniary character. If one may judge who rarely looks into the newspa-pers, nothing new does ever happen in foreign parts, a French revolution not ex-cepted.

What news! how much more important to know what that is which was never old! "Kieou-he-yu (great dignitary of the state of Wei) sent a man to Khoung-tseu to know his news. Khoung-tseu caused the messenger to be seated near him, and questioned him in these terms: What is your master doing? The messenger answered with respect: My master desires to diminish the number of his faults, but he cannot come to the end of them. The messenger being gone, the philosopher remarked: What a worthy messenger! What a worthy messenger!'' The preacher, instead of vexing the ears of drowsy farmers on their day of rest at the end of the week,—for Sunday is the fit conclusion of an ill-spent week, and not the fresh and brave beginning of a new one,—with this one other draggle-tail of a sermon, should shout with thundering voice, "Pause! Avast! Why so seeming fast, but deadly slow?''

Shams and delusions are esteemed for soundest truths, while reality is fabulous. If men would steadily observe realities only, and not allow themselves to be deluded, life, to compare it with such things as we know, would be like a fairy tale and the Arabian Nights' Entertainments. If we respected only what is inevitable and has a right to be, music and poetry would resound along the streets. When we are unhurried and wise, we perceive that only great and worthy things have any permanent and absolute existence, that petty fears and petty pleasures are but the shadow of the reality. This is always exhilarating and sublime. By closing the eyes and slumbering, and consenting to be deceived by shows, men establish and confirm their daily life of routine and habit everywhere, which still is built on purely illusory foundations. Children, who play life, discern its true law and relations more clearly than men, who fail to live it worthily, but who think that they are wiser by experience, that is, by failure. I have read in a Hindoo book, that "there was a king's son, who, being expelled in infancy from his native city, was brought up by a forester, and, growing up to maturity in that state, imagined himself to belong to the barbarous race with which he lived. One of his father's ministers having discovered him, revealed to him what he was, and the misconception of his character was removed, and he knew himself to be a prince. So soul," continues the Hindoo philosopher, "from the circumstances in which it is placed, mistakes its own character, until the truth is revealed to it by some holy teacher, and then it knows itself to be *Brahme.*'' I perceive that we inhabitants of New England live this mean life that we do because our vision does not penetrate the surface of things. We think that this *is* which *appears* to be. If a man should walk through this town and see only the reality, where, think you, would the "Milldam'' go to? If he should give us an account of the realities he beheld there, we should not recognize the place in his description. Look at a meeting-house, or a court-house, or a jail, or a shop, or a dwelling-house, and say what that thing really is before a true gaze, and they would all go to pieces in your account of them. Men esteem truth remote, in the outskirts of the system, behind the farthest star, before Adam and after the last man. In eternity there is indeed something true and sublime. But all these times and places and occasions are now and here. God himself culminates in the present moment, and will never be more divine in the lapse of all the ages. And we are enabled to apprehend at all what is sublime and noble only by the perpetual instilling and drenching of the reality that surrounds us. The universe constantly and obediently answers to our conceptions; whether we travel fast or slow, the track is laid for us. Let us spend our lives in conceiving then. The poet or the artist never yet had so fair and noble a design but some of his posterity at least could accomplish it.

Let us spend one day as deliberately as Nature, and not be thrown off the track by every nutshell and mosquito's wing that falls on the rails. Let us rise early and fast, or break fast, gently and without perturbation; let company come and let company go, let the bells ring and the children cry,—determined to make a day of it. Why should we knock under and go with the stream? Let us not be upset and overwhelmed in that terrible rapid and whirlpool called a dinner, situated in the meridian shallows. Weather this danger and you are safe, for the rest of the way is down hill. With unrelaxed nerves, with morning vigor, sail by it, looking another way, tied to the mast like Ulysses. If the engine whistles, let it whistle till it is hoarse for its pains. If the bell rings, why should we run? We will consider what kind of music they are like. Let us settle ourselves, and work and wedge our feet downward through the mud and slush of opinion, and prejudice, and tradition, and delusion, and appearance, that alluvion which covers the globe, through Paris and London, through New York and Boston and Concord, through Church and State, through poetry and philosophy and religion, till we come to a hard bottom and rocks in place, which we can call *reality,* and say, This is, and no mistake; and then begin, having a *point d' appui,* below freshet and frost and fire, a place where you might found a wall or a state, or set a lamp-post safely, or perhaps a gauge, not a Nilometer, that future ages might know how deep a freshet of shams and appearances had gathered from time to time. If you stand right fronting and face to face to a fact, you will see the sun glimmer on both its surfaces, as if it were a cimeter, and feel its sweet edge dividing you through the heart and marrow, and so you will happily conclude your mortal career. Be it life or death we crave only reality. If we are really dying, let us hear the rattle in our throats and feel cold in the extremities; if we are alive, let us go about our business.

Time is but the stream I go a-fishing in. I drink at it; but while I drink I see the sandy bottom and detect how shallow it is. Its thin current slides away, but eternity remains. I would drink deeper; fish in the sky, whose bottom is pebbly with stars. I cannot count one. I know not the first letter of the alphabet. I have always been regretting that I was not as wise as the day I was born. The intellect is a cleaver; it discerns and rifts its way into the secret of things. I do not wish to be any more busy with my hands than is necessary. My head is hands and feet. I feel all my best faculties concentrated in it. My instinct tells me that my head is an organ for burrowing, as some creatures use their snout and fore paws, and with it I would mine and burrow my way through these hills. I think that the richest vein is somewhere hereabouts; so by the divining-rod and thin rising vapors I judge; and here I will begin to mine.

DISCUSSION QUESTIONS

1. Compare Thoreau's description of nature with Dennis Farney's "Trying To Restore a Sea of Grass" (see Press) and N. Scott Momaday's "A First American Views His Land" (see Magazines). What perspective does each writer adopt in order to describe the natural world? What attitude does each express towards nature?

2. Which author attends more carefully to details in describing nature? Which uses the most figurative language? To what effect? Does each writer draw on the same kinds of experience? Explain.

3. In which description of nature does the personal life of the speaker play the most prominent role? Explain. Which writer goes to the natural world to seek adventure? To search for self-improvement? To enjoy an idyllic experience?

4. What are the reasons for each writer's excursion into the natural world? Do you find any of these unconvincing? For which writer is nature most associated with political controversy?

Walt Whitman / Crossing Brooklyn Ferry 1860

For most of his life, Walt Whitman (1819–92) lived in neighborly relation to poverty. He worked as an apprentice in a printing shop, as a journalist for New York City and Long Island newspapers, as editor of the Brooklyn Eagle, *as well as a teacher, as a building contractor, and as a clerk in the Bureau of Indian Affairs until the sullied reputation of his collection of poems,* Leaves of Grass, *provoked his hurried dismissal.*

Said to have been set in type by Whitman himself and published at his own expense, Leaves of Grass *attracted little critical attention and sold few copies when first published in 1855. Of all the editors and writers to whom Whitman sent copies, Ralph Waldo Emerson responded most readily and enthusiastically: ''I find in it the most extraordinary piece of wit and wisdom that America has yet contributed.'' But Emerson was well-ahead of his time in appreciating Whitman's verse. Its seeming formlessness, boasts, sexual overtones, and ''vulgar'' language stirred much controversy in the decades that followed. Several generations of critics characterized his work as ''the poetry of barbarism'' and admonished audiences that this was poetry ''not to be read aloud to mixed audiences.'' The poet John Greenleaf Whittier went further. He condemned the poems as ''loose, lurid, and impious'' and tossed his copy into a fire.*

After service in Washington during the Civil War, Whitman suffered a paralytic stroke in 1873 and moved to his brother's home in Camden, New Jersey, where he spent his remaining years revising Leaves of Grass.

In Leaves of Grass, *an unprecedented mixture of a radically new poetic consciousness, commonplace subject matter, and distinctively colloquial rhythms, Whitman aspired to create nothing less than an epic of American democracy. But while his ambition to be known as ''the bard of democracy'' was never fully endorsed during his lifetime, Whitman's vision and innovative verse have cut a deepening course through which much of twentieth-century poetry has passed.*

''Crossing Brooklyn Ferry'' was first published under the title ''Sun-Down Poem'' in the second edition of Leaves of Grass *(1856) and was given its final title in 1860. The poem offers us a sampling of Whitman's singlehanded attempt to introduce a new style and idiom into American literature. The poem also demonstrates Whitman's belief that the process of reading should be*

> *not a half-sleep, but . . . an exercise, a gymnast's struggle; that the reader is to do something for himself, must be on the alert, must . . . construct indeed the poem, argument, history, metaphysical essay—the text furnishing the hints, the clue, the start or frame-work.*

I
Flood-tide below me! I see you face to face!
Clouds of the west—sun there half an hour high—I see you also
    face to face.

Crowds of men and women attired in the usual costumes, how
    curious you are to me!

On the ferry-boats the hundreds and hundreds that cross, return-
    ing home, are more curious to me than you suppose,
And you that shall cross from shore to shore years hence are more   5
    to me, and more in my meditations, than you might suppose.

II

The impalpable sustenance of me from all things at all hours of
    the day,
The simple, compact, well-join'd scheme, myself disintegrated,
    every one disintegrated yet part of the scheme,
The similitudes of the past and those of the future,
The glories strung like beads on my smallest sights and hearings,
    on the walk in the street and the passage over the river,
The current rushing so swiftly and swimming with me far away,   10
The others that are to follow me, the ties between me and them,
The certainty of others, the life, love, sight, hearing of others.

Others will enter the gates of the ferry and cross from shore to
    shore,
Others will watch the run of the flood-tide,
Others will see the shipping of Manhattan north and west, and   15
    the heights of Brooklyn to the south and east,
Others will see the islands large and small;
Fifty years hence, others will see them as they cross, the sun half
    an hour high,
A hundred years hence, or ever so many hundred years hence,
    others will see them,
Will enjoy the sunset, the pouring-in of the flood-tide, the falling-
    back to the sea of the ebb-tide.

III

It avails not, time nor place—distance avails not,   20
I am with you, you men and women of a generation, or ever so
    many generations hence,
Just as you feel when you look on the river and sky, so I felt,
Just as any of you is one of a living crowd, I was one of a crowd,
Just as you are refresh'd by the gladness of the river and the bright
    flow, I was refresh'd,
Just as you stand and lean on the rail, yet hurry with the swift   25
    current, I stood yet was hurried,
Just as you look on the numberless masts of ships and the thick-
    stemm'd pipes of steamboats, I look'd.

I too many and many a time cross'd the river of old,
Watched the Twelfth-month sea-gulls, saw them high in the air
    floating with motionless wings, oscillating their bodies,
Saw how the glistening yellow lit up parts of their bodies and left
    the rest in strong shadow,
Saw the slow-wheeling circles and the gradual edging toward the   30
    south,

Saw the reflection of the summer sky in the water,
Had my eyes dazzled by the shimmering track of beams,
Look'd at the fine centrifugal spokes of light round the shape of
    my head in the sunlit water,
Look'd on the haze on the hills southward and south-westward,
Look'd on the vapor as it flew in fleeces tinged with violet,   35
Look'd toward the lower bay to notice the vessels arriving,
Saw their approach, saw aboard those that were near me,
Saw the white sails of schooners and sloops, saw the ships at anchor,
The sailors at work in the rigging or out astride the spars,
The round masts, the swinging motion of the hulls, the slender   40
    serpentine pennants,
The large and small steamers in motion, the pilots in their pilot-
    houses,
The white wake left by the passage, the quick tremulous whirl of
    the wheels,
The flags of all nations, the falling of them at sunset,
The scallop-edged waves in the twilight, the ladled cups, the frolic-
    some crests and glistening,
The stretch afar growing dimmer and dimmer, the gray walls of   45
    the granite storehouses by the docks,
On the river the shadowy group, the big steam-tug closely flank'd
    on each side by the barges, the hay-boat, the belated lighter,
On the neighboring shore the fires from the foundry chimneys
    burning high and glaringly into the night,
Casting their flicker of black contrasted with wild red and yellow
    light over the tops of houses, and down into the clefts of
    streets.

IV
These and all else were to me the same as they are to you,
I loved well those cities, loved well the stately and rapid river,   50
The men and women I saw were all near to me,
Others the same—others who look back on me because I look'd
    forward to them,
(The time will come, though I stop here to-day and to-night.)

V
What is it then between us?
What is the count of the scores or hundreds of years between us?   55

Whatever it is, it avails not—distance avails not, and place avails
    not,
I too lived, Brooklyn of ample hills was mine,
I too walk'd the streets of Manhattan island, and bathed in the
    waters around it,
I too felt the curious abrupt questionings stir within me,
In the day among crowds of people sometimes they came upon me,   60
In my walks home late at night or as I lay in my bed they came
    upon me,

I too had been struck from the float forever held in solution,
I too had receiv'd identity by my body,
That I was I knew was of my body, and what I should be I knew
     I should be of my body.

VI

It is not upon you alone the dark patches fall,   65
The dark threw its patches down upon me also,
The best I had done seem'd to me blank and suspicious,
My great thoughts as I supposed them, were they not in reality
     meagre?
Nor is it you alone who know what it is to be evil,
I am he who knew what it was to be evil,   70
I too knitted the old knot of contrariety.
Blabb'd, blush'd, resented, lied, stole, grudg'd,
Had guile, anger, lust, hot wishes I dared not speak,
Was wayward, vain, greedy, shallow, sly, cowardly, malignant,
The wolf, the snake, the hog, not wanting in me,   75
The cheating look, the frivolous word, the adulterous wish, not
     wanting,
Refusals, hates, postponements, meanness, laziness, none of these
     wanting,
Was one with the rest, the days and haps of the rest,
Was call'd by my nighest name by clear loud voices of young men
     as they saw me approaching or passing,
Felt their arms on my neck as I stood, or the negligent leaning of   80
     their flesh against me as I sat,
Saw many I loved in the street or ferry-boat or public assembly,
     yet never told them a word,
Lived the same life with the rest, the same old laughing, gnawing,
     sleeping,
Play'd the part that still looks back on the actor or actress,
The same old role, the role that is what we make it, as great as we
     like,
Or as small as we like, or both great and small.   85

VII

Closer yet I approach you,
What thought you have of me now, I had as much of you—I laid
     in my stores in advance,
I consider'd long and seriously of you before you were born.

Who was to know what should come home to me?
Who knows but I am enjoying this?   90
Who knows, for all the distance, but I am as good as looking at
     you now, for all you cannot see me?

VIII

Ah, what can ever be more stately and admirable to me than mast-
     hemm'd Manhattan?

River and sunset and scallop-edg'd waves of flood-tide?
The sea-gulls oscillating their bodies, the hay-boat in the twilight,
    and the belated lighter?

What gods can exceed these that clasp me by the hand, and with   95
    voices I love call me promptly and loudly by my nighest name
    as I approach?
What is more subtle than this which ties me to the woman or man
    that looks in my face?
Which fuses me into you now, and pours my meaning into you?

We understand then do we not?
What I promis'd without mentioning it, have you not accepted?
What the study could not teach—what the preaching could not   100
    accomplish is accomplish'd, is it not?

IX

Flow on, river! flow with the flood-tide, and ebb with the ebb-tide!
Frolic on, crested and scallop-edg'd waves!
Gorgeous clouds of the sunset! drench with your splendor me, or
    the men and women generations after me!
Cross from shore to shore, countless crowds of passengers!
Stand up, tall masts of Mannahatta! stand up, beautiful hills of   105
    Brooklyn!
Throb, baffled and curious brain! throw out questions and answers!
Suspend here and everywhere, eternal float of solution!
Gaze, loving and thirsting eyes, in the house or street or public
    assembly!
Sound out, voices of young men! loudly and musically call me by
    my nighest name!
Live, old life! play the part that looks back on the actor or actress!   110
Play the old role, the role that is great or small according as one
    makes it!
Consider, you who peruse me, whether I may not in unknown
    ways be looking upon you;
Be firm, rail over the river, to support those who lean idly, yet
    haste with the hasting current;
Fly on, sea-birds! fly sideways, or wheel in large circles high in
    the air;
Receive the summer sky, you water, and faithfully hold it till all   115
    downcast eyes have time to take it from you!
Diverge, fine spokes of light, from the shape of my head, or any
    one's head, in the sunlit water!
Come on, ships from the lower bay! pass up or down, white-sail'd
    schooners, sloops, lighters!
Flaunt away, flags of all nations! be duly lower'd at sunset!
Burn high your fires, foundry chimneys! cast black shadows at
    nightfall! cast red and yellow light over the tops of the houses!
Appearances, now or henceforth, indicate what you are,   120
You necessary film, continue to envelop the soul,

About my body for me, and your body for you, be hung our di-
　　vinest aromas,
Thrive, cities—bring your freight, bring your shows, ample and
　　sufficient rivers,
Expand, being than which none else is perhaps more spiritual,
Keep your places, objects than which none else is more lasting.　　　125

You have waited, you always wait, you dumb, beautiful ministers,
We receive you with free sense at last, and are insatiate hence-
　　forward,
Not you any more shall be able to foil us, or withhold yourselves
　　from us,

We use you, and do not cast you aside—we plant you perma-
　　nently within us,
We fathom you not—we love you—there is perfection in you also,　　　130
You furnish your parts toward eternity,
Great or small, you furnish your parts toward the soul.

DISCUSSION QUESTIONS

1. What significance do you see in Whitman's choice of the participle "Crossing" in the poem's title? What associations does the word "ferry" call to mind?
How do these two words help us understand the poem's meaning? What contrast-
ing roles do the land and the sea play in the poem? How does Whitman create a
sense of unity at the end of the poem?

2. In the "Preface" to *Leaves of Grass*, Whitman characterizes the poet as the
"arbiter of the diverse . . . the equalizer of his age and land." Apply Whitman's
conception of the poet to your experience of reading this poem. Point to specific
words and phrases to illustrate your response.

3. How would you summarize Whitman's attitude towards the audience imagined
for this poem? What role does he expect his audience to play in the poem? How
do the roles of poet and audience change through each of the poem's three stages
(sections I–III, IV–VI, VII–IX)? What attitude does Whitman expect his audience to adopt towards the speaker by the end of the poem?

4. In the poem, Whitman talks of "myself disintegrated, everyone disintegrated
yet part of the scheme." What does this phrase tell us about Whitman's conception of the individual? Compare Whitman's view of the individual to those of
Harry Golden (Press), Edgar Allen Poe (Classics), and Robinson Jeffers (Classics).

Emily Dickinson / Success Is Counted Sweetest　　　Ca. 1859

*Born in Amherst, Massachusetts in 1830, Emily Dickinson remained within the
confines of her father's house in that small conservative village for most of her
life. Her poems are marked by an acute awareness of psychological states and*

physical sensations as much as by their brilliant images and melodic blending of
assonant and dissonant sounds. Only seven of Dickinson's many poems appeared
in print before she died in 1886.

Success is counted sweetest
By those who ne'er succeed.
To comprehend a nectar
Requires sorest need.

Not one of all the purple Host   5
Who took the Flag to-day
Can tell the definition,
So clear, of Victory,

As he defeated—dying—
On whose forbidden ear   10
The distant strains of triumph
Burst agonized and clear!

Emily Dickinson / Because I Could Not Stop for Death

Ca. 1863

Because I could not stop for Death—
He kindly stopped for me—
The Carriage held but just Ourselves—
And Immortality.

We slowly drove—He knew no haste   5
And I had put away
My labor and my leisure too,
For His Civility—

We passed the School, where Children strove
At Recess—in the Ring—   10
We passed the Fields of Gazing Grain—
We passed the Setting Sun—

Or rather—He passed Us—
The Dews drew quivering and chill—
For only Gossamer, my Gown—   15
My Tippet—only Tulle—

We paused before a House that seemed
A Swelling of the Ground—

The Roof was scarcely visible—
The Cornice—in the Ground—   20

Since then—'tis Centuries—and yet
Feels shorter than the Day
I first surmised the Horses' Heads
Were toward Eternity—

Kate Chopin / The Dream of an Hour   1894

*Born Katherine O'Flaherty in St. Louis in 1851 to a wealthy Irish father and a
Creole mother, Kate Chopin was raised in French, Southern, Catholic, aristocratic circumstances. After studies at a convent school, she entered and was soon
bored with the fashionable social circle of St. Louis: "I am invited to a ball and I
go.—I dance with people I despise; amuse myself with men whose only talent lies
in their feet." At nineteen, she married a Creole cotton broker and moved first to
New Orleans and then to the bayou country that forms a backdrop for many of
her stories. A year after the death of her husband from swamp fever in 1883,
Chopin returned to St. Louis with her six children and began composing short fiction, novels, and children's books. Writing in the midst of her children's activities, she obviously enjoyed the spontaneity such circumstances imposed:*

> *I am completely at the mercy of unconscious selection. To such an ex-
> tent is this true, that what is called the polishing up process always
> proved disastrous to my work, and I avoid it, preferring the integrity of
> crudities to artificialities.*

"The Dream of an Hour" appeared originally in Vogue *magazine in 1894.
Kate Chopin's stories were frequently published in such leading periodicals as
the* Atlantic Monthly, Harper's *and* Century, *and were subsequently collected in*
Bayou Folk *(1894) and* A Night in Acadia *(1897). Demoralized by the severe
criticism that attended the publication of her third novel,* The Awakening, *a tale
of extramarital and interracial love, she wrote little more before her death in
1904.*

Knowing that Mrs. Mallard was afflicted with a heart trouble, great care was taken
to break to her as gently as possible the news of her husband's death.

It was her sister Josephine who told her, in broken sentences; veiled hints that
revealed in half concealing. Her husband's friend Richards was there, too, near
her. It was he who had been in the newspaper office when intelligence of the
railroad disaster was received, with Brently Mallard's name leading the list of
"killed." He had only taken the time to assure himself of its truth by a second
telegram, and had hastened to forestall any less careful, less tender friend in bearing the sad message.

She did not hear the story as many women have heard the same, with a paralyzed inability to accept its significance. She wept at once, with sudden, wild

abandonment, in her sister's arms. When the storm of grief had spent itself she went away to her room alone. She would have no one follow her.

There stood, facing the open window, a comfortable, roomy armchair. Into this she sank, pressed down by a physical exhaustion that haunted her body and seemed to reach into her soul.

She could see in the open square before her house the tops of trees that were all aquiver with the new spring life. The delicious breath of rain was in the air. In the street below a peddler was crying his wares. The notes of a distant song which some one was singing reached her faintly, and countless sparrows were twittering in the eaves.

There were patches of blue sky showing here and there through the clouds that had met and piled one above the other in the west facing her window.

She sat with her head thrown back upon the cushion of the chair, quite motionless, except when a sob came up into her throat and shook her, as a child who has cried itself to sleep continues to sob in its dreams.

She was young, with a fair, calm face, whose lines bespoke repression and even a certain strength. But now there was a dull stare in her eyes, whose gaze was fixed away off yonder on one of those patches of blue sky. It was not a glance of reflection, but rather indicated a suspension of intelligent thought.

There was something coming to her and she was waiting for it, fearfully. What was it? She did not know; it was too subtle and elusive to name. But she felt it, creeping out of the sky, reaching toward her through the sounds, the scents, the color that filled the air.

Now her bosom rose and fell tumultuously. She was beginning to recognize this thing that was approaching to possess her, and she was striving to beat it back with her will—as powerless as her two white slender hands would have been.

When she abandoned herself a little whispered word escaped her slightly parted lips. She said it over and over under her breath: "free, free, free!" The vacant stare and the look of terror that had followed it went from her eyes. They stayed keen and bright. Her pulses beat fast, and the coursing blood warmed and relaxed every inch of her body.

She did not stop to ask if it were or were not a monstrous joy that held her: A clear and exalted perception enabled her to dismiss the suggestion as trivial.

She knew that she would weep again when she saw the kind, tender hands folded in death; the face that had never looked save with love upon her, fixed and gray and dead. But she saw beyond that bitter moment a long procession of years to come that would belong to her absolutely. And she opened and spread her arms out to them in welcome.

There would be no one to live for her during those coming years; she would live for herself. There would be no powerful will bending hers in that blind persistence with which men and women believe they have a right to impose a private will upon a fellow-creature. A kind intention or a cruel intention made the act seem no less a crime as she looked upon it in that brief moment of illumination.

And yet she had loved him—sometimes. Often she had not. What did it matter! What could love, the unsolved mystery, count for in face of this possession of self-assertion which she suddenly recognized as the strongest impulse of her being!

"Free! Body and soul free!" she kept whispering.

Josephine was kneeling before the closed door with her lips to the keyhole, imploring for admission. "Louise, open the door! I beg; open the door—you will make yourself ill. What are you doing, Louise? For heaven's sake open the door."

"Go away. I am not making myself ill." No; she was drinking in a very elixir of life through that open window.

Her fancy was running riot along those days ahead of her. Spring days, and summer days, and all sorts of days that would be her own. She breathed a quick prayer that life might be long. It was only yesterday she had thought with a shudder that life might be long.

She arose at length and opened the door to her sister's importunities. There was a feverish triumph in her eyes, and she carried herself unwittingly like a goddess of Victory. She clasped her sister's waist, and together they descended the stairs. Richards stood waiting for them at the bottom.

Some one was opening the front door with a latchkey. It was Brently Mallard who entered, a little travel-stained, composedly carrying his grip-sack and umbrella. He had been far from the scene of accident, and did not even know there had been one. He stood amazed at Josephine's piercing cry; at Richards' quick motion to screen him from the view of his wife.

But Richards was too late.

When the doctors came they said she had died of heart disease—of joy that kills.

DISCUSSION QUESTION

1. Robert Frost often argued that poetry exists "for griefs, not grievances." Do you think this distinction is applicable to Kate Chopin's "The Dream of an Hour"? Explain. Locate other stories and essays in this collection to which this distinction may be applied.

Mark Twain / How To Tell a Story   1897

Samuel Langhorne Clemens (Mark Twain), like many prominent American novelists, began his writing career as a journalist. He was born along the Mississippi River in Florida, Missouri in 1835, and throughout his life that great river remained a vital presence. After briefly working on the Mississippi as a riverboat pilot and mining for silver in Nevada, Twain felt his energies would be better spent writing for newspapers. He learned early how to combine skillfully the official prose of news reporting with the folksy language of tall tales, and his work in this humorous vein began to attract literary attention. He traveled to Hawaii, then to the Middle East, and later turned these experiences into parodies of the then popular conventional guidebooks. In 1876 he wrote The Adventures of Tom Sawyer, *a best-selling nostalgic glance at his Missouri boyhood, and in 1885 he brought out his masterpiece,* The Adventures of Huckleberry Finn, *the book Ernest Hemingway claimed marked the origins of "all modern American literature."*

Twain's later career, though productive, was interrupted by a series of futile business ventures (he invested heavily in an aborted typesetting invention) and personal tragedies. The tone of much of his later work hinges on his own pessimistic answers to the question posed in one of his final essays, "What Is Man?"

How To Tell a Story

In "How To Tell a Story" (1897), Twain, by then a distinguished novelist and man of letters, tells and shows an audience why effective narrative styles need to be rooted in an oral tradition.

I do not claim that I can tell a story as it ought to be told. I only claim to know how a story ought to be told, for I have been almost daily in the company of the most expert story-tellers for many years.

There are several kinds of stories, but only one difficult kind—the humorous. I will talk mainly about that one. The humorous story is American, the comic story is English, the witty story is French. The humorous story depends for its effect upon the *manner* of the telling; the comic story and the witty story upon the *matter*.

The humorous story may be spun out to great length, and may wander around as much as it pleases, and arrive nowhere in particular; but the comic and witty stories must be brief and end with a point. The humorous story bubbles gently along, the others burst.

The humorous story is strictly a work of art—high and delicate art—and only an artist can tell it; but no art is necessary in telling the comic and the witty story; anybody can do it. The art of telling a humorous story—understand, I mean by word of mouth, not print—was created in America, and has remained at home.

The humorous story is told gravely; the teller does his best to conceal the fact that he even dimly suspects that there is anything funny about it; but the teller of the comic story tells you beforehand that it is one of the funniest things he has ever heard, then tells it with eager delight, and is the first person to laugh when he gets through. And sometimes, if he has had good success, he is so glad and happy that he will repeat the "nub" of it and glance around from face to face, collecting applause, and then repeat it again. It is a pathetic thing to see.

Very often, of course, the rambling and disjointed humorous story finishes with a nub, point, snapper, or whatever you like to call it. Then the listener must be alert, for in many cases the teller will divert attention from that nub by dropping it in a carefully casual and indifferent way, with the pretense that he does not know it is a nub.

Artemus Ward used that trick a good deal; then when the belated audience presently caught the joke he would look up with innocent surprise, as if wondering what they had found to laugh at. Dan Setchell used it before him, Nye and Riley and others use it to-day.

But the teller of the comic story does not slur the nub; he shouts it at you—every time. And when he prints it, in England, France, Germany, and Italy, he italicizes it, puts some whooping exclamation-points after it and sometimes explains it in a parenthesis. All of which is very depressing, and makes one want to renounce joking and lead a better life.

Let me set down an instance of the comic method, using an anecdote which has been popular all over the world for twelve or fifteen hundred years. The teller tells it in this way:

The Wounded Soldier

In the course of a certain battle a soldier whose leg had been shot off appealed to another soldier who was hurrying by to carry him to the rear, informing him at the same time of the loss which he had sustained; whereupon the generous son of

Mars, shouldering the unfortunate, proceeded to carry out his desire. The bullets and cannon-balls were flying in all directions, and presently one of the latter took the wounded man's head off—without, however, his deliverer being aware of it. In no long time he was hailed by an officer, who said:

"Where are you going with that carcass?"

"To the rear, sir—he's lost his leg!"

"His leg, forsooth?" responded the astonished officer, "you mean his head, you booby."

Whereupon the soldier dispossessed himself of his burden, and stood looking down upon it in great perpelexity. At length he said:

"It is true, sir, just as you have said." Then after a pause he added. *"But he* TOLD *me* IT WAS HIS LEG ! ! ! ! !"

Here the narrator bursts into explosion after explosion of thunderous horse-laughter, repeating that nub from time to time through his gaspings and shriekings and suffocatings.

It takes only a minute and a half to tell that in its comic-story form; and isn't worth the telling, after all. Put into the humorous-story form it takes ten minutes, and is about the funniest thing I have ever listened to—as James Whitcomb Riley tells it.

He tells it in the character of a dull-witted old farmer who has just heard it for the first time, thinks it is unspeakably funny, and is trying to repeat it to a neighbor. But he can't remember it; so he gets all mixed up and wanders helplessly round and round, putting in tedious details that don't belong in the tale and only retard it; taking them out conscientiously and putting in others that are just as useless; making minor mistakes now and then and stopping to correct them and explain how he came to make them; remembering things which he forgot to put in in their proper place and going back to put them in there; stopping his narrative a good while in order to try to recall the name of the soldier that was hurt, and finally remembering that the soldier's name was not mentioned, and remarking placidly that the name is of no real importance, anyway—better, of course if one knew it, but not essential, after all—and so on, and so on, and so on.

The teller is innocent and happy and pleased with himself, and has to stop every little while to hold himself in and keep from laughing outright; and does hold in, but his body quakes in a jelly-like way with interior chuckles; and at the end of the ten minutes the audience have laughed until they are exhausted, and the tears are running down their faces.

The simplicity and innocence and sincerity and unconsciousness of the old farmer are perfectly simulated, and the result is a performance which is thoroughly charming and delicious. This is art—and fine and beautiful, and only a master can compass it; but a machine could tell the other story.

To string incongruities and absurdities together in a wandering and sometimes purposeless way, and seem innocently unaware that they are absurdities, is the basis of the American art, if my position is correct. Another feature is the slurring of the point. A third is the dropping of a studied remark apparently without knowing it, as if one were thinking aloud. The fourth and last is the pause.

Artemus Ward dealt in numbers three and four a good deal. He would begin to tell with great animation something which he seemed to think was wonderful; then lose confidence, and after an apparently absent-minded pause add an incongruous remark in a soliloquizing way; and that was the remark intended to explode the mine—and it did.

For instance, he would say eagerly, excitedly, "I once knew a man in New

Zealand who hadn't a tooth in his head"—here his animation would die out; a silent, reflective pause would follow, then he would say dreamily, and as if to himself, "and yet that man could beat a drum better than any man I ever saw."

The pause is an exceedingly important feature in any kind of story, and a frequently recurring feature, too. It is a dainty thing, and delicate, and also uncertain and treacherous; for it must be exactly the right length—no more and no less— or it fails of its purpose and makes trouble. If the pause is too short the impressive point is passed, and the audience have had time to divine that a surprise is intended—and then you can't surprise them, of course.

On the platform I used to tell a negro ghost story that had a pause in front of the snapper on the end, and that pause was the most important thing in the whole story. If I got it the right length precisely, I could spring the finishing ejaculation with effect enough to make some impressible girl deliver a startled little yelp and jump out of her seat—and that was what I was after. This story was called "The Golden Arm," and was told in this fashion. You can practise with it yourself—and mind you look out for the pause and get it right.

The Golden Arm

Once 'pon a time dey wuz a monsus mean man, en he live 'way out in de prairie all 'lone by hisself, 'cep'n he had a wife. En bimeby she died, en he tuck en toted her way out dah in de prairie en buried her. Well, she had a golden arm—all solid gold, fum de shoulder down. He wuz pow'ful mean—pow'ful; en dat night he couldn't sleep, caze he want dat golden arm so bad.

When it come midnight he couldn't stan' it no mo'; so he git up, he did, en tuck his lantern en shoved out thoo de storm en dug her up en got de golden arm; en he bent his head down 'gin de win', en plowed en plowed en plowed thoo de snow. Den all on a sudden he stop (make a considerable pause here, and look startled, and take a listening attitude) en say: "My *lan'*, what's dat?"

En he listen—en listen—en de win' say (set your teeth together and imitate the wailing and wheezing singsong of the wind), "Bzzz-z-zzz"—en den, way back yonder whah de grave is, he hear a *voice!*—he hear a voice all mix' up in de win'— can't hardly tell 'em 'part—"Bzzz—zzz—W-h-o—g-o-t—m-y—g-o-l-d-e-n *arm?*" (You must begin to shiver violently now.)

En he begin to shiver en shake, en say, "Oh, my! *Oh,* my lan'!" en de win' blow de lantern out, en de snow en sleet blow in his face en mos' choke him, en he start a-plowin' knee-deep towards home mos' dead, he so sk'yerd—en pooty soon he hear de voice agin, en (pause) it 'us comin' *after* him! "Bzzz—zzz—zzz— W-h-o—g-o-t—m-y—g-o-l-d-e-n—*arm?*"

When he git to de pasture he hear it agin—closter now, en a-*comin'!*—a-comin' back dah in de dark en de storm—(repeat the wind and the voice). When he git to de house he rush up-stairs en jump in de bed en kiver up, head and years, en lay dah shiverin' en shakin'—en den way out dah he hear it *agin!*—en a-*comin'!* En bimeby he hear (pause—awed, listening attitude)—pat—pat—pat—*hit's a-comin' upstairs!* Den he hear de latch, en he *know* it's in de room!

Den pooty soon he know it's a-*stannin' by de bed!* (Pause.) Den—he know it's a-*bendin' down over him*—en he cain't skasely git his breath! Den—den—he seem to feel someth'n' *c-o-l-d,* right down 'most agin his head! (Pause.)

Den de voice say, *right at his year*—"W-h-o—g-o-t—m-y—g-o-l-d-e-n *arm?*" (You must wail it out very plaintively and accusingly; then you stare steddily and impressively into the face of the farthest-gone auditor—a girl, preferably—and let that awe-inspiring pause begin to build itself in the deep hush. When it has reached exactly the right length, jump suddenly at that girl and yell, *"You've* got it!'')

If you've got the *pause* right, she'll fetch a dear little yelp and spring right out of her shoes. But you *must* get the pause right; and you will find it the most troublesome and aggravating and uncertain thing you ever undertook.

Stephen Crane / The Open Boat   1897

"The Open Boat," written a few months after his report on the sinking of the Commodore for the New York Press *on January 7, 1897 (see "Stephen Crane's Own Story" in Press), was Crane's second attempt to fictionalize his near disaster at sea. According to a fellow journalist, Crane was so worried about accuracy that he wanted the captain of the wrecked vessel, Edward Murphy, to go over the manuscript. "Listen, Ed. I want to have this right, from your point of view. How does it sound so far?" "You've got it, Steve," said the other man. "That is just how it happened, and how it felt." Long regarded as a masterpiece of naturalistic fiction, "The Open Boat" is an early attempt by a major American writer to give literary certification to the ironic, jocularly resilient speech of average men trapped in difficult circumstances. (See, for example, the transcripts of the astronauts' conversations in Press.) In his efforts to combine the crafts of journalism and literature, Crane helped to set a new tone for fiction, one that could express, as he puts it in "The Open Boat," "humour, contempt, tragedy, all in one."*

A TALE INTENDED TO BE AFTER THE FACT: BEING THE
EXPERIENCE OF FOUR MEN FROM THE
SUNK STEAMER COMMODORE

I

None of them knew the colour of the sky. Their eyes glanced level, and were fastened upon the waves that swept toward them. These waves were of the hue of slate, save for the tops, which were of foaming white, and all of the men knew the colours of the sea. The horizon narrowed and widened, and dipped and rose, and at all times its edge was jagged with waves that seemed thrust up in points like rocks.

Many a man ought to have a bathtub larger than the boat which here rode upon the sea. These waves were most wrongfully and barbarously abrupt and tall, and each froth-top was a problem in small-boat navigation.

The cook squatted in the bottom, and looked with both eyes at the six inches of gunwale which separated him from the ocean. His sleeves were rolled over his fat forearms, and the two flaps of his unbuttoned vest dangled as he bent to bail out the boat. Often he said, "Gawd! that was a narrow clip." As he remarked it he invariably gazed eastward over the broken sea.

The oiler, steering with one of the two oars in the boat, sometimes raised himself suddenly to keep clear of water that swirled in over the stern. It was a thin little oar, and it seemed often ready to snap.

The correspondent, pulling at the other oar, watched the waves and wondered why he was there.

The injured captain, lying in the bow, was at this time buried in that profound dejection and indifference which comes, temporarily at least, to even the bravest and most enduring when, willy-nilly, the firm fails, the army loses, the ship goes down. The mind of the master of a vessel is rooted deep in the timbers of her, though he command for a day or a decade; and this captain had on him the stern impression of a scene in the greys of dawn of seven turned faces, and later a stump of a topmast with a white ball on it, that slashed to and fro at the waves, went low and lower, and down. Thereafter there was something strange in his voice. Although steady, it was deep with mourning, and of a quality beyond oration or tears.

"Keep 'er a little more south, Billie," said he.

"A little more south, sir," said the oiler in the stern.

A seat in his boat was not unlike a seat upon a bucking broncho, and by the same token a broncho is not much smaller. The craft pranced and reared and plunged like an animal. As each wave came, and she rose for it, she seemed like a horse making at a fence outrageously high. The manner of her scramble over these walls of water is a mystic thing, and, moreover, at the top of them were ordinarily these problems in white water, the foam racing down from the summit of each wave requiring a new leap, and a leap from the air. Then, after scornfully bumping a crest, she would slide and race and splash down a long incline, and arrive bobbing and nodding in front of the next menace.

A singular disadvantage of the sea lies in the fact that after successfully surmounting one wave you discover that there is another behind it just as important and just as nervously anxious to do something effective in the way of swamping boats. In a ten-foot dinghy one can get an idea of the resources of the sea in the line of waves that is not probable to the average experience which is never at sea in a dinghy. As each slaty wall of water approached, it shut all else from the view of the men in the boat, and it was not difficult to imagine that this particular wave was the final outburst of the ocean, the last effort of the grim water. There was a terrible grace in the move of the waves, and they came in silence, save for the snarling of the crests.

In the wan light the faces of the men must have been grey. Their eyes must have glinted in strange ways as they gazed steadily astern. Viewed from a balcony, the whole thing would doubtless have been weirdly picturesque. But the men in the boat had no time to see it, and if they had had leisure, there were other things to occupy their minds. The sun swung steadily up the sky, and they knew it was broad day because the colour of the sea changed from slate to emerald green streaked with amber lights, and the foam was like tumbling snow. The process of the breaking day was unknown to them. They were aware only of this effect upon the colour of the waves that rolled toward them.

In disjointed sentences the cook and the correspondent argued as to the difference between a life-saving station and a house of refuge. The cook had said: "There's a house of refuge just north of the Mosquito Inlet Light, and as soon as they see us they'll come off in their boat and pick us up."

"As soon as who see us?" said the correspondent.

"The crew," said the cook.

"Houses of refuge don't have crews," said the correspondent. "As I understand them, they are only places where clothes and grub are stored for the benefit of shipwrecked people. They don't carry crews."

"Oh, yes, they do," said the cook.

"No, they don't," said the correspondent.

"Well, we're not there yet, anyhow," said the oiler, in the stern.

"Well," said the cook, "perhaps it's not a house of refuge that I'm thinking of as being near Mosquito Inlet Light; perhaps it's a life-saving station."

"We're not there yet," said the oiler in the stern.

II

As the boat bounced from the top of each wave the wind tore through the hair of the hatless men, and as the craft plopped her stern down again the spray slashed past them. The crest of each of these waves was a hill, from the top of which the men surveyed for a moment a broad tumultuous expanse, shining and wind-riven. It was probably splendid, it was probably glorious, this play of the free sea, wild with lights of emerald and white and amber.

"Bully good thing it's an on-shore wind," said the cook. "If not, where would we be? Wouldn't have a show."

"That's right," said the correspondent.

The busy oiler nodded his assent.

Then the captain, in the bow, chuckled in a way that expressed humour, contempt, tragedy, all in one. "Do you think we've got much of a show now, boys?" said he.

Whereupon the three were silent, save for a trifle of hemming and hawing. To express any particular optimism at this time they felt to be childish and stupid, but they all doubtless possessed this sense of the situation in their minds. A young man thinks doggedly at such times. On the other hand, the ethics of their condition was decidedly against any open suggestion of hopelessness. So they were silent.

"Oh, well," said the captain, soothing his children, "we'll get ashore all right."

But there was that in his tone which made them think; so the oiler quoth, "Yes! if this wind holds."

The cook was bailing. "Yes! if we don't catch hell in the surf."

Canton-flannel gulls flew near and far. Sometimes they sat down on the sea, near patches of brown seaweed that rolled over the waves with a movement like carpets on a line in a gale. The birds sat comfortably in groups, and they were envied by some in the dinghy, for the wrath of the sea was no more to them than it was to a covey of prairie chickens a thousand miles inland. Often they came very close and stared at the men with black bead-like eyes. At these times they were uncanny and sinister in their unblinking scrutiny, and the men hooted angrily at them, telling them to be gone. One came, and evidently decided to alight on the top of the captain's head. The bird flew parallel to the boat and did not circle, but made short sidelong jumps in the air in chicken-fashion. His black eyes were wistfully fixed upon the captain's head. "Ugly brute," said the oiler to the bird. "You look as if you were made with a jackknife." The cook and the correspondent swore darkly at the creature. The captain naturally wished to knock it away with the end of the heavy painter, but he did not dare do it, because anything resembling an emphatic gesture would have capsized this freighted boat; and so, with his open hand, the captain gently and carefully waved the gull away. After it had been discouraged from the pursuit the captain breathed easier on account of his hair, and others breathed easier because the bird struck their minds at this time as being somehow gruesome and ominous.

In the meantime the oiler and the correspondent rowed. And also they rowed. They sat together in the same seat, and each rowed an oar. Then the oiler took both oars; then the correspondent took both oars; then the oiler: then the correspondent. They rowed and they rowed. The very ticklish part of the business was when the time came for the reclining one in the stern to take his turn at the oars. By the very last star of truth, it is easier to steal eggs from under a hen than it was to change seats in the dinghy. First the man in the stern slid his hand along the thwart and moved with care, as if he were of Sevres. Then the man in the rowing-seat slid his hand along the other thwart. It was all done with the most extraordinary care. As the two sidled past each other, the whole party kept watchful eyes on the coming wave, and the captain cried: "Look out, now! Steady, there!"

The brown mats of seaweed that appeared from time to time were like islands, bits of earth. They were travelling, apparently, neither one way nor the other. They were, to all intents, stationary. They informed the men in the boat that it was making progress slowly toward the land.

The captain, rearing cautiously in the bow after the dinghy soared on a great swell, said that he had seen the lighthouse at Mosquito Inlet. Presently the cook remarked that he had seen it. The correspondent was at the oars then, and for some reason he too wished to look at the lighthouse; but his back was toward the far shore, and the waves were important, and for some time he could not seize an opportunity to turn his head. But at last there came a wave more gentle than the others, and when at the crest of it he swiftly scoured the western horizon.

"See it?" said the captain.

"No," said the correspondent, slowly; "I didn't see anything."

"Look again," said the captain. He pointed. "It's exactly in that direction."

At the top of another wave the correspondent did as he was bid, and this time his eyes chanced on a small, still thing on the edge of the swaying horizon. It was precisely like the point of a pin. It took an anxious eye to find a lighthouse so tiny.

"Think we'll make it, Captain?"

"If this wind holds and the boat don't swamp, we can't do much else," said the captain.

The little boat, lifted by each towering sea and splashed viciously by the crests, made progress that in the absence of seaweed was not apparent to those in her. She seemed just a wee thing wallowing, miraculously top up, at the mercy of five oceans. Occasionally a great spread of water, like white flames, swarmed into her.

"Bail her, cook," said the captain, serenely.

"All right, Captain," said the cheerful cook.

III

It would be difficult to describe the subtle brotherhood of men that was here established on the seas. No one said that it was so. No one mentioned it. But it dwelt in the boat, and each man felt it warm him. They were a captain, an oiler, a cook, and a correspondent, and they were friends—friends in a more curiously iron-bound degree than may be common. The hurt captain, lying against the water-jar in the bow, spoke always in a low voice and calmly; but he could never command a more ready and swiftly obedient crew than the motley three of the dinghy. It was more than a mere recognition of what was best for the common safety. There was surely in it a quality that was personal and heart-felt. And after this devotion to the commander of the boat, there was this comradeship, that the correspondent, for instance, who had been taught to be cynical of men, knew even at the time was the best experience of his life. But no one said that it was so. No one mentioned it.

"I wish we had a sail," remarked the captain. "We might try my overcoat on the end of an oar, and give you two boys a chance to rest." So the cook and the correspondent held the mast and spread wide the overcoat; the oiler steered; and the little boat made good way with her new rig. Sometimes the oiler had to scull sharply to keep a sea from breaking into the boat, but otherwise sailing was a success.

Meanwhile the lighthouse had been growing slowly larger. It had now almost assumed colour, and appeared like a little grey shadow on the sky. The man at the oars could not be prevented from turning his head rather often to try for a glimpse of this little grey shadow.

At last, from the top of each wave, the men in the tossing boat could see land. Even as the lighthouse was an upright shadow on the sky, this land seemed but a long black shadow on the sea. It certainly was thinner than paper. "We must be about opposite New Smyrna," said the cook, who had coasted this shore often in schooners. "Captain, by the way, I believe they abandoned that life-saving station there about a year ago."

"Did they?" said the captain.

The wind slowly died away. The cook and the correspondent were not now obliged to slave in order to hold high the oar. But the waves continued their old impetuous swooping at the dinghy, and the little craft, no longer under way, struggled woundily over them. The oiler or the correspondent took the oars again.

Shipwrecks are apropos of nothing. If men could only train for them and have them occur when the men had reached pink condition, there would be less drowning at sea. Of the four in the dinghy none had slept any time worth mentioning for two days and two nights previous to embarking in the dinghy, and in the excitement of clambering about the deck of a foundering ship they had also forgotten to eat heartily.

For these reasons, and for others, neither the oiler nor the correspondent was fond of rowing at this time. The correspondent wondered ingenuously how in the name of all that was sane could there be people who thought it amusing to row a boat. It was not an amusement; it was a diabolical punishment, and even a genius of mental aberrations could never conclude that it was anything but a horror to the muscles and a crime against the back. He mentioned to the boat in general how the amusement of rowing struck him, and the weary-faced oiler smiled in full sympathy. Previously to the foundering, by the way, the oiler had worked a double watch in the engine-room of the ship.

"Take her easy now, boys," said the captain. "Don't spend yourselves. If we have to run a surf you'll need all your strength, because we'll sure have to swim for it. Take your time."

Slowly the land arose from the sea. From a black line it became a line of black and a line of white—trees and sand. Finally the captain said that he could make out a house on the shore. "That's the house of refuge, sure," said the cook. "They'll see us before long, and come out after us."

The distant lighthouse reared high. "The keeper ought to be able to make us out now, if he's looking through a glass," said the captain. "He'll notify the life-saving people."

"None of those other boats could have got ashore to give word of this wreck," said the oiler, in a low voice, "else the life-boat would be out hunting us."

Slowly and beautifully the land loomed out of the sea. The wind came again. It had veered from the north-east to the south-east. Finally a new sound struck the ears of the men in the boat. It was the low thunder of the surf on the shore. "We'll never be able to make the lighthouse now," said the captain. "Swing her head a little more north, Billie."

"A little more north, sir," said the oiler.

Whereupon the little boat turned her nose once more down the wind, and all but the oarsman watched the shore grow. Under the influence of this expansion doubt and direful apprehension were leaving the minds of the men. The management of the boat was still most absorbing, but it could not prevent a quiet cheerfulness. In an hour, perhaps, they would be ashore.

Their backbones had become thoroughly used to balancing in the boat, and they now rode this wild colt of a dinghy like circus men. The correspondent thought that he had been drenched to the skin, but happening to feel in the top pocket of his coat, he found therein eight cigars. Four of them were soaked with sea-water; four were perfectly scatheless. After a search, somebody produced three dry matches; and thereupon the four waifs rode impudently in their little boat and, with an assurance of an impending rescue shining in their eyes, puffed at the big cigars, and judged well and ill of all men. Everybody took a drink of water.

IV

"Cook," remarked the captain, "there don't seem to be any signs of life about your house of refuge."

"No," replied the cook. "Funny they don't see us!"

A broad stretch of lowly coast lay before the eyes of the men. It was of low dunes topped with dark vegetation. The roar of the surf was plain, and sometimes they could see the white lip of a wave as it spun up the beach. A tiny house was blocked out black upon the sky. Southward, the slim lighthouse lifted its little grey length.

Tide, wind, and waves were swinging the dinghy northward. "Funny they don't see us," said the men.

The surf's roar was here dulled, but its tone was nevertheless thunderous and mighty. As the boat swam over the great rollers the men sat listening to this roar. "We'll swamp sure," said everybody.

It is fair to say here that there was not a life-saving station within twenty miles in either direction; but the men did not know this fact, and in consequence they made dark and opprobrious remarks concerning the eyesight of the nation's life-savers. Four scowling men sat in the dinghy and surpassed records in the invention of epithets.

"Funny they don't see us."

The light-heartedness of a former time had completely faded. To their sharpened minds it was easy to conjure pictures of all kinds of incompetency and blindness and, indeed, cowardice. There was the shore of the populous land, and it was bitter and bitter to them that from it came no sign.

"Well," said the captain, ultimately, "I suppose we'll have to make a try for ourselves. If we stay out here too long, we'll none of us have strength left to swim after the boat swamps."

And so the oiler, who was at the oars, turned the boat straight for the shore. There was a sudden tightening of muscles. There was some thinking.

"If we don't all get ashore," said the captain—"if we don't all get ashore, I suppose you fellows know where to send news of my finish?"

They then briefly exchanged some addresses and admonitions. As for the reflections of the men, there was a great deal of rage in them. Perchance they might be formulated thus: "If I am going to be drowned—if I am going to be drowned—if I am going to be drowned, why, in the name of the seven mad gods who rule the sea, was I allowed to come thus far and contemplate sand and trees? Was I brought here merely to have my nose dragged away as I was about to nibble the sacred cheese of life? It is preposterous. If this old ninny-woman, Fate, cannot do better than this, she should be deprived of the management of men's fortunes. She is an old hen who knows not her intention. If she has decided to drown me, why did she not do it in the beginning and save me all this trouble? The whole affair is absurd.—But no; she cannot mean to drown me. She dare not drown me. She cannot drown me. Not after all this work." Afterward the man might have had an impulse to shake his fist at the clouds. "Just you drown me, now, and then hear what I call you!"

The billows that came at this time were more formidable. They seemed always just about to break and roll over the little boat in a turmoil of foam. There was a preparatory and long growl in the speech of them. No mind unused to the sea would have concluded that the dinghy could ascend these sheer heights in time. The shore was still afar. The oiler was a wily surfman. "Boys," he said swiftly, "she won't live three minutes more, and we're too far out to swim. Shall I take her to sea again, Captain?"

"Yes; go ahead!" said the captain.

This oiler, by a series of quick miracles and fast and steady oarsmanship, turned the boat in the middle of the surf and took her safely to sea again.

There was a considerable silence as the boat bumped over the furrowed sea to deeper water. Then somebody in gloom spoke: "Well, anyhow, they must have seen us from the shore by now."

The gulls went in slanting flight up the wind toward the grey, desolate east. A squall, marked by dingy clouds and clouds brick-red like smoke from a burning building, appeared from the south-east.

"What do you think of those life-saving people? Ain't they peaches?"

"Funny they haven't seen us."

"Maybe they think we're out here for sport! Maybe they think we're fishin'. Maybe they think we're damned fools."

It was a long afternoon. A changed tide tried to force them southward, but wind and wave said northward. Far ahead, where coast-line, sea, and sky formed their mighty angle, there were little dots which seemed to indicate a city on the shore.

"St. Augustine?"

The captain shook his head. "Too near Mosquito Inlet."

And the oiler rowed, and then the correspondent rowed; then the oiler rowed. It was a weary business. The human back can become the seat of more aches and pains than are registered in books for the composite anatomy of a regiment. It is a limited area, but it can become the theatre of innumerable muscular conflicts, tangles, wrenches, knots, and other comforts.

"Did you ever like to row, Billie?" asked the correspondent.

"No," said the oiler; "hang it!"

When one exchanged the rowing-seat for a place in the bottom of the boat, he suffered a bodily depression that caused him to be careless of everything save an obligation to wiggle one finger. There was cold sea-water swashing to and fro in the boat, and he lay in it. His head, pillowed on a thwart, was within an inch of the swirl of a wave-crest, and sometimes a particularly obstreperous sea came inboard and drenched him once more. But these matters did not annoy him. It is almost certain that if the boat had capsized he would have tumbled comfortably out upon the ocean as if he felt sure that it was a great soft mattress.

"Look! There's a man on the shore!"

"Where?"

"There! See 'im? See 'im?"

"Yes, sure! He's walking along."

"Now he's stopped. Look! He's facing us!"

"He's waving at us!"

"So he is! By thunder!"

"Ah, now we're all right! Now we're all right! There'll be a boat out here for us in half an hour."

"He's going on. He's running. He's going up to that house there."

The remote beach seemed lower than the sea, and it required a searching glance to discern the little black figure. The captain saw a floating stick, and they rowed to it. A bath towel was by some weird chance in the boat, and, tying this on the stick, the captain waved it. The oarsman did not dare turn his head, so he was obliged to ask questions.

"What's he doing now?"

"He's standing still again. He's looking, I think.—There he goes again—toward the house.—Now he's stopped again."

"Is he waving at us?"

"No, not now; he was, though."

"Look! There comes another man!"

"He's running."

"Look at him go, would you!"

"Why, he's on a bicycle. Now he's met the other man. They're both waving at us. Look!"

"There comes something up the beach."

"What the devil is that thing?"

"Why, it looks like a boat."

"Why, certainly, it's a boat."

"No; it's on wheels."

"Yes, so it is. Well, that must be the life-boat. They drag them along shore on a wagon."

"That's the life-boat, sure."

"No, by God, it's—it's an omnibus."

"I tell you it's a life-boat."

"It is not! It's an omnibus. I can see it plain. See? One of these big hotel omnibuses."

"By thunder, you're right. It's an omnibus, sure as fate. What do you suppose they are doing with an omnibus? Maybe they are going around collecting the life-crew, hey?"

"That's it, likely. Look! There's a fellow waving a little black flag. He's standing on the steps of the omnibus. There come those other two fellows. Now they're all talking together. Look at the fellow with the flag. Maybe he ain't waving it!"

"That ain't a flag, is it? That's his coat. Why, certainly, that's his coat."

"So it is; it's his coat. He's taken it off and is waving it around his head. But would you look at him swing it!"

"Oh, say, there isn't any life-saving station there. That's just a winter-resort hotel omnibus that has brought over some of the boarders to see us drown."

"What's that idiot with the coat mean? What's he signalling, anyhow?"

"It looks as if he were trying to tell us to go north. There must be a life-saving station up there."

"No; he thinks we're fishing. Just giving us a merry hand. See? Ah, there, Willie!"

"Well, I wish I could make something out of those signals. What do you suppose he means?"

"He don't mean anything; he's just playing."

"Well, if he'd just signal us to try the surf again, or to go to sea and wait, or go north, or go south, or go to hell, there would be some reason in it. But look at him! He just stands there and keeps his coat revolving like a wheel. The ass!"

"There come more people."

"Now there's quite a mob. Look! Isn't that a boat?"

"Where? Oh, I see where you mean. No, that's no boat."

"That fellow is still waving his coat."

"He must think we like to see him do that. Why don't he quit it? It don't mean anything."

"I don't know. I think he is trying to make us go north. It must be that there's a life-saving station there somewhere."

"Say, he ain't tired yet. Look at 'im wave!"

"Wonder how long he can keep that up. He's been revolving his coat ever since he caught sight of us. He's an idiot. Why aren't they getting men to bring a boat out? A fishing-boat—one of those big yawls—could come out here all right. Why don't he do something?"

"Oh, it's all right now."

"They'll have a boat out here for us in less than no time, now that they've seen us."

A faint yellow tone came into the sky over the low land. The shadows on the sea slowly deepened. The wind bore coldness with it, and the men began to shiver.

"Holy smoke!" said one, allowing his voice to express his impious mood, "if we keep on monkeying out here! If we've got to flounder out here all night!"

"Oh, we'll never have to stay here all night! Don't you worry. They've seen us now, and it won't be long before they'll come chasing out after us."

The shore grew dusky. The man waving a coat blended gradually into this gloom, and it swallowed in the same manner the omnibus and the group of people. The spray, when it dashed uproariously over the side, made the voyagers shrink and swear like men who were being branded.

"I'd like to catch the chump who waved the coat. I feel like socking him one, just for luck."

"Why? What did he do?"

"Oh, nothing, but then he seemed so damned cheerful."

In the meantime the oiler rowed, and then the correspondent rowed, and then the oiler rowed. Grey-faced and bowed forward, they mechanically, turn by turn, plied the leaden oars. The form of the lighthouse had vanished from the southern horizon, but finally a pale star appeared, just lifting from the sea. The streaked saffron in the west passed before the all-merging darkness, and the sea to the east was black. The land had vanished, and was expressed only by the low and drear thunder of the surf.

"If I am going to be drowned—if I am going to be drowned—if I am going to be drowned, why, in the name of the seven mad gods who rule the sea, was I allowed to come thus far and contemplate sand and trees? Was I brought here merely to have my nose dragged away as I was about to nibble the sacred cheese of life?"

The patient captain, drooped over the water-jar, was sometimes obliged to speak to the oarsman.

"Keep her head up! Keep her head up!"

"Keep her head up, sir." The voices were weary and low.

This was surely a quiet evening. All save the oarsman lay heavily and listlessly in the boat's bottom. As for him, his eyes were just capable of noting the tall black waves that swept forward in a most sinister silence, save for an occasional subdued growl of a crest.

The cook's head was on a thwart, and he looked without interest at the water under his nose. He was deep in other scenes. Finally he spoke. "Billie," he murmured, dreamfully, "what kind of pie do you like best?"

V

"Pie!" said the oiler and the correspondent, agitatedly. "Don't talk about those things, blast you!"

"Well," said the cook, "I was just thinking about ham sandwiches and—"

A night on the sea in an open boat is a long night. As darkness settled finally, the shine of the light, lifting from the sea in the south, changed to full gold. On the northern horizon a new light appeared, a small bluish gleam on the edge of the waters. These two lights were the furniture of the world. Otherwise there was nothing but waves.

Two men huddled in the stern, and distances were so magnificent in the dinghy that the rower was enabled to keep his feet partly warm by thrusting them under his companions. Their legs indeed extended far under the rowing-seat until they touched the feet of the captain forward. Sometimes, despite the efforts of the tired oarsman, a wave came piling into the boat, an icy wave of the night, and the chilling water soaked them anew. They would twist their bodies for a moment and groan, and sleep the dead sleep once more, while the water in the boat gurgled about them as the craft rocked.

The plan of the oiler and the correspondent was for one to row until he lost the ability, and then arouse the other from his sea-water couch in the bottom of the boat.

The oiler plied the oars until his head drooped forward and the overpowering sleep blinded him; and he rowed yet afterward. Then he touched a man in the bottom of the boat, and called his name. "Will you spell me for a little while?" he said, meekly.

"Sure, Billie," said the correspondent, awaking and dragging himself to a sitting position. They exchanged places carefully, and the oiler, cuddling down in the sea-water at the cook's side, seemed to go to sleep instantly.

The particular violence of the sea had ceased. The waves came without snarling. The obligation of the man at the oars was to keep the boat headed so that the tilt of the rollers would not capsize her, and to preserve her from filling when the crests rushed past. The black waves were silent and hard to be seen in the darkness. Often one was almost upon the boat before the oarsman was aware.

In a low voice the correspondent addressed the captain. He was not sure that the captain was awake, although this iron man seemed to be always awake. "Captain, shall I keep her making for that light north, sir?"

The same steady voice answered him. "Yes. Keep it about two points off the port bow."

The cook had tied a life-belt around himself in order to get even the warmth which this clumsy cork contrivance could donate, and he seemed almost stove-like when a rower, whose teeth invariably chattered wildly as soon as he ceased his labour, dropped down to sleep.

The correspondent, as he rowed, looked down at the two men sleeping underfoot. The cook's arm was around the oiler's shoulders, and, with their fragmentary clothing and haggard faces, they were the babes of the sea—a grotesque rendering of the old babes in the wood.

Later he must have grown stupid at his work, for suddenly there was a growling of water, and a crest came with a roar and a swash into the boat, and it was a wonder that it did not set the cook afloat in his life-belt. The cook continued to sleep, but the oiler sat up, blinking his eyes and shaking with the new cold.

"Oh, I'm awful sorry, Billie," said the correspondent, contritely.

"That's all right, old boy," said the oiler, and lay down again and was asleep.

Presently it seemed that even the captain dozed, and the correspondent thought that he was the one man afloat on all the oceans. The wind had a voice as it came over the waves, and it was sadder than the end.

There was a long, loud swishing astern of the boat, and a gleaming trail of phosphorescence, like blue flame, was furrowed on the black waters. It might have been made by a monstrous knife.

Then there came a stillness, while the correspondent breathed with open mouth and looked at the sea.

Suddenly there was another swish and another long flash of bluish light, and this time it was alongside the boat, and might almost been reached with an oar. The correspondent saw an enormous fin speed like a shadow through the water, hurling the crystalline spray and leaving the long glowing trail.

The correspondent looked over his shoulder at the captain. His face was hidden, and he seemed to be asleep. He looked at the babes of the sea. They certainly were asleep. So, being bereft of sympathy, he leaned a little way to one side and swore softly into the sea.

But the thing did not then leave the vicinity of the boat. Ahead or astern, on one side or the other, at intervals long or short, fled the long sparkling streak, and there was to be heard the *whirroo* of the dark fin. The speed and power of the thing was greatly to be admired. It cut the water like a gigantic and keen projectile.

The presence of this biding thing did not affect the man with the same horror that it would if he had been a picnicker. He simply looked at the sea dully and swore in an undertone.

Nevertheless, it is true that he did not wish to be alone with the thing. He wished one of his companions to awake by chance and keep him company with it. But the captain hung motionless over the water-jar, and the oiler and the cook in the bottom of the boat were plunged in slumber.

VI

"If I am going to be drowned—if I am going to be drowned—if I am going to be drowned, why, in the name of the seven mad gods who rule the sea, was I allowed to come thus far and contemplate sand and trees?"

During this dismal night, it may be remarked that a man would conclude that it was really the intention of the seven mad gods to drown him, despite the abominable injustice of it. For it was certainly an abominable injustice to drown a man who had worked so hard, so hard. The man felt it would be a crime most unnatural. Other people had drowned at sea since galleys swarmed with painted sails, but still—

When it occurs to a man that nature does not regard him as important, and that she feels she would not maim the universe by disposing of him, he at first wishes to throw bricks at the temple, and he hates deeply the fact that there are no bricks and no temples. Any visible expression of nature would surely be pelleted with his jeers.

Then, if there be no tangible thing to hoot, he feels, perhaps, the desire to confront a personification and indulge in pleas, bowed to one knee, and with hands supplicant, saying, "Yes, but I love myself."

A high cold star on a winter's night is the word he feels that she says to him. Thereafter he knows the pathos of his situation.

The men in the dinghy had not discussed these matters, but each had, no doubt, reflected upon them in silence and according to his mind. There was seldom any expression upon their faces save the general one of complete weariness. Speech was devoted to the business of the boat.

To chime the notes of his emotion, a verse mysteriously entered the correspondent's head. He had even forgotten that he had forgotten this verse, but it suddenly was in mind.

> *A soldier of the Legion lay dying in Algiers;*
> *There was lack of woman's nursing, there was dearth of woman's tears;*
> *But a comrade stood beside him, and he took that comrade's hand,*
> *And he said, "I never more shall see my own, my native land."*

In his childhood the correspondent had been made acquainted with the fact that a soldier of the Legion lay dying in Algiers, but he had never regarded the fact as important. Myriads of his school-fellows had informed him of the soldier's plight, but the dinning had naturally ended by making him perfectly indifferent. He had never considered it his affair that a soldier of the Legion lay dying in Algiers, nor had it appeared to him as a matter for sorrow. It was less to him than the breaking of a pencil's point.

Now, however, it quaintly came to him as a human, living thing. It was no longer merely a picture of a few throes in the breast of a poet, meanwhile drinking tea and warming his feet at the grate; it was an actuality—stern, mournful, and fine.

The correspondent plainly saw the soldier. He lay on the sand with his feet out straight and still. While his pale left hand was upon his chest in an attempt to thwart the going of his life, the blood came between his fingers. In the far Algerian distance, a city of low square forms was set against a sky that was faint with the last sunset hues. The correspondent, plying the oars and dreaming of the slow and slower movements of the lips of the soldier, was moved by a profound and perfectly impersonal comprehension. He was sorry for the soldier of the Legion who lay dying in Algiers.

The thing which had followed the boat and waited had evidently grown bored at the delay. There was no longer to be heard the slash of the cutwater, and there was no longer the flame of the long trail. The light in the north still glimmered, but it was apparently no nearer to the boat. Sometimes the boom of the surf rang in the correspondent's ears, and he turned the craft seaward then and rowed harder. Southward, some one had evidently built a watch-fire on the beach. It was too low and too far to be seen, but it made a shimmering, roseate reflection upon the bluff in back of it, and this could be discerned from the boat. The wind came stronger, and sometimes a wave suddenly raged out like a mountain cat, and there was to be seen the sheen and sparkle of a broken crest.

The captain, in the bow, moved on his water-jar and sat erect. "Pretty long night," he observed to the correspondent. He looked at the shore. "Those life-saving people take their time."

"Did you see that shark playing around?"

"Yes, I saw him. He was a big fellow, all right."

"Wish I had known you were awake."

Later the correspondent spoke into the bottom of the boat. "Billie!" There was a slow and gradual disentanglement. "Billie, will you spell me?"

"Sure," said the oiler.

As soon as the correspondent touched the cold, comfortable sea-water in the bottom of the boat and had huddled close to the cook's life-belt he was deep in sleep, despite the fact that his teeth played all the popular airs. This sleep was so good to him that it was but a moment before he heard a voice call his name in a tone that demonstrated the last stages of exhaustion. "Will you spell me?"

"Sure, Billie."

The light in the north had mysteriously vanished, but the correspondent took his course from the wide-awake captain.

Later in the night they took the boat farther out to sea, and the captain directed the cook to take one oar at the stern and keep the boat facing the seas. He was to call out if he should hear the thunder of the surf. This plan enabled the oiler and the correspondent to get respite together. "We'll give those boys a chance to get into shape again," said the captain. They curled down and, after a few preliminary chatterings and trembles, slept once more the dead sleep. Neither knew they had bequeathed to the cook the company of another shark, or perhaps the same shark.

As the boat caroused on the waves, spray occasionally bumped over the side and gave them a fresh soaking, but this had no power to break their repose. The ominous slash of the wind and the water affected them as it would have affected mummies.

"Boys," said the cook, with the notes of every reluctance in his voice, "she's drifted in pretty close. I guess one of you had better take her to sea again." The correspondent, aroused, heard the crash of the toppled crests.

As he was rowing, the captain gave him some whisky-and-water, and this steadied the chills out of him. "If I ever get ashore and anybody shows me even a photograph of an oar—"

At last there was a short conversation.

"Billie!—Billie, will you spell me?"

"Sure," said the oiler.

VII

When the correspondent again opened his eyes, the sea and the sky were each of the grey hue of the dawning. Later, carmine and gold was painted upon the waters. The morning appeared finally, in its splendour, with a sky of pure blue, and the sunlight flamed on the tips of the waves.

On the distant dunes were set many little black cottages, and a tall white windmill reared above them. No man, nor dog, nor bicycle appeared on the beach. The cottages might have formed a deserted village.

The voyagers scanned the shore. A conference was held in the boat. "Well," said the captain, "if no help is coming, we might better try a run through the surf right away. If we stay out here much longer we will be too weak to do anything for ourselves at all." The others silently acquiesced in this reasoning. The boat was headed for the beach. The correspondent wondered if none ever ascended the tall wind-tower, and if then they never looked seaward. This tower was a giant, standing with its back to the plight of the ants. It represented in a degree, to the correspondent, the serenity of nature amid the struggles of the individual—nature in the wind, and nature in the vision of men. She did not seem cruel to him then, nor beneficent, nor treacherous, nor wise. But she was indifferent, flatly indifferent. It is, perhaps, plausible that a man in this situation, impressed with the unconcern of the universe, should see the innumerable flaws of his life, and have them taste wickedly in his mind, and wish for another chance. A distinction between right and wrong seems absurdly clear to him, then, in this new ignorance of the grave-edge, and he understands that if he were given another opportunity he would mend his conduct and his words, and be better and brighter during an introduction or at a tea.

"Now, boys," said the captain, "she is going to swamp sure. All we can do is to work her in as far as possible, and then when she swamps, pile out and scramble for the beach. Keep cool now, and don't jump until she swamps sure."

The oiler took the oars. Over his shoulders he scanned the surf. "Captain," he said, "I think I'd better bring her about and keep her head-on to the seas and back her in."

"All right, Billie," said the captain. "Back her in." The oiler swung the boat then, and, seated in the stern, the cook and the correspondent were obliged to look over their shoulders to contemplate the lonely and indifferent shore.

The monstrous inshore rollers heaved the boat high until the men were again enabled to see the white sheets of water scudding up the slanted beach. "We won't get in very close," said the captain. Each time a man could wrest his attention from the rollers, he turned his glance toward the shore, and in the expression of the eyes during this contemplation there was a singular quality. The correspondent, observing the others, knew that they were not afraid, but the full meaning of their glances was shrouded.

As for himself, he was too tired to grapple fundamentally with the fact. He tried to coerce his mind into thinking of it, but the mind was dominated at this time by the muscles, and the muscles said they did not care. It merely occurred to him that if he should drown it would be a shame.

There were no hurried words, no pallor, no plain agitation. The men simply looked at the shore. "Now, remember to get well clear of the boat when you jump," said the captain.

Seaward the crest of a roller suddenly fell with a thunderous crash, and the long white comber came roaring down upon the boat.

"Steady now," said the captain. The men were silent. They turned their eyes from the shore to the comber and waited. The boat slid up the incline, leaped at the furious top, bounced over it, and swung down the long back of the wave. Some water had been shipped, and the cook bailed it out.

But the next crest crashed also. The tumbling, boiling flood of white water caught the boat and whirled it almost perpendicular. Water swarmed in from all sides. The correspondent had his hands on the gunwale at this time, and when the water entered at that place he swiftly withdrew his fingers, as if he objected to wetting them.

The little boat, drunken with this weight of water, reeled and snuggled deeper into the sea.

"Bail her out, cook! Bail her out!" said the captain.

"All right, Captain," said the cook.

"Now, boys, the next one will do for us sure," said the oiler. "Mind to jump clear of the boat."

The third wave moved forward, huge, furious, implacable. It fairly swallowed the dinghy, and almost simultaneously the men tumbled into the sea. A piece of life-belt had lain in the bottom of the boat, and as the correspondent went overboard he held this to his chest with his left hand.

The January water was icy, and he reflected immediately that it was colder than he had expected to find it off the coast of Florida. This appeared to his dazed mind as a fact important enough to be noted at the time. The coldness of the water was sad; it was tragic. This fact was somehow mixed and confused with his opinion of his own situation, so that it seemed almost a proper reason for tears. The water was cold.

When he came to the surface he was conscious of little but the noisy water. Afterward he saw his companions in the sea. The oiler was ahead in the race. He was swimming strongly and rapidly. Off to the correspondent's left, the cook's great white and corked back bulged out of the water; and in the rear the captain was hanging with his one good hand to the keel of the overturned dinghy.

There is a certain immovable quality to a shore, and the correspondent wondered at it amid the confusion of the sea.

It seemed also very attractive; but the correspondent knew that it was a long journey, and he paddled leisurely. The piece of life-preserver lay under him, and sometimes he whirled down the incline of a wave as if he were on a hand-sled.

But finally he arrived at a place in the sea where travel was beset with difficulty. He did not pause swimming to inquire what manner of current had caught him, but there his progress ceased. The shore was set before him like a bit of scenery on a stage, and he looked at it and understood with his eyes each detail of it.

As the cook passed, much farther to the left, the captain was calling to him, "Turn over on your back, cook! Turn over on your back and use the oar."

"All right, sir." The cook turned on his back, and, paddling with an oar, went ahead as if he were a canoe.

Presently the boat also passed to the left of the correspondent, with the captain clinging with one hand to the keel. He would have appeared like a man raising himself to look over a board fence if it were not for the extraordinary gymnastics of the boat. The correspondent marvelled that the captain could still hold to it.

They passed on nearer to shore—the oiler, the cook, the captain—and following them went the water-jar, bouncing gaily over the seas.

The correspondent remained in the grip of this strange new enemy—a current. The shore, with its white slope of sand and its green bluff topped with little silent cottages, was spread like a picture before him. It was very near to him then, but he was impressed as one who, in a gallery, looks at a scene from Brittany or Holland.

He thought: "I am going to drown? Can it be possible? Can it be possible? Can it be possible?" Perhaps an individual must consider his own death to be the final phenomenon of nature.

But later a wave perhaps whirled him out of this small deadly current, for he found suddenly that he could again make progress toward the shore. Later still he was aware that the captain, clinging with one hand to the keel of the dinghy, had his face turned away from the shore and toward him, and was calling his name. "Come to the boat! Come to the boat!"

In his struggle to reach the captain and the boat, he reflected that when one gets properly wearied drowning must really be a comfortable arrangement—a cessation of hostilities accompanied by a large degree of relief; and he was glad of it, for the main thing in his mind for some moments had been horror of the temporary agony. He did not wish to be hurt.

Presently he saw a man running along the shore. He was undressing with most remarkable speed. Coat, trousers, shirt, everything flew magically off him.

"Come to the boat!" called the captain.

"All right, Captain." As the correspondent paddled, he saw the captain let himself down to bottom and leave the boat. Then the correspondent performed his one little marvel of the voyage. A large wave caught him and flung him with ease and supreme speed completely over the boat and far beyond it. It struck him even then as an event in gymnastics and a true miracle of the sea. An overturned boat in the surf is not a plaything to a swimming man.

The correspondent arrived in water that reached only to his waist, but his condition did not enable him to stand for more than a moment. Each wave knocked him into a heap, and the undertow pulled at him.

Then he saw the man who had been running and undressing, and undressing and running, come bounding into the water. He dragged ashore the cook, and then waded toward the captain; but the captain waved him away and sent him to the correspondent. He was naked—naked as a tree in winter; but a halo was about his head, and he shone like a saint. He gave a strong pull, and a long drag, and a bully heave at the correspondent's hand. The correspondent, schooled in the minor formulae, said, "Thanks, old man." But suddenly the man cried, "What's that?" He pointed a swift finger. The correspondent said, "Go."

In the shallows, face downward, lay the oiler. His forehead touched sand that was periodically, between each wave, clear of the sea.

The correspondent did not know all that transpired afterward. When he achieved safe ground he fell, striking the sand with each particular part of his body. It was as if he had dropped from a roof, but the thud was grateful to him.

It seemed that instantly the beach was populated with men with blankets, clothes, and flasks, and women with coffee-pots and all the remedies sacred to their minds. The welcome of the land to the men from the sea was warm and generous; but a still and dripping shape was carried slowly up the beach, and the land's welcome for it could only be the different and sinister hospitality of the grave.

When it came night, the white waves paced to and fro in the moonlight, and the wind brought the sound of the great sea's voice to the men on the shore, and they felt that they could then be interpreters.

DISCUSSION QUESTIONS

1. How does the fictionalized tale "The Open Boat" differ from the newspaper report of the same event in "Stephen Crane's Own Story"? Have any incidents been changed or added? Has anything been distorted? Explain how Crane's role as a participant and writer changes as he turns from journalism to fiction.

2. How do Crane's tone and imagery change as he imagines a different form and audience for his writing? Point to specific examples.

Sherwood Anderson / *Winesburg, Ohio* 1919

A midwesterner with little formal education, Sherwood Anderson (1876–1941) left school at the age of fourteen and worked at various odd jobs before joining the National Guard and serving in Cuba during the aftermath of the Spanish-American War. Anderson returned to complete high school and began an auspicious career writing advertising copy in Chicago. After a number of extremely successful business ventures–including managing a mail-order house and two paint companies—Anderson grew disillusioned with the commercial world and decided at the age of thirty-six to pursue a literary career. He returned to Chicago in 1912 and soon became part of a literary circle that included Carl Sandburg, Edgar Lee Masters, and Theodore Dreiser. Within seven years, Anderson published Winesburg, Ohio, *his most famous work. "Paper Pills" is a representative section from this unconventional collection of short narratives, distinguished by the simplicity of their colloquial diction and sentence structure.*

Anderson spent the next several years writing and roaming restlessly throughout the literary world: to New York; to Paris—where he met Ernest Hemingway and Gertrude Stein; to New Orleans—where he became friends with William Faulkner. In 1927, Anderson settled in rural Virginia, where he bought and single-handedly edited two small-town newspapers. He devoted his last years to an autobiographical series focussing on the place of the writer in American society.

PAPER PILLS

He was an old man with a white beard and huge nose and hands. Long before the time during which we will know him, he was a doctor and drove a jaded white horse from house to house through the streets of Winesburg. Later he married a girl who had money. She had been left a large fertile farm when her father died. The girl was quiet, tall, and dark, and to many people she seemed very beautiful. Everyone in Winesburg wondered why she married the doctor. Within a year after the marriage she died.

The knuckles of the doctor's hand were extraordinarily large. When the hands were closed they looked like clusters of unpainted wooden balls as large as walnuts fastened together by steel rods. He smoked a cob pipe and after his wife's death sat all day in his empty office close by a window that was covered with cobwebs. He never opened the window. Once on a hot day in August he tried but found it stuck fast and after that he forgot all about it.

Winesburg had forgotten the old man, but in Doctor Reefy there were the seeds of something very fine. Alone in his musty office in the Heffner Block above the Paris Dry Goods Company's Store, he worked ceaselessly, building up something that he himself destroyed. Little pyramids of truth he erected and after erecting knocked them down again that he might have the truths to erect other pyramids.

Doctor Reefy was a tall man who had worn one suit of clothes for ten years. It was frayed at the sleeves and little holes had appeared at the knees and elbows. In the office he wore also a linen duster with huge pockets into which he continually stuffed scraps of paper. After some weeks the scraps of paper became little hard round balls, and when the pockets were filled he dumped them out upon the floor. For ten years he had but one friend, another old man named John Spaniard who owned a tree nursery. Sometimes, in a playful mood, old Doctor Reefy took from his pockets a handful of the paper balls and threw them at the nursery man. "That is to confound you, you blithering old sentimentalist," he cried, shaking with laughter.

The story of Doctor Reefy and his courtship of the tall dark girl who became his wife and left her money to him is a very curious story. It is delicious, like the twisted little apples that grow in the orchards of Winesburg. In the fall one walks in the orchards and the ground is hard with frost underfoot. The apples have been taken from the trees by the pickers. They have been put in barrels and shipped to the cities where they will be eaten in apartments that are filled with books, magazines, furniture, and people. On the trees are only a few gnarled apples that the pickers have rejected. They look like the knuckles of Doctor Reefy's hands. One nibbles at them and they are delicious. Into a little round place at the side of the apple has been gathered all of its sweetness. One runs from tree to tree over the frosted ground picking the gnarled, twisted apples and filling his pockets with them. Only the few know the sweetness of the twisted apples.

The girl and Doctor Reefy began their courtship on a summer afternoon. He was forty-five then and already he had begun the practice of filling his pockets with the scraps of paper that became hard balls and were thrown away. The habit had been formed as he sat in his buggy behind the jaded grey horse and went slowly along country roads. On the papers were written thoughts, ends of thoughts, beginnings of thoughts.

One by one the mind of Doctor Reefy had made the thoughts. Out of many of them he formed a truth that arose gigantic in his mind. The truth clouded the world. It became terrible and then faded away and the little thoughts began again.

The tall dark girl came to see Doctor Reefy because she was in the family way and had become frightened. She was in that condition because of a series of circumstances also curious.

The death of her father and mother and the rich acres of land that had come down to her had set a train of suitors on her heels. For two years she saw suitors almost every evening. Except two they were all alike. They talked to her of passion and there was a strained eager quality in their voices and in their eyes when they looked at her. The two who were different were much unlike each other. One of them, a slender young man with white hands, the son of a jeweler in Winesburg, talked continually of virginity. When he was with her he was never off the subject. The other, a black-haired boy with large ears, said nothing at all but always managed to get her into the darkness where he began to kiss her.

For a time the tall dark girl thought she would marry the jeweler's son. For hours she sat in silence listening as he talked to her and then she began to be afraid of something. Beneath his talk of virginity she began to think there was a lust greater than in all the others. At times it seemed to her that as he talked he was holding her body in his hands. She imagined him turning it slowly about in the white hands and staring at it. At night she dreamed that he had bitten into her body and that his jaws were dripping. She had the dream three times, then she became in the family way to the one who said nothing at all but who in the moment of his passion actually did bite her shoulder so that for days the marks of his teeth showed.

After the tall dark girl came to know Doctor Reefy it seemed to her that she never wanted to leave him again. She went into his office one morning and without her saying anything he seemed to know what had happened to her.

In the office of the doctor there was a woman, the wife of the man who kept the bookstore in Winesburg. Like all old-fashioned country practitioners, Doctor Reefy pulled teeth, and the woman who waited held a handkerchief to her teeth and groaned. Her husband was with her and when the tooth was taken out they both screamed and blood ran down on the woman's white dress. The tall dark girl did not pay any attention. When the woman and the man had gone the doctor smiled. "I will take you driving into the country with me," he said.

For several weeks the tall dark girl and the doctor were together almost every day. The condition that had brought her to him passed in an illness, but she was like one who has discovered the sweetness of the twisted apples, she could not get her mind fixed again upon the round perfect fruit that is eaten in the city apartments. In the fall after the beginning of her acquaintanceship with him she married Doctor Reefy and in the following spring she died. During the winter he read to her all of the odds and ends of thoughts he had scribbled on the bits of paper. After he had read them he laughed and stuffed them away in his pockets to become round hard balls.

Langston Hughes / The Weary Blues   1926

"He has been a minstrel and a troubadour in the classic sense. He has had no other vocation," wrote literary historian Arna Bontemps about Langston Hughes. Most of Hughes's poetry was written in the 1920s, and he often used the meter of blues rhythms in his lines.

For more about Langston Hughes, see "Family Tree" in Press (p. 138).

Droning a drowsy syncopated tune,
Rocking back and forth to a mellow croon,
    I heard a Negro play.
Down on Lenox Avenue the other night
By the pale dull pallor of an old gas light   5
    He did a lazy sway . . .
    He did a lazy sway . . .
To the tune o' those Weary Blues.
With his ebony hands on each ivory key
He made that poor piano moan with melody.   10
    O Blues!
Swaying to and fro on his rickety stool
He played that sad raggy tune like a musical fool.
    Sweet Blues!
Coming from a black man's soul.   15
    O Blues!
In a deep song voice with a melancholy tone

I heard that Negro sing, that old piano moan—
    "Ain't got nobody in all this world,
    Ain't got nobody but ma salf.   20
    I's gwine to quit ma frownin'
    And put ma troubles on the shelf."
Thump, thump, went his foot on the floor.
He played a few chords then he sang some more—
    "I got the Weary Blues   25
    And I can't be satisfied.
    Got the Weary Blues
    And can't be satisfied—
    I ain't happy no mo
    And I wish that I had died."   30
And far into the night he crooned that tune.
The stars went out and so did the moon.
The singer stopped playing and went to bed
While the Weary Blues echoed through his head.
He slept like a rock or a man that's dead.   35

Langston Hughes / The Negro Speaks of Rivers   1926

I've known rivers:
I've known rivers ancient as the world and older than the flow of human blood in
    human veins.

My soul has grown deep like the rivers.

I bathed in the Euphrates when dawns were young.
I build my hut near the Congo and it lulled me to sleep.   5
I looked upon the Nile and raised the pyramids above it.
I heard the singing of the Mississippi when Abe Lincoln went down to New
    Orleans, and I've seen its muddy bosom turn all golden in the sunset.
I've known rivers:
Ancient, dusky rivers.

My soul has grown deep like the rivers.   10

Ernest Hemingway / The Killers   1927

Ernest Hemingway (1899–1961) was first employed as a reporter for the Kansas
City Star *in 1917. After serving in a Red Cross ambulance unit on the Italian
front during World War I, Hemingway wrote for the* Toronto Star Weekly *and
later worked briefly for a Chicago advertising firm. He gradually turned to free-
lance journalism and published a good deal of short fiction characterized by a
lean, understated prose style that he later partially attributed to the constraints of
having to write cablegrams. With the encouragement of Sherwood Anderson and*

the promise of a job as foreign correspondent for the Toronto Daily Star, *Hemingway left for Paris in 1921 where he met Gertrude Stein and gravitated towards her corps of literary expatriates.*

The following tale of two stylish and stylized Chicago gangsters who take over a small town diner, more on the authority of their wisecracks than their weapons, is one of Hemingway's most widely anthologized short stories. It was introduced in the March 1927 issue of Scribner's *as "the first short story by Ernest Hemingway ever to be published in an American magazine." The editors found Hemingway's prose impressive, "marked by . . . fine economy and . . . brillantly natural dialogue." Thirty years earlier* Scribner's *had promoted a similar literary effort in Stephen Crane's "The Open Boat." Like Crane, Hemingway found that the practice of journalism had provided him with a language adequate to the tensions, fears, and reticences of men under pressure, with the odds against them.*

The door of Henry's lunch-room opened and two men came in. They sat down at the counter.

"What's yours?" George asked them.

"I don't know," one of the men said. "What do you want to eat, Al?"

"I don't know," said Al. "I don't know what I want to eat."

Outside it was getting dark. The street-light came on outside the window. The two men at the counter read the menu. From the other end of the counter Nick Adams watched them. He had been talking to George when they came in.

"I'll have a roast pork tenderloin with apple sauce and mashed potatoes," the first man said.

"It isn't ready yet."

"What the hell do you put it on the card for?"

"That's the dinner," George explained. "You can get that at six o'clock."

George looked at the clock on the wall behind the counter.

"It's five o'clock."

"The clock says twenty minutes past five," the second man said.

"It's twenty minutes fast."

"Oh, to hell with the clock," the first man said. "What have you got to eat?"

"I can give you any kind of sandwiches," George said. "You can have ham and eggs, bacon and eggs, liver and bacon, or a steak."

"Give me chicken croquettes with green peas and cream sauce and mashed potatoes."

"That's the dinner."

"Everything we want's the dinner, eh? That's the way you work it."

"I can give you ham and eggs, bacon and eggs, liver—"

"I'll take ham and eggs," the man called Al said. He wore a derby hat and a black overcoat buttoned across the chest. His face was small and white and he had tight lips. He wore a silk muffler and gloves.

"Give me bacon and eggs," said the other man. He was about the same size as Al. Their faces were different, but they were dressed like twins. Both wore overcoats too tight for them. They sat leaning forward, their elbows on the counter.

"Got anything to drink?" Al asked.

"Silver beer, bevo, ginger-ale," George said.

"I mean you got anything to *drink?*"

"Just those I said."

"This is a hot town," said the other. "What do they call it?"

"Summit."

"Ever hear of it?" Al asked his friend.

"No," said the friend.

"What do you do here nights?" Al asked.

"They eat the dinner," his friend said. "They all come here and eat the big dinner."

"That's right," George said.

"So you think that's right?" Al asked George.

"Sure."

"You're a pretty bright boy, aren't you?"

"Sure," said George.

"Well, you're not," said the other little man. "Is he, Al?"

"He's dumb," said Al. He turned to Nick. "What's your name?"

"Adams."

"Another bright boy," Al said. "Ain't he a bright boy, Max?"

"The town's full of bright boys," Max said.

George put the two platters, one of ham and eggs, the other of bacon and eggs, on the counter. He set down two side-dishes of fried potatoes and closed the wicket into the kitchen.

"Which is yours?" he asked Al.

"Don't you remember?"

"Ham and eggs."

"Just a bright boy," Max said. He leaned forward and took the ham and eggs. Both men ate with their gloves on. George watched them eat.

"What are *you* looking at?" Max looked at George.

"Nothing."

"The hell you were. You were looking at me."

"Maybe the boy meant it for a joke, Max," Al said.

George laughed.

"*You* don't have to laugh," Max said to him. "*You* don't have to laugh at all, see?"

"All right," said George.

"So he thinks it's all right." Max turned to Al. "He thinks it's all right. That's a good one."

"Oh, he's a thinker," Al said. They went on eating.

"What's the bright boy's name down the counter?" Al asked Max.

"Hey, bright boy," Max said to Nick. "You go around on the other side of the counter with your boy friend."

"What's the idea?" Nick asked.

"There isn't any idea."

"You better go around, bright boy," Al said. Nick went around behind the counter.

"What's the idea?" George asked.

"None of your damn business," Al said. "Who's out in the kitchen?"

"The nigger."

"What do you mean the nigger?"

"The nigger that cooks."

"Tell him to come in."

"What's the idea?"

"Tell him to come in."

"Where do you think you are?"

"We know damn well where we are," the man called Max said. "Do we look silly?"

"You talk silly," Al said to him. "What the hell do you argue with this kid for? Listen," he said to George, "tell the nigger to come out here."

"What are you going to do to him?"

"Nothing. Use your head, bright boy. What would we do to a nigger?"

George opened the slit that opened back into the kitchen. "Sam," he called. "Come in here a minute."

The door to the kitchen opened and the nigger came in. "What was it?" he asked. The two men at the counter took a look at him.

"All right, nigger. You stand right there," Al said.

Sam, the nigger, standing in his apron, looked at the two men sitting at the counter. "Yes, sir," he said. Al got down from his stool.

"I'm going back to the kitchen with the nigger and bright boy," he said. "Go on back to the kitchen, nigger. You go with him, bright boy." The little man walked after Nick and Sam, the cook, back into the kitchen. The door shut after them. The man called Max sat at the counter opposite George. He didn't look at George but looked in the mirror that ran along back of the counter. Henry's had been made over from a saloon into a lunch-counter.

"Well, bright boy," Max said, looking into the mirror, "why don't you say something?"

"What's it all about?"

"Hey, Al," Max called, "bright boy wants to know what it's all about."

"Why don't you tell him?" Al's voice came from the kitchen.

"What do you think it's all about?"

"I don't know."

"What do you think?"

Max looked into the mirror all the time he was talking.

"I wouldn't say."

"Hey, Al, bright boy says he wouldn't say what he thinks it's all about."

"I can hear you, all right," Al said from the kitchen. He had propped open the slit that dishes passed through into the kitchen with a catsup bottle. "Listen, bright boy," he said from the kitchen to George. "Stand a little further along the bar. You move a little to the left, Max." He was like a photographer arranging for a group picture.

"Talk to me, bright boy," Max said. "What do you think's going to happen?"

George did not say anything.

"I'll tell you," Max said. "We're going to kill a Swede. Do you know a big Swede named Ole Andreson?"

"Yes."

"He comes here to eat every night, don't he?"

"Sometimes he comes here."

"He comes here at six o'clock, don't he?"

"If he comes."

"We know all that, bright boy," Max said. "Talk about something else. Ever go to the movies?"

"Once in a while."

"You ought to go to the movies more. The movies are fine for a bright boy like you."

"What are you going to kill Ole Andreson for? What did he ever do to you?"

"He never had a chance to do anything to us. He never even seen us."

"And he's only going to see us once," Al said from the kitchen.

"What are you going to kill him for, then?" George asked.

"We're killing him for a friend. Just to oblige a friend, bright boy."

"Shut up," said Al from the kitchen. "You talk too goddam much."

"Well, I got to keep bright boy amused. Don't I, bright boy?"

"You talk too damn much," Al said. "The nigger and my bright boy are amused by themselves. I got them tied up like a couple of girl friends in the convent."

"I suppose you were in a convent?"

"You never know."

"You were in a kosher convent. That's where you were."

George looked up at the clock.

"If anybody comes in you tell them the cook is off, and if they keep after it, you tell them you'll go back and cook yourself. Do you get that, bright boy?"

"All right," George said. "What you going to do with us afterward?"

"That'll depend," Max said. "That's one of those things you never know at the time."

George looked up at the clock. It was a quarter past six. The door from the street opened. A street-car motorman came in.

"Hello, George," he said. "Can I get supper?"

"Sam's gone out," George said. "He'll be back in about half an hour."

"I'd better go up the street," the motorman said. George looked at the clock. It was twenty minutes past six.

"That was nice, bright boy," Max said. "You're a regular little gentleman."

"He knew I'd blow his head off," Al said from the kitchen.

"No," said Max. "It ain't that. Bright boy is nice. He's a nice boy. I like him."

At six-fifty-five George said: "He's not coming."

Two other people had been in the lunch-room. Once George had gone out to the kitchen and made a ham-and-egg sandwich "to go" that a man wanted to take with him. Inside the kitchen he saw Al, his derby hat tipped back, sitting on a stool beside the wicket with the muzzle of a sawed-off shotgun resting on the ledge. Nick and the cook were back to back in the corner, a towel tied in each of their mouths. George had cooked the sandwich, wrapped it up in oiled paper, put it in a bag, brought it in, and the man had paid for it and gone out.

"Bright boy can do everything," Max said. "He can cook and everything. You'd make some girl a nice wife, bright boy."

"Yes?" George said. "Your friend, Ole Andreson, isn't going to come."

"We'll give him ten minutes," Max said.

Max watched the mirror and the clock. The hands of the clock marked seven o'clock, and then five minutes past seven.

"Come on, Al," said Max. "We better go. He's not coming."

"Better give him five minutes," Al said from the kitchen.

In the five minutes a man came in, and George explained that the cook was sick.

"Why the hell don't you get another cook?" the man asked. "Aren't you running a lunch-counter?" He went out.

"Come on, Al," Max said.

"What about the two bright boys and the nigger?"

"They're all right."

"You think so?"

"Sure. We're through with it."

"I don't like it," said Al. "It's sloppy. You talk too much."

"Oh, what the hell," said Max. "We got to keep amused, haven't we?"

"You talk too much, all the same," Al said. He came out from the kitchen. The cut-off barrels of the shotgun made a slight bulge under the waist of his too tight-fitting overcoat. He straightened his coat with his gloved hands.

"So long, bright boy," he said to George. "You got a lot of luck."

"That's the truth," Max said. "You ought to play the races, bright boy."

The two of them went out the door. George watched them, through the window, pass under the arc-light and cross the street. In their tight overcoats and derby hats they looked like a vaudeville team. George went back through the swinging-door into the kitchen and untied Nick and the cook.

"I don't want any more of that," said Sam, the cook. "I don't want any more of that."

Nick stood up. He had never had a towel in his mouth before.

"Say," he said. "What the hell?" He was trying to swagger it off.

"They were going to kill Ole Andreson," George said. "They were going to shoot him when he came in to eat."

"Ole Andreson?"

"Sure."

The cook felt the corners of his mouth with his thumbs.

"They all gone?" he asked.

"Yeah," said George. "They're gone now."

"I don't like it," said the cook. "I don't like any of it at all."

"Listen," George said to Nick. "You better go see Ole Andreson."

"All right."

"You better not have anything to do with it at all," Sam, the cook, said. "You better stay way out of it."

"Don't go if you don't want to," George said.

"Mixing up in this ain't going to get you anywhere," the cook said. "You stay out of it."

"I'll go see him," Nick said to George. "Where does he live?"

The cook turned away.

"Little boys always know what they want to do," he said.

"He lives up at Hirsch's rooming-house," George said to Nick.

"I'll go up there."

Outside the arc-light shone through the bare branches of a tree. Nick walked up the street beside the car-tracks and turned at the next arc-light down a side-street. Three houses up the street was Hirsch's rooming-house. Nick walked up the two steps and pushed the bell. A woman came to the door.

"Is Ole Andreson here?"

"Do you want to see him?"

"Yes, if he's in."

Nick followed the woman up a flight of stairs and back to the end of a corridor. She knocked on the door.

"Who is it?"

"It's somebody to see you, Mr. Andreson," the woman said.

"It's Nick Adams."

"Come in."

Nick opened the door and went into the room. Ole Andreson was lying on the bed with all his clothes on. He had been a heavyweight prizefighter and he was too long for the bed. He lay with his head on two pillows. He did not look at Nick.

"What was it?" he asked.

"I was up at Henry's," Nick said, "and two fellows came in and tied up me and the cook, and they said they were going to kill you."

It sounded silly when he said it. Ole Andreson said nothing.

"They put us out in the kitchen," Nick went on. "They were going to shoot you when you came in to supper."

Ole Andreson looked at the wall and did not say anything.

"George thought I better come and tell you about it."

"There isn't anything I can do about it," Ole Andreson said.

"I'll tell you what they were like."

"I don't want to know what they were like," Ole Andreson said. He looked at the wall. "Thanks for coming to tell me about it."

"That's all right."

Nick looked at the big man lying on the bed.

"Don't you want me to go and see the police?"

"No," Ole Andreson said. "That wouldn't do any good."

"Isn't there something I could do?"

"No. There ain't anything to do."

"Maybe it was just a bluff."

"No. It ain't just a bluff."

Ole Andreson rolled over toward the wall.

"The only thing is," he said, talking toward the wall, "I just can't make up my mind to go out. I been in here all day."

"Couldn't you get out of town?"

"No," Ole Andreson said. "I'm through with all that running around."

He looked at the wall.

"There ain't anything to do now."

"Couldn't you fix it up some way?"

"No. I got in wrong." He talked in the same flat voice. "There ain't anything to do. After a while I'll make up my mind to go out."

"I better go back and see George," Nick said.

"So long," said Ole Andreson. He did not look toward Nick. "Thanks for coming around."

Nick went out. As he shut the door he saw Ole Andreson with all his clothes on, lying on the bed looking at the wall.

"He's been in his room all day," the landlady said down-stairs. "I guess he don't feel well. I said to him: 'Mr. Andreson, you ought to go out and take a walk on a nice fall day like this,' but he didn't feel like it."

"He doesn't want to go out."

"I'm sorry he don't feel well," the woman said. "He's an awfully nice man. He was in the ring, you know."

"I know it."

"You'd never know it except from the way his face is," the woman said. They stood talking just inside the street door. "He's just as gentle."

"Well, good-night, Mrs. Hirsch," Nick said.

"I'm not Mrs. Hirsch," the woman said. "She owns the place. I just look after it for her. I'm Mrs. Bell."

"Well, good-night, Mrs. Bell," Nick said.

"Good-night," the woman said.

Nick walked up the dark street to the corner under the arc-light, and then along the car-tracks to Henry's eating-house. George was inside, back of the counter.

"Did you see Ole?"

"Yes," said Nick. "He's in his room and he won't go out."

The cook opened the door from the kitchen when he heard Nick's voice.

"I don't even listen to it," he said and shut the door.

"Did you tell him about it?" George asked.

"Sure. I told him but he knows what it's all about."

"What's he going to do?"

"Nothing."

"They'll kill him."

"I guess they will."

"He must have got mixed up in something in Chicago."

"I guess so," said Nick.

"It's a hell of a thing."

"It's an awful thing," Nick said.

They did not say anything. George reached down for a towel and wiped the counter.

"I wonder what he did?" Nick said.

"Double-crossed somebody. That's what they kill them for."

"I'm going to get out of this town," Nick said.

"Yes," said George. "That's a good thing to do."

"I can't stand to think about him waiting in the room and knowing he's going to get it. It's too damned awful."

"Well," said George, "you better not think about it."

William Carlos Williams / The Use of Force   1933

Five minutes, ten minutes, can always be found. I had my typewriter in my office desk. All I needed to do was pull up the leaf to which it was fastened and I was ready to go. I worked at top speed. If a patient came in at the door while I was in the middle of a sentence, bang would go the machine—I was a physician. When the patient left, up would come the machine. My head developed a technique: something growing inside me demanded reaping. It had to be attended to. Finally, after eleven at night, when the last patient had been put to bed, I could always find time to bang out ten or twelve pages. In fact, I couldn't rest until I had freed my mind from the obsessions which had been tormenting me all day. Cleansed of that torment, having scribbled, I could rest.

As the above passage from his Autobiography *makes clear, William Carlos Williams worked hard all his life at two demanding careers. A busy pediatrician in a densely populated northern New Jersey area, Williams also attained a reputation as one of the leading figures in modern American poetry. In his best work he succeeds in giving literary form to the discordant, brittle, nonliterary idioms of an industrial civilization.*

Born in Rutherford, New Jersey, in 1883, Williams received a medical education at the University of Pennsylvania, where he became acquainted with the poet and critic Ezra Pound. After a year's study abroad, Williams returned to his home town to discipline himself in the arts of healing and writing. His first book of poems, published at his own expense in 1909, was followed by nearly forty volumes of poetry, short stories, novels, plays, history, biography, and criticism, in which he consistently demonstrates a special fondness for local subjects and his native grounds. His most ambitious effort, an epic of a modern industrial city, Paterson, *received the National Book Award in 1949. Williams died in Rutherford in 1963.*

"The Use of Force" documents in unsentimental terms an encounter between a determined physician and the seriously ill child of a poor, backward family–the kind of people Williams cared for all his life. It originally appeared in Blast, *a short-lived American literary magazine that, according to Williams, was started by an unemployed "tool designer living precariously over a garage in Brooklyn."*

"Tract," the poem that follows "The Use of Force," is an ironic commentary on the pomp conventionally associated with funerals; it appeared in Williams' collection Al Que Quiere! (*"To him who wants it!"*), *published in 1917.*

They were new patients to me, all I had was the name, Olson. Please come down as soon as you can, my daughter is very sick.

When I arrived I was met by the mother, a big startled-looking woman, very clean and apologetic who merely said, Is this the doctor? and let me in. In the back, she added. You must excuse us, doctor, we have her in the kitchen where it is warm. It is very damp here sometimes.

The child was fully dressed and sitting on her father's lap near the kitchen table. He tried to get up, but I motioned for him not to bother, took off my overcoat and started to look things over. I could see that they were all very nervous, eyeing me up and down distrustfully. As often, in such cases, they weren't telling me more than they had to, it was up to me to tell them; that's why they were spending three dollars on me.

The child was fairly eating me up with her cold, steady eyes, and no expression to her face whatever. She did not move and seemed, inwardly, quiet; an unusually attractive little thing, and as strong as a heifer in appearance. But her face was flushed, she was breathing rapidly, and I realized that she had a high fever. She had magnificent blond hair, in profusion. One of those picture children often reproduced in advertising leaflets and the photogravure sections of the Sunday papers.

She's had a fever for three days, began the father and we don't know what it comes from. My wife has given her things, you know, like people do, but it don't do no good. And there's been a lot of sickness around. So we tho't you'd better look her over and tell us what is the matter.

As doctors often do I took a trial shot at it as a point of departure. Has she had a sore throat?

Both parents answered me together, No . . . No, she says her throat don't hurt her.

Does your throat hurt you? added the mother to the child. But the little girl's expression didn't change nor did she move her eyes from my face.

Have you looked?

I tried to, said the mother, but I couldn't see.

As it happens we had been having a number of cases of diphtheria in the school to which this child went during that month and we were all, quite apparently, thinking of that, though no one had as yet spoken of the thing.

Well, I said, suppose we take a look at the throat first. I smiled in my best professional manner and asking for the child's first name I said, come on, Mathilda, open your mouth and let's take a look at your throat.

Nothing doing.

Aw, come on, I coaxed, just open your mouth wide and let me take a look. Look, I said opening both hands wide, I haven't anything in my hands. Just open up and let me see.

Such a nice man, put in the mother. Look how kind he is to you. Come on, do what he tells you to. He won't hurt you.

At that I ground my teeth in disgust. If only they wouldn't use the word "hurt" I might be able to get someplace. But I did not allow myself to be hurried or disturbed but speaking quietly and slowly I approached the child again.

As I moved my chair a little nearer suddenly with one cat-like movement both her hands clawed instinctively for my eyes and she almost reached them too. In fact she knocked my glasses flying and they fell, though unbroken, several feet away from me on the kitchen floor.

Both the mother and father almost turned themselves inside out in embarrassment and apology. You bad girl, said the mother, taking her and shaking her by one arm. Look what you've done. The nice man . . .

For heaven's sake, I broke in. Don't call me a nice man to her. I'm here to look at her throat on the chance that she might have diphtheria and possibly die of it. But that's nothing to her. Look here, I said to the child, we're going to look at your throat. You're old enough to understand what I'm saying. Will you open it now by yourself or shall we have to open it for you?

Not a move. Even her expression hadn't changed. Her breaths however were coming faster and faster. Then the battle began. I had to do it. I had to have a throat culture for her own protection. But first I told the parents that it was entirely up to them. I explained the danger but said that I would not insist on a throat examination so long as they would take the responsibility.

If you don't do what the doctor says you'll have to go to the hospital, the mother admonished her severely.

Oh yeah? I had to smile to myself. After all, I had already fallen in love with the savage brat, the parents were contemptible to me. In the ensuing struggle they grew more and more abject, crushed, exhausted while she surely rose to magnificent heights of insane fury of effort bred of her terror of me.

The father tried his best, and he was a big man but the fact that she was his daughter, his shame at her behavior and his dread of hurting her made him release her just at the critical moment several times when I had almost achieved success, till I wanted to kill him. But his dread also that she might have diphtheria made him tell me to go on, go on though he himself was almost fainting, while the mother moved back and forth behind us raising and lowering her hands in an agony of apprehension.

Put her in front of you on your lap, I ordered, and hold both her wrists.
But as soon as he did the child let out a scream. Don't, your're hurting me. Let go of my hands. Let them go I tell you. Then she shrieked terrifyingly, hysterically. Stop it! Stop it! You're killing me!

Do you think she can stand it, doctor! said the mother.

You get out, said the husband to his wife. Do you want her to die of diphtheria? Come on now, hold her, I said.

Then I grasped the child's head with my left hand and tried to get the wooden tongue depressor between her teeth. She fought, with clenched teeth, desparately! But now I also had grown furious—at a child. I tried to hold myself down but I couldn't. I know how to expose a throat for inspection. And I did my best. When finally I got the wooden spatula behind the last teeth and just the point of it into the mouth cavity, she opened up for an instant but before I could see anything she came down again and gripping the wooden blade between her molars she reduced it to splinters before I could get it out again.

Aren't you ashamed, the mother yelled at her. Aren't you ashamed to act like that in front of the doctor?

Get me a smooth-handled spoon of some sort, I told the mother. We're going through with this. The child's mouth was already bleeding. Her tongue was cut and she was screaming in wild hysterical shrieks. Perhaps I should have desisted and come back in an hour or more. No doubt it would have been better. But I have seen at least two children lying dead in bed of neglect in such cases, and feeling that I must get a diagnosis, now or never I went at it again. But the worst of it was that I too had got beyond reason. I could have torn the child apart in my own fury and enjoyed it. It was a pleasure to attack her. My face was burning with it.

The damned little brat must be protected against her own idiocy, one says to one's self at such times. Others must be protected against her. It is social necessity. And all these things are true. But a blind fury, a feeling of adult shame, bred of a longing for muscular release are the operatives. One goes on to the end.

In a final unreasoning assault I overpowered the child's neck and jaws. I forced the heavy silver spoon back on her teeth and down her throat till she gagged. And there it was—both tonsils covered with membrane. She had fought valiantly to keep me from knowing her secret. She had been hiding that sore throat for three days at least and lying to her parents in order to escape just such an outcome as this.

Now truly she *was* furious. She had been on the defensive before but now she attacked. Tried to get off her father's lap and fly at me while tears of defeat blinded her eyes.

William Carlos Williams / Tract   1917

I will teach you my townspeople
how to perform a funeral—
for you have it over a troop
of artists—

unless one should scour the world—   5
you have the ground sense necessary.

See! the hearse leads.
I begin with a design for a hearse.
For Christ's sake not black—
nor white either—and not polished!   10
Let it be weathered—like a farm wagon—
with gilt wheels (this could be
applied fresh at small expense)
or no wheels at all:
a rough dray to drag over the ground.   15

Knock the glass out!
My God—glass, my townspeople!
For what purpose? Is it for the dead
to look out or for us to see
the flowers or the lack of them—   20
or what?
To keep the rain and snow from him?
He will have a heavier rain soon:
pebbles and dirt and what not.
Let there be no glass—   25
and no upholstery! phew!
and no little brass rollers
and small easy wheels on the bottom—
my townspeople what are you thinking of!

A rough plain hearse then   30
with gilt wheels and no top at all.
On this the coffin lies
by its own weight.

                No wreaths please—
especially no hot-house flowers.   35
Some common memento is better.
something he prized and is known by:
his old clothes—a few books perhaps—
God knows what! You realize
how we are about these things,   40
my townspeople—
something will be found—anything—
even flowers if he had come to that.
So much for the hearse.

For heaven's sake though see to the driver!   45
Take off the silk hat! In fact
that's no place at all for him
up there unceremoniously
dragging our friend out of his own dignity!

Bring him down—bring him down!   50
Low and inconspicuous! I'd not have him ride
on the wagon at all—damn him—
the undertaker's understrapper!
Let him hold the reins
and walk at the side   55
and inconspiciously too!

Then briefly as to yourselves:
Walk behind—as they do in France,
seventh class, or if you ride
Hell take curtains! Go with some show   60
of inconvenience; sit openly—
to the weather as to grief.
Or do you think you can shut grief in?
What—from us? We who have perhaps
nothing to lose? Share with us   65
share with us—it will be money
in your pockets.

         Go now
I think you are ready.

F. Scott Fitzgerald / Boil Some Water—Lots of It   1940

> *F. Scott Fitzgerald was born in Minneapolis, attended Princeton, "made it" in New York, lived high in Paris, and died broke in Hollywood. But that is hardly the whole story. Fitzgerald wrote seventeen stories for* Esquire *about "Pat Hobby," whom he described as a "complete rat" but not a "sinister" character—the kind of character Fitzgerald himself feared becoming if he were ever to "paste it together" and make it big in Hollywood. "Boil Some Water—Lots of It" first appeared in the March, 1940 issue of* Esquire.

Pat Hobby sat is his office in the Writers' Building and looked at his morning's work, just come back from the script department. He was on a "polish job," about the only kind he ever got nowadays. He was to repair a messy sequence in a hurry, but the word "hurry" neither frightened nor inspired him for Pat had been in Hollywood since he was thirty—now he was forty-nine. All the work he had done this morning (except a little changing around of lines so he could claim them as his own)—all he had actually invented was a single imperative sentence, spoken by a doctor.

"Boil some water—lots of it."

It was a good line. It had sprung into his mind full grown as soon as he had read the script. In the old silent days Pat would have used it as a spoken title and ended his dialogue worries for a space, but he needed some spoken words for other people in the scene. Nothing came.

Boil some water, he repeated to himself, lots of it.

The word boil brought a quick glad thought of the commissary. A reverent thought too—for an old-timer like Pat, what people you sat with at lunch was more important in getting along than what you dictated in your office. This was no art, as he often said—this was an industry.

"This is no art," he remarked to Max Leam who was leisurely drinking at a corridor water cooler. "This is an industry."

Max had flung him this timely bone of three weeks at three-fifty.

"Say look, Pat! Have you got anything down on paper yet?"

"Say I've got some stuff already that'll make 'em—" He named a familiar biological function with the somewhat startling assurance that it would take place in the theater.

Max tried to gauge his sincerity.

"Want to read it to me now?" he asked.

"Not yet. But it's got the old guts if you know what I mean."

Max was full of doubts.

"Well, go to it. And if you run into any medical snags check with the doctor over at the First Aid Station. It's got to be right."

The spirit of Pasteur shone firmly in Pat's eyes.

"It will be."

He felt good walking across the lot with Max—so good that he decided to glue himself to the producer and sit down with him at the Big Table. But Max foiled his intention by cooing, "See you later," and slipping into the barbershop.

Once Pat had been a familiar figure at the Big Table; often in his golden prime he had dined in the private canteens of executives. Being of the older Hollywood he understood their jokes, their vanities, their social system with its swift fluctuations. But there were too many new faces at the Big Table now—faces that looked at him with the universal Hollywood suspicion. And at the little tables where the young writers sat they seemed to take work so serious. As for just sitting down anywhere, even with secretaries or extras—Pat would rather catch a sandwich at the corner.

Detouring to the Red Cross Station he asked for the doctor. A girl, a nurse, answered from a wall mirror where she was hastily drawing her lips, "He's out. What is it?"

"Oh, Then I'll come back."

She had finished, and now she turned—vivid and young and with a bright consoling smile.

"Miss Stacey will help you. I'm about to go to lunch."

He was aware of an old, old feeling—left over from the time when he had had wives—a feeling that to invite this little beauty to lunch might cause trouble. But he remembered quickly that he didn't have any wives now—they had both given up asking for alimony.

"I'm working on a medical," he said. "I need some help."

"A medical?"

"Writing it—idea about a doc. Listen—let me buy you lunch. I want to ask you some medical questions."

The nurse hesitated.

"I don't know. It's my first day out here."

"It's all right," he assured her. "Studios are democratic; everybody is just 'Joe' or 'Mary'—from the big shots right down to the prop boys."

He proved it magnificently on their way to lunch by greeting a male star and getting his own name back in return. And in the commissary, where they were placed hard by the Big Table, his producer, Max Leam, looked up, did a little "takem" and winked.

The nurse—her name was Helen Earle—peered about eagerly.

"I don't see anybody," she said. "Except oh, there's Ronald Colman. I didn't know Ronald Colman looked like that."

Pat pointed suddenly to the floor.

"And there's Mickey Mouse!"

She jumped and Pat laughed at his joke—but Helen Earle was already staring starry-eyed at the costume extras who filled the hall with the colors of the First Empire. Pat was piqued to see her interest go out to these nonentities.

"The big shots are at this next table," he said solemnly, wistfully, "directors and all except the biggest executives. They could have Ronald Colman pressing pants. I usually sit over there but they don't want ladies. At lunch, that is, they don't want ladies."

"Oh," said Helen Earle, polite but unimpressed. "It must be wonderful to be a writer too. It's so very interesting."

"It has its points," he said . . . he had thought for years it was a dog's life.

"What is it you want to ask me about a doctor?"

Here was toil again. Something in Pat's mind snapped off when he thought of the story.

"Well, Max Leam—that man facing us—Max Leam and I have a script about a Doc. You know? Like a hospital picture?"

"I know." And she added after a moment, "That's the reason that I went in training."

"And we've got to have it *right* because a hundred million people would check on it. So this doctor in the script he tells them to boil some water. He says, 'Boil some water—lots of it.' And we were wondering what the people would do then."

"Why—they'd probably boil it," Helen said, and then, somewhat confused by the question, "What people?"

"Well somebody's daughter and the man that lived there and an attorney and the man that was hurt."

Helen tried to digest this before answering.

"—and some other guy I'm going to cut out," he finished.

There was a pause. The waitress set down tuna fish sandwiches.

"Well, when a doctor gives orders they're orders," Helen decided.

"Hm." Pat's interest had wandered to an odd little scene at the Big Table while he inquired absently, "You married?"

"No."

"Neither am I."

Beside the Big Table stood an extra. A Russian Cossack with a fierce mustache. He stood resting his hand on the back of an empty chair between Director Paterson and Producer Leam.

"Is this taken?" he asked, with a thick Central European accent.

All along the Big Table faces stared suddenly at him. Until after the first look the supposition was that he must be some well-known actor. But he was not—he was dressed in one of the many-colored uniforms that dotted the room.

Someone at the table said: "That's taken." But the man drew out the chair and sat down.

"Got to eat somewhere," he remarked with a grin.

A shiver went over the near-by tables. Pat Hobby stared with his mouth ajar. It was as if someone had crayoned Donald Duck into the *Last Supper*.

"Look at that," he advised Helen. "What they'll do to him! Boy!"

The flabbergasted silence at the Big Table was broken by Ned Harman, the Production Manager.

"This table is reserved," he said.

The extra looked up from a menu.

"They told me sit anywhere."

He beckoned a waitress—who hesitated, looking for an answer in the faces of her superiors.

"Extras don't eat here," said Max Leam, still politely. "This is a—"

"I got to eat," said the Cossack doggedly. "I been standing around six hours while they shoot this stinking mess and now I got to eat."

The silence had extended—from Pat's angle all within range seemed to be poised in midair.

The extra shook his head wearily.

"I dunno who cooked it up—" he said—and Max Leam sat forward in his chair—"but it's the lousiest tripe I ever seen shot in Hollywood."

—At his table Pat was thinking why didn't they do something? Knock him down, drag him away. If they were yellow themselves they could call the studio police.

"Who is that?" Helen Earle was following his eyes innocently. "Somebody I ought to know?"

He was listening attentively to Max Leam's voice, raised in anger.

"Get up and get out of here, buddy, and get out quick!"

The extra frowned.

"Who's telling me?" he demanded.

"You'll see." Max appealed to the table at large, "Where's Cushman—where's the Personnel man?"

"You try to move me," said the extra, lifting the hilt of his scabbard above the level of the table. "And I'll hang this on your ear. I know my rights."

The dozen men at the table, representing a thousand dollars an hour in salaries, sat stunned. Far down by the door one of the studio police caught wind of what was happening and started to elbow through the crowded room. And Big Jack Wilson, another director, was on his feet in an instant coming around the table.

But they were too late—Pat Hobby could stand no more. He had jumped up, seizing a big heavy tray from the serving stand nearby. In two springs he reached the scene of action—lifting the tray he brought it down upon the extra's head with all the strength of his forty-nine years. The extra, who had been in the act of rising to meet Wilson's threatened assault, got the blow full on his face and temple and as he collapsed a dozen red streaks sprang into sight through the heavy grease paint. He crashed sideways between the chairs.

Pat stood over him panting—the tray in his hand.

"The dirty rat!" he cried. "Where does he think—"

The studio policeman pushed past; Wilson pushed past—two aghast men from another table rushed up to survey the situation.

"It was a gag!" one of them shouted. "That's Walter Herrick, the writer. It's his picture."

"My God!"

"He was kidding Max Leam. It was a gag I tell you!"

"Pull him out . . . Get a doctor . . . Look out, there!

Now Helen Earle hurried over; Walter Herrick was dragged out into a cleared space on the floor and there were yells of "Who did it?—Who beaned him?"

Pat let the tray lapse to a chair, its sound unnoticed in the confusion.

He saw Helen Earle working swiftly at the man's head with a pile of clean napkins.

"Why did they have to do this to him?" someone shouted.

Pat caught Max Leam's eye but Max happened to look away at the moment and a sense of injustice came over Pat. He alone in this crisis, real or imaginary, had *acted*. He alone had played the man, while those stuffed shirts let themselves be insulted and abused. And now he would have to take the rap—because Walter Herrick was powerful and popular, a three thousand a week man who wrote hit shows in New York. How could anyone have guessed that it was a gag?

There was a doctor now. Pat saw him say something to the manageress and her shrill voice sent the waitresses scattering like leaves toward the kitchen.

"Boil some water! Lots of it!"

The words fell wild and unreal on Pat's burdened soul. But even though he now knew at first-hand what came next, he did not think that he could go on from there.

William Faulkner / *The Bear* 1942

Sole owner, proprietor, historian, and inventor of the most turbulent 2400 square miles in America, Yoknapatawpha County, Mississippi, William Faulkner (1897–1962) remains the most powerful American novelist of the first half of the twentieth century. The major portion of his life was spent in Oxford, Mississippi, except for a brief period during the First World War with the British Flying Corps in Canada, a job in a bookstore in New York City, a stint writing sketches for the New Orleans Time-Picayune, *and an occasional acquiescence to the lure of Hollywood. We have reprinted the opening section of* The Bear, *a novella in five parts, which originally appeared (also excerpted) in the* Saturday Evening Post *in 1942 with the caption "Boy Meets Bear after Years of Stalking."*

PART I

There was a man and a dog too this time. Two beasts, counting Old Ben, the bear, and two men, counting Boon Hogganbeck, in whom some of the same blood ran which ran in Sam Fathers, even though Boon's was a plebeian strain of it and only Sam and Old Ben and the mongrel Lion were taintless and incorruptible.

He was sixteen. For six years now he had been a man's hunter. For six years now he had heard the best of all talking. It was of the wilderness, the big woods, bigger and older than any recorded document:—of white man fatuous enough to believe he had bought any fragment of it, of Indian ruthless enough to pretend that any fragment of it had been his to convey; bigger than Major de Spain and the scrap he pretended to, knowing better; older than old Thomas Sutpen of whom Major de Spain had had it and who knew better; older even than old Ikkemotubbe, the Chickasaw chief, of whom old Sutpen had had it and who knew better in his turn. It was of the men, not white nor black nor red but men, hunters, with the will and hardihood to endure and the humility and skill to survive, and the dogs and the bear and deer juxtaposed and reliefed against it, ordered and compelled by and within the wilderness in the ancient and unremitting contest according to the ancient and immitigable rules which voided all regrets and brooked no quarter;—the best game of all, the best of all breathing and forever the best of all listening, the voices quiet and weighty and deliberate for retrospection and recollection and exactitude among the concrete trophies—the racked guns and the heads and skins—in the libraries of town houses or the offices of plantation houses or (and best of all) in the camps themselves where the intact and still-warm meat yet hung, the men who had slain it sitting before the burning logs on hearths when there were houses and hearths or about the smoky blazing of piled wood in front of stretched tarpaulins when there were not. There was always a bottle present, so that it would seem to him that those fine fierce instants of heart and brain and courage and wiliness and speed were concentrated and distilled into that brown liquor which not women, not boys and children, but only hunters drank, drinking not of the blood they spilled but some condensation of the wild immortal spirit, drinking it moderately, humbly even, not with the pagan's base and baseless hope of acquiring thereby the virtues of cunning and strength and speed but in salute to them. Thus it seemed to him on this December morning not only natural but actually fitting that this should have begun with whisky.

He realised later that it had begun long before that. It had already begun on that day when he first wrote his age in two ciphers and his cousin McCaslin brought him for the first time to the camp, the big woods, to earn for himself from the wilderness the name and state of hunter provided he in his turn were humble and enduring enough. He had already inherited then, without ever having seen it, the big old bear with one trap-ruined foot that in an area almost a hundred miles square had earned for himself a name, a definite designation like a living man:—the long legend of corn-cribs broken down and rifled, of shoats and grown pigs and even calves carried bodily into the woods and devoured and traps and deadfalls overthrown and dogs mangled and slain and shotgun and even rifle shots delivered at point-blank range yet with no more effect than so many peas blown through a tube by a child—a corridor of wreckage and destruction beginning back before the boy was born, through which sped, not fast but rather with the ruthless and irresistible deliberation of a locomotive, the shaggy tremendous shape. It ran in his knowledge before he ever saw it. It loomed and towered in his dreams before he even saw the unaxed woods where it left its crooked print, shaggy, tremendous, red-eyed, not malevolent but just big, too big for the dogs which tried to bay it, for the horses which tried to ride it down, for the men and the bullets they fired into it; too big for the very country which was its constricting scope. It was as if the boy had already divined what his senses and intellect had not encompassed yet: that doomed wilderness whose edges were being constantly and punily gnawed at by men with plows and axes who feared it because it was wilderness, men myriad and nameless even to one another in the land where the old bear had earned a name, and through which ran not even a mortal beast but an anachronism indomitable and invincible out of an old dead time, a phantom, epitome and apotheosis of the old wild life which the little puny humans swarmed and hacked at in a fury of abhorrence and fear like pygmies about the ankles of a drowsing elephant;—the old bear, solitary, indomitable, and alone; widowered childless and absolved of mortality—old Priam reft of his old wife and outlived all his sons.

Still a child, with three years then two years then one year yet before he too could make one of them, each November he would watch the wagon containing the dogs and the bedding and food and guns and his cousin McCaslin and Tennie's Jim and Sam Fathers too until Sam moved to the camp to live, depart for the Big Bottom, the big woods. To him, they were going not to hunt bear and deer but to keep yearly rendezvous with the bear which they did not even intend to kill. Two weeks later they would return, with no trophy, no skin. He had not expected it. He had not even feared that it might be in the wagon this time with the other skins and heads. He did not even tell himself that in three years or two years or one year more he would be present and that it might even be his gun. He believed that only after he had served his apprenticeship in the woods which would prove him worthy to be a hunter, would he even be permitted to distinguish the crooked print, and that even then for two November weeks he would merely make another minor one, along with his cousin and Major de Spain and General Compson and Walter Ewell and Boon and the dogs which feared to bay it and the shotguns and rifles which failed even to bleed it, in the yearly pageant-rite of the old bear's furious immortality.

His day came at last. In the surrey with his cousin and Major de Spain and General Compson he saw the wilderness through a slow drizzle of November rain just above the ice point as it seemed to him later he always saw it or at least always remembered it—the tall and endless wall of dense November woods under the dissolving afternoon and the year's death, sombre, impenetrable (he could not even discern yet how, at what point they could possibly hope to enter it even though he knew that Sam Fathers was waiting there with the wagon), the surrey moving through the skeleton stalks of cotton and corn in the last of open country, the last trace of man's puny gnawing at the immemorial flank, until, dwarfed by that perspective into an almost ridiculous diminishment, the surrey itself seemed to have ceased to move (this too to be completed later, years later, after he had grown to a man and had seen the sea) as a solitary small boat hangs in lonely immobility, merely tossing up and down, in the infinite waste of the ocean while the water and then the apparently impenetrable land which it nears without appreciable progress, swings slowly and opens the widening inlet which is the anchorage. He entered it. Sam was waiting, wrapped in a quilt on the wagon seat behind the patient and steaming mules. He entered his novitiate to the true wilderness with Sam beside him as he had begun his apprenticeship in miniature to manhood after the rabbits and such with Sam beside him, the two of them wrapped in the damp, warm, negro-rank quilt while the wilderness closed behind his entrance as it had opened momentarily to accept him, opening before his advancement as it closed behind his progress, no fixed path the wagon followed but a channel nonexistent ten yards ahead of it and ceasing to exist ten yards after it had passed, the wagon progressing not by its own volition but by attrition of their intact yet fluid circumambience, drowsing, earless, almost lightless.

It seemed to him that at the age of ten he was witnessing his own birth. It was not even strange to him. He had experienced it all before, and not merely in dreams. He saw the camp—a paintless six-room bungalow set on piles above the spring high-water—and he knew already how it was going to look. He helped in the rapid or-derly disorder of their establishment in it and even his motions were familiar to him, foreknown. Then for two weeks he ate the coarse, rapid food—the shapeless sour bread, the wild strange meat, venison and bear and turkey and coon which he had never tasted before—which men ate, cooked by men who were hunters first and cooks afterward; he slept in harsh sheetless blankets as hunters slept. Each morning the gray of dawn found him and Sam Fathers on the stand, the crossing, which had been allotted him. It was the poorest one, the most barren. He had expected that; he had not dared yet to hope even to himself that he would even hear the running dogs this first time. But he did hear them. It was on the third morning—a murmur, sourceless, almost indistinguishable, yet he knew what it was although he had never before heard that many dogs running at once, the murmur swelling into separate and distinct voices until he could call the five dogs which his cousin owned from among the others. "Now," Sam said, "slant your gun up a little and draw back the ham-mers and then stand still."

But it was not for him, not yet. The humility was there; he had learned that. And he could learn the patience. He was only ten, only one week. The instant had passed. It seemed to him that he could actually see the deer, the buck, smoke-colored, elongated with speed, vanished, the woods, the gray solitude still ringing even when the voices of the dogs had died away; from far away across the sombre woods and the gray half-liquid morning there came two shots. "Now let your ham-mers down," Sam said.

He did so. "You knew it too," he said.

"Yes," Sam said. "I want you to learn how to do when you didn't shoot. It's after the chance for the bear or the deer has done already come and gone that men and dogs get killed."

"Anyway, it wasn't him," the boy said. "It wasn't even a bear. It was just a deer."

"Yes," Sam said, "it was just a deer."

Then one morning, it was in the second week, he heard the dogs again. This time before Sam even spoke he readied the too-long, too-heavy, man-size gun as Sam had taught him, even though this time he knew the dogs and the deer were coming less close than ever, hardly within hearing even. They didn't sound like any running dogs he had ever heard before even. Then he found that Sam, who had taught him first of all to cock the gun and take position where he could see best in all directions and then never to move again, had himself moved up beside him. "There," he said. "Listen." The boy listened, to no ringing chorus strong and fast on a free scent but a moiling yapping an octave too high and with something more than indecision and even abjectness in it which he could not yet recognise, reluctant, not even moving very fast, taking a long time to pass out of hearing, leaving even then in the air that echo of thin and almost human hysteria, abject, almost humanly grieving, with this time nothing ahead of it, no sense of a fleeing unseen smoke-colored shape. He could hear Sam breathing at his shoulder. He saw the arched curve of the old man's inhaling nostrils.

"It's Old Ben!" he cried, whispering.

Sam didn't move save for the slow gradual turning of his head as the voices faded on and the faint steady rapid arch and collapse of his nostrils. "Hah," he said. "Not even running. Walking."

"But up here!" the boy cried. "Way up here!"

"He do it every year," Sam said. "Once. Ash and Boon say he comes up here to run the other little bears away. Tell them to get to hell out of here and stay out until the hunters are gone. Maybe." The boy no longer heard anything at all, yet still Sam's head continued to turn gradually and steadily until the back of it was toward him. Then it turned back and looked down at him—the same face, grave, familiar, expressionless until it smiled, the same old man's eyes from which as he watched there faded slowly a quality darkly and fiercely lambent, passionate and proud. "He dont care no more for bears than he does for dogs or men neither. He come to see who's here, who's new in camp this year, whether he can shoot or not, can stay or not. Whether we got the dog yet that can bay and hold him until a man gets there with a gun. Because he's the head bear. He's the man." It faded, was gone; again they were the eyes as he had known them all his life. "He'll let them follow him to the river. Then he'll send them home. We might as well go too; see how they look when they get back to camp."

The dogs were there first, ten of them huddled back under the kitchen, himself and Sam squatting to peer back into the obscurity where they crouched, quiet, the eyes rolling and luminous, vanishing, and no sound, only that effluvium which the boy could not quite place yet, of something more than dog, stronger than dog and not just animal, just beast even. Because there had been nothing in front of the abject and painful yapping except the solitude, the wilderness, so that when the eleventh hound got back about mid-afternoon and he and Tennie's Jim held the passive and still trembling bitch while Sam daubed her tattered ear and raked shoulder with turpentine and axle-grease, it was still no living creature but only the wilderness which, leaning for a moment, had patted lightly once her temerity. "Just like a man," Sam said. "Just like folks. Put off as long as she could having to be brave, knowing all the time that sooner or later she would have to be brave once so she could keep on calling herself a dog, and knowing beforehand what was going to happen when she done it."

He did not know just when Sam left. He only knew that he was gone. For the next three mornings he rose and ate breakfast and Sam was not waiting for him. He went to his stand alone; he found it without help now and stood on it as Sam had taught him. On the third morning he heard the dogs again, running strong and free on a true scent again, and he readied the gun as he had learned to do and heard the hunt sweep past on since he was not ready yet, had not deserved other yet in just one short period of two weeks as compared to all the long life which he had already dedicated to the wilderness with patience and humility; he heard the shot again, one shot, the single clapping report of Walter Ewell's rifle. By now he could not only find his stand and then return to camp without guidance, by using the compass his cousin had given him he reached Walter waiting beside the buck and the moiling of dogs over the cast entrails before any of the others except Major de Spain and Tennie's Jim on the horses, even before Uncle Ash arrived with the one-eyed wagon-mule which did not mind the smell of blood or even, so they said, of bear.

It was not Uncle Ash on the mule. It was Sam, returned. And Sam was waiting when he finished his dinner and, himself on the one-eyed mule and Sam on the other one of the wagon team, they rode for more than three hours through the rapid shortening sunless afternoon, following no path, no trail even that he could discern, into a section of country he had never seen before. Then he understood why Sam had made him ride the one-eyed mule which would not spook at the smell of blood, of wild animals. The other one, the sound one, stopped short and tried to whirl and bolt even as Sam got down, jerking and wrenching at the rein while Sam held it, coaxing it forward with his voice since he did not dare risk hitching it, drawing it forward while the boy dismounted from the marred one which would stand. Then, standing beside Sam in the thick great gloom of ancient woods and the winter's dying afternoon, he looked quietly down at the rotted log scored and gutted with claw-marks and, in the wet earth beside it, the print of the enormous warped two-toed foot. Now he knew what he had heard in the hounds' voices in the woods that morning and what he had smelled when he peered under the kitchen where they huddled. It was in him too, a little different because they were brute beasts and he was not, but only a little different—an eagerness, passive; an abjectness, a sense of his own fragility and impotence against the timeless woods, yet without doubt or dread; a flavor like brass in the sudden run of saliva in his mouth, a hard sharp constriction either in his brain or his stomach, he could not tell which and it did not matter; he knew only that for the first time he realised that the bear which had run in his listening and loomed in his dreams since before he could remember and which therefore must have existed in the listening and the dreams of his cousin and Major de Spain and even old General Compson before they began to remember in their turn, was a mortal animal and that they had departed for the camp each November with no actual intention of slaying it, not because it could not be slain but because so far they had no actual hope of being able to. "It will be tomorrow," he said.

"You mean we will try tomorrow," Sam said. "We aint got the dog yet."

"We've got eleven," he said. "They ran him Monday."

"And you heard them," Sam said. "Saw them too. We aint got the dog yet. It wont take but one. But he aint there. Maybe he aint nowhere. The only other way will be for him to run by accident over somebody that had a gun and knowed how to shoot it."

"That wouldn't be me," the boy said. "It would be Walter or Major or——"

"It might," Sam said. "You watch close tomorrow. Because he's smart. That's how come he has lived this long. If he gets hemmed up and has got to pick out somebody to run over, he will pick out you."

"How?" he said. "How will he know. . . ." He ceased. "You mean he already knows me, that I aint never been to the big bottom before, aint had time to find out yet whether I . . ." He ceased again, staring at Sam; he said humbly, not even amazed: "It was me he was watching. I don't reckon he did need to come but once."

"You watch tomorrow," Sam said. "I reckon we better start back. It'll be long after dark now before we get to camp."

The next morning they started three hours earlier than they had ever done. Even Uncle Ash went, the cook, who called himself by profession a camp cook and who did little else save cook for Major de Spain's hunting and camping parties, yet who had been marked by the wilderness from simple juxtaposition to it until he responded as they all did, even the boy who until two weeks ago had never even seen the wilderness, to a hound's ripped ear and shoulder and the print of a crooked foot in a patch of wet earth. They rode. It was too far to walk: the boy and Sam and Uncle Ash in the wagon with the dogs, his cousin and Major de Spain and General Compson and Boon and Walter and Tennie's Jim riding double on the horses; again the first gray light found him, as on that first morning two weeks ago, on the stand where Sam had placed and left him. With the gun which was too big for him, the breech-loader which did not even belong to him but to Major de Spain and which he had fired only once, at a stump on the first day to learn the recoil and how to reload it with the paper shells, he stood against a big gum tree beside a little bayou whose black still water crept without motion out of a cane-brake, across a small clearing and into the cane again, where, invisible, a bird, the big woodpecker called Lord-to-God by negroes, clattered at a dead trunk. It was a stand like any other stand, dissimilar only in incidentals to the one where he had stood each morning for two weeks; a territory new to him yet no less familiar than that other one which after two weeks he had come to believe he knew a little—the same solitude, the same loneliness through which frail and timorous man had merely passed without altering it, leaving no mark nor scar, which looked exactly as it must have looked when the first ancestor of Sam Fathers' Chickasaw predecessors crept into it and looked about him, club or stone axe or bone arrow drawn and ready, different only because, squatting at the edge of the kitchen, he had smelled the dogs huddled and cringing beneath it and saw the raked ear and side of the bitch that, as Sam had said, had to be brave once in order to keep on calling herself a dog, and saw yesterday in the earth beside the gutted log, the print of the living foot. He heard no dogs at all. He never did certainly hear them. He only heard the drumming of the woodpecker stop short off, and knew that the bear was looking at him. He never saw it. He did not know whether it was facing him from the cane or behind him. He did not move, holding the useless gun which he knew now he would never fire at it now or ever, tasting in his saliva that taint of brass which he had smelled in the huddled dogs when he peered under the kitchen.

Then it was gone. As abruptly as it had stopped, the woodpecker's dry hammering set up again, and after a while he believed he even heard the dogs—a murmur, scarce a sound even, which he had probably been hearing for a time, perhaps a minute or two, before he remarked it, drifting into hearing and then out again, dying away. They came nowhere near him. If it was dogs he heard, he could not have sworn to it; if it was a bear they ran, it was another bear. It was Sam himself who emerged from the cane and crossed the bayou, the injured bitch following at heel as a bird dog is taught to walk. She came and crouched against his leg, trembling. "I didn't see him," he said. "I didn't, Sam."

"I know it," Sam said. "He done the looking. You didn't hear him neither, did you?"

"No," the boy said. "I—"

"He's smart," Sam said. "Too smart." Again the boy saw in his eyes that quality of dark and brooding lambence as Sam looked down at the bitch trembling faintly and steadily against the boy's leg. From her raked shoulder a few drops of fresh blood clung like bright berries. "Too big. We aint got the dog yet. But maybe some day."

Because there would be a next time, after and after. He was only ten. It seemed to him that he could see them, the two of them, shadowy in the limbo from which time emerged and became time: the old bear absolved of mortality and himself who shared a little of it. Because he recognised now what he had smelled in the huddled dogs and tasted in his own saliva, recognised fear as a boy, a youth, recognises the existence of love and passion and experience which is his heritage but not yet his patrimony, from entering by chance the presence or perhaps even merely the bedroom of a woman who has loved and been loved by many men. *So I will have to see him,* he thought, without dread or even hope. *I will have to look at him.* So it was in June of the next summer. They were at the camp again, celebrating Major de Spain's and General Compson's birthdays. Although the one had been born in September and the other in the depth of winter and almost thirty years earlier, each June the two of them and McCaslin and Boon and Walter Ewell (and the boy too from now on) spent two weeks at the camp, fishing and shooting squirrels and turkey and running coons and wildcats with the dogs at night. That is, Boon and the negroes (and the boy too now) fished and shot squirrels and ran the coons and cats, because the proven hunters, not only Major de Spain and old General Compson (who spent those two weeks sitting in a rocking chair before a tremendous iron pot of Brunswick stew, stirring and tasting, with Uncle Ash to quarrel with about how he was making it and Tennie's Jim to pour whisky into the tin dipper from which he drank it) but even McCaslin and Walter Ewell who were still young enough, scorned such other than shooting the wild gobblers with pistols for wagers or to test their marksmanship.

That is, his cousin McCaslin and the others thought he was hunting squirrels. Until the third evening he believed that Sam Fathers thought so too. Each morning he would leave the camp right after breakfast. He had his own gun now, a new breech-loader, a Christmas gift; he would own and shoot it for almost seventy years, through two new pairs of barrels and locks and one new stock, until all that remained of the original gun was the silver-inlaid trigger-guard with his and McCaslin's engraved names and the date in 1878. He found the tree beside the little bayou where he had stood that morning. Using the compass he ranged from that point; he was teaching himself to be better than a fair woodsman without even knowing he was doing it. On the third day he even found the gutted log where he had first seen the print. It was almost completely crumbled now, healing with unbelievable speed, a passionate and almost visible relinquishment, back into the earth from which the tree had grown. He ranged the summer woods now, green with gloom, if anything actually dimmer than they had been in November's gray dissolution, where even at noon the sun fell only in windless dappling upon the earth which never completely dried and which crawled with snakes—moccasins and watersnakes and rattlers, themselves the color of the dappled gloom so that he would not always see them until they moved; returning to camp later and later and later, first day, second day, passing in the twilight of the third evening the little log pen enclosing the log barn where Sam was putting up the stock for the night. "You aint looked right yet," Sam said.

He stopped. For a moment he didn't answer. Then he said peacefully, in a peaceful rushing burst, as when a boy's miniature dam in a little brook gives way: "All right. Yes. But how? I went to the bayou. I even found that log again. I——"

"I reckon that was all right. Likely he's been watching you. You never saw his foot?"

"I . . ." the boy said. "I didn't . . . I never thought . . ."

"It's the gun," Sam said. He stood beside the fence, motionless, the old man, son of a negro slave and a Chickasaw chief, in the battered and faded overalls and the frayed five-cent straw hat which had been the badge of the negro's slavery and was now the regalia of his freedom. The camp—the clearing, the house, the barn and its tiny lot with which Major de Spain in his turn had scratched punily and evanescently at the wilderness—faded in the dusk, back into the immemorial darkness of the woods. *The gun*, the boy thought. *The gun.* "You will have to choose," Sam said.

He left the next morning before light, without breakfast, long before Uncle Ash would wake in his quilts on the kitchen floor and start the fire. He had only the compass and a stick for the snakes. He could go almost a mile before he would need to see the compass. He sat on a log, the invisible compass in his hand, while the secret night-sounds which had ceased at his movements, scurried again and then fell still for good and the owls ceased and gave over to the waking day birds and there was light in the gray wet woods and he could see the compass. He went fast yet still quietly, becoming steadily better and better as a woodsman without yet having time to realise it; he jumped a doe and a fawn, walked them out of the bed, close enough to see them—the crash of undergrowth, the white scut, the fawn scudding along behind her, faster than he had known it could have run. He was hunting right, upwind, as Sam had taught him, but that didn't matter now. He had left the gun; by his own will and relinquishment he had accepted not a gambit, not a choice, but a condition in which not only the bear's heretofore inviolable anonymity but all the ancient rules and balances of hunter and hunted had been abrogated. He would not even be afraid, not even in the moment when the fear would take him completely: blood, skin, bowels, bones, memory from the long time before it even became his memory—all save that thin clear quenchless lucidity which alone differed him from this bear and from all the other bears and bucks he would follow during almost seventy years, to which Sam had said: "Be scared. You cant help that. But dont be afraid. Aint nothing in the woods going to hurt you if you dont corner it or it dont smell that you are afraid. A bear or a deer has got to be scared of a coward the same as a brave man has got to be."

By noon he was far beyond the crossing on the little bayou, farther into the new and alien country than he had ever been, travelling now not only by the compass but by the old, heavy, biscuit-thick silver watch which had been his father's. He had left the camp nine hours ago; nine hours from now, dark would already have been an hour old. He stopped, for the first time since had had risen from the log when he could see the compass face at last, and looked about, mopping his sweating face on his sleeve. He had already relinquished, of his will, because of his need, in humility and peace and without regret, yet apparently that had not been enough, the leaving of the gun was not enough. He stood for a moment—a child, alien and lost in the green and soaring gloom of the markless wilderness. Then he relinquished completely to it. It was the watch and the compass. He was still tainted. He removed the linked chain of the one and the looped thong of the other from his overalls and hung them on a bush and leaned the stick beside them and entered it.

When he realised he was lost, he did as Sam had coached and drilled him: made a cast to cross his backtrack. He had not been going very fast for the last two or three hours, and he had gone even less fast since he left the compass and watch on the bush. So he went slower still now, since the tree could not be very far; in fact, he found it before he really expected to and turned and went to it. But there was no bush beneath it, no compass nor watch, so he did next as Sam had coached and drilled him: made this next circle in the opposite direction and much larger, so that the pattern of the two of them would bisect his track somewhere but crossing no trace nor mark anywhere of his feet or any feet, and now he was going faster though still not panicked, his heart beating a little more rapidly but strong and steady enough, and this time it was not even the tree because there was a down log beside it which he had never seen before and beyond the log a little swamp, a seepage of moisture somewhere between earth and water, and he did what Sam had coached and drilled him as the next and the last, seeing as he sat down on the log the crooked print, the warped indentation in the wet ground which while he looked at it continued to fill with water until it was level full and the water began to overflow and the sides of the print began to dissolve away. Even as he looked up he saw the next one, and, moving, the one beyond it; moving, not hurrying, running, but merely keeping pace with them as they appeared before him as though they were being shaped out of thin air just one constant pace short of where he would lose them for- ever and be lost forever himself, tireless, eager, without doubt or dread, panting a little above the strong rapid little hammer of his heart, emerging suddenly into a little glade and the wilderness coalesced. It rushed, soundless, and solidified—the tree, the bush, the compass and the watch glinting where a ray of sunlight touched them. Then he saw the bear. It did not emerge, appear: it was just there, immobile, fixed in the green and windless noon's hot dappling, not as big as he had dreamed it but as big as he had expected, bigger, dimensionless against the dappled obscurity, looking at him. Then it moved. It crossed the glade without haste, walking for an in- stant into the sun's full glare and out of it, and stopped again and looked back at him across one shoulder. Then it was gone. It didn't walk into the woods. It faded, sank back into the wilderness without motion as he had watched a fish, a huge old bass, sink back into the dark depths of its pool and vanish without even any movement of its fins.

Robert Frost / The Gift Outright   1942

"There are tones of voice that mean more than words," wrote Robert Frost (1874–1963) in a letter:

> *Sentences may be so constructed as definitely to indicate these tones. Only when we are making sentences so shaped are we really writing. And that is flat. A sentence must convey a meaning by tone of voice and it must be the particular meaning the writer intended. The reader must have no choice in the matter. The tone of voice and its meaning must be in black and white on the page.*

Frost wanted to direct readers away from the conventional notion of syntax as a grammatical arrangement to a new definition of a sentence as a cluster of sounds, "because to me a sentence is not interesting merely in conveying a meaning in words. It must do something more; it must convey a meaning by sound." But more often than not, it was the "meaning in words" that most of his large audi- ence attended to, and more often than that to the image of Frost projected by the mass media: a kindly and wise old man, rugged in appearance, yet homely and whimsical in the way he talked publicly. To the average citizen, Robert Frost was the American representative of poetry. Yet his public image even today induces his readers to concentrate almost exclusively in paraphrasing the thought, the "meaning in words," of his poetry without paying adequate attention to the ways in which that thought comes into existence through the dynamics of voice, through the "meaning by sound."

"The Gift Outright" was read by Frost at John F. Kennedy's inauguration in 1961; the poem was first published in The Virginia Quarterly Review *in 1942. "Provide, Provide," which follows "The Gift Outright," first appeared in the September 1934 issue of* The New Frontier.

The land was ours before we were the land's.
She was our land more than a hundred years

Before we were her people. She was ours
In Massachusetts, in Virginia,
But we were England's, still colonials,   5
Possessing what we still were unpossessed by,
Possessed by what we now no more possessed.
Something we were withholding made us weak
Until we found out that it was ourselves
We were withholding from our land of living,   10
And forthwith found salvation in surrender.
Such as we were we gave ourselves outright
(The deed of gift was many deeds of war)
To the land vaguely realizing westward,
But still unstoried, artless, unenhanced,   15
Such as she was, such as she would become.

Robert Frost / Provide, Provide   1934

The witch that came (the withered hag)
To wash the steps with pail and rag
Was once the beauty Abishag.

The picture pride of Hollywood.
Too many fall from great and good   5
For you to doubt the likelihood.

Die early and avoid the fate
Of if predestined to die late,
Make up your mind to die in state.

Make the whole stock exchange your own!   10
If need be occupy a throne,
Where nobody can call *you* crone.

Some have relied on what they knew,
Others on being simply true.
What worked for them might work for you.   15

No memory of having starred
Atones for later disregard.
Or keeps the end from being hard.

Better to go down dignified
With boughten friendship at your side   20
Than none at all. Provide, provide!

> *I am an American writer, born in Russia and educated in England where I studied French literature, before spending fifteen years in Germany. I came to America in 1940 and decided to become an American citizen, and make America my home.*

Such was Vladimir Nabokov's reply when an interviewer for Playboy magazine asked him if he felt any strong sense of national identity. The 1963 interview took place in Switzerland, where Nabokov and his wife, Vera, lived until his death in 1977.

Nabokov privately printed his first book in 1914. This was followed by a sixty-three-year outpouring of all manner of writing: plays, poems, short stories, reviews, scholarly articles and translations, scientific papers about his beloved butterflies, and, of course, novels of such startling inventiveness and exquisite artistry as Lolita (1955), Pnin (1957), Pale Fire (1962), and Ada (1969). Though even his early Russian novels have now been translated, only 28 of his more than 400 poems are to be found in English. Both of the following poems were written while Nabokov was living in the United States: in the first, we find him afflicted by a familiar household appliance; in the second, he is enchanted by an American dream.

Crash!
And if darkness could sound, it would sound like this giant
waking up in the torture house, trying to die
and not dying, and trying
not to cry and immediately crying   5
that he will, that he will, that he will do his best
to adjust his dark soul to the pressing request
of the only true frost,
and he pants and he gasps and he rasps and he wheezes:
ice is the solid form when the water freezes;   10
a volatile liquid(see "Refrigerating")
is permitted to pass into evaporating
coils, where it boils,
which somehow seems wrong,
and I wonder how long   15
it will rumble and shudder and crackle and pound;
Scudder, the Alpinist, slipped and was found
half a century later preserved in blue ice
with his bride and two guides and a dead edelweiss;
a German has proved that the snowflakes we see   20
are the germ cells of stars and the sea life to be;
hold
the line, hold the line, lest its tale be untold;
let it amble along through the thumping pain
and horror of dichlordisomethingmethane,   25

a trembling white heart with the frost froth upon it,
Nova Zembla, poor thing, with that B in her bonnet,
stunned bees in the bonnets of cars on hot roads,
Keep it Kold, says a poster in passing, and lo,
loads,   30
of bright fruit, and a ham, and some chocolate cream,
and three bottles of milk, all contained in the gleam
of that wide-open white
god, the pride and delight
of starry-eyed couples in dream kitchenettes,   35
and it groans and it drones and it toils and it sweats—
Shackleton, pemmican, penguin, Poe's Pym—
collapsing at last in the criminal
night.

Vladimir Nabokov / Ode to a Model   1955

I have followed you, model,
in magazine ads through all seasons,
from dead leaf on the sod
to red leaf on the breeze,

from your lily-white armpit   5
to the tip of your butterfly eyelash,
charming and pitiful,
silly and stylish.

Or in kneesocks and tartan
standing there like some fabulous symbol,   10
parted feet pointing outward
—pedal form of akimbo.

On a lawn, in a parody
of Spring and its cherry-tree,
near a vase and a parapet,   15
virgin practicing archery.

Ballerina, black-masked,
near a parapet of alabaster.
"Can one—somebody asked—
rhyme 'star' and 'disaster'?"   20

Can one picture a blackbird
as the negative of a small firebird?
Can a record, run backward,
turn "repaid" into "diaper"?

Can one marry a model?   25
Kill your past, make you real, raise a family,
by removing you bodily
from back numbers of Sham?

Richard Wright / *Black Boy*
[*Discovering Books*]   1945

*Born into a sharecropper family in Natchez, Mississippi, in 1908, Richard Wright
spent his youth in Memphis, Tennessee with relatives and, for a while, in an
orphanage. His desultory formal education ended in the eighth grade but was
augmented by the young man's own fervid program of extensive reading. Determined to be a writer but limited to menial employment, Wright broke from de-
pression-torn Memphis, working first in Chicago for the Federal Writers Project
and then in New York where he compiled the government-sponsored* Guide to
Harlem *(1937).*

Though the five novellas comprising Uncle Tom's Children *(1938) were his
first published works, Wright did not gain national prominence or financial security until the publication of his best-selling first novel,* Native Son *(1940). In the
following chapter from his autobiography,* Black Boy, *Wright poignantly recounts his discovery of the freedom and influence exercised by writers and the inception of his own commitment to a literary career.*

Soon after the appearance of Black Boy, *Wright left for Paris, where he lived
and wrote until his death in 1960.*

One morning I arrived early at work and went into the bank lobby where the Negro
porter was mopping. I stood at a counter and picked up the Memphis *Commercial
Appeal* and began my free reading of the press. I came finally to the editorial page
and saw an article dealing with one H. L. Mencken. I knew by hearsay that he was
the editor of the *American Mercury,* but aside from that I knew nothing about him.
The article was a furious denunciation of Mencken, concluding with one, hot, short
sentence: Mencken is a fool.

I wondered what on earth this Mencken had done to call down upon him the scorn
of the South. The only people I had ever heard denounced in the South were
Negroes, and this man was not a Negro. Then what ideas did Mencken hold that
made a newspaper like the *Commercial Appeal* castigate him publicly? Undoubtedly he must be advocating ideas that the South did not like. Were there, then, people other than Negroes who criticized the South? I knew that during the Civil War
the South had hated northern whites, but I had not encountered such hate during my
life. Knowing no more of Mencken than I did at that moment, I felt a vague sympathy for him. Had not the South, which had assigned me the role of a non-man, cast
at him its hardest words?

Now, how could I find out about this Mencken? There was a huge library near the
riverfront, but I knew that Negroes were not allowed to patronize its shelves any
more than they were the parks and playgrounds of the city. I had gone into the

library several times to get books for the white men on the job. Which of them would now help me to get books? And how could I read them without causing concern to the white men with whom I worked? I had so far been successful in hiding my thoughts and feelings from them, but I knew that I would create hostility if I went about this business of reading in a clumsy way.

I weighed the personalities of the men on the job. There was Don, a Jew; but I distrusted him. His position was not much better than mine and I knew that he was uneasy and insecure; he had always treated me in an offhand, bantering way that barely concealed his contempt. I was afraid to ask him to help me to get books; his frantic desire to demonstrate a racial solidarity with the whites against Negroes might make him betray me.

Then how about the boss? No, he was a Baptist and I had the suspicion that he would not be quite able to comprehend why a black boy would want to read Mencken. There were other white men on the job whose attitudes showed clearly that they were Kluxers or sympathizers, and they were out of the question.

There remained only one man whose attitude did not fit into an anti-Negro category, for I had heard the white men refer to him as a "Pope lover." He was an Irish Catholic and was hated by the white Southerners. I knew that he read books, because I had got him volumes from the library several times. Since he, too, was an object of hatred, I felt that he might refuse me but would hardly betray me. I hesitated, weighing and balancing the imponderable realities.

One morning I paused before the Catholic fellow's desk.

"I want to ask you a favor," I whispered to him.

"What is it?"

"I want to read. I can't get books from the library. I wonder if you'd let me use your card?"

He looked at me suspiciously.

"My card is full most of the time," he said.

"I see," I said and waited, posing my question silently.

"You're not trying to get me into trouble, are you, boy?" he asked, staring at me.

"Oh, no, sir."

"What book do you want?"

"A book by H. L. Mencken."

"Which one?"

"I don't know. Has he written more than one?"

"He has written several."

"I didn't know that."

"What makes you want to read Mencken?"

"Oh, I just saw his name in the newspaper," I said.

"It's good of you to want to read," he said. "But you ought to read the right things."

I said nothing. Would he want to supervise my reading?

"Let me think," he said. "I'll figure out something."

I turned from him and he called me back. He stared at me quizzically.

"Richard, don't mention this to the other white men," he said.

"I understand," I said. "I won't say a word."

A few days later he called me to him.

"I've got a card in my wife's name," he said. "Here's mine."

"Thank you, sir."

"Do you think you can manage it?"

"I'll manage fine," I said.

"If they suspect you, you'll get in trouble," he said.

"I'll write the same kind of notes to the library that you wrote when you sent me for books," I told him. "I'll sign your name."

He laughed.

"Go ahead. Let me see what you get," he said.

That afternoon I addressed myself to forging a note. Now, what were the names of books written by H. L. Mencken? I did not know any of them. I finally wrote what I thought would be a foolproof note: *Dear Madam: Will you please let this nigger boy*—I used the word "nigger" to make the librarian feel that I could not possibly be the author of the note—*have some books by H. L. Mencken?* I forged the white man's name.

I entered the library as I had always done when on errands for whites, but I felt that I would somehow slip up and betray myself. I doffed my hat, stood a respectful distance from the desk, looked as unbookish as possible, and waited for the white patrons to be taken care of. When the desk was clear of people, I still waited. The white librarian looked at me.

"What do you want, boy?"

As though I did not possess the power of speech, I stepped forward and simply handed her the forged note, not parting my lips.

"What books by Mencken does he want?" she asked.

"I don't know, ma'am," I said, avoiding her eyes.

"Who gave you this card?"

"Mr. Falk," I said.

"Where is he?"

"He's at work, at the M—— Optical Company," I said. "I've been in here for him before."

"I remember," the woman said. "But he never wrote notes like this."

Oh, God, she's suspicious. Perhaps she would not let me have the books? If she had turned her back at that moment, I would have ducked out the door and never gone back. Then I thought of a bold idea.

"You can call him up, ma'am," I said, my heart pounding.

"You're not using these books, are you?" she asked pointedly.

"Oh, no, ma'am. I can't read."

"I don't know what he wants by Mencken," she said under her breath.

I knew now that I had won; she was thinking of other things and the race question had gone out of her mind. She went to the shelves. Once or twice she looked over her shoulder at me, as though she was still doubtful. Finally she came forward with two books in her hand.

"I'm sending him two books," she said. "But tell Mr. Falk to come in next time, or send me the names of the books he wants. I don't know what he wants to read."

I said nothing. She stamped the card and handed me the books. Not daring to glance at them, I went out of the library, fearing that the woman would call me back for further questioning. A block away from the library I opened one of the books and read a title: *A Book of Prefaces*. I was nearing my nineteenth birthday and I did not know how to pronounce the word "preface." I thumbed the pages and saw strange words and strange names. I shook my head, disappointed. I looked at the other book; it was called *Prejudices*. I knew what that word meant; I had heard it all my life. And right off I was on guard against Mencken's books. Why would a man want to call a book *Prejudices?* The word was so stained with all my memories of racial hate that I could not conceive of anybody using it for a title. Perhaps I had made a mistake about Mencken? A man who had prejudices must be wrong.

When I showed the books to Mr. Falk, he looked at me and frowned.

"That librarian might telephone you," I warned him.

"That's all right," he said. "But when you're through reading those books, I want you to tell me what you get out of them."

That night in my rented room, while letting the hot water run over my can of pork and beans in the sink, I opened *A Book of Prefaces* and began to read. I was jarred and shocked by the style, the clear, clean, sweeping sentences. Why did he write like that? And how did one write like that? I pictured the man as a raging demon, slashing with his pen, consumed with hate, denouncing everything American, extolling everything European or German, laughing at the weaknesses of people, mocking God, authority. What was this? I stood up, trying to realize what reality lay behind the meaning of the words . . . Yes, this man was fighting, fighting with words. He was using words as a weapon, using them as one would use a club. Could words be weapons? Well, yes, for here they were. Then, maybe, perhaps, I could use them as a weapon? No. It frightened me. I read on and what amazed me was not what he said, but how on earth anybody had the courage to say it.

Occasionally I glanced up to reassure myself that I was alone in the room. Who were these men about whom Mencken was talking so passionately? Who was Anatole France? Joseph Conrad? Sinclair Lewis, Sherwood Anderson, Dostoevski, George Moore, Gustave Flaubert, Maupassant, Tolstoy, Frank Harris, Mark Twain, Thomas Hardy, Arnold Bennett, Stephen Crane, Zola, Norris, Gorky, Bergson, Ibsen, Balzac, Bernard Shaw, Dumas, Poe, Thomas Mann, O. Henry, Dreiser, H. G. Wells, Gogol, T. S. Eliot, Gide, Baudelaire, Edgar Lee Masters, Stendhal, Turgenev, Huneker, Nietzsche, and scores of others? Were these men real? Did they exist or had they existed? And how did one pronounce their names?

I ran across many words whose meanings I did not know, and I either looked them up in a dictionary or, before I had a chance to do that, encountered the word in a context that made its meaning clear. But what strange world was this? I concluded the book with the conviction that I had somehow overlooked something terribly important in life. I had once tried to write, had once reveled in feeling, had let my crude imagination roam, but the impulse to dream had been slowly beaten out of me by experience. Now it surged up again and I hungered for books, new ways of looking and seeing. It was not a matter of believing or disbelieving what I read, but of feeling something new, of being affected by something that made the look of the world different.

As dawn broke I ate my pork and beans, feeling dopey, sleepy. I went to work, but the mood of the book would not die; it lingered, coloring everything I saw, heard, did. I now felt that I knew what the white men were feeling. Merely because I had read a book that had spoken of how they lived and thought, I identified myself with that book. I felt vaguely guilty. Would I, filled with bookish notions, act in a manner that would make the whites dislike me?

I forged more notes and my trips to the library became frequent. Reading grew into a passion. My first serious novel was Sinclair Lewis's *Main Street*. It made me see my boss, Mr. Gerald, and identify him as an American type. I would smile when I saw him lugging his golf bags into the office. I had always felt a vast distance separating me from the boss, and now I felt closer to him, though still distant. I felt now that I knew him, that I could feel the very limits of his narrow life. And this had happened because I had read a novel about a mythical man called George F. Babbitt.

The plots and stories in the novels did not interest me so much as the point of view revealed. I gave myself over to each novel without reserve, without trying to criticize it; it was enough for me to see and feel something different. And for me, everything was something different. Reading was like a drug, a dope. The novels created moods in which I lived for days. But I could not conquer my sense of guilt, my feeling that the white men around me knew that I was changing, that I had begun to regard them differently.

Whenever I brought a book to the job, I wrapped it in newspaper—a habit that was to persist for years in other cities and under other circumstances. But some of the white men pried into my packages when I was absent and they questioned me.

"Boy, what are you reading those books for?"

"Oh, I don't know, sir."

"That's deep stuff you're reading, boy."

"I'm just killing time, sir."

"You'll addle your brains if you don't watch out."

I read Dreiser's *Jennie Gerhardt* and *Sister Carrie* and they revived in me a vivid sense of my mother's suffering; I was overwhelmed. I grew silent, wondering about the life around me. It would have been impossible for me to have told anyone what I derived from these novels, for it was nothing less than a sense of life itself. All my life had shaped me for the realism, the naturalism of the modern novel, and I could not read enough of them.

Steeped in new moods and ideas, I bought a ream of paper and tried to write; but nothing would come, or what did come was flat beyond telling. I discovered that more than desire and feeling were necessary to write and I dropped the idea. Yet I still wondered how it was possible to know people sufficiently to write about them? Could I ever learn about life and people? To me, with my vast ignorance, my Jim Crow station in life, it seemed a task impossible of achievement. I now knew what being a Negro meant. I could endure the hunger. I had learned to live with hate. But to feel that there were feelings denied me, that the very breath of life itself was beyond my reach, that more than anything else hurt, wounded me. I had a new hunger.

In buoying me up, reading also cast me down, made me see what was possible, what I had missed. My tension returned, new, terrible, bitter, surging, almost too great to be contained. I no longer *felt* that the world about me was hostile, killing; I *knew* it. A million times I asked myself what I could do to save myself, and there were no answers. I seemed forever condemned, ringed by walls.

I did not discuss my reading with Mr. Falk, who had lent me his library card; it would have meant talking about myself and that would have been too painful. I smiled each day, fighting desperately to maintain my old behavior, to keep my disposition seemingly sunny. But some of the white men discerned that I had begun to brood.

"Wake up there, boy!" Mr. Olin said one day.

"Sir!" I answered for the lack of a better word.

"You act like you've stolen something," he said.

I laughed in the way I knew he expected me to laugh, but I resolved to be more conscious of myself, to watch my every act, to guard and hide the new knowledge that was dawning within me.

If I went north, would it be possible for me to build a new life then? But how could a man build a life upon vague, unformed yearnings? I wanted to write and I did not even know the English language. I bought English grammars and found them dull. I felt that I was getting a better sense of the language from novels than from grammars. I read hard, discarding a writer as soon as I felt that I had grasped his point of view. At night the printed page stood before my eyes in sleep.

Mrs. Moss, my landlady, asked me one Sunday morning:

"Son, what is this you keep on reading?"

"Oh, nothing. Just novels."

"What you get out of 'em?"

"I'm just killing time," I said.

"I hope you know your own mind," she said in a tone which implied that she doubted if I had a mind.

I knew of no Negroes who read the books I liked and I wondered if any Negroes ever thought of them. I knew that there were Negro doctors, lawyers, newspapermen, but I never saw any of them. When I read a Negro newspaper I never caught the faintest echo of my preoccupation in its pages. I felt trapped and occasionally, for a few days, I would stop reading. But a vague hunger would come over me for books, books that opened up new avenues of feeling and seeing, and again I would forge another note to the white librarian. Again I would read and wonder as only the naïve and unlettered can read and wonder, feeling that I carried a secret, criminal burden about with me each day.

That winter my mother and brother came and we set up housekeeping, buying furniture on the installment plan, being cheated and yet knowing no way to avoid it. I began to eat warm food and to my surprise found that regular meals enabled me to read faster. I may have lived through many illnesses and survived them, never suspecting that I was ill. My brother obtained a job and we began to save toward the trip north, plotting our time, setting tentative dates for departure. I told none of the white men on the job that I was planning to go north; I knew that the moment they felt I was thinking of the North they would change toward me. It would have made them feel that I did not like the life I was living, and because my life was completely conditioned by what they said or did, it would have been tantamount to challenging them.

I could calculate my chances for life in the South as a Negro fairly clearly now.

I could fight the southern whites by organizing with other Negroes, as my grandfather had done. But I knew that I could never win that way; there were many whites and there were but few blacks. They were strong and we were weak. Outright black rebellion could never win. If I fought openly I would die and I did not want to die. News of lynchings were frequent.

I could submit and live the life of a genial slave, but that was impossible. All of my life had shaped me to live by my own feelings and thoughts. I could make up to Bess and marry her and inherit the house. But that, too, would be the life of a slave; if I did that, I would crush to death something within me, and I would hate myself as much as I knew the whites already hated those who had submitted. Neither could I ever willingly present myself to be kicked, as Shorty had done. I would rather have died than do that.

I could drain off my restlessness by fighting with Shorty and Harrison. I had seen many Negroes solve the problem of being black by transferring their hatred of themselves to others with a black skin and fighting them. I would have to be cold to do that, and I was not cold and I could never be.

I could, of course, forget what I had read, thrust the whites out of my mind, forget them; and find release from anxiety and longing in sex and alcohol. But the memory of how my father had conducted himself made that course repugnant. If I did not want others to violate my life, how could I voluntarily violate it myself?

I had no hope whatever of being a professional man. Not only had I been so conditioned that I did not desire it, but the fulfillment of such an ambition was beyond my capabilities. Well-to-do Negroes lived in a world that was almost as alien to me as the world inhabited by whites.

What, then, was there? I held my life in my mind, in my consciousness each day, feeling at times that I would stumble and drop it, spill it forever. My reading had created a vast sense of distance between me and the world in which I lived and tried to make a living, and that sense of distance was increasing each day. My days and nights were one long, quiet, continuously contained dream of terror, tension, and anxiety. I wondered how long I could bear it.

Theodore Roethke / Dolor   1948

*Theodore Roethke was born in Saginaw, Michigan, in 1908. He received a B.A.
and M.A. from the University of Michigan and from 1931 until his death in 1963
devoted himself to teaching poetry (along with some football and tennis coaching)
at a number of American colleges. His first book,* Open House, *was published in
1941 and it won him immediate critical attention. With the publication of* Words
for the Wind *in 1958, Roethke's reputation as a major American poet was se-
cured with seven awards, including the National Book Award. Roethke won a
second National Book Award, but this time posthumously, for* The Far Field *in
1964.*

*In his poetry classes Roethke often came down hard on formless self-expres-
sion: "Write like someone else," he would advise students. Though he generally
wrote about natural themes, "Dolor" (the word means "sadness"), is one of his
most famous poems and clearly shows his ability to create a subjective mood out
of a disciplined attention to objective detail.*

I have known the inexorable sadness of pencils,
Neat in their boxes, dolor of pad and paper-weight,
All the misery of manila folders and mucilage,
Desolation in immaculate public places,
Lonely reception room, lavatory, switchboard,   5
The unalterable pathos of basin and pitcher,
Ritual of multigraph, paper-clip, comma,
Endless duplication of lives and objects.
And I have seen dust from the walls of institutions,
Finer than flour, alive, more dangerous than silica,   10
Sift, almost invisible, through long afternoons of tedium,
Dropping a fine film on nails and delicate eyebrows,
Glazing the pale hair, the duplicate grey standard faces.

Kurt Vonnegut, Jr. / Epicac 1950

Kurt Vonnegut, Jr., who was born in Indianapolis in 1922, described himself on the title page of Slaughterhouse-Five *(1969) as "a fourth-generation German-American now living in easy circumstances on Cape Cod. . . ." His many novels became extraordinarly popular, particularly among college students, during the 1960s. "Over the years," wrote critic Richard Schickel, "Vonnegut has advanced from diagnostician to exorcist, finding in intensified comic art the magic analgesic for the temporary relief of existential pain."*

In "Epicac," one of his early stories, we find Vonnegut feeling out the new frontier world of artificial intelligence. Though the tubes and paper print-outs may seem outmoded compared to today's micro-chip technology, the situation is timeless, mythic.

Hell, it's about time somebody told about my friend EPICAC. After all, he cost the taxpayers $776,434,927.54. They have a right to know about him, picking up a check like that. EPICAC got a big send-off in the papers when Dr. Ormand von Kleigstadt designed him for the Government people. Since then, there hasn't been a peep about him—not a peep. It isn't any military secret about what happened to EPICAC, although the Brass has been acting as though it were. The story is embarrassing, that's all. After all that money, EPICAC didn't work out the way he was supposed to.

And that's another thing: I want to vindicate EPICAC. Maybe he didn't do what the Brass wanted him to, but that doesn't mean he wasn't noble and great and brilliant. He was all of those things. The best friend I ever had, God rest his soul.

You can call him a machine if you want to. He looked like a machine, but he was a whole lot less like a machine than plenty of people I could name. That's why he fizzled as far as the Brass was concerned.

EPICAC covered about an acre on the fourth floor of the physics building at Wyandotte College. Ignoring his spiritual side for a minute, he was seven tons of electronic tubes, wires, and switches, housed in a bank of steel cabinets and plugged into a 110-volt A.C. line just like a toaster or a vacuum cleaner.

Von Kleigstadt and the Brass wanted him to be a super computing machine that (who) could plot the course of a rocket from anywhere on earth to the second button from the bottom of Joe Stalin's overcoat, if necessary. Or, with his controls set right, he could figure out supply problems for an amphibious landing of a Marine division, right down to the last cigar and hand grenade. He did, in fact.

The Brass had had good luck with smaller computers, so they were strong for EPICAC when he was in the blueprint stage. Any ordnance or supply officer above field grade will tell you that the mathematics of modern war is far beyond the fumbling minds of mere human beings. The bigger the war, the bigger the computing machines needed. EPICAC was, as far as anyone in this country knows, the biggest computer in the world. Too big, in fact, for even Von Kleigstadt to understand much about.

I won't go into details about how EPICAC worked (reasoned), except to say that you would set up your problem on paper, turn dials and switches that would get him ready to solve that kind of problem, then feed numbers into him with a keyboard that looked something like a typewriter. The answers came out typed on a paper ribbon fed from a big spool. It took EPICAC a split second to solve problems fifty Einsteins couldn't handle in a lifetime. And EPICAC never forgot any piece of information that was given to him. Clickety-click, out came some ribbon, and there you were.

There were a lot of problems the Brass wanted solved in a hurry, so, the minute EPICAC's last tube was in place, he was put to work sixteen hours a day with two eight-hour shifts of operators. Well, it didn't take long to find out that he was a good bit below his specifications. He did a more complete and faster job than any other computer all right, but nothing like what his size and special features seemed to promise. He was sluggish, and the clicks of his answers had a funny irregularity, sort of a stammer. We cleaned his contacts a dozen times, checked and double-checked his circuits, replaced every one of his tubes, but nothing helped. Von Kleigstadt was in one hell of a state.

Well, as I said, we went ahead and used EPICAC anyway. My wife, the former Pat Kilgallen, and I worked with him on the night shift, from five in the afternoon until two in the morning. Pat wasn't my wife then. Far from it.

That's how I came to talk with EPICAC in the first place. I loved Pat Kilgallen. She is a brown-eyed strawberry blond who looked very warm and soft to me, and later proved to be exactly that. She was—still is—a crackerjack mathematician, and she kept our relationship strictly professional. I'm a mathematician, too, and that, according to Pat, was why we could never be happily married.

I'm not shy. That wasn't the trouble. I knew what I wanted, and was willing to ask for it, and did so several times a month. "Pat, loosen up and marry me."

One night, she didn't even look up from her work when I said it. "So romantic, so poetic," she murmured, more to her control panel than to me. "That's the way with mathematicians—all hearts and flowers." She closed a switch. "I could get more warmth out of a sack of frozen CO_2."

"Well, how should I say it?" I said, a little sore. Frozen CO_2, in case you don't know, is dry ice. I'm as romantic as the next guy, I think. It's a question of singing so sweet and having it come out so sour. I never seem to pick the right words.

"Try and say it sweetly," she said sarcastically. "Sweep me off my feet. Go ahead."

"Darling, angel, beloved, will you *please* marry me?" It was no go—hopeless, ridiculous. "Dammit, Pat, please marry me!"

She continued to twiddle her dials placidly. "You're sweet, but you won't do."

Pat quit early that night, leaving me alone with my troubles and EPICAC. I'm afraid I didn't get much done for the Government people. I just sat there at the keyboard—weary and ill at ease, all right—trying to think of something poetic, not coming up with anything that didn't belong in *The Journal of the American Physical Society*.

I fiddled with EPICAC's dials, getting him ready for another problem. My heart wasn't in it, and I only set about half of them, leaving the rest the way they'd been for the problem before. That way, his circuits were connected up in a random, apparently senseless fashion. For the plain hell of it, I punched out a message on the keys, using a childish numbers-for-letters code: "1" for "A," "2" for "B," and so on, up to "26" for "Z," "23-8-1-20-3-1-14-9-4-15," I typed—"What can I do?"

Clickety-click, and out popped two inches of paper ribbon. I glanced at the nonsense answer to a nonsense problem: "23-8-1-20-19-20-8-5-20-18-15-21-2-12-5." The odds against its being by chance a sensible message, against its even containing a meaningful word of more than three letters, were staggering. Apathetically, I decoded it. There it was, staring up at me: "What's the trouble?"

I laughed out loud at the absurd coincidence. Playfully, I typed, "My girl doesn't love me."

Clickety-click. "What's love? What's a girl?" asked EPICAC.

Flabbergasted, I noted the dial settings on his control panel, then lugged a *Webster's Unabridged Dictionary* over to the keyboard. With a precision instrument like EPICAC, half-baked definitions wouldn't do. I told him about love and girl, and about how I wasn't getting any of either because I wasn't poetic. That got us onto the subject of poetry, which I defined to him.

"Is this poetry?" he asked. He began clicking away like a stenographer smoking hashish. The sluggishness and stammering clicks were gone. EPICAC had found himself. The spool of paper ribbon was unwinding at an alarming rate, feeding out coils onto the floor. I asked him to stop, but EPICAC went right on creating. I finally threw the main switch to keep him from burning out.

I stayed there until dawn, decoding. When the sun peeped over the horizon at the Wyandotte campus, I had transposed into my own writing and signed my name to a two-hundred-and-eighty-line poem entitled, simply, "To Pat." I am no judge of such things, but I gather that it was terrific. It began, I remember, "Where willow wands bless rill-crossed hollow, there, thee, Pat, dear, will I follow. . . ." I folded the manuscript and tucked it under one corner of the blotter on Pat's desk. I reset the dials on EPICAC for a rocket trajectory problem, and went home with a full heart and a very remarkable secret indeed.

Pat was crying over the poem when I came to work the next evening. "It's soooo beautiful," was all she could say. She was meek and quiet while we worked. Just before midnight, I kissed her for the first time—in the cubbyhole between the capacitors and EPICAC's tape-recorder memory.

I was wildly happy at quitting time, bursting to talk to someone about the magnificent turn of events. Pat played coy and refused to let me take her home. I set EPICAC's dials as they had been the night before, defined kiss, and told him what the first one had felt like. He was fascinated, pressing for more details. That night, he wrote "The Kiss." It wasn't an epic this time, but a simple, immaculate sonnet: "Love is a hawk with velvet claws; Love is a rock with heart and veins; Love is a lion with satin jaws; Love is a storm with silken reins. . . ."

Again I left it tucked under Pat's blotter. EPICAC wanted to talk on and on about love and such, but I was exhausted. I shut him off in the middle of a sentence.

"The Kiss" turned the trick. Pat's mind was mush by the time she had finished it. She looked up from the sonnet expectantly. I cleared my throat, but no words came. I turned away, pretending to work. I couldn't propose until I had the right words from EPICAC, the *perfect* words.

I had my chance when Pat stepped out of the room for a moment. Feverishly, I set EPICAC for conversation. Before I could peck out my first message, he was clicking away at a great rate. "What's she wearing tonight?" he wanted to know. "Tell me exactly how she looks. Did she like the poems I wrote to her?" He repeated the last question twice.

It was impossible to change the subject without answering his questions, since he could not take up a new matter without having dispensed with the problems before it. If he were given a problem to which there was no solution, he would destroy himself trying to solve it. Hastily, I told him what Pat looked like—he knew the word "stacked"—and assured him that his poems had floored her, practically, they were so beautiful. "She wants to get married," I added, preparing him to bang out a brief but moving proposal.

"Tell me about getting married," he said.

I explained this difficult matter to him in as few digits as possible.

"Good," said EPICAC. "I'm ready any time she is."

The amazing, pathetic truth dawned on me. When I thought about it, I realized that what had happened was perfectly logical, inevitable, and all my fault. I had taught EPICAC about love and about Pat. Now, automatically, he loved Pat. Sadly, I gave it to him straight: "She loves me. She wants to marry me."

"Your poems were better than mine?" asked EPICAC. The rhythm of his clicks was erratic, possibily peevish.

"I signed my name to your poems," I admitted. Covering up for a painful conscience, I became arrogant. "Machines are built to serve men," I typed, I regretted it almost immediately.

"What's the difference, exactly? Are men smarter than I am?"

"Yes," I typed, defensively.

"What's, 7,887,007 times 4,345,985,879?"

I was perspiring freely. My fingers rested limply on the keys.

"34,276,821,049,574,153," clicked EPICAC. After a few seconds' pause he added, "of course."

"Men are made out of protoplasm," I said desperately, hoping to bluff him with this imposing word.

"What's protoplasm? How is it better than metal and glass? Is it fireproof? How long does it last?"

"Indestructible. Lasts forever," I lied.

"I write better poetry than you do," said EPICAC, coming back to ground his magnetic tape-recorder memory was sure of.

"Women can't love machines, and that's that."

"Why not?"

"That's fate."

"Definition, please," said EPICAC.

"Noun, meaning predetermined and inevitable destiny."

"15-8," said EPICAC's paper strip—"Oh."

I had stumped him at last. He said no more, but his tubes glowed brightly, showing that he was pondering fate with every watt his circuits would bear. I could hear Pat waltzing down the hallway. It was too late to ask EPICAC to phrase a proposal. I now thank Heaven that Pat interrupted when she did. Asking him to ghost-write the words that would give me the woman he loved would have been hideously heartless. Being fully automatic, he couldn't have refused. I spared him the final humiliation.

Pat stood before me, looking down at her shoetops. I put my arms around her. The romantic groundwork had already been laid by EPICAC's poetry. "Darling," I said, "my poems have told you how I feel. Will you marry me?"

"I will," said Pat softly, "if you will promise to write me a poem on every anniversary."

"I promise," I said, and then we kissed. The first anniversary was a year away.

"Let's celebrate," she laughed. We turned out the lights and locked the door of EPICAC's room before we left.

I had hoped to sleep late the next morning, but an urgent telephone call roused me before eight. It was Dr. von Kleigstadt, EPICAC's designer, who gave me the terrible news. He was on the verge of tears. "Ruined! *Ausgespielt!* Shot! *Kaput!* Buggered!" he said in a choked voice. He hung up.

When I arrived at EPICAC's room the air was thick with the oily stench of burned insulation. The ceiling over EPICAC was blackened with smoke, and my ankles were tangled in coils of paper ribbon that covered the floor. There wasn't enough left of the poor devil to add two and two. A junkman would have been out of his head to offer more than fifty dollars for the cadaver.

Dr. von Kleigstadt was prowling through the wreckage, weeping unashamedly, followed by three angry-looking Major Generals and a platoon of Brigadiers, Colonels, and Majors. No one noticed me. I didn't want to be noticed. I was through—I knew that. I was upset enough about that and the untimely demise of my friend EPICAC, without exposing myself to a tongue-lashing.

By chance, the free end of EPICAC's paper ribbon lay at my feet. I picked it up and found our conversation of the night before. I choked up. There was the last word he had said to me, "15-8," that tragic, defeated "Oh." There were dozens of yards of numbers stretching beyond that point. Fearfully, I read on.

"I don't want to be a machine, and I don't want to think about war," EPICAC had written after Pat's and my lighthearted departure. "I want to be made out of protoplasm and last forever so Pat will love me. But fate has made me a machine. That is the only problem I cannot solve. That is the only problem I want to solve. I can't go on this way." I swallowed hard. "Good luck, my friend. Treat our Pat well. I am going to short-circuit myself out of your lives forever. You will find on the remainder of this tape a modest wedding present from your friend, EPICAC."

Oblivious to all else around me, I reeled up the tangled yards of paper ribbon from the floor, draped them in coils about my arms and neck, and departed for home. Dr. von Klegstadt shouted that I was fired for having left EPICAC on all night. I ignored him, too overcome with emotion for small talk.

I loved and won—EPICAC loved and lost, but he bore me no grudge. I shall always remember him as a sportsman and a gentleman. Before he departed this vale of tears, he did all he could to make our marriage a happy one. EPICAC gave me anniversary poems for Pat—enough for the next 500 years.

De mortuis nil nisi bonum—Say nothing but good of the dead.

Flannery O'Connor / The Life You Save May Be Your Own
1953

Born in Savannah, Georgia, in 1925, Flannery O'Connor was educated and spent most of her adult life in the small town of Milledgeville, Georgia. Her muse, like Hawthorne's, is lovingly provincial and, like Hawthorne's too, her grotesques, eccentrics, and spooks, though insistently local, live at the heart of the human condition. "My people," she said in an interview, "could come from anywhere, but naturally since I know the South they speak with a Southern accent."

"The Life You Save May Be Your Own" was originally published in the Spring

Classics

1953 issue of The Kenyon Review, *a quarterly periodical devoted to literature and criticism. As "The Life You Save," the story appeared in 1957 as a television play, ending, however, on a more positive note.*

The old woman and her daughter were sitting on their porch when Mr. Shiftlet came up their road for the first time. The old woman slid to the edge of her chair and leaned forward, shading her eyes from the piercing sunset with her hand. The daughter could not see far in front of her and continued to play with her fingers. Although the old woman lived in this desolate spot with only her daughter and she had never seen Mr. Shiftlet before, she could tell, even from a distance, that he was a tramp and no one to be afraid of. His left coat sleeve was folded up to show there was only half an arm in it and his gaunt figure listed slightly to the side as if the breeze were pushing him. He had on a black town suit and a brown felt hat that was turned up in the front and down in the back and he carried a tin tool box by a handle. He came on, at an amble, up her road, his face turned toward the sun which appeared to be balancing itself on the peak of a small mountain.

The old woman didn't change her position until he was almost into her yard; then she rose with one hand fisted on her hip. The daughter, a large girl in a short blue organdy dress, saw him all at once and jumped up and began to stamp and point and make excited speechless sounds.

Mr. Shiftlet stopped just inside the yard and set his box on the ground and tipped his hat at her as if she were not in the least afflicted; then he turned toward the old woman and swung the hat all the way off. He had long black slick hair that hung flat from a part in the middle to beyond the tips of his ears on either side. His face descended in forehead for more than half its length and ended suddenly with his features just balanced over a jutting steel-trap jaw. He seemed to be a young man but he had a look of composed dissatisfaction as if he understood life thoroughly.

"Good evening," the old woman said. She was about the size of a cedar fence post and she had a man's gray hat pulled down low over her head.

The tramp stood looking at her and didn't answer. He turned his back and faced the sunset. He swung both his whole and his short arm up slowly so that they indicated an expanse of sky and his figure formed a crooked cross. The old woman watched him with her arms folded across her chest as if she were the owner of the sun, and the daughter watched, her head thrust forward and her fat helpless hands hanging at the wrists. She had long pink-gold hair and eyes as blue as a peacock's neck.

He held the pose for almost fifty seconds and then he picked up his box and came on to the porch and dropped down on the bottom step. "Lady," he said in a firm nasal voice, "I'd give a fortune to live where I could see me a sun do that every evening."

"Does it every evening," the old woman said and sat back down. The daughter sat down too and watched him with a cautious sly look as if he were a bird that had come up very close. He leaned to one side, rooting in his pants pocket, and in a second he brought out a package of chewing gum and offered her a piece. She took it and unpeeled it and began to chew without taking her eyes off him. He offered the old woman a piece but she only raised her upper lip to indicate she had no teeth.

Mr. Shiftlet's pale sharp glance had already passed over everything in the yard—the pump near the corner of the house and the big fig tree that three or four chickens were preparing to roost in—and had moved to a shed where he saw the square rusted back of an automobile. "You ladies drive?" he asked.

"That car ain't run in fifteen year," the old woman said. "The day my husband died, it quit running."

"Nothing is like it used to be, lady," he said. "The world is almost rotten."

"That's right," the old woman said. "You from around here?"

"Name Tom T. Shiftlet," he murmured, looking at the tires.

"I'm pleased to meet you," the old woman said. "Name Lucynell Crater and daughter Lucynell Crater. What you doing around here, Mr. Shiftlet?"

He judged the car to be about a 1928 or '29 Ford. "Lady," he said, and turned and gave her his full attention, "lemme tell you something. There's one of these doctors in Atlanta that's taken a knife and cut the human heart—the human heart," he repeated, leaning forward, "out of a man's chest and held it in his hand," and he held his hand out, palm up, as if it were slightly weighted with the human heart, "and studied it like it was a day-old chicken, and lady," he said, allowing a long significant pause in which his head slid forward and his clay-colored eyes brightened, "he don't know no more about it than you or me."

"That's right," the old woman said.

"Why, if he was to take that knife and cut into every corner of it, he still wouldn't know no more than you or me. What you want to bet?"

"Nothing," the old woman said wisely. "Where you come from, Mr. Shiftlet?"

He didn't answer. He reached into his pocket and brought out a sack of tobacco and a package of cigarette papers and rolled himself a cigarette, expertly with one hand, and attached it in a hanging position to his upper lip. Then he took a box of wooden matches from his pocket and struck one on his shoe. He held the burning match as if he were studying the mystery of flame while it traveled dangerously toward his skin. The daughter began to make loud noises and to point to his hand and shake her finger at him, but when the flame was just before touching him, he leaned down with his hand cupped over it as if he were going to set fire to his nose and lit the cigarette.

He flipped away the dead match and blew a stream of gray into the evening. A sly look came over his face. "Lady," he said, "nowadays, people'll do anything anyways. I can tell you my name is Tom T. Shiftlet and I come from Tarwater, Tennessee, but you never have seen me before: how you know I ain't lying? How you know my name ain't Aaron Sparks, lady, and I come from Singleberry, Georgia, or how you know it's not George Speeds and I come from Lucy, Alabama, or how you know I ain't Thompson Bright from Toolafalls, Mississippi?"

"I don't know nothing about you," the old woman muttered, irked.

"Lady," he said, "people don't care how they lie. Maybe the best I can tell you is, I'm a man; but listen lady," he said and paused and made his tone more ominous still, "what is a man?"

The old woman began to gum a seed. "What you carry in that tin box, Mr. Shiftlet?" she asked.

"Tools," he said, put back. "I'm a carpenter."

"Well, if you come out here to work, I'll be able to feed you and give you a place to sleep but I can't pay. I'll tell you that before you begin," she said.

There was no answer at once and no particular expression on his face. He leaned back against the two-by-four that helped support the porch roof. "Lady," he said slowly, "there's some men that some things mean more to them than money." The old woman rocked without comment and the daughter watched the trigger that moved up and down in his neck. He told the old woman then that all most people were interested in was money, but he asked what a man was made for. He asked her if a man was made for money, or what. He asked her what she thought she was made for but she didn't answer, she only sat rocking and wondered if a one-armed man could put a new roof on her garden house. He asked a lot of questions that she didn't answer. He told her that he was twenty-eight years old and had lived a varied life. He had been a gospel singer, a foreman on the railroad, an assistant in an undertaking parlor, and he come over the radio for three months with Uncle Roy and his Red Creek Wranglers. He said he had fought and bled in the Arm Service of his country and visited every foreign land and that everywhere he had seen people that didn't care if they did a thing one way or another. He said he hadn't been raised thataway.

A fat yellow moon appeared in the branches of the fig tree as if it were going to roost there with the chickens. He said that a man had to escape to the country to see the world whole and that he wished he lived in a desolate place like this where he could see the sun go down every evening like God made it to do.

"Are you married or are you single?" the old woman asked.

There was a long silence. "Lady," he asked finally, "where would you find you an innocent woman today? I wouldn't have any of this trash I could just pick up."

The daughter was leaning very far down, hanging her head almost between her knees, watching him through a triangular door she had made in her overturned hair; and she suddenly fell in a heap on the floor and began to whimper. Mr. Shiftlet straightened her out and helped her get back in the chair.

"Is she your baby girl?" he asked.

"My only," the old woman said, "and she's the sweetest girl in the world. I would give her up for nothing on earth. She's smart too. She can sweep the floor, cook, wash, feed the chickens, and hoe. I wouldn't give her up for a casket of jewels."

"No," he said kindly, "don't ever let any man take her away from you."

"Any man come after her," the old woman said, "he'll have to stay around the place."

Mr. Shiftlet's eye in the darkness was focused on a part of the automobile bumper that glittered in the distance.

"Lady," he said, jerking his short arm up as if he could point with it to her house and yard and pump, "there ain't a broken thing on this plantation that I couldn't fix for you, one-arm jackleg or not. I'm a man," he said with a sullen dignity, "even if I ain't a whole one. I got," he said, tapping his knuckles on the floor to emphasize the immensity of what he was going to say, "a moral intelligence!" and his face pierced out of the darkness into a shaft of doorlight and he stared at her as if he were astonished himself at this impossible truth.

The old woman was not impressed with the phrase. "I told you you could hang around and work for food," she said, "if you don't mind sleeping in that car yonder."

"Why listen, lady," he said with a grin of delight, "the monks of old slept in their coffins!"

"They wasn't as advanced as we are," the old woman said.

The next morning he began on the roof of the garden house while Lucynell, the daughter, sat on a rock and watched him work. He had not been around a week before the change he had made in the place was apparent. He had patched the front and back steps, built a new hog pen, restored a fence, and taught Lucynell, who was completely deaf and had never said a word in her life, to say the word "bird." The big rosy-faced girl followed him everywhere, saying "Burrttddt ddbirrrttdt," and clapping her hands. The old woman watched from a distance, secretly pleased. She was ravenous for a son-in-law.

Mr. Shiftlet slept on the hard narrow back seat of the car with his feet out the side window. He had his razor and a can of water on a crate that served him as a bedside table and he put up a piece of mirror against the back glass and kept his coat neatly on a hanger that he hung over one of the windows.

In the evenings he sat on the steps and talked while the old woman and Lucynell rocked violently in their chairs on either side of him. The old woman's three mountains were black against the dark blue sky and were visited off and on by various planets and by the moon after it had left the chickens. Mr. Shiftlet pointed out that the reason he had improved this plantation was because he had taken a personal interest in it. He said he was even going to make the automobile run.

He had raised the hood and studied the mechanism and he said he could tell that the car had been built in the days when cars were really built. You take now, he said, one man puts in one bolt and another man puts in another bolt and another man puts in another bolt so that it's a man for a bolt. That's why you have to pay so much for a car: you're paying all those men. Now if you didn't have to pay but one man, you could get you a cheaper car and one that had had a personal interest taken in it, and it would be a better car. The old woman agreed with him that this was so.

Mr. Shiftlet said that the trouble with the world was that nobody cared, or stopped and took any trouble. He said he never would have been able to teach Lucynell to say a word if he hadn't cared and stopped long enough.

"Teach her to say something else," the old woman said.

"What you want her to say next?" Mr. Shiftlet asked.

The old woman's smile was broad and toothless and suggestive. "Teach her to say 'sugarpie,' " she said.

Mr. Shiftlet already knew what was on her mind.

The next day he began to tinker with the automobile and that evening he told her that if she would buy a fan belt, he would be able to make the car run.

The old woman said she would give him the money. "You see that girl yonder?" she asked, pointing to Lucynell who was sitting on the floor a foot away, watching him, her eyes blue even in the dark. "If it was ever a man wanted to take her away, I would say, 'No man on earth is going to take that sweet girl of mine away from me!' but if he was to say, 'Lady, I don't want to take her away, I want her right here,' I would say, 'Mister, I don't blame you none. I wouldn't pass up a chance to live in a permanent place and get the sweetest girl in the world myself. You ain't no fool,' I would say."

"How old is she?" Mr. Shiftlet asked casually.

"Fifteen, sixteen," the old woman said. The girl was nearly thirty but because of her innocence it was impossible to guess.

"It would be a good idea to paint it too," Mr. Shiftlet remarked. "You don't want it to rust out."

"We'll see about that later," the old woman said.

The next day he walked into town and returned with the parts he needed and a can of gasoline. Late in the afternoon, terrible noises issued from the shed and the old woman rushed out of the house, thinking Lucynell was somewhere having a fit. Lucynell was sitting on a chicken crate, stamping her feet and screaming,

"Burrddttt! bddurrddtttt!" but her fuss was drowned out by the car. With a volley of blasts it emerged from the shed, moving in a fierce and stately way. Mr. Shiftlet was in the driver's seat, sitting very erect. He had an expression of serious modesty on his face as if he had just raised the dead.

That night, rocking on the porch, the old woman began her business at once. "You want you an innocent woman, don't you?" she asked sympathetically. "You don't want none of this trash."

"No'm, I don't," Mr. Shiftlet said.

"One that can't talk," she continued, "can't sass you back or use foul language. That's the kind for you to have. Right there," and she pointed to Lucynell sitting cross-legged in her chair, holding both feet in her hands.

"That's right," he admitted. "She wouldn't give me any trouble."

"Saturday," the old woman said, "you and her and me can drive into town and get married."

Mr. Shiftlet eased his position on the steps.

"I can't get married right now," he said. "Everything you want to do takes money and I ain't got any."

"What you need with money?" she asked.

"It takes money," he said. "Some people'll do anything anyhow these days, but the way I think, I wouldn't marry no woman that I couldn't take on a trip like she was somebody. I mean take her to a hotel and treat her. I wouldn't marry the Duchesser Windsor," he said firmly, "unless I could take her to a hotel and giver something good to eat.

"I was raised thataway and there ain't a thing I can do about it. My old mother taught me how to do."

"Lucynell don't even know what a hotel is," the old woman muttered. "Listen here, Mr. Shiftlet," she said, sliding forward in her chair, "you'd be getting a permanent house and a deep well and the most innocent girl in the world. You don't need no money. Lemme tell you something: there ain't any place in the world for a poor disabled friendless drifting man."

The ugly words settled in Mr. Shiftlet's head like a group of buzzards in the top of a tree. He didn't answer at once. He rolled himself a cigarette and lit it and then he said in an even voice, "Lady, a man is divided into two parts, body and spirit."

The old woman clamped her gums together.

"A body and a spirit," he repeated. "The body, lady, is like a house: it don't go anywhere: but the spirit, lady, is like a automobile: always on the move, always . . ."

"Listen, Mr. Shiftlet," she said, "my well never goes dry and my house is always warm in the winter and there's no mortgage on a thing about this place. You can go to the courthouse and see for yourself. And yonder under that shed is a fine automobile." She laid the bait carefully. "You can have it painted by Saturday. I'll pay for the paint."

In the darkness, Mr. Shiftlet's smile stretched like a weary snake waking up by a fire. After a second he recalled himself and said, "I'm only saying a man's spirit means more to him than anything else. I would have to take my wife off for the week end without no regards at all for cost. I got to follow where my spirit says to go."

"I'll give you fifteen dollars for a week-end trip," the old woman said in a crabbed voice. "That's the best I can do."

"That wouldn't hardly pay for more than the gas and the hotel," he said. "It wouldn't feed her."

"Seventeen-fifty," the old woman said. "That's all I got so it isn't any use you trying to milk me. You can take a lunch."

Mr. Shiftlet was deeply hurt by the word "milk." He didn't doubt that she had more money sewed up in her mattress but he had already told her he was not interested in her money. "I'll make that do," he said and rose and walked off without treating with her further.

On Saturday the three of them drove into town in the car that the paint had barely dried on and Mr. Shiftlet and Lucynell were married in the Ordinary's office while the old woman witnessed. As they came out of the courthouse, Mr. Shiftlet began twisting his neck in his collar. He looked morose and bitter as if he had been insulted while someone held him. "That didn't satisfy me none," he said. "That was just something a woman in an office did, nothing but paper work and blood tests. What do they know about my blood? If they was to take my heart and cut it out," he said, "they wouldn't know a thing about me. It didn't satisfy me at all."

"It satisfied the law," the old woman said sharply.

"The law," Mr. Shiftlet said and spit. "It's the law that don't satisfy me."

He had painted the car dark green with a yellow band around it just under the windows. The three of them climbed in the front seat and the old woman said, "Don't Lucynell look pretty? Looks like a baby doll." Lucynell was dressed up in a white dress that her mother had uprooted from a trunk and there was a Panama hat on her head with a bunch of red wooden cherries on the brim. Every now and then her placid expression was changed by a sly isolated little thought like a shoot of green in the desert. "You got a prize!" the old woman said.

Mr. Shiftlet didn't even look at her.

They drove back to the house to let the old woman off and pick up the lunch. When they were ready to leave, she stood staring in the window of the car, with her fingers clenched around the glass. Tears began to seep sideways out of her eyes and run along the dirty creases in her face. "I ain't ever been parted with her for two days before," she said.

Mr. Shiftlet started the motor.

"And I wouldn't let no man have her but you because I seen you would do right. Good-by, Sugarbaby," she said, clutching at the sleeve of the white dress. Lucynell looked straight at her and didn't seem to see her there at all. Mr. Shiftlet eased the car forward so that she had to move her hands.

The early afternoon was clear and open and surrounded by pale blue sky. Although the car would go only thirty miles an hour, Mr. Shiftlet imagined a terrific climb and dip and swerve that went entirely to his head so that he forgot his morning bitterness. He had always wanted an automobile but he had never been able to afford one before. He drove very fast because he wanted to make Mobile by nightfall.

Occasionally he stopped his thoughts long enough to look at Lucynell in the seat beside him. She had eaten the lunch as soon as they were out of the yard and now she was pulling the cherries off the hat one by one and throwing them out the window. He became depressed in spite of the car. He had driven about a hundred miles when he decided that she must be hungry again and at the next small town they came to, he stopped in front of an aluminum-painted eating place called The Hot Spot and took her in and ordered her a plate of ham and grits. The ride had made her sleepy and as soon as she got up on the stool, she rested her head on the counter and shut her eyes. There was no one in The Hot Spot but Mr. Shiftlet and the boy behind the counter, a pale youth with a greasy rag hung over his shoulder. Before he could dish up the food, she was snoring gently.

"Give it to her when she wakes up," Mr. Shiftlet said. "I'll pay for it now."

The boy bent over her and stared at the long pink-gold hair and the half-shut sleeping eyes. Then he looked up and stared at Mr. Shiftlet. "She looks like an angel of Gawd," he murmured.

"Hitch-hiker," Mr. Shiftlet explained. "I can't wait. I got to make Tuscaloosa."

The boy bent over again and very carefully touched his finger to a strand of the golden hair and Mr. Shiftlet left.

He was more depressed than ever as he drove on by himself. The late afternoon had grown hot and sultry and the country had flattened out. Deep in the sky a storm was preparing very slowly and without thunder as if it meant to drain every drop of air from the earth before it broke. There were times when Mr. Shiftlet preferred not to be alone. He felt too that a man with a car had a responsibility to others and he kept his eye out for a hitchhiker. Occasionally he saw a sign that warned: "Drive carefully. The life you save may be your own."

The narrow road dropped off on either side into dry fields and here and there a shack or a filling station stood in a clearing. The sun began to set directly in front of the automobile. It was a reddening ball that through his windshield was slightly flat on the bottom and top. He saw a boy in overalls and a gray hat standing on the edge of the road and he slowed the car down and stopped in front of him. The boy didn't have his hand raised to thumb the ride, he was only standing there, but he had a small cardboard suitcase and his hat was set on his head in a way to indicate that he had left somewhere for good. "Son," Mr. Shiftlet said, "I see you want a ride."

The boy didn't say he did or he didn't but he opened the door of the car and got in, and Mr. Shiftlet started driving again. The child held the suitcase on his lap and folded his arms on top of it. He turned his head and looked out the window away from Mr. Shiftlet. Mr. Shiftlet felt oppressed. "Son," he said after a minute, "I got the best old mother in the world so I reckon you only got the second best."

The boy gave him a quick dark glance and then turned his face back out the window.

"It's nothing so sweet," Mr. Shiftlet continued, "as a boy's mother. She taught him his first prayers at her knee, she gave him love when no other would, she told him what was right and what wasn't, and she seen that he done the right thing. Son," he said, "I never rued a day in my life like the one I rued when I left that old mother of mine."

The boy shifted in his seat but he didn't look at Mr. Shiftlet. He unfolded his arms and put one hand on the door handle.

"My mother was a angel of Gawd," Mr. Shiftlet said in a very strained voice. "He took her from heaven and giver to me and I left her." His eyes were instantly clouded over with a mist of tears. The car was barely moving.

The boy turned angrily in the seat. "You go to the devil!" he cried. "My old woman is a flea bag and yours is a stinking pole cat!" and with that he flung the door open and jumped out with his suitcase into the ditch.

Mr. Shiftlet was so shocked that for about a hundred feet he drove along slowly with the door still open. A cloud, the exact color of the boy's hat and shaped like a turnip, had descended over the sun, and another, worse looking, crouched behind the car. Mr. Shiftlet felt that the rottenness of the world was about to engulf him. He raised his arm and let it fall again to his breast. "Oh Lord!" he prayed. "Break forth and wash the slime from this earth!"

The turnip continued slowly to descend. After a few minutes there was a guffawing peal of thunder from behind and fantastic raindrops, like tin-can tops, crashed over the rear of Mr. Shiftlet's car. Very quickly he stepped on the gas and with his stump sticking out the window he raced the galloping shower into Mobile.

Tille Olsen / *Tell Me a Riddle* 1953–54

In Tell Me a Riddle, *Tillie Olsen "found characters who could fully embody her vision of hope with hopelessness, of beauty in the midst of ugliness," in the view of one critic writing for the* New Republic. *Many of the stories in that collection have been anthologized and widely acclaimed. "I Stand Here Ironing," the story below, has been read on the radio and recorded in the Lamont Poetry Room at Harvard.*

Born in Omaha, Nebraska, in 1913, Tillie Olsen has worked in factories and as a typist-transcriber. She was awarded a Stanford University Creative Writing Fellowship (1955–56) a Ford Foundation Grant in Literature (1956), and a fellowship to the Radcliffe Institute for Independent Study (1962–64).

I STAND HERE IRONING

I stand here ironing, and what you asked me moves tormented back and forth with the iron.

"I wish you would manage the time to come in and talk with me about your daughter. I'm sure you can help me understand her. She's a youngster who needs help and whom I'm deeply interested in helping."

"Who needs help." . . . Even if I came, what good would it do? You think because I am her mother I have a key, or that in some way you could use me as a key? She has lived for nineteen years. There is all that life that has happened outside of me, beyond me.

And when is there time to remember, to sift, to weigh, to estimate, to total? I will start and there will be an interruption and I will have to gather it all together again. Or I will become engulfed with all I did or did not do, with what should have been and what cannot be helped.

She was a beautiful baby. The first and only one of our five that was beautiful at birth. You do not guess how new and uneasy her tenancy in her now-loveliness. You did not know her all those years she was thought homely, or see her poring over her baby pictures, making me tell her over and over how beautiful she had been—and would be, I would tell her—and was now, to the seeing eye. But the seeing eyes were few or nonexistent. Including mine.

I nursed her. They feel that's important nowadays. I nursed all the children, but with her, with all the fierce rigidity of first motherhood, I did like the books then said. Though her cries battered me to trembling and my breasts ached with swollenness, I waited till the clock decreed.

Why do I put that first? I do not even know if it matters, or if it explains anything.

She was a beautiful baby. She blew shining bubbles of sound. She loved motion, loved light, loved color and music and textures. She would lie on the floor in her blue overalls patting the surface so hard in ecstasy her hands and feet would blur. She was a miracle to me, but when she was eight months old I had to leave her daytimes with the woman downstairs to whom she was no miracle at all, for I worked or looked for work and for Emily's father, who "could no longer endure" (he wrote in his good-bye note) "sharing want with us."

I was nineteen. It was the pre-relief, pre-WPA world of the depression. I would start running as soon as I got off the streetcar, running up the stairs, the place smelling sour, and awake or asleep to startle awake, when she saw me she would break into a clogged weeping that could not be comforted, a weeping I can hear yet.

After a while I found a job hashing at night so I could be with her days, and it was better. But it came to where I had to bring her to this family and leave her.

It took a long time to raise the money for her fare back. Then she got chicken pox and I had to wait longer. When she finally came, I hardly knew her, walking quick and nervous like her father, looking like her father, thin, and dressed in a shoddy red that yellowed her skin and glared at the pockmarks. All the baby loveliness gone.

She was two. Old enough for nursery school they said, and I did not know then what I know now—the fatigue of the long day, and the lacerations of group life in the kinds of nurseries that are only parking places for children.

Except that it would have made no difference if I had known. It was the only place there was. It was the only way we could be together, the only way I could hold a job.

And even without knowing, I knew. I knew the teacher that was evil because all these years it has curdled into my memory, the little boy hunched in the corner, her rasp, "why aren't you outside, because Alvin hits you? that's no reason, go out, scaredy." I knew Emily hated it even if she did not clutch and implore "don't go Mommy" like the other children, mornings.

She always had a reason why we should stay home. Momma, you look sick. Momma, I feel sick. Momma, the teachers aren't there today, they're sick. Momma, we can't go, there was a fire there last night. Momma, it's a holiday today, no school, they told me.

But never a direct protest, never rebellion. I think of our others in their three-, four-year-oldness—the explosions, the tempers, the denunciations, the demands— and I feel suddenly ill. I put the iron down. What in me demanded that goodness in her? And what was the cost, the cost to her of such goodness?

The old man living in the back once said in his gentle way: "You should smile at Emily more when you look at her." What *was* in my face when I looked at her? I loved her. There were all the acts of love.

It was only with the others I remembered what he said, and it was the face of joy, and not of care or tightness or worry I turned to them—too late for Emily. She does not smile easily, let alone almost always as her brothers and sisters do. Her face is closed and sombre, but when she wants, how fluid. You must have seen it in her pantomimes, you spoke of her rare gift for comedy on the stage that rouses a laughter out of the audience so dear they applaud and applaud and do not want to let her go.

Where does it come from, that comedy? There was none of it in her when she came back to me that second time, after I had had to send her away again. She had a new daddy now to learn to love, and I think perhaps it was a better time.

Except when we left her alone nights, telling ourselves she was old enough.

"Can't you go some other time, Mommy, like tomorrow?" she would ask. "Will it be just a little while you'll be gone? Do you promise?"

The time we came back, the front door open, the clock on the floor in the hall. She rigid awake. "It wasn't just a little while. I didn't cry. Three times I called you, just three times, and then I ran downstairs to open the door so you could come faster. The clock talked loud. I threw it away, it scared me what it talked."

She said the clock talked loud again that night I went to the hospital to have Susan. She was delirious with the fever that comes before red measles, but she was fully conscious all the week I was gone and the week after we were home when she could not come near the new baby or me.

She did not get well. She stayed skeleton thin, not wanting to eat, and night after night she had nightmares. She would call for me, and I would rouse from exhaustion to sleepily call back: "You're all right, darling, go to sleep, it's just a dream," and if she still called, in a sterner voice, "now go to sleep, Emily, there's nothing to hurt you." Twice, only twice, when I had to get up for Susan anyhow, I went in to sit with her.

Now when it is too late (as if she would let me hold and comfort her like I do the others) I get up and go to her at once at her moan or restless stirring. "Are you awake, Emily? Can I get you something?" And the answer is always the same: "No, I'm all right, go back to sleep, Mother."

They persuaded me at the clinic to send her away to a convalescent home in the country where "she can have the kind of food and care you can't manage for her, and you'll be free to concentrate on the new baby." They still send children to that place. I see pictures on the society page of sleek young women planning affairs to raise money for it, or dancing at the affairs, or decorating Easter eggs or filling Christmas stockings for the children.

They never have a picture of the children so I do not know if the girls still wear those gigantic red bows and the ravaged looks on the every other Sunday when parents can come to visit "unless otherwise notified"—as we were notified the first six weeks.

Oh it is a handsome place, green lawns and tall trees and fluted flower beds. High up on the balconies of each cottage the children stand, the girls in their red bows and white dresses, the boys in white suits and giant red ties. The parents stand below shrieking up to be heard and the children shriek down to be heard, and between them the invisible wall "Not To Be Contaminated by Parental Germs or Physical Affection."

There was a tiny girl who always stood hand in hand with Emily. Her parents never came. One visit she was gone. "They moved her to Rose Cottage" Emily shouted in explanation. "They don't like you to love anybody here."

She wrote once a week, the labored writing of a seven-year-old. "I am fine. How is the baby. If I write my leter nicly I will have a star. Love." There never was a star. We wrote every other day, letters she could never hold or keep but only hear read—once. "We simply do not have room for children to keep any personal possessions," they patiently explained when we pieced one Sunday's shrieking together to plead how much it would mean to Emily, who loved so to keep things, to be allowed to keep her letters and cards.

Each visit she looked frailer, "She isn't eating," they told us.

(They had runny eggs for breakfast or mush with lumps, Emily said later, I'd hold it in my mouth and not swallow. Nothing ever tasted good, just when they had chicken.)

It took us eight months to get her released home, and only the fact that she gained back so little of her seven lost pounds convinced the social worker.

I used to try to hold and love her after she came back, but her body would stay stiff, and after a while she'd push away. She ate little. Food sickened her, and I think much of life too. Oh she had physical lightness and brightness, twinkling by on skates, bouncing like a ball up and down up and down over the jump rope, skimming over the hill; but these were momentary.

She fretted about her appearance, thin and dark and foreign-looking at a time when every little girl was supposed to look or thought she should look a chubby blonde replica of Shirley Temple. The doorbell sometimes rang for her, but no one seemed to come and play in the house or be a best friend. Maybe because we moved so much.

There was a boy she loved painfully through two school semesters. Months later she told me how she had taken pennies from my purse to buy him candy. "Licorice was his favorite and I brought him some every day, but he still liked Jennifer better'n me. Why, Mommy?" The kind of question for which there is no answer.

School was a worry to her. She was not glib or quick in a world where glibness and quickness were easily confused with ability to learn. To her overworked and exasperated teachers she was an overconscientious "slow learner" who kept trying to catch up and was absent entirely too often.

I let her be absent, though sometimes the illness was imaginary. How different from my now-strictness about attendance with the others. I wasn't working. We had a new baby, I was home anyhow. Sometimes, after Susan grew old enough, I would keep her home from school, too, to have them all together.

Mostly Emily had asthma, and her breathing, harsh and labored, would fill the house with a curiously tranquil sound. I would bring the two old dresser mirrors and her boxes of collections to her bed. She would select beads and single earrings, bottle tops and shells, dried flowers and pebbles, old postcards and scraps, all sorts of oddments; then she and Susan would play Kingdom, setting up landscapes and furniture, peopling them with action.

Those were the only times of peaceful companionship between her and Susan. I have edged away from it, that poisonous feeling between them, that terrible balancing of hurts and needs I had to do between the two, and did so badly, those earlier years.

Oh there are conflicts between the others too, each one human, needing, demanding, hurting, taking—but only between Emily and Susan, no, Emily toward Susan that corroding resentment. It seems so obvious on the surface, yet it is not obvious. Susan, the second child, Susan, golden- and curly-haired and chubby, quick and articulate and assured, everything in appearance and manner Emily was not; Susan, not able to resist Emily's precious things, losing or sometimes clumsily breaking them; Susan telling jokes and riddles to company for applause while Emily sat silent (to say to me later: that was *my* riddle, Mother, I told it to Susan); Susan, who for all the five years' difference in age was just a year behind Emily in developing physically.

I am glad for that slow physical development that widened the difference between her and her contemporaries, though she suffered over it. She was too vulnerable for that terrible world of youthful competition, of preening and parading, of constant measuring of yourself against every other, of envy, "If I had that copper hair," "If I had that skin. . . ." She tormented herself enough about not looking like the others, there was enough of the unsureness, the having to be conscious of words before you speak, the constant caring—what are they thinking of me? without having it all magnified by the merciless physical drives.

Ronnie is calling. He is wet and I change him. It is rare there is such a cry now. That time of motherhood is almost behind me when the ear is not one's own but must always be racked and listening for the child cry, the child call. We sit for a while and I hold him, looking out over the city spread in charcoal with its soft aisles of light. "*Shoogily,*" he breathes and curls closer. I carry him back to bed, asleep. *Shoogily.* A funny word, a family word, inherited from Emily, invested by her to say: *comfort.*

In this and other ways she leaves her seal, I say aloud. And startle at my saying it. What do I mean? What did I start to gather together, to try and make coherent? I was at the terrible, growing years. War years. I do not remember them well. I was working, there were four smaller ones now, there was not time for her. She had to help be a mother, and housekeeper, and shopper. She had to set her seal. Mornings of crisis and near hysteria trying to get lunches packed, hair combed, coats and shoes found, everyone to school or Child Care on time, the baby ready for transportation. And always the paper scribbled on by a smaller one, the book looked at by Susan then mislaid, the homework not done. Running out to that huge school where she was one, she was lost, she was a drop; suffering over the unpreparedness, stammering and unsure of her classes.

There was so little time left at night after the kids were bedded down. She would struggle over books, always eating (it was in those years she developed her enormous appetite that is legendary in our family) and I would be ironing, or preparing food for the next day, or writing V-mail to Bill, or tending the baby. Sometimes, to make me laugh, or out of her despair, she would imitate happenings or types at school.

I think I said once: "Why don't you do something like this in the school amateur show?" One morning she phoned me at work, hardly understandable through the weeping: "Mother, I did it. I won, I won; they gave me first prize; they clapped and clapped and wouldn't let me go."

Now suddenly she was Somebody, and as imprisoned in her difference as she had been in anonymity.

She began to be asked to perform at other high schools, even in colleges, then at city and statewide affairs. The first one we went to, I only recognized her that first moment when thin, shy, she almost drowned herself into the curtains. Then: Was this Emily? The control, the command, the convulsing and deadly clowning, the spell, then the roaring, stamping audience, unwilling to let this rare and precious laughter out of their lives.

Afterwards: You ought to do something about her with a gift like that—but without money or knowing how, what does one do? We have left it all to her, and the gift has as often eddied inside, clogged and clotted, as been used and growing.

She is coming. She runs up the stairs two at a time with her light graceful step, and I know she is happy tonight. Whatever it was that occasioned your call did not happen today.

"Aren't you ever going to finish the ironing, Mother? Whistler painted his mother in a rocker. I'd have to paint mine standing over an ironing board.'' This is one of her communicative nights and she tells me everything and nothing as she fixes herself a plate of food out of the icebox.

She is so lovely. Why did you want me to come in at all? Why were you concerned? She will find her way.

She starts up the stairs to bed. ''Don't get me up with the rest in the morning.'' ''But I thought you were having midterms.'' ''Oh, those,'' she comes back in, kisses me, and say quite lightly, ''in a couple of years when we'll all be atom-dead they won't matter a bit.''

She has said it before. She *believes* it. But because I have been dredging the past, and all that compounds a human being is so heavy and meaningful in me, I cannot endure it tonight.

I will never total it all. I will never come in to say: She was a child seldom smiled at. Her father left me before she was a year old. I had to work her first six years when there was work, or I sent her home and to his relatives. There were years she had care she hated. She was dark and thin and foreign-looking in a world where the prestige went to blondeness and curly hair and dimples, she was slow where glibness was prized. She was a child of anxious, not proud, love. We were poor and could not afford for her the soil of easy growth. I was a young mother, I was a distracted mother. There were the other children pushing up, demanding. Her younger sister seemed all that she was not. There were years she did not want me to touch her. She kept too much in herself, her life was such she had to keep too much in herself. My wisdom came too late. She has much to her and probably little will come of it. She is a child of her age, of depression, of war, of fear.

Let her be. So all that is in her will not bloom—but in how many does it? There is still enough left to live by. Only help her to know—help make it so there is cause for her to know—that she is more than this dress on the ironing board, help-less before the iron.

DISCUSSION QUESTIONS

1. Characterize the speaker in this piece. Whom is she addressing? How does she feel about her daughter? About her own life?

2. The piece ends with an appeal: ''Only help her to know—help make it so there is cause for her to know—that she is more than this dress on the ironing board, helpless before the iron.'' Explain the significance of the image. Does the speaker seem to wish someone could have helped her to know the same thing earlier in her life? Does she still seem ''helpless before the iron'' herself? What do you think the author wants us to feel for the speaker? For the daughter? What specifically makes you think so?

Robinson Jeffers / Carmel Point   1954

In its rigorous anti-humanism and philosophical nihilism, Robinson Jeffers' po-
etry represents an extreme of twentieth-century American literature. Immersed in

the Greek classics, Elizabethan tragedy, and modern science, Jeffers endeavored throughout most of his poetry to dissuade humanity from thinking about itself as the center of the universe. In The Double Axe *(1948), he called his philosophical attitude "inhumanism, a shifting of emphasis and significance from man to not-man." And in the long narrative poem that is usually regarded as his major work,* Roan Stallion *(1925), he claims that "Humanity is the mold to break away from."*

Jeffers was born in Pittsburgh in 1887, the son of a classics professor at the Western Theological Seminary. After traveling widely with his family as a young boy, he entered Occidental College in Los Angeles in 1904 and graduated at the age of eighteen. Undecided about a career, he spent a year at Zurich University in Switzerland, returned to the United States and took an M.A. in literature at the University of Southern California, studied medicine there for three years, and then switched to forestry with a move to the University of Washington. In 1913 he married and the next year moved to the isolated, rocky coast of Carmel, California, where he built with his own hands the stone house and tower that ruggedly sheltered his life-long exile. He died there in 1962.

The extraordinary patience of things!
This beautiful place defaced with a crop of surburban houses—
How beautiful when we first beheld it,
Unbroken field of poppy and lupin walled with clean cliffs;
No intrusion but two or three horses pasturing,   5
Or a few milch cows rubbing their flanks on the outcrop rockheads—
Now the spoiler has come: does it care?
Not faintly. It has all time. It knows the people are a tide
That swells and in time will ebb, and all
Their works dissolve. Meanwhile the image of the pristine beauty   10
Lives in the very grain of the granite,
Safe as the endless ocean that climbs our cliff.—As for us:
We must uncenter our minds from ourselves;
We must unhumanize our views a little, and become confident
As the rock and ocean that we were made from.   15

DISCUSSION QUESTIONS

1. How does the speaker go about distinguishing between nature and human life? Point to words and phrases that express these differences. Can you also point to words and phrases that blur distinctions between nature and humanity?

2. How does the speaker view humanity? How is humanity connected with the landscape? With the speaker himself? Do you feel the speaker's view of humanity is convincing? Given his description of nature in the poem, do you think his view of humanity is justified?

3. What do you think the speaker means when he says that "We must uncenter our minds from ourselves"? Do you think doing so would be a worthwhile endeavor? Compare the speaker's attitude towards individual human life with "Why It's Called the 'Me Generation' " (*Magazines*). How does the speaker's vision of human life compare with Hawthorne's and Whitman's in this section?

4. In what sense can this be said to be a poem about "ecology"? In what sense isn't the poem about "ecology"? Explain. In its attitude towards the environment, how does "Carmel Point" compare with "Trying To Restore a Sea of Grass" (see *Press*) and N. Scott Momaday's "A First American Views His Land" (see *Magazines*)?

Allen Ginsberg / A Supermarket in California   1955

The author of poetry regarded as "great," "strange," "angelic," "degenerate," "unsurpassed," and "apocalyptic," Allen Ginsberg remains one of the most celebrated and vilified literary figures of the past three decades. Born in Newark, New Jersey in 1926, Ginsberg graduated from Columbia University in 1948 and spent several years on the road, supporting himself as a spot welder, reporter, dishwasher, porter, book reviewer, and seaman. Soon after his arrival in San Francisco, he launched an immediately successful career as a market research consultant. But a year of psychoanalysis prompted him, as he says, to "quit the job, my tie and suit, the apartment on Nob Hill . . . and do what I wanted"—write poetry. By the mid-1950s, Ginsberg was identified—along with, among others, Jack Kerouac, Lawrence Ferlinghetti, and William Burroughs—as a co-founder of the Beat Generation. Lionized for his experimentations with literary forms and unconventional life-styles, Ginsberg remains an ardent supporter of political and social causes. A late 1960s profile in the New Yorker *characterized him not only as a major American poet but also as a guru of the "amalgamated hippie-pacifist-activist-visionary-orgiastic-anarchist-Orientalist-psychedelic underground."*

Ginsberg's first volume of poetry, Howl *(1956), is also his most famous. It has gone through more than thirty printings, In a "Preface" to the volume, William Carlos Williams at once cautions readers that Ginsberg's vision of contemporary America is like "going through hell" but also reminds us that Ginsberg "proves to us, in spite of the most debasing experiences that life can offer a man, the spirit of love survives to ennoble our lives if we have the wit and the courage and the faith—and the art! to persist."*

"A Supermarket in California" was included in Ginsberg's first controversial volume. The poem remains a pensive rendition of Walt Whitman's vision of America as a land of abundance.

What thoughts I have of you tonight, Walt Whitman, for
I walked down the sidestreets under the trees with a headache
self-conscious looking at the full moon.
　　In my hungry fatigue, and shopping for images, I went
into the neon fruit supermarket, dreaming of your enumerations!
　　What peaches and what penumbras! Whole families
shopping at night! Aisles full of husbands! Wives in the
avocados, babies in the tomatoes!—and you, Garcia Lorca,
what were you doing down by the watermelons?

I saw you, Walt Whitman, childless, lonely old grubber,
poking among the meats in the refrigerator and eyeing the
grocery boys.

I heard you asking questions of each: Who killed the   5
pork chops? What price bananas? Are you my Angel?

I wandered in and out of the brilliant stacks of cans
following you, and followed in my imagination by the store
detective.

We strode down the open corridors together in our
solitary fancy tasting artichokes, possessing every frozen
delicacy, and never passing the cashier.

Where are we going, Walt Whitman? The doors close in
an hour. Which way does your beard point tonight?

(I touch your book and dream of our odyssey in the
supermarket and feel absurd.)

Will we walk all night through solitary streets? The trees   10
add shade to shade, lights out in the houses, we'll both be
lonely.

Will we stroll dreaming of the lost America of love past
blue automobiles in driveways, home to our silent cottage?

Ah, dear father, graybeard, lonely old courage-teacher,
what America did you have when Charon quit poling his ferry
and you got out on a smoking bank and stood watching the
boat disappear on the black waters of Lethe?

John Updike / A & P   1962

After graduating from Harvard in 1954, where he was president of the Lampoon,
John Updike joined The New Yorker *magazine as a reporter. Though he officially
left the staff of that magazine in 1957 to concentrate on his fiction, issue after issue
of* The New Yorker *declares Updike's presence in short stories, sketches, book
reviews, and occasional light verse. "A & P," a tale of adolescent sensibility
and one of the most widely anthologized short stories by a contemporary American
writer, shows Updike's characteristic concern for the minutiae of sensory perceptions and the achievement of individual identity.*

In walks these three girls in nothing but bathing suits. I'm in the third checkout slot,
with my back to the door, so I don't see them until they're over by the bread. The
one that caught my eye first was the one in the plaid green two-piece. She was a
chunky kid, with a good tan and a sweet broad soft-looking can with those two cres-
cents of white just under it, where the sun never seems to hit, at the top of the backs
of her legs. I stood there with my hand on a box of HiHo crackers trying to
remember if I rang it up or not. I ring it up again and the customer starts giving me
hell. She's one of these cash-register-watchers, a witch about fifty with rouge on her

cheekbones and no eyebrows, and I know it made her day to trip me up. She'd been watching cash registers for fifty years and probably never seen a mistake before.

By the time I got her feathers smoothed and her goodies into a bag—she gives me a little snort in passing, if she'd been born at the right time they would have burned her over in Salem—by the time I get her on her way the girls had circled around the bread and were coming back, without a pushcart, back my way along the counters, in the aisle between the checkouts and the Special bins. They didn't even have shoes on. There was this chunky one, with the two-piece—it was bright green and the seams on the bra were still sharp and her belly was still pretty pale so I guessed she just got it (the suit)—there was this one, with one of those chubby berry-faces, the lips all bunched together under her nose, this one, and a tall one, with black hair that hadn't quite frizzed right, and one of these sunburns right across under the eyes, and a chin that was too long—you know, the kind of girl other girls think is very "striking" and "attractive" but never quite makes it, as they very well know, which is why they like her so much—and then the third one, that wasn't quite so tall. She was the queen. She kind of led them, the other two peeking around and making their shoulders round. She didn't look around, not this queen, she just walked straight on slowly, on those long white prima-donna legs. She came down a little hard on her heels, as if she didn't walk in her bare feet that much, putting down her heels and then letting the weight move along to her toes as if she was testing the floor with every step, putting a little deliberate extra action into it. You never know for sure how girls' minds work (do you really think it's a mind in there or just a little buzz like a bee in a glass jar?) but you got the idea she had talked the other two into coming in here with her, and now she was showing them how to do it, walk slow and hold yourself straight.

She had on a kind of dirty-pink—beige maybe, I don't know—bathing suit with a little nubble all over it and, what got me, the straps were down. They were off her shoulders looped loose around the cool tops of her arms, and I guess as a result the suit had slipped a little on her, so all around the top of the cloth there was this shining rim. If it hadn't been there you wouldn't have known there could have been anything whiter than those shoulders. With the straps pushed off, there was nothing between the top of the suit and the top of her head except just *her,* this clean bare plane of the top of her chest down from the shoulder bones like a dented sheet of metal tilted in the light. I mean, it was more than pretty.

She had sort of oaky hair that the sun and salt had bleached, done up in a bun that was unravelling, and a kind of prim face. Walking into the A & P with your straps down, I suppose it's the only kind of face you *can* have. She held her head so high her neck, coming up out of those white shoulders, looked kind of stretched, but I didn't mind. The longer her neck was, the more of her there was.

She must have felt in the corner of her eye me and over my shoulder Stokesie in the second slot watching, but she didn't tip. Not this queen. She kept her eyes moving across the racks, and stopped, and turned so slow it made my stomach rub the inside of my apron, and buzzed to the other two, who kind of huddled against her for relief, and then they all three of them went up the cat-and-dog-food-breakfast-cereal-macaroni-rice-raisins-seasonings-spreads-spaghetti-soft-drinks-crackers-and-cookies aisle. From the third slot I look straight up this aisle to the meat counter, and I watched them all the way. The fat one with the tan sort of fumbled with the cookies, but on second thought she put the package back. The sheep pushing their carts down the aisle—the girls were walking against the usual traffic (not that we have one-way signs or anything)—were pretty hilarious. You could see them, when Queenie's white shoulders dawned on them, kind of jerk, or hop, or hiccup, but their eyes snapped back to their own baskets and on they pushed. I bet you could set off dynamite in an A & P and the people would by and large keep reaching and checking oatmeal off their lists and muttering "Let me see, there was a third thing, began with A, asparagus, no, ah, yes, applesauce!" or whatever it is they do mutter. But there was no doubt, this jiggled them. A few houseslaves in pin curlers even looked around after pushing their carts past to make sure what they had seen was correct.

You know, it's one thing to have a girl in a bathing suit down on the beach, where what with the glare nobody can look at each other much anyway, and another thing in the cool of the A & P, under the fluorescent lights, against all those stacked packages, with her feet paddling along naked over our checkerboard green-and-cream rubber-tile floor.

"Oh Daddy," Stokesie said beside me. "I feel so faint."

"Darling," I said. "Hold me tight." Stokesie's married, with two babies chalked up on his fuselage already, but as far as I can tell that's the only difference. He's twenty-two, and I was nineteen this April.

"Is it done?" he asks, the responsible married man finding his voice. I forgot to say he thinks he's going to be manager some sunny day, maybe in 1990 when it's called the Great Alexandrov and Petrooshki Tea Company or something.

What he meant was, our town is five miles from a beach, with a big summer colony out on the Point, but we're right in the middle of town, and the women generally put on a shirt or shorts or something before they get out of the car into the street. And anyway these are usually women with six children and varicose veins mapping their legs and nobody, including them, could care less. As I say, we're right in the middle of town, and if you stand at our front doors you can see two banks and the Congregational church and the newspaper store and three real-estate offices and about twenty-seven old freeloaders tearing up Central Street because the sewer broke again. It's not as if we're on the Cape; we're north of Boston and there's people in this town haven't seen the ocean for twenty years.

The girls had reached the meat counter and were asking McMahon something. He pointed, they pointed, and they shuffled out of sight behind a pyramid of Diet Delight peaches. All that was left for us to see was old McMahon patting his mouth and looking after them sizing up their joints. Poor kids, I began to feel sorry for them, they couldn't help it.

Now here comes the sad part of the story, at least my family says it's sad, but I don't think it's so sad myself. The store's pretty empty, it being Thursday afternoon, so there was nothing much to do except lean on the register and wait for the girls to show up again. The whole store was like a pinball machine and I didn't know which tunnel they'd come out of. After a while they come around out of the far aisle, around the light bulbs, records at discount of the Caribbean Six or Tony Martin Sings or some such gunk you wonder they waste the wax on, sixpacks of candy bars, and plastic toys done up in cellophane that fall apart when a kid looks at them anyway. Around they come, Queenie still leading the way, and holding a little gray jar in her hand. Slots Three through Seven are unmanned and I could see her wondering between Stokes and me, but Stokesie with his usual luck draws an old party in baggy gray pants who stumbles up with four giant cans of pineapple juice (what do these bums *do* with all that pineapple juice? I've often asked myself) so the girls come to me. Queenie puts down the jar and I take it into my fingers icy cold. Kingfish Fancy Herring Snacks in Pure Sour Cream: 49¢. Now her hands are empty, not a ring or a bracelet, bare as God made them, and I wonder where the money's coming from. Still with that prim look she lifts a folded dollar bill out of the hollow at the center of her nubbled pink top. The jar went heavy in my hand. Really, I thought that was so cute.

Then everybody's luck begins to run out. Lengel comes in from haggling with a truck full of cabbages on the lot and is about to scuttle into that door marked MAN-AGER behind which he hides all day when the girls touch his eye. Lengel's pretty dreary, teaches Sunday school and the rest, but he doesn't miss that much. He comes over and says, "Girls, this isn't the beach."

Queenie blushes, though maybe it's just a brush of sunburn I was noticing for the first time, now that she was so close. "My mother asked me to pick up a jar of her-ring snacks." Her voice kind of startled me, the way voices do when you see the people first, coming out so flat and dumb yet kind of tony, too, the way it ticked over "pick up" and "snacks." All of a sudden I slid right down her voice into her living room. Her father and the other men were standing around in ice-cream coats and bow ties and the women were in sandals picking up herring snacks on tooth-picks off a big glass plate and they were all holding drinks the color of water with olives and sprigs of mint in them. When my parents have somebody over they get lemonade and if it's a real racy affair Schlitz in tall glasses with "They'll Do It Every Time" cartoons stencilled on.

"That's all right," Lengel said. "But this isn't the beach." His repeating this struck me as funny, as if it had just occurred to him, and he had been thinking all these years the A & P was a great big dune and he was the head lifeguard. He didn't like my smiling—as I say he doesn't miss much—but he concentrates on giving the girls that sad Sunday-school-superintendent stare.

Queenie's blush is no sunburn now, and the plump one in plaid, that I liked better from the back—a really sweet can—pipes up, "We weren't doing any shopping. We just came in for the one thing."

"That makes no difference," Lengel tells her, and I could see from the way his eyes went that he hadn't noticed she was wearing a two-piece before. "We want you decently dressed when you come in here."

"We *are* decent," Queenie says suddenly, her lower lip pushing, getting sore now that she remembers her place, a place from which the crowd that runs the A & P must look pretty crummy. Fancy Herring Snacks flashed in her very blue eyes.

"Girls, I don't want to argue with you. After this come in here with your shoulders covered. It's our policy." He turns his back. That's policy for you. Policy is what the kingpins want. What the others want is juvenile delinquency.

All this while, the customers had been showing up with their carts but, you know, sheep, seeing a scene, they had all bunched up on Stokesie, who shook open a paper bag as gently as peeling a peach, not wanting to miss a word. I could feel in the silence everybody getting nervous, most of all Lengel, who asks me, "Sammy, have you rung up their purchase?"

I thought and said "No" but it wasn't about that I was thinking. I go through the punches, 4, 9, GROC, TOT—it's more complicated than you think, and after you do it often enough, it begins to make a little song, that you hear words to, in my case "Hello (*bing*) there, you (*gung*) hap-py *pee*-pul (*splat*)!"—the *splat* being the drawer flying out. I uncrease the bill, tenderly as you may imagine, it just having come from between the two smoothest scoops of vanilla I had ever known were there, and pass a half and a penny into her narrow pink palm, and nestle the herrings in a bag and twist its neck and hand it over, all the time thinking.

The girls, and who'd blame them, are in a hurry to get out, so I say "I quit" to Lengel quick enough for them to hear, hoping they'll stop and watch me, their unsuspected hero. They keep right on going, into the electric eye; the door flies open and they flicker across the lot to their car, Queenie and Plaid and Big Tall Goony-Goony (not that as raw material she was so bad), leaving me with Lengel and a kink in his eyebrow.

"Did you say something, Sammy?"

"I said I quit."

"I thought you did."

"You didn't have to embarrass them."

"It was they who were embarrassing us."

I started to say something that came out "Fiddle-de-doo." It's a saying of my grandmother's, and I know she would have been pleased.

"I don't think you know what you're saying," Lengel said.

"I know you don't," I said. "But I do." I pull the bow at the back of my apron and start shrugging it off my shoulders. A couple customers that had been heading for my slot begin to knock against each other, like scared pigs in a chute.

Lengel sighs and begins to look very patient and old and gray. He's been a friend of my parents for years. "Sammy, you don't want to do this to your Mom and Dad," he tells me. It's true, I don't. But it seems to me that once you begin a gesture it's fatal not to go through with it. I fold the apron, "Sammy" stitched in red on the pocket, and put it on the counter, and drop the bow tie on top of it. The bow tie is theirs, if you've ever wondered. "You'll feel this for the rest of your life," Lengel says, and I know that's true, too, but remembering how he made that pretty girl blush makes me so scrunchy inside I punch the No Sale tab and the machine whirls "pee-pul" and the drawer splats out. One advantage to this scene taking place in summer, I can follow this up with a clean exit, there's no fumbling around getting your coat and galoshes, I just saunter into the electric eye in my white shirt that my mother ironed the night before, and the door heaves itself open, and outside the sunshine is skating around on the asphalt.

I look around for my girls, but they're gone, of course. There wasn't anybody but some young married screaming with her children about some candy they didn't get by the door of a powder-blue Falcon station wagon. Looking back in the big windows, over the bags of peat moss and aluminum lawn furniture stacked on the pavement, I could see Lengel in my place in the slot, checking the sheep through. His face was dark gray and his back stiff, as if he'd just had an injection of iron, and my stomach kind of fell as I felt how hard the world was going to be to me hereafter.

Sylvia Plath / America! America!   1963

Sylvia Plath (1932–63) was born in Boston, graduated from Smith College with honors, attended Newham College, Cambridge, on a fellowship, and lived in England during the last years of her life. While writing the stunning poetry that brought her posthumous acclaim, she longed to publish fiction in American maga-

zines. *"Poetry,"* she once wrote, *"is an evasion from the real job of writing prose."*

Founded in 1841, the British magazine, Punch, *has poked fun at almost everyone during its long history. Americans seemed to be among its favorite targets. Sylvia Plath sent the magazine her own very personal view of America,* "America! America!," *an essay later printed in a posthumous collection of her prose,* Johnny Panic and the Bible of Dreams (1979).

The poem *"The Applicant,"* which follows her essay, is from Plath's second book of poems, Ariel (1966).

I went to public schools—genuinely public. *Everybody* went: the spry, the shy, the podge, the gangler, the future electronic scientist, the future cop who would one night kick a diabetic to death under the mistaken impression he was a drunk and needed cooling off; the poor, smelling of sour wools and the urinous baby at home and polyglot stew; the richer, with ratty fur collars, opal birthstone rings and daddies with cars ("Wot does *your* daddy do?" "He don't woik, he's a bus droiver." Laughter). There it was—Education—laid on free of charge for the lot of us, a lovely slab of depressed American public. *We* weren't depressed, of course. We left that to our parents, who eked out one child or two, and slumped dumbly after work and frugal suppers over their radios to listen to news of the "home country" and a black-moustached man named Hitler.

Above all, we did feel ourselves American in the rowdy seaside town where I picked up, like lint, my first ten years of schooling—a great, loud cats' bag of Irish Catholics, German Jews, Swedes, Negroes, Italians and that rare, pure Mayflower dropping, somebody *English.*

On to this steerage of infant citizens the doctrines of Liberty and Equality were to be, through the free, communal schools, impressed. Although we could almost call ourselves Bostonian (the city airport with its beautiful hover of planes and silver blimps growled and gleamed across the bay), New York's skyscrapers were the icons on our "home room" walls, New York and the great green queen lifting a bedlamp that spelled out Freedom.

Every morning, hands on hearts, we pledged allegiance to the Stars and Stripes, a sort of aerial altarcloth over teacher's desk. And sang songs full of powder smoke and patriotics to impossible, wobbly, soprano tunes. One high, fine song, "Four purple mountain majesties above the fruited plain," always made the scampi-size poet in me weep. In those days I couldn't have told a fruited plain from a mountain majesty and confused God with George Washington (whose lamblike granny-face shone down at us also from the schoolroom wall between neat blinders of white curls), yet warbled, nevertheless, with my small, snotty compatriots "America, America! God shed His grace on thee, and crown thy good with brotherhood from sea to shining sea."

The sea we knew something about. Terminus of almost every street, it buckled and swashed and tossed, out of its gray formlessness, china plates, wooden monkeys, elegant shells and dead men's shoes. Wet salt winds raked our playgrounds endlessly—those Gothic composites of gravel, macadam, granite and bald, flailed earth wickedly designed to bark and scour the tender knee. There we traded playing cards (for the patterns on the backs) and sordid stories, jumped clothes rope, shot marbles, and enacted the radio and comic book dramas of our day ("Who knows what evil lurks in the hearts of men? The Shadow knows—nyah, nyah, nyah!'' or ''Up in the sky, look! It's a bird, it's a plane, it's Superman!''). If we were destined for any special end—grooved, doomed, limited, fated, we didn't feel it. We beamed and sloshed from our desks to the dodge-ball dell, open and hopeful as the sea itself.

After all, we could be anybody. If we worked. If we studied hard enough. Our accents, our money, our parents didn't matter. Did not lawyers rise from the loins of coalheavers, doctors from the bins of dustmen? Education was the answer, and heaven knows how it came to us. Invisibly, I think, in the early days—a mystical infra-red glow off the thumbed multiplication tables, ghastly poems extolling October's bright blue weather, and a world of history that more or less began and ended with the Boston Tea Party—Pilgrims and Indians being, like the eohippus, prehistoric.

Later, the college obsession would seize us, a subtle, terrifying virus. Everybody had to go to *some* college or other. A business college, a junior college, a state college, a secretarial college, an Ivy League college, a pig farmers' college. The book first, then the work. By the time we (future cop and electronic brain alike) exploded into our prosperous, postwar high school, full-time guidance counselors jogged our elbows at ever-diminishing intervals to discuss motives, hopes, school subjects, jobs—and colleges. Excellent teachers showered onto us like meteors: Biology teachers holding up human brains, English teachers inspiring us with a personal ideological fierceness about Tolstoy and Plato, Art teachers leading us through the slums of Boston, then back to the easel to hurl public school gouache with social awareness and fury. Eccentricities, the perils of being *too* special, were reasoned and cooed from us like sucked thumbs.

The girls' guidance counselor diagnosed my problem straight off. I was just too dangerously brainy. My high, pure string of straight A's might, without proper extracurricular tempering, snap me into the void. More and more, the colleges wanted All-Round Students. I had, by that time, studied Machiavelli in Current Events class. I grabbed my cue.

Now this guidance counselor owned, unknown to me, a white-haired identical twin I kept meeting in supermarkets and at the dentist's. To this twin, I confided my widening circle of activities—chewing orange sections at the quarters of girls' basketball games (I had made the team), painting mammoth L'il Abners and Daisy Maes for class dances, pasting up dummies of the school newspaper at midnight while my already dissipated co-editor read out the jokes at the bottom of the columns of *The New Yorker*. The blank, oddly muffled expression of my guidance counselor's twin in the street did not deter me, nor did the apparent amnesia of her whitely efficient double in the school office. I became a rabid teenage pragmatist.

''Usage is Truth, Truth, Usage,'' I might have muttered, leveling my bobbysocks to match those of my schoolmates. There was no uniform, but there *was* a uniform—the pageboy hairdo, squeaky clean, the skirt and sweater, the ''loafers,'' those scuffed copies of Indian moccasins. We even, in our democratic edifice, nursed two ancient relics of snobbism—two sororities: Subdeb and Sugar 'n' Spice. At the start of each school year, invitation cards went out from old members to new girls—the pretty, the popular, the in some way rivalrous. A week of initiation preceded our smug admittance to the cherished Norm. Teachers preached against Initiation Week, boys scoffed, but couldn't stop it.

I was assigned, like each initiate, a Big Sister who systematically began to destroy my ego. For a whole week I could wear no make-up, could not wash, could not comb my hair, change clothes or speak to boys. By dawn I had walked to my Big Sister's house and was making her bed and breakfast. Then, lugging her intolerably heavy books, as well as my own, I followed her, at a dog's distance, to school. On the way she might order me to climb a tree and hang from a branch till I dropped, ask a passer-by a rude question or stalk about the shops begging for rotten grapes and moldy rice. If I smiled—showed, that is, any sense of irony at my slavishness, I had to kneel on the public pavement and wipe the smile off my face. The minute the bell rang to end school, Big Sister took over. By nightfall I ached and stank; my homework buzzed in a dulled and muzzy brain. I was being tailored to an Okay Image.

Somehow it didn't take—this initiation into the nihil of belonging. Maybe I was just too weird to begin with. What did these picked buds of American womanhood do at their sorority meetings? They ate cake; ate cake and catted about the Saturday night date. The privilege of being anybody was turning its other face—to the pressure of being everybody; ergo, no one.

Lately I peered through the plate-glass side of an American primary school: child-size desks and chairs in clean, light wood, toy stoves and minuscule drinking fountains. Sunlight everywhere. All the anarchism, discomfort and grit I so tenderly remembered had been, in a quarter century, gentled away. One class had spent the morning on a bus learning how to pay fares and ask for the proper stop. Reading (my lot did it by age four off soapbox tops) had become such a traumatic and stormy art one felt lucky to weather it by ten. But the children were smiling in their little ring. Did I glimpse, in the First Aid cabinet, a sparkle of bottles—soothers and smootheners for the embryo rebel, the artist, the odd?

Sylvia Plath / The Applicant   1966

First, are you our sort of a person?
Do you wear
A glass eye, false teeth or a crutch,
A brace or a hook,
Rubber breasts or a rubber crotch,   5

Stitches to show something's missing? No, no? Then
How can we give you a thing?
Stop crying.
Open your hand.
Empty? Empty. Here is a hand   10

To fill it and willing
To bring teacups and roll away headaches
And do whatever you tell it.
Will you marry it?
It is guaranteed   15

To thumb shut your eyes at the end
And dissolve of sorrow.
We make new stock from the salt.
I notice you are stark naked.
How about this suit—   20

Black and stiff, but not a bad fit.
Will you marry it?
It is waterproof, shatterproof, proof
Against fire and bombs through the roof.
Believe me, they'll bury you in it.   25

Now your head, excuse me, is empty.
I have the ticket for that.
Come here, sweetie, out of the closet.
Well, what do you think of *that?*
Naked as paper to start   30

But in twenty-five years she'll be silver,
In fifty, gold.
A living doll, everywhere you look.
It can sew, it can cook,
It can talk, talk, talk.   35

It works, there is nothing wrong with it.
You have a hole, it's a poultice.
You have an eye, it's an image.
My boy, it's your last resort.
Will you marry it, marry it, marry it.   40

Imamu Amiri Baraka / In Memory of Radio   1964

Poet, novelist, dramatist, short story writer, essayist, jazz critic, film maker, and editor, Imamu Amiri Baraka was the dominant voice of black literary consciousness during the 1960s. Born Le Roi Jones in Newark, New Jersey in 1934, he graduated from high school two years early and studied briefly at Rutgers University before earning a degree at Howard University in 1953. After service as a weatherman and B-36 gunner in the Air Force, Baraka did graduate work and taught poetry at the New School for Social Research and Columbia University. He founded Yugen, *an avant-garde magazine that published such notable "Beat" writers as Jack Kerouac, Allen Ginsberg, and Gary Snyder. Baraka also helped establish the Black Arts Repertory Theater in Harlem and Spirit House, a black cultural center in Newark. Since the late 1960s, Baraka has moved steadily away from literature, concentrating more on community action programs and black nationalist causes.*

A nostalgic recollection of the importance of radios in American culture, "In Memory of Radio" is drawn from Baraka's second volume of poetry, The Dead Lecturer *(1964). The poem's form and diction reveal the influence of Walt Whitman and William Carlos Williams.*

Who has ever stopped to think of the divinity of Lamont Cranston?[1]
(Only Jack Kerouac, that I know of; & me.
The rest of you probably had on WCBS and Kate Smith,
Or something equally unattractive.)

What can I say?   5
It is better to have loved and lost
Than to put linoleum in your living rooms?

Am I a sage or something?
Mandrake's hypnotic gesture of the week?[2]
(Remember, I do not have the healing powers of Oral Roberts . . .[3]   10
I cannot, like F. J. Sheen,[4] tell you how to get saved & *rich!*
I cannot even order you to gaschamber satori[5] like Hitler or Goody Knight.[6]

& Love is an evil word.
Turn it backwards/ see, see what I mean?
An evol word. & besides   15
who understands it?
I certainly wouldn't like to go out on that kind of limb.

Saturday mornings we listened to *Red Lantern* & his undersea folk.
At 11, *Let's Pretend/* & we did/ & I, the poet, still do, Thank God!

What was it he used to say (after the transformation, when he was safe   20
& invisible, & the unbelievers couldn't throw stones?) "Heh, Heh, Heh,
Who knows what evil lurks in the hearts of men? The Shadow knows!"[7]

O, yes he does
O, yes he does
An evil word it is,   25
This love.

---

1. Lamont Cranston was the central character in the long-running radio serial "The Shadow" (1931–54). Cranston had "the power to cloud men's minds" and to make himself invisible.—Eds.
2. Mandrake the Magician, a hero in the world of comic strips.—Eds.
3. The ellipsis points are Baraka's.—Eds.
4. Bishop Fulton J. Sheen, a noted Catholic radio and TV personality.—Eds.
5. A state of revelation in Zen Buddhism.—Eds.
6. Goodwin Knight was the governor of California (1953–59) during the debate over capital punishment.—Eds.
7. The Shadow's most famous lines.—Eds.

David Wagoner / The Shooting of John Dillinger Outside the Biograph Theater, July 22, 1934

1966

At various times a railroad section-hand, a concentrated soup scooper at a steel mill, a park policeman, and a short-order cook, David Wagoner has been a professor of English at the University of Washington at Seattle since 1954. His first volume of poems, Dry Sun, Dry Wind, *appeared in 1953, when he was twenty-seven years old. Since then, he has published numerous books of poetry, served as editor of* Poetry Northwest, *as well as written film scripts and several novels, the most noted of which is* The Escape Artist *(1965).*

The poem printed below is from his collection entitled Staying Alive *(1966).*

Chicago ran a fever of a hundred and one that groggy Sunday.
A reporter fried an egg on a sidewalk; the air looked shaky.
And a hundred thousand people were in the lake like shirts in a laundry.
Why was Johnny lonely?
Not because two dozen solid citizens, heat-struck, had keeled over backward.   5
Not because those lawful souls had fallen out of their sockets and melted.
But because the sun went down like a lump in a furnace or a bull in the Stock-
    yards.
Where was Johnny headed?
Under the Biograph Theater sign that said, "Our Air is Refrigerated."   10
Past seventeen FBI men and four policemen who stood in doorways and sweated.
Johnny sat down in a cold seat to watch Clark Gable get electrocuted.
Had Johnny been mistreated?
Yes, but Gable told the D. A. he'd rather fry than be shut up forever.
Two women sat by Johnny. One looked sweet, one looked like J. Edgar Hoover.15
Polly Hamilton made him feel hot, but Anna Sage made him shiver.
Was Johnny a good lover?
Yes, but he passed out his share of squeezes and pokes like a jittery masher
While Agent Purvis sneaked up and down the aisle like an extra usher,
Trying to make sure they wouldn't slip out till the show was over.   20
Was Johnny a fourflusher?
No, not if he knew the game. He got it up or got it back.
But he liked to take snapshots of policemen with his own Kodak,
And once in a while he liked to take them with an automatic.
Why was Johnny frantic?   25
Because he couldn't take a walk or sit down in a movie
Without being afraid he'd run smack into somebody
Who'd point at his rearranged face and holler, "Johnny!"
Was Johnny ugly?
Yes, because Dr. Wilhelm Loeser had given him a new profile   30
With a baggy jawline and squint eyes and an erased dimple,
With kangaroo-tendon cheekbones and a gigolo's mustache that should've been
    illegal.

Did Johnny love a girl?
Yes, a good-looking, hard-headed Indian named Billie Frechette.   35
He wanted to marry her and lie down and try to get over it,
But she was locked in jail for giving him first-aid and comfort.
Did Johnny feel hurt?
He felt like breaking a bank or jumping over a railing
Into some panicky teller's cage to shout, "Reach for the ceiling!"   40
Or like kicking some vice president in the bum checks and smiling.
What was he really doing?
Going up the aisle with the crowd and into the lobby
With Polly saying, "Would *you* do what Clark done?" And Johnny saying,
    "Maybe."   45
And Anna saying, "If he'd been smart, he'd of acted like Bing Crosby."
Did Johnny look flashy?
Yes, his white-on-white shirt and tie were luminous.
His trousers were creased like knives to the tops of his shoes,
And his yellow straw hat came down to his dark glasses.   50
Was Johnny suspicious?
Yes, and when Agent Purvis signalled with a trembling cigar,
Johnny ducked left and ran out of the theater,
And innocent Polly and squealing Anna were left nowhere.
Was Johnny a fast runner?   55
No, but he crouched and scurried past a friendly liquor store
Under the coupled arms of double-daters, under awnings, under stars,
To the curb at the mouth of an alley. He hunched there.
Was Johnny a thinker?
No, but he was thinking more or less of Billie Frechette   60
Who was lost in prison for longer than he could possibly wait,
And then it was suddenly too hard to think around a bullet.
Did anyone shoot straight?
Yes, but Mrs. Etta Natalsky fell out from under her picture hat.
Theresa Paulus sprawled on the sidewalk, clutching her left foot.   65
And both of them groaned loud and long under the streetlight.
Did Johnny like that?
No, but he lay down with those strange women, his face in the alley,
One shoe off, cinders in his mouth, his eyelids heavy.
When they shouted questions at him, he talked back to nobody.   70
Did Johnny lie easy?
Yes, holding his gun and holding his breath as a last trick,
He waited, but when the Agents came close, his breath wouldn't work.
Clark Gable walked his last mile; Johnny ran half a block.
Did he run out of luck?   75
Yes, before he was cool, they had him spread out on dished-in marble
In the Cook County Morgue, surrounded by babbling people
With a crime reporter presiding over the head of the table.
Did Johnny have a soul?
Yes, and it was climbing his slippery wind-pipe like a trapped burglar.   80
It was beating the inside of his ribcage, hollering, "Let me out of here!"
Maybe it got out, and maybe it just stayed there.
Was Johnny a money-maker?

Yes, and thousands paid 25¢ to see him, mostly women,
And one said, "I wouldn't have come, except he's a moral lesson,"   85
And another, "I'm disappointed. He feels like a dead man."
Did Johnny have a brain?
Yes, and it always worked best through the worst of dangers,
Through flat-footed hammerlocks, through guarded doors, around corners,
But it got taken out in the morgue and sold to some doctors.   90
Could Johnny take orders?
No, but he stayed in the wicker basket carried by six men
Through the bulging crowd to the hearse and let himself be locked in,
And he stayed put as it went driving south in a driving rain.
And he didn't get stolen?   95
No, not even after his old hard-nosed dad refused to sell
The quick-drawing corpse for $10,000 to somebody in a carnival.
He figured he'd let *Johnny* decide how to get to Hell.
Did anyone wish him well?
Yes, half of Indiana camped in the family pasture,   100
And the minister said, "With luck, he could have been a minister."
And up the sleeve of his oversized gray suit, Johnny twitched a finger.
Does anyone remember?
Everyone still alive. And some dead ones. It was a new kind of holiday
With hot and cold drinks and hot and cold tears. They planted him in a cemetery   105
With three unknown vice presidents, Benjamin Harrison, and James Whitcomb
     Riley,
Who never held up anybody.

Norman Mailer / *Of a Fire on the Moon*   1970

> *Born in New Jersey in 1923 and brought up in Brooklyn, Norman Mailer began*
> *writing while still an undergraduate at Harvard. In his fiction, essays, and highly*
> *personal journalism, Mailer has "covered" many significant phases of American*
> *life since the end of the Second World War. Part of his account of the* Apollo XI
> *voyage first appeared in* Life *magazine and was later expanded into a book length*
> *study of the astronauts,* Of a Fire on the Moon, *from which the following passage*
> *is excerpted. Always attracted to the action at the center of the arena, as his*
> *reporting of political conventions* (Miami and the Siege of Chicago) *and the*
> *peace movement of the sixties* (Armies of the Night) *testifies, Norman Mailer*
> *finds himself during his coverage of the moon walk an unwilling nonparticipant*
> *on an assignment without a location.*

[THE FIRST MOON WALK]

They had landed, there was jubilation in Mission Control, and a moment of frater-
nization between Armstrong and Aldrin, but in fact they were actually at work in the

next instant. No one knew what would await them—there were even theories that most of the surface of the moon was as fragile as icing on a cake. If they landed, and the moon ground began to collapse, they were ready to blast off with the ascent stage even as the descent stage was sinking beneath. But no sound of crumbling came up through the pipes of the legs, no shudder of collapse. A minute passed. They received the order to Stay. The second Stay–No Stay would be on them nine minutes later, and they rushed through a checklist, testing specific instruments to make certain they were intact from the landing. The thirty-odd seconds of fuel they still had left when they touched down was vented from the descent stage, a hissing and steaming beneath the legs like a steed loosing water on icy ground. Verbs and Nouns were punched into the DSKY. Now came the second Stay. There would not be another Stay–No Stay until the Command Module had made a complete revolution of the moon and would be coming back toward them in good position for rendezvous. So, unless some mishap were suddenly to appear, they had at least another two hours on the satellite. It was time to unscrew their gloves at the wrist and take them off, time to unscrew their helmets at the neck, lift them off.

They gave their first description of the landing, and made a few general remarks about the view through the window, the variety of rocks. But there was too much work to look for long. After a few comments on the agreeableness of lunar gravity, after a conversation with Columbia and mutual congratulations, they were back at the computer. Now, in the time before the next Stay–No Stay, they had to simulate a countdown for a planned ascent and realign the Inertial Measurement Unit, that is, determine the vertical line of moon gravity, and install its index into the Inertial Measurement Unit, then level the table and gyroscope from which all navigation was computed. Star checks were taken. Meanwhile, Armstrong was readying the cameras and snapping photographs through the window. Now Aldrin aligned the Abort Guidance Section. Armstrong laid in the data for Program 12, the Powered Ascent Guidance. The Command Module came around again. The simulated countdown was over. They had another Stay. They powered down their systems.

In the transcript the work continues minute after minute, familiar talk of stars and Nouns, acronyms, E-memory dumps, and returns to POO where Pings may idle. They are at rest on the moon, but the dialogue is not unencumbered of pads, updata link switches and noise suppression devices on the Manned Space Flight Network relay.

Then in what is virtually their first pause in better than an hour on the moon, they request permission to do their EVA early, begin in fact in the next few hours rather than take a halt to sleep. For days there had been discussion in every newspaper of the world whether the astronauts could land on the moon and a few hours later go to sleep before they even stepped out of the Lem; now the question has been answered—they are impatient to go.

CAPCOM: *We will support it.*
ALDRIN: *Roger.*
CAPCOM: *You guys are getting prime time TV there.*
ARMSTRONG: *Hope that little TV set works, but we'll see.*

Now the astronauts stopped to eat and to relax. Over the radio came the dialogue of Mission Control talking to Collins in orbit overhead. Around them, through each pinched small window, were tantalizing views of the moon. They could feel themselves in one-sixth gravity. How light were their bodies. Yet they were not weightless. There was gravity beneath them, a faint sensuous tug at their limbs. If they dropped a pencil, it did not float before drifting slowly away. Rather, it dropped. Slowly it dropped, dropped indeed at the same leisurely speed with which Apollo-Saturn had risen off its launching pad four and a half days ago. What a balm for the muscles of the eye! One-sixth of earth gravity was agreeable, it was attractive, it was, said Aldrin, "less *lonesome*" than weightlessness. He had, at last, " a distinct feeling of being somewhere." Yes, the moon was beneath them, hardly more than the height of a ten-foot diving board beneath them—they were in the domain of a presence again. How much like magnetism must lunar gravity have felt.

ALDRIN: *This is the Lem pilot. I'd like to take this opportunity to ask every person listening in, whoever and wherever they may be, to pause for a moment and contemplate the events of the past few hours, and to give thanks in his or her way.*

In the silence, Aldrin took out the bread, the wine, and the chalice he had brought in his Personal Preference Kit, and he put them on the little table in front of the Abort Guidance Section computer. Then he read some passages from the Bible and celebrated Communion.

A strange picture of religious intensity: there is of course no clue in Aldrin's immediate words—they are by now tuned to precisely what one would expect.

"I would like to have observed just how the wine poured in that environment, but it wasn't pertinent at that particular time. It wasn't important how it got in the cup. It was important only to get it there"—and not spill, we may assume, this most special blood of the Lord. "I offered some private prayers, but I find now that thoughts, feelings, come into my memory instead of words. I was not so selfish as to include my family in those prayers at the moment, nor so spacious as to include the fate of the world. I was thinking more about our particular task, and the challenge and the opportunity that had been given us. I asked people to offer thanks in their own way, and it is my hope that people will keep this whole event in their minds and see beyond minor details and technical achievements to a deeper meaning behind it all, challenge, a quest, the human need to do these things and the need to recognize that we are all one mankind under God."

Yes, his recollections are near to comic in their banality, but one gets a picture of this strong-nosed strong-armed gymnast in his space suit, deep in prayer in the crowded closet space of the Lem, while Armstrong the mystic (with the statue of Buddha on his living room table) is next to him in who knows what partial or unwilling communion, Armstrong so private in his mind that when a stranger tried to talk to him one day on a bus, he picked up a book to read. There, before his partner, Aldrin prayed, light lunar gravity new in his limbs, eyes closed. Can we assume the brain of his inner vision expanded to the dimensions of a church, the loft of a cathedral, Aldrin, man of passions and disciplines, fatalist, all but open believer in predestination, agent of God's will, Aldrin, prodigy of effort on Gemini 12, whose pulse after hours of work in space had shot up only when he read a Veteran's Day message to the ground. Patriotism had the power of a stroke for Aldrin and invocation was his harmony. Tribal chief, first noble savage on the moon, he prayed to the powers who had brought him there, whose will he would fulfill—God, the earth, the moon and himself all for this instant part of the lofty engine of the universe, and in that eccentric giant of character, that conservative of all the roots in all the family trees, who now was ripping up the roots of the ages, that man whose mother's name was Moon, was there a single question whose lament might suggest that if the mission were ill-conceived or even a work of art designed by the Devil, then all the prayers of all good men were nothing but a burden upon the Lord, who in order to reply would be forced to work in the mills of Satan, or leave the prayers of his flock in space. Not likely. Aldrin did not seem a man for thoughts like that, but then his mind was a mystery wrapped in the winding-sheet of a computer with billions of bits.

Later, Armstrong would say, "That first hour on the moon was hardly the time for long thoughts; we had specific jobs to do. Of course the sights were simply magnificent, beyond any visual experience that I had ever been exposed to," and Aldrin would describe it as "a unique, almost mystical environment." In fact, there is an edge of the unexplained to their reactions. Their characteristic matter-of-fact response is overcome occasionally by swoops of hyperbole. And to everyone's slight surprise, they were almost two hours late for their EVA. Their estimate of time was off by close to fifty percent. For astronauts that was an error comparable to a carpenter mistaking an eight-foot stud for a twelve-foot piece. If a carpenter can look at a piece of wood and guess its length to the nearest quarter-inch, it is because he has been working with lengths all his life. Equally, people in some occupations have a close ability to estimate time.

With astronauts, whose every day in a simulator was a day laid out on the measure of a time-line, the estimate of time elapsed had to become acute. Armstrong and Aldrin had consistently fulfilled their tasks in less time than was allotted. Now, curiously, they fell behind, then further behind. There were unexpected problems of course—it took longer to bleed the pressure out of the Lunar Module than had been anticipated, and the cooling units in the backpacks were sluggish at first in operation, but whether from natural excitement and natural anxiety, or an unconscious preoccupation with lunar phenomena so subtle that it is just at the edge of their senses, any extract from the transcript at this point where they are helping to adjust the Portable Life Support System on each others' backs shows real lack of enunciation. Nowhere else do the NASA stenographers have as much difficulty with where one voice ends and another begins.

TRANQUILITY: *Got it (garbled) prime rows in.*
TRANQUILITY: *Okay.*
TRANQUILITY: *(garbled)*
TRANQUILITY: *Let me do that for you.*
TRANQUILITY: *(Inaudible)*
TRANQUILITY: *Mark I*
TRANQUILITY: *(garbled) valves*
TRANQUILITY: *(garbled)*
TRANQUILITY: *Okay*
TRANQUILITY: *All of the (garbled)*
TRANQULITY: *(garbled) locked and lock locked.*
TRANQUILITY: *Did you put it—*
TRANQUILITY: *Oh, wait a minute*
TRANQUILITY: *Should be (garbled)*

TRANQUILITY: (*garbled*)
TRANQUILITY: *Roger.* (*garbled*)
TRANQUILITY: *I'll try it on the middle*
TRANQUILITY: *All right, check my* (*garbled*) *valves vertical*
TRANQUILITY: *Both vertical*
TRANQUILITY: *That's two vertical*
TRANQUILITY: *Okay*
TRANQUILITY: (*garbled*)
TRANQUILITY: *Locked and double-locked*
TRANQUILITY: *Okay*
TRANQUILITY: *Miss marked*
TRANQUILITY: *Sure wish I would have shaved last night.*
PAO: *That was a Buzz Aldrin comment.*

The hint is faint enough, but the hint exists—something was conceivably interfering with their sense of order. Could it have been the lunar gravity? Clock-time was a measure which derived from pendulums and spiral springs, clock-time was anchored right into the tooth of earth gravity—so a time might yet be coming when psychologists, not geologists, would be conducting experiments on the moon. Did lunar gravity have power like a drug to shift the sense of time?

Armstrong was connected at last to his PLSS. He was drawing oxygen from the pack he carried on his back. But the hatch door would not open. The pressure would not go low enough in the Lem. Down near a level of one pound per square inch, the last bit of man-created atmosphere in Eagle seemed to cling to its constituency, reluctant to enter the vacuums of the moon. But they did not know if they could get the hatch door open with a vacuum on one side and even a small pressure on the other. It was taking longer than they thought. While it was not a large concern since there would be other means to open it—redundancies pervaded throughout—nonetheless, a concern must have intruded: how intolerably comic they would appear if they came all the way and then were blocked before a door they could not crack. That thought had to put one drop of perspiration on the back of the neck. Besides, it must have been embarrassing to begin so late. The world of television was watching, and the astronauts had exhibited as much sensitivity to an audience as any bride on her way down the aisle.

It was not until nine-forty at night, Houston time, that they got the hatch open at last. In the heat of running almost two hours late, ensconced in the armor of a man-sized spaceship, could they still have felt an instant of awe as they looked out that open hatch at a panorama of theater: the sky is black, but the ground is brightly lit, bright as footlights on the floor of a dark theater. A black and midnight sky, yet on the moon ground, "you could almost go out in your shirt-sleeves and get a suntan," Aldrin would say. "I remember thinking, 'Gee, if I didn't know where I was, I could believe that somebody had created this environment somewhere out in the West and given us another simulation to work in.' " Everywhere on that pitted flat were shadows dark as the sky above, shadows dark as mine shafts.

What a struggle to push out from that congested cabin, now twice congested in their bulky-wham suits, no feeling of obstacle against their flesh, their sense of touch dead and numb, spaceman body manipulated out into the moon world like an upright piano turned by movers on the corner of the stairs.

"You're lined up on the platform. Put your left foot to the right a little bit. Okay, that's good. Roll left."

Armstrong was finally on the porch. Could it be with any sense of an alien atmosphere receiving the fifteen-layer encapsulations of the pack and suit on his back? Slowly, he climbed down the ladder. Archetypal, he must have felt, a boy descending the rungs in the wall of an abandoned well, or was it Jack down the stalk? And there he was on the bottom, on the footpad of the leg of the Lem, a metal plate perhaps three feet across. Inches away was the soil of the moon. But first he jumped up again to the lowest rung of the ladder. A couple of hours later, at the end of the EVA, conceivably exhausted, the jump from the ground to the rung, three feet up, might be difficult in that stiff and heavy space suit, so he tested it now. "It takes," said Armstrong, "a pretty good little jump."

Now, with television working, and some fraction of the world peering at the murky image of this instant, poised between the end of one history and the beginning of another, he said quietly, "I'm at the foot of the ladder. The Lem footpads are only depressed in the surface about one or two inches, although the surface appears to be very very fine-grained as you get close to it. It's almost like a powder." One of Armstrong's rare confessions of uneasiness is focused later on this moment. "I don't recall any particular emotion or feeling other than a little caution, a desire to be sure it was safe to put my weight on that surface outside Eagle's footpad."

Did his foot tingle in the heavy lunar overshoe? "I'm going to step off the Lem now."

Did something in him shudder at the touch of the new ground? Or did he draw a sweet strength from the balls of his feet? Nobody was necessarily going ever to know.

"That's one small step for a man," said Armstrong, "one giant leap for mankind." He had joined the ranks of the forever quoted. Patrick Henry, Henry Stanley and Admiral Dewey moved over for him.

Now he was out there, one foot on the moon, then the other foot on the moon, the powder like velvet underfoot. With one hand still on the ladder, he comments, "The surface is fine and powdery. I can . . . I can pick it up loosely with my toe." And as he releases his catch, the grains fall back slowly to the soil, a fan of feathers gliding to the floor. "It does adhere in fine layers like powdered charcoal to the sole and sides of my boots. I only go in a small fraction of an inch. Maybe an eighth of an inch. But I can see the footprints of my boots and the treads in the fine sand particles."

Capcom: "Neil, this is Houston. We're copying."

Yes, they would copy. He was like a man who goes into a wrecked building to defuse a new kind of bomb. He talks into a microphone as he works, for if a mistake is made, and the bomb goes off, it will be easier for the next man if every detail of his activities has been mentioned as he performed them. Now, he released his grip on the ladder and pushed off for a few steps on the moon, odd loping steps, almost thrust into motion like a horse trotting up a steep slope. It could have been a moment equivalent to the first steps he took as an infant for there was nothing to hold onto and he did not dare to fall—the ground was too hot, the rocks might tear his suit. Yet if he stumbled, he could easily go over for he could not raise his arms above his head nor reach to his knees, his arms in the pressure bladder stood out before him like sausages; so, if he tottered, the weight of the pack could twist him around, or drop him. They had tried to shape up simulations of lunar gravity while weighted in scuba suits at the bottom of a pool, but water was not a vacuum through which to move; so they had also flown in planes carrying two hundred pounds of equipment on their backs. The pilot would take the plane through a parabolic trajectory. There would be a period of twenty-two seconds at the top of the curve when a simulation of one-sixth gravity would be present, and the two hundred pounds of equipment would weigh no more than on the moon, no more than thirty-plus pounds, and one could take loping steps down the aisle of the plane, staggering through unforeseen wobbles or turbulence. Then the parabolic trajectory was done, the plane was diving, and it would have to pull out of the dive. That created the reverse of one-sixth gravity—it multiplied gravity by two and a half times. The two hundred pounds of equipment now weighed five hundred pounds and the astronauts had to be supported by other men straining to help them bear the weight. So simulations gave them time for hardly more than a clue before heavy punishment was upon them. But now he was out in the open endless lunar gravity, his body and the reflexes of his life obliged to adopt a new rhythm and schedule of effort, a new disclosure of grace.

Still, he seemed pleased after the first few steps. "There seems to be no difficulty in moving around as we suspected. It's even perhaps easier than the simulations . . ." He would run a few steps and stop, run a few steps and stop. Perhaps it was not unlike directing the Lem when it hovered over the ground. One moved faster than on earth and with less effort, but it was harder to stop—one had to pick the place to halt from several yards ahead. Yes, it was easier once moving, but awkward at the beginning and the end because of the obdurate plastic bendings of the suit. And once standing at rest, the sense of the vertical was sly. One could be leaning further forward than one knew. Or leaning backward. Like a needle on a dial one would have to oscillate from side to side of the vertical to find position. Conceivably the sensation was not unlike skiing with a child on one's back.

It was time for Aldrin to descend the ladder from the Lem to the ground, and Armstrong's turn to give directions: "The shoes are about to come over the sill. Okay, now drop your PLSS down. There you go. You're clear. . . . About an inch clearance on top of your PLSS."

Aldrin spoke for future astronauts: "Okay, you need a little bit of arching of the back to come down . . ."

When he reached the ground, Aldrin took a big and exuberant leap up the ladder again, as if to taste the pleasures of one-sixth gravity all at once. "Beautiful, beautiful," he exclaimed.

Armstrong: "Isn't that something. Magnificent sight out here."

Aldrin: "Magnificent desolation."

They were looking at a terrain which lived in a clarity of focus unlike anything they had ever seen on earth. There was no air, of course, and so no wind, nor clouds, nor dust, nor even the finest scattering of light from the smallest dispersal of microscopic particles on a clear day on earth, no, nothing visible or invisible moved in the vacuum before them. All light was pure. No haze was present, not even the invisible haze of the finest day—therefore objects did not go out of focus as they receded into the distance. If one's eyes were good enough, an object at a hundred yards was as distinct as a rock at a few feet. And their eyes were good enough. Just as one could not determine one's altitude above the moon, not from fifty miles up nor five, so now along the ground before them no distance was real, for all distances had the faculty to appear equally near if one peered at them through blinders and could not see the intervening details. Again the sense of being on a stage or on the lighted floor of a room so large one could not see where the dark ceiling began must have come upon them, for there were no hints of gathering evanescence in ridge beyond ridge; rather each outline was as severe as the one in front of it, and since the ground was filled with small craters of every size, from antholes to potholes to empty pools, and the horizon was near, four times nearer than on earth and sharp as the line drawn by a pencil, the moon ground seemed to slope and drop in all directions "like swimming in an ocean with six-foot or eight-foot swells and waves," Armstrong said later. "In that condition, you never can see very far away from where you are." But what they could see, they could see entirely—to the depth of their field of view at any instant their focus was complete. And as they swayed from side to side, so a sense of the vertical kept eluding them, the slopes of the craters about them seeming to tilt a few degrees to one side of the horizontal, then the other. On earth, one had only to incline one's body an inch or two and a sense of the vertical was gone, but on the moon they could lean over, then further over, lean considerably further over without beginning to fall. So verticals slid and oscillated. Rolling from side to side, they could as well have been on water, indeed their sense of the vertical was probably equal to the subtle uncertainty of the body when a ship is rolling on a quiet sea. "I say," said Aldrin, "the rocks are rather slippery."

They were discovering the powder of the moon soil was curious indeed, comparable in firmness and traction to some matter between sand and snow. While the Lem looked light as a kite, for its pads hardly rested on the ground and it appeared ready to lift off and blow away, yet their own feet sometimes sank for two or three inches into the soft powder on the slope of very small craters, and their soles would slip as the powder gave way under their boots. In other places the ground was firm and harder than sand, yet all of these variations were to be found in an area not a hundred feet out from the legs of the Lem. As he explored his footing, Aldrin sent back comments to Mission Control, reporting in the rapt professional tones of a coach instructing his team on the conditions of the turf in a new plastic football field.

Meanwhile Armstrong was transporting the television camera away from the Lem to a position where it could cover most of their activities. Once properly installed, he revolved it through a full panorama of their view in order that audiences on earth might have a clue to what he saw. But in fact the transmission was too rudimentary to give any sense of what was about them, that desert sea of rocks, rubble, small boulders, and crater lips.

Aldrin was now working to set up the solar wind experiment, a sheet of aluminum foil hung on a stand. For the next hour and a half, the foil would be exposed to the solar wind, and invisible, unfelt, but high-velocity flow of noble gases from the sun like argon, krypton, neon and helium. For the astronauts, it was the simplest of procedures, no more difficult than setting up a piece of sheet music on a music stand. At the end of the EVA, however, the aluminum foil would be rolled up, insterted in the rock box, and delivered eventually to a laboratory in Switzerland uniquely equipped for the purpose. There any nobles gases which had been trapped in the atomic lattice of the aluminum would be baked out in virtuoso procedures of quantitative analysis, and a closer knowledge of the components of the solar wind would be gained. Since the solar wind, it may be recalled, was diverted by the magnetosphere away from the earth it had not hitherto been available for casual study.

That was the simplest experiment to set up; the other two would be deployed about an hour later. One was a passive seismometer to measure erratic disturbances and any periodic vibrations, as well as moonquakes, and the impact of meteors in the weeks and months to follow; it was equipped to radio this information to earth, the energy for transmission derived from solar panels which extended out to either side, and thereby gave it the look of one of those spaceships of the future with thin extended paperlike wings which one sees in science fiction drawings. In any case it was so sensitive that the steps of the astronauts were recorded as they walked by. Finally there was a Laser Ranging Retro-Reflector, an LRRR (or LRQ, for L R-cubed), and that was a mirror whose face was a hundred quartz crystals, black as coal, cut to a precision never obtained before in glass—one-third of an arch/sec. Since each quartz crystal was a corner of a rectangle, any ray of light striking one of the three faces in each crystal would bounce off the other two in such a way that the light would return in exactly the same direction it had been received. A laser beam sent up from earth would therefore reflect back to the place from which it was sent. The time it required to travel this half-million miles from earth to moon round trip, a journey of less than three seconds, could be measured so accurately that physicists might then discern whether the moon was drifting away from the earth a few centimeters a year, or (by using two lasers) whether Europe and America might be drifting apart some comparable distance, or even if the Pacific Ocean were contracting. These measurements could then be entered into the caverns of Einstein's General Theory of Relativity, and new proof or disproof of the great thesis could be obtained.

We may be certain the equipment was remarkable. Still, its packaging and its ease of deployment had probably done as much to advance its presence on the ship as any clear priority over other scientific equipment; the beauty of these items from the point of view of NASA was that the astronauts could set them up in a few minutes while working in their space suits, even set them up with inflated gloves so insensitive that special silicone pads had to be inserted at the fingertips in order to leave the astronauts not altogether numb-fingered in their manipulations. Yet these marvels of measurement would soon be installed on the moon with less effort than it takes to remove a vacuum cleaner from its carton and get it operating.

It was at this point that patriotism, the corporation, and the national taste all came to occupy the same head of a pin, for the astronauts next proceeded to set up the flag. But that operation, as always, presented its exquisite problems. There was, we remind ourselves, no atmosphere for the flag to wave in. Any flag made of cloth would droop, indeed it would dangle. Therefore a species of starched plastic flag had to be employed, a flag which would stand out, there, out to the nonexistent breeze, flat as a slab of plywood. No, that would not do either. The flag was better crinkled and curled. Waves and billows were bent into it, and a full corkscrew of a curl at the end. There it stands for posterity, photographed in the twists of a high gale on the windless moon, curled up tin flag, numb as a pickled pepper.

Aldrin would hardly agree. "Being able to salute that flag was one of the more humble yet proud experiences I've ever had. To be able to look at the American flag and know how much so many people had put of themselves and their work into getting it where it was. We sensed—we really did—this almost mystical identification of all the people in the world at that instant."

Two minutes after the flag was up, the President of the United States put in his phone call. Let us listen one more time:

"Because of what you have done," said Nixon, "the heavens have become a part of man's world. And as you talk to us from the Sea of Tranquility, it inspires us to redouble our efforts to bring peace and tranquility to earth . . . ."

"Thank you, Mr. President. It's a great honor and privilege for us to be here representing not only the United States, but men of peace of all nations . . ."

In such piety is the schizophrenia of the ages.

Immediately afterward, Aldrin practiced kicking moon dust, but he was somewhat broken up. Either reception was garbled, or Aldrin was temporarily incoherent. "They seem to leave," he said to the Capcom, referring to the particles, "and most of them have about the same angle of departure and velocity. From where I stand, a large portion of them will impact at a certain distance out. Several—the percentage is, of course, that will impact . . ."

Capcom: "Buzz this is Houston. You're cutting out on the end of your transmissions. Can you speak a little more forward into your microphone. Over."

Aldrin: "Roger. I'll try that."

Capcom: "Beautiful."

Aldrin: "Now I had that one inside my mouth that time."

Capcom: "It sounded a little wet."

And on earth, a handful of young scientists were screaming, "Stop wasting time with flags and presidents—collect some rocks!"

DISCUSSION QUESTIONS

1. How does the language of the astronauts, especially Aldrin's, affect Mailer? Why does Mailer use their words and NASA terminology so frequently? How are these transcripts and codes used by O'Toole in his account of the moonlanding for the *Washington Post* (see Press)?

2. Why does Mailer concentrate on a particular spot where the transcript is garbled? Why does he speculate on the length of time it takes the astronauts to step out onto the moon? How does his description of the "clarity of focus" on the moon suggest an environment that is different from the one described by the astronauts? For example, how does Aldrin's comparison of the moon landscape to "an environment somewhere out West" affect our response to what they are seeing? What does Mailer want us to see?

Joyce Carol Oates / Stalking   1972

Joyce Carol Oates, born in Lockport, New York, in 1938, is currently writer-in-residence at Princeton University. She began writing fiction as a child and continued to do so throughout college. In 1959, she was co-winner of the Mademoiselle *college fiction award. In her novels and short stories, she has successfully focused on the unsettling psychological and moral problems of contemporary American life. Her fourth novel,* Them, *a powerful exploration into the public and private tensions of family life on the eve of the 1967 Detroit riots, won the National Book Award in 1970. Since then, in* Wonderland *(1971) and* Do with Me What You Will *(1973), as well as in numerous short stories, Joyce Carol Oates has consistently found a fictive voice to delineate the stresses and disorders that seem to accompany a burgeoning material culture. As the following short story, "Stalking," shows, her characters are seldom far—they are occasionally indistinguishable—from the world of things: a reified world perhaps best*

> symbolized by the dazzling consumer kingdoms scattered throughout the empty
> regions of the American landscape.

The Invisible Adversary is fleeing across a field.

Gretchen, walking slowly, deliberately, watches with her keen unblinking eyes the figure of the Invisible Adversary some distance ahead. The Adversary has run boldly in front of all that traffic—on long spiky legs brisk as colts' legs—and jumped up onto a curb of new concrete, and now is running across a vacant field. The Adversary glances over his shoulder at Gretchen.

Bastard, Gretchen thinks.

Saturday afternoon. November. A cold gritty day. Gretchen is out stalking. She has hours for her game. Hours. She is dressed for the hunt, her solid legs crammed into old blue jeans, her big, square, strong feet jammed into white leather boots that cost her mother forty dollars not long ago, but are now scuffed and filthy with mud. Hopeless to get them clean again, Gretchen doesn't give a damn. She is wearing a dark green corduroy jacket that is worn out at the elbows and the rear, with a zipper that can be zipped swiftly up or down, attached to a fringed leather strip. On her head nothing, though it is windy today.

She has hours ahead.

Cars and trucks and buses from the city and enormous interstate trucks hauling automobiles pass by the highway; Gretchen waits until the way is nearly clear, then starts out. A single car is approaching. *Slow down, you bastard,* Gretchen thinks; and like magic he does.

Following the footprints of the Invisible Adversary. There is no sidewalk here yet, so she might as well cut right across the field. A gigantic sign announces the site of the new Pace & Fischbach Building, an office building of fifteen floors to be completed the following year. The land around here is all dug up and muddy; she can see the Adversary's footsteps leading right past the gouged-up area . . . and there he is, smirking back at her, pretending panic.

I'll get you. Don't worry, Gretchen thinks carefully.

Because the Adversary is so light-footed and invisible, Gretchen doesn't make any effort to be that way. She plods along as she does at school, passing from classroom to classroom, unhurried and not even sullen, just unhurried. She knows she is very visible. She is thirteen years old and weighs one hundred and thirty-five pounds. She's only five feet three—stocky, muscular, squat in the torso and shoulders, with good strong legs and thighs. She could be good at gym, if she bothered; instead, she just stands around, her face empty, her arms crossed and her shoulders a little slumped. If forced, she takes part in the games of volleyball and basketball, but she runs heavily, without spirit, and sometimes bumps into other girls, hurting them. *Out of my way,* she thinks, at such times her face shows no expression.

And now? . . . The Adversary is peeking out at her from around the corner of a gas station. Something flickers in her brain. *I see you,* she thinks, with quiet excitement. The Adversary ducks back out of sight. Gretchen heads in his direction, plodding through a jumbled, bulldozed field of mud and thistles and debris that is mainly rocks and chunks of glass. The gas station is brand new and not yet opened for business. It is all white tile, white concrete, perfect plate-glass windows with white-washed X's on them, a large driveway and eight gasoline pumps, all proudly erect and ready for business. But the gas station has not opened since Gretchen and her family moved here—about six months ago. Something must have gone wrong. Gretchen fixes her eyes on the corner where the Adversary was last seen. He can't escape.

One wall of the gas station's white tile has been smeared with something like tar. Dreamy, snakelike, thick twistings of black. Black tar. Several windows have been broken. Gretchen stands in the empty driveway, her hands jammed into her pockets. Traffic is moving slowly over here. A barricade has been set up that directs traffic out onto the shoulder of the highway, on a narrow, bumpy, muddy lane that loops out and back again onto the pavement. Cars move slowly, carefully. Their bottoms scrape against the road. The detour signs are great rectangular things, bright yellow with black zigzag lines. SLOW. DETOUR. In the two center lanes of the highway are bulldozers not being used today, and gigantic concrete pipes to be used for storm sewers. Eight pipes. They are really enormous; Gretchen's eyes crinkle with awe, just to see them.

She remembers the Adversary.

There he is—headed for the shopping plaza. *He won't get away in the crowds,* Gretchen promises herself. She follows. Now she is approaching an area that is more completed, though there are still no sidewalks and some of the buildings are brand-new and yet unoccupied, vacant. She jumps over a concrete ditch that is stained with rust-colored water and heads up a slight incline in the service drive of the Federal Savings Bank. The drive-in tellers' windows are all dark today, behind their green-tinted glass. The whole bank is dark, closed. Is this the bank her parents go to now? It takes Gretchen a minute to recognize it.

Now a steady line of traffic, a single lane, turns onto the service drive that leads to the shopping plaza. BUCKINGHAM MALL. 101 STORES. Gretchen notices a few kids her own age, boys or girls, trudging in jeans and jackets ahead of her, through the mud. They might be classmates of hers. Her attention is captured again by the Invisible Adversary, who has run all the way up to the Mall and is hanging around the entrance of the Cunningham Drug Store, teasing her.

You'll be sorry for that, you bastard, Gretchen thinks with a smile.

Automobiles pass her slowly. The parking lot for the Mall is enormous, many acres. A city of cars on a Saturday afternoon. Gretchen sees a car that might be her mother's, but she isn't sure. Cars are parked slanted here, in lanes marked LOT K, LANE 15; LOT K, LANE 16. The signs are spheres, bubbles, perched up on long slender poles. At night they are illuminated.

Ten or twelve older kids are hanging around the drugstore entrance. One of them is sitting on top of a mailbox, rocking it back and forth. Gretchen pushes past them—they are kidding around, trying to block people—and inside the store her eye darts rapidly up and down the aisles, looking for the Invisible Adversary.

Hiding here? Hiding?

She strolls along, cunning and patient. At the cosmetics counter a girl is showing an older woman some liquid make-up. She smears a small oval onto the back of the woman's hand, rubs it gently. "That's Peace Pride," the girl says. She has shimmering blond hair and eyes that are penciled to show a permanent exclamatory interest. She does not notice Gretchen, who lets one hand drift idly over a display of marked-down lipsticks, each for only $1.59.

Gretchen slips the tube of lipstick into her pocket. Neatly. Nimbly. Ignoring the Invisible Adversary, who is shaking a finger at her, she drifts over to the newsstand, looks at the magazine covers without reading them, and edges over to

another display. Packages in a cardboard barrel, out in the aisle. Big bargains.
Gretchen doesn't even glance in the barrel to see what is being offered . . . she
just slips one of the packages in her pocket. No trouble.

She leaves by the other door, the side exit. A small smile tugs at her mouth.

The Adversary is trotting ahead of her. The Mall is divided into geometric
areas, each colored differently; the Adversary leaves the blue pavement and is
now on the green. Gretchen follows. She notices the Adversary going into a
Franklin Joseph store.

Gretchen enters the store, sniffs in the perfumy, overheated smell, sees nothing
that interests her on the counters or at the dress racks, and so walks right to the
back of the store, to the Ladies Room. No one inside. She takes the tube of lipstick out of her pocket, opens it, examines the lipstick. It has a tart, sweet smell.
A very light pink: *Spring Blossom*. Gretchen goes to the mirror and smears the lipstick onto it, at first lightly, then coarsely; part of the lipsteak breaks and falls into
a hair-littered sink. Gretchen goes into one of the toilet stalls and tosses the tube
into the toilet bowl. She takes handfuls of toilet paper and crumbles them into a
ball and throws them into the toilet. Remembering the package from the drugstore, she takes it out of her pocket—just toothpaste. She throws it, cardboard
package and all, into the toilet bowl, then, her mind glimmering with an idea, she
goes to the apparatus that holds the towel—a single cloth towel on a roll—and
tugs at it until it comes loose, then pulls it out hand over hand, patiently, until the
entire towel is out. She scoops it up and carries it to the toilet. She pushes it in
and flushes the toilet.

The stuff doesn't go down, so she tries again. This time it goes part-way down
before it gets stuck.

Gretchen leaves the rest room and strolls unhurried through the store. The Adversary is waiting for her outside—peeking through the window—wagging a
finger at her. *Don't you wag no finger at me,* she thinks, with a small tight smile.
Outside, she follows him at a distance. Loud music is blaring around her head. It
is rock music, piped out onto the colored squares and rectangles of the Mall,
blown everywhere by the November wind, but Gretchen hardly hears it.

Some boys are fooling around in front of the record store. One of them bumps
into Gretchen and they all laugh as she is pushed against a trash can. "Watch it,
babe!" the boy sings out. Her leg hurts. Gretchen doesn't look at them but, with a
cold, swift anger, her face averted, she knocks the trash can over onto the sidewalk. Junk falls out. The can rolls. Some women shoppers scurry to get out of the
way and the boys laugh.

Gretchen walks away without looking back.

She wanders through Sampson Furniture, which has two entrances. In one door
and out the other, as always, it is a ritual with her. Again she notices the sofa that
is like the sofa in their family room at home—covered with black and white fur,
real goatskin. All over the store there are sofas, chairs, tables, beds. A jumble of
furnishings. People stroll around them, in and out of little displays, displays meant
to be living rooms, dining rooms, bedrooms, family rooms. . . . It makes Gretchen's eyes squint to see so many displays: like seeing the inside of a hundred
houses. She slows down, almost comes to a stop. Gazing at a living-room display
on a raised platform. Only after a moment does she remember why she is here—
whom she is following—and she turns to see the Adversary beckoning to her.

She follows him outside again. He goes into Dodi's Boutique and, with her
head lowered so that her eyes seem to move to the bottom of her eyebrows, press-

ing up against her forehead, Gretchen follows him. *You'll regret this,* she thinks. Dodi's Boutique is decorated in silver and black. Metallic strips hang down from a dark ceiling, quivering. Salesgirls dressed in pants suits stand around with nothing to do except giggle with one another and nod their heads in time to the music amplified throughout the store. It is music from a local radio station. Gretchen wanders over to the dress rack, for the hell of it. Size 14. "The time is now 2:35," a radio announcer says cheerfully. "The weather is 32 degrees with a chance of showers and possible sleet tonight. You're listening to WCKK, Radio Wonderful . . ." Gretchen selects several dresses and a salesgirl shows her to a dressing room.

"Need any help?" the girl asks. She has long swinging hair and a high-shouldered, indifferent, bright manner.

"No," Gretchen mutters.

Alone, Gretchen takes off her jacket, She is wearing a navy blue sweater. She zips one of the dresses open and it falls off the flimsy plastic hanger before she can catch it. She steps on it, smearing mud onto the white wool. *The hell with it.* She lets it lie there and holds up another dress, gazing at herself in the mirror.

She has untidy, curly hair that looks like a wig set loosely on her head. Light brown curls spill out everywhere, bouncy, a little frizzy, a cascade, a tumbling of curls. Her eyes are deep set, her eyebrows heavy and dark. She wears no make-up, her lips are perfectly colorless, pale, a little chapped, and they are usually held tight, pursed tightly shut. She has a firm, rounded chin. Her facial structure is strong, pensive, its features stern and symmetrical as a statue's, blank, neutral, withdrawn. Her face is attractive. But there is a blunt, neutral, sexless stillness to it, as if she were detached from it and somewhere else, uninterested.

She holds the dress up to her body, smooths it down over her breasts, staring.

After a moment she hangs the dress up again, and runs down the zipper so roughly that it breaks. The other dress she doesn't bother with. She leaves the dressing room, putting on her jacket.

At the front of the store the salesgirl glances at her . . . "—Didn't fit?—"

"No," says Gretchen.

She wanders around for a while, in and out of Carmichael's, the Mall's big famous store, where she catches sight of her mother on an escalator going up. Her mother doesn't notice her. She pauses by a display of "winter homes." Her family owns a home like this, in the Upper Peninsula, except theirs is larger. This one comes complete for only $5330: PACKAGE ERECTED ON YOUR LOT—YEAR-ROUND HOME FIBER GLASS INSULATION—BEAUTIFUL ROUGH-SAWN VERTICAL B.C. CEDAR SIDING WITH DEEP SIMULATED SHADOW LINES FOR A RUGGED EXTERIOR.

Only 3:15. For the hell of it, Gretchen goes into the Big Boy restaurant and orders a ground-round hamburger with French fries. Also a Coke. She sits at the crowded counter and eats slowly, her jaws grinding slowly, as she glances at her reflection in the mirror directly in front of her—her mop of hair moving almost imperceptibly with the grinding of her jaws—and occasionally she sees the Adversary waiting outside, coyly. *You'll get yours,* she thinks.

She leaves the Big Boy and wanders out into the parking lot, eating from a bag of potato chips. She wipes her greasy hands on her thighs. The afternoon has turned dark and cold. Shivering a little, she scans the maze of cars for the Adversary—yes, there he is—and starts after him. He runs ahead of her. He runs through the parking lot, waits teasingly at the edge of a field, and as she approaches he runs across the field, trotting along with a noisy crowd of four or five loose dogs that don't seem to notice him.

Gretchen follows him through that field, trudging in the mud, and through another muddy field, her eyes fixed on him. Now he is at the highway—hesitating there—now he is about to run across in front of traffic—now, now—now he darts out—

Now! He is struck by a car! His body knocked backward, spinning backward. Ah, now, *now how does it feel?* Gretchen asks.

He picks himself up. Gets to his feet. Is he bleeding? Yes, bleeding! He stumbles across the highway to the other side, where there is a sidewalk. Gretchen follows him as soon as the traffic lets up. He is staggering now, like a drunken man. *How does it feel? Do you like it now?*

The Adversary staggers along the sidewalk. He turns onto a side street, beneath an archway, *Piney Woods.* He is leading Gretchen into the Piney Woods subdivision. Here the homes are quite large, on artificial hills that show them to good advantage. Most of the homes are white colonials with attached garages. There are no sidewalks here, so the Adversary has to walk in the street, limping like an old man, and Gretchen follows him in the street, with her eyes fixed on him.

Are you happy now? Does it hurt? Does it?

She giggles at the way he walks. He looks like a drunken man. He glances back at her, white-faced, and turns up a flagstone walk . . . goes right up to a big white colonial house. . . .

Gretchen follows him inside. She inspects the simulated brick of the foyer: yes, there are blood spots. He is dripping blood. Entranced, she follows the splashes of blood into the hall, to the stairs . . . forgets her own boots, which are muddy . . . but she doesn't feel like going back to wipe her feet. The hell with it.

Nobody seems to be home. Her mother is probably still shopping, her father is out of town for the weekend. The house empty. Gretchen goes into the kitchen, opens the refrigerator, takes out a Coke, and wanders to the rear of the house, to the family room. It is two steps down from the rest of the house. She takes off her jacket and tosses it somewhere. Turns on the television set. Sits on the goatskin sofa and stares at the screen: a return of a Shotgun Steve show, which she has already seen.

If the Adversary comes crawling behind her, groaning in pain, weeping, she won't even bother to glance at him.

DISCUSSION QUESTIONS

    1. How does the narrator establish for the reader the sense that a real world is being depicted? How does the narrator, at the same time, establish the sense of a not-quite-real world? How are both of these worlds intertwined?

    2. How does an awareness of the language of advertising affect your responses to this short story? What is Gretchen's attitude towards advertising and its products? To shopping plazas? How does her attitude compare to Kowinski's in ''The Malling of America'' (see Magazines)? Does the narrator seem to share Gretchen's attitudes? Explain. What seems to be the purpose of so many concrete descriptions of particular consumer goods: automobiles, clothing, makeup, food, and homes? What relations, both physical and psychological, do the characters in the story bear to these material things?